Public Administration in a Globalized World: Theories and Practices between the US and Korea

Marc Holzer, PhD

Dean and Board of Governors Professor
School of Public Affairs and Administration
Rutgers University-Newark, New Jersey

Richard W. Schwester, PhD

Associate Professor
John Jay College of Criminal Justice
The City University of New York(CUNY)

Seok-Hwan Lee, PhD

Professor
Public Administration and Public Policy
Kookmin University, Seoul

M.E.Sharpe
Armonk, New York
London, England

Daeyoung Moonhwasa
Seoul, Korea

ISBN 978-89-7644-479-0
Published by Choon Hwan Lim
Daeyoung Moonhwasa Publishing Co.
5, Cheongpa-ro 61-gil, Yongsan-gu, Seoul, 140-869, Korea
TEL (02) 716-3883, (02) 714-3062
FAX (02) 703-3839
Published on 10 June, 2014

Price ₩35,000

About the Authors

Marc Holzer

Dean Holzer (MPA, PhD University of Michigan) is Dean of the School of Public Affairs and Administration, and Board of Governors Professor of Public Affairs and Administration, at Rutgers University's Newark Campus. He is a Fellow of the National Academy of Public Administration and a Past President of the American Society of Public Administration. Since 1975, he has directed the National Center for Public Performance, and he is the founder and editor-in-chief of the journals *Public Performance and Management Review* and *Public Voices*, and is the co-founder/co-editor of the *Chinese Public Administration Review*. He has also recently founded the Public Performance Measurement and Reporting Network. His research, service, and teaching has been honored by awards from the National Association of Schools of Public Affairs and Administration, the American Society of Public Administration, and the Chinese Public Administration Society. He has published well over one hundred books, monographs, chapters and articles.

Richard W. Schwester

Professor Schwester (MA, PhD Rutgers University) is an Associate Professor at John Jay College of Criminal Justice at the City University of New York. His research interests include the use of technology in government, e-government, prison privatization, critical incidents, and inter-local shared services. Some of Professor Schwester's most recent work appears in *Public Budgeting and Finance, Public Performance and Management Review, Public Administration Quarterly, International Journal of Public Administration*, and the *International Journal of Organization Theory and Behavior*.

Seok-Hwan Lee

Seok-Hwan Lee (MPA. Korea University, Ph.D. Rutgers University－Newark) is Professor of Public Administration and Public Policy at Kookmin University, Seoul, Korea where he specializes in public performance measurements and management. He formerly taught in the Doctor of Public Administration program at the University of Illinois at Springfield. His research interests include strategic performance management in the public sector, and organization theory and behavior. He previously served as an Assistant Editor of the *Public Performance and Management Review* (formerly the *Public Productivity and Management Review*) from 1998-2000. He also sits on editorial boards of major public administration journals, including the *Public Performance and Management Review*, the *Review of Public Personnel Administration*, and the *International Review of Public Administration*. His published works appear in the *Public Administration Review*, the *Review of Public Personnel Administration*, the *Public Productivity & Management Review*, the *International Journal of Organizational Analysis, the International Review of Public Administration, and International Journal of Public Administration*, among others. He is co-editor with Marc Holzer on the second edition of *Public Productivity Handbook* (Marcel Dekker Inc., 2004) and his most recent publication includes *UOFO (Unreasonable Objectives－focused Organization): Strategic Performance Management for Governments and Business Enterprises* (Seoul: Bubmoon Publishers, 2008, in Korean).

PREFACE

This text is an extended and edited version of the original textbook titled 'Public Administration: An Introduction (M.E. Sharpe, 2011)' by Marc Holzer and Richard Schwester.

Unlike previous public administration textbooks, this book focuses on a dynamic learning system rather than a static volume. This has made this textbook received very well by students, scholars and practitioners in the public sector. In the meantime, there have been a growing number of requests among students, scholars, practitioners to share foreign countries' government experience and further develop a stronger and more effective model for effective public administration on a global context.

Public administration, in general, deals with the role of the public sector and seeks effective solutions for social problems at the same time. As social problems are intertwined and complicated in nature, to search out effective solutions for specific situations in a country presents a great challenge to public managers. In this difficult situation, the most effective, enduring way to provide high performing solutions is to benchmark against what other governments or countries have done in similar situations. Of course, different contextsand cultures have to be considered in order to make realistic decisions. It is to be noted, however, that diagnosing current public sector situations and pondering over specific solutions certainly require public managers to view all problems from a comparative perspective. Effective public mangers should see social problems from viewpoints both of unique situations and comparative perspectives. They have to understand what has been learned from other governments' cases before they reach a final decision on their own case.

Our public sector environments are rapidly changing, thereby forcing public managers to make accurate and speedy decisions, which is very difficult in nature. However, to adapt to the change of environment and survive, public sector managers should put on multiple lenses with which to view social phenomena. They have to be equipped with knowledge of multiple cases in order to precisely diagnose and solve social problems. The starting point is that we need to learn what other countries (governments) have done and have been doing in similar situations.

This textbook is a response to requests from practitioners in the field. Although the importance of a comparative perspective in the field of public administration has often been overlooked for the past few decades, we still believe that comparative perspectivesare a necessary first step to under-standingpublic administration phenomena and identifying effective solutions.

While introducing and discussing American public administration issues, this textbook provides critical views of parallel Korean public administration issues for each chapter. In this regard, not only will students and practitioners be able to more deeply understand their own countries' public sector issues, but they also will be able to improve and extend their knowledge of effective solutions based on lessons learned from different countries' experiences. From this perspective, this book is for both American and Korean students studying public administration at the initial stage.

While there have been many public administration textbooks in the field (both in Korean and in English), there has been few books introducing public administration issues from a comparative perspective based on the two countries.

American public administration has been the mainstream in the field, and thus has had great impact on other countries' public administration throughout the world. In the meantime, Korean public administration, although its modern history is relatively short, has rapidly grownin terms of practical solutionsand theoretical implications in the field.

Tradition, cultures, behaviors, and attitudes that Korean public administration is based on are different from what American public administration is based upon. However, there are also many similarities between the two countries.

We hope that this textbook will serve as a main basis for sharing different experiences and discussing effective solutions among students, practitioners, and scholars between the two countries.

This book could not have been completed without the assistance of a number of dedicated individuals. In particular, we wish to thank Taehee Kim, Soojin Kim, and Mirae Kim, who are doctoral students at Rutgers-Newark, for their tremendous efforts to collect Korean cases and data for this book.

Special thanks go to Mr. Choonhwan Lim, President of Daeyoung Moonhwasa

Publisher, who supported us to publish this volume in Korea and Harry Briggs, Executive Editor of M.E. Sharpe, who helped us start reworking the original book published in the US from a comparative perspective.

Finally, we always are indebted to our famillies,—Madeleine Holzer, and our sons, Ben and Matt and his wife Wendy; my wife Serena and my mother Judith; Kyung-Yeon, and our sons, Joshua and Donghyun—who patiently tolerated our compulsive attention to this effort.

Marc Holzer,
Richard W. Schwester
Seok-Hwan Lee

Table of Contents

CHAPTER 1

CHAPTER 2

Organizational Theory and Management 54

CHAPTER 3

Managing Human Resources 104

CHAPTER 4

CHAPTER 5

CHAPTER 6

CHAPTER 7

CHAPTER 8

CHAPTER 9

CHAPTER 10

CHAPTER 11

CHAPTER 12

CHAPTER 13

CHAPTER 14

Public Administration in a Globalized World: Theories and Practices between the US and Korea

CHAPTER 1

Public Administration: An Indispensable Part of Society

This chapter introduces the reader to the foundational elements of government and public administration. It reviews many of the essential characteristics of government, such as revenue collection, government expenditures, and government workforce. It also presents an overview of the services that government provides and how those services affect citizens on a daily basis. Furthermore, this chapter constructs a working definition of public administration and discusses key concepts that are essential to the field.

"The care of human life and happiness... is the first and only legitimate object of good government."

THOMAS JEFFERSON
Third President of the United States
(1743–1846)

Environmental Police Unit Officers with the Department of Sanitation of New York take precautions when dealing with hazardous waste.

GOVERNMENT REQUIRES RESOURCES

There is no question that government spends a great deal of money. And theoretically—just like any other organization—the government must make money before it can spend money. So, where does government get its money and how does it spend it? How does this process affect people on a daily basis? These are just some of the questions we will answer in this introductory chapter.

Let's start with the basics. Like all organizations, the government typically must take in money before expending it. In rare situations, government can spend money it did not collect; that will be discussed in Chapter 9, "Public Budgeting." Unlike organizations in the private or nonprofit sectors, government has the power to tax. Taxation, one of the federal government's constitutional rights under the founding documents of the United States, is necessary to support the three branches of government, particularly the executive branch with its wide array of functions. State constitutions extend that taxing power to states, which then authorize counties, cities, towns, villages, and special districts to levy taxes.

> "What made you choose this career is what made me go into politics—a chance to serve, to make a difference. It is not just a job. It is a vocation."
>
> **TONY BLAIR**
> Prime Minister of GreatBritain

Governments are considered sovereign bodies, holding the highest authority in a specific region; therefore, government is granted unique powers under which it may implement its authority. Taxation is one of those unique powers. Unlike companies, which make money by selling a product or a service, the government takes in funds by taxing its citizenry. These taxes are collected by local, state, and federal agencies and pay for a broad range of services that meet citizens' daily needs. The nature of these needs will be discussed throughout this chapter, but first we will sketch out the amount of money government spends on a yearly basis.

In 2007 (the latest year for which the actual state and local spending figures were available at the time this book was written) the federal, state, and local governments in the United States spent over $4 trillion. Federal spending represented about 63 percent of all spending by governments. The U.S. federal government spent about $2.7 trillion, and state and local governments spent about $1.6 trillion.

To understand the impact that government spending has on the economy of the United States, it is sometimes helpful to use economic terms. One often-used term for gauging the nation's economy is the gross domestic product (GDP). The GDP is a measure based on the amount of goods and services produced within the borders of the United States. There are numerous ways to measure this figure, but the most straightforward is simply to add together the total amount of money spent on pro-

FIGURE 1.1 – U.S. GOVERNMENT ORGANIZATIONAL CHART

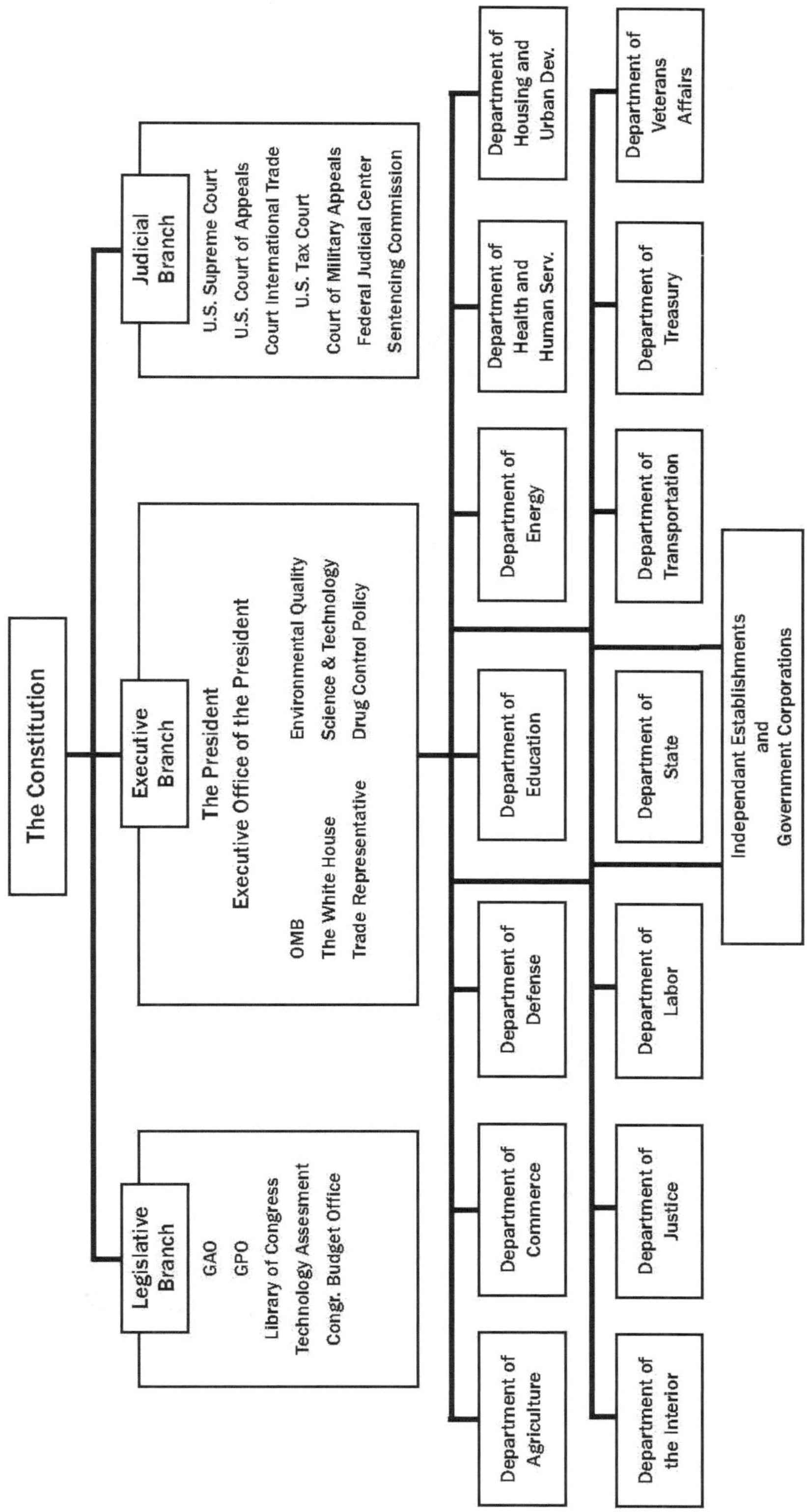

Source: Washburn University School of Law, U.S. Federal Resources, www.washlaw.edu/doclaw/orgchart/mainog.html.

ducing these goods and services. Understandably, one may think that the GDP measures only the private sector's economic activity; in reality, however, public sector activity makes up a large percentage of the GDP. Federal, state, and local government spending was approximately 32 percent of the U.S. GDP in 2007 (see

FIGURE 1.2 – TOTAL GOVERNMENT EXPENDITURES (IN BILLIONS OF DOLLARS)

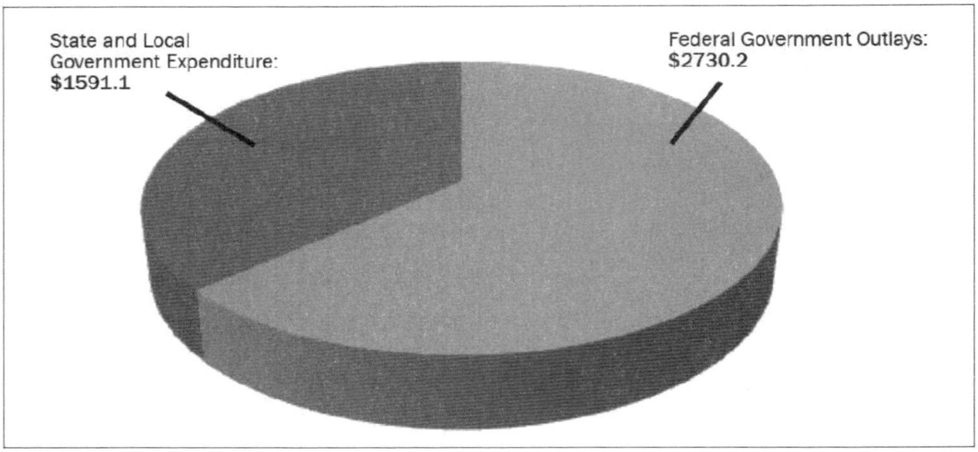

Source: U.S. Government Printing Office, Office of Management and Budget (OMB). 200. "Budget of the U.S. Government: Historical Tables Fiscal Year 2009." www.gpoaccess.gov/usbudget/fy09/hist.html.

FIGURE 1.3 – GOVERNMENT SPENDING AS A PERCENTAGE OF GDP (IN BILLIONS OF DOLLARS)

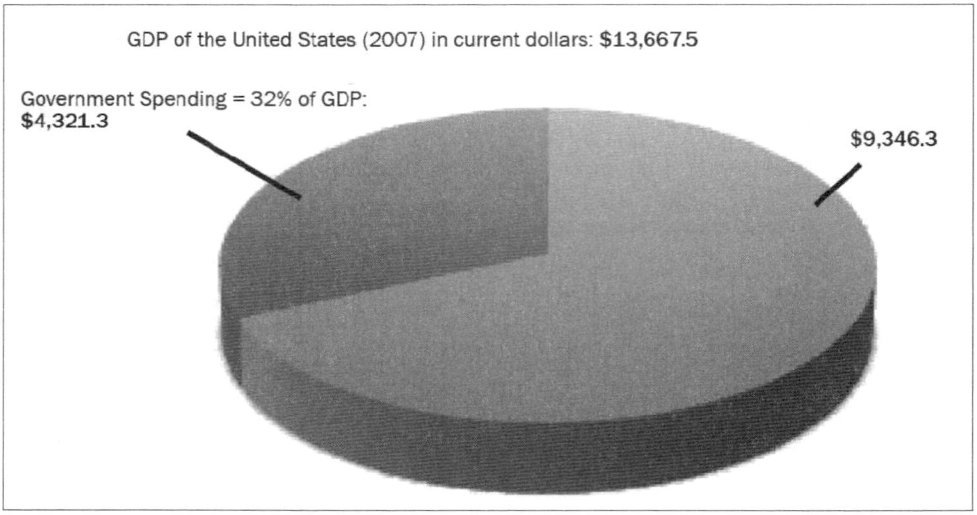

Source: U.S. Government Printing Office, Office of Management and Budget (OMB). 200. "Budget of the U.S. Government: Historical Tables Fiscal Year 2009." www.gpoaccess.gov/usbudget/fy09/hist.html.

Figures 1.2 and 1.3). It is important to remember that government not only provides an array of services with the money it spends but that such spending contributes significantly to the health and stability of the nation's economy.

To spend trillions of dollars, governments need to take in as much money every year—a feat that is accomplished through both taxation and fee-based services. Among the various taxes government collects from its citizens is the sales tax, which is typically levied by states. Sales taxes are encountered at most retail stores when a good is sold to the final customer in a transaction. A majority of states do not tax food purchases, and many other goods and services such as medical care, landscaping, salon, and taxi and courier services are exempt from taxation in some states. In 2008 sales taxes ranged from zero in states such as New Hampshire and Alaska to 7.25 percent in California; county or local sales taxes often add to those taxes at the cash register. Other common levies—including the income tax, property tax, inheritance tax, and excise tax—are used to create the revenue needed to provide the public services that citizens expect and demand. In addition, tolls on roads, bridges, and tunnels are considered a direct tax for the use of integrated transportation networks.

A large part of government funding at the federal level comes from employment taxes,

FIGURE 1.4 – COMPOSITION OF SOCIAL INSURANCE AND RETIREMENT RECEIPTS, 2000–2007

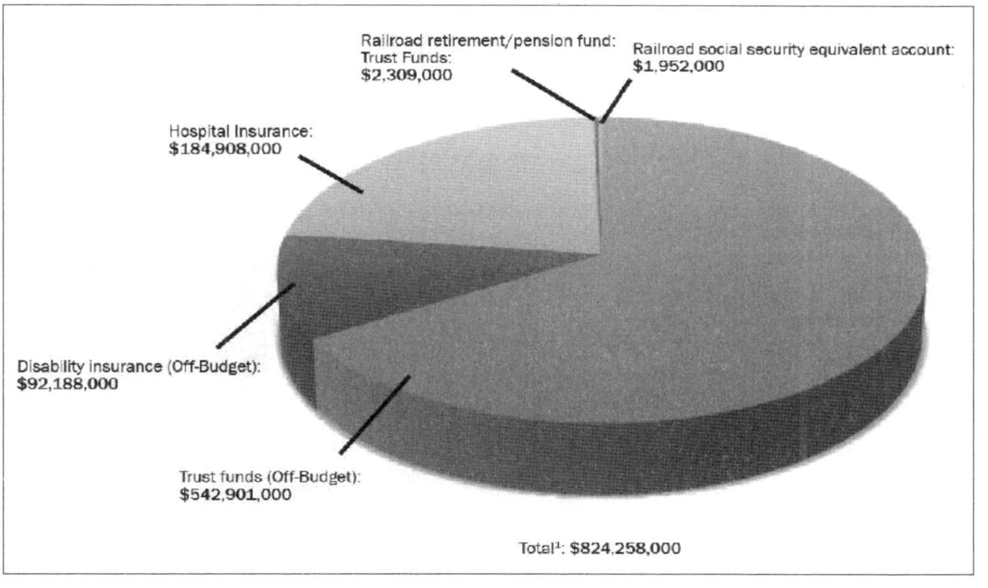

Source: U.S. Government Printing Office, Office of Management and Budget (OMB). 2008. "Budget of the U.S. Government: Historical Tables Fiscal Year 2009." www.gpoaccess.gov/usbudget/fy09/hist.html. Note: Unless otherwise noted, all receipts shown in this figure are trust funds and on-budget.
[1]On-budget and off-budget.

which are directed toward specific social programs that generally provide support for citizens when they have reached the age of retirement or are disabled. Among the programs covered by payroll taxes are Social Security benefits and Medicaid and Medicare insurance. Employees also contribute to U.S. unemployment insurance and to the pension funds of the federal workforce. These revenue sources are collected and used in a

FIGURE 1.5 – 2007 TOTAL GOVERNMENT RECEIPTS (IN BILLIONS OF DOLLARS)

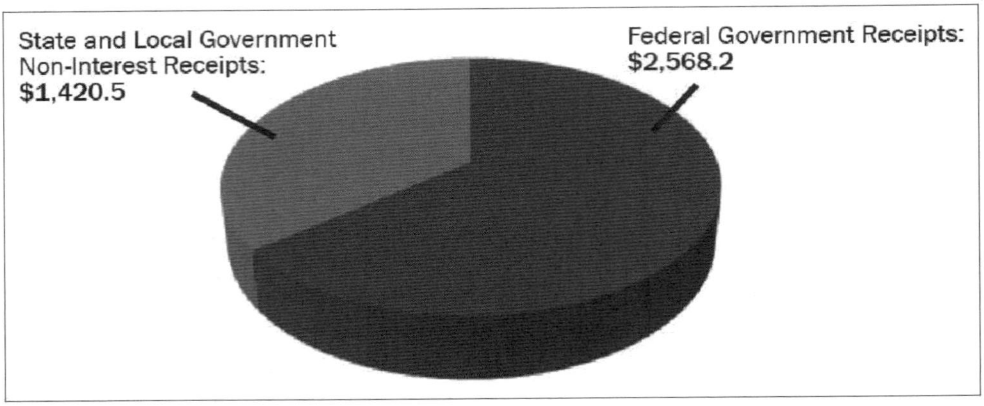

Source: U.S. Government Printing Office, Office of Management and Budget (OMB). 2008. "Budget of the U.S. Government: Historical Tables Fiscal Year 2009." http://www.gpoaccess.gov/usbudget/fy09/hist.html.

FIGURE 1.6 – 2007 GOVERNMENT RECEIPTS BY SOURCE (IN MILLIONS OF DOLLARS)

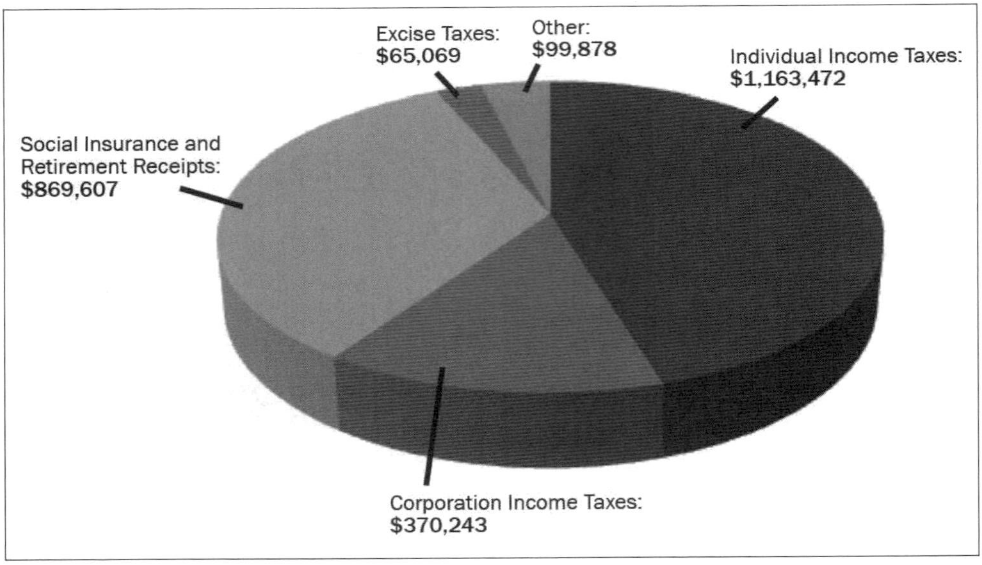

Source: U.S. Government Printing Office, Office of Management and Budget (OMB). 2008. "Budget of the U.S. Government: Historical Tables Fiscal Year 2009." http://www.gpoaccess.gov/usbudget/fy09/hist.html.

different manner than other revenue sources: They are earmarked, or set aside, as trust funds for the benefit of those who paid in (see Figure 1.4). The money put in by users will be taken out by users when they are in need of various insurance programs.

Government funds also come from fees. These fees make up a smaller portion of a government's income and tend to be more significant on the state and local levels. Fees are charged for access to certain desirable locations, such as public beaches or state parks. Fees may also be charged for obtaining a driver's license, a passport, or

FIGURE 1.7 – 2008 U.S. MILITARY SPENDING VS. THE WORLD (IN BILLIONS OF DOLLARS AND % OF WORLD TOTAL)

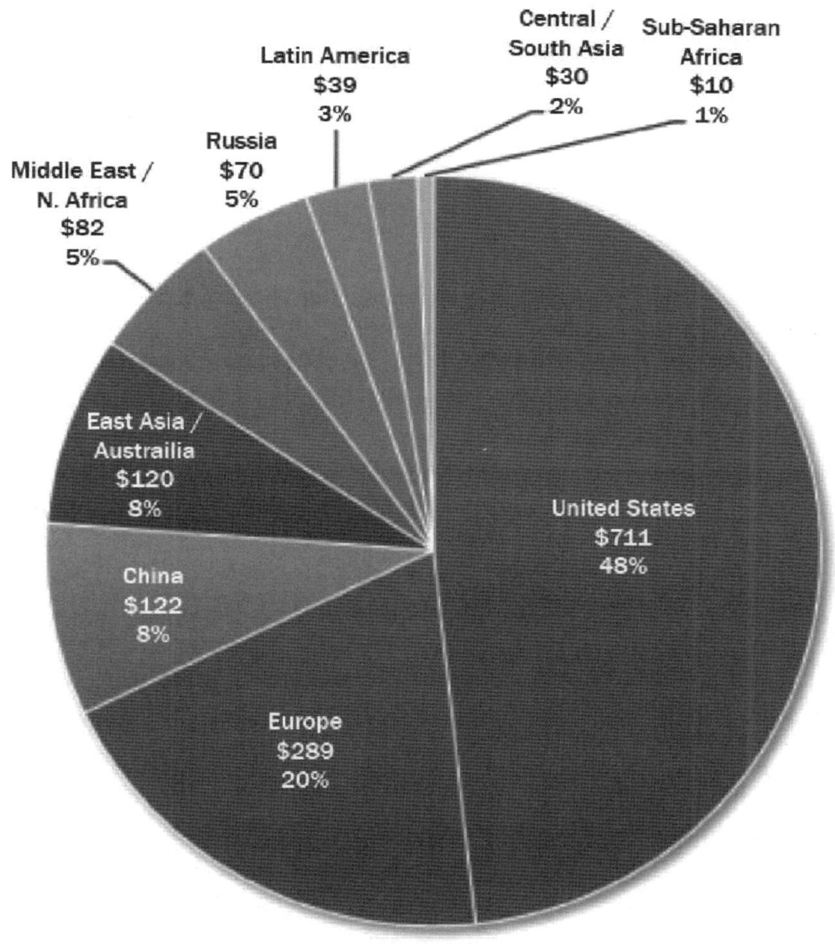

2008 Total Military Spending: $1.473 Trillion

Source: Global Issues. 2010. "World Military Spending." http://www.globalissues.org/article/75/world-military-spending#WorldMilitarySpending.

to get a building permit for an addition to a house or to build in a certain location. Figures 1.5 and 1.6 indicate the total extent of government revenue.

What exactly does the public sector spend money on? A large portion of federal expenditures go toward defense and other international programs. In 2007 the U.S. Department of Defense (DoD) had a budget of about $600 billion. Half of the entire world's military expenditures are spent by the United States alone (see Figure 1.7). In comparison to other expenditures made by the federal government, DoD spending accounts for about 22 percent of the federal budget. Another large portion of the federal government's spending goes toward the insurance programs mentioned earlier, such as Social Security and Medicare. Because the government is required by law to pay for such programs, they are often referred to as mandatory expenditures. In 2007 the federal government spent about $1 trillion on Social Security and Medicare. That accounts for almost 40 percent of the federal budget. In total, funds spent on defense, Social Security, and Medicare make up about 60 percent of all federal expenditures.

Federal spending makes up about 65 percent of all government expenditures, with state and local governments accounting for the other 35 percent. In 2007 state and local government budgets in the United States exceeded $1.5 trillion—money used by government to provide a range of services its citizens access on a daily basis. This spending contributes significantly to the country's economy and employment, and it allows government to provide selected services that would otherwise be challenging to provide on a private basis. Figure 1.8 shows a breakdown of all government spending.

FIGURE 1.8 – 2007 TOTAL GOVERNMENT EXPENDITURES BY MAJOR CATEGORY (IN BILLIONS OF DOLLARS)

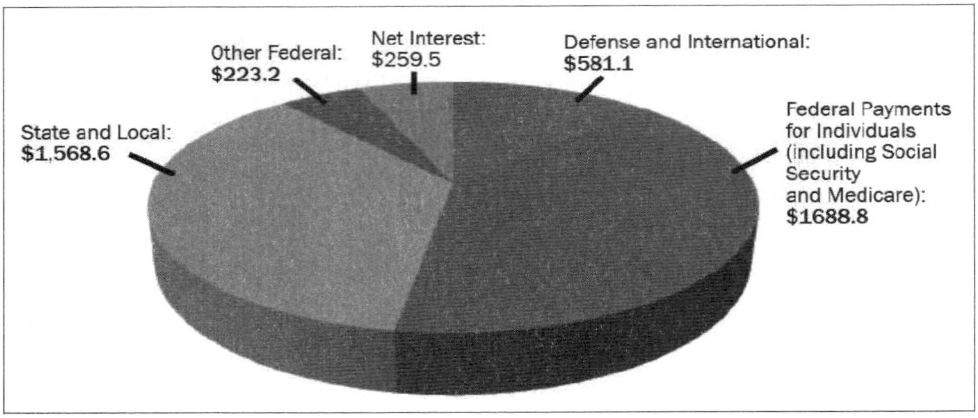

Source: U.S. Government Printing Office, Office of Management and Budget (OMB). 2008. "Budget of the U.S. Government: Historical Tables Fiscal Year 2009." http://www.gpoaccess.gov/usbudget/fy09/hist.html.

The federal, state, and local governments in the United States employed about 23 million people in 2007. Millions of others were employed to fill public sector positions via contractual relationships with private organizations: management consultants, temporary workers, technicians, and the like. According to the Bureau of Labor Statistics (BLS) as of September 2007, this amounts to approximately 17 percent of all employed individuals in the United States, not including farm payroll (BLS 2007). According to Paul Light, the Paulette Goddard Professor of Public Service at New York University and the former director of Governmental Studies at the Brookings Institution, as of 2002 the number of people employed by federal contracts was about 8 million (Light 2003). This underscores the importance of government employment in relationship to the U.S. economy."

The federal government, while the largest single government employer, employs far fewer people than the combined state and local governments throughout the nation. In addition, over the past several decades, the federal labor force has been decreasing steadily, while the state and local labor forces have been increasing in size. In 1980, for example, the federal government employed more than 4.9 million people (military and civilian); nine years later, its ranks peaked at nearly 5.3 million employees. Since then, the federal government has been scaling back the size of its labor force. As a percentage of the U.S. workforce, it declined from about 5 percent in 1989 to 3 percent in 2007, meaning more than a million jobs were shed in less than 20

FIGURE 1.9 – GOVERNMENT EMPLOYMENT AND PERCENTAGE OF POPULATION, 2007

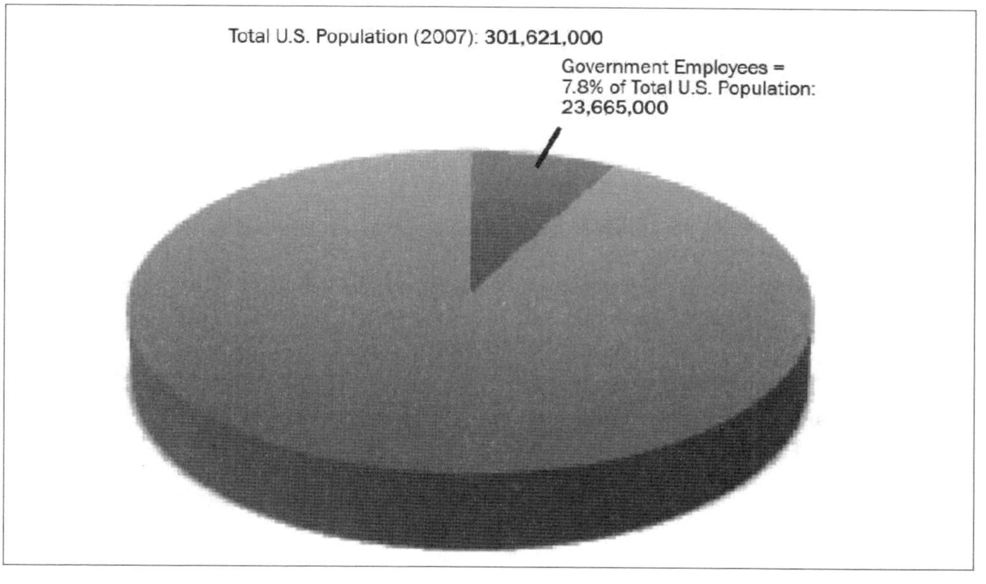

Source: U.S. Government Printing Office, Office of Management and Budget (OMB). 2008. "Budget of the U.S. Government: Historical Tables Fiscal Year 2009." http://www.gpoaccess.gov/usbudget/fy09/hist.htm.

years. At the same time, state and local levels have been behaving in just the opposite manner. In 1980 state and local governments employed nearly 13.4 million people. This number increased to over 19 million in 2007, accounting for about 14 percent of the total U.S. workforce. Although state and local governments increased their labor force by about 6 million people over three decades, in comparison to the growth of the U.S. population, this number is not out of proportion, and as a percent of the total workforce it constitutes about 13 percent. Thus, total government employment (federal, state, local) has stayed somewhat consistent—on average—since 1980, representing about 17 percent of the total workforce, with a high in 1980 of 18.4 percent. It is now (as of 2007) about 16 percent of the entire workforce. Figure 1.9 summarizes personnel figures for local, state, and federal governments.

Clearly, a significant portion of the U.S. workforce is employed by the government.

FIGURE 1.10 – FEDERAL GOVERNMENT CIVILIAN EMPLOYEES BY FUNCTION, DECEMBER 2007

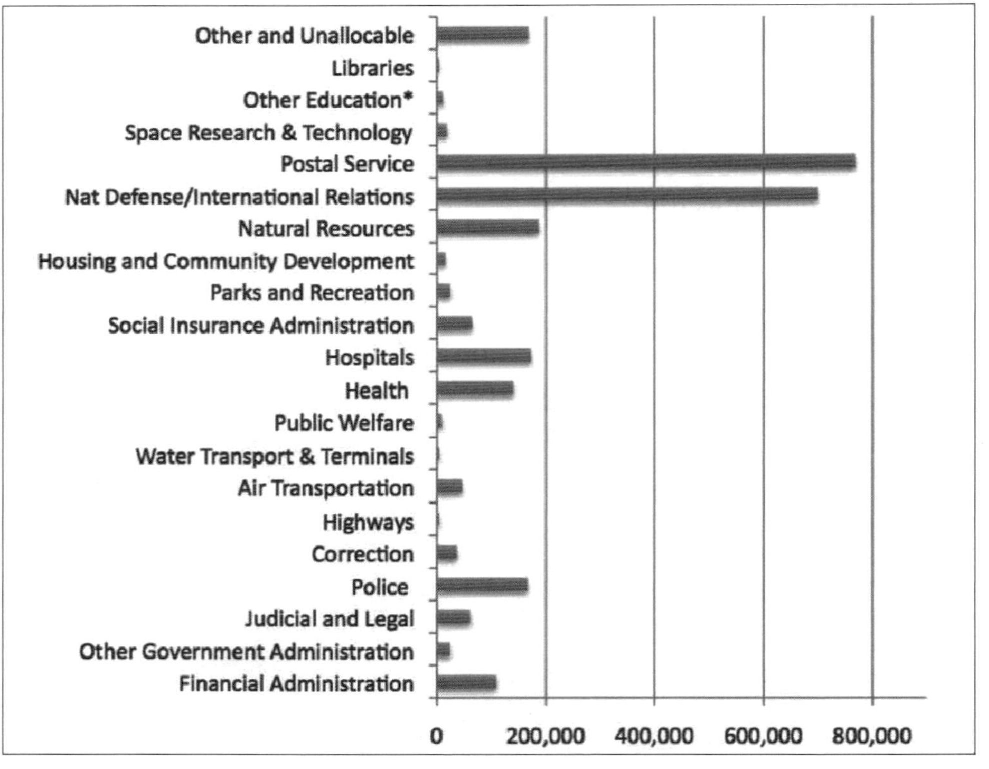

Source: U.S. Census Bureau, Governments Division Employment and Payroll. 2010. "Historical Data" http://www2.census.gov/govs/apes/07fedfun.pdf.

**Includes Department of Education and the National Science Foundation, plus parts of the Bureau of Indian Affairs.*

What do all of these people do? On the state and local levels it is more challenging to identify how the numbers break down exactly, but on the federal level we can classify employees by their designated function. Figure 1.10 illustrates that the two largest employee categories, by far, are National Security and the U.S Postal Service.

What Do We Get for All of These Resources?

Citizens of the United States come in contact with government on a daily basis—often without even realizing it. From the moment you wake up in the morning, government helps ensures your health, safety, and well-being. It continues to do so while you sleep.

In the morning you expect to wake to your alarm clock rather than some pesky noise such as a lawnmower, construction, or a barking dog. Typically, you will not hear such noises because government helps to regulate such activities. In New York City, for example, construction activity is not allowed to begin until 7:00 a.m. Likewise, a citizen may not use equipment such as a lawnmower or a leaf blower before 7:00 a.m. Such policies go a long way toward fostering respect among neighbors. In addition to noise ordinances, thousands of other ordinances facilitate the creation and maintenance of a livable environment. They range from how citizens should deal with waste removal to whether or not they may purchase and use fireworks. Ordinances—enforced by public servants—help to establish reasonable norms by which we conduct our daily activities.

> "And so, my fellow Americans, ask not what your country can do for you; ask what you can do for your country."
>
> **JOHN F. KENNEDY**
> 35th President of the United States

Beyond municipal ordinances, broader laws and regulations help us function in our daily activities. The simple act of obeying a stop sign may seem commonplace—and sensible—but what might happen if we did not have laws in place that require us to drive in a certain manner? Government has codified these very basic rules of the road. We know that drivers must stop their vehicles when approaching a red light and slow down when approaching a yellow light. These rules allow traffic to flow in an organized manner.

What about water consumption? It seems like second nature to turn on a water faucet and get a glass of cold drinkable water, or to request a glass of water with your meal while dining at a restaurant. Although we typically do not think about the cleanliness and safety of this water, it is clear that somebody must. That is why we rely on government. The federal Environmental Protection Agency (EPA) is responsible for setting a national standard for drinking water and ensuring that none of the 90 different types of banned contaminants taint our water system. In total, the United States has over 170,000 water systems and on average delivers about 100,000 gallons of water annually to each residence (EPA 2010). Most Americans rarely think about the complexity of this infrastructure and the amount of support and control required to keep the supply of drinkable water safe and easily accessible. It is important to remember, though, that access to clean, safe water is not cheap; according to the United Nations (2010), nearly 20 percent of the world's population does not benefit from having clean drinking water.

The government not only establishes these ordinances, laws, and regulations but also serves as a major provider of services such as public education. From the moment you enter kindergarten until you graduate at the end of your senior year of high school, the U.S. education system provides the tools you need to become a responsible adult. Throughout the United States in any given year, there are about 50 million school-age children attending elementary, middle, or high schools—a total of 97,000 public schools. To maintain such an expansive system requires a great deal of pooled resources in the form of public sector budgets.

While children are at school, adults are generally at work. Although we may rarely think twice about the dangers that might occur at the workplace, the Occupational Safety and Health Administration (OSHA) does. This federal agency is charged with ensuring that any given workplace provides a safe and healthy environment for all its employees. Since OSHA's creation in 1971, on-the-job injuries have decreased by 61 percent and fatalities by 44 percent. A decrease on such a large scale cannot happen without a great deal of planning and work. In 2006 OSHA inspected over 35,000 workplaces. In addition to the federal government, many state agencies conduct inspections, and an additional 58,000 were completed on the state level that same year. Although most of us are not concerned with work-related injuries on a daily basis, it is important to remember that one of the main reasons we can afford to be so complacent about workplace safety is the government's vigilance in ensuring our protection.

Water Tunnel Is Spectacular Feat of Engineering—and Hard Work

Mayor Rudolph W. Giuliani

Mayor's WINS Address, Sunday, August 16, 1998 (New York City, 1998)

"New York City has always been a place where seemingly impossible things are made possible—in business, art, literature and so many other realms—because no other City can match the ambition, hard work, and perseverance of our people. This Thursday [August 13, 1998], these qualities were on full display in Central Park for the opening of the Third Water Tunnel—which represents the culmination of decades of hard work and sacrifice by thousands of New Yorkers."

There are literally thousands of additional programs, services, and interventions that government initiates and that we encounter every day. Some of the key public sector services are listed in the section that follows. Although we might not access many on a daily basis, the safety net they provide allows us to go about our daily routines.

How Government Is Organized to Deliver Services

The Interstate Highway System

"Although the Federal-Aid Highway Act of 1944 authorized designation of a 'National System of Interstate Highways,' the legislation did not authorize an initiating program to build it. This act started the initial design of the system, but it was not until the Federal-Aid Highway Act of 1956 that the system started to be constructed. Currently, the Interstate System is 46,876 miles long. The final estimate of the cost of the Interstate System was issued in 1991. It estimated that the total cost would be $128.9 billion, with a Federal share of $114.3 billion."

(Source: U.S. Department of Transportation, Federal Highway Administration, "Frequently Asked Questions," http://www.fhwa.dot.gov/interstate/faq.htm.)

Federal Housing Administration

"The Federal Housing Administration, generally known as 'FHA,' is the largest government insurer of mortgages in the world. A part of the United States Department of Housing and Urban Development (HUD), FHA provides mortgage insurance on single-family, multifamily, manufactured homes and hospital loans made by FHA-approved lenders throughout the United States and its territories. While borrowers must meet certain requirements established by FHA to qualify for the insurance, lenders bear less risk because FHA will pay the lender if a homeowner defaults on his or her loan. FHA has insured over 37 million home mortgages and 47,205 multifamily project mortgages since 1934. Currently, FHA has 5.2 million insured single-family mortgages and 13,000 insured multifamily projects in its portfolio."

(Source: U.S. Department of Housing and Urban Development, "Federal Housing Administration Overview," http://portal.hud.gov/portal/page/portal/HUD/federal_housing_administration.)

Consumer Protection

"If you exercise your right to receive a free credit report, use the National Do Not Call Registry to block unwanted telemarketing calls, or refer to product warranties, care labels in your clothes, or stickers showing the energy costs of home appliances, you are taking advantage of laws enforced by the FTC's [Federal Trade Commission's] Bureau of Consumer Protection. The Bureau of Consumer Protection works to protect consumers against unfair, deceptive, or fraudulent practices in the marketplace. The Bureau conducts investigations, sues companies and people who violate the law, develops rules to protect consumers, and educates consumers and businesses about their rights and responsibilities. The Bureau also collects complaints about consumer fraud and identity theft and makes them available to law enforcement agencies across the country."

(Source: Federal Trade Commission, "About the Bureau of Consumer Protection," www.ftc.gov/bcp/about.shtm.)

National Weather Service

"The National Weather Service is a component of the National Oceanic and Atmospheric Administration (NOAA). NOAA is an Operating Unit of the U.S. Department of Commerce.... The National Weather Service (NWS) provides weather, hydrologic, and climate forecasts and warnings for the United States, its territories, adjacent waters and ocean areas, for the protection of life and property and the enhancement of the national economy. NWS data and products form a national information database and infrastructure which can be used by other governmental agencies, the private sector, the public, and the global community."

(Source: National Oceanic and Atmospheric Administration's National Weather Service, "About NOAA's National Weather Service," www.nws.noaa.gov/admin.php.)

Federal Student Financial Aid Programs

"Federal Student Aid's core mission is to ensure that all eligible individuals benefit from federal financial assistance—grants, loans and work-study programs—for education beyond high school. The programs we administer comprise the nation's largest source of student aid. Every year we provide more than $100 billion in new aid to nearly 14 million postsecondary students and their families. Our staff of 1,100 is based in 10 cities in addition to our Washington headquarters."

(Source: Federal Student Aid, "About Us," http://studentaid.ed.gov/PORTALSWebApp/students/english/aboutus.jsp.)

EXERCISE 1.1

Create a New Government (Simulation)

Working as a team, create a new governing body for your university using the strategy established to create the Iraqi National Assembly as highlighted in the following simulation. Establish a list of the key principles upon which this new governance structure is based, and explain why each principle is important.

Sarah Kavanagh and Javaid Khan, "A Good Government Is Hard to Build," *The New York Times*: The Learning Network, March 30, 2005, http://learning.blogs.nytimes.com/2005/03/30/a-good-government-is-hard-to-build

Food and Drug Safety Programs

"FDA [the Food and Drug Administration] is an agency within the Department of Health and Human Services and...is responsible for protecting the public health by assuring the safety, efficacy, and security of human and veterinary drugs, biological products, medical devices, our nation's food supply, cosmetics, and products that emit radiation. The FDA is also responsible for advancing the public health by helping to speed innovations that make medicines and foods more effective, safer, and more affordable; and helping the public get the accurate, science-based information they need to use medicines and foods to improve their health."

(Source: U.S. Department of Health and Human Services, U.S. Food and Drug Administration, "Centers and Offices," www.fda.gov/AboutFDA/CentersOffices/default.htm.)

Federal Emergency Response

"FEMA's mission is to support our citizens and first responders to ensure that as a nation we work together to build, sustain, and improve our capability to prepare for, protect against, respond to, recover from, and mitigate all hazards."

"FEMA has more than 3,700 full time employees. They work at FEMA headquarters in Washington D.C., at regional and area offices across the country, the Mount Weather Emergency Operations Center, and the National Emergency Training Center in Emmitsburg, Maryland. FEMA also has nearly 4,000 standby disaster assistance employees who are available for deployment after disasters. Often FEMA works in partnership with other organizations that are part of the nation's emergency management system. These partners include state and local emergency management agencies, 27 federal agencies and the American Red Cross."

(Source: U.S. Department of Homeland Security, Federal Emergency Management Agency, "About FEMA," http://www.fema.gov/about/index.shtm#o.)

AMTRAK

"As the nation's intercity passenger rail operator, Amtrak connects America in safer, greener and healthier ways. With 21,000 route miles in 46 states, the District of Columbia and three Canadian provinces, Amtrak operates more than 300 trains each day—at speeds up to 150 mph—to more than 500 destinations. Amtrak also is the operator of choice for state-supported corridor services in 15 states and for four commuter rail agencies."

(Source: AMTRAK, "Amtrak Information and Facts," www.amtrak.com/servlet/ContentServer/Page/1241256467960/1237608345018.)

United States Post Office

"The United States Postal Service delivers more mail to more addresses in a larger geographical area than any other post in the world. We deliver to more than 150 million homes, businesses and Post Office boxes in every state, city, town and borough in this country. Everyone living in the U.S. and its territories has access to postal services and pays the same postage regardless of his or her location."

(Source: United States Postal Service, "Postal Facts 2010," www.usps.com/communications/newsroom/postalfacts.htm.)

Organizational Chart of Municipality—City of Burlington, New Jersey

"The City of Burlington operates in accordance with the Mayor-Council form of government. The Mayor is the chief executive of the municipality, while the legislative powers of the City are exercised by the Common Council. The Common Council consists of seven members, three at-large Councilpersons and one from each of the four wards, who shall serve for a term of four years. Various boards, committees, and departments comprise other areas of the City's government."

FIGURE 1.11 - CITY OF BURLINGTON ORGANIZATIONAL CHART

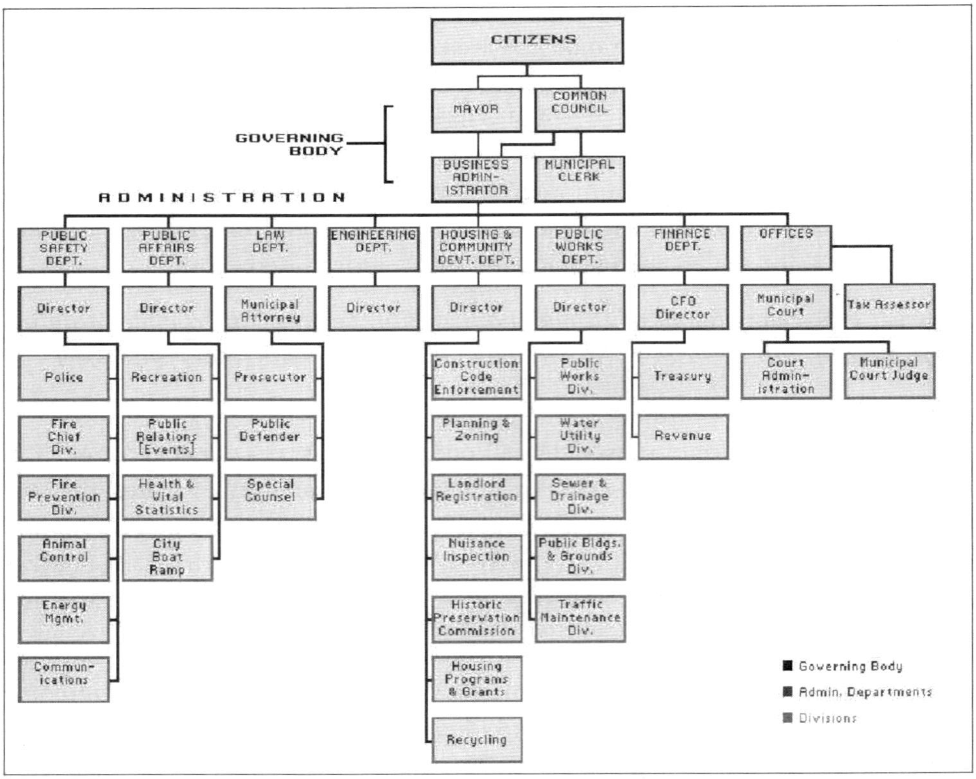

Source: City of Burlington, New Jersey, USA Website. 2008. "The Administration: City Government, Departments & Divisions Organization Chart." www.burlingtonnj.us/Organiz.html.

How Government Serves Others

It is clear that government affects us on a daily basis, but it is important to remember that government not only serves the individual; it lends its resources to a number of efforts that aid the common good.

Government support for the not-for-profit sector is one example of the public sector promoting the common good. The not-for-profit sector or nonprofit sector is generally viewed as the charitable arm of American society. What differentiates it from the private sector? Unlike for-profit companies, organizations in the nonprofit sector are not driven to increase revenue by an economic bottom line. Rather, they are driven by a unique mission upon which all of their organizational programs and activities are focused. Nonprofit organizations typically try to limit their spending on administrative functions and use the bulk of their funding for mission-specific activities.

According to the Urban Institute (2010), about 1.4 million nonprofit organizations account for 5.2 percent of the national GDP. Nonprofit organizations range widely in size and scope of activities. Some nonprofits provide arts, culture, education, environmental monitoring, health care, human services and seemingly endless lists of services that promote the common good. Not only do nonprofits give to the community, they also enable citizens to give of their time and energy to others. The Bureau of Labor Statistics (2010) estimates that approximately 27 percent of adults (more than 60 million individuals) volunteered at a nonprofit organization in 2009. To some degree, many people believe that nonprofits hold society together.

> "The call to service is one of the highest callings you will hear and your country can make."
>
> **LEE H. HAMILTON**
> Former U.S. Congressman; Vice Chairman, 9/11 Commission

How does this have anything to do with government? The government supports the nonprofit sector in two primary ways: First, it has created a special tax status for nonprofit organizations that allows them to operate outside of the typical tax structure. Second, government makes direct contributions to nonprofit organizations through grant funding for specific programs.

The special tax status developed by the Internal Revenue Service (IRS) for public charities—known as 501(c)(3)—provides nonprofit organizations with an exemption from paying federal income tax. It also ensures that all individuals who make contributions to such organizations can deduct those donations from their own income. To qualify as an exempt organization, nonprofits must follow certain rules. According to the guidelines listed on the IRS website, they must be organized specifically for an exempt purpose, as outlined in the following text:

> The exempt purposes set forth in section 501(c)(3) are charitable, religious, educational, scientific, literary, testing for public safety, fostering national or international amateur sports competition, and preventing cruelty to

> children or animals. The term *charitable* is used in its generally accepted legal sense and includes relief of the poor, the distressed, or the underprivileged; advancement of religion; advancement of education or science; erecting or maintaining public buildings, monuments, or works; lessening the burdens of government; lessening neighborhood tensions; eliminating prejudice and discrimination; defending human and civil rights secured by law; and combating community deterioration and juvenile delinquency. (IRS.gov, "Exempt Purposes—Internal Revenue Code Section 501(c)(3)," updated December 7, 2009, www.irs.gov/charities/charitable/article/0,,id=175418,00.html).

Furthermore, IRS rules indicate that nonprofit organizations cannot be owned by any private shareholder or individual, and the goal of such organizations cannot be to increase the wealth of such a person or persons. In addition, to meet this exempt status, nonprofit organizations cannot exist to promote a specific political campaign, and they must restrict their lobbying and advocacy activities.

> "No one is useless in this world who lightens the burden of it for someone else."
>
> **BENJAMIN FRANKLIN**
> American Statesman; Ambassador; Patriot

Aside from granting a special tax status to not-for-profit charitable organizations, government also contributes a great deal of money outright to the nonprofit sector. In 2005 the U.S. government provided about $18 billion in direct payments to nonprofits; that translates into about 30 percent of all revenue for nonprofit organizations in 2005 (Wing, Pollack, and Blackwood 2008). Some of the recipients of these funds are well-known organizations and typically have a strong presence in our communities. For instance, the Boys and Girls Clubs of America received about $81 million in 2005. Their mission is to "enable all young people, especially those who need us most, to reach their full potential as productive, caring, responsible citizens" (www.bgca.org). For over 40 years, the community-based organization Experience Works, originally called Green Thumb, Inc., has received about $85 million in government dollars to "improve the lives of older people through employment, community service, and training" (www.experienceworks.org). By promoting the nonprofit sector, government is strengthening the fabric of American civil society.

Another effort by government to enhance the common good is the promotion of research. Although this may sound like an abstract concept that rarely affects the lives of everyday people, it is just the opposite. One of the main avenues through which research funding has a broad public impact is the National Institutes of Health, or the NIH. The NIH was formed in 1887 and is now composed of 27 different research institutions and groups. It is one of the largest funders of scientific research worldwide. In 2007 the NIH made over 47,000 research awards at a total cost of about $20 billion. Over its history, the NIH has provided funding for groundbreaking dis-

Accountability

Accountability in the public sector most often boils down to dual aspects: accountability for what and accountability to whom. Typically, accountability is a political construction. Public managers are accountable to their legislative counterparts. The delegation of power takes place when Congress assigns its constitutional Article I, Section 8 powers to the executive branch. Clause 18 of this section specifies that Congress has the power "to make all laws which shall be necessary and proper for carrying into execution the foregoing powers, and all other powers vested by this Constitution in the government of the United States, or in any department or office thereof." While the courts have shifted back and forth on the issue of congressional delegation, it is clearly stated in the "delegation doctrine" that Congress can delegate its power to the executive branch as long as the power is accompanied by sufficient standards or guidelines so the executive branch is controlled by Congress. Therefore, the chief executive is accountable to the legislature from which power was granted.

In a 2000 article for *Public Administration Review,* David Rosenbloom highlights the dimensions of accountability implemented to link public administration to a constitutional framework. Traditionally, the executive branch was seen as being under the purview of the executive (president) in a top-down accountability scheme. However, as Rosenbloom points out, this is not in line with the U.S. constitutional framework or with the interpretations handed down by the Supreme Court over the years. As Congress delegates its power, Congress provides oversight for that delegated power. Rosenbloom (2000) cites four acts passed by Congress to ensure this constitutional accountability: the Administrative Procedures Act, the Federal Advisory Committee Act (FACA), the Negotiated Rulemaking Act, and the Small Business Regulatory Enforcement Fairness Act.

Other observers divide accountability into a number of schemes and categories such as Bureaucratic, Legal, Professional and Political (Romzek and Dubnick 1987). Robert Behn (2001), in his text *Rethinking Democratic Accountability,* provides further insight into the question of professional accountability. Behn argues that accountability among public administrators should be based on their performance. He claims that systems of accountability should not be set up to deter behavior; they should be set up to provide incentives for desirable behavior (Behn 2001).

Implementation

Implementation is a concept that seems straightforward initially but raises many questions upon further examination. When, for instance, does implementation

(continued)

(continued)

begin? Who is responsible for implementation? Can the implementers change the mode of implementation? We look to the formation of the term implementation from the classic text by Pressman and Wildavsky (1973), *Implementation*. They write, "Implementation, to us, means just what Webster and Roget say it does: to carry out, accomplish, fulfill, produce, complete." They authors state that it is a policy that is being implemented, but they go further, providing a context for implementation. Implementation must have a clear goal; otherwise, it is difficult to determine the success of the implementation efforts. The challenge in defining implementation in this manner is that often the environment and conditions change. While initially stipulated with a clear goal, the process may change due to the environment in which the implementation is taking place. Ultimately, "implementers become responsible both for the initial conditions and for the objectives toward which they are supposed to lead" (Pressman and Wildavsky 1973).

Those responsible for implementation are sometime referred to as "street-level bureaucrats"—a term coined by Lipsky (1980). These men and women are implementing state policies; they are responsible for providing everyday services, including police, education, and waste disposal. Lipsky believes this aspect of implementation has grave consequences for society. He writes, "Thus, in a sense, street-level bureaucrats implicitly mediate aspects of constitutional relationships of citizens to the state. In short, they hold the key to a dimension of citizenship."

According to Merriam-Webster's Collegiate Dictionary, 11th ed., the verb implement means to "CARRY OUT, ACCOMPLISH; especially: to give practical effect to and ensure of actual fulfillment by concrete measures."

coveries throughout the scientific community (NIH, 2010). Since 1998 NIH research has contributed to increased prevention of type 2 diabetes, advanced treatments for breast cancer, and new knowledge about the transmission and suppression of HIV/AIDS. Table 1.1 summarizes some of the scientific breakthroughs made possible by NIH funding (NIH, 2009). This research—funded or conducted by the NIH—has saved millions of lives. Many other federal agencies have made similar advancements that dramatically improve our quality of life, including for example the National Science Foundation (2010), the National Institute of Food and Agriculture (2010), and the National Office of Public Health Genomics of the Centers for Disease Control and Prevention (2010).

In a world that becomes smaller each day in a technological sense—with, for instance, the ability to transmit information from the United States to China in a mat-

TABLE 1.1 – THE NIH ALMANAC—HISTORICAL DATA

Year	Discoveries
1998	Results from a National Cancer Institute (NCI) sponsored clinical trial showed that women at high risk of developing breast cancer who took the drug tamoxifen had 49 percent fewer cases of breast cancer than those who did not. Tamoxifen was hailed as the first drug to prevent breast cancer in women at high risk for the disease.
1999	A team of investigators led by a National Institute of Allergy and Infectious Diseases (NIAID) grantee discovered that a subspecies of chimpanzees native to west Africa are the origin of HIV-1, the virus responsible for the global AIDS pandemic.
2000	Researchers supported by National Institute of General Medical Sciences (NIGMS) demonstrated that a simple and inexpensive change in basic surgical procedures—giving patients more oxygen during and immediately after surgery—can cut the rate of wound infections in half, thus saving millions of dollars in hospital costs by helping to prevent postsurgical wound infection, nausea, and vomiting.
2001	A team composed of scientists from National Human Genome Research Institute (NHGRI) and National Institute of Neurological Disorders and Stroke (NINDS), grantees of National Heart, Lung, and Blood Institute (NHLBI) and National Institute on Aging (NIA), and others demonstrated that adult stem cells isolated from mouse bone marrow could become functioning heart muscle cells when injected into a damaged mouse heart. The new cells at least partially restored the heart's ability to pump blood.
2002	People with elevated levels of the amino acid homocysteine in the blood had nearly double the risk of Alzheimer's disease (AD), according to a team of scientists supported by NIA and NINDS. The findings, in a group of participants in NHLBI's long-running Framingham Study, are the first to tie homocysteine levels measured several years before with a later diagnosis of AD and the other dementias, providing some of the most powerful evidence yet of an association between high plasma homocysteine and later significant memory loss.
2003	Researchers supported by National Institute of Mental Health (NIMH) found a gene called 5-HTT that influences whether people become depressed when faced with major life stresses such as relationship problems, financial difficulties and illness. The gene by itself does not cause depression, but it does affect how likely people are to get depressed when faced with major life stresses. Another study led by National Institute on Alcohol Abuse and Alcoholism (NIAAA) researchers found that this same gene affects drinking habits in college students. These studies are major contributions toward understanding how a person's response to their environment is influenced by their genetic makeup.

(continued)

TABLE 1.1 – THE NIH ALMANAC—HISTORICAL DATA

(continued)

Year	Discoveries
2004	An international clinical trial concluded that women should consider taking letrozole after five years of tamoxifen treatment to continue to reduce the risk of recurrence of breast cancer. This advance in breast cancer treatment will improve the outlook for many thousands of women. NCI supported the U.S. portion of the study, which offered one more example of the ability to interrupt the progression of a cancer using a drug that blocks a crucial metabolic pathway in the tumor cell.
2005	An HIV/AIDS vaccine developed by scientists at NIAID's Dale and Betty Bumpers Vaccine Research Center moved into its second phase of clinical testing in October. This vaccine contains synthetic genes representing HIV subtypes found in Europe, North America, Africa, and Asia that account about 85 percent of HIV infections worldwide.
2006	NCI-funded research spanning nearly two decades helped lead to U.S. Food and Drug Administration (FDA) approval for a vaccine to prevent cervical cancer, a disease that claims the lives of nearly 4,000 women each year in the United States. It is the first cancer vaccine approved by the FDA.
2007	An experimental vaccine—originally created and tested over the past two decades by NIAID scientists—appears safe and effective in preventing hepatitis E, a sometimes deadly viral disease prevalent in developing countries. A clinical trial involving nearly 2,000 healthy adults in Nepal, where the virus is widespread, found that the vaccine was nearly 96 percent effective in preventing hepatitis E during a follow-up period of about two years.

Source: National Institutes of Health, "The NIH Almanac—Historical Data," September 1, 2009, www.nih.gov/about/almanac/historical/chronology_of_events.htm.

ter of seconds—one must also consider the common good outside U.S. borders. Since the 1980s, globalization has increased at a particularly rapid pace, resulting in both positive and negative effects. Globalization has changed how Americans do business and has turned a national economy into a global economy. It has opened up markets for American products and has allowed for the importation of less expensive goods from developing markets—i.e., China, India, Brazil.

At the same time, U.S. citizens have also witnessed how globalization might affect their health and safety. Foodborne illnesses such as mad cow disease have traveled across borders. H1N1 and avian flu strains have entered the United States with relative ease. Globalization has made it easier for terrorists to attack American interests both within and outside the borders of the United States. This new global environment stresses the need for the U.S. government to increase national security while improving defensive measures on an international scale as well.

FIGURE 1.12 – NET COST OF OPERATIONS (DOLLARS IN THOUSANDS)

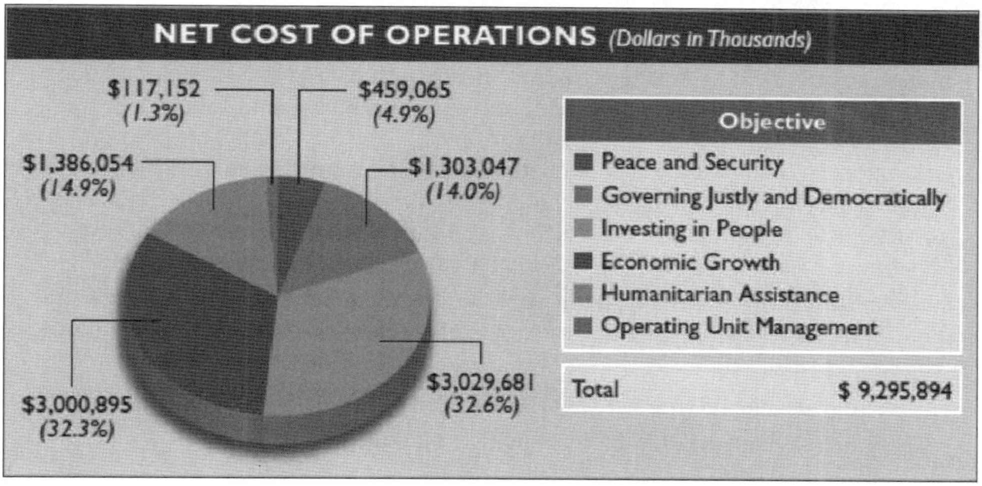

Source: USAID Policy. 2007. "Analysis of USAID's Financial Statements. Overview of Financial Position." www.usaid.gov/policy/afr07/mda_0400.html.

One of the federal government's most powerful tools in the international arena is the United States Agency for International Development, or USAID. Created in 1961 with the primary responsibility of providing long-range social and economic assistance, USAID has a vision of "accelerat[ing] the advance of democracy, prosperity and human well-being in developing countries." According to the agency, its mission is to facilitate "human progress in developing countries by reducing poverty, advancing democracy, building market economies, promoting security, responding to crises, and improving quality of life. Working with governments, institutions, and civil society, we assist individuals to build their own futures by mobilizing the full range of America's public and private resources through our expert presence overseas" (USAID 2008). To accomplish that mission, USAID has five strategic goals around which it organizes its operations: Peace and Security, Governing Justly and Democratically, Investing in People, Economic Growth, and Humanitarian Assistance. As displayed in Figure 1.12, in FY 2007 the total net cost of USAID operations was about $9.3 billion, and less than 2 percent of that was spent on management. More than $8 billion was spent on foreign aid.

Since its inception in 1961, USAID has revolutionized the concept of foreign assistance programs. According to the USAID website:

- More than 3 million lives are saved every year through USAID immunization programs.
- Oral rehydration therapy, a low cost and easily administered solution

EXERCISE 1.2

Jennifer Government: NationStates (Simulation)

In this nation-building simulation game, students take charge of a country and test their ability to improve its performance. Your decisions may reduce crime, improve educational achievement, lift people out of poverty, and accelerate economic growth. But improving performance is dependent upon the performance metrics you chose to establish. After completing the simulation, students will summarize the plan of action they have taken, justify those actions, and assess the outcomes of their decisions. In groups of three to five students, compare their strategies and results.

Jennifer Government: NationStates, www.nationstates.net

developed through USAID programs in Bangladesh, is credited with saving tens of millions of lives around the globe.

- There were 58 democratic nations in 1980. By 1995, this number had jumped to 115 nations.
- Life expectancy in the developing world has increased by about 33 percent, smallpox has been eradicated worldwide, and as of 2009, the number of the world's chronically undernourished has been reduced by 50 percent.
- The United Nations Drinking Water Supply and Sanitation Decade, in which USAID played a major role, resulted in 1.3 billion people receiving safe drinking water sources, and 750 million people receiving sanitation for the first time.
- With the help of USAID, 21,000 farm families in Honduras have been trained in improved land cultivation practices that have reduced soil erosion by 70,000 tons.
- Agricultural research sponsored by the United States sparked the "Green Revolution" in India. These breakthroughs in agricultural technology and practices resulted in the most dramatic increase in agricultural yields and production in the history of humankind, allowing nations like India and Bangladesh to become nearly food self-sufficient.
- In the past 50 years, infant and child death rates in the developing world have been reduced by 50 percent, and health conditions around the world have improved more during this period than in all previous human history.
- Early USAID action in southern Africa in 1992 prevented massive famine in the region, saving millions of lives.

- Literacy rates are up 33 percent worldwide in the last 25 years, and primary school enrollment has tripled in that period.

(Source: www.usaid.gov/policy/afro8/afro8_brochure.pdf)

Some observers may question the amount of money the U.S. government spends on foreign assistance. Some may think that money can be better spent within the borders of the United States. Ultimately, the answers to those questions remain a political decision. Nevertheless, it is clear that without U.S. assistance, the world would be a much different place. Whether through supporting the nonprofit community, investing in research, or providing assistance to the international community, federal government support enhances the quality of life as we know it. But what about local governments? What efforts can we identify that improve the quality of our lives on a local level?

Governments around the country continually take innovative initiatives to deliver public services as promised in their charters, by their elected officials, and by the appointed public servants who are committed to continuous improvement. For example, the city of Chicago makes enormous investments in police services. In 2002 the Chicago Police Department (CPD) launched the Citizen and Law Enforcement Analysis and Reporting (CLEAR) program. CLEAR is a broad database of crime statistics. The data are, in general, openly accessible through websites and provide both police officers and citizens detailed crime information in response to their inquiries. CLEAR data are displayed utilizing Geographic Information Systems (GIS) technology. Citizens may engage the system in multiple ways: First, they can report incidents through CLEAR. According to the website, those reports "should be criminal, quality of life or neighborhood disorder in nature, which affects more than one person and should be addressed by the police, city services and the community" (Chicago Police Department 2008). Second, citizens may sign up to receive regular updates of crime statistics within a certain area. Areas can be defined by ward, beat, district, etc. Finally, citizens can form block groups, such as those associated with small, geographically defined communities, or they can be represented as vertical block groups for residents of one building. Once a block group is formed, data about that specific block will then be posted in the CLEAR database. The database can also be useful to police officers. According to *Governing* magazine, police officer Brian Joseph Tierney claimed it has helped him deal with criminals as he walks the beat: "It's very deflating to them," he says, "when some character finds out that I know he's lying to me because I was able to pull up his picture with the touch of a finger." Tierney's experience must be felt by others. Crime in Chicago has been decreasing by about 6 percent each year

> "Government is a trust, and the officers of the government are trustees; and both the trust and the trustees are created for the benefit of the people."
>
> **HENRY CLAY**
> American Statesman

since the system was initiated in 2002. Based upon Chicago's success, similar systems are being implemented throughout the United States.

Public Services Are Provided by Dedicated Public Servants

It is ironic that the many deeply personal services of government, only a few of which have been described here, are often provided by anonymous public servants who rarely gain personal recognition. That is the government with which most Americans are familiar—a bureaucracy staffed by civil servants with no faces and no names. Every day millions of public servants provide the services that make our lives more secure, healthy, and vibrant.

Dr. Rajiv Jain is the Chief of Staff and Methicillin-Resistant Staphylococcus Aureus (MRSA) Program Director within the Department of Veterans Affairs. Jain received his Doctor of Medicine from Saurashtra University in India. He then continued his training at the University of Connecticut and at the University of Virginia Hospital in Charlottesville, Virginia. He has won many awards for his outstanding work dealing with MSRA.

In the United States, about 100,000 people die each year from infections contracted during hospital stays. MRSA is one of the major causes of those infections. Dr. Jain's work has led to the reduction of MRSA-caused infections by about 60 percent. If implemented throughout the United States, his techniques would reduce the number of deaths by about 60,000 people and decrease the number of infections (which has now reached about 2 million) by 1.2 million. Many other medical personnel—though unrecognized—are helping him implement this program: "I think the [Service to America] award should really go to the people [working in the hospitals] because, although we came up with the idea, they are the ones carrying it out every day" (Lu 2009). What was originally intended to be a short stint at Veterans Affairs has turned into 29 years—a dedicated life of serving the public. Jain believes, "The fact that you are serving the public to me is absolutely the icing on the cake" (Service to America 2008).

EXERCISE 1.3

Harness the Power of Public Service (Video)

President Bill Clinton addresses Rutgers University students regarding the value of public service and civic engagement. Access the following website and watch the video. What key messages would you deliver concerning the importance of public service? Augment your answer with information from other videos on this site that deal with the impact of public service on community building.

Rutgers Newark Public Service, "Harness the Power of Public Service," September 29, 2009, www.youtube.com/RUPubServe

Rarely do we acknowledge a particular public servant who keeps our community safe or teaches our children on a daily basis. World War II veteran Osceola L. Fletcher (Ozzie) is a public servant whose career spans 60 years. Not only did he serve as an officer in the New York Police Department for 24 years, but he continued to work another 15 years as a teacher in the New York City Public Schools and then went on to become a community relations specialist in the Brooklyn District Attorney's office. He was honored with a Sloan Public Service Award, at which time the Brooklyn District Attorney stated: "Ozzie Fletcher's long and distinguished career epitomizes what it means to be a public servant" (Fund for the City of New York 2009, p. 2). In Ozzie's own words, "Everything I have done is a continuum of the kind of public service I believe in. I have had the opportunity to work with such a wonderful diversity of people—something that was not possible when I was growing up. It is important to connect generations to each other; otherwise we lose perspective on the meaning of what came before and what lies ahead, and how to achieve a less contentious world" (Fund for the City of New York 2009).

> "We know that government can't solve all our problems—and we don't want it to. But we also know that there are some things we can't do on our own. We know that there are some things we do better together."
>
> **BARACK OBAMA**
> 44th President of the United States

Bureaucracy—Functional or Not?

Bureaucracy is the structure within which virtually all government organizations operate and is characteristic of large, private concerns, as well. The concept of a bureaucracy is to ensure that goods and services can be produced or provided in the most efficient manner possible. Max Weber (1922/2004), an eminent German sociologist and organizational theorist, defined bureaucracy as having the following characteristics:

I. Jurisdictional boundaries—which are typically prescribed by laws or administrative regulations.

II. Hierarchy—which ensures an ordered system where superiors monitor subordinates.

III. Reliance on written documents (or the preservation of files).

IV. Expertly trained managers.

V. The management of the organization subscribes to general rules, which can be learned and applied uniformly more or less.

It has become commonplace to associate negative stereotypes with bureaucrats. These are often perpetuated by groups seeking smaller government, politicians looking to place blame, or citizens involved in uncomfortable interactions or transactions. But these stereotypes often have little basis in fact. The career officials who work for government are typically productive, dedicated members of society. Politicians will often blame an incompetent bureaucracy when a policy fails but rarely credit the same bureaucratic officials when a policy is successfully implemented.

A common claim is that those who work in the public sector receive too much money for the amount of time that they work. This is especially common in discussions of teachers. The assumption is that they work fewer hours a day than other professionals and have long vacations throughout the year and in the summer. But a recent study by the Time Committee (2007)—established by the State of Hawaii Board of Education—found that teachers in Hawaii work an extra 1,780 hours a year preparing for class, grading papers, attending school events, etc. Even if that figure is somewhat exaggerated, the study suggests that teachers are actually underpaid for the amount of hours they spend working in a professional capacity (Joint Hawaii State Teachers Association and Board of Education Time Committee 2007).

Not only do teachers spend more time working in a professional capacity than is typically acknowledged, but they work in a far more turbulent environment than many other professionals. During the 2006–2007 school year, students aged 12 to 18 were the victims of 1.7 million nonfatal crimes, and about 10 percent of teachers in urban schools were threatened with harm or violence (National Center for Education Statistics 2009). In the 2003–2004 school year, more than 120,000 teachers reported being physically attacked by a student. That vulnera-

At Age 112, Montana Resident Reflects on More Than a Century of Changes

WILLIAM MARCUS [PBS]: And who, of all those presidents, who's your favorite?

WALTER BREUNING: Well, I think Roosevelt done the most when he created Social Security and made several changes. But, you know, the second war, if he hadn't opened up at that time, Roosevelt would have had a tough time.

WILLIAM MARCUS [PBS]: How would you counsel future generations to be a part of their country?

WALTER BREUNING: Everybody learns from life what's going on. And if they pay attention to everything that people do, especially helping people, that's one big thing. A lot of people think they're born for themselves; I don't think that. I believe that we're here to help other people all the way through.

Source: PBS NewsHour, online transcript, February 16, 2009, www.pbs.org/newshour/bb/social_issues/jan-june09/walter_02-16.html.

bility is not specific to teachers, however. In 2002, about 35 percent of social workers reported being attacked. Other public servants such as police officers and firefighters face even greater risk to their lives. On average about 62,000 police officers are assaulted and 95,000 firefighters are injured each year. The contributions provided by dedicated public professionals in dangerous settings certainly deserve our appreciation.

What, Then, Is Public Administration?

Among the many depictions of the field of public administration (PA) is that of the administrator as an impartial implementer. This view gained much of its credibility from some of the original scholars in the field of public administration, including Woodrow Wilson (1887/2004) and Frank Goodnow (1906/2004). Both scholars viewed the field as being separate from the everyday clashes and compromises of politics. They defined a field in which politics and administration could and should be separated from each other. Wilson held that "the business of government is to organize the common interest against the special interest" (1887/2004). Goodnow advocated for a distinction between the functions of the politics and the administration of government, noting that politics had to do with policies and the administration dealt with their execution (1906/2004). Although this view of a "dichotomy" has long been disputed and is commonly viewed as overly narrow and simplistic, its legacy still partly defines public administration.

An overly narrow understanding of public administration can be challenged quite easily by examining the many facets of responsibility for the public administrator. Although impartial implementer may be one legitimate role, it does not fully define a field so vast and influential in its actions. In 1926 Leonard White—a renowned public administration scholar—defined public administration as "the management of men and materials in the accomplishment of the purpose of the state." He went on to say, "The objective of public administration is the most efficient utilization of the resources at the disposal of officials and employees." Absent from this definition, though, is the idea of democracy and social equity (White 1926/2004).

A narrower view of public administration is as public management, generally considered the management of organizations within the government or nonprofit sector. Unlike private management, public management is driven by its need to reach its goals or mission rather than its need to make a profit. Public management's inherent attachment to democratic principles affects the dynamics of management policies. Public management has to do with some of the key responsibilities of the executive as defined by Luther Gulick's (1937/2004) formulation of PODSCORB—Planning, Organizing, Directing, Staffing, Coordinating, Recruiting, and Budgeting. In the twenty-first century, public management also deals with broad organizational objectives through strategic planning, budgeting, and human resource implementation.

The Encyclopedia Britannica Online defines public administration as "the implementation of government policies. Today public administration is often regarded as including also some responsibility for determining the policies and programs of governments. Specifically, it is the planning, organizing, directing, coordinating, and controlling of government operations" (www.britannica.com/EBchecked/topic/482290/public-administration).

Since the 1930s, the field of public administration has changed significantly. One of the largest changes came in the 1960s and 1970s with the ideas that grew out of the New Public Administration movement. Eminent scholar H. George Frederickson wrote: "The rationale for public administration is almost always better (more efficient or economical) management. New Public Administration adds social equity to the classical objectives and rationale" (1971/2004). The concept of social equity—and its adoption as an integral element of government's mission—has transformed the field of public administration.

Our own definition incorporates some of the classical and more recent concepts associated with public administration. We define public administration as *the formation and implementation of public policy. It is an amalgamation of management-based strategies such as planning, organizing, directing, coordinating, and controlling. It incorporates behaviorally based practices adopted from fields such as psychology and sociology. All of those strategies and practices are utilized within a democratic framework of accountability. The formation and implementation of policy, while formally controlled by government managers, has since been expanded to include the nonprofit and for-profit communities.*

HISTORY OF KOREAN PUBLIC ADMINISTRATION AND CENTRAL GOVERNMENT

Comparing Government's Organizational Chart

Similar to American government system (federal level, state level, and local level), Korean governments also have three levels (central level, provincial level, and city level). The functions and responsibilities of Korean government at each level are not always consistent with those of the American government at the corresponding level. Korean central government takes care of national issues as a whole, while provincial and city levels work at the local level. The followings is an organizational chart of central government in Korea, as well as some statistics as to government expenditures. Try to compare the US and Korean Governments. What are the similarities and differences?

FIGURE 1.13 – KOREAN CENTRAL GOVERNMENT'S ORGANIZATIONAL CHART

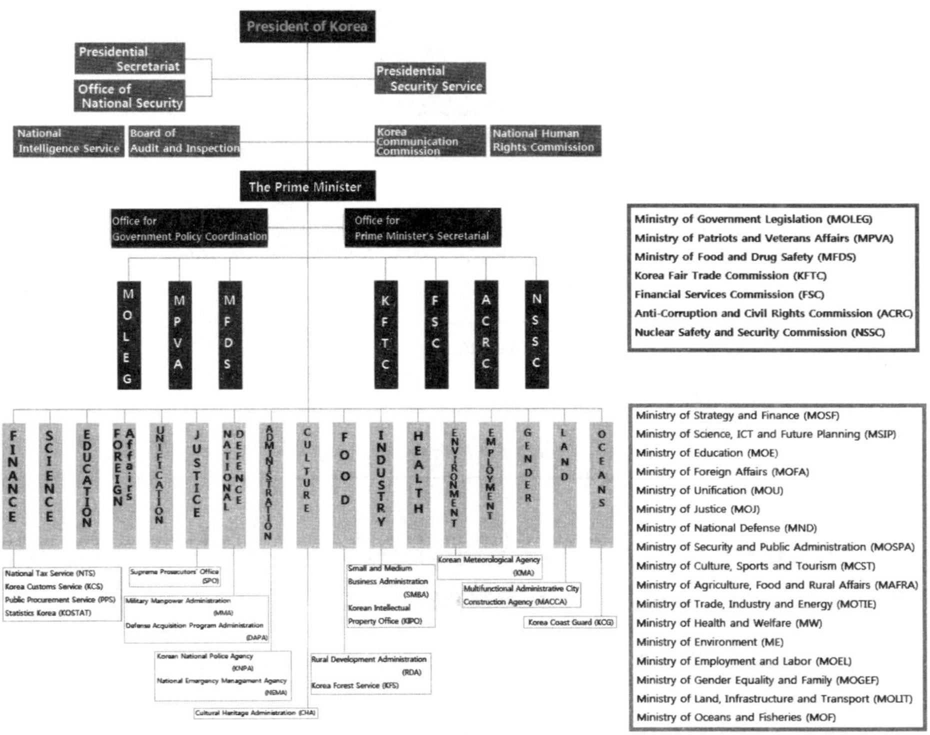

Comparing Total Government Expenditures

The Korean central government works closely with local governments in Korea. As noted above, both the US and Korean governments spend a huge amount of money to support each nation's economy and the health of the population. Do you see any difference in terms of proportions of expenditure shared by the US federal and state/local governments? Please discuss why the central government spends more money than local governments.

FIGURE 1.14 – Total GOVERNMENT EXPENDITURES: FISCAL YEAR 2009
(CURRENT PRICES, MILLIONS WON)

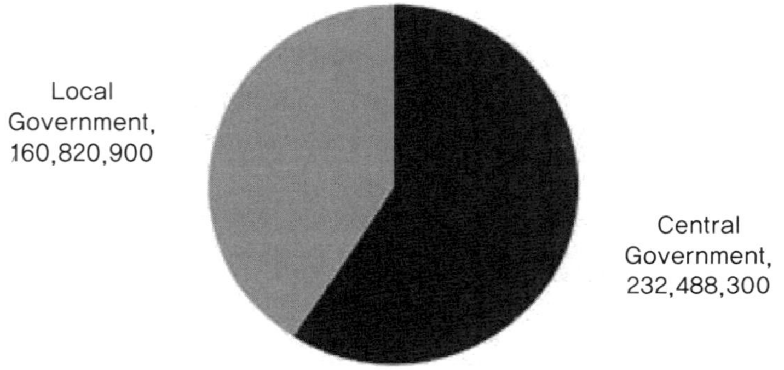

Source: http://stats.oecd.org/Index.aspx?DataSetCode=SNA_TABLE11

TABLE 1.2 – TOTAL GOVERNMENT EXPENDITURES: FISCAL YEAR 2009
(CURRENTPRICES, MILLIONS WON)

	Central Government	Local Government
Total Expenditure	232,488,300	160,820,900

Source: http://stats.oecd.org/Index.aspx?DataSetCode=SNA_TABLE11

Comparing the Composition of Social Insurance and Retirement Receipts

As both Tables 1.3 and 1.4 indicate, the Korean government also takes care of the health of citizens as well as their retirement plans. Like the US, the Korean central government also operates various funds (off–budget) to support citizens who reached the age of retirement, and such funds are supposed to generate a significant amount of profit based on good pension management. However, pension management is often in trouble because profit depends heavily on business cycles and the ability to invest in the right places. Do you see any difference in proportions when comparing the US composition of Social Insurance and Retirement Receipts? Try to identify the difference in terms of items and proportions.

TABLE 1.3– SOCIAL INSURANCE: NATIONAL HEALTH INSURANCE(UNIT: ONE TRILLION WON)

Receipts	33.6
–Health Insurance	28.7
–Government Subsidies	4.9

Source: E–National Indicators, accessed at http://sgis.kostat.go.kr/intro/smain.html

TABLE 1.4– RETIREMENT RECEIPTS: NATIONAL PENSION(UNIT: ONE MILLION WON)

Receipts	554,822
–Annuity Insurance	252,857
–Profit on Pension Management	301,467
–Government Subsidies	498

Source: E–National Indicators, accessed at http://sgis.kostat.go.kr/intro/smain.html

Comparing Total Government Receipts

Compared to the US case, what would be the difference in terms of receipt

FIGURE 1.15 – TOTAL GOVERNMENT RECEIPTS IN 2010(UNIT: ONE BILLION WON)

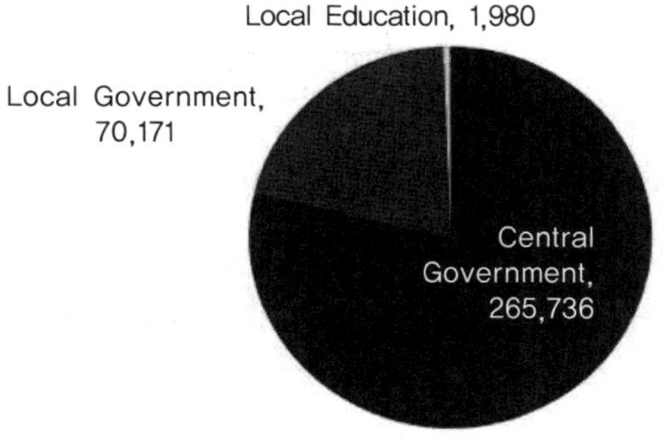

Source: Digital Budget and Accounting System, accessed at https://www.digitalbrain.go.kr/kor/view/statis/statis03_01_01.jsp?code=DB0103

proportions? It looks like the central government has much more in receipts than local government. How about the situation of US governments? Do you think the central government has to provide more funds to local governments? Please discuss why.

Comparing Total Government Receipts by Source

In comparison to the US case, what are differences in items and proportions? It seems that the Korean government collects a small portion from individual income tax and corporation income tax as a revenue source. Take a look at the US government receipts by source. Can you argue that the Korean government must raise more income taxes and corporation income taxes?

FIGURE 1.16 – TOTAL GOVERNMENT RECEIPTS BY SOURCE(UNIT: ONE BILLION WON)

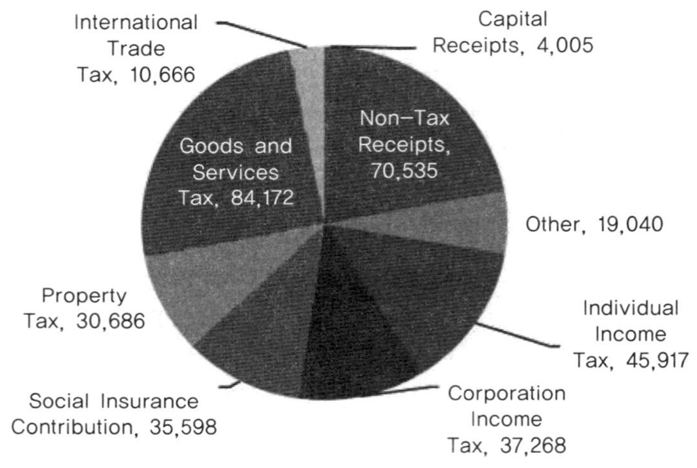

Source: Digital Budget and Accounting System, accessed at https://www.digitalbrain.go.kr/kor/view/statis/statis03_01_02.jsp?code=DB01030102

Comparing Government Employment and Percentage of Population

Information identified in Figure 1.17 is interesting. Government employment in Korea consists of 2% of the population, while in the US government employees at all levels represent 7.8% of total US population. Do you think Korean government is too small? Please discuss whether or not you agree with this question.

TABLE 1.5 – FIXED NUMBER OF CIVIL SERVANTS BY INSTITUTION IN 2010 (UNIT: NUMBER)

Total	Political Service	Extraordinary Civil Service	Contractual Service	Special Service	General Service	Technical Service	Others
979,583	145	7,811	112	504,162	346,102	119,181	2,070

Source: Ministry of Public Administration and Security (2010), accessed at http://sgis.kostat.go.kr/intro/smain.html

TABLE 1.6 – TOTAL POPULATION AND TOTAL GOVERNMENT EMPLOYMENT IN 2010 (UNIT: NUMBER)

Total Population	Total Government Employment
49,410,000	979,583

Source: e-National indicators/ Ministry of Korean Administration and Security(2010), accessed at http://sgis.kostat.go.kr/intro/smain.html

FIGURE 1.17 – GOVERNMENT EMPLOYMENT AS A PERCENTAGE OF TOTAL POPULATION IN 2010

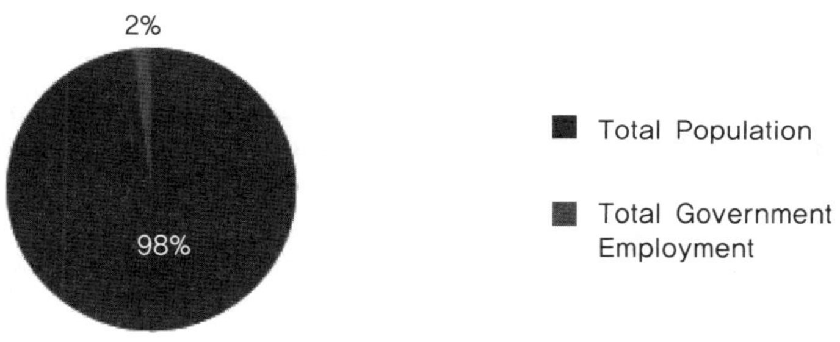

Source: e-National indicators/ Ministry of Korean Administration and Security(2010), accessed at http://sgis.kostat.go.kr/intro/smain.html

Comparing Military Spending as a Percentage of Total Budget

In relation to military spending, due to tensions with North Korea, the Korean government has placed a top priority on its military budget. Figure 1.18 shows that Korean government military spending accounts for about 12% of the total budget. In contrast, US military spending (Department of Defense) accounts for about 22 % of the federal budget. Also US military spending, in comparison with the world, accounts for 48% of the total defense budgets spent by all countries worldwide. Given this situation, do you think the Korean government should increase the portion of its budget allocated to the military in order to be a stronger nation in the world? Please discuss.

TABLE 1.7 – KOREAN MILITARY SPENDING AS A PERCENTAGE OF GDP

	$billion	%GDP	$ Per Capita
South Korea	27.6	2.9	569

Note: US $billions at 2010 prices and exchange rates.
Source: http://milexdata.sipri.org/result.php4

TABLE 1.8 – KOREAN MILITARY SPENDING AS A PERCENTAGE TOTAL BUDGET

Total Budget	Korean Military Spending
2.09161E+11	27,600,000,000

Source: Total Budget, accessed at
http://www.index.go.kr/egams/stts/jsp/potal/stts/PO_STTS_IdxMain.jsp?idx_cd=1045b.
Korean Military Spending: http://milexdata.sipri.org/result.php4

FIGURE 1.18 – KOREAN MILITARY SPENDING AS A PERCENTAGE OF TOTAL BUDGET

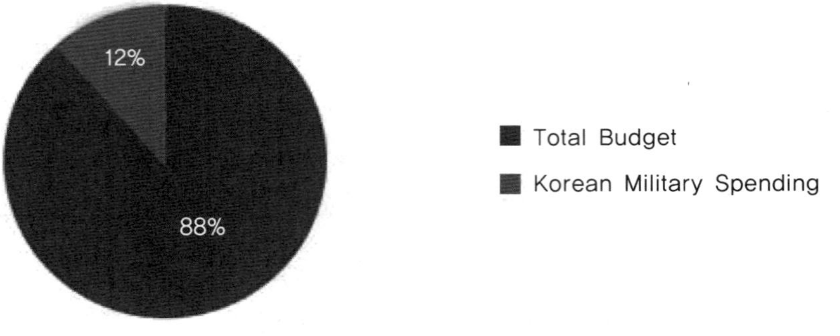

Source: Total Budget, accessed at
http://www.index.go.kr/egams/stts/jsp/potal/stts/PO_STTS_IdxMain.jsp?idxcd=1045b.
Korean Military Spending: http://milexdata.sipri.org/result.php4

KEY TERMS

501(c)(3)

Bureaucracy

Employment taxes

Globalization

Gross domestic product (GDP)

Nonprofit sector

Private sector

Public administration (PA)

Public management

Public sector

Sales taxes

Taxation

REFERENCES

Behn, R.D. 2001. *Rethinking Democratic Accountability*. Washington, DC: Brookings Institution Press.

Boys and Girls Clubs of America. 2010. "Who We Are." http://www.bgca.org/whoweare/mission.asp.

Bureau of Labor Statistics. 2010. "Economic News Release. Volunteering in the United States, 2009." http://www.bls.gov/news.release/volun.nro.htm.

Chicago Police Department. 2008. "CLEARpath. Community Concerns." https://portal.chicagopolice.org/portal/page/portal/ClearPath/Communities/Community%20Concerns.

Environmental Protection Agency. 2010. "EPA Office of Water." http://water.epa.gov/.

Experience Works. 2010. "What We Do." http://www.experienceworks.org.

Frederickson, H.G. 1971/2004. "Toward a New Public Administration." In *Classics of Public Administration*, ed. A.C. Hyde, J.M. Shafritz, and S.J. Parkes, 315–27. Belmont, CA: Wadsworth/Thomson Learning.

Fund for the City of New York. 2009. "Sloan Public Service Awards." New York: Alfred P. Sloan Foundation/Fund for the City of New York. www.fcny.org/fcny/core/sloan/.

Goodnow. F. 1906/2004. "Politics and Administration." In *Classics of Public Administration*, ed. A.C. Hyde, J.M. Shafritz, and S.J. Parkes, 35–37. Belmont, CA: Wadsworth/Thomson Learning.

Greene, J.P., and M. Winters. 2005. "The Teacher-Pay Myth." *New York Post*, September 22.

Gulick, L. 1937/2004. "Notes on the Theory of Organization." In *Classics of Public Administration*, ed. A.C. Hyde, J.M. Shafritz, and S.J. Parkes, 90–98. Belmont, CA: Wadsworth/Thomson Learning.

Howe, S. 2008. "Eight Stand-out Public Servants Receive Coveted Service to America Medals at Washington, DC Gala." *Partnership for Public Service*, September 16. http://ourpublicservice.org/OPS/pressroom/releases/release_080917_sammies.shtml.

Joint Hawaii State Teachers Association and Board of Education Time Committee. 2007. *Time Committee Preliminary Report*. Honolulu: Hawaii Board of Education, http://www.focusmauinui.com/pdf/TimeCommittee%20PreliminaryReport_3–15–07.pdf.

Light, P.C. 2002. "Fact Sheet on the New True Size of Government." Brookings Institution website. www.brookings.edu/~/media/Files/rc/articles/2003/0905politics_light/light20030905.pdf.

Lipsky, M. 1980. *Street-level Bureacracy: Dilemmas of the Individual in Public Services*. New York: Russell Sage Foundation.

Lu, Y. 2009. "Pittsburgh Doctor Wins Service to America Medal." *The Tartan Online*, January 26. www.thetartan.org/2009/1/26/scitech/serviceaward.

National Center for Education Statistics. 2009. "Indicators of School Crime and Safety: 2008." http://nces.ed.gov/programs/crimeindicators/crimeindicators2008/key.asp.

National Institute of Food and Agriculture. 2010. "About NIFA." http://www.csrees.usda.gov/about/about.html.

National Institutes of Health. 2009. "The NIH Almanac—Historical Data," September 1. www.nih.gov/about/almanac/historical/chronology_of_events.htm.

National Institutes for Health. 2010. "About the National Institutes of Health." May 18. http://www.nih.gov/about/index.html.

National Office of Public Health Genomics of the Centers for Disease Control and Prevention. 2010. "Public Health Genomics. About Us." http://www.cdc.gov/genomics/about/index.htm.

National Science Foundation. 2010. "About the National Science Foundation." http://www.nsf.gov/about/.

New York City. 1998. Archives of Rudolph W. Giuliani. Mayor's WINS Address, Sunday, August 16. http://www.nyc.gov/html/records/rwg/html/98b/me980816.html.

Partnership for Public Service. 2008. "Service to America Medal Recipients."

http://servicetoamericamedals.org/SAM/recipients/sam08/sam08a.shtml.

Pressman, J.L., and A.B. Wildavsky. 1973. *Implementation: How Great Expectations in Washington Are Dashed in Oakland; Or, Why It's Amazing That Federal Programs Work at All, This Being a Saga of the Economic Development Administration as Told by Two Sympathetic Observers Who Seek to Build Morals on a Foundation of Ruined Hopes*. The Oakland Project series. Berkeley: University of California Press.

Romzek, B.S., and M.J. Dubnick. 1987. "Accountability in the Public Sector: Lessons from the Challenger Tragedy." In *Democracy, Bureaucracy, and the Study of Administration*, ed. C. Stivers, 182–204. Boulder, CO: Westview Press.

Rosenbloom, D.H. 2000. "Retrofitting the Administrative State to the Constitution: Congress and the Judiciary's Twentieth-Century Progress." *Public Administration Review* 60: 39–46.

United Nations. 2010. "International Water for Life Decade. Factsheet on Water and Sanitation." http://www.un.org/waterforlifedecade/factsheet.html.

Urban Institute. 2010. "Nonprofits." http://www.urban.org/nonprofits/index.cfm.

USAID.2008. "Fiscal Year 2008. USAID Annual Performance Report. Overview." http://www.usaid.gov/policy/budget/apr08/apr08_overview.pdf.

Walters, Johnathan.2007. "Data on the Beat." *Governing* magazine, July 31. www.governing.com/topics/public-justice-safety/Data-on-the-Beat.html.

Weber, M. 1922/2004. "Bureaucracy." In *Classics of Public Administration*, ed. A.C. Hyde, J.M. Shafritz, and S.J. Parkes, 50–55. Belmont, CA: Wadsworth/Thomson Learning.

White, L. 1926/2004. "Introduction to the Study of Public Administration." In *Classics of Public Administration*, ed. A.C. Hyde, J.M. Shafritz, and S.J. Parkes, 56–63. Belmont, CA: Wadsworth/Thomson Learning.

Wilson, W. 1887/2004. "The Study of Administration." In *Classics of Public Administration*, ed. A.C. Hyde, J.M. Shafritz, and S.J. Parkes, 22–34. Belmont, CA: Wadsworth/Thomson Learning.

SUPPLEMENTARY READINGS

Bozeman, Barry. 2007. *Public Values and Public Interest*. Washington, DC: Georgetown University Press.

Denhardt, Janet V., and Robert B. Denhardt. 2007. *The New Public Service: Serving, not Steering*. Armonk, NY: M.E. Sharpe.

Gargan, John J., ed. 2000. *Handbook of State Government Administration.* New York: Marcel Dekker.

Laurence E. Lynn. 2006. *Public Management: Old and New.* New York: Routledge.

Nicholas Henry. 2009. *Public Administration and Public Affairs.* Upper Saddle River, NJ: Pearson/Prentice-Hall.

Peters, B. Guy and Jon Pierre, eds. 2003. *Handbook of Public Administration.* Thousand Oaks, CA: Sage.

Philip H. Jos and Mark E. Tompkins. 2009. "Keeping It Public: Defending Public Service Values in a Customer Service Age." *Public Administration Review* 69, no. 6: 1077-1086.

Richard T. Green, Gary L. Wamsley and Lawrence F. Keller. 1993. "Reconstituting a Profession for American Public Administration." *Public Administration Review* 53, no. 6: 516-524.

Tina Nabatchi, Holly T. Goerdel, and Shelly Peffer. 2011. "Public Administration in Dark Times: Some Questions for the Future of the Field." *Journal of Public Administration and Research* 21: i29-i43.

Wamsley, Gary L., Robert N. Bacher, Charles T. Goodsell, Philip S. Kronenberg, John A. Rohr, Camilla M. Stivers, Orion F. White, and James F. Wolf. 1990. *Refounding Public Administration.* Newbury Park, CA: Sage.

Wing, K., Pollack, T.H., and Blackwood, A. 2008. *The Nonprofit Almanac,* 7th ed. Washington, DC: The Urban Institute Press.

ELECTRONIC RESOURCES

Fred Thompson. "What Public Managers Should Study." Atkinson Graduate School of Management, Willamette University, http://www.willamette.edu/~fthompso/Public_MANAGEMENT.html

Robert Behn. 2005, "M-Gov, E-Gov, and I-Gov" Public Management report, 2-10, http://www.hks.harvard.edu/thebehnreport/June2005.pdf

Russell W. Mills. 2010. "The Promise of Collaborative Voluntary Partnerships: Lessons from the Federal Aviation Administration." *Collaborating Across Boundaries Series.* IBM Center for The Business of Government, http://www.businessofgovernment.org/sites/default/files/The%20Promise%20of%20Collaborative%20Voluntary%20Partnerships.pdf

CASE STUDIES

Building Commissioning for Better Public Buildings Case Study, "Bainbridge Island High School—Assuring HVAC Comfort and Efficiency," Washington State Department of General Administration, Fall 2003, www.ga.wa.gov/eas/bcx/BainbridgeIsland%20HighSchool-cx.pdf.

Fuchs, Ester R., Rachel Hare, and Hannah Nudell. "Innovations in City Government: The Case of New York City's Workforce Development System." Columbia School of International and Public Affairs Case Study, November 5, 2008, www.nyc.gov/html/sbs/wib/downloads/pdf/columbia_case_study.pdf.

Government-Bashing: Seven Myths

Claim 1:

Government exerts too much control over our lives. Every time private citizens allow "government" to enact a new law, or new regulation, we cede a little bit more power to it. We give up a little bit more of our privacy, a bit more control over our future, and enable this huge impersonal force called government to make more decisions for us.

Answer: Ask yourself the following questions: What goes into our ears? Sounds provided by Clear Channel and an ever-shrinking number of privately owned radio conglomerates answerable to no one. What goes into our eyes? TV shows and movies and news broadcasts provided by a small group of ever more powerful private entities whose goal is to increase their bottom line. Who tells us what foods to eat and medicines to take? Privately owned companies like McDonald's and Coke and Pfizer and Johnson & Johnson. Who tells our children what constitutes "cool behavior" and gives our kids daily examples of what is fair and moral? Does [President Barack] Obama get on TV and say that premarital sex and swearing are great ways to make friends? No, but private industries do—in that case, the entertainment industry, which makes money selling kids extremely nonfamily values. Who tells us what cars we need to drive in order to feel manly, what gadgets we need to buy for our children, and where to shop? Private industry does. Who tells our children that it's much better to spend money on trinkets and fancy cars to impress girls than it is to save for college? Who tells our kids to drink Budweiser and smoke cigarettes? Private industries do, industries that make billions of dollars from your children's future addictions. Who collects data on the websites we visit, what we buy online, and whom we chat with? Well, my friend, that would be Google, Microsoft and Facebook, not "government." Who reports the identities of political dissidents to repressive governments like China, sells our personal data to the highest bidder, and spies on our Internet activity? You're thinking, that's gotta be Obama and those wicked Democrats? No. Once again, that would be Yahoo, Facebook and Google, respectively. Does government make the schoolbooks our children learn from? No. Private industries do, companies like Pearson, McGraw-Hill, Reed Elsevier, and Houghton Mifflin. Check your child's textbook. Did "government" make it? Nope. Mostly likely, it came from one of the companies I just named. Does government make the voting machines we vote on? No. Private industries do, companies like Diebold, Sequoia, and the Nebraska-based Election Systems, who are answerable to no one but their shareholders. And who has the largest financial stake in you ignoring the above paragraph, and wants you to please, please get back to the business of complaining about government? Private industry does.

Claim 2:

When government steps in to fix a problem, they never get it right. They should just leave business to fix itself.

Answer: It's quite true that government's fixes never seem to work, but that's by design. We don't want a government with absolute power to dictate policies, even if those policies seem good for the short term. We're too smart for that. We know very well that giving government lots of power to fix today's crises would create rules that, later on, would be burdensome. This is true by and large, but there are times we should rethink that notion. Take the example of the BP oil mess. For decades, America has let Big Oil pretty much have its own way, let them sign off on their own safety reports, accept their verbal assurances that they will play nice and not hurt the pretty fishes when they drill. Now, BP has created a crisis they can't control, so we want [President] Obama to step up and take over. But since America has always let oil companies manage their own problems, we lack the expertise to come in behind BP and play cleanup. Obama will now try his best to jump in and fix things, and the results will appear clumsy and poorly thought out, simply because a spill of this magnitude is quite new to all of us, and we'll have to learn as we go. One might say that the government should have been keeping closer watch of Big Oil all along, so as not to be caught in this sort of mess. But then, Republicans would have seized that opportunity to whine even more about "government" interference. Another example of government's partial solutions to big problems is Obama's foreclosure prevention plan. It's a flop. Why? Because the plan is voluntary. Obama's plan would work just fine if Congress forced the banks to play, but who has the political stomach for that? Force the banks to take pennies on the dollar? There'd be cries of "socialism." Very few people want to grant the government the broad powers and regulatory teeth required to craft a workable solution to the foreclosure problem. Such a plan would be very good for the economy, but enacting it is a matter of political will. Who wants to tell the banks that they need to take a haircut for the good of the nation? Obama could, if he had enough political support to weather the Glenn Beck character assassination that is sure to follow. But since Americans want Obama to be both "in charge," but also let the private sector run its own ship, then he's bound to fail in many people's eyes. Americans seem destined to accept ineffective half-solutions to the problems we want the government to address, rather than give the President the mandate to enact something far-reaching and comprehensive. So pick your poison: Give government the wide-ranging power to fix a problem, or live with that problem and feel "free" from government oppression. But don't just complain that "government can't fix things."

(continued)

(continued)

Claim 3:

Government can't do anything right.

Answer: Everything you do is protected by government. We drive on paved highways, eat food, drink water, breath air, and take medicines that are relatively safe and contain ingredients that bear some similarity to what's on the label, all because of government. The dealer who sold you a car can't sell you a lemon, because of government. The restaurant where you eat can't serve you spoiled food, because of government. We live in homes that are built according to legal codes, codes that punish builders who use shoddy workmanship and toxic materials. These benefits also come from government. We are paid regular wages by employers who are obligated to do so by law. Because of government oversight, the police [officer] who pulls you over can't punch you in the stomach just because he's in a bad mood. When we go to the hospital, we are treated according to standards that carry the force of regulations that come from government. When we hire a lawyer, he or she must do the same, or risk disbarment. The elderly among us are not obliged to beg, or die in the streets when they get sick, because a government program takes care of them. When we turn on the radio or TV, the airwaves broadcast as expected. Programs not suitable for families are labeled accordingly, and aired only when the kids are (supposed to be) in bed. Despite all our complaints, our lives are improved greatly by that evil boogeyman, "government," the institution we love to hate, those mousy regulators that are the butt of everyone's jokes. These faceless, plodding, uninspiring bureaucrats that we endlessly make fun of actually make it so that our lives run relatively smoothly.

Claim 4:

Before [President Ronald] Reagan came along and reduced government and lowered taxes, America was worse off. Although it's true that in the 1950s–70s, America enjoyed a heyday, with a healthy middle class, lots of well-paying union jobs, few economic worries, where the average worker could raise a family in a nice neighborhood, buy a home, and afford to send his kids to college. However, these salad days were built on comfortable union deals and high taxes that were only sustainable because America was the sole economic engine of the West. Enter the mid-1970s, with its crippling inflation, expensive foreign aid commitments, and the resulting Carter-era "stagflation," and it became clear that America's experiment with high taxes and liberal big government was coming to an end. The allies America helped rebuild were challenging our economic dominance, and no Democrat had the guts to propose scaling back government and union power. When President Reagan was elected, he bucked all trends and lowered taxes, especially on the wealthy, and on corporations. Reagan ordered The Fed to tighten money, which unfortunately ushered in three years of painful unemployment, but the final result was an unprecedented economic boom that made money for everyone and generated wealth in all quarters. There can be no doubt that Reagan's brave medicine of tax cuts in the face of almost universal Democratic opposition turned the nation around, so that the America that Reagan left us, awash in national pride and wealth, bore no resemblance to the sorry state given him by the outgoing President Carter in 1980.

Answer: There's certainly some truth to the above. It's true that by 1980, America's allies were becoming industrial powerhouses, and wiser heads predicted a day when the world would no longer buy all our cars, absorb our exports, and thus finance Big Labor's expectation of cradle-to-grave comfort for America's workers. Reagan's answer was to radically cut taxes. In doing so, he created massive deficits. America quickly learned that deficits would balloon and become unmanageable, so in 1983, Reagan backed off his tax cuts and raised the amount that each worker had to contribute to Social Security. He also raised the Social Security deduction ceiling to $90,000 (before this, you didn't have to pay Social Security tax on yearly income over $30,000). However, Reagan continued to cut corporate taxes and taxes for the very wealthy, so the deficit grew. To curb it, he borrowed hundreds of billions from the Social Security trust fund, the first president to do so in significant amounts. Americans still pay 100 billion dollars a year in interest on the money that Reagan took from Social Security. This deficit-fear and all the creative bookkeeping required to paper over the deficit has clouded every presidency since. There was, however, lots of money floating around in the '80s. The shifting of the tax burden to regular workers and away from corporations and their owners resulted in a rush of new cash that required investment, capital that had to be stashed in some way. What's more, other nations were coming into their own, flush with cash, and were eager to loan it to us so America could skip down its merry high-borrowing ways. Thus began the now-familiar scenario of foreign investors owning an ever-increasing portion of the American pie. And around this time, since banks and corporations and the wealthy were flush with cash, common-sense investment regulations were tossed aside. Capitalization/reserve requirements of banks were reduced. Banks began bundling debts from various sources and swapping them for other commodities (sound familiar?), making billions of dollars in the process. Wealthy players were encouraged to bet on energy futures, and one result was the collapse of Enron, half a generation later, which cost taxpayers billions. Thus, Reagan's newly minted billionaires played Wall Street like a casino, and Wall Street's character changed from the stolid, relatively boring institution it had become in the postwar world. We see the results of such gambling today, when Goldman Sachs testified before Congress that they thrived

(continued)

(continued)

during the 2008 meltdown by betting that their own investors would fail. And under Reagan, for the first time, pension funds and bond markets were encouraged to begin playing these risky financial games. These staid pillars of prudence were no longer content with slow growth, while the rest of the big players were making billions. So they tossed money into the pot as well, and one result was the financial near-collapse of Orange County, California, in 1994. All of this was presaged by the Reagan-era Savings & Loan scandal, which was but the first of the now-familiar bankers' games that cost the taxpayer hundreds of billions of dollars. The 2008 and 2009 "bailouts" were not the first time the taxpayers footed the bill for Wall Street's betting frenzy. They were only the first giveaways to be called what they really were. But it was under Reagan that taxpayers began shoring up bankers after they failed at dice. Before his presidency, such a practice was unheard of.

What else did the Reagan-rich do with their newly minted billions? Buy other companies. The phenomena of eliminating companies and product lines because they weren't profitable enough, of forcing every company to do what it must to maximize profits or risk being taken over, all that started under Reagan. The Reagan billionaires didn't buy other companies for the good of the nation, so that America could run fit and trim on the open seas of tough competition, but instead, they treated newly acquired firms as if they were ATMs, firing employees, gutting communities, stripping legacy businesses of their assets, and draining money to the new corporate headquarters. The resulting dearth of small businesses, the lack of local flavor, the corporate bigness that reduces every town to a series of strip malls each with a Starbucks and a Subway and a Blockbuster Video, that all started under Reagan. The mega-rich reasoned that the purpose for all the easy money Reagan gave them was to make more. We Americans didn't notice the trends right away, the corporate acquisitions that gradually touched every corner of America over three decades. Therefore, it's hard for us to imagine an America that doesn't resemble an ever-shrinking portfolio of corporate logos dotting the highway. There was a time when a community's livelihood had a lot more to do with what actually happened in that community (no matter how small), not a corporate boardroom in a different state, or different country. Can you imagine a world in which CEOs could grow their company at a manageable pace over a number of years, focusing on sustainability rather than obsessing over quarterly profits? Before Reagan, such goals were the norm. Of course in 2010, in the wake of the Enron scandal and the 2008 Meltdown, we are careful to lament the obsession for fast profits at the expense of common sense, but such wariness is only hindsight. Beginning under Reagan and through today, profit-mania is viewed as a patriotic duty. Many have also lamented the loss of small, local industries, local food and power production—but these had been deemed "inef-

(continued)

ficient" by the still-popular Reagan business model, and so, we find that they've gone the way of the typewriter and the dial-up modem. This notion that maximum profitability must be the Golden Mean for all commerce was not popular until the Reagan presidency sanctioned pure profitability for its own sake. A local industry that employs perhaps a few hundred people can seldom compete with the profitability of its global brethren. But so what? Should that assessment be regarded as the final word on its value? Reagan convinced America that it was.

In the short run though, Reagan's America was indeed awash in cash. We were wealthy on paper, but those billions created relatively few jobs, and the ones created were usually not robust. The 1980s saw the decline of well-paying manufacturing jobs and the rise of the "service sector." American workers emerged from early 1980s recession to find themselves wearing aprons and colorful hats and serving hamburgers. But rather than invest in industries that would create good jobs, rather than building industries that required highly educated workers in a multi-step production chain that would put lots of people to work, the Reagan-rich invested in financial schemes that created a quick buck. Why didn't the rich invest in stable, multifaceted industries that created a vast array of products that regular people could actually buy? Because during the Reagan years, regular people couldn't afford to buy much of anything. During Reagan's first term, 10 percent of all working Americans had no job, and the jobs they found later didn't pay very well. Thus, industry had little incentive to re-invent the Boom Years of 1955–75, during which products and all their parts were made at home. During that era, regular Americans could afford to buy the things they manufactured, a dual role which encouraged industry to manufacture more, creating a healthy cycle. But under Reagan, the middle class lost buying power, making up for this loss only by going into debt. The result was that the Reagan-rich saw little incentive to finance what might have been a rejuvenated industrial base, a new economy that created long-term, nonexportable jobs, rather than electronic trinkets that could just as well be manufactured overseas.

It's quite true that in 1980, taxes needed to be cut, but America had other options besides setting the rich loose on some sort of extended Las Vegas vacation at our expense. What if Reagan had cut taxes but created strong incentives to reinvest in America? By now, we'd be energy-independent, a nation of producers as well as consumers, and this notion of America going bankrupt because the Chinese market blinks would be the subject of a novel, not our reality. How? By doing what America does best: invent what is next. Ever hear of Bell & Howell? A joint business-government think tank that developed technologies that shaped the world. We got there first. America did it by combining brains and skill with manufacturing know-how. We could

(continued)

(continued)

do that again by developing renewable energy sources, for example biomass fuels, which only need a bit of tweaking to be profitable. America under Reagan, flush with cash from tax cuts, could have begun such a partnership, getting a jump on fuel-efficient cars (by now, we'd all have one, and oil-producing nations would have no power over us at all). Under Reagan, we could have used all that cash to develop small industries with minimal environmental impact that could be controlled locally, which matches the goal of both the Right and Left—to keep our affairs small and controllable. If Reagan hadn't simply handed over tax cuts to the rich, giving them play-money to manipulate stocks and housing, but had instead put America first, today, we'd have broadband in every corner of America, we'd have small rural industries efficiently run off biomass fuels and computer technology, and students that could look forward to jobs in these new burgeoning sectors, instead of working at Starbucks and flipping houses. Under Reagan, America's prisons grew by 90 percent. Imagine if the percentage of Reagan Youth that spent its years behind bars could have, instead, been given a low-cost education, then put to work developing tomorrow's technologies. Expensive? Not as expensive as incarceration. Incarceration is much, much more expensive than education. The rush to lock up citizens is a problem of mindset, a problem that results when you listen to an actor, not a thinker. We can do better.

Claim 5:

Small government is good government.

Answer: Because of the atmosphere described in the above paragraphs, the need to squeeze every dollar spent for maximum profit, businesses can't function with a lot of common sense. In such a go-getter environment, a company is tempted to make-believe that their employees can actually live on 8 dollars per hour, or that, by cutting health insurance, their employees will magically stay healthy and productive. A company is tempted to pretend that water runoff from animal waste will magically avoid the lettuce crops nearby, or that customers who purchase your pharmaceuticals will magically not notice the nasty side-effects that you've been hiding for years. The breakneck rush for profits, the need to avoid being taken over by a larger company who's willing to be nastier than you are—well, those realities make it too tempting for a large business to engage in predatory and unsafe practices. Business critics on the Left often characterize corporate leaders as evil human beings. That's not fair. They're just people who want their companies to survive, who believe that by firing 300 employees today, they're doing right by the 800 employees who remain. Today's corporate heads did not make these rules. Reagan and his cronies did, and today's businesses must survive by them. I once worked at a fiber-optic cable company, and one day, a particular salesman was lauded for making our product the dominant player in Australia and Oceana. "Good show," everyone said. "Now, go out and do it again. And we'll fire all your colleagues that can't keep up with you." For a moment, you could see the weariness in his eyes, the realization that his own demise was only a matter of time, the realization that this is not a way to do business.

But, regardless of whose fault it is, it's fair to say that, given the atmosphere described above, big companies cannot function with our best interests at heart—"our" meaning the regular people who drive their cars and buy their products and work at their factories and offices. Therefore, some entity needs to watch for stuff, watch for the salmonella in the lettuce, the shoddy workmanship in the cars, the pollutants in the air, the side effects in the medications, and so forth. Of course, a person might live each day eating food that's relatively free of poisons, living in a home constructed with safe materials, and believe that the world of commerce proceeds smoothly as if by magic. That's not true. It's because of "government." This fact won't be obvious until you become one of those sad statistics whose plane trip ended in tragedy, whose liver was ruined from unlabeled medication, whose shoreline is covered with oil, whose daughter died from E. coli in the cheese. You see them on TV, and it's easy to assume they're just trying to squeeze money from a company that made an honest mistake. But when you find yourself in a similar situation, you realize how easy it is for big companies to get away with... well, murder. You realize it is perfectly fair to expect government to protect us from these economic entities that have such control over our daily lives. Such "government" oversight is indeed necessary.

Of course, if you read the news, you'd think all big companies practice careless disregard for our lives. That's silly. People are people. But regardless of the exaggerations, it should be obvious America needs corporate watchdogs, unless you believe that CEOs are saints who would never cut corners on safety reports or produce shoddy ingredients. That, too, is silly. Society just runs much better if somebody's keeping the big guys honest. And not just anybody. The task requires a powerful entity outside a company's corporate structure, an entity accountable only to "the people" (at least on paper), and not corporate boardrooms. We would call that "government." Now, does all this mean government should be "big?" Not necessarily. But regulatory agencies should be well-funded and staffed, empowered with the right technology and skills to do their job, and enough regulatory teeth to make their findings legally binding and enforceable. If regulation agencies are not "big," then they are no match for the corporations they much watch over, who are getting bigger and more concentrated by the minute. Still, in America, we don't like to interfere with a man and his right to make a dollar. We're inclined to side with the bloke who made the machine, rather than the guy who wants to burden him down with "safety"

(continued)

(continued)

this and "safety" that. What this means, then, is that the public supports regulations, but unfortunately, only toothless ones, regulations with huge loopholes. If politicians try to design regulations that honestly do the job, for example, force oil companies to install safety mechanisms so that oil spills can be contained, the companies complain of overregulation and start ragging on "government," and usually get the support of the public. From there, it gets worse: these toothless, ineffective regulations give the public more reason to complain "government can't do anything right." Sometimes, it all seems like a game of cat and mouse, and it's only after you've been screwed out of your life savings, lost your house, a limb, or a family member, or had your coastline polluted by oil that you realize that it's not a game at all.

Claim 6:

Government is more secretive and less answerable to the people than business.

Answer: In reality, businesses routinely hide data that would be of great interest to the general public. Goldman Sachs claims that they had no obligation to reveal that they were betting against their own investors. During the recent financial meltdown, firms routinely cooked the books to hide their losses, claiming such deceptions were legal. Food companies claim they have the right to call their products "organic" when they are anything but, and bottled water companies can legally lie about the source of their natural spring (city tap) water. Car companies will hide data about their unsafe vehicles until the resulting injuries and deaths can no longer be plausibly denied. Companies routinely hide the anticompetitive results of their mergers and acquisitions, and mask the deceitful means they use to drive competitors out of business. Businesses claim these rights because they don't want to reveal trade secrets, or reveal their true financial health to competitors. In any event, right or wrong, big corporations believe they don't have to reveal facts that might be harmful to their bottom line, regardless of the central roles their products play in our lives. Government, however, does have an obligation to be transparent, and when it refuses, we can fire officeholders who refuse to be accountable. Whistleblowers at government agencies are protected by law and have at least some recourse when they are harassed for speaking up. Although government regulators lie as much as anyone, there are pathways for concerned citizens to get to the bottom of these deceptions. Raise similar charges against a large private company, and they can stonewall until the money runs out (forever).

Claim 7:

Anything government can do, business can do better.

Answer: In America, we don't look to government to take on money-making, potentially profitable ventures. We leave that for the private sector, with its healthy, profit-seeking motivation. We look to government to do things that all citizens require, even those citizens that can't pay. The postal service delivers mail to everyone, because not everyone can afford UPS and Fed Ex. Public schools have to let in all the kids, even those who might never read or write or do math very well. Not everyone can afford a car, so you have to have busses. Not all goods can be delivered on airplanes, so you have to have trains, even though they're not profitable. Since we haven't found a way to keep germs on the poor side of town, we have to have hospitals where poor people can get treated. Notice every institution I just mentioned is the frequent butt of anti-government jokes. It's true that none of these ventures make money, because they're not allowed to choose whom they treat, educate, deliver mail to, or drive around town. Now, businesses often say that they can run these ventures "at a profit," and do them "better than government." What they mean is that they can cut people off who can't pay. But profitability is not the point of these services. They are necessities and are provided by government, for everybody, without regard to profit. Therefore, they will forever be considered "money losers" and "inefficient."

Source: Cohen, Gail. 2010. "Government-Bashing: 7 Myths." Daily Freep, June 4. http://dailyfreep.blogspot.com/2010/06/government-bashing-7-myths.html.

CHAPTER 2

Organizational Theory and Management

Chapter 2 presents the literature on administrative and organizational theory and behavior relating to the challenges and opportunities of public management. The information in this chapter will enable students to identify and discuss major authors, concepts, and terms associated with organizational theory and management. Some of these theories relate to efficient administration of an organization—the so-called classical and neo-classical management theories that introduce readers to Max Weber's idea of bureaucracy, Frederick Taylor's assembly-line approach to managing organizations, as well as Herbert Simon's skepticism of these approaches. The discussion then shifts to the human side of organizations, where Mary Parker Follett, Abraham Maslow, and Douglas McGregor show us that organizational management must take into account the feelings and needs of people. We conclude with an examination of more modern organizational theories.

“When in charge, ponder; when in trouble, delegate; when in doubt, mumble.”

JAMES H. BOREN
Author; Founder of the International Association of Professional Bureaucrats, 1970

Postal Workers Sorting Mail – Mural, Ariel Rios Building, Federal Triangle, Washington DC.

THEORIES OF MANAGERIAL EFFICIENCY

The Classical Management Movement

Frederick Taylor

Frederick Taylor's 1911 monograph, *The Principles of Scientific Management*, revolutionized the idea of optimizing productivity. His four principles of scientific management are the hallmark of the classical management period of public administration. The first principle encompasses the adoption of laws and formulas to determine the most efficient ways of completing tasks. Standard work procedures were believed to engender productivity—and more importantly profit. Taylor, a mechanical engineer by profession, implemented the use of time-and-motion studies to determine the highest level of worker output in accordance with a particular procedure. To motivate workers and maximize output, Taylor advocated adherence to stringent working procedures and tied employee production levels to earnings: he paid workers on a piece-rate basis.

The second principle of Taylor's scientific management theory entails studying the capabilities of workers. By doing so, management can better identify the inherent strengths and limitations of each worker and offer special training to maximize his or her capabilities. Specialization is paramount within the context of Taylorism, a notion first embraced by the eighteenth-century Scottish economist Adam Smith in *The Wealth of Nations* (1776/2003). Smith believed that specialized work increased organizational productivity by increasing the "dexterity" of its workers, allowing them to become as proficient as possible in completing their task. Also, according to Smith, much time is saved by eliminating the need to change tasks, tools, and the like.

Taylor's third principle of scientific management is the fusing together of work procedures and specialized training. "You may develop all the science that you please," noted Taylor (1911), "and you may scientifically select and train workmen just as much as you please, but unless some man or some men bring the science and the workmen together all your labor will be lost." The fusion of procedures and training is arguably the most important responsibility of management, and the success of scientific management is contingent upon an equal division of responsibility between management and workers. This is the fourth, and final, principle of Taylorism. An equal division of labor is advantageous, given the fact that management can better supervise its workers, thereby ensuring adherence to standard procedures. Moreover, according to Taylor, dividing labor promotes cooperation and interdependence, which reduces the likelihood of serious disputes. Productivity and efficiency are the primary ends of scientific management. Standard work procedures, as developed through empirical examination, specialized training, and divided labor serve as the means to those ends. Taylor's organizational components, and the subsequent relationships they manifest, correspond to a bureaucratic framework defined by Weber and discussed later in this chapter.

Frank and Lillian Gilbreth: Stewards of Scientific Management

As associates of Frederick Taylor, Frank and Lillian Gilbreth operated their own management consulting firm, Gilbreth, Inc., from 1910 to 1924. They taught workers how to be more productive and efficient. The Gilbreths were employed as efficiency experts by several major industries both domestically and internationally. Frank Gilbreth's work as a building contractor inspired him to conduct time-and-motion studies in order to decrease the number of motions a worker would need to complete a given task. The results of his studies led to the redesign of machinery operated by factory workers. Lillian Gilbreth was an engineer and a trained psychol-

Workers on the first moving assembly line put together magnetos and flywheels for 1913 Ford autos. By an unknown photographer, Highland Park, Michigan, 1913.

Source: National Archives, Records of the U.S. Information Agency (306-PSE-73-1534).

ogist, and she and Frank coauthored several books on motion studies, including *Fatigue Study: The Elimination of Humanity's Greatest Unnecessary Waste; A First Step in Motion Study* (1919). The Gilbreths had twelve children—most likely a motivating factor in their work on efficiency and time management. Two of their children, Frank Gilbreth, Jr., and Ernestine Gilbreth Carey, chronicled their parents' use of scientific management principles in the context of child rearing in the book *Cheaper by the Dozen*, which was first made into a film in 1950.

> "We don't have plush office space. For many years we weren't treated as professionals, but this office is very professional... We have to take everybody who comes here. Unlike private agencies, we cannot pick and choose our clientele. You've got to love it to stay... I've been here 25 years."
>
> **MARY VIRGINIA DOUGLASS**
> Social Worker

Frank Gilbreth believed that what worked in a factory could work as effectively in a household. For example, he adapted industry process charts for use in the home. These charts listed each of his children's duties and when they were to be done. Throughout the film version of *Cheaper by the Dozen*, one can see Taylorism at work. Particularly memorable scenes include showing his children's school principal the most efficient way to take a bath (fully clothed, of course), as well as the application of motion studies to reduce the recovery time required for his children's tonsillectomies. Frank Gilbreth died in 1924, only days before he was scheduled to lead an assembly of the World Congress of Scientific Management in Prague. At this assembly, Gilbreth was to be honored for his work on the elimination of fatigue in industry through motion study. Lillian Gilbreth ultimately attended the conference in his place. The story of the Gilbreth family subsequent to Frank's death is told in the book *Belles on Their Toes*, which was adapted for film as well.

Lillian Gilbreth had trouble continuing the work of Gilbreth, Inc.—not for a lack of expertise, but because many clients in the 1920s doubted that a woman could command the respect of factory foremen and workers. She started a motion study school in her home in Montclair, New Jersey, believing that even if companies felt she was incapable of implementing scientific management theories within the workplace, they might be willing to send their engineers to her for training. Gilbreth reached out to women, as well, designing blueprints for an efficiency kitchenette that remains the standard for studio apartments even today. She was awarded a contract from General Electric, and the publicity from her kitchenette design caused enrollment in her motion study school to increase substantially. Gilbreth later became a professor of management at Purdue University, and during World War II she was recruited by the War Manpower Commission to help with the rehabilitation of amputees. The American Society of Mechanical Engineers awarded the Henry Laurence Gantt medal to Lillian Gilbreth, and posthumously to Frank Gilbreth, in 1944. This medal recognizes exemplary work in management and community service. In 1966 Lillian Gilbreth became the first woman elected to the National Academy of Engineering.

The Weberian Bureaucracy

Max Weber was a German sociologist and educator. His model of bureaucracy includes several components that mirror Taylor's principles. According to Weber in his influential book *Economy and Society* (1922, published in English translation in 1978), bureaucratic models possess stringent hierarchical components, whereby authority is centralized. Bureaucracies are "jurisdictional" structures that afford modest, if any, individual latitude (1922/1978). This notion of bureaucracy mandates uniform procedures, which are to be executed in an impersonal fashion. For example, Weber advocated the use of written documents as a means of establishing formal lines of communication, which ultimately reinforce a member's powers and responsibilities within the context of the organization's hierarchical structure.

The viability of a bureaucracy is contingent upon technical expertise and appropriate training. While this notion of expertise is thought to be common within corporate structures, Weber believed it was paramount that governmental bureaucracies follow suit. In addition to technical expertise, bureaucracies function best when responsibilities are divided in accordance with competence. Weber championed a bureaucratic model where hierarchy, technical expertise, and merit-based appointments, in conjunction with uniform and impersonal procedures, produce greater organizational output. The Weberian bureaucracy is a machine-like structure under which efficiency is paramount (1922/1978).

Luther Gulick, Lyndall Urwick, and Henri Fayol

Building on the principles of Taylor and Weber, Luther Gulick and Lyndall Urwick (1937) developed the notion of POSDCORB—a set of organizational processes that offer executives a tangible understanding of administration. POSDCORB stands for planning, organizing, staffing, directing, coordinating, reporting, and budgeting, all of which are functional responsibilities of a chief executive. Gulick and Urwick's major goal was to develop the framework for designing and running the most effective organizations. Besides POSDCORB, other equally important principles of administration are discussed by the French executive engineer Henri Fayol in his major work, *General and Industrial Management* (1916, published in English translation in 1949).

Henri Fayol's 14 Principles of Management

1. **Division of work.** Specialization allows for continuous improvement in skills and methods, which leads to increased productivity.

2. **Authority.** The right to give orders and the expectation that they will be followed comes with responsibility.

THE PAPER "STREAM"

Artist: V. Kunnap; Poet: V. Suslov; "The Fighting Pencil" group, 1960.

Look! This is the method of a conveyer belt,
But it seems to resemble more of a red tape,
And if we want to be more precise and less cautious,
We can call the method what it is – just VICIOUS.

3. **Discipline.** Employees are expected to obey the rules. At the same time, the management should provide good leadership.

4. **Unity of command.** This is the "one master principle." That is, a worker should answer to one superior and only one superior to avoid conflicting lines of command.

5. **Unity of direction.** A single mind establishes a single plan that everybody in the organization has a role in. Unity of direction assumes a strategic planning focus.

6. **Subordination of individual interest to the common interest.** When at work, employees must focus only on work-related activities, while the management ensures that they stay focused on achievement of organizational goals.

7. **Remuneration of personnel.** Payment is an important motivator and should be fair, although Fayol points out that there is no perfect system of remuneration.

8. **Centralization** refers to the consolidation of management functions. Decisions flow from top to bottom.

9. **Scalar chain** (or line of authority) is a formal chain of command running from top to bottom of the organization whereby superiors have authority over and responsibility for a number of subordinates, while the span of control suggests that a manager should not have authority over and responsibility for too many subordinates, as this can adversely impact the reach of a manager. Hierarchy is necessary for unity of direction. However, lateral communication is also important as long as superiors know that it is taking place. Scalar chain should not be overstretched or consist of too many levels.

10. **Order.** All materials and personnel have a proper place.

11. **Equity** means equality of treatment (not to be confused with identical treatment). In running a business, a "combination of kindliness and justice" is needed. Treating personnel "well" is paramount for achieving equity.

12. **Stability of personnel tenure.** Employees work better if they have some measure of job security and future career prospects. High employee turnover will deleteriously affect the organization.

> "Leaders work on the culture of the organization, creating it or changing it. Managers work within the culture of the organization."
>
> **EDGAR H. SCHEIN**
> Author, *Organizational Culture and Leadership*

13. **Initiative.** Affording employees opportunities to take initiative is a means of building a strong organization.

14. **Esprit de corps or unity of employed people.** Management must foster the morale, harmony, and cohesion among its employees. As Fayol suggests, "Real talent is needed to coordinate effort, encourage keenness, use each person's abilities, and reward each one's merit without arousing possible jealousies and disturbing harmonious relations" (1916/1949).

Fayol believed his principles of management were universal and applicable to any type of organization. The most important among them are specialization, unity of command, scalar chain, authority, and unity of direction (the last two are referred to as "coordination" by managers).

Drawing from and building on Fayol's theories, Urwick (1952) established "Ten

EXERCISE 2.1

Managerial Priorities

The principal responsibilities usually assigned to a manager are listed below. Review the list and add any responsibilities that you think are missing. Then, rate the five most important managerial responsibilities in descending order from 1 to 5.

_____ Communicate to each worker what the organization expects from him or her.
_____ Interpret policies and procedures.
_____ Plan the work.
_____ Assign the work, providing instructions and explanations to employees.
_____ Provide ongoing guidance to workers.
_____ Maintain quality standards.
_____ Observe and evaluate worker performance.
_____ Correct difficulties as they arise.
_____ Use criticism constructively to improve performance.
_____ Keep records and do required paperwork.
_____ Provide incentives.
_____ Administer and maintain discipline.
_____ Train and orient personnel.
_____ Plan and carry out programs to stimulate employee improvement and growth.
_____ Communicate employees' feelings up the line.
_____ Communicate management's feelings to employees.
_____ Display a keen interest in the work.
_____ Improve your own effectiveness.

Principles," which are now regarded as classical guidelines for organizational management.

1. **Principle of the Objective:** Organizations and each organizational subdivision must be guided by a central purpose.
2. **Principle of Specialization:** Limiting workers to a single responsibility engenders greater productivity.
3. **Principle of Coordination:** The purpose of organizations is to unify workers' efforts.
4. **Principle of Authority:** In any organization, it is imperative that ultimate authority rest with someone. Further, there should be a clear command chain that runs from supreme authority to each individual in the organization.

"A good plan is like a road map: it shows the final destination and usually the best way to get there."

H. STANLEY JUDD
Author; Communications Consultant

5. **Principle of Responsibility:** Managers must be held accountable for their subordinates.
6. **Principle of Definition:** All workers must be informed, in writing, as to the nature of their respective positions. This includes ensuring that workers understand their duties and responsibilities, as well as their working relationship with other positions, both superior and subordinate.
7. **Principle of Correspondence:** There should be continuity between responsibility and authority. In other words, the more authority an individual is given, the more responsibility that individual has.
8. **Span of Control:** The number of subordinates a manager oversees should not exceed six.
9. **Principle of Balance:** Organizational subdivisions must be kept in balance.
10. **Principle of Continuity:** Organizations must recognize that "organizing" is a never-ending process.

Fayol, Urwick, and Gulick's theoretical principles were put into action through the Committee on Administrative Management, also called the *Brownlow Commission,* which was established by Congress in 1936. Under the direction of Gulick, the recommendations set forth in the Brownlow Commission Report (1937) sought to apply classical management principles to public sector institutions. Highlighting the need for reorganization within the executive branch of the federal government, the report recommended an expansion of the White House staff. Additional executive officers would serve in an administrative capacity, providing the president with necessary information so that decisions could be made more responsibly and efficiently. Other Brownlow Commission recommendations included the consolidation of government agencies, an alteration of the fiscal system, and civil service reformation that called for greater emphasis on attracting the most capable individuals for administrative posts.

The Neo-Classical School

Herbert Simon's Skepticism

Widely accepted classical management principles suggest that productivity and efficiency are a function of specialization, hierarchy, a limited span of control, and unity of command and direction. According to Herbert Simon (1946), however, these principles are merely "proverbs," as they are not grounded in scientific research. Simon believed that the classical management principles of administration should be tested empirically, embracing the quasi-scientific methods of controlled experimentation and quantitative analysis. "It is necessary that the objectives of the administrative organization under study be defined in concrete terms so that results, expressed in terms of these objectives, can be accurately measured," Simon wrote in his now-famous article for *Public Administration Review*, "The Proverbs of Administration." He further noted that "sufficient experimental control be exercised to make possible the isolation of the particular effect under study from other disturbing factors that might be operating on the organization at the same time" (1946). Descriptive summaries and best practices research, according to Simon, were inadequate. In particular, Simon argued, "What does it mean, for example, to say: 'The department is made up of three bureaus. The first has a function of..., the second the function of..., and the third a function of....' What can be learned from such a description about the workability of the organizational arrangement? Very little, indeed... Administrative description suffers currently from superficiality, oversimplification, [and] lack of realism" (1946). Best practices introduce the notion of subjective realism, whereby one operates under the assumption that an organization is a model of success, regardless of whether there is a factual basis for such an assumption.

> "Anything that gives us new knowledge gives us an opportunity to be more rational."
>
> **HERBERT A. SIMON**
> Nobel Laureate; Artificial Intelligence Expert

Simon further advocated what became known as the *fact-value dichotomy* (1946), based on the premise that management science inquiry be concerned only with facts. The employment of quasi-scientific methods would afford scholars and practitioners an enhanced understanding of public administration's most productive and efficient practices, and thus the so-called "proverbs" of administration could be replaced with true principles. Simon's quasi-scientific approach to the study of administration—and especially his fact-value dichotomy—engendered significant criticism.

Public administration scholars like Robert Dahl (1989) argued that values were important to the study of public administration, while Dwight Waldo maintained that value-free research undermines the inherent importance of morality and ethics. Underscoring this point, Waldo wrote the following in *American Political Science Review*: "To maintain that efficiency is value-neutral and to propose at the same time that it be used as the central concept in a 'science' of administration is to commit one's self to nihilism, so long as the prescription is actually followed" (1952). Earlier, he had criticized Simon's fact-value dichotomy as implausible, arguing that "administrative study, as any 'social science,' is concerned primarily with human beings, a type of being characterized by thinking and valuing. Thinking implies creativeness, free will. Valuing implies morality" (Waldo, 1948).

> "The threat of people acting in their own enlightened and rational self-interest strikes bureaucrats, politicians and social workers as ominous and dangerous."
>
> **W.G. HILL**

Robert Merton's Challenge

Like Simon's challenge of the classical principles, Robert Merton challenged the Weberian model of bureaucracy during this neo-classical period. As discussed in the context of classical management, the Weberian model of bureaucracy is hierarchical: power is centralized, individual responsibilities are jurisdictional, and uniform procedures are executed in the interest of efficiency. Weber championed rationalization and legal order. According to his model, control and power are sources of stability, and they exist within the context of a dominant-subordinate relationship. The inherent complexity of interpersonal relationships necessitates a measure of coordination, and the Weberian model serves as a means of that coordination.

Merton acknowledged the inherent tension between bureaucratic and democratic principles, most notably because the Weberian model is predicated on secrecy. Transparency and citizen participation are seemingly nonexistent within the context of Weber's model, as Merton points out in his book *Social Theory and Social Structure* (1957, p. 102): "Bureaucracy is administration which almost avoids public discussion of its techniques." Merton considers this condition antithetical to democratic governance. He further contends that the Weberian bureaucracy engenders organizational rigidity, whereby an organization's members are unable to adapt to changing conditions because patterns of behavior are programmed. While programmed patterns of behavior foster greater administrative efficiency, consistency, and precision, there is a disadvantage: behavior that is programmed to the point of being machine-like severely compromises an individual's administrative capacity, perhaps to the point where nothing can be accomplished. Merton refers to this as "trained incapacity" (1957). For example, police officers trained to faithfully cite all traffic violators are unlikely to be successful in enforcing more serious laws.

Merton emphasizes the administrative implications of overconformity; that is, the nature of Weber's bureaucracy cultivates a culture of conformity to the point where *groupthink* is omnipresent. Organizations, then, become overly conservative and resistant to change. Irving L. Janis (1972) describes "groupthink" as a specialized kind of conformity. It occurs only in highly cohesive groups that operate in an environment where there is a feeling of security. The primary goal of this particular decision-making group is to maintain its power and cohesiveness. Groupthink is characterized by extreme conformity that gets in the way of any critical analysis. In the wake of September 11, 2001, the U.S. intelligence community was criticized in this regard, especially the Central Intelligence Administration (CIA), where secrecy and conformity are believed to be pervasive. Further, the standardization of the Weberian model creates a tendency toward depersonalized relationships, the implications of which are felt most at the grassroots level. The routine and depersonalized nature of street-level bureaucrats propagates the impression that public administrators are altogether haughty and uncaring, which reflects poorly on government in general.

> "What you cannot enforce, do not command."
>
> **SOPHOCLES**
> Greek playwright
> (c. 496–406 B.C.)

A recurring theme throughout public administration is reconciling the inherent conflict between administrative bureaucracy and democratic governance. Bureaucracies are synonymous with a managerial approach, which is predicated upon a hierarchical structure, formalization, and uniform procedures that are carried out rather impersonally. Representative bodies are political in nature, which suggests a certain measure of transparency and accountability. This is in contrast to the Weberian bureaucratic model, where a premium is placed upon secrecy. Furthermore, expertise is the hallmark of a bureaucracy, which affords bureaucrats a monopoly of power. Bureaucracies are closed systems that execute policies in a technical rationalist manner—a manner antithetical to the nature of democratic institutions, which ideally emphasize openness and citizen participation.

Philip Selznick

Philip Selznick's discussion of informal organizations within the formal organization departs from classical principles (1949). Selznick notes that the "classical" formal organization is comprised of a certain number of managers and staff, each of whom has specific duties and responsibilities, a chain of command, and some hierarchical arrangement that is reinforced through formal rules and procedures. However, according to Selznick, embedded within this "formal" organization are informal organizations that can either buttress the formal organization's goals and functions, or in some cases serve as tools of resistance, impeding what the formal organization is trying to accomplish (1949). In simplest terms, informal organizations are cliques that are grounded in personal relationships. These cliques can cut across the formal organizational hierarchy—as vice presidents, managers, and rank-and-file employees can form an informal organization.

Selznick also introduces the concept of organizational co-optation (1949). Co-optation deals with bringing new or outside elements into an organization's leadership or decision-making structure. The purpose of doing so is to protect the organization from potential threats. A concrete example will help clarify the idea: Suppose that a state's department of transportation (DOT) has plans to construct an additional highway to alleviate traffic congestion from the suburbs to one of its major cities. Let us assume that this highway project will cut through several residential areas and some parkland throughout a number of municipalities. Even though the new highway is thought to be largely positive in that it will help shorten commute times for workers, its construction will displace a certain number of residents and destroy park land. This is very likely to spark some controversy from local residents and environmentalists. In an effort to minimize the controversy, the DOT will co-opt local residents and environmentalists by giving them a formal voice within the DOT's decision-making and planning structures relating to the highway project. This could be done by simply creating a temporary (or ad hoc) advisory committee that provides input and expresses their concerns regarding the highway project. By having a voice, certain concession from the DOT might be gained. For example, environmental representatives on the ad hoc committee may influence the DOT to pay for the planting of three trees for every one tree destroyed by the highway's construction; or, perhaps the DOT could partially fund the construction of a new park altogether.

Chester Barnard

Chester Barnard's management insights stem from his experiences as president of New Jersey Bell Telephone Company. Barnard differs from the classical theorists in that he stresses the importance of monetary and nonmonetary work incentives in an effort to secure greater worker cooperation. This, in turn, leads to greater organizational stability and improved worker performance. Classical theory assumes that worker cooperation is a function of money and negative reinforcement (e.g., wage reductions, punishment, threats of punishment). In *The Functions of the Executive* (1938), Barnard discusses eight types of worker incentives:

- Material inducements
- Personal nonmaterial opportunities
- Desirable physical conditions of work
- Ideal benefactions
- Habit and attitude conformity
- Opportunity for participation
- Associational attractiveness
- Condition of communion

A material inducement refers to money. Personal nonmaterial opportunities are synonymous with work-related power, prestige, and the opportunity to distinguish oneself. Desirable physical conditions of work can be taken at face value: If an individual works in a factory, a safe working environment may be an important incentive. If an individual works in a white-collar setting, a comfortable office or workspace might be important. The notion of ideal benefactions refers to the belief that your work makes a difference or has a societal purpose. Pride in your work is central to this notion. Habit and attitude conformity is Barnard's way of suggesting that organizational members need to embrace a core set of beliefs. The opportunity for participation coincides with the feeling that one's voice is being heard. And while most workers would not expect to have significant influence in decision making, knowing that their concerns and ideas do not completely fall upon deaf ears can prove to be a cooperative incentive. Associational attractiveness and condition of communion refer to the interpersonal dynamics at work in an organization. Specifically, associational attractiveness assumes that creating a good work environment is a function of everyone "getting along," despite any personality or com-

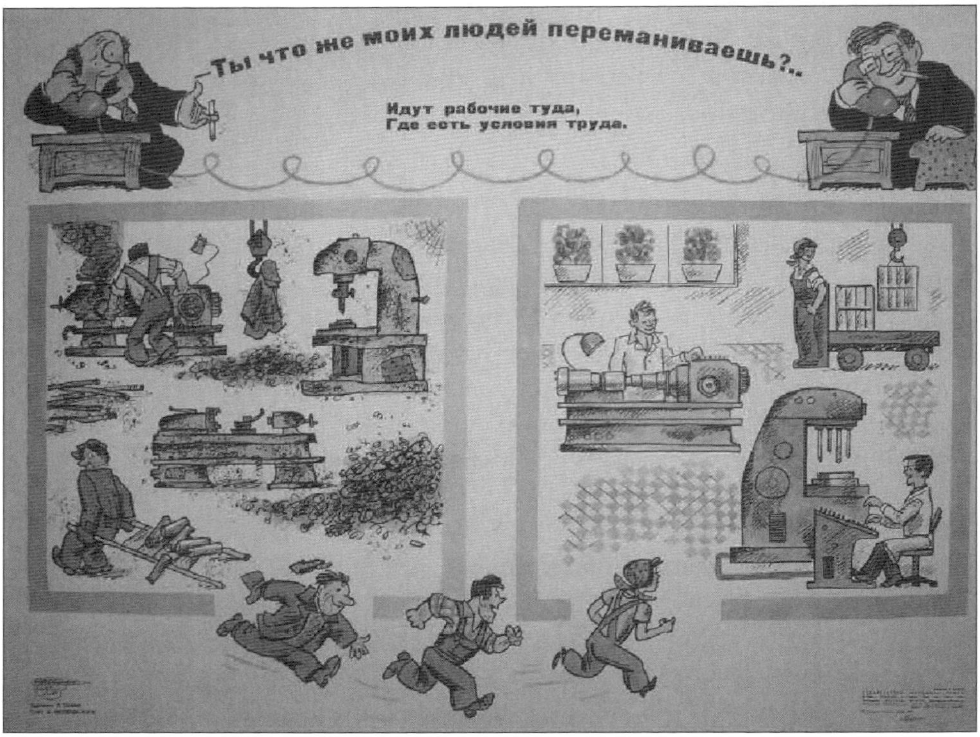

– WHY ARE YOU LURING MY PEOPLE AWAY FROM ME?
Artist: V. Travin; Poet: V. Shkliarinsky; "The Fighting Pencil" group, 1973.

The people choose to work in those places
That have well-organized and clean workspaces.

patibility differences that could be a source of friction. Condition of communion takes things a step further. Instead of merely getting along, an optimal work environment can be created if workers are afforded the "opportunity for comradeship." Associational attractiveness and condition of communion is the difference between getting along with your coworkers and actually liking them (Barnard 1938).

Barnard's notions are a departure from classical management principles. Barnard acknowledges that workers are motivated by more than money, as workers have more complex needs and those needs should be addressed in the interest of fostering cooperation and loyalty to the organization and its goals. It is important to note that while Barnard injects more humanistic views into the broader management literature, the organization remains of paramount importance (1938). People are still thought to be cogs—albeit more complex cogs that can be motivated to cooperate through nonmonetary incentives.

The Human Side of Organizational Management

Mary Parker Follett

Throughout history, friction between upper management and the proletariat has been common. This friction, if not mitigated through proper leadership, can adversely influence the productivity and efficiency of an organization. Organizational leaders are responsible not only for overseeing operations but also for delegating authority. According to Mary Parker Follett in "The Giving of Orders" (1926/2008), authority must be exercised in an impersonal fashion if a leader is to avoid being perceived as overly authoritative or obsequious, as both extremes are counterproductive. The notion of depersonalized orders originated from scientific management. The depersonalization of orders coincided with the notion that workers were like machines. Follett sought a way to reduce management-worker conflict, recognizing that negative behavioral responses are more likely to emerge with superiors who embrace an overly authoritative leadership style. More specifically, Follett wrote:

> What happens to a man, in a man, when an order is given in a disagreeable manner by foreman, head of department, his immediate superior at the store, bank or factory? The man addressed feels that his self-respect has been attacked, that one of his most inner sanctuaries is invaded. He loses his temper or becomes sullen or is on the defensive... the wrong behavior pattern has been set.... He is now set to act in a way which is not going to benefit the enterprise in which he is engaged.

Follett stressed the importance of effective leadership. Organizational leaders must be able to unify individuals, resolve conflicts, demand performance, and delegate authority without dehumanizing an individual. Having written during the height of the classical management movement, Follett interjected humanistic considerations into classical principles.

Stumbling Upon Human Relations Theory

Human relations theory emerged with the *Hawthorne experiments*, which were conducted for studying productivity in accordance with Taylor's scientific management principles. For example, the Western Electric Company conducted an experiment that examined the impact of light amplification differences on worker productivity. Workers were divided into two groups: the treatment group and the control group. The treatment group was exposed to changing light amplifications, while the control group was exposed to a constant light amplification. Curiously, productivity increased in both groups. Further examination by Elton Mayo and Fritz Roethlisberger determined that social-psychological factors impact worker productivity. In other words, the workers at Western Electric were more productive because of the attention paid to them.

> "Nearly all men can stand adversity, but if you want to test a man's character, give him power."
>
> **ABRAHAM LINCOLN**
> 16th President of the United States

The Hawthorne experiments further demonstrated that, under Taylorism, worker-management relationships fostered behaviors that adversely affected organizational efficiency and productivity. The solution was not to increase wages, as Taylor would have prescribed. On the contrary, it was discovered that workers' needs extend beyond economic considerations. Organizations are social institutions, and the classical management theories proved inadequate for satisfactorily explaining organizational dynamics. Such theories failed to acknowledge how complex human nature can be and how a changing environment can impact workers' performance.

Abraham Maslow and Douglas McGregor

The unanticipated results of the Hawthorne experiments engendered a scholarly movement that altered the dynamics of organizational theory. This, in turn, fostered the ascendance of scholars such as Abraham Maslow (1943) and Douglas McGregor (1960), whose theories of motivation were credible enough to rival the orthodoxy. Maslow's theories pertaining to human motivation have been recognized as a hallmark of the human relations movement. In his 1943 article "A Theory of Human Motivation," Maslow states that motivation is predicated upon five fundamental needs, known as the *needs hierarchy*. At the lowest level of the hierarchy are the physiological needs necessary to sustain life (e.g., shelter, food, and clothing). Given the fulfillment of physiological needs, safety needs emerge. Safety needs refer not only to personal security but also to the desire for an "ordered" and "predictable world." Should one's physiological and safety needs be fulfilled, the need for love is next on the hierarchy. In this instance, love refers to acceptance, affection, and a sense of belonging. Fulfillment of an individual's need for love and affection gives way to esteem needs, which are divided into two subgroups. The first accounts for a person's need to be recognized as strong, confident, and autonomous, while the second encompasses a desire for prestige and appreciation. Gratification of esteem needs produces feelings of self-worth and efficacy. Representing the apex of the needs hierarchy is the desire for self-actualization. Individual happiness, according to Maslow, requires that an individual recognize his or her societal niche. As Maslow wrote in "A Theory of Human Motivation" (1943), "A musician must make music, an artist must paint, a poet write, if he is to be ultimately happy. What a man can be, he must be. This need we may call self-actualization." Proving to be the most complex need, the fulfillment of one's inherent potential epitomizes self-actualization.

Classical management theories assume that individuals are motivated primarily by money. Maslow undermined this notion. He contended that individuals are motivated by social and psychological needs, which served to reaffirm what was observed during the Hawthorne experiments. Maslow's needs hierarchy legitimized the human relations school as an alternative to classical management. Several human relations theorists were propelled to the forefront of the management arena, most notably McGregor. Regarded as one of the most influential organizational humanists, McGregor offered two conflicting management theories, each of which

FIGURE 2.1 – CHANGES IN PUBLIC PERSONNEL MANAGEMENT

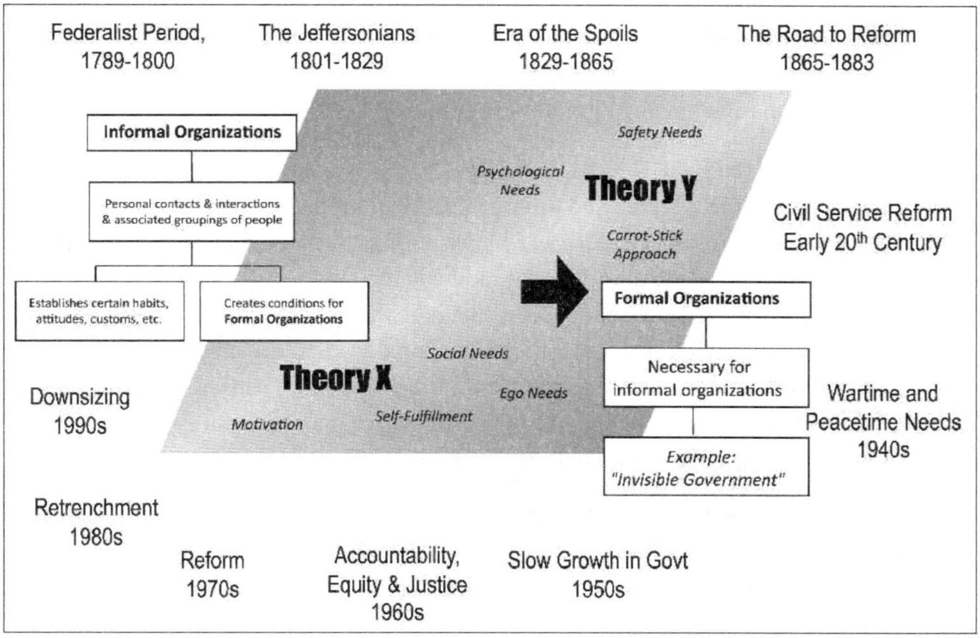

Source: P. Diñoso (2006). School of Public Affairs and Administration, Rutgers University-Newark.

makes specific assumptions regarding human nature. They are *Theories X* and *Y*. *Theory X* assumes that individuals dislike work, and they avoid it whenever possible. This makes intense supervision necessary, because workers typically shun responsibility and are frequently incapable of solving problems. Under *Theory X*, workers are motivated by economic factors, threats, and punishment. This theory represents a classical Weberian closed model, which is reminiscent of a quasi-military structure.

> "Never tell people how to do things. Tell them what to do and they will surprise you with their ingenuity."
>
> **GEORGE S. PATTON**
> U.S. Army General, 1944

Theory Y is an open model that assumes individuals enjoy work and they embrace responsibility. Most people are capable of self-direction and prefer not to be micromanaged. *Theory Y* further assumes that individuals possess the ingenuity to solve complex problems through creative means. According to this theory, management should afford its workers the latitude to achieve individual goals through self-directed efforts. This will help to achieve organizational goals. McGregor embraced *Theory Y*, as it offers more realistic assumptions regarding human nature and human motivation. *Theory X* places a premium upon "external controls," while *Theory Y* relies heavily upon "self-direction." In other words, the difference between *Theories X* and *Y* is "the difference between treating people like children and treating them as mature adults" (McGregor 1960). *Theory X* management principles hinder individual capabilities and discourage personal responsibility through excessive control and worker manipulation. As organizations become more complex, managing becomes more complicated. As such, *Theory X* assumptions are less helpful, and *Theory Y* styles of management that recognize delegation of authority, job enlargement, and participation must receiver greater attention.

Rensis Likert and Chris Argyris

Rensis Likert (1961) developed an organizational model consisting of participative work groups. These work groups were envisioned as important sources of individuals' need satisfaction. Central to Likert's model is the creation of "supportive relationships," which better allow managers to facilitate the productivity of such groups. Likert also constructed a typology of organizational leadership, distinguishing among four types of management: (1) exploitative authoritative, (2) benevolent authoritative, (3) participative consultative, and (4) participative management systems. Systems three and four are ideal from both productivity and human relations standpoints.

Chris Argyris (1957) emphasized the importance of the human condition within organized settings. He viewed the individual and the formal organization as two elements that are often in conflict, ultimately seeking separate goals. Argyris argued that the formal organization—with its chain of command, span of control, and task specialization—can create individual feelings of failure and frustration. Employees may feel deprived of their potential for growth and self-fulfillment. In place of in-

EXERCISE 2.2

X-Y Theory Questionnaire

Score the statements (5 = always, 4 = mostly, 3 = often, 2 = occasionally, 1 = rarely, 0 = never) to indicate whether your current work situation is X or Y:

1. My boss asks me politely to do things, gives me reasons why, and invites my suggestions.
2. I am encouraged to learn skills outside of my immediate area of responsibility.
3. I am left to work without interference from my boss, but help is available if I want it.
4. I am given credit and praise when I do good work or put in extra effort.
5. People leaving the company are given exit interviews to hear their views on the organization.
6. I am incentivized to work hard and well.
7. If I want extra responsibility, my boss will find a way to give it to me.
8. If I want extra training, my boss will help me find how to get it or will arrange it.
9. I call my boss and my boss's boss by their first names.
10. My boss is available for me to discuss my concerns or worries or suggestions.
11. I know what the company's aims and targets are.
12. I am told how the company is performing on a regular basis.
13. I am given an opportunity to solve problems connected with my work.
14. My boss tells me what is happening in the organization.
15. I have regular meetings with my boss to discuss how I can improve and develop.

Total score [___]

60–75 = strongly Y-theory management (effective short- and long-term)
45–59 = generally Y-theory management
16–44 = generally X-theory management
0–15 = strongly X-theory management (autocratic; may be effective short-term, poor long-term)

Score the statements (5 = always, 4 = mostly, 3 = often, 2 = occasionally, 1 = rarely, 0 = never) to indicate whether the person prefers being managed by X or Y style:

1. I like to be involved and consulted by my boss about how I can best do my job.
2. I want to learn skills outside of my immediate area of responsibility.
3. I like to work without interference from my boss, but be able to ask for help if I need it.
4. I work best and most productively without pressure from my boss or the threat of losing my job.
5. When I leave the company, I would like an exit interview to give my views on the organization.
6. I like to be incentivized and praised for working hard and well.

(continued)

EXERCISE 2.2

(continued)

7. I want to increase my responsibility.
8. I want to be trained to do new things.
9. I prefer to be friendly with my boss and the management.
10. I want to be able to discuss my concerns, worries, or suggestions with my boss or another manager.
11. I like to know what the company's aims and targets are.
12. I like to be told how the company is performing on a regular basis.
13. I like to be given opportunities to solve problems connected with my work.
14. I like to be told by my boss what is happening in the organization.
15. I like to have regular meetings with my boss to discuss how I can improve and develop.

Total score [___]

60–75 = strongly prefers Y-theory management
45–59 = generally prefers Y-theory management
16–44 = generally prefers X-theory management
0–15 = strongly prefers X-theory management

Source: Copyright © Alan Chapman 2002–7. With permission from www.businessballs.com. Based on the work of Douglas McGregor.

centives to produce, there are often pressures to be mediocre. Otherwise intelligent and enthusiastic new employees quickly receive messages not to overwork or outperform their superiors. Most important, bureaucrats do not "rock the boat." This attitude is often reinforced by the knowledge that underperformers are seldom fired, a consequence of Weberian-like bureaucratic mechanisms. Argyris suggests that a worker's participation in decisions affecting his or her work gives that individual greater job satisfaction, which, in turn, will have a positive impact on productivity.

One other unanticipated consequence of bureaucracy is the creation of what is known as the "organization man or woman." The organization man is one who has bartered his or her conscience for security. These individuals are survivors in that they are products of the necessity "to go along to get along," which means compromising and complying in the interest of protecting one's position and work. They are cooperative, adept at embracing colleagues, effective in establishing informal links within an organization, and protective of their subordinates. In short, they are successful "bureaucrats."

Others who may not be suited to bureaucracy include the "technical expert." The organizational roles of technical experts are unique; they share a special commitment to their skills and a primary identification with their professional peers. Their professional values may conflict with bureaucratic claims for organizational loyalty and adaptability. As a result, they often find it difficult to play the roles required to compete for organizational success and power. These technical experts differ from so-called "locals" who identify with and stress loyalty to the bureaucracy.

Human relations theorists were critical of classical management approaches, particularly Taylorism, because they ignored the social and emotional impacts these theories exerted on workers. Classical management underestimated the inherent complexity of human nature; consequently, workers were not treated as human beings. Rather, they were thought to be interchangeable cogs working within the framework of a hierarchically rigid, machine-like organizational structure.

CONTEMPORARY ORGANIZATIONAL THEORIES

Structural Theory

Structural theory assumes that organizations are rational in that they function to accomplish specific goals and objectives. Further, for every organization there is believed to be a "best structure," and organizational dysfunction can be corrected through structural changes. Structural theory is, by and large, grounded in classical principles of efficiency, effectiveness, and productivity. In their research on electronics firms in the United Kingdom, Tom Burns and G.M. Stalker (1961) describe two disparate but complementary organizational management systems: *mechanistic* and *organic* systems. Mechanistic systems are Weberian in nature, and they are ideally suited for stable environments. In mechanistic systems, worker roles and responsibilities are clearly defined, communication is formal and top-down, the organizational structure is hierarchical, and the decision-making processes are authoritative. Emphasis is placed on being able to efficiently repeat procedures, an example of which is mass production or mass service delivery. Organic systems are better suited for environments where instability and change are frequent. Worker roles and responsibilities are less clearly defined and more flexible. Communication is informal, and workers of different ranks exchange ideas through consultative networks. The organizational structure is horizontal, and decisions are made on the basis of knowledge and expertise as opposed to hierarchical position. Organic systems emphasize adaptability and innovation over efficient repetition, example of which may include IT systems. Burns and Stalker (1961) note that mechanistic and organic systems are not mutually exclusive. In other words, the best organizations try to incorporate the best of both systems.

Henry Mintzberg (1979) identifies five fundamental parts of an organization. They include: (1) the operating core, (2) the strategic apex, (3) the middle line, (4) the technostructure, and (5) the support staff. The operating core represents the frontline workers who are responsible for an organization's production of goods or services. The strategic apex—the organization's upper-level or executive leadership—includes the chief executive officer, board of directors, and related executive level staff. Primarily responsible for ensuring that the organization runs smoothly and in accordance with a broader organizational strategy, the strategic apex is further charged with managing outside stakeholder relationships that are critical to the organization's work. The third fundamental part of an organization, the middle line, represents middle management. These workers are charged with supervising the operating core while simultaneously supporting and taking direction from the strategic apex. The middle line is also responsible for managing relations with the technostructure and support staff.

The technostructure and support staff are removed from the hierarchical structure that encompasses the operating core, the strategic apex, and the middle line. The technostructure represents analysts responsible for training, standardizing work procedures, and general planning. This typically would include engineers, trainers, accountants, and budget analysts. Finally, support staff ranges from public relations, legal aid, and personnel staff to mailroom, custodial, and foodservice work-

— *Укажите конкретно, чем мы ограничиваем вашу инициативу!*

Рисунок Э. ПИХО
(из эстонского сатирического журнала «Пиккер»)

– TELL US EXACTLY IN WHAT WAY WE LIMIT YOUR INITIATIVE!
Artist: E. Piho; Pikker (Estonia), the 1970s.

TABLE 2.1 – MECHANISTIC VS. ORGANIC MANAGEMENT SYSTEMS

	Mechanistic Organization Form/ Management System	**Organic Organization Form/ Management System**
Conditions	**Stable**	**Changing**
Distribution of tasks	Specialized differentiation of functional tasks into which the problems and tasks facing a concern as a whole are broken down	Contributive nature of special knowledge and experience to the common task of the concern
Nature of individual task	The abstract nature of each individual task, which is pursued with techniques and purposes more or less distinct from those of the concern as a whole: i.e., the functionaries tend to pursue the technical improvements of means, rather than the accomplishment of the ends of the concern	The "realistic" nature of the individual task, which is seen as set by the total situation of the concern
Who (re)defines tasks	The reconciliation, for each level in the hierarchy, of these distinct performances by the immediate superiors, who are also, in turn, responsible for seeing that each is relevant in his own special part of the main task	The adjustment and continual redefinition of individual tasks through interaction with others
Task scope	The precise definition of rights and obligations and technical methods attached to each functional role	The shedding of "responsibility" as a limited field of rights, obligations and methods (problems may not be posted upwards, downwards or sideways as being someone else's responsibility)
How is task conformance ensured	The translation of rights and obligations and methods into the responsibilities of a functional position	The spread of commitment to the concern beyond any technical definition
Structure of control, authority and communication	Hierarchic, Contractual	Network, Presumed Community of Interest
Locating of knowledge	Reinforcement of the hierarchic structure by the location of knowledge of actualities exclusively at the top of the hierarchy, where the final reconciliation of distinct tasks and assessment of relevance is made	Omniscience no longer imputed to the head of the concern; knowledge about the technical or commercial nature of the here and now may be located anywhere in the network
Communication between members of concern	Vertical; i.e., between superior and subordinate	Lateral; i.e., between people of different rank, resembling consultation rather than command
Governance for operations and working behavior	Instructions and decisions issued by superiors	Information and advice rather than instructions and decisions
Values	Insistence on loyalty to the concern and obedience to superiors as a condition of membership	Commitment to the concern's task and to the "technological ethos" of material progress and expansion is more highly valued than loyalty and obedience
Prestige	Greater importance and prestige attaching to internal (local) than to general (cosmopolitan) knowledge, experience, and skill	Importance and prestige attach to affiliations and expertise valid in the industrial and technical and commercial milieus external to the firm

Source: Based on Tom Burns and G.M. Stalker, The Management of Innovation. Value-Based Management.net. www.valuebasedmanagement.net/.

ers. When comparing technostructure jobs with support staff jobs, the distinction we draw is that while members of the technostructure could, more than likely, do the work of the support staff, the support staff would probably require some specialized training to do the work of the technostructure. Consistent with Taylor's principles of scientific management, organizations placed greater emphasis on standardization following World War II, and thus the importance of the technostructure grew. The advent and growth of operations research and strategic planning further enhanced the importance of the technostructure.

Systems Theory

Systems theory is based on the premise that the organization is comprised of several interconnected parts, each of which is designed to achieve broader organizational goals and objectives. Systems theory looks at the organization in terms of inputs, processes, outputs, and feedback mechanisms. Inputs refer to an organization's resources, and processes refer to what an organization does with its resources, while outputs are the goods or services that an organization produces. Feedback mechanisms are the means by which an organization collects and analyzes data regarding the impacts of its outputs. Inputs feed into processes, which feed into outputs. Outputs generate feedback, which cycle around and feed into the organization's inputs. Systems theory is cyclical, and it assumes that organizations are ever changing in order to respond effectively to environmental and intra-organizational changes. In other words, systems theorists argue that organizations must be able to adapt to changing conditions.

W. Edwards Deming and Japanese Management

Following World War II, General Douglas MacArthur, commander of the U.S. forces occupying Japan, sought to do all he could to revive the Japanese economy as quickly as possible. He saw that Japan, as an island economy, needed to trade with other nations rather than rely upon its own natural resources. However, he also saw that Japan's poor reputation for quality would seriously hurt its trade efforts. MacArthur asked the U.S. government to assign someone to teach better quality control methods to Japanese industrial leaders. American quality management expert Dr. W. Edwards Deming, a statistician for the U.S. government, was sent overseas to train Japanese managers in continued process improvement. Deming served in this function from 1948 to 1950, and he performed his job so successfully that he was asked repeatedly to train more engineers and scientists in statistical methods. In 1951, the Japanese government honored his services by establishing the Deming prize. Dr. Deming's philosophy, also known as the Deming wheel, says that everyone should plan, collect data, analyze, construct the work, and keep the circle rotating to maintain quality properly in a company.

The "Quality Circle"

Deming (1986) introduced the Japanese to the concept of statistical quality control (SQC), which was immediately adopted by the union of Japanese scientists and engineers (JUSE) as the cornerstone of their improvement program. Then, in 1952, at a conference in Syracuse, New York, Dr. Deming introduced the founder of JUSE,

– WHY ISN'T YOUR NEW EMPLOYEE SLEEPING?
– HE'S A CLIMBER.
Artist: O. Kornev; *Krokodil* [*Crocodile*] satirical magazine, 1970s.

FIGURE 2.2 – A COLLEGE THROUGH MINZBERG'S LENS

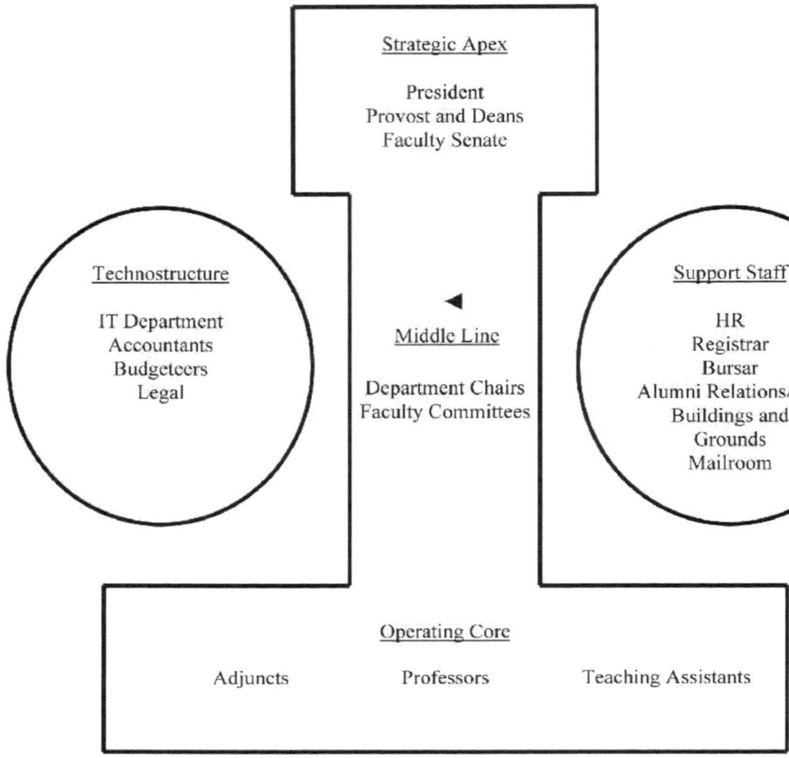

Mr. Koyanagi, to another American expert on quality control, Dr. Joseph Juran. (2004) Over the next few years, Juran visited Japan several times, teaching the Japanese his approach to quality improvement, an approach that stressed participative decision making (2004). Juran's ideas served as the basis for the so-called "quality circles" program that followed several years later. Dr. Juran lectured and preached what is known as total quality control, which says that quality begins in the design stage and ends after satisfactory services are provided to the customer. An organization's success depends, therefore, on "total quality," not simply manufacturing quality (Juran 2004).

In order for an agency or organization to increase its effectiveness and productivity, careful attention must be paid to the nature and quality of employee commitment and participation. Thus, the concept of the "quality circle" (or QC) emerged as a management concept. A quality circle is a small group of employees who perform similar tasks and meet regularly and voluntarily to solve work-related problems. The overriding purpose of these meetings is to improve the quality of an organization's services or products by systematically involving employees in the decision-making process. The underlying concept is that the employee is an expert: the person closest to the work knows the problems best and can be trained to solve them. Employees share with management the commitment to identifying and solving problems related to coordination and productivity. Decisions are made by consensus, with broad participation and a long-term view. For some organizations, QCs formalize informal or sporadic efforts already under way. They provide structure, continuity, and recognition to ad hoc attempts at employee involvement. Their appeal and potential is in offering a theory and set of practices for effecting organizational change.

QCs are not gripe sessions, social hours, alternatives to unions, or substitutes for regular staff meetings. They do not focus on union or personnel issues such as wages, benefits, and grievances. Discussion of specific personalities is usually forbidden, although some QC programs allow it if the purpose is to solve a problem and not simply to vent. QCs address problems related to work processes: expediting the work flow (processing of cases, forms, requests, complaints, and the like); bureaucratic rigidity (e.g., unrealistic, time-consuming procedures); organizing physical facilities and resources more efficiently; overstaffing/understaffing; lateness and absenteeism; communication bottlenecks among work units/levels; clarifying organizational goals, objectives, and methods; reducing costs in specific program areas; reducing waste; and improving on-the-job safety. As the most widely used method of participatory management, QCs have been instituted under various names, among them:

- Quality teams
- Employee teams
- Task force management
- Operations improvement
- Performance circles
- Z teams
- Employee participation groups
- Participative decision making

Potential Benefits of QC Programs

Performance improves for the following reasons: Quality of information improves because employees are typically closer to the problems than management. When employees solve their own work-related problems, management has access to a different set of information and a wider range of problems can be addressed. Usually a small percentage of the people in an organization are responsible for the vast majority of the problem solving. With QCs, however, problems become the responsibility of the entire organization. Quality of decisions improves, time is better spent, and more and better information about a wider range of problems that everyone works to solve gives management more time to manage.

Employees are more committed to decisions that they make for themselves. Most organizations have to spend too much time "selling" their decisions to resistant employees. But if employees see the connection between their own performance and the organization's success, they feel invested in the outcome and commit more of themselves to it. Attitudes change and the quality of services and products improves as emphasis shifts away from performance. Quality improvement is the raison d'être for QCs. Organizational tensions decrease when employees gain a stronger voice in determining their work environment. Likewise, when the burden of problem solving becomes shared, managers' attitudes change. A "win-win" orientation develops. Both sides benefit from an atmosphere of cooperation, mutual interest, and trust.

Through QCs, an organizational mission develops—a genuine mission, not just a paper mandate. Employees develop a clear sense of purpose in terms of their specific jobs. High performance standards emerge; communication increases and actually

FIGURE 2.3 – THE DEMING WHEEL

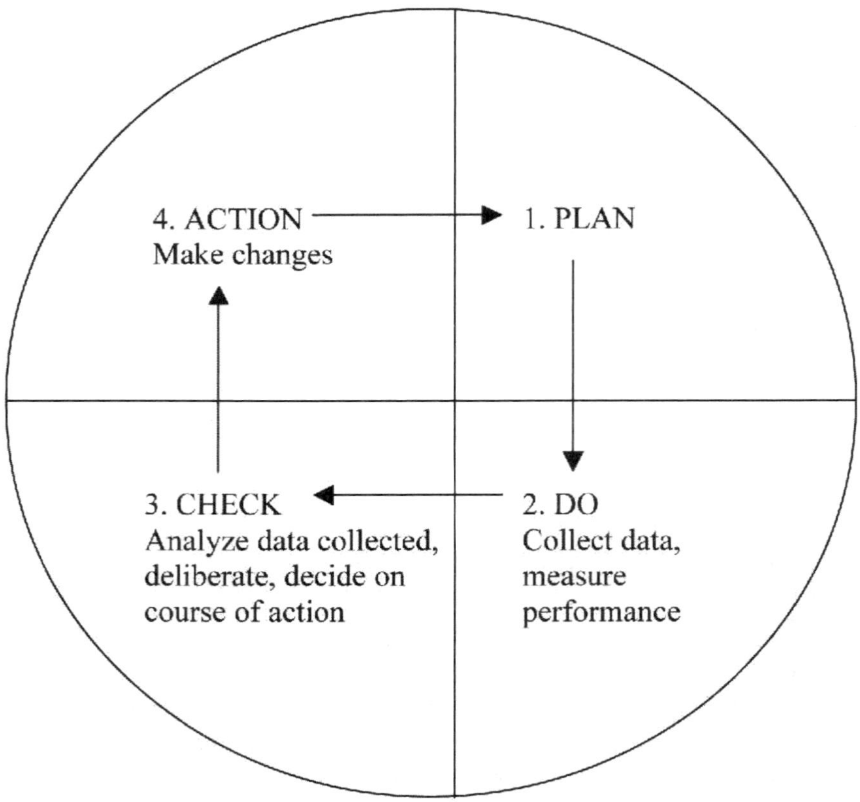

improves as problems arise; and more people are consulted to create ongoing consensus and ensure that the best ideas are implemented. Career development becomes a dynamic process by expanding skills. QCs promote personal growth by enlarging the bounds of routine work. They provide job enrichment. These benefits are particularly important in organizations with limited avenues of vertical mobility. Pride in performance increases, and employees gain a sense of autonomy: they realize that they can influence how the job is done and that management will help. Any dissatisfaction with the status quo motivates them toward further improvement. At the same time, managers feel better about their role by spending less time "managing by exception"—that is, emphasizing the negative side of employees' performance.

> "The disease which inflicts bureaucracy ar what they usua die from is routine."
>
> **JOHN STUART MII**
> Nineteenth-centur English Philosophe

Organizational Economic Theory

Organizational economic theory is primarily concerned with ensuring that managers and rank-and-file employees are working for the betterment of the organization. In other words, economic theory strives to ensure that worker interests coincide with the organization's interests, which are embodied in the organization's "owner." This idea is best captured in what is known as *principal-agent theory*. Principal-agent theory deals with the inherent challenges of motivating workers and controlling cooperative action. It holds that an organization's principals—owners, stockholders, CEOs, government agency heads—desire some organizational achievement. From a private sector perspective, this could include greater profits and market share or higher stock prices. From a public sector perspective, this could include more efficient and effective service delivery or improved citizen satisfaction. Regardless of what the principals hope to achieve, they need help from "agents." Agents usually represent an organization's employees, but they also include external players that provide services to the organization but are not a part of the formal structure.

A fundamental problem is that both principals and agents are motivated by self-interest. Principals are concerned about themselves in the context of how the organization is performing, while agents are simply concerned about themselves. Another problem for principals is that they seldom know whether agents are behaving in a way that benefits the organization. In short, principals are at a significant disadvantage in terms of information. Principal-agent theory attempts to reconcile the inherent conflict between principal and agent interests, while at the same time addressing the information disadvantage of principals. This is accomplished by (1) monetarily compensating agents in a manner that influences the interests of the agents to converge with interests of the principals, and (2) implementing oversight mechanisms that make sure agents are performing as expected.

Organizational Culture

What is organizational culture? Does it refer to the customs and rituals that go on within an organization? Does it refer to behavioral norms or the way people interact with one another? Can organizational culture be defined as the values that underpin how an organization operates? Or, as Joanne Martin (2002) suggests, does it refer to "how things are done" within any organization? In short, organizational culture is all of these things and much more. Edgar Schein (1993) believes that organizational culture refers to shared notions that bind together members of an organization, some of which include:

- Behavioral regularities when people interact: This could include greeting a coworker with a "good morning" or asking about someone's family or weekend.
- Group norms and values.
- A guiding mission and formal rules that dictate what is and is not appropriate behavior.
- Climate and environment. This typically refers to an organization's physical layout.
- Shared skills and modes of thinking.

An organization's physical layout can tell someone a great deal about an organization's culture. New York City mayor and media mogul Michael Bloomberg believes that the layout of an organization's workspace significantly impacts worker morale and performance. As former chief executive of Bloomberg, L.P., Mayor Bloomberg does not believe in private, individual offices or closed-in cubicles; rather, he champions an open layout, whereby rank-and-file and upper-level employees are given small, open workspaces within a large chamber. Dubbed the "bullpen," Bloomberg's open layout is reminiscent of the trading floor of the New York Stock Exchange. From an organizational culture standpoint, what does this convey? Most notably, it conveys the importance of transparency and accountability. Furthermore, the open layout is conducive to employee interaction. City Hall employees are not forced to schedule time with the mayor to ask his opinion or gain approval for something. All they need to do is stop by his desk, which is in the middle of the bullpen, and talk to him face to face. When there is a need for privacy, the mayor and his associates can retreat to conference rooms that are surrounded by glass. Mayor Bloomberg does not believe in executive dining halls or private parking spaces, as these types of things serve only to create class culture, which can have a negative impact on employee morale (Bloomberg 1997, 2001).

The importance of organizational culture was thrust center stage following the terrorist attacks on New York City's Twin Towers on September 11, 2001. Specifically, the CIA and FBI were highly criticized for their failure to cooperate with one another regarding domestic terrorism. Any effort to get the CIA and FBI to work together goes beyond mere edicts. The organizational cultures of the CIA and FBI differ fundamentally, and this cultural rift makes collaboration and communication inherently difficult. From an outsider's perspective, it would appear that an ongoing clash exists between the CIA and FBI—a clash that manifests itself in petty turf battles that are simply a part of interagency competition. This, according to experts, would be oversimplifying the problem, as members of the CIA and FBI view the world very differently.

The FBI's mission is law enforcement, and success is measured in terms of the number of arrests, prosecutions, and convictions made. FBI agents tend to process information in a linear fashion; that is, they have tunnel vision, only concerning themselves with facts that are relevant to a specific case. Like all domestic law enforcement agencies, the FBI is guided by strict rules with regard to information gathering (refer to the Fifth Amendment of the U.S. Constitution), while the CIA is not bound by the same legal standards given its operations abroad. The FBI is case driven, whereby emphasis is placed on gathering facts that lead to a suspect. In contrast, the CIA is concerned not with facts of specific cases but rather with the relationship or connection between facts and cases. This ideally enables the CIA to predict what might happen in the future. The FBI's world is real and tangible, while the CIA's world is hypothetical and predictive. In other words, FBI agents are not trained to predict where the next bank robbery will take place; they are trained to react to the situation once it occurs. In contrast, CIA agents are trained to be proactive, not reactive.

National Performance Review

Given the public pressure on government organizations to perform more effectively, Osborne and Gaebler's *Reinventing Government* (1992) provides recommendations

EXERCISE 2.3

Organization Effectiveness Simulator (Simulation)

Test your understanding of organizational theory through a series of exercises provided on the Booz & Company website. Identify the organizational flash points and create a strategy to address them. Using this simulator, test your strategy and evaluate the results. After you have completed this exercise, analyze the process for diagnosing the flash points, for creating the strategy, and for assessing the results. Would you have done anything differently?

Booz & Company, Inc., "Organization Effectiveness Simulator"
www.simulator-orgeffectiveness.com/booz

for improvements. The "reinventing government" movement is a synthesis of varying approaches. Specifically, Osborne and Gaebler (1992) argue that government should:

- Act as a catalyst
- Empower rather than simply serve
- Be competitive
- Be mission-driven as opposed to rule-driven
- Be results-oriented
- Be customer-driven
- Be enterprising
- Anticipate social problems
- Be decentralized
- Be market-oriented

As much as reinventing government has become part of the public management lexicon, it is far from a new invention. For instance, the ideas of decentralization and competition were taken from the public-choice school of thought (in the mid-1960s). The reinventing government school of thought is more pro-government than public choice, whose supporters tended to view government as inherently problematic. Reinventing government calls for more discretion for public administrators, praise for entrepreneurial government, and support for preventive rather than reactive government.

Central to reinventing government is competition. Competition, however, is not limited to private sector organizations bidding to do the work of government organizations. Rather, the idea calls for competition within the public sector itself—public organizations competing with other public organizations. Osborne and Gaebler advocate competition as a means for improving government performance. They further point out the strengths and weaknesses not only of the public sector but also of the private and nonprofit sectors. The public sector, they argue, is better suited toward policy management, regulation, enforcement of regulations, prevention of discrimination and exploitation, and promoting social cohesion. The private sector is better suited for generating profit and fostering self-sufficiency. The nonprofit sector (which generates no profit and relies on huge numbers of volunteers) is ideal for promoting social welfare, individual responsibility, community, and commitment to society's general welfare.

UNDERSTANDING DIFFERENT CULTURES AND HISTORY BETWEEN THE TWO COUNTRIES

Comparing Different Cultures between the Two Countries

According to Geert Hofstede, we can divide national cultures along five dimensions: Power distance, Individualism, Masculinity/Femininity, Uncertainty avoidance, and Long-term orientation. A definition of each dimension is listed in the box below:

Power distance

This dimension deals with the fact that all individuals in societies are not equal —it expresses the attitude of the culture towards these inequalities amongst us. Power distance is defined as *the extent to which the less powerful members of institutions and organisations within a country expect and accept that power is distributed unequally*. It has to do with the fact that a society's inequality is endorsed by the followers as much as by the leaders.

Individualism

The fundamental issue addressed by this dimension is *the degree of interdependence a society maintains among its members*. It has to do with whether a peoples' self-image is defined in terms of "I" or "We." In Individualist societies people are supposed to look after themselves and their direct family only. In Collectivist societies people belong to "in groups" that take care of them in exchange for loyalty.

Masculinity / Femininity

A high score (masculine) on this dimension indicates that the society will be driven by competition, achievement and success, with success being defined by the "winner" or "best-in-the-field." This value system starts in school and continues throughout one's life- both in work and leisure pursuits. A low score (feminine) on this dimension means that the dominant values in society are caring for others and quality of life. A feminine society is one where quality of life is the sign of success and standing out from the crowd is not admirable. *The fundamental issue here is what motivates people, wanting to be the best (masculine) or liking what you do (feminine).*

(continued)

(continued)

Uncertainty avoidance

The dimension Uncertainty Avoidance has to do with the way that a society deals with the fact that the future can never be known: should we try to control the future or just let it happen? This ambiguity brings with it anxiety and different cultures have learned to deal with this anxiety in different ways. *The extent to which the members of a culture feel threatened by ambiguous or unknown situations and have created beliefs and institutions that try to avoid these* is reflected in the UAI score.

Long-term orientation

The long-term orientation dimension is closely related to the teachings of Confucius and can be interpreted as dealing with society's search for virtue, *the extent to which a society shows a pragmatic future-oriented perspective rather than a conventional historical short-term point of view.*

Source: http://geert-hofstede.com/united-states.html

FIGURE 2.4 – CULTURE COMPARISONS BETWEEN THE US AND SOUTH KOREA

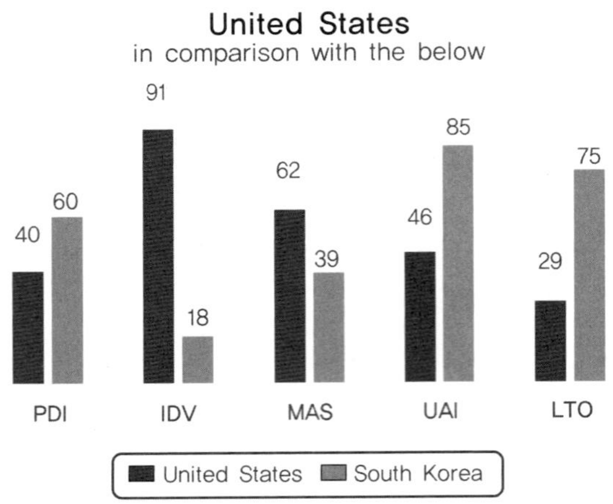

As Figure 2.4 shows, we can find out real differences in culture dimensions between the two countries. Korea is higher on the power distance index, uncertainty avoidance index, and long-term orientation. It is obvious that the US is significantly higher than Korea on individualism. Based on this information, what can you conclude in terms of motivation and organization theories as applied to public managers? Please discuss what caused these differences between the two nations.

Different Nations, Different History

Below are some diagnoses on two countries' different settings. Do you agree with these analyses? Can you imagine how different types of organizational culture affect public managers' behaviors? After reading the following diagnoses in the box, please discuss different strategies to motivate public managers in each country.

The United States: Individualism-Based Bureaucratic Culture

LEGACIES OF LIBERALISM, PLURALISM, AND CHRISTIAN VALUES

Liberalism has played a vital role in American history (Garry 1992, p.43). The American liberal tradition reflects a consistent belief in the two basic concepts of liberalism — individual freedom and dignity and democratic rule of society (Garry 1992, p.81). The liberalism of Jefferson and Jackson sought to expand the American democracy and equip more Americans with political freedoms and power.

Political liberals historically have had close connections with religion and have gleaned many of their political values from religious values (Garry 1992, p.126). Religion in America has been historically liberal in its political messages. Many of the virtues of liberal pluralism, such as a respect for individual dignity and a belief in the equality of all persons, have strong roots in Judeo-Christian beliefs. Unlike Marxism, the Judeo-Christian theology believes that every individual matters and possesses incalculable worth (Garry 1992, p.177). As Patricia Bonomi put it,

> The Great-Awakening of the eighteenth century fostered a strong individualism in spiritual matters and had a spill over effect in the political world by inspiring individuals to throw off corrupt, traditional forms of authority and to attack the doctrines of divine right and passive obedience to rulers that had propped up despotic bishops as well as tyrannous kings. Thus, by encouraging liberal colonial leaders to rebel against traditional hierarchical rulers in the name of individual freedom, the American colonial churches exerted a strong and vital hand in forming the American liberal political tradition (Quoted from Garry 1992, pp. 126-127).

Garry also adds to American Liberalism:

> Besides the influence of religious ideas and values upon liberalism, the acceptance and support of civil religion also characterizes American Liberalism. The concept of civil religion refers to the political recognition of the influence and tradition of religion in America's public life. Civil religion recognizes the strong influence on American liberal democratic principles of the Judeo-Christian values and heritage, and expresses the correlation between religious and political behavior that has always prevailed (Garry 1992, pp.127-128). *(continued)*

(continued)

In addition, Lutrin and Settle emphasize the legacy of pluralism in America's public bureaucracy as follows:

> Pluralism has long provided the dominant description and ideal of American politics. As description, it portrays the system as a balance of power among overlapping economies, religious, ethnic, and geographic groups. Each group has some voice in shaping socially-binding decisions; each constraint and is constrained through processes of mutual group adjustments; and all major groups share a broad system of beliefs and values which encourages conflict to proceed within established channels and allows initial disagreements to dissolve into compromise solutions (Lutrin and Settle 1976, p.293).

Page also describes pluralism as follows:

> Pluralism, as a theory and practice, assumes that groups are good: that citizens have the right to organize to advance their interests; that groups with differing interests will bargain and compete; and that the result of bargaining and competition among group interests is in the interest of the whole community or nation — the public interest (Page 1971, p.61).

Directly related to individualism and pluralism is the notion of political and economic competition, primarily among groups but also among individuals. Limited government suggests that competition will be loosely regulated by government; in theory, competition itself will establish boundaries of acceptable behavior among the competitors, and allocate the fruits of victory (Gordon 1978).

In a sense, both pluralism and individualism are closely related to the spirit of representativeness in American government. As Kaufman argues, "the quest for representativeness in this generation centers primarily on administrative agencies" (Kaufman 1969, p.5).

According to Gordon (1978), the United States has defined itself politically as a "liberal democracy," and economically as a capitalist system. Two political concepts, popular sovereignty and limited government, are central to the notion of liberal democracy. In particular, the concept of limited government reflects the predominant view held by those who framed the Constitution that government posed a basic threat to individual liberties. Limited government was to be achieved through four devices working concurrently: (1) separation of powers among the executive, legislative, and judicial branches of government; (2) a system of checks and balances, (3) federalism, and (4) judicial review.

Almond and Verba described American political culture as a civic culture that is participant-based and pluralistic, "based on communication and persuasion, a culture of consensus and diversity, a culture that permitted change but moderated it" (Almond and Verba 1963, p.8). This participant political culture is one in which the members of the society tend to be explicitly oriented to the system as a whole and to both the political and administrative structures and processes: in other words, to both the input and output aspects of the political system (Almond and Verba 1963, p.19). In this situation, in general one can expect that the extent to which the local government is open to citizen participation in decisions would be closely related to the extent of local autonomy (Almond and Verba 1963, p.168).

As Gordon points out, two related concepts widely reflected in American society are individualism and pluralism. The emphasis on the individual is evident in the complex of civil rights and liberties protections, but individualism also implies the right to participate meaningfully in the political process in pursuit of the goals one considers important. Pluralism, on the other hand, stresses the appropriateness of group organization as a means of securing protection for broad group interests in society (Gordon 1978, p.34).

Lowi defined "interest-group liberalism" as follows:

> It may be called liberalism because it expects to use government in a positive and expansive role, it is motivated by the highest sentiments and it possesses strong faith that what is good for government is good for society. It is interest-group liberalism because it sees as both necessary and good that the policy agenda and the public interest be defined in terms of the organized interests in society (Lowi 1969, p.71).

Interest-group liberalism, as a model for public policy, is derived from a more inclusive conceptualization of power relations and the role of the government in American society, namely pluralism. Government institutions, according to the early proponents of pluralism, were created by a voluntary social contract among members of society. The contract was based on mutual consensus regarding certain fundamental rights and norms of public order which government is entrusted to protect. From this perspective, it is maintained that the multi-influence process provides checks and balances among the numerous private interest groups outside government as well as among the institutions of government themselves (Nachmias and Rosenbloom 1980).

THE IDEA OF AMERICAN FEDERALISM: NON-CENTRALIZATION

In The Federalist (1788), Madison, Hamilton, and Jay were particularly concerned with the concept of the separation of powers, which they hoped would be established through the ratification of the Constitution. Furthermore, "Dispersion

(continued)

(continued)

of authority among diverse decision structures in any one unit of government is a necessary condition if the rules of constitutional law are to be enforceable as against those who exercise governmental authority"(*Federalist* 47 and 80, requoted from Ostrom, 1974).

In this regard, the primary purpose of a constitutional system is to limit the powers of government.

It should be noted that the starting point of the American government system was the idea of the separation of powers, and these premises still dominate American bureaucracy.

The most elementary definition of federalism suggests that it is a constitutional division of governmental power between a central or national government and a set of regional units, where both the national and regional governments have some independent as well as some shared powers over their citizens (Gordon 1978). These ideas have been reflected in the American constitution. In fact, the framers of the American constitution devised a number of ways — separation of powers, checks and balances, judicial review, and federalism — to prevent the abuse of power in the system they were creating and at the same time to preserve the largest possible area of independent action for the individual (Leach 1970, p.57). Leach also points out that the "new federalism" asserted by President Richard Nixon stresses responsible decentralization. In other words, it places greater emphasis on the effective implementation of government policies, particularly at the state and local levels (Leach 1970, p.16). In its simplest form, federalism means national unification through the maintenance of sub-national systems (Elazar 1972, p.3). In fact, federalism is everywhere a compromise between centralizing and decentralizing forces (Schlesinger 1945, p.11). Federalism can be defined as the mode of political organization that unites separate polities within an overarching political system by distributing power among general and constituent governments in a manner designed to protect the existence and authority of both (Elazar 1972, 1987; Hicks 1978; Leach 1970). Elazar distinguishes noncentralization, which is the major characteristic of federalism, from decentralization as follows:

> The idea of the federal union as a partnership is a key concept of federalism …. Partnership implies that distribution of real power among several centers that must negotiate cooperative arrangements with one another in order to achieve common goals. This arrangement is often mislabeled decentralization but more appropriately should be called noncentralization (Elazar 1972, p.3).

However, the roles and effects of decentralization seem similar to those of

"Concentralization" in that both focus on the responsiveness of subnational units. Therefore, this study assumes that both decentralization and noncentralization are basically identical. In this context, Fredrich's comment is appropriate for the ambiguity of the difference between decentralization and federalism: "If one were to contrast federalism and decentralization, as is often done in political studies, the conclusion is rather equivocal" (Fredrich 1968 p. 5).

Federalism can be meaningful only if a set of political communities coexist and interact as autonomous entities, united in a common order with an autonomy of its own (Fredrich 1968, pp.7–8). Elazar points out that "although the centralization–decentralization problem is common to all political systems, it takes on special characteristics in federal systems because of their noncentralized character" (Elazar 1987, p. 198). In fact, decentralization is a device to reduce generalized dissatisfaction with "big government"(Elazar 1987, p.204).

From this point of view, Elazar, in his book, *Exploring Federalism* (1987), suggests recent tendencies in American federal system:

> Had this book been written in the early 1970's, it would still emphasize the centralizing tendencies in contemporary federal systems, although qualifying that emphasis with the caveats regarding noncentralization and the matrix model presented above. For the moment, the tendency seems to be in the other direction (Elazar 1987, pp. 221–222).

In this regard, Nachmais & Rosenbloom describe the attitudes and values of federal bureaucrats as representative and democratic. As they put it,

> The federal bureaucracy is characterized by fragmentation, and federal bureaucrats tend to adhere to democratic attitudes and values. Although bureaucrats are not elected, they are broadly representative of the nation's population, and so is the bureaucracy in a structural sense. In the United States, there is no federal administrative elite in the European tradition (Nachmais & Rosenbloom 1980, p.66).

As Heady also argues,

> Because the Unites States is a relatively open society without pronounced class distinctions, and because of appointment and advancement methods used in the civil service, the upper echelons of the bureaucracy have been reasonably representative of the society, without much of a caste or elite quality (Heady 1992, p.235).

As already noted, the legacies of pluralism, liberalism and Christian values, which mainly emphasize individual value, have dominated the way of thinking of American bureaucracy. Furthermore, the ideas of federalism have also contributed

(continued)

(continued)

to preventing centralization by a bureaucratic elite group. In this situation, it seems to be appropriate to say that American bureaucracy places an emphasis on individualism values rather than on elite group values.

South Korea: Elite Group-Based Bureaucratic Culture

CONFUCIANISM AND FAMILY VALUES

Historically, Korea has long been a strict Confucian society. In Korea, Confucianism was made the state ideology during the Yi Dynasty (1392–1910). Based on the Confucian kinship, it was emphasized that, due to his ancestors' virtue, Heaven had conferred the mandate upon the Yi Dynasty, and it appealed to officials for their help in discharging the awesome responsibilities of governing in accordance with Heaven's will, promising the people that the ruler, though unworthy and deficient in virtue, would toil for their benefit and share their joys and sorrows (Haboush 1988, p.11).

Unlike the American situation, Korea was ruled by gentlemen–scholars — the *Yangban* class. The lowest class, that of *Chonmin*, were in effect slaves who could be bought or sold by their masters. The civil service examination, which was the route to government service and the highest status positions, was open only to members of the *Yangban* class. By all accounts, pre–modern society in Korea was extremely stagnant, inert and internally rigid, and closed off to foreign influences (Fukuyama 1995, p.132). In this situation, there prevailed a phenomenon of putting government above people, which is called *Kwanjon-Minbi*.

As mentioned above, the governing class of Joseon (Yi Dynasty) were known as *Yangbans*. Originally, *Yangbans* were civilians and military bureaucrats who gradually became the ruling governing class. They enjoyed many privileges (KBS et al. 1995, p.89). Among *Yangbans*, civilians were given preferential treatment over military men. *Yangbans* did not engage in productive labor. They read the Confucian classics or history books and lived their lives according to Confucian rites (KBS et al. 1995, p.90).

The family system was extremely important in Confucianism, with the head of the family as the center exercising absolute powers. He presided over the ceremony of offering sacrifices to the ancestors of the family shrines and offered sacrifices on memorial days (KBS et al. 1995, p.94). The Joseon dynasty utilized a Confucian–based politics founded in metaphysics. The political ideal of the era was the realization of a King–centered state (KBS et al. 1995, p.93). The strong emphasis in Confucianism on the family as the intellectual and ideological analogy for state governance and the institution of primary loyalty reinforced an earlier buffeted by superior military pressures, Korea has survived as a relatively small Korean emphasis on family and clan. With few intermediate institutions between the state and family, the family protected the individual against the outside world. The result, reinforced by Confucianism as a form of ancestor reverence, has been the submerging of individual identity within the family context. This collectivity is a pervasive phenomenon and is illustrated linguistically by the useof the Korean "we" when the American would normally say "I" ("our house," "our country," even "our wife") (Steinberg 1989, p.99).

This collectivity exists at the national as well as the family level. Constantly nation because of its collective cultural concepts (*uri*-ism or "we-ism"). (Steinberg 1989). However, as Steinberg points out, it should be noted that the degree of government and administrative collectivity is far different from that in Japan. Group consensus in Japan reaches extremes, but in Korea it is often replaced by strong, often unquestioned, leadership at the top, with subordinate groups bent on implementing top decisions rather than formulating them (Steinberg 1989, pp.99-100).

In the Confucian-oriented Korean society, people have thought of themselves as part of an organic whole that included human society and the world around it, hierarchically arranged, related in a family-like pattern, with eternally ordained responsibilities for everyone. Individuals found their identity not so much in themselves as in their relationships and mutual obligations within their extended families, and above all, in their relationships with their parents. In this situation, order and harmony, rather than competition and adversarial relations, have been supreme values, to be upheld by the conduct and example of superior men.

Government officials were expected to be such men, with superior benevolence and wisdom derived from study of the classics and tested by state examination. Government and scholarship were the highest callings; industry and commerce were looked down upon (MacDonald 1988).

Although Koreans had an individualistic, ambitious element that clashed with the Confucian norms, it cannot be denied that those thoughts still prevail in the minds of the average Koreans.

For Korean bureaucrats, there have been strong customs of making much of government and little of the people. Those deplorable customs have been regarded as the natural thing by the people. Confucianism provides the basis for social order and hierarchy: emperor and nation, government and people, manager and subordinate, senior and junior (Jun and Muto 1995, p.127). For these reasons, everyone wanted to enter the world of bureaucracy.

(continued)

(continued)

THE EXPERIENCE OF CENTRALIZED MILITARY GOVERNMENT

In addition, the aspiration to be bureaucrats has been reinforced much more through periods of military government than ever. Experience in Korea since the early 1960s manifests several of the characteristics commonly found in a military-dominated regime with an emphatic law-and-order orientation (Heady 1991, p.329). In 1961, a military coup ousted a short lived civilian government which in turn had replaced a year earlier the presidency of Rhee Seungman, who had been in office since the founding of the republic in 1948. Judging from the situation at that time when economic deterioration, social unrest, and political instability were rampant, the coup probably was inevitable. As a result, General Park Chung-Hee became President. The main officials were replaced by military high-level officers who participated in the coup. In this situation, the main initiative was to achieve economic development in Korea. The Korean state could control corporate behavior through more direct authoritarian methods by putting out-of-favor executives on trial and letting their businesses fail (Fukuyama 1995, p.139). The close ties between government and the business community were based on fear and the implicit threat that the state would use its coercive power if entrepreneurs did not take its' direction. The willingness of the Korean state to intervene in the economy with these instruments meant that the broad course of that country's post 1961 economic development was very much dictated by the visionof economic bureaucrats rather than by the market (Fukuyama 1995, p.139). In fact, during the period from 1953 to 1986, the growth of the Korean economy (since independence and after the vast destruction caused by the Korean War) is the most remarkable instance of national economic developmental success in the contemporary world (Steinberg 1989). The leader, Park Chung-Hee was elected president in 1963 and was successively elected several times before his assassination. After his assassination, the ruling military elite selected Chun Doo Hwan, another military man, as his successor and Chun was later elected to a full seven year term in 1981. And then Noh Tae Woo, another military man, was subsequently elected President in 1987. As the decade of the 1990s began, South Korea had seen progress toward a civilian-led government based on open political competition, but was in fact still led by politicians with military backgrounds (Heady 1992, p.330).

In addition, Heady describes the appearance of the Korean military government in the following context:

> An assumption of political sovereignty by the military is alien to Korea's deep seated Confucian political culture. Military politics is regarded with contempt. The coup leaders themselves claimed no superiority and their lowly origins were

generally acknowledged. Thus, in pursuit of their goals, they were keenly aware of their limitations and consciously tried to compensate for them (Heady 1992, p.331).

Through these processes, the prestige of the public sector was firmed up more than ever. The overall political culture of South Korea is well described by MacDonald (1988). He points out that Confucianism has extremely influenced the political culture of South Korea. In other words, It became an integral and dominant part of Korean political culture. Those elements of political culture include:

- belief that human society was an integral part of the whole universe, interrelated with it in maintaining order and harmony;
- acceptance of harmony, order, and consensus as major political values and purposes;
- acceptance of duty toward family and associated group (such as the court factions) as more important than individual satisfaction;
- concurrently, a strong individual drive for power and position, often manifested as a struggle among factions of rival leaders and their supporters;
- loyalty of subject to the person of the ruler, rather than to the whole state as such;
- belief that the proper model for political behavior was the ideal kingdom of the ancients, the principles of which were to be found in the Chinese classics;
- a static view of the human condition, in which nations and dynasties and families rose and fell in cyclical fashion, but life's potentialities remained basically the same;
- acceptance of hierarchical relations among people within the society, and among nations, so that everyone was inferior or superior to everyone else except for friends of the same age;
- a view of the ruler as responsible to Heaven (through China) for the order and well-being of all aspects of his kingdom — political, economic, and social — and possessing the Mandate of Heaven to rule so long as he fulfilled this responsibility;
- disparagement of industrial and commercial activity, and encouragement of agriculture as the central activity;
- emphasis on form and procedure, as well as substantive performance, as key elements in maintaining order;
- preference for decision-making by consensus, rather than by majority vote

(continued)

(continued)

or force of arms; yet at thesame time, unwillingness to compromise on matters perceived to involve principle;

- respect and honor to scholar-officials, passers of the examinations, as a class possessing superior benevolence, wisdom, and administrative ability, and therefore entitled to special status;
- self-governance of the agricultural majority of the population in their villages, except for governmental collection of taxes and labor and punishment of particular heinous crimes;
- reluctance to involve governmental institutions in personal or family quarrels, which were settled wherever possible within families or communities; (McDonald 1988, p.116).

McDonald goes on to assert that these values are opposite in many respects to those of the West, which (at least from the latter eighteenth century, particularly in the United States) emphasizes progress, change, individual freedom, equality of all persons, adversary relations, government by consent of the people, separation of political from economic and social affairs, and the importance of civic duty (McDonald 1988).

It should be noted, however, that not all elements mentioned above fit the current Korean situation, especially during the period that public organizations at all levels in Korea are experiencing significant government reform. Of course, Korean bureaucrats are now suffering from the change which replaces traditional values with modern organizational values. In these processes, they may be experiencing significant cultural changes in their organizations. Nevertheless, one cannot deny that, still, those traditional values dominate average people in Korea.

Source: Seok-Hwan Lee (2000). A Multidimensional View of Employee Commitment and Willingness to Improve Productivity Improvement Strategies (pp.30-43): Unpublished doctoral dissertation, NJ: Rutgers University-Newark

KEY TERMS

Brownlow Commission Report
Bureaucracy
Co-optation
Fact-value dichotomy
Groupthink
Hawthorne experiments
Informal organizations
Mechanistic systems
Needs hierarchy
Organic systems
Organizational culture
POSDCORB
Principal-agent theory
Proverbs of administration
Quality Circles (QCs)
Reinventing government
Scalar chain
Scientific management
Span of control
Systems theory
Theory X
Theory Y
Total Quality
Unity of command
Unity of direction

REFERENCES

Almond, G.A., and S. Verba 1963. *The civic culture: Political attitudes and democracy in five nations*. Princeton, NJ: Princeton University Press.

Argyris, C. 1957. *Personality and Organization*. New York: Harper.

Barnard, C.I. 1938. *The Functions of the Executive*. Cambridge, MA: Harvard University Press.

Bloomberg, M.R. 1997, 2001. *Bloomberg by Bloomberg*. Hoboken, NJ: Wiley.

Brownlow Commission. 1937. *Report of the President's Committee on Administrative Management (The Brownlow Report)*. U.S. Government Printing Office.

Dahl, R. 1989. *Democracy and Its Critics*. New Haven, CT: Yale University Press.

Deming, W.E. 1986. *Out of the Crisis*. Cambridge, MA: MIT Center for Advanced Engineering Study.

Elazar, D.J. 1972. *American federalism: A view from the states*. 2d edition, New York: Thomas Y. Crowell Company.

———. 1987. *Exploring federalism.* AL: University of Alabama Press.

Fayol, H. 1916. *General and Industrial Management.* Trans. C. Storrs. London: Pitman Publishing, 1949.

Follett, M.P. 1926/2008. "The Giving of Orders." In *Classics of Public Administration*, ed. A.C. Hyde, J.M. Shafritz, and S.J. Parkes. Belmont, CA: Wadsworth/Thomson Learning.

Friedrich, C.J. 1968. *Trends of federalism in theory and practice.* New York: Frederick A. Praeger.

Fukuyama, F. 1995. *Trust: The social virtues and the creation of prosperity.* New York, NY: The Free Press.

Garry, P.M. 1992. *Liberalism and American identity.* Kent, OH: The Kent State University Press.

Gordon, G.J. 1978. *Public administration in America.* New York, NY: St. Martin's Press.

Gulick, L.H., and L. Urwick, eds. 1937. *Papers on the Science of Administration.* New York: Institute for Public Administration. See especially: "Notes on the Theory of Organization," pp. 1-46.

Haboush, J.K. 1988. *A heritage of kings: One man's monarchy in the Confucian world.* New York, NY: Columbia University Press.

Heady, F. 1992. *Public administration: A comparative perspective.* 4th edition, New York, NY: Marcel Dekker, Inc.

Hicks, K.U. 1978. *Federalism: Failure and success: A comparative study.* New York: Oxford University Press.

Janis, I.L. 1972. *Victims of Groupthink: A Psychological Study of Foreign-Policy Decisions and Fiascoes.* Boston: Houghton Mifflin.

Jun, J.S., & H. Muto 1995. The hidden dimensions of Japanese Administration: Culture and its impact. *Public Administration Review* 55: 125-134.

Juran, J.M. 2004. *Architect of Quality.* New York: McGraw-Hill.

Kaufman, H. 1969. Administrative decentralization and political power. *Public Administration Review* 29: 3-15.

Leach, H.R. 1970. *American federalism: A searching examination of conflict and cooperation between the federal government and the separate states.* New York:

W.W. Norton & Company, Inc.

Likert, R. 1961. *New Patterns of Management*. New York: McGraw-Hill.

Lutin, C.E., & A.K. Settle 1976. *American public administration: Concepts & cases*. Palo Alto, CA: Mayfield Publishing Co.

Martin, J. 2002. "Organizational Culture: Pieces of the Puzzle." In *Classics of Organizational Theory*, ed. J.M. Shafritz, J.S. Ott, and Yong Suk Jang, 6th ed. Belmont, CA: Wadsworth Publishing.

Maslow, A.H. 1943. "A Theory of Human Motivation." *Psychology Review* 50: 370-396.

McGregor, D. 1960. *The Human Side of Enterprise*. New York: McGraw-Hill.

Merton, R. 1957. *Social Theory and Social Structure*. New York: Free Press.

Minzberg, H. 1979. *The Structuring of Organizations: A Synthesis of the Research*. Upper Saddle River, NJ: Prentice-Hall.

MacDonald, D.S. 1988. *The Koreans: Contemporary politics and society*. Boulder, CO: Westview Press.

Nachmias, D., and D. H. Rosenbloom 1980. *Bureaucratic government* USA. New York, NY: St. Martin's Press.

Osborne, D., and T. Gaebler. 1992. *Reinventing Government: How the Entrepreneurial Spirit Is Transforming the Public Sector*. Reading, MA: Addison-Wesley.

Radio Korea International, KBS, National Institute for International Education Development, & Ministry of Korea 1995. *The history of Korea.* Seoul, Korea: Jungmoon Printing Co..

Schein, E.H. 1993. *Organizational Culture and Leadership*, 2d ed. San Francisco: Jossey-Bass.

Selzick, P. 1949. *TVA and the Grass Roots: A Study in the Sociology of Formal Organizations*. Berkley, CA: University of California Press.

Simon, H.A. 1946. "The Proverbs of Administration." *Public Administration Review* 6, no. 1: 53-67.

_____. 1947/1997. *Administrative Behavior*. New York: Simon and Schuster.

Smith, A. 1776/2003. *The Wealth of Nations*. New York: Bantam.

Steinberg, D.I. 1989. *The Republic of Korea: Economic transformation and social change*. Boulder, CO: Westview Press.

Taylor, F. 1911. *The Principles of Scientific Management*. New York: W.W. Norton.

Urwick, L.F. 1952. *Notes on the Theory of Organization*. New York: American Management Association.

Waldo, D. 1948. *The Administrative State: A Study of the Political Theory of American Public Administration*. New York: The Ronald Press Co.

———. 1952. "Development of Theory of Democratic Administration." *American Political Science Review* 46 (March): 97.

Weber, M. 1978/1922. *Economy and Society: An Outline of Interpretive Sociology*. Trans. and ed. Guenther Roth and Claus Wittich. Berkeley: University of California Press.

SUPPLEMENTARY READINGS

Etzioni, A. 1964. *Modern Organizations*. Englewood Cliffs, NJ: Prentice-Hall.

Gilbreth, F., and L.M. Gilbreth. 1919. *Fatigue Study: The Elimination of Humanity's Greatest Unnecessary Waste; A First Step in Motion Study*, 2d ed. New York: MacMillan.

Kanigel, R. 1997. *The One Best Way: Frederick Winslow Taylor and the Enigma of Efficiency*. New York: Viking.

Rainey, H. 2003. *Understanding and Managing Public Organizations*, 3d ed. San Francisco, CA: Jossey-Bass.

Robbins, S.P. 2005. *Essentials of Organizational Behavior*, 8th ed. Upper Saddle River, NJ: Pearson/Prentice-Hall.

Waldo, D. 1961. "Organization Theory: An Elephantine Problem." *Public Administration Review* 21, no. 4: 210-215.

Weber, M. 1958. *From Max Weber: Essays in Sociology*. New York: Oxford University Press.

ELECTRONIC RESOURCES

Carnegie Mellon School of Computer Science, "A Tribute to Herbert Simon," http://www.cs.cmu.edu/simon/index.html

The Department of Economics of the New School for Social Research, "Max Weber, 1864–920," The History of Economic Thought Website http://homepage.newschool.edu/het//profiles/weber.htm

Huitt, W. 2007. "Maslow's Hierarchy of Needs." Educational Psychology Interactive Website. Valdosta, GA: Valdosta State University, 2007 www.edpsycinteractive.org/topics/regsys/maslow.html

CHAPTER 3

Managing Human Resources

Chapter 3 examines the management of an organization's most important resource—its people. Upon reading this chapter, students will be able to discuss the major concepts associated with human resource management. Productive human resource management and the cultivation of a high-quality and diverse workforce are discussed, with emphasis on the importance of recruiting the best and brightest workers and devising employee development strategies. The chapter then transitions into a discussion of employee motivation theories, touching on employee assessment and counseling techniques. To conclude, strategies for creating a quality work environment are addressed.

“No duty the Executive had to perform was so trying as to put the right man in the right place.”

THOMAS JEFFERSON
Third President of the United States
(1743–1846)

— Мне нужны подходящие — под эту мерку... Рисунок Ю. ЧЕРЕПАНОВА

– I NEED THOSE WHO FIT THIS MEASURE...
Artist: Y. Cherepanov; *Krokodil* [*Crocodile*] satirical magazine, 1965.

HUMAN RESOURCES MANAGEMENT

Twenty-first-century management is dynamic. It is characterized by competition, increasing demands for improved and new services, budgetary constraints, calls for higher performance, increased citizen involvement, and a variety of political pressures. These demands present new challenges for managers within the public sector. Public managers must attend to demands for responsive and effective government, the citizenry's demands for greater involvement in public decision making and governance, and an evolving workforce that holds new attitudes and higher expecta-

Source: www.cartoonstock.com

tions. In addition, there exists a political-administrative dynamic that is embodied in the demand for open and transparent governance, while simultaneously charged with providing more and better services with fewer resources. Public managers are now forced to respond with novel and groundbreaking ways of managing their human resources. High-performing public organizations are using innovative approaches to create and maintain a productive workforce.

The most important resource of any public organization—indeed, the public sector's most critical investment—is its people. In fact, employee salaries and benefits make up between 50 and 85 percent of government budgets. Guy (1992a) underscores the importance of people in high-performing public organizations: "The easiest way to make quick productivity gains is to mechanize a process. The most difficult, but most enduring, way to make productivity gains is to develop each worker's desire and ability to be maximally productive. The reason is simple: It is people who, in the long term, control the productivity of any organization" (p. 307).

> "Leadership is all about people. It is not about organizations. It is not about plans. It is not about strategies. It is all about people—motivating people to get the job done. You have to be people-centered."
>
> **COLIN POWELL**
> U.S. Army General; Former Secretary of State

According to Mintzberg (1996), an organization without commitment to its human resources is analogous to a body that has no soul. Flesh, bones, and blood may be able to consume and to exert energy, but without a soul there is no life force. Public organizations, notes Mintzberg, need a life force, so to speak. Thus, acknowledging and responding to emerging human resource management needs is directly tied into improving government performance. High-performing organizations are compassionate and demonstrate concern for meeting the needs of their employees. This coincides with the view that productive organizations have a vested interest in satisfying human needs. In other words, productive human resource management balances a worker's needs and an organization's goals.

Human resource management encompasses managing people's concerns. Managers who deal effectively with these concerns are more likely to achieve organizational goals, in addition to satisfying employee needs, which range from job satisfaction, to recognition for personal and group achievements, to a competitive salary and a safe work environment. Public organizations are dependent on knowledgeable, industrious, enthusiastic workers and harmonious relations between managers and employees (Isaacs 1996).

At one time, human resource management dealt with standardizing personnel processes. Twenty-first-century human resource management, however, is not just about safeguarding employees and upholding the integrity of personnel systems from management exploitation. With more traditional management models, adherence to strict processes was paramount. Under more contemporary public management paradigms, where performance improvement and the achievement of organizational goals are vital, the focus of human resource management is to enable managers and employees to better serve the public (Cooper 1998). This requires the traditional human resource elements of

- Hiring the right workers to achieve an organization's goals and fulfill its mandate;
- Training and developing workers; and
- Rewarding workers using monetary, as well as non-monetary, psychological rewards—i.e., creating an organizational environment that engenders loyalty and cooperation.

> "The growth and development of people is the highest calling of leadership."
>
> **HARVEY S. FIRESTONE**
> Industrialist; Founder of Firestone Tire and Rubber Co.

In this era of scarce resources, increasing cynicism and distrust of government, and demands for improved performance, human resource management systems have additional concerns. Key among those concerns, notes Naff (1993), are:

- Creating and maintaining a diverse workforce;
- Affording workers a measure of power in the workplace;
- Enabling workers to fulfill and balance both work and family responsibilities;
- Enabling workers to hold their managers accountable for merit principles;
- Taking into account different ways of motivating workers; and
- Identifying ways of fostering a culture of cooperation and teamwork in the workplace.

Productive Human Resource Management

Overall, productive human resource management can be thought of as a lively, open system (Cooper 1998) in which external and internal environments are interconnected. Such a system is likely to influence a public organization's capacity to attract and hold on to workers who take on new and more complex responsibilities. This occurs in an environment where the public sector often competes with private sector organizations for human resources. Also, ongoing changes in and increasing reliance upon technology have resulted in a greater need for knowledge workers and information systems that support management decisions. Sherman, Bohlander, and Schnell (1998) argue that rapid technology change requires a superior workforce. Productive human resource management reflects societal demographic changes as well. As society becomes more diverse, it is imperative that public sector employees reflect a similar measure of diversity. Human resource management systems must embrace all employee differences. This view is supported by Sherman, Bohlander, and Schnell (1998). Public organizations have been shown to benefit from diversity by acknowledging and embracing the differences and concerns of their employees. The increasing presence of females and racial and ethnic minorities in public administration has led to a significant amount of academic work on the value of diversity in organizations (Golembiewski 1995; Rainey 1997).

Porous department and unit boundaries of public organizations pose human resource challenges that can best be met by adopting a "team player" approach. Human resources must work with other departments and units in achieving organization-wide goals. Clearly, internal factors—most notably the values held by an organization's upper management and by extension the organization's culture—

—THE WORK IS IN FULL SWING, BUT THERE'S A SHORTAGE OF PEOPLE!
Artist and Date Unknown; "The Fighting Pencil" group.

influence human resource management. Upper-management leadership determines the extent to which human resource management is viewed as important. Schuler and Huber (1993) argue that if upper managers downplay the importance of workers to the organization's overall success, so will line managers. If line managers do the same, then the human resource department will be less likely to embrace innovative and productive human resource policies. On the other hand, upper management's support of and commitment to employee-centric human resource policies does not necessarily ensure that the organization will be productive. Performance improvement in public organizations requires a commitment from all employees.

> "You know the type. They bank vacation days. They hand in slips of paper noting how many half-days or holidays they've worked. They remind bosses and colleagues of company policies regarding over-time. They are little technocrats who show time and time again that they are not working for fun or the passion to win. They're just logging hours."
>
> **JACK WELCH**
> Retired CEO of General Electric

The culture of an organization embodies its value system. Individual-level and organizational-level performance can only be understood if that organization's culture is taken into account (Schein 1988). As one of the key factors influencing employee motivation (Romzek 1990), organizational culture, to some measure, indicates how organizations treat their employees (Schuler and Huber 1993). Organizations possessing a culture of concern and respect for individuals are likely to have policies that address employee needs specifically. Employees, too, learn a great deal about an organization's culture through human resource practices—for example, how the organization chooses people for hiring and promotion, what criteria are used to evaluate employees, and how well it compensates its employees both monetarily and nonmonetarily. These indicate a great deal about an organization.

The political-administrative interconnection has profound human resource implications. Thompson (1990) is among the theorists who maintain that human resource management may well have political consequences. Processes such as hiring and firing are no longer clandestine activities; such policies must now withstand public and interorganizational scrutiny. Depending on the human resource issue, several public agencies may have a role to play. For example, when policy questions are raised regarding employee performance appraisal in the federal government, the Equal Employment Opportunity Commission, the Office of Personnel Management, the Federal Labor Relations Authority, and the Merit Systems Protection Board all have a vested interest in the issue. In such organizations, politicization must be balanced with principles of merit and equal opportunity for employment.

An organization's environment—both internal and external—influences human resource management. Recognizing internal and external environmental factors prepares human resource managers to address the challenges inherent in their field. In high-performing organizations, human resource managers look at these factors as opportunities, not problems. Responsibilities for human resource (HR) management are spread out in the organization: organization heads and their upper managers, middle managers, and HR managers share these responsibilities. According to Naff (1993), virtually all managers are dependent on human resource management. In fact, managers are an HR department's most important customers. Human resources support enables managers to cultivate and sustain a quality workforce; develop and prepare employees for more advanced positions; and preserve the principles of merit and fair play within the organization. Human resource departments provide invaluable support services so that managers may deliver more efficient and effective services.

Among the strategies to effectively manage human resources in high-performing organizations are:

- Cultivating and maintaining a high quality of work environment, and
- Creating satisfying work relations through teamwork and collaboration.

Cultivating and Maintaining a High-Quality Diverse Workforce

While challenging and time-consuming, the task of improving performance requires the capacity and motivation of the workforce to operate at high levels. Innovative public sector strategies for managing human resources show that cultivating and sustaining a high-quality and diverse workforce is indeed an attainable goal. Doing so entails identifying and hiring the right people, systematically preparing them for their roles, providing them with sources of motivation, and then evaluating them fairly. Workforce planning involves more than estimating the number of workers needed in various capacities now and in the future; it deals with personnel development, the optimal utilization of each worker, and employee retention. Workforce planning also has prospective and evaluative components, as it addresses the future impacts of employment based on present-day decisions.

> "People often say that motivation doesn't last. Well, neither does bathing—that's why we recommend it daily."
>
> **ZIG ZIGLAR**
> Corporate Trainer; Motivational Speaker

Recruiting the Best and the Brightest

Sustained attacks on public servants dissuade the best and the brightest students from pursuing public sector careers (Holzer and Rabin 1987). The importance of recruiting and retaining exceptional employees cannot be overstated; yet, public organizations risk losing many of their most talented people to alternative employment (Romzek 1990, p. 374). According to research conducted by Jurkiewicz, Massey, and Brown (1998), there are 15 factors relevant to the motivation of public employees. Of those factors, high prestige and social status ranked fifteenth (Jurkiewicz, Massey, and Brown 1998, p. 235).

Identifying and hiring the right people have emerged as significant issues that warrant innovative approaches. Public organizations need to woo the so-called "best and brightest" from multiple recruiting pools—from new graduates, to private sector employees who have been "downsized," to older workers looking for a second career, to civic-minded volunteers. Some organizations have implemented innovative hiring practices that are more user friendly. Holzer (1991) recommends several strategies for persuading the best and the brightest into government, namely advocacy activities that keep the idea of public service on the forefront of people's minds. Central to this is educating and reminding people that public service is both a necessary investment and a civic duty. Of course, appealing to an individual's civic virtues will accomplish only so much. More competitive salaries, increased employee discretion, and the power of resources all play important roles in attracting the best and the brightest to government.

Employee Development

In high-performing public organizations, training and development are never-ending processes. Twenty-first-century organizations operate in a climate that requires constant organizational learning (Mills 1994). Training begins with employee orientation as an individual begins work, and it continues throughout that individual's career in order to fulfill the need for new knowledge, skills, and attitudes—commonly referred to as KSAs. Employee development encompasses a long-term agenda of activities (that is, training and education) to prepare workers for career advancement within the organization. Training is central to improving performance and lessens the probability of employees becoming obsolete in an increasingly changing environment. Training and development are vital to accomplishing workforce plans, as well as improving individual competencies.

> "There are incalculable resources in the human spirit, once it has been set free."
>
> **HUBERT H. HUMPHREY**
> 38th Vice President of the United States

Training employees is of the utmost importance, as public employees work within politically charged environments. Because of the traditional separation between politics and administration, the legislative—or lawmaking—environment is often unfamiliar to public employees, and they tend not to work as effectively in it. Public employees will perform better if they have a better understanding of the legislative environment (Lewis and Raffel 1996). Clearly, according to Isaacs (1996), the effectiveness of training and development programs affects employee performance. Not to be overlooked, however, is how receptive trainees are to training and development programs. The training program design, delivery, and evaluation—as well as whether employees are afforded opportunities to use their newly acquired skills—also affect organizational performance.

New in Hiring Practices—
A Strategic Approach to Hiring

A MAKEOVER THAT MATTERS: THE EXTREME HIRING MAKEOVER

Current events have raised the stakes on government's success—and to perform effectively, government needs top talent. But the federal government is in double jeopardy: More than half of all federal employees will be eligible to retire within the next five years, and there is a very thin pipeline of talent waiting in the wings to replace the skilled and experienced workers who will walk out the door. Worse yet, the way the federal government hires is often inadequate—it takes too long, is cumbersome, and may fail to produce quality results.

The federal hiring process is one of the biggest impediments to attracting new employees to government service. In some cases, federal job application instructions run 35 pages long—and applicants often have to wait six months to a year before getting a federal job offer, sometimes with little or no communication from agencies. There is also growing concern that methods used by federal employers for assessing the skills of potential employees are among the least effective available. If it takes federal agencies a year to hire, and they don't properly assess applicant skills, they will lose the most highly qualified candidates to more nimble organizations.

Project Overview

Modeled after the popular Extreme Makeover television shows, this project united some of the nation's premier experts on recruiting and assessment with three federal agencies to implement some of the most effective hiring practices used in any sector. Like the television shows, participating agencies boldly and bravely came forward with a simple desire to improve. But unlike the TV show participants, their measure of success is not cosmetic, but something far more important: bringing the best talent into the federal government by improving the way the government works. This is a makeover that matters.

Agencies

The three participating agencies are the Centers for Medicare & Medicaid Services (CMS), within the Department of Health and Human Services (HHS); the Department of Education (ED); and the National Nuclear Security Administration (NNSA), within the Department of Energy.

Partners

The Extreme Hiring Makeover project was enhanced by the participation of world-

(continued)

(continued)

class experts in the area of recruiting and hiring. Whether the issue is planning, marketing, assessment, or selection, the Extreme Hiring Makeover (EHM) team has the skills and knowledge to help participating agencies improve their practices. In addition to the Partnership for Public Service, this team included: Monster Government Solutions, ePredix, CPS Human Resource Services, AIRS, Brainbench, the Human Capital Institute and Korn/Ferry International.

Approach

This project was launched in the summer of 2004 with a phased approach. From July to January, the EHM team helped agencies diagnose the key issues they face through a series of interviews and by mapping the hiring process. Also, "quick wins" were implemented to demonstrate rapid progress. Those included creating new looks and marketing appeal for vacancy announcements, targeting passive candidates for existing positions, helping to script communications for job fairs, and providing interview guides for managers. From January through the end of April, the project participants constructed short-term fixes—designing the new hiring process, creating a new front-end toolkit to facilitate better planning for managers and HR teams, tightening up the pre-screening and assessment process, designing new recruiting materials, and training the agency's recruiting experts. The remaining portion of the project focused on long-term planning for building on and sustaining change.

At all three organizations, mapping the hiring process allowed them to gain a realistic and practical understanding of their hiring issues. While it is difficult to prescribe the optimal number of steps for any given agency, this exercise highlighted areas where non-value added steps had crept into the process over a period of years. Many of those steps were not generated by statute or regulation, but through a layered history of Department, agency, and functional practice. Most important, it allowed the collective leadership of the organization to understand each other's activities and where to hunt for real process improvements. The simple visual of this multi-step process evoked enthusiastic commitments for change from all the Makeover teams.

Key Lessons

While this project illustrated several areas where rapid improvement can be achieved, it also underscored the obstacles facing government agencies as they try to implement and manage change initiatives. To improve their hiring results, each agency could improve the planning phase of their process, better sell their job opportunities, and focus on quality. To enable these changes, the involvement of top leadership was clearly the most critical factor leading to success, but it was also apparent that staff members implementing such efforts must support the project. In effect, agencies need to change from the inside out. Though the Extreme Makeover showed focus on the surface, this project pushed agencies to review their deeper internal practices to find better ways to present themselves to the public. Some team members called this "battling inertia," daring to do things differently.

Even with notable accomplishments at all three participating organizations, each agency team can identify specific areas where they could have improved their results. Team members agreed that enhanced internal communication, extending to those outside the project, would have benefited the outcome. Further, there was consensus that dedicated project resources, specifically assigning staff members solely to this effort, would have eliminated competing priorities and allowed the team to focus exclusively on their intended goals.

Across government, agencies post vacancy announcements and assume top-flight candidates will apply. Each agency in this project has benefited from outreach to candidates who may not regularly seek government work, broadening their reach and expanding their organizational capabilities. Through a variety of means, agencies can market their job openings to new and diverse sources of candidates, often with exceptional results. While targeted recruiting promotes agencies, it also demonstrates the appeal of serving our nation. When Uncle Sam calls, top talent answers.

THE SCIENCE OF MARKETING: NATIONAL NUCLEAR SECURITY ADMINISTRATION

While almost every organization sees itself as unique, the National Nuclear Security Administration (NNSA) is truly one of a kind. Where else can you harness nuclear energy for security and scientific advancement, and save the world from nuclear proliferation and terrorism? Established in March 2000, NNSA merged the efforts of several federal programs responsible for nuclear security: defense nuclear weapons, nuclear non-proliferation, the naval nuclear propulsion program and other supporting efforts.

Just as NNSA's mission is highly specialized, so are the skills and talents that it needs in its federal workforce. Given the critical shortages in scientific and technical talent in America and a rapidly changing security environment, recruiting needed talent presents a major challenge for NNSA.

For national security reasons, NNSA did not maintain a highly visible public posture. Potential candidates for employment were not aware of NNSA's exciting and

(continued)

(continued)

challenging programs. Compounding the difficulty of hiring the right talent is the challenge of finding people to work in remote locations. To overcome these challenges, NNSA needs world-class recruiting capabilities. Agency leaders recognized that old methods would not allow them to compete effectively for their highly sought-after talent.

Challenges

NNSA leaders had already begun to take a close look at their hiring process when the Extreme Hiring Makeover (EHM) team arrived.

The multiple-page job announcements did not capture the power of the critical mission that NNSA serves, did provide an overly extensive list of job duties that obscured the major features and selling points of the job, and did not highlight the most important skills and experience that the candidate needed to bring to the organization.

As a result, some of NNSA's critical positions went unfilled. In launching the Extreme Hiring Makeover effort, Mike Kane, the Associate Administrator for Management and Administration, used the example of a nonproductive effort for a senior scientific position as a proxy for their larger issues. After looking for months, using the current, longstanding, job announcement formats, they had only three candidates and none fit the bill. How could the Makeover turn that situation around?

Solutions

Extreme Makeover Team members rose to the challenge. After reviewing the prior vacancy announcement for the senior scientific position and meeting with the hiring manager and HR team, the root of the problem became clear: NNSA was not selling or marketing its unique employment opportunities. When asked about the vacancy, the hiring manager could describe the position at length in technical terms but had not considered how to convey the job in such a way as to excite a potential applicant. So, the Extreme team led him through a series of questions to elicit what the position really entailed, why a candidate would want to work there, and what competencies and credentials were most important for the job.

NNSA Gets a Face Lift

Following the manager interview, the team worked with NNSA to produce a marketing pitch and targeting strategy. Monster Government Solutions helped to create a new look and language for their position announcement that conveyed the importance and excitement of the position. Not only did the new announcement start with a description of why NNSA is a great place to work, but it utilized a user-friendly, five-tab vacancy announcement format developed for the Office of Personnel Management's (OPM's) USA Jobs website. The announcement was also written in plain English—no government jargon. The web-based posting also included photos of the unique work environment at NNSA that would appeal to the scientists and engineers it sought to attract.

To further improve NNSA's odds of attracting highly qualified applicants, AIRS helped to implement an Internet-based targeted recruiting strategy. They searched various job boards and other Internet sources for experienced candidates who met the highly skilled NNSA criteria. A senior NNSA official then called the most desirable candidates that came out of this targeted search to encourage them to apply. The new look for the announcement and the proactive outreach approach produced a slate of 28 qualified candidates.

Emboldened by this success, NNSA leaders took up their own sales and marketing efforts. They developed an advertisement that ran in *Government Executive* magazine featuring the new face of NNSA—"Where Engineering, Science and National Security Intersect in a Challenging Career."

Engaging the Next Generation

To build a pipeline of future leaders, NNSA also launched an emerging leaders program that took the recruiting message to a new level. NNSA recruiters targeted fifteen universities, many in the South and West, with an emphasis on diversity. Building on some of the lessons from the EHM, professional recruitment materials, including a state-of-the art Flash presentation, were prepared for use in on-campus

(continued)

(continued)

recruiting efforts. NNSA developed a core intern-training program built around three separate functional curricula tracks in facility oversight, business functions, and information technology.

To compete successfully with private sector organizations, NNSA now aggressively employs a wide range of recruiting flexibilities and benefits. They tackle the money issues head-on by offering candidates the possibility of student loan repayment, signing bonuses and relocation assistance.

Partnering with Managers Effectively

The NNSA HR team is constantly looking for ways to enhance their service to managers and forge a collaborative working partnership. They have worked with managers to reexamine their hiring process to reduce the time and effort required to bring someone on board while improving the quality of candidates delivered by the process. Extreme Makeover sponsor CPS assisted NNSA in mapping their existing process and identifying areas for improvement. Managers and HR representatives agreed that engaging in a comprehensive strategic conversation at the outset would speed the process, eliminate redundancies and guarantee improved quality of outcomes.

Providing Great Recruiting Resources

Also in the course of the diagnostic phase, NNSA determined that they needed to enhance their human resources staff, and the HR Director took action. As part of their targeted approach to address that issue, a new position was created to lead HR operations. Additionally, the HR team embarked on renewed workforce planning to identify current and future skills gaps; provide training where needed; and improve its use of automated HR systems and tools, including a new, consolidated approach to performance management and recognition.

Results

Science and marketing do mix to create a potent force.

- The pilot project to fill a senior scientific position yielded an eight-fold increase in the number of applicants.
- Selecting officials have chosen the first class of about 30 interns, and their feedback indicates that the candidate pool was of a very high quality. Having heard about the success of this program, leaders recruiting candidates in other functional areas have asked for a custom program of their own.

Perhaps the best example of success comes from the HR Director himself. Having participated in the first pilot effort to recruit the senior scientist, Ray Greenberg decided to set an example by revamping his own approach to hiring. He needed an HR operating executive who was ready to embrace a challenge and help make change happen in this new organization. Ray spent time upfront in developing a clear position description and an effective marketing pitch, job announcement and recruiting strategy. It worked. His final candidates were so good that he faced an entirely new kind of challenge: how to select the best from a range of outstanding candidates.

Lessons Learned

Top Leadership Commitment Is Critical

As with the other participating agencies, NNSA witnessed how the commitment of top leadership within their organization could advance the goals of the project.

Everything Flows from Strategy

The HR staff saw the benefits of having a deeper knowledge of the business of NNSA, including the type of talent they need to attract, where to look for ideal candidates, and what top talent would find attractive about working at NNSA. This foundational understanding of the organization helps the HR team enhance its partnership and collaboration with management. By building their own organization, they help build NNSA in its entirety.

New Ideas Fuel Innovation

Openness to external assistance and seeking outside expertise is extremely valuable when tackling major change initiatives. Many agencies don't have the resources to hire outside consultants or expand their operational practices. In this project, NNSA had access to both the pro-bono assistance provided by the EHM partners as well as to further outside assistance to produce recruitment materials for the intern program. This openness to outside assistance helped to improve its internal practices.

A Picture Speaks a Thousand Words

Mapping the hiring process provided a shared understanding of current activities across the HR and management teams. The visual of the process facilitated efforts to develop a shared vision for improvement, and enabled NNSA to smartly target areas for training and development—for both HR staff and hiring managers—as they seek to make improvements in the recruitment process.

Recruiting Flexibilities Make a Difference

NNSA has committed to optimizing its use of available flexibilities. In each component of this project, where applicable, NNSA has interwoven the application of student loan repayments, recruitment bonuses and relocation payments along with

(continued)

(continued)

special hiring authorities. This both heightens NNSA's appeal to potential applicants and brings the agency toward its goal of recruiting and retaining top talent.

What's Next?

As with many federal agencies, NNSA has seen that successful transformational efforts require follow-up and follow-through. To achieve the goals outlined in this effort, and to encourage enduring change, the team is prepared to make a long-term commitment to improvement. NNSA will map a plan to institutionalize the changes, folding them into their standard hiring process and spreading their knowledge throughout the agency by communicating more broadly with agency staff.

Inspired by their own progress in this effort, NNSA has launched an "Employer of Choice" initiative, demonstrating its commitment to recruiting and retaining top talent. The agency will begin with a survey of all employees, using the Partnership for Public Service's Best Places to Work in the Federal Government analysis of employee satisfaction data as one benchmark. From those results, the team will assess its strengths and weaknesses and craft corresponding efforts to address key issues.

Building on the foundational elements of the Extreme Hiring Makeover project, the NNSA team also plans to expand and address efforts central to human capital issues, including a major workforce planning effort. This will help identify the skills and competencies needed in the workforce, identify skills gaps, and fine-tune future workforce planning. On a parallel track, the team is developing a "one-NNSA" approach to HR systems that emphasizes linkages between HR initiatives and the organization's strategic goals. This will include implementation of a single performance management system to replace eight different legacy systems. To deepen collaboration with managers, the HR team will also begin to use additional automated tools.

NNSA may be unique in many ways, but its experiences in the Extreme Hiring Makeover and its additional efforts to improve its practices offer lessons that are applicable to any agency across government.

PRESCRIPTION FOR HIRING SUCCESS: CENTERS FOR MEDICARE & MEDICAID SERVICES

Responsible for programs like Medicare, Medicaid, the State Children's Health Insurance Program, and the Health Insurance Portability and Accountability Act (HIPAA), CMS touches the lives of nearly 1 in 4 Americans. CMS processes more than 1 billion claims per year, providing service to nearly 42 million beneficiaries who receive Medicare benefits.

The agency's mandate was recently expanded with the enactment of the Medicare

Modernization Act (MMA)—the most extensive modification to the Medicare program since its inception in 1965. The MMA includes a drug discount card in 2004, new preventive benefits including a "Welcome to Medicare" physical for new Medicare beneficiaries in 2005 and a prescription drug benefit plan by 2006.

Challenges

CMS had a pressing need for change in staffing to meet the requirements of the MMA. Implementation of the new law demanded significantly increased hiring, growing the size of the workforce by approximately 500 professionals within two years. This increase constituted 10 percent of the existing workforce and twice the agency's normal annual hiring. Such changes involved not only consideration of new lines of business but also new skills and competencies to effectively rollout provisions of the MMA.

Among other hiring challenges, the agency's managers were very vocal about their dissatisfaction with both the length of time it took to hire and the quality of applicants that emerged through the certification process. Moreover, like the rest of government, CMS has an aging workforce and will likely face significant retirements in coming years. It must attract and retain a highly skilled workforce to address the increasing pressures of America's aging population.

Hiring challenges were further compounded by the introduction of a new automated staffing system and the transition to a new human resources servicing model as the Department of Health and Human Services consolidated staffing and other services at the Department level. Given the considerable amount of change taking place in the organization, volume hiring for MMA and anticipated retirement turnover, it was clear the old system would not meet the needs of the new CMS.

Solutions

At CMS, a focus on effective selection and assessment processes was central to addressing managers' concerns. They wanted to ensure that the CMS of the future would have top talent to meet changing circumstances and their increasing mission requirements. With high volumes of applicants for many CMS positions and an automated staffing system that few understood how to use effectively, screening and assessing candidates for quality were often a challenge.

Analyzing the Process

All of the Makeover efforts included an "end to end" mapping of the hiring process and identification of short-term and long-term fixes. With resources from across the agency and partners at CPS Human Resources Services, the hiring process was

(continued)

(continued)

mapped from end to end—starting when a manager identifies his or her need and concluding when the person reports for duty. That is notable because the effort extends well beyond the traditional HR functions.

Focusing on Quality

Concurrent with the process mapping and diagnosis, CMS conducted a demonstration hiring process for one of its components. This demonstration process employed a selection of successful pre-screening and assessment processes from best practice organizations, thereby providing a model on which other CMS groups could base their practices. This demonstration also presented the opportunity to test category rating, demonstrating greater flexibility in considering a range of qualified candidates.

CMS identified the position of health insurance specialist as the best candidate for the test process for several reasons:

- It was the most common occupation series across the organization. There will always be hiring needs in this area.
- There were immediate hiring needs for multiple positions.
- Many of the projected retirements are expected to deplete these positions going forward, so the work done in this area could benefit future hiring.
- There were no special flexibilities or direct hiring authorities for these positions, so positive results might benefit all hiring efforts and be even more significant for MMA positions.

The EHM team began the demonstration effort with a strategic conversation with the hiring manager to clearly define the needs of the position. Information gathered during this critical discussion and during job analysis enabled the team to:

- Market the position using a visually appealing, plain-English vacancy announcement,
- Proactively target qualified candidates via a number of Internet accessible resume databases, and
- Build tools to effectively screen applicants and assess their skills and fit for the position, combining several different approaches to enhance results.

Results

Results from the demonstration process were very impressive. In the first round, more than 200 people applied for the GS-13 health insurance specialist position (the average number of applicants for similar positions in HHS was slightly more than 50). Of that population, 33 applicants were a direct result of the team's proactive recruiting efforts using Internet-accessible resume databases.

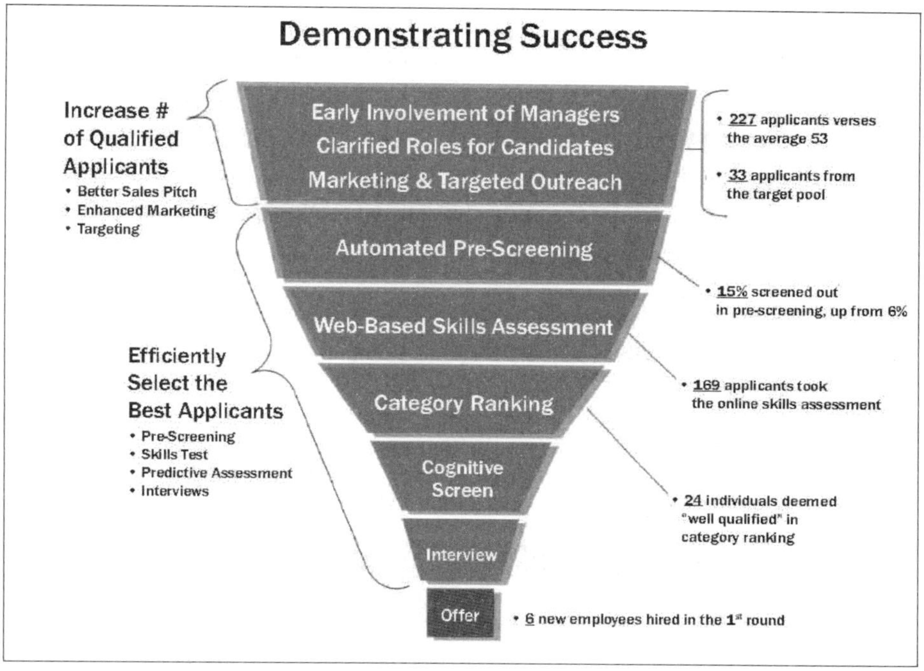

Pursuing a phased approach to screening and assessment, CMS required the applicants to complete a questionnaire in QuickHire. The well-crafted questions screened-out about 15 percent of applicants, a significantly higher percentage than in most other CMS efforts. The remaining applicants were then required to complete an online skills test. Applicants were ranked based on the combined score from the questionnaire and skills test.

Applying category rating, the hiring manager was presented with 24 applicants to consider rather than three as in the conventional process. Finally, candidates invited to interview were required to complete an additional assessment. Whereas the first online skills test reviewed specific knowledge and writing skills, the final assessment was predictive, reviewing behavioral competencies and cognitive abilities.

In the final analysis, the hiring manager was able to hire seven people—the first within

(continued)

(continued)

22 business days of closing the vacancy announcement—and was extremely pleased with the caliber of candidates. Having committed significant time to the project, he stated, "The process produced great candidates and was well worth the effort!"

In addition to conducting the pilot, CMS also implemented some "quick fixes" to the hiring process. This included modifying the vacancy announcements to better market the agency and streamlining the hiring process to eliminate redundancies and unnecessary handoffs. In streamlining the hiring process, more than 60 steps were identified that represented a series of actions involving the hiring managers, their executive officers, budget resources, agency and HHS executives, EEO and multiple HR resources. Illustrating the steps highlighted some of the inefficiencies that had crept into their practices over time and helped each function better understand its involvement in the overall process.

The illustration also led to a focus on accountability. Experts helped CMS reduce the steps in their hiring process by more than 20 percent. The agency has since taken steps to further streamline the process.

Source: This is an abridged and modified version of the case studies published 02/20/2004 by the Partnership for Public Service. The full version can be found at the following web address: http://www.ourpublicservice.org/OPS/publications/viewcontentdetails.php?id=85.

High-performing organizations tailor their training and development programs with emphasis on satisfying the needs of both the organization and the individual. In an ideal world, these programs are not based on imagined needs or "a wish list" (Isaacs 1996). Instruction must be carefully monitored to make sure that stated training objectives are met. Experience dictates that when organizations make use of employees' new skills and knowledge, the employees will perform at higher levels. Similarly, performance will likely suffer when there is resistance to applying these skills or employees are made to feel powerless and discouraged in their efforts to utilize the skills (Isaacs 1996).

On-the-Job Methods of Employee Development

On-the-job methods for development can be very effective if used properly by the supervisor. Five techniques are available: delegation, coaching, special assignments, job rotation, and understudy.

1. **Delegation:** Can be utilized when an employee exhibits potential. The supervisor can delegate as much authority and commensurate responsibility as possible to his or her subordinate. Exercising authority helps an individual to grow. This technique also encourages self-confidence.

2. **Coaching:** Giving an individual an assignment and then personally assisting them in its completion allows the subordinate to learn by doing. It further encourages the subordinate to seek advice from the supervisor as often as needed. Coaching is a delicate art and must be practiced with a keen sense of understanding. A good coach reviews the subordinate's progress and provides constructive criticism and praise when needed.

3. **Special assignments:** Can increase an employee's usefulness and self-confidence. Presenting a plan to a group or the department, correcting office or production problems, and helping to develop new product ideas are examples of special projects that can be assigned. The challenges of a special assignment can stimulate the subordinate.

4. **Job rotation:** Refers to moving an employee from one responsible job to another. Job rotation can expose him or her to different problems, decision processes, and solutions.

5. **Understudy:** Is a term that refers to the supervisor's choice of a subordinate to succeed him or her. When the supervisor receives advancement, the subordinate chosen for this type of development must possess the skills, ability, and common sense necessary to fill a leadership position.

Delegation

There are several reasons why supervisors should delegate more. For one, it frees them of time-consuming tasks that would otherwise keep them from supervisory work and overall planning. In addition, delegation demonstrates trust. By delegating, supervisors show that they have confidence in their subordinates. Developing one's subordinates is, perhaps, the most important skill a manager can have. Delegation allows a supervisor to take time off for business or just a vacation. Delegation also helps in the process of compiling performance appraisals, giving a manager tangible ways to observe and measure the performance of delegated assignments. Similarly, delegation facilitates promotions. An organization runs more smoothly when subordinates can step into other positions. Supervisors may get some good ideas by delegating work to their employees. Subordinates may approach a task with a fresh eye, coming up with ways to do things better or faster. Delegation also increases the efficiency of the manager, since he or she is forced to communicate the assignment clearly and precisely.

> "Government is only as good as the men in it."
>
> **DREW PEARSON**
> Journalist

The Role of the Boss in Delegating. A delegator must accept the fact that effective delegation is critical to agency success and a key factor in improving organizational performance and productivity. He or she must communicate goals and tasks clearly; set high performance standards; know employees' work backgrounds, strengths, and interests; encourage participation in objectives and gain commitment to them;

establish communication (or feedback) systems and expectations; provide necessary supports (i.e., coaching and training); exhibit confidence and trust at all stages; be aware of progress and be available for backup help; review results, not methods; and evaluate the completion of each task and provide feedback to the workers.

The Role of the Employee in Delegating. Employees must know organizational and unit goals and priorities; take the initiative and determine personal goals; be sure the delegation is realistic; check for complete understanding of the following: (a) resources available, (b) performance standards, (c) potential problems, (d) new ideas/techniques to use, and (e) possible personal outcomes; establish a communication (or feedback) system; report to the boss (i.e., allow for no surprises); and submit completed project, including all paperwork.

Why Supervisors Do Not Delegate. Supervisors who are reluctant to delegate are usually fearful of the consequences of delegation, do not realize the benefits of delegating, or do not know how to delegate effectively. The reasons why supervisors do not delegate enough typically include:

- **Fear of mistakes:** Since supervisors are still accountable, they will likely be blamed for mistakes made by their subordinates. However, by learning through experience, employees will make fewer mistakes with time.
- **A supervisor may delegate him or herself out of a job:** However, by being indispensable, workers at all levels are actually less likely to be promoted.
- **The job can be done faster by the supervisor than by subordinates:** Perhaps, but the supervisor is robbing him or herself of time that could be spent doing managerial tasks—for instance, planning ahead.
- **A supervisor will lose prestige by foregoing certain decisions:** A supervisor who must make all decisions—even minor ones—usually earns a reputation for lacking confidence in his or her subordinates.
- **A supervisor will not be able to check up on delegated assignments:** This is a flimsy excuse—a supervisor should establish deadlines, set performance standards, keep in touch, ask for progress reports, etc.
- **Delegation forces a supervisor to give up favorite parts of the job:** Supervisors do not have to give up everything. However, all of their tasks should be cast in the role of the supervisor.
- **Subordinates will have too much to do if more work is dele-**

> "Our progress as a nation can be no swifter than our progress in education... The human mind is our fundamental resource."
>
> **JOHN F. KENNEDY**
> 35th President of the United States

The Knowledge Transfer Dilemma

Although we can't train people in relationship management or create an instant history, there are structured, methodical approaches we can employ to accomplish the transfer of knowledge.

- **Job Analysis**—This helps identify job duties and the skills, knowledge, and abilities needed to accomplish those duties. There are a number of methods for conducting a job analysis, including observations, questionnaires, and work logs. Some models are quite complex, but for the purpose of knowledge transfer, a simple questionnaire and interview will probably suffice.
- **Job Shadowing**—This is something that we haven't always been able to do in the public sector. Typically, budget constraints and human resource policies present problems in hiring a replacement before the retiree has departed. However, many organizations are recognizing the value in overlapping the incumbent with the newcomer and HR offices are developing methods for accomplishing the overlap.
- **Process Documentation**—Clear process documentation can be very helpful in both storing and passing on job requirements. Process flow charts, desk procedure manuals, critical event calendars, and other documents can be very helpful for passing information from a more experienced worker to their replacement. With jobs that are very dependent on relationship management, a network journal can be helpful. This document is a method for capturing whom the incumbent deals with and for what purpose.

To be successful, there must be several factors at play in making knowledge transfer part of the culture of your organization.

- Performance appraisals for managers should include objectives focused on succession planning and knowledge transfer plans.
- Retiring and TERI employees should be required to develop and implement structured knowledge transfer plans.
- Training departments should be co-opted to help with conducting job analysis and developing learning plans.
- The organization's policies and procedures should be reviewed to ensure that they support knowledge transfer.

(continued)

(continued)

So far we have not seen a mass exodus of retirees. Many of our retired employees have returned to the workplace. However, that will not always be the case, and we need to focus on the processes needed to transfer knowledge from our experienced workforce to our newer employees. Not only do we risk the inability to carry out our missions when people do leave our organizations, we may struggle to retain talented potential leaders. When employees don't see an opportunity for moving into leadership roles because retirees are staying in key roles, these potential leaders will move on to other organizations, exacerbating the current problem.

Source: Reprinted from article appearing in Impact—The South Carolina State Government Improvement Network Newsletter, September 2007. http://www.scsgin.org/newsletter/XVI_III.pdf.

gated to them: Supervisors who think this way should ask themselves the question: Since I have been doing the job instead of supervising it, am I sure that I have reviewed my operations to determine if it is really operating efficiently?

- **A supervisor does not really know how or what to delegate:** Anyone can learn how to delegate from articles, books, a boss, or seminars.
- **A supervisor's boss will be annoyed if he or she delegates the job instead of doing it:** Bosses are typically most interested that a job is done well, not in who does it.
- **Subordinates don't really want more work:** A supervisor who gives people an opportunity to make decisions themselves may find that many of them actually enjoy it.

Delegating Effectively. Meaning what you say is imperative. In other words, once you have given someone full authority through delegation, that authority should never be taken back without good cause. Ensure that subordinates know exactly what tasks have been delegated. Soliciting a subordinate's ideas regarding the delegated task can be helpful in this regard. Managers with knowledge on how best to accomplish a given task can use delegation as a way to develop alternative skill sets and workplace proficiencies. Similarly, delegating tasks that subordinates are not necessarily familiar with can prove useful in long run; that is, this enables workers to cultivate new skills. Not insisting that the delegating task be done "your" way is important to effective delegation. People have their own ways of working. A manager may find that a subordinate's way of doing things is, perhaps, a better way. Delegation must be a sustained process—a way of doing business in the department. Those who delegate must show that they want feedback. Managers must work to create an organizational climate where subordinates will seek assistance when stymied, confused, or apprehensive about proceeding. Finally, following up after the task is completed is necessary. Managers must inform subordinates precisely how well they have performed.

> "No executive has ever suffered because his subordinates were strong and effective."
>
> **PETER DRUCKER**
> Economist; Author

Employee Motivation

Motivating employees to perform at a high level goes beyond competitive pay and benefits. What Carl Stone's *Work Attitude Survey* (1982) emphasized more than two decades ago still holds true today: greater numbers of workers are driven by the desire to find a societal niche where their talents are recognized, where they are treated as human beings who have deeply held desires, where they view their work as having a greater purpose, and where they are afforded the opportunity to be consulted on those matters that have influence on their work lives. Healthy worker-management relationships, clear lines of communication, more training to cultivate and improve skills, and an attractive physical work environment may all motivate the workers in high-performing organizations.

Managers should hold responsibility, punctuality, and the yearning for accomplishment in high regard. Most managers feel that they underscore these qualities when supervising their workers. All too often, however, workers fail to

EXERCISE 3.1

What Motivates You?

Complete the following sentences with the first words or phrases that come to mind:

1. I go to work because . . .
2. Work to me means . . .
3. The best part about work is . . .
4. The worst part about work is . . .
5. My job is . . .
6. Motivation to work comes from . . .
7. If I made one change to make my work more interesting, I would . . .
8. My motivation at work would improve if . . .
9. My motivation would decline if . . .
10. My ambition is to . . .

execute their tasks as effectively or efficiently as a manager might like. The concept of motivation can be thought as "something" that triggers a person to act in a certain way. From a manager's perspective, motivation means coexisting with workers in a way that causes them to be responsible, punctual, and productive

Job Satisfaction and Fulfillment

This article offers some simple suggestions to facilitate "Joy Building" within the work environment:

1. Be here now. Employee appreciation days do not make up for otherwise insincere or abusive behavior. What do you do every other day of the week?
2. Don't be a fair weather friend. Keep your employees engaged in good times and bad.
3. See team members as individuals. Define your goal and use each employee's strengths to get there.
4. Remember that silence is not golden. Talking to employees only when they make a mistake alienates them.
5. Let friendship ring. When employees find friends at work, they feel connected to their jobs and will likely be happier and more productive employees.
6. Let the outside world in. Asking employees about their weekends or their kids shows that you see them as people, not just slots on an organizational chart.
7. Be yourself. What works for celebrity CEOs doesn't always work for everybody else. An honest, low-key chat can be as effective as a high-voltage pep rally.
8. Make it meaningful. Tell the mailroom clerk why that package is so important. Let people know The Big Picture. Everyone wants to feel that their work matters.

Take a few minutes to rediscover your employees and customers before you tackle the next crisis. Who knows, you might approach things from a different perspective and achieve a greater sense of fulfillment, even happiness, with your accomplishments.

Source: Walter Caudel, Impact—The South Carolina State Government Improvement Network Newsletter, Spring 2005, XIV, I. http://www.scsgin.org/newsletter/XIV_I.pdf.

when completing job-specific tasks. Workers' "lack of ambition," absence from work, and lackluster performance are outgrowths of negative job experiences. Workers need to experience on-the-job rewards. This will foster more positive worker behaviors. In order to use effective motivational techniques, a manager need not know every detail about every worker; rather, the manager must understand that worker motivation is tied to workers' needs, and motivational techniques that enable workers to have positive experiences will help cultivate a sense of responsibility on the job.

Public organizations increasingly employ a host of innovative approaches motivating people. These organizations recognize that money, while no doubt an important source of employee motivation, is certainly not the only source. Such high-achieving organizations embrace an approach to human resource management that links HR management policies, plans, and processes. According to Isaacs (2003), employees' work needs and expectations must be given constant attention from the time they begin working in an organization until the time they leave. Humanistic management approaches that account for employee needs, expectations, and attitudes and recognize employees' differing abilities and knowledge likely improve worker performance.

> "Most important, leaders can conceive and articulate goals that lift people out of their petty preoccupations and unite them in pursuit of objectives worthy of their best efforts."
>
> **JOHN W. GARDNER**
> Government Official; Leadership Expert

Hierarchy of Human Needs

Abraham Maslow, author of the groundbreaking 1943 article "A Theory of Human Motivation," states that motivation is predicated upon five fundamental needs. . At the lowest level of the needs hierarchy are physiological needs, which deal with anything that is necessary to sustain life (for example, shelter, food, and clothing). Given the fulfillment of physiological needs, safety needs emerge. Safety needs refer not only to personal security but also the desire for an "ordered" and "predictable world" (Maslow 1943). This includes job security, financial security, and emotional security. Should one's physiological and safety needs be fulfilled, the need for love emerges in the hierarchy. In this instance, love refers to acceptance, friendship, affection, and a sense of belonging. Fulfillment of an individual's need for love gives way to esteem needs, which are divided into two subgroups. The first refers to one's desire to be recognized as strong, confident, and autonomous—in other words, feeling independent is central in this case. The second encompasses a desire for prestige and appreciation—in other words, anything that enhances one's self-image. Representing the apex of the needs hierarchy is the desire for self-actualization. Individual happiness, according to Maslow, requires that an individual recognize his or her societal niche; fulfilling one's inherent potential epitomizes self-actualization.

FIGURE 3.1 – MASLOW'S NEEDS HIERARCHY

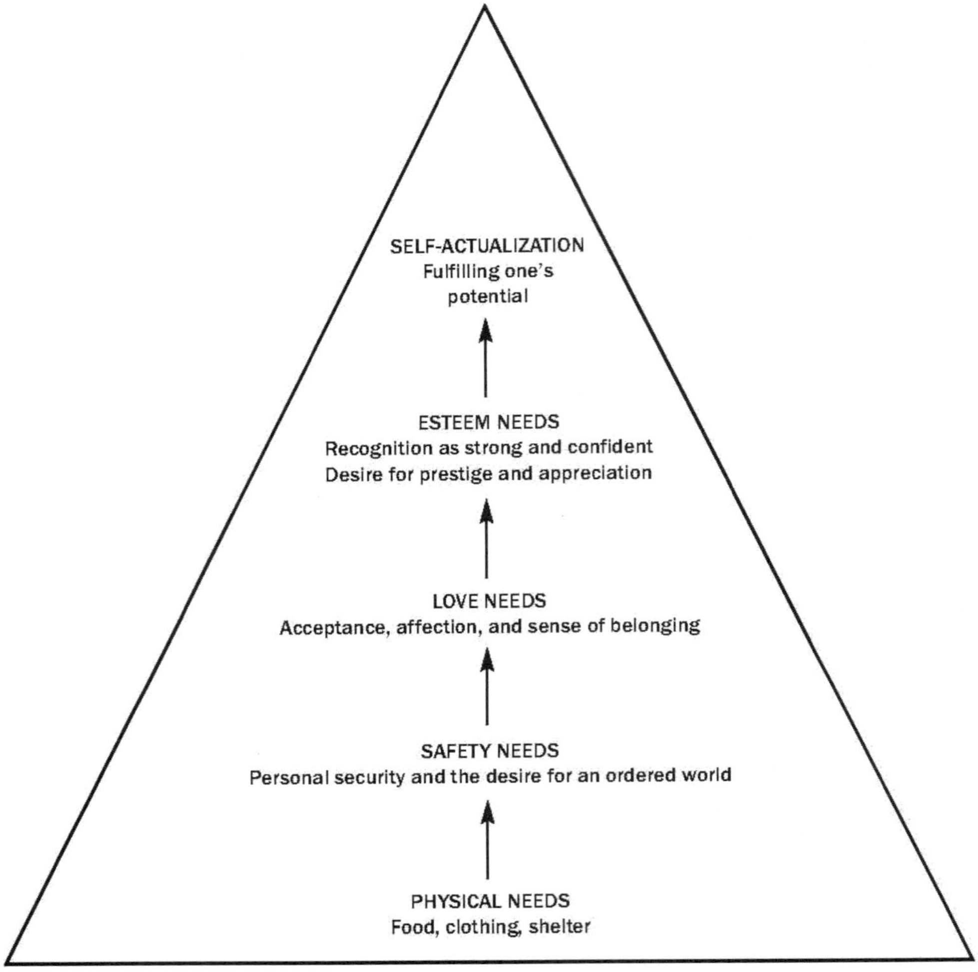

Herzberg's Satisfiers and Dissatisfiers

In a 1959 study directed by Frederick Herzberg, psychologists interviewed 200 Pittsburgh-area engineers and accountants. Each was asked the following:

1. Think of a recent experience that made you feel particularly good about your job.
2. Think of a recent experience that made you feel particularly bad about your job.
3. What effects did these incidents have on your attitudes and performance?
4. How long did these effects last?

TABLE 3.1 – HERZBERG'S TWO-FACTOR THEORY

Satisfiers	Dissatisfiers
Achievement	Company policy and administration
Recognition	Supervision
Work itself	Working conditions
Responsibility	Interpersonal relations
Advancement	Salary
Growth	Status
	Job security

Herzberg (1966) found that when people felt good about their jobs, it was because some event had revealed that they were doing their jobs well or becoming more expert in their field. Bad feelings, on the other hand, usually resulted from unfair treatment rather than a factor specifically related to the content of the job. These findings led Herzberg to conclude that two sets of factors affect performance:

- Job content factors (satisfiers) and
- Hygiene or maintenance factors (dissatisfiers)

Employee Motivation and Theories X and Y

Regarded as one of the most influential organizational humanists, McGregor (1960) offered two conflicting management theories, each of which makes specific assumptions regarding human nature. According to Theory X, the average person dislikes work and will avoid it if possible. Because of this, most people need to be coerced, controlled, or even threatened with reprimand to motivate the effort needed for the achievement of organizational goals. Theory X further argues that people prefer being directed, avoid responsibility at all costs, have few ambitions, and desire job security above all else. In contrast, Theory Y argues that work comes naturally to most people. Under this theory, external control and coercive threats of reprimand are not necessary for the achievement of organizational goals; rather, workers will exercise self-direction in the interest of achieving organizational goals to which they are committed. Commitment to organizational goals is a function of the rewards associated with goal attainment; that is, the opportunity and capacity to exercise high levels of imagination, ingenuity, and creativity in

> "Management is nothing more than motivating other people."
>
> **LEE IACOCCA**
> American Automobile-industry Leader

solving organizational problems. Finally—according to Theory Y—the intellectual potential of the average person is only partially developed.

How might the above assumptions affect employees' behaviors? Let's take a specific example. Let's suppose that we—the authors—are supervising you—the reader. As your supervisor, we make the following assumptions about you:

- You dislike work.
- You are lazy and avoid responsibility.
- You are incapable of directing your own behavior and prefer to be led.
- You avoid making decisions.
- You are unconcerned about organizational goals and objectives.

We may not actually say such things to you, but the following behaviors make our attitudes quite clear:

- We don't tell you anything.

FIGURE 3.2 – SATISFIERS AND DISSATISFIERS

SATISFACTION SCALE		MOTIVATION SCALE
	Fully Satisfied	100% motivated
<u>Satisfiers</u> Achievement Recognition The Work Responsibility Status Advancement Opportunity for Growth	Can fully satisfy or dissatisfy if absent	
		50% motivated
<u>Dissatisfiers</u> Agency Policy Supervision Skill Salary Working Conditions	Can only dissatisfy or move the worker to zero on the satisfaction scale	
	Fully Dissatisfied	0% motivated

Source: From Frederick Herzberg. 1966. Work and the Nature of Man. Cleveland, OH: World Publishing.

- We don't allow you much latitude in your work: we tell you what to do, how to do it, and when to do it.
- We accept your ideas, but only when they agree with our ideas.
- We take care of all important communications.
- In order to minimize favoritism, we communicate with all employees individually.

Our various acts or behaviors will have a direct effect on your behavior. It is likely that you will react in the following ways:

- Since we don't tell you anything, you begin to "leak" information to prove your own importance.

TABLE 3.2 – ACTIONS/NEEDS ANALYSIS TABLE

Actions that reveal needs	Needs revealed by actions
Does extra work	Self-actualization
Takes fixed positions and refuses to evaluate others' positions	Esteem
Overly agreeable	Love, affection, belongingness
Wants step-by-step instructions	Safety
Uses new or difficult methods to complete assignments	Self-actualization
Resists control and structure	Esteem
Aloof, inwardly directed	Safety
Volunteers for group work	Love, affection, belongingness
Argues rather than listens	Esteem
Keeps low profile	Safety
Brags about accomplishments	Esteem
Asks for feedback on progress	Self-actualization and love, affection, and belongingness
Asks for lots of structure	Safety

- Since we determine what you do on the job, you don't develop new work interests.
- Since we reject your ideas, you stop giving them.
- Since we accept your recommendations only if they agree with ours, you try to anticipate what our position will be.
- Since we don't communicate with your group, you and your coworkers develop informal coalitions to "keep us guessing."

It would be natural for you to become frustrated, apathetic, and resistant to organizational goals in such an atmosphere. As a result—to complete the circle—we will see you as lazy, incapable of making decisions for yourself, and unwilling to assume responsibility. Through a self-fulfilling prophesy, you will have proved our original assumptions. This example illustrates how behavioral assumptions held by managers have a direct influence on the organizational climate. These attitudes, behaviors, and communication characteristics essentially make up the organizational climate.

Assessing Employee Performance

High-performing organizations implement well-conceived and well-managed performance appraisal systems to act as developmental and motivational tools. These systems recognize that mutually dependent factors help create a work environment conducive to high performance (Guy 1992b). Among these factors are an organizational culture that depends on team building, takes advantage of employee

EXERCISE 3.2

Appraisal Communication Role Plays

1. You are Supervisor John Samuels. Your secretary has informed you that Mike Adams has requested to see you immediately concerning his performance evaluation. You rated him unsatisfactory for the following reasons:
   - He is consistently late, thereby holding up unit production.
   - He has not gotten along well with his coworkers, thus creating morale and assignment problems.
   - His unit assignments are oftentimes late and of poor quality.
2. You are Supervisor Jim Thompson. Henry Johnson requested an appointment to see you four days ago concerning his performance evaluation, which you rated satisfactory. You have no information as to the reason for Henry's request to see you.
3. You are Supervisor Michele Davis. You have asked to speak to Amy Brennan concerning her performance evaluation, which you rated "satisfactory." You do not have any problems with Ms. Brennan as her work is always done in a satisfactory manner; however, you feel you should give all your workers an opportunity to discuss their performance evaluation.

EXERCISE 3.3

Identifying When Counseling Is Necessary

1. Mr. Brown always arrives 10 to 15 minutes early for work and starts his assignments immediately. Frequently, he stays at least a half an hour after working hours to complete a special project. Despite the extra time he works, the quality and quantity of his work is average.

   [__] Counsel *[__] Do Not Counsel*

2. Ms. Jones is a clerk in a small office that faces frequent deadlines. There is constant pressure on the staff to increase production. Very often there are arguments among the staff; more often than not, Ms. Jones seems to be the instigator of the arguments. Although Ms. Jones's work is satisfactorily completed, the unit's production is often late and incomplete, and morale is very low.

   [__] Counsel *[__] Do Not Counsel*

3. Mr. Kavech is a professional employee who is assigned to travel within New York State, auditing work for the local social services districts. This auditing requires a team of three employees. It is rumored that Mr. Kavech is gay. His work is satisfactory. However, because of these rumors, certain employees do not want to travel with Mr. Kavech.

   [__] Counsel *[__] Do Not Counsel*

4. Ms. Carey is always volunteering to help other workers catch up on their assignments. The staff seems to seek her guidance constantly. She also appears to be very effective in assisting new employees. Additionally, Ms. Carey's own assignments consistently far exceed the standard.

   [__] Counsel *[__] Do Not Counsel*

5. Mr. Ett is responsible for traveling within New York State to implement an automated eligibility system in the local Social Security districts. Because of the political ramifications involved in the process of a state organization working with a county organization, Mr. Ett is required to be courteous, tactful, and aware of the sensitive nature of his position. Although Mr. Ett's work as a technician is excellent, he is discourteous and abrupt with the county employees, including some of the local district commissioners.

   [__] Counsel *[__] Do Not Counsel*

6. Ms. Caliber is a longtime employee of your office. You are her newly appointed supervisor. Ms. Caliber is an average employee who gets the work done. She does not practice the personal hygiene habits that would normally be accepted in an office setting. It is apparent that she doesn't bathe regularly and she does not use deodorant. Ms. Caliber has been around for so long, the other employees have learned to work around her offensive nature.

   [__] Counsel *[__] Do Not Counsel*

strengths while compensating for employee weaknesses, maintains open and transparent communication channels, and balances organizational needs with employee needs.

Organizational mandates at the operational level equate to on-the-job tasks for work teams or individuals. These tasks serve as a starting point for the performance assessment process. Now, both employer and employee may discuss and settle on the distribution of these tasks to the employee's work team or position. When a performance standard for completion of those tasks is established, an opportunity is provided for an inventory of the skills or training that the employee

Purposes of Performance Appraisals

1. To assure an employee a regular, formal opportunity to discuss his/her performance, achievements, difficulties, and goals.
2. To provide a regular, formal opportunity for a supervisor to discuss his/her view of an employee's performance and present standing.
3. To improve employee performance through recognition, encouragement, constructive criticism, or personal counseling.
4. To establish goals or performance standards to be followed until the next evaluation.
5. To offer a periodic, formal means of identifying training needs and fostering employee development.
6. To offer a periodic, formal means of gathering employee suggestions for improving methods, procedures, performance, or morale.
7. To demonstrate that the employee's contribution matters, and that the supervisor is concerned about him/her as an individual.
8. To deepen the employee's job satisfaction and his/her commitment to the organization.
9. To help determine employee potential for advancement.
10. To help provide an objective, equitable basis for making compensation, transfer, and other decisions.

needs. After this, the appropriate employee developmental plans are established and implemented (McDonald 1995).

In high-performing organizations. performance assessment is used to cultivate first-class employees and improve performance. The success of performance assessment as a developmental tool relies on sincerity between manager and employee. Assessment is a way of identifying employee strengths and weaknesses on a continual basis, providing performance feedback to employees regularly, counseling employees, and identifying ways to improve performance. If carried out effectively, performance assessments make employees aware of whether or not they are fulfilling job expectations. Successful performance assessments may bolster an employee's confidence and morale, both of which are likely to positively affect performance (Isaacs 1996).

> "Not surprisingly, work-life moaners tend to be a phenomenon of below-average performers."
>
> **JACK WELCH**
> Retired CEO of General Electric

Inherent to the assessment process is conflict. There are, however, ways of minimizing this conflict. To begin with, employees must have an understanding of their job expectations. This can be done by: providing job descriptions that underscore expectations; having discussions with employees regarding reachable performance standards; and developing performance standards that measure work quality, work quantity, and the timeliness of the work to be completed. According to McDonald (1995), identifying performance standards is an essential precursor to the performance assessment process in that it gives the employee a framework within which to conduct self-assessments. It also establishes the agenda for the formal assessment session. Delineating clear job expectations and per-

EXERCISE 3.4

Appraisal Communication—Exercise in Counseling

Supervisor Role

You are Jo Davis. You have arranged to meet with Sandy Donaldson, your subordinate, to follow up on his/her performance appraisal interview of two months ago; you had rated him/her satisfactory at that time. Lately, though, you have been noticing that Sandy has not been returning to work after lunch on the average of twice a week and passed out at work just the other day. Rumor has it that Sandy has been drinking heavily.

Employee Role

You are Sandy Donaldson. You have agreed to meet with your supervisor, Jo Davis, to follow up on your performance appraisal interview. You are anxious because you know you haven't been at your desk during the busy time of the day lately. You have not been feeling well and are bit bored with work. Only an innocent drink or two at lunch seems to dull the strain of the workday.

formance standards removes the subjectivity and ambiguity that all too often undermine the performance appraisal process. Clear goals, then, reduce the likelihood of manager-worker conflict. In an effort to reduce conflict even further, some organizations may hire professional appraisers to assess performance accurately. Professional appraisers champion a problem-solving approach to formal assessment (Isaacs 1996).

Employee Counseling

Performance problems need to be faced as early as possible before they turn into disasters. Usually when a supervisor counsels with a subordinate, it is about a particular problem such as the worker's tardiness, inability to complete assigned work, or his or her personality conflict with a coworker. Counseling may also be used to give feedback on performance and to plan for employee development when those opportunities exist. As in all management, counseling involves having an impact on others so that the task of the group is accomplished. The purpose of the counseling session is to determine the cause of an employee's behavior, give feedback, and guide subsequent efforts. Counseling should not be viewed as punitive, but as a problem-solving session. The supervisor's goal is to help employees to help themselves in resolving existing problems, avoiding potential problems, and making future decisions. When the supervisor approaches the counseling situation, he or she stands to benefit for many reasons: Counseling can accomplish many objectives that fall within supervisor's responsibility. It provides:

- The most direct and efficient means available to improve employee performance;
- A vehicle for planning and monitoring staff development;
- An effective way of identifying necessary avenues for improvement (e.g., training);
- An excellent means to get to know employees and build credibility into the employer-employee relationship;
- A way to reduce on-the-job anxiety;
- A means for recognizing serious employee problems that require referrals;
- A means of identifying and offsetting potential problems.

On the other hand, the counseling situations contain many risks. Counseling can:

- Be time consuming;
- Be personally unpleasant;

- Uncover deep-rooted problems that are difficult to cope with;
- Reveal problems that both the employer and employee contribute to;
- Worsen the problem if mismanaged.

There is always a risk of mismanaging counseling when the supervisor miscon-

– GOOD WORK, PETROV. YOU WENT A WHOLE MONTH WITHOUT MAKING A SINGLE DEFECTIVE PART!
– YEAH, I WAS ON VACATION!
Artist: V. Bokovnia; *Krokodil* [*Crocodile*] satirical magazine, mid-1980s.

Sample Counseling Sessions

Example 1

Circumstances: Supervisor Jackson discovers that employee Wray is late for work again. This is the sixth time in the last month that the employee has been late. Wray did not call to inform Jackson that she would be late.

Scene: Outer office about 3 minutes after Wray gets back to her desk, Jackson enters as Wray is assembling some of her typing materials. The rest of the secretarial staff are at their desks, and three or four other individuals wander in and out of the office during the following discussion.

Wray: Hi, Ms. Jackson. Sorry I'm late. The subways were really slow this morning.

Jackson: Look, Wray, I don't know why you can't get in here on time. Everyone else does.

Wray: Well, you know I live way out . . .

Jackson: (Interrupting) Don't give me that. You're just irresponsible. Do you know what is going to happen if you don't straighten out?

Wray: No, not really.

Jackson: Sure, you do. Don't ever let this happen again.

Wray: But I really have a good explanation... Can't you...?

Jackson:(Interrupting) I've heard all I'm going to. Don't give me any more excuses. Just get to work.

Example 2

Circumstances: Supervisor Jackson discovers that employee Wray is late for work again. This is the sixth time in the last month that Wray has been late. Wray did not inform Jackson that she would be late.

Scene: Supervisor's office.

Jackson: Come in.

Wray: You wanted to see me?

Jackson: Yes. I noticed that you were late again this morning. I'm quite concerned.

Wray: Why? I got in. Didn't I?

Jackson: Well, not on time.

Wray: Other employees are late sometimes. Why are you picking on me?

Jackson: Because you are making it a habit. This is the sixth time this month. Do you have a particular problem?

Wray: Well, I live up in the Bronx where the trains get backed up during rush hour. It takes a lot longer time to get here. All the others live a lot closer than I do.

Jackson: You are aware that you have a responsibility under the attendance rules to be here on time no matter where you live. Aren't you?

Wray: You mean I don't get any consideration?

Jackson: I've given you plenty of consideration to this point, but I cannot let you slip into a habit of arriving tardy. We have work to do, and sometimes other employees are unable to begin their work until you arrive.

Wray: Look. The subway is frustrating. If I leave any earlier, I will have to get up at five in the morning. Do you want me to come to work exhausted?

Jackson: No. But if you have to get up earlier in order to get here on time, I would suggest that you go to sleep earlier at night. If that poses too much of a problem, then you may want to consider transferring to an office closer to your home.

Wray: Does that mean you want me to leave?

Jackson: No. In fact, I'd hate to lose you.

Wray: Then why can't I just start later and take a shorter lunch hour?

Jackson: Because, rules just don't permit that and until they do, you have to be here on time. If your tardiness doesn't improve, I will be forced to recommend that you be disciplined. You are too good an employee to go that route.

Wray: Okay. I get the message.

Jackson: I'll tell you what. Let's get together in about a month. I will review your promptness record before that meeting. I think by that time you will have corrected the problem.

Wray: Okay.

Jackson: Thanks for dropping by to speak with me.

strues his or her role. Furthermore, it must be remembered that counseling is not therapy. It is inappropriate for the manager to function as therapist. It is, however, appropriate for the manager to arrange for help from someone else if and when the employee's problem warrants—such as when a worker has a drug or alcohol problem that interferes with job performance. Also, counseling is not discipline: it should not be threatening or punitive in tone. It is appropriate to inform an employee that performance is below standard and that continued failure to perform adequately could lead to disciplinary measures. However, the discussion's main objective should be to uncover the causes for the undesirable behaviors, and to spell out future courses of constructive action. Finally, counseling is not coaching. Coaching employees is a day-to-day supervisory job that involves giving employees clear directions and guidance in how to complete specific tasks. On the other hand, counseling is a discussion between employer and employee that focuses more broadly on the employee's performance and how it can be improved.

Before you counsel a subordinate, you should plan an approach that will effectively move the employee's behavior in the desired direction. Although each counseling session is unique, the following guidelines are always relevant:

- Conduct counseling sessions in private surroundings.
- Never schedule a counseling session when you are in a hurry.
- Be direct. Do not "beat around the bush" when talking to employees. Be candid.
- Give an employee the opportunity to explain his or her version of the incident or circumstances about which you are concerned. Be a good listener.
- Keep an open mind. If after talking to the employee you determine that your concern was misplaced, then say so.
- Explore means by which an employee can overcome a performance shortcoming.
- Some employees may be hostile. In these cases, you should remain calm, constantly trying to return the attention to your concerns. In other words, refocus on what happened, why it happened, and what can be done to improve it.
- Never characterize counseling sessions as "discipline."
- Do not speak in a punitive or derogatory manner.
- At the conclusion of the session, thank the employee for seeing you and establish an open-door policy should further problems arise.

The Problem Performer

Most employees want to do a good job and intend to correct behavior that is unproductive or unacceptable to their superiors. Some reasons why change does not always occur include:

- Conscious and unconscious forces may interfere with the change, e.g., the need to be liked by a group;
- Rewards may reinforce old behaviors, e.g., the need to repeat pleasurable activity;
- Situational factors may control behavior, e.g., an employee feels that a work situation calls for behavior that causes him or her discomfort.

> "There are three main ways managers get firing wrong—moving too fast, not using enough candor, and taking too long."
>
> **JACK WELCH**
> Retired CEO of General Electric

Managers often need to have a job done correctly as soon as possible, with no time for the effects of long-term positive reinforcement to kick in. We know through behavioral research that people behave differently in different situations. For example, we behave one way when we feel safe and another when we feel threatened. The following situational controls can be used by managers to encourage behavioral change on the job:

1. **Blend a new element into the situation**—e.g., a change in work location that places the problem employee closer to the foreman or perhaps near a highly productive fellow employee.
2. **Create discomfort in the current situation**—e.g., in a work area where loitering takes place, constrict the area so no more than one or two can be comfortable in the area.
3. **Generate conditions that create mild fear**—e.g., remind a worker that a drop in productivity may lead to the loss of business orders and eventually to possible layoffs.
4. **Assign a task that requires change**—e.g., if one employee is working slowly and holding back the person who has the final piece of a task, the slow worker should be given the end part of the assignment. A change in behavior may be necessary to complete the final project, or the individual may be indicated as the one holding up the work.
5. **Eliminate situational supports for the undesirable behavior**—"As long as an employee receives rewards—e.g., group approval/attention for behavior—the behavior will continue. When rewards are given coincidentally with hostile or aggressive behavior, the employee experiences this as management support for the negative behavior" (Adapted from Donaldson 1928).

Getting Along with People

Theodore Roosevelt once said, "The most important single ingredient in the formula of success is knowing how to get along with people." I guess this depends on what you call success. For me, success is about relationships. People. So how do you get along with people?

1. First, you must be curious. Human beings are amazing works of art. Each one has his or her own unique history. Just ask someone you don't know a couple of open-ended questions like, "What gets your best?" or "What kinds of things do you do in your free time?" and actively listen to their response. You'll be amazed at what you will learn. Listen and learn.

2. Second, be willing to share. How can we expect to get to know people if we aren't willing to share information about ourselves? Let people see the real you. A great way to reveal the real you is through a personal story. A personal story gives the listener a chance to visit a moment in time in your life. People love stories.

3. Third, be compassionate. Practice the "platinum" rule: "Do unto to others as they would have done unto themselves." Breaking news . . . everybody is not like me! We each have individual preferences and paradigms that make us who we are. The more we understand, embrace, and respect the preferences and paradigms of others the better we can connect with others—which leads me to the next point.

4. Fourth, become a student of human behavior. Participate in a Myers-Briggs Type Indicator (MBTI) workshop. Swiss physician-psychologist Carl Jung believed people could be identified by their different and equally valuable preferences for understanding and viewing both the world and themselves. An understanding of type preference fosters self-awareness and increases appreciation of others. The MBTI enables us to more easily see similarities and differences in the mental processing preferences of others—their decision styles, approaches to team work, relationships with co-workers, and communication styles. Seemingly chance variation in human behavior in fact is not due to chance; it is the logical result of a few basic, observable preferences.

5. Fifth, practice positive talk with yourself and others. When engaged in daily conversation with others, be a source of positive dialogue. Talk in terms of solutions and what's going right. Speak of the positives of every situation.

Turn the negative side of a situation around by practicing the "flipside" technique, a humorous approach useful in warding off the "negativity" virus. For example, if someone cuts you off in traffic say, "Where have you been, I've been saving this safe place in front of me for you for 10 minutes." You get the idea. Diffuse a bad situation with humor—which leads me to my last point...

6. Laugh! Nothing builds relationships with people better than a shared laugh. Research supports the point that laughter is actually a primal form of relationship building. Laughter is universal. It's easy, contagious, good for you, and fun. Make someone laugh and you make a connection.

In conclusion, be curious, share, be compassionate, be a student, be positive and laugh. Now, get out there and get along with people. Please? Thank you!

Source: Bobby George. "Getting Along with People." Impact—The South Carolina State Government Improvement Network, XIII (IV) (December 2004), www.scsgin.org/newsletter/XIII_IV.pdf.

Creating a Quality Work Environment

Creating a Team Mentality

An organization's upper management, middle and line managers, and human resource managers must cultivate and sustain teams in order to create a quality work environment, thereby leading to organizational productivity. Productive human resource management fosters cooperative work relationships, a high-value and diverse workforce, and a work environment that enhances—or at least does not detract from—an employee's quality of life. Work relations in high-performing organizations require clear and open communication between employees and employers, as well as a working partnership. This ensures that employees understand their rights, obligations to the organization, and job expectations. Balancing employee and organizational need is paramount. In this context, it is becoming more obvious that high-performing organizations use "work teams" to complete tasks and achieve objectives. As its name suggests, individuals within work teams work cooperatively. They do not work as individuals competing against each other. Work teams typically embrace a supportive philosophy for their members and can accomplish more than a group of individuals working independently.

Fostering Labor-Management Cooperation

Public administration scholars tend to agree that harmonious labor-management relationships are central to improving employee performance (Coleman 1990; Hodes 1991; Grace and Holzer 1992; Herrick 1990). Obviously, labor and management tension exists because of complicated workplace relationships, impasses, or other disagreements. Adversarial relations between employer and employee present the classic "no win" situation. Munroe (1992) argues that the development of partnerships must replace adversarial factions and that cooperative work systems must replace antagonistic ones. Building partnerships is likely to be difficult, as it requires persistence, determination, time, and diplomacy. Munroe advocates for Employee Involvement Programs, which are designed to bring all employees into the fold when important decisions need to be made. These programs are likely to minimize workforce demotivation, improve morale, and marshal human resources for exigent labor-management problem solving.

Holzer and Lee (1999) maintain that employer-employee strain is likely to occur when each views the other as an adversarial "out-group." Harmonious labor-management partnerships might be established through a mindset change; that is, viewing the dynamic between labor and management not as a "conflict" but rather as a mutually dependent and mutually beneficial "partnership." This mindset change can be accomplished only through open communication, the full support of upper management, and a large supply of previous success stories. Open communications will enable labor and management to better understand mutual problems. Providing success stories on labor-management partnerships will engender optimistic beliefs that labor and management can, despite their inherent differences, work toward equally beneficial resolutions. Finally, upper-management support will lend needed credibility about the seriousness of creating labor-management partnerships.

Although employer-employee cooperation is a condition for productive public man-

EXERCISE 3.5

Case Study: The Electronic Hallway Budget Reorganization in the Urbanopolis Human Resource Department (Simulation)

As the human resource manager for an urban city, you are mandated by the mayor to reduce your budget. In this exercise you will tackle present-day human resource management decisions based on a myriad of both city government and human resource management priorities, and civil service regulations. Read the case study and develop a staff reduction plan. This plan should include the positions you would eliminate and why. Also include the total dollar impact of your reduction plan. Compare your recommendations with other students in class and discuss your results.

The Electronic Hallway, Case Teaching Resources from the Evans School of Public Affairs https://hallway.org/cases/index.php

agement, tension will continue to be part of the labor-management relationship. It should be noted, however, that labor-management partnerships are possible, an example of which is the Department of Public Works in the City of Portland, Maine. Despite significant resource constraints, labor-management cooperation in the construction of a sports venue enabled the project to be completed under budget and in record time. In order to facilitate open communication, the city manager created a 26-person labor-management working group, which included an equipment operator, a working foreman, an assistant city manager, an administrative assistant, an engineer, an arborist, and the head of the department, in addition to the president of American Federation of State, County, and Municipal Employees (AFSCME) Local 481. As a result, employees came to view management as part of their team rather than as outsiders and adversaries. No longer was the dynamic between labor and management characterized as "us versus them." Central to this success story was strong leadership on the part of the mayor of Portland (U.S. Department of Labor 1996).

> "You may be the boss, but you're only as good as the people who work for you."
>
> **WILLIAM LEAHY**
> U.S. Naval Officer; White House Chief of Staff during World War II

Among the key factors in overcoming labor-management tensions is the formation of partnerships—partnerships facilitated by open communication, the sharing of previous success stories, and the support of upper management. It is important that public managers appreciate the magnitude of labor-management partnerships and emphasize these three factors for productive human resource management. Fruitful human resource management is unlikely to exist without a harmonious labor-management relationship.

Productive working relationships are not limited to employer-employee relations. Relations between public organizations and the citizens they serve are important as well. Productive relationships with both internal and external clients are important in order to circumvent potential problems. Quality work relationships are necessary to improve problem situations that may burgeon into conflict and become the basis for litigation. It is vital that managers emphasize the importance of this relationship to employees.

Productive human resource management exists in an open system in which internal and external factors are connected. People are the primary means to improving organizational performance in the public sector. It is critical to be aware of how to develop and effectively manage public employees, as well as to recognize what motivates these people to work at a high level. Effectively managing people will remain a critical issue in public personnel administration. This chapter has presented strategies relevant to creating and maintaining a quality and diverse workforce and creating and maintaining a high quality of work-life environment.

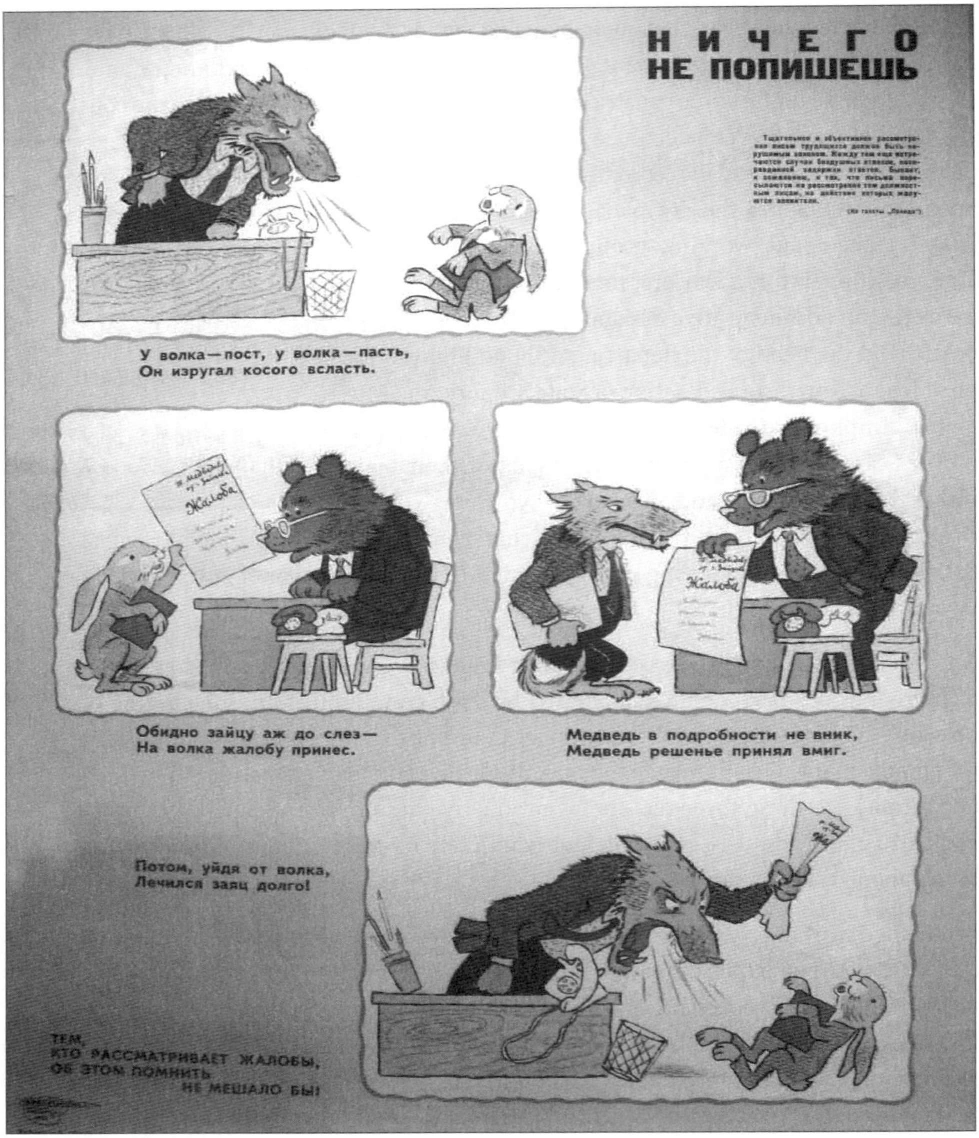

NOTHING YOU CAN DO
Artist: V. Kunnap; Poet: G. Tumarinson; "The Fighting Pencil" group, 1968.

The Wolf has an office and mouth very loud,
He scolded the Hare and started to shout.
Offended, the weeping Hare
Brought his petition to the Bear.
The Bear did not probe too deeply in the act,
He resolved the problem as a matter of fact.
The end is obvious for the Hare:
He needed intensive health care.
PEOPLE WHO EXAMINE GRIEVANCES
SHOULDN'T FORGET INCIDENTS LIKE THIS.

In terms of creating and maintaining a quality and diverse workforce, discovering ways to attract the so-called "best and brightest" is paramount to productive human resource management. The next step is to provide these individuals with training and development, enabling them to work effectively within what can be at times both a rapidly changing and a politically charged environment. At the same time, public managers must be mindful of a number of factors that have significant impacts on employee motivation. In addition to rudimentary factors such as rewarding workers (using monetary as well as nonmonetary, psychological rewards), public managers must recognize that employee commitment is not universal; that is, workers may be differentially committed to their managers, work group, unions, upper management, and clients. This multidimensional outlook on employee commitment enables managers to better identify what type of employee commitment serves as a source of motivation at a given time within the organization. Employee commitment also varies with differences in organizational culture.

> "Our chief want is someone who will inspire us to be what we know we could be."
>
> **RALPH WALDO EMERSON**
> Author; Poet; Philosopher (1803–1882)

Creating and maintaining a high quality of work life is crucial. The significance of a worker's physical surroundings—workplace safety, ergonomically sound workstations, a clean place to have lunch—are challenges for high-performing organizations. Accidents, diseases and hazards, and poor amenities generally result in lower performance, inefficiencies, higher rates of worker turnover and absenteeism, and increased numbers of medical claims. In dealing with these problems, it is necessary to have a variety of programs available to assist employees. By taking steps to lessen the likelihood and severity of these problems in the first place, both the workers and the organization benefit.

Finally, creating a cooperative workplace culture is essential. Organizational performance improvement is not the product of one employee's efforts. A collaborative atmosphere helps employees to be more productive, making labor-management partnerships imperative. These partnerships thrive on open communication, supplying success stories, and upper management leadership. While no doubt difficult, successful partnerships can be achieved when these factors are working simultaneously. Productive human resource management is more likely to occur when multiple strategies are pursued simultaneously, and throughout the rest of the twenty-first century, such management must be alert, responsive, and committed to its employees and to the demands of an ever-changing environment.

DIFFERENT MOTIVATIONAL BASES BETWEEN THE TWO COUNTRIES

Employee commitment, along with top management support, is the key to enhancing the level of performance in any type of organization. Employee commitment can be defined as a worker's psychological attachment to the workplace. It should be noted that recent research identified multiple dimensions in organizational commitment. Workers can be differentially committed to their supervisor, coworkers, and organization. And these multiple dimensions differentially explain employees' willingness to make an extra effort and desire to remain in the organization. Please read the following box and discuss how these three types of commitment differentially explain employees' motivations in each country and try to identify which type is stronger in each country depending upon different nation's cultures as mentioned in Chapter 2.

A Multidimensional View of Commitment: Individual, Group, and Organizational Levels

Conventional views of commitment have exclusively focused on commitment to the organization. It should be noted, however, that in contrast to these conventional views, a number of researchers have begun to view employee commitment as having multiple foci and bases (Becker, Randall, and Riegel 1995; Reichers 1985, 1986; Becker 1992; Gordon, Philpot, Burt, Thomson, and Spiller 1980; Meyer, Allen, and Smith 1993). Distinctions among foci and bases of commitment are not made in the more conventional views of commitment (Becker Randall, and Riegel, 1995).

In response to such deficiencies of organizational commitment research, O' Reilly and Chatman (1986) proposed an alternative approach in which commitment is defined as the psychological attachment felt by the person for the organization, reflecting the degree to which the person internalizes or adopts the characteristics or perspectives of the organization. They also suggested three bases of commitment to an organization: compliance, identification, and internalization commitments. Here, compliance occurs when people adopt attitudes and behaviors in order to obtain specific rewards or to avoid specific punishments. Identification occurs when people adopt attitudes and behaviors in order to be associated with a satisfying, self-defining relationship with another person or group. Internalization occurs when people adopt attitudes and behaviors because their content is congruent with the individuals' value systems (Kelman 1958). Using these three dimensions of commitment, Balfour and Wechsler (1991) examined two aspects of organizational commitment as it relates to public organizations: (1) identification of the antecedents of compliance, identification, and internalization commitment; and (2) determination of the effects of these dimensions on three hypothesized outcome measures: desire to remain with the organization, extra-role behaviors, and in-role behaviors. According to their findings, increased commitment among public employees showed a strong relation to their desire to remain with the organization but did not increase their willingness to make extra efforts on behalf of the organization. They argue that increased commitment, therefore, may produce valuable results such as reducing turnover, but may not increase productivity and performance.

It should be noted, however, that distinguishing among employee commitments within organizational commitment does not tell us the whole story about why employees are motivated to enhance performance and productivity and why they would like to remain with and to make an extra effort on behalf of their organization. It is necessary to distinguish among employee commitments above and beyond organizational commitment. Furthermore, Vandenberg and McCullin (1989) questioned the construct validity of O'Reilly and Chatman's measures of organizational commitment. "In a confirmatory factor analysis, they found a very strong relationship between the identification and internalization items and discovered that the compliance items had relatively low internal consistency coefficients" (Quoted from Balfour and Wechsler 1991, p.357).

As Reichers argues, the theory underlying the multiple commitments literature holds that an employee's commitment to the workplace cannot be adequately explained by commitment to the organization alone, because the coalitional nature of organizations leads employee commitment to be multidimensional (Reichers 1985).

Becker, Randall, and Riegel (1995) examined the relative ability of the multidimensional view of commitment and the theory of reasoned action to explain employee intentions and predict work behavior. In their study, they found that the commitment variables explain significant variance in each of the intentions and behaviors, controlling for the demographic variables.

In a study that employed a multiple constituency framework to examine the correlates of organizational commitment among a sample of 124 mental health professionals, Reichers (1986) found that only commitment to top management's goals was positively associated with commitment to the organization.

Meyer, Allen, and Smith (1993) also found that organizational and occupational

(continued)

(continued)

commitment contributed independently to the predictionof important organization–relevant outcome variables (e.g., turnover intention, performance, and citizenship). In particular, occupational commitment significantly contributed to predicting such outcome variables even when organizational commitment was controlled.

Gordon, Philpot, Burt, Thomson, and Spiller (1980) tried to describe the development of a criterion for union commitment because the commitment to union can explain a variety of variables. Gordon, Beauvais, and Ladd (1984), in their study of the job satisfaction and union commitment of unionized engineers, found that the engineers and technicians did not differ markedly in union commitment or job satisfaction, but that engineers expressed greater union commitment than did the nonprofessional workers.

There is growing evidence that the attitudinal commitment of employees to the workplace is multidimensional and that the foci and bases of commitment can improve the prediction of employee intentions and behaviors (Reichers 1985; Becker, Radall, and Riegel 1995).

Foci of commitment are the individuals and groups to whom an employee is attached (Reichers 1985). It has been found that employees can be committed to such foci as professions (Morrow 1983; Aranya and Ferris, 1983; Gouldner 1958) and unions (Angle and Perry 1986; Gordon, Beauvais, and Ladd 1984), as well as commitment to organizations (Mowday et al. 1982). In addition, recent research suggests that workers can also be differentially committed to occupations, top management, supervisors, co–workers, and customers (Becker 1992; Meyer, Allen, and Smith, 1993; Reichers 1986).

Morrow (1983) discussed the fact that there are several different foci for work commitment, including (a) value or personal ethic (e.g., protestant work ethic); (b) career; (c) job (e.g., job involvement and job orientation) and (d) union, in addition to a focus on one's organization.

Reichers (1985) advanced a similar position and argued for a multiple constituency model of organizational commitment.

Becker et al. (1996) pointed out that previous research has found that employee commitment and job performance are largely unrelated because prior work has not distinguished among individual foci (targets) and bases (motives) of commitment. Based on their empirical findings, they argued that commitment to supervisors was positively related to performance and was more strongly associated with performance than was commitment to organization (Becker, Billings, Eveleth, and Gilbert 1996).

Becker and Billings (1993) also divided profiles of commitment into two types: the locally committed (employees who are attached to their supervisor and work group) and the globally committed (employees who are attached to top management and organization). They found that these profiles of commitment were differentially related to intent to quit, job satisfaction, prosocial organizational behaviors, and certain demographic and contextual variables (Becker and Billings 1993).

Meyer et al. found that occupational and organizational commitment contributed independently to the prediction of professional activity and work behavior (Meyer, Allen, and Smith 1993).

Becker (1992) also discovered that commitment to top management, supervisor, and work group were important factors affecting job satisfaction, intent to quit, and prosocial organizational behaviors over and above commitment to an organization. In particular, they found that "commitment to foci other than an employing organization, specifically to top management, supervisors, and work groups, were negatively related to intent to quit and positively related to satisfaction and prosocial organizational behaviors and explained variance in these dependent variables over and above that explained by commitment to organization" (Becker 1992, p. 232).

Taking all into account, Reichers' comment is noteworthy:

> It has been argued that current approaches to organizational commitment ignore the multifaced conceptions of organization that have been prominent among organizational theorists. The addition of this macro perspective on organizations, coupled with what is known regarding reference group and role theories, suggests that commitment should be reconceptualized to reflect multiple commitments to the goal orientations of the multiple groups that constitute the organization (Reichers 1985, p.474).

Randall also points out the problem of OC and emphasizes the need for a multidimensional view of employee commitment:

> Thus advances in understanding the OC-work outcome relationship are likely to proceed, not through methodological advances, but through model development and refinement. To refine the model, researchers may need to seek closer contact with the participants they are studying and develop an understanding of what they mean by OC, how they express it, and if the meaning attached to OC varies across different professions and work groups. To illustrate, there is notable lack of specificity in the commitment literature about the object of the individual's commitment. Questions about commitment are a global construct. OC may actually be a collection of multiple commitment

(continued)

(continued)

to various groups and values that comprise the organization (Randall 1990, p.376).

In this regard, as Becker et al. (1996) argue, it should be noted that distinguishing among individual foci of commitment helps to explain variance in key dependent variables above and beyond that explained by commitment to organizations.

Source: Seok-Hwan Lee (2000). A Multidimensional View of Employee Commitment and Willingness to Improve Productivity Improvement Strategies (pp.30–43): Unpublished doctoral dissertation, NJ: Rutgers University-Newark

KEY TERMS

Coaching
Delegation
Dissatisfiers
Employee development
Equal Employment Opportunity Commission (EEOC)
Federal Labor Relations Authority
Human capital
Human resource management
Job rotation
Merit Systems Protection Board
Office of Personnel Management (OPM)
Performance appraisal
Personnel selection
Satisfiers
Understudy
Workforce planning
Workforce retention

REFERENCES

Angle, H.L., and J.L. Perry 1986. Dual commitment and labor-management relationship climates. *Academy of Management Journal* 29: 31-50.

Aranya, N., and K.R. Ferris 1983. Organizational-professional conflict among U.S. and Israeli professional accountants. *Journal of Social Psychology* 119: 153-161.

Balfour, D.L., and B. Wechsler 1991. Commitment, performance, and productivity in public organizations. *Public Productivity & Management Review* 14: 355-368.

Becker, T.E. 1992. Foci and bases of commitment: Are they distinctions worth making? *Academy of Management Journal* 35: 232-244.

Becker, T.E., and R.S. Billings 1993. Profiles of commitment: An empirical test. *Journal of Organizational Behavior* 14: 177-190.

Becker, T.E., R.S. Billings, D.M. Eveleth, and N.L. Gilbert 1996. Foci and bases of employee commitment: Implications for job performance. *Academy of Management Journal* 39: 464-482.

Becker, T.E., D.M. Randall, and C.D. Riegel 1995. The multidimensional view of commitment and the theory of reasoned action: A comparative evaluation. *Journal of Management* 21: 617-638.

Coleman, C.J. 1990. *Managing Labor Relations in the Public Sector*. San Francisco, CA: Jossey-Bass.

Cooper, P.J. 1998. *Public Administration for the Twenty-First Century*. Fort Worth, TX: Harcourt Brace.

Donaldson, L. 1928. *Behavioral Supervision*. Addison-Wesley Publishing Company, Inc.

Golembiewski, R.T. 1995. *Managing Diversity in Organizations*. Tuscaloosa: University of Alabama Press.

Gordon, M.E., L.L. Beauvais, and R.T. Ladd 1984. The job satisfaction and union commitment of unionized engineers. *Industrial and Labor Relations Review* 37: 359-370.

Gordon, M.E., J.W. Philpot, R.E. Burt, C.A. Thompson, and W.E. Spiller 1980. Commitment to union: Development of a measure and an examination of its correlates. *Journal of Applied Psycholog* 65: 479-499.

Gouldner, A.W. 1958. Cosmopolitans and locals: Toward and analysis of latent social roles. *Administrative Science Quarterly* 2: 444-480.

Grace, S.L., and M. Holzer. 1992. "Labor-Management Cooperation: An Opportunity for Change." *In Public Productivity Handbook*, ed. M. Holzer, 487-498. New York: Marcel Dekker.

Guy, M.E. 1992a. "Managing People." In *Public Productivity Handbook*, ed. M.

Holzer, 307–20. New York: Marcel Dekker.

_____. 1992b. "Productive Work Environment." In *Public Productivity Handbook*, ed. M. Holzer, 321-344. New York: Marcel Dekker.

Herrick, N. 1990. *Joint Management and Employee Participation: Labor and Management at the Crossroads*. San Francisco, CA: Jossey-Bass.

Herzberg, F. 1966. *Work and the Nature of Man*. Cleveland, OH: World Publishing.

Hodes, N. 1991. "Achieving Quality through Labor-Management Participation in New York State." *Public Productivity and Management Review* 15, no. 2: 163-168.

Holzer, M. 1991. "Attracting the Best and the Brightest to Government Service." In *Public Personnel Management: Current Concerns-Future Challenges*, ed. C. Ban and N. Riccucci, 3-6. White Plains, NY: Longman.

Holzer, M., and S.-H. Lee. 1999. "Labor-Management Tension and Partnership: Where Are We? What Should We Do?" *International Review of Public Administration* 4, no. 2: 33-44.

Holzer, M., and J. Rabin. 1987. "Public Service: Problems, Professionalism, and Policy

Recommendations." *Public Productivity and Management Review* 11: 3-13.

Isaacs, H. 1996. *Personnel Management and Industrial Relations MS488 Study Guide.* Kingston, Jamaica: University of the West Indies Press.

_____. 2003. "Nonmonetary Incentives and Productivity." In *Encyclopedia of Public Administration and Public Policy.* New York: Marcel Dekker.

Jurkiewicz, C.L., T.K. Massey, Jr., and R.G. Brown. 1998. "Motivation in Public and Private Organizations: A Comparative Study." *Public Productivity and Management Review* 21: 230-250.

Kelman, H.C. 1958. Compliance, identification, and internalization: Three processes of attitude change. *Journal of Conflict Resolution*, 2: 51-60.

Lewis, J.R., and J. Raffel. 1996. "Training Public Administrators to Work with Legislators." *Case Studies in Productive Public Management: From the Public Productivity and Management Review*, ed. M. Holzer and V. Gabrielian, 301-9. Burke, VA: Chatelaine Press.

Lowi, T.J. 1969. *The end of liberalism.* New York, NY: Norton.

Maslow, A.H. 1943. "A Theory of Human Motivation." *Psychology Review* 50: 370-96.

McDonald, N. 1995. "The Importance and Role of Performance Appraisal." In *Personnel Management and Industrial Relations MS488 Study Guide*, 71-72. Kingston, Jamaica: University of the West Indies Press.

McGregor, D. 1960. *Human Side of Enterprise.* New York: McGraw-Hill.

Meyer, J.P., Allen, N.J., and C.A. Smith, 1993. Commitment to organizations and occupations: Extension and test of a three-component conceptualization. *Journal of Applied Psychology* 78: 538-551.

Mills, O. 1994. "Leadership and the Culture of Change." *Caribbean Labour Journal.* 4, no. 1: 29-31.

Mintzberg, H. 1996. "Managing Government, Governing Management." *Harvard Business Review* 74: 75-83.

Morrow, P.C. 1983. Concept redundancy in organizational research: The case of work commitment. *Academy of Management Review* 8: 486-500.

Mowday, R.T., L.W. Porter, and R.M. Steers 1982. *Employee-organization linkages: The psychology of commitment, absenteeism, and turnover.* New York, NY: Academic Press.

Munroe, T. 1992. "Partnership in Labor Relations." *Caribbean Labour Journal* 3

(September): 27.

Naff, K.C. 1993. "Human Resources Management Support." In *Public Administration for the Twenty-First Century*, ed. P. Cooper, 285. Fort Worth, TX: Harcourt Brace.

National Partnership for Reinventing Government. 1998. "Vice President Gore's National Partnership for Reinventing Government Summary of Accomplishments: 1993-1998." http://govinfo.library.unt.edu/npr/whoweare/historyofnpr.html, accessed August 1, 2010.

O'Reilly, C.A., & J. Chatman. (1986). Organizational commitment and psychological attachment: The effects of compliance, identification, and internalization on prosocial behavior. *Journal of applied psychology* 71: 492-499.

Rainey, H.G. 1997. *Understanding and Managing Public Organizations*. 2d ed. San Francisco, CA: Jossey-Bass.

Randall, D.M. 1990. The consequences of organizational commitment: methodological investigation. *Journal of Organizational Behavior* 11: 361-378.

Reichers, A.E. 1985. A review and reconceptualization of organizational commitment. *Academy of Management Review* 10: 476-485.

_____. 1986. Conflict and organizational commitments. *Journal of Applied Psychology* 71: 508-514.

"Report of Task Force on Work Attitudes to the Right Honourable Edward Seaga, Prime Minister of Jamaica." (March 1983): 11-12.

Romzek, B. 1990. "Employee Investment and Commitment: The Ties That Bind." *Public Administration Review* 50: 374-382.

Schein, E.H. 1988. *Organizational Culture and Leadership: A Dynamic View*. San Francisco, CA: Jossey-Bass.

Schuler, R.S., and V.L. Huber. 1993. *Personnel and Human Resource Management*, 5th ed. Eagan, MN: West Publishing Co.

Sherman, A., G. Bohlander, and S. Snell. 1998. *Managing Human Resources*. Cincinnati, OH: South-Western College Publishing.

Stone, C. 1982. *Work Attitude Survey: A Report to the Jamaican Government*. St. Anne, Jamaica: Earle Publisher's Ltd.

_____. 1983. *Findings of the Stone Survey*. Kingston, Jamaica: JIS Press.

Thompson, F. 1990. "The Politics of Public Personnel Management." In *Public Personnel Administration: Problems and Prospects*, ed. S. W. Hays and R. Kearny.

U.S. Department of Labor. 1996. *Working Together for Public Service*. Washington, DC: U.S. Government Printing Office.

SUPPLEMENTARY READINGS

Ban, C., and N. Riccucci, eds. 2002. *Public Personnel Management*. 3d ed. New York: Longman.

Berman, E., J. Bowman, J. West, and M. Van Wart. 2001. *Human Resources Management in the Public Service*. Thousand Oaks, CA: Sage Publications.

Condrey, S.E., and R. Maranto, eds. 2001. *Radical Reform of the Civil Service*. Lanham, MD: Lexington Books.

Gore, A. 1993. *Creating a Government That Works Better and Costs Less: Reinventing Human Resource Management*. Washington, DC: Government Printing Office.

Lewis, G., and S. Frank. 2002. "Who Wants to Work for the Government?" *Public Administration Review* 62 (July/August): 395-404.

Mosher, F.C. 1982. *Democracy and the Public Service*, 2d ed. Oxford, UK, and New York: Oxford University Press.

Perry, J.L., and L.R. Wise. 1990. "The Motivational Bases of Public Service." *Public Administration Review* 50, no. 3: 367-373.

Shafritz, J.M., N. Riccucci, D.H. Rosenbloom, K. Naff, and A. Hyde. 2001. *Personnel Management in Government*. 5th ed. New York: Marcel Dekker.

ELECTRONIC RESOURCES

Partnership for Public Service
http://www.ourpublicservice.org/OPS/

Society for Human Resource Management
http://www.shrm.org/

Uniform Guidelines.com—Free Service for Human Resources Professionals
http://www.uniformguidelines.com/

U.S. Department of Labor Employment and Training Administration
http://www.doleta.gov/

U.S. Office of Personnel Management
http://www.opm.gov/

CHAPTER 4

Public Decision Making

We are confronted with a relentless need to make decisions. Virtually every day, a situation arises that does not conform to our expectations. We then ask ourselves: What should we do? How do we decide what to do? Each person has his or her own approach to decision making. Some people panic, while others automatically respond in a specific way. Some individuals try one solution after another before they find the right one. This chapter dissects the decision-making process and examines each step in it. It further underscores various theoretical models of decision making and concludes with a discussion of dysfunctional decision making.

"Decision-making processes hold the key to understanding organizations."

HERBERT A. SIMON
Economist; Nobel Prize Winner

During the Cuban Missile Crisis in 1962, President John F. Kennedy authorized the creation of ExComm—or the Executive Committee of the President.

HOW DECISIONS ARE MADE

The Nature of Decision Making

In simplest terms, decision making entails choosing one course of action among other competing courses of action. The decision process includes the following steps: (1) pinpointing the problem; (2) identifying causes; (3) setting objectives; (4) formulating alternative courses of action; (5) evaluating alternatives against organizational objectives; (6) choosing the best course of action; and (7) implementing and evaluating the decision.

Step 1: Pinpointing the Problem

In pinpointing the problem (Step 1), the decision maker compares an expected standard of performance to the actual standard of performance. In other words, what is happening, and what should be happening? It is important to have a clear definition of a problem before looking for its solution. The analysis of a problem should be specific and should indicate the desired behavior, as well as the present behavior. This can be stated as follows:

Actual condition	Desired condition
What is happening?	What should be happening?
Where it is happening?	Where should it be happening?
When is it happening?	When should it be happening?
To what extent is it happening?	To what extent should it be happening?

The goals (desired condition) should be realized. One should also pinpoint the possible cause or causes for the disparity between the existing condition and the desired condition, and then decide the most likely cause for the situation (Step 2).

Step 2: Identifying Causes

In identifying possible causes, one may ask: "What are the causes for the deviation between the actual and desired condition?" The most likely cause of the problem is the one that most precisely explains all the facts about that problem.

- Has all the available information been gathered?
- Are there specific barriers to be faced in the process?
    - Do strong individual member attitudes exist toward the situation?
    - Are there important points of view not yet represented?

Step 3: Setting Objectives

After the problem and its causes have been identified, the decision maker must set objectives that the decision must achieve (Step 3). Effective objectives should:

- Be specific
- Be measurable (this implies an empirically-based performance criteria)
- Indicate who, what, how much, when, and where

Examples of objectives:

- *Ineffective objective*—Each respondent will receive an appropriate financial evaluation interview.
- *Effective objective*—To decide the respondent's support payments, the caseworker will interview him or her to determine his or her: age, marital status, employment status, number of other children, financial resources, and eligibility for assistance.

After listing the objectives for a given course of action, those objectives should be separated into objectives that are absolutely necessary ("must" objectives)

FIGURE 4.1 – DECISION-MAKING STEPS

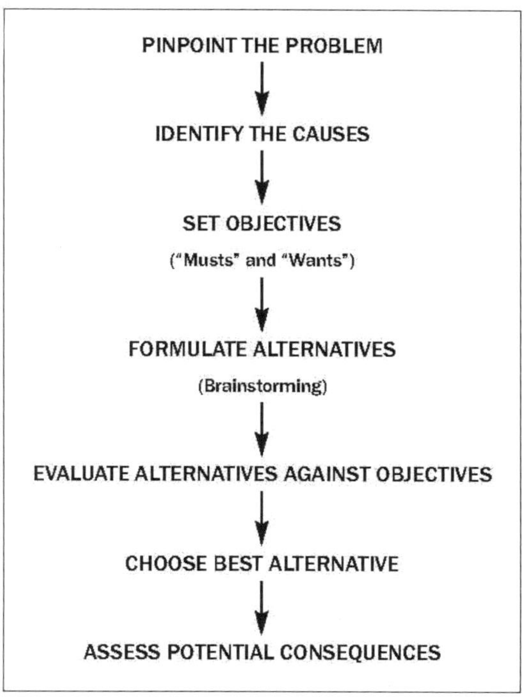

and those that are desirable but less pressing ("want" objectives). "Must" objectives set limits that are nonnegotiable. "Want" objectives set limits that are, to some extent, flexible.

Example:

"Must" objective—All staff will remain with the unit for a minimum of two years.

"Want" objective—All staff will remain with the unit for three to five years.

"Want" objectives need to be weighted as to their relative importance. There are two methods for doing this: One method is to decide which objective is the least important and give it a numerical weight of 1. Then, decide how much more important another "want" objective is compared to the one deemed least essential and give the second objective a weight in accordance with that decision, for example a 2 or a 3. Continue on with each want objective, comparing it to the least important one and ranking it accordingly. The other method is to use a straight interval scale ranging from 1 to 10 as a means of rating the importance of "want" objectives. Less important objectives are given scores of less than five, while more important objectives are given scores greater than five. The idea here is to establish a criterion for determining which "want" objectives a decision maker should consider when making a final decision.

Step 4: Formulating Action Alternatives

When formulating alternative courses of action (Step 4), a decision maker should ask whether the problem has existed before. If so, what was done and what was the outcome? Has a related problem occurred? If so, what elements were similar? How were they handled and to what effect? A primary method of formulating courses of action includes brainstorming, which was developed to help generate ideas in the field of advertising. The term means to use the brain to "storm" a creative problem. Effective brainstorming entails the following:

- Criticisms of ideas must be postponed temporarily.
- Freewheeling is encouraged; that is, the wilder the idea, the better—the logic being that it is easier to tone down wild ideas than to liven up lackluster ones.
- Quantity is stressed over quality. The greater the number of ideas, the more likely there will be potential winners in the pack.
- Combination and improvement are pursued. Not only should participants contribute ideas of their own, but also they should strive to use other people's ideas to make better ideas—i.e., combining two or more ideas into an alternative idea.

In conducting effective brainstorming sessions, the problem should not be revealed before the session. The idea is to create an environment conducive to spontaneity, which will help generate a free flow of ideas. During the session, however, the problem should be defined clearly. Within a brainstorming discussion group, it is advantageous to include people with experience and people new to the specific problem. An eclectic group of participants is more likely to trigger a range of innovative ideas. The flow of ideas can sometimes be increased by presenting idea-spinning questions such as, How can we adapt (modify, rearrange, reverse, combine, minimize, maximize) any general solution? Finally, when the discussion group seems to have run out of ideas, try reviewing the list quickly, and then ask for a precise number of additional suggestions.

> "Indecision is debilitating; it feeds upon itself; it is, one might almost say, habit-forming. Not only that, but it is contagious; it transmits itself to others."
>
> **H.A. HOPF**
> Author

Creativity and Formulating Decision Alternatives

Creativity is an innate human capacity, not a gift of the talented elite. To become creative in our work and personal lives, we must unlearn a range of limiting behaviors and attitudes and foster creative organizational sets. Creativity is synonymous with seeing things in a new way; going outside of our own experiences for solutions; challenging assumptions—which encompasses flexibility of thought, going beyond stereotypical interpretations, questioning self-evident truths, and developing a healthy skepticism. Making connections between seemingly unrelated ideas and/or events is central to creativity. Taking risks is also central to creative decision making.

Several personality traits affect individual creativity. These traits include: a tolerance for ambiguity, a healthy self-concept, a reasonable focus of control, and a moderate level of comfort regarding risk taking. The higher an individual's tolerance for ambiguity, the more patience he or she will have for systematically working through the elements of the situation and then formulating and assessing alternatives. The lower an individual's self-concept, the more anxiety that individual will have about how he or she is viewed by others. This leads to stress, preventing a thorough search for decision alternatives. Also, the lower the self-concept, the more sensitive a person will be to social pressure, causing that person to side with the majority. Additionally, people who believe they have little control over outcomes will be less exhaustive in searching for alternatives. They may ask themselves, Why do anything when the result is beyond my control, anyway? Finally, a person who is neither a high risk taker nor a low risk taker will be the best decision maker. A high risk taker is an inefficient decision maker because it is unlikely that the risky alternative will solve the problem. The low risk taker, on the other hand, plays it too safe and is less likely to come up with a sufficient number of decision alternatives.

Blocks to Creativity. Creativity is an innate human capacity. People differ in the degree, not the kind, of creative resources available to them. In order for us to cultivate our creative resources, we must overcome numerous creative blocks, among them:

- Overdominance of left side of brain
- Organizational and individual mindsets that impose immediate judgment and evaluation of ideas
- Internal conflict between experimental and safekeeping selves
- Childhood conditioning
- Fear of mistakes
- Fear of risking self-esteem
- Need for control and conditioned responses
- Overly narrow or broad definitions of problems
- Competition
- Perfectionism

FIGURE 4.2 – DECISION PROCESS MODEL

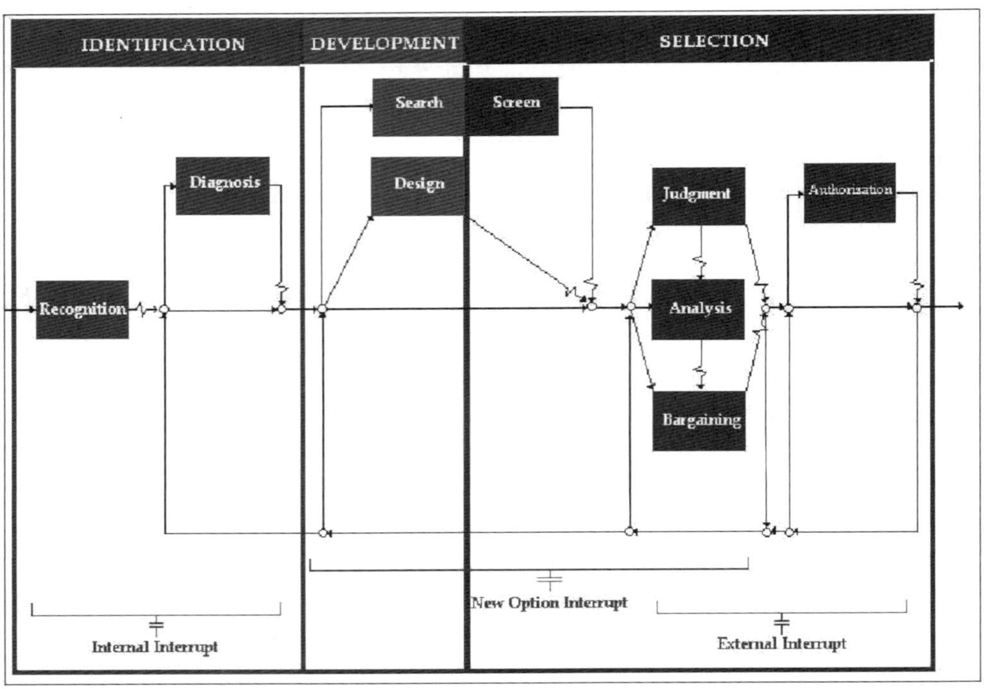

Source: Choo, C.W. 2006. The Knowing Organization: How Organizations Use Information to Construct Meaning, Create Knowledge, and Make Decisions (2nd ed.). New York: Oxford University Press.

Costs of Creativity. Developing our creative resources may cause certain strains. Recognizing these potential stresses can help minimize blocks to our creative efforts. Creative individuals face new frustrations because of increased problem awareness. People who are highly sensitive to problems are likely to expose themselves to more and greater despair because they are struck by the full complexity of the issues before them, as well as the full scope of their new responsibilities.

> "If you chase two rabbits, both will escape."
>
> **CHINESE PROVERB**

Creative individuals face new frustrations because of increased opportunity awareness. For example, they see new opportunities to improve agency effectiveness, but often no one in authority seems willing to dedicate the time or resources to mine the gold that is there. Others will say that the opportunities are not gold ore, but chunks of rock.

Creativity adds up to a lot of hard work. Many individuals feel overworked already. Often, however, they have become overly busy with the 80 percent of the work that—if done perfectly—accounts for only 20 percent of the results. They keep busy to avoid the pain, frustration, and worry of tackling the important work, that is, the 20 percent that matters. Reweighing priorities is hard work. Implementing ideas is even harder.

Creativity adds new risks to life, which brings new tensions and new anxieties. Some individuals crave creativity and innovation, yet they are uncomfortable with change. This is a contradiction, of course, as creativity implies something new, nonconforming, or different. Also, the more confidence a person builds with creativity tools, the more pioneering that person becomes. He or she will be taking the initiative, knowing full well who is accountable if the idea fails. An idea can fail. There are no magic bullets for solving problems or making decisions creatively; there are no magic potions for developing imaginative opportunities. A first try may be a disaster—but that does not mean a second try will not bring success.

Steps 5 and 6: Evaluating Alternatives and Choosing the Best One

Evaluating each course of action against the objectives (Step 5) allows the decision maker to choose the best course of action (Step 6). To remain in the running, a course of action should meet all of the "must" objectives, and it should meet some of the "want" objectives. Moreover, it is important that decision makers take into account the potential impacts each course of action may have on the organization and its people. Some questions to consider include:

- Will the workers' motivation, skills, or growth be affected?
- Will relationships among units, communication, responsibility, or delegation be affected?

- Will the organization's image be affected, or will there be legal and/or political ramifications of choosing one course of action over another?

By and large, the best course of action is the one that meets all of the "must" objectives and the most number of "want" objectives, while at the same time engendering the fewest disadvantages to the organization and its people. Using a balance sheet is a good way of visually representing the benefits and burdens of one course of action versus another. The balance sheet helps individuals to make more comprehensive appraisals of competing courses of action, as decision makers are better able to think about possible trade-offs, concentrate on the major differences between the choices, and think about the degree of importance of each pro and con. Table 4.1 is an example of a balance sheet created by a manager who is considering moving to a different job. The balance sheet is meant to evaluate his present position. The matrix details the positives and negatives of staying with the current job.

TABLE 4.1 – BALANCE SHEET

Expected consequences	Positives	Negatives
Gains and losses for self	1. Satisfactory pay 2. More opportunities to use skills 3. Current status within the organization is good	1. Long hours 2. Constant time pressure 3. Unpleasant paperwork 4. Poor prospects for advancement
Gains and losses for others	1. Adequate income for family 2. Family receives perks given my position	1. Not enough free time for family 2. Spouse forced to deal with my work-related irritability
Self-approval or disapproval	1. This position allows me to make use of full potential 2. Proud of my achievements 3. Sense of meaningful accomplishments	1. Feel like a fool at times for putting up with unreasonable deadlines and other work-related red tape
Social approval or disapproval	1. Approval of members of my team—who look up to me. 2. Approval of my superior—who is a friend and desires that I stay	1. Very slight skeptical reaction from spouse 2. A friend who has wanted to wangle a new job for me will be disappointed

Decision-Making Example:

"Must" objective: All unit staff will remain with the unit for at least two years.

"Want" objectives: (1) All unit staff will remain with the unit for at least three years.

Weight = 3 (on a scale of 1–5, with 5 being the highest)

(2) All unit staff will remain with the unit for at least five years.

Weight = 1 (on a scale of 1–5, with 5 being the highest)

From the "must" and "want" objectives listed above, the following decision alternatives are formulated and evaluated.

Decision Alternatives: (1) Staff will sign two-year renewable contracts.

(2) Staff will sign one-year renewable contracts.

(3) Staff will sign three-year renewable contracts.

Decision alternative 2 does not meet the "must" objective sufficiently.

Rank of decision alternative 1 against "want" objective 1 = 4 (on scale of 1–5, with 5 being the highest).

Rank of decision alternative 1 against "want" objective 2 = 2.

Rank of decision alternative 3 against "want" objective 1 = 5.

Rank of decision alternative 3 against "want" objective 2 = 5.

Relative score of decision alternative 1 = (4*3) + (2*1) = 14

Relative score of decision alternative 3 = (5*3) + (5*1) = 20

Decision alternative 3 should be chosen.

Theoretical Models of Decision Making

Rational Model

The rational decision-making model is grounded in economic principles. The concept of marginal utility, according to Verne Lewis (1952), brings pure rationality into public decision making. Relative value, effectiveness, and incremental comparisons should determine which decision alternative is chosen. Relative value refers to the "opportunity cost" of a particular policy decision. The opportunity cost of a choice reflects the difference between one's first and second choices. Consider, for example, that Thomas chooses to pursue a Master of Public Administration (MPA) degree after college. The cost of tuition and living expenses amount to

$40,000 per year for two years ($80,000 total). This $80,000 total, however, does not reflect opportunity cost. Let us further assume that by going to graduate school for two years, Tom turned down a job that would have paid him $50,000 a year with a 5 percent raise after the first year ($102,500 total). This $102,500 reflects the opportunity cost of choosing graduate school instead of the job, and therefore the total real cost of graduate school equals $182,500. So, why pursue an MPA degree? The idea is that more education will afford Tom more earning potential long-term, which will offset any lost wages in the short-term.

Effectiveness deals with evaluating a decision in terms of achieving a common purpose. Lewis's notion of incremental comparisons (1952) refers to comparing marginal value and costs, assuming that the value of anything decreases with increasing quantity. In other words, as one acquires additional units of anything, an added unit has decreasing value. Consider this: you need four tires on a car. You may need a fifth due to the occasional flat tire. Having a sixth tire, however, does not seem worth the cost relative to its value. While the policymaking process deals with value-laden questions, economic and cost-benefit principles must remain dominant, ac-

FIGURE 4.3 – DECISION MAKING BY HERBERT SIMON

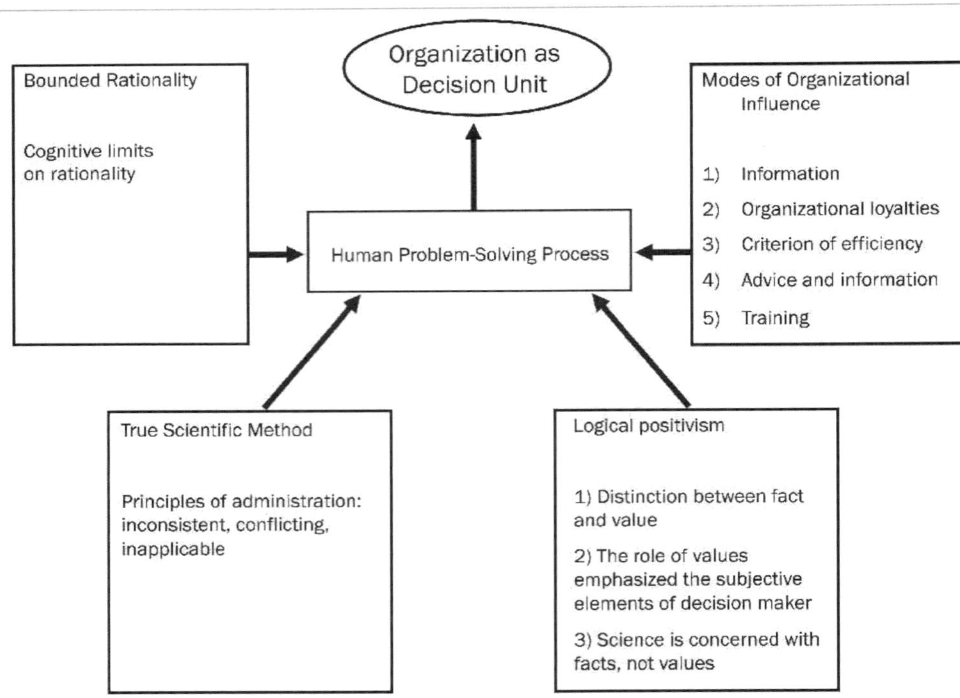

Source: S-Y, Rho. 1998. School of Public Affairs and Administration, Rutgers University, Newark, NJ.

cording to Lewis (1952). Much like Lewis, J.L. Mikesell (1978) maintains that the decision-making process should try to identify valuable government activities. In doing so, cost-benefit analysis (CBA) serves as a primary tool of the rational decision maker.

CBA is predicated on comparing the primary and secondary costs of a program or policy, and comparing those costs to direct and indirect benefits. Both costs and benefits are expressed in monetary terms. Typically, results are expressed in terms of a benefit-cost ratio, which is equal to the benefits of a program divided by its costs. If the benefit-cost ratio is greater than one, it can be said that the benefits of a program outweigh its costs. CBA can be conducted on either an ex ante or ex post basis. Ex ante analyses are prospective in that they try to estimate costs and benefits of a program or policy prior to development or implementation. In contrast, ex post analyses are retrospective, as they examine costs and benefits of programs and policies that have existed for some time. Both ex ante and ex post analyses aid the rational decision maker in determining whether a program or policy should be pursued or continued. CBA is covered in greater depth in Chapter 8.

Herbert Simon (1947/1997) was somewhat critical of the rational model given his belief that people's cognitive limitations make it impossible to consider the full range of decision-making alternatives and the information corresponding to each

FIGURE 4.4 – BOUNDED RATIONAL DECISION MAKING

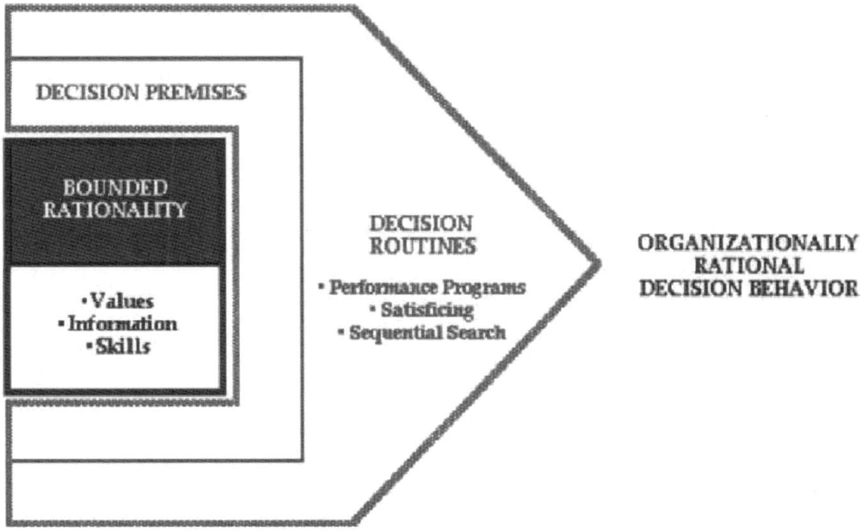

Source: Choo, C.W. 2006. The Knowing Organization: How Organizations Use Information to Construct Meaning, Create Knowledge, and Make Decisions (2d ed.). New York: Oxford University Press.

alternative. This concept is known as bounded rationality. Decision makers are, therefore, limited to a few courses of action and ultimately choose the one that is most satisfactory or "good enough." Simon terms this *satisficing* (1947/1997).

Satisficing and Incrementalism

Policy changes occur little by little. According to Lindblom (1959), individuals tend not to follow the rational model when making decisions. Instead, they avoid "rational" decision making through satisficing and incrementalism. From a practical standpoint, Simon's concept of satisficing entails lowering the bar in terms of goal attainment, and then choosing a policy alternative that satisfies this lower standard. Furthermore, decision makers who satisfice choose policies that are thought to be "good enough" for the time being, until a better policy alternative can be found. The incremental decision-making model suggests that: (1) realistically, only

The Administrative (or Behavioral) Model

- Is descriptive in that it describes how decisions are actually made.
- Decision makers seek to simplify problems and make them less complex because they are constrained by their individual capabilities (e.g., limited information-processing ability) and by organizational conditions (e.g., availability of resources).
- Assumes that decision makers operate with limited (or "bounded") rationality; this means that decision makers are rational within a simplified model that contains fewer components (e.g., fewer decision-making criteria, fewer options, and so on).
- Assumes that decision makers identify a limited number of decision-making criteria, that they examine a limited range of alternatives (only those that are easy to find, highly visible, have been tried before, or are only slightly different from the status quo) and that they do not possess all the information needed to make a decision.
- The decision maker selects a satisficing alternative. This is an alternative that is "good enough" or satisfactory in that it meets the minimum criteria established for a desired solution.
- Decision making proceeds sequentially: alternatives are examined one at a time and the first satisfactory alternative that is found is selected.

Source: CSWT Papers, "Group Decision Making Within the Organization: Can Models Help?" by Ryan K. Lahti (Center for the Study of Work Teams, University of North Texas).

a few policy alternatives can be considered at one time, and (2) these policies do not differ radically from existing policies. Change, therefore, occurs through decisions that have an incremental effect. The incremental model is a more realistic approach to public decision making, as it provides greater flexibility in coping with time-sensitive policy problems (Lindblom 1959).

Incrementalism is often criticized, given that it perpetuates and condones the status quo. In more extreme cases, it allows failing government agencies and programs to continue and even expand. Fundamental change is difficult to achieve via incrementalism (Dror 1964). One response to incrementalism is the use of sunset provisions, under which an agency, program, or law expires automatically following a specified period, unless the legislature votes to reenact it. This was the case with many of the provisions of the USA Patriot Act, which was passed in the wake of the 9/11 terrorist attacks on the United States.

Revised Garbage Can Model

In contrast to the rational decision-making model, Kingdon (2003) defies conventional wisdom by claiming that the decision-making process is neither systematic nor neatly defined within the context of the political arena. Rather, public admin-

The Implicit Favorite Model

- Is descriptive in that it describes how decisions are actually made.
- The decision maker seeks to simplify the decision making process by identifying an "implicit favorite" before alternatives are evaluated; this often occurs subconsciously.
- The decision maker is neither rational nor objective and unbiased.
- After a "favorite" is selected, the decision maker tries to appear rational and objective by developing decision criteria and by identifying and evaluating various alternatives; however, this is done in a biased way so as to ensure that the favorite appears superior on these criteria and thus, can legitimately be selected as the "best" solution.
- In this model, "decision making" is essentially a process of confirming a choice/decision that has already been made. The actual decision was made in an intuitive and unscientific fashion.

Source: CSWT Papers, "Group Decision Making Within the Organization: Can Models Help?" by Ryan K. Lahti (Center for the Study of Work Teams, University of North Texas).

istration decision making is chaotic. According to the revised garbage can model, the decision-making process can be understood in the context of three separate "streams" that operate independently. Specifically, the problem, political, and policy streams steer the decision-making process. The problem stream refers to an understanding of "how and why one set of problems rather than another comes to occupy officials' attention" (Kingdon 2003, p. 87). The political stream represents the pulse of the nation as conveyed through public opinion, election results, or ideological shifts as evidenced through public and special interest campaigns. Finally, within the policy stream, administrators, technocrats, researchers, and political

FIGURE 4.5 – GARBAGE CAN MODEL

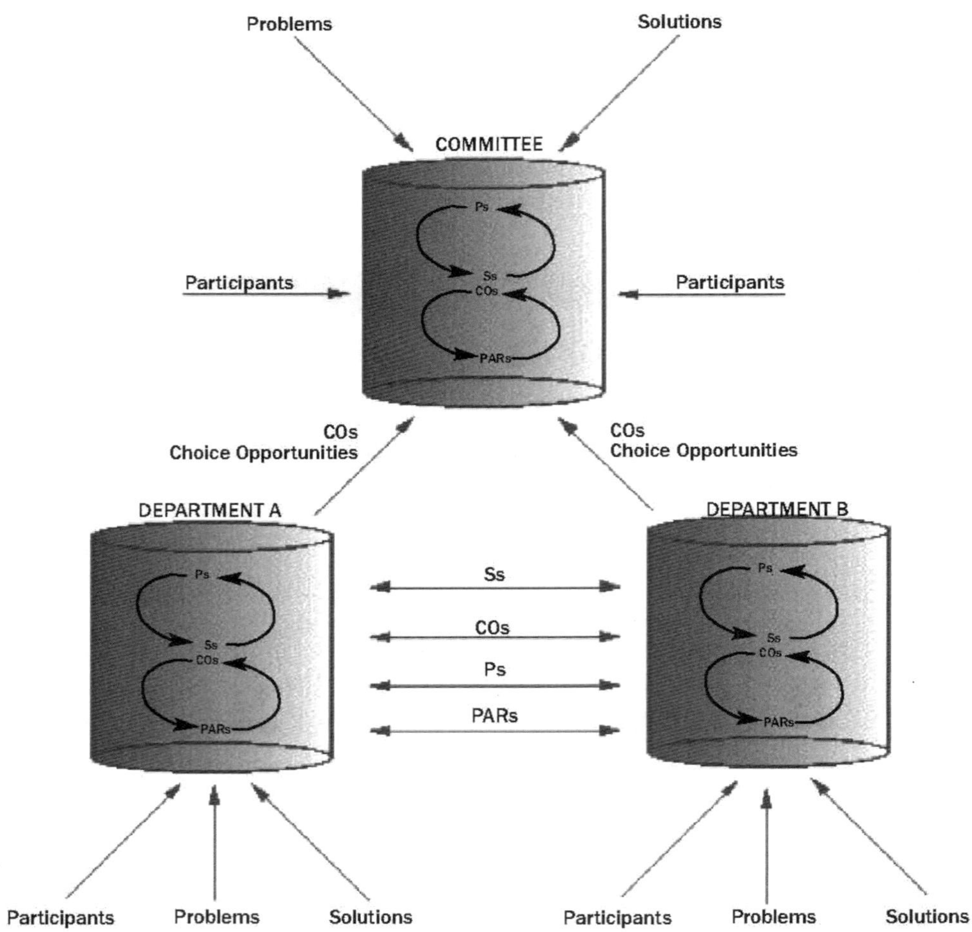

Source: Choo, C.W. 2006. The Knowing Organization: How Organizations Use Information to Construct Meaning, Create Knowledge, and Make Decisions (2nd ed.). New York: Oxford University Press.

staffers formulate policy proposals. Policy advocates who have crafted specific proposals wait for a compelling problem to emerge and present their respective proposals as plausible solutions. In the absence of a societal problem with which advocates can link their respective proposals, a change in the political climate is necessary for certain policies to be given consideration. Policy advocates increase their chances of influencing the agenda-setting process given the convergence of the problem, political, and policy streams. That is, the policy window widens (i.e., the likelihood that a policy will be given consideration) when a problem emerges and the political climate is ripe for certain policy preferences. The three streams converge at "critical times" (e.g., a crisis), according to Kingdon (2003).

The gun control movement moved to the forefront subsequent to the near-fatal injury of White House press secretary James Brady during an assassination attempt on President Ronald Reagan in 1981. Arguably, it was this focusing event that served as the impetus for more widespread gun control measures. In the context of Kingdon's framework, the problem was the availability of firearms. The existing solution (or policy preference) was the Brady bill (now the Brady law), which requires a five-day waiting period and mandatory background checks prior to the purchase of certain firearms. It was believed that these measures would reduce crimes of passion and ensure that convicted felons or the mentally ill were not able to purchase firearms. The policy window for the Brady bill widened with the election of President Bill Clinton, as the bill was originally introduced in 1987 and was signed in November 1993.

> "For every complex problem, there is a simple solution that is wrong."
>
> **GEORGE BERNARD SHAW**
> Irish Critic; Poet
> (1856–1950)

The passage and implementation of the USA Patriot Act fits within the context of Kingdon's garbage can model. Passed shortly after the terrorist attacks on the World Trade Center and the Pentagon in 2001, the Patriot Act expanded the authority of U.S. law enforcement agencies to intensify the fight against terrorism in the United States and abroad. The most notable provisions of the Patriot Act deal with the federal government's enhanced power in gathering information. For example, the Patriot Act gives law enforcement agencies greater authority to search telephone and e-mail communications, as well as medical and financial records. Other surveillance provisions include what are called roving wiretaps—which give the U.S. government the authority to wiretap all types of communication devices. Previously, the government would need to obtain permission from a court to tap each device (filing a separate request, for instance, for a phone, cell phone, personal computer, iPhone, and so on). With roving wiretaps, however, the government can tap into any and all of a subject's communications devices after receiving blanket authority from a court. Now, consider this: The Patriot Act was written and passed into law on October 24, 2001—only six weeks after the terrorist attacks. This piece of legislation was a hefty 342 pages. How on earth could this have been written and passed so quickly? The answer is that many of the Patriot Act's provisions were failed legislative proposals that were still floating around the legislature. These ideas and proposals did not have any traction, so to speak, because there was never any problem serious enough to warrant putting such ideas into place—not until September 11, 2001, anyway. The problem, therefore, was domestic terrorism, and the political window widened given the fear of another attack and people's desire for concrete action. The solution became a compilation of policies that previously had not taken root but were nevertheless repackaged as the USA Patriot Act.

Participatory Model

Participatory decision making assumes that a diverse group of individuals (or individuals representing a diverse set of interests) will act in a consultative capacity. Typically, those people affected by a particular problem or a potential course of action are afforded the opportunity to provide input. This input is documented through public meetings or hearings, advisory boards, and citizen advocacy groups.

> "By failing to prepare, you are preparing to fail."
>
> **BENJAMIN FRANKLIN**
> American Statesman; Ambassador; Patriot

A classical example of participatory decision making deals with the writing of federal regulations. Federal regulatory agencies such as the Environmental Protection Agency (EPA), the Food and Drug Administration (FDA), and the Occupational Safety and Health Administration (OSHA) are responsible for writing and rewriting what are known as "rules." Rules have the same impact as laws, and they exist for purpose of protecting the citizenry. For example, some rules stipulate that tests, trials, and other safety precautions be met prior to a new drug's release; others mandate that automobile plants must meet certain environmental and safety standards. Even though rules are not passed by Congress (or the legislature at the state level), they possess the effect of law. As a result, individuals or corporations who, for instance, violate environmental rules by dumping toxic waste into the oceans will be held accountable for their actions. The federal government alone writes and rewrites thousands of rules each year. Agencies like the EPA, FDA, and OSHA rely upon information and expertise from private individuals and business owners to craft these rules. In 2005 the federal government launched Regulations.gov, an Internet-based clearinghouse that allows anyone to read and comment on proposed federal rules through an electronic template. From a more local perspective, participatory decision making occurs when a parent-teacher association advises a school board or the superintendent of schools. Binding referenda represent more extreme cases of participatory decision making. Through referenda, citizens are given the authority to accept or reject specific policy actions through the ballot box.

The participatory model is advantageous insofar as interest groups provide decision makers with a wealth of information. Decision makers too dependent on informa-

Public Involvement Techniques for Transportation Decision Making: Citizens on Decision and Policy Bodies

Who are citizens on decision and policy boards?

Community people serve on policy and decision-making committees and boards. They represent groups organized around civic, environmental, business, or community interests, or specific geographic areas, or they serve as individual experts in a field. They need not be elected officials or agency staff. The Connecticut Department of Transportation (ConnDOT) appointed a community committee to develop and recommend alternatives for reconstruction of a large I-95 bridge.

Some boards make decisions; others help formulate policy. Regional residents sit on the decision-making Great Falls City/County Planning Board in Montana, and on Washington's Puget Sound Regional Council. The head of Georgia's Chatham County-Savannah Metropolitan Planning Committee sits on the Metropolitan Planning Organization's (MPO's) Project Committee. Citizens on such boards are distinct from purely advisory groups, such as civic advisory committees, that are often part of planning and project development.

These boards are established by statute, regulation, or political decision. Ad hoc committees are set up by legislative acts or executive decision to investigate specific subjects. They may be temporary or permanent. In Portland, Oregon, a committee of community members works with the Metropolitan Planning Organization (MPO) staff to develop scopes of service for projects and to review and select consultants. For the U.S. 301 corridor study, Maryland's governor created a 76-member task force to address regional transportation issues, develop and evaluate possible transportation and land-use solutions, and recommend public policies. The majority of members were private citizens.

The composition of a board varies, depending on its assigned task. A board may include citizens and elected or appointed officials or be composed entirely of citizens. It may be assisted in its task by staff members assigned from elected officials or agency representatives. The Airport Policy Committee of the San Diego, California, MPO has a mixed representation of citizens and professionals. The Metro Council, MPO for Minneapolis-St. Paul, Minnesota, has both citizens and elected officials on its 30-member Transportation Board, including 10 municipal elected officials, 7 elected county officials, 9 private citizens (including the chair), and 4 representatives of state or regional agencies.

People are appointed to boards in a variety of ways. They are nominated or appointed

(continued)

(continued)

to these positions by public officials, or they volunteer or are elected by their peers. The ways they come to serve depend on the rules and nature of the policy body.

The board's role establishes the amount of influence these citizens wield. The 76-member task force overseeing the U.S. 301 Corridor Planning Study in Maryland has virtually total decision-making power. Composed entirely of citizens appointed by the governor, Arizona DOT's Transportation Board has final say on the state's five-year plan, the transportation improvement program, and state transportation planning projects.

Why are they useful?

Community people bring new points of view, new ideas, and a community perspective directly into the decision-making process. Little Rock, Arkansas, MPO found that people were able to integrate political and technical engineering issues in solving problems. They focused on whether an idea made sense to them, their neighbors, and the people most affected by the decision. Ad hoc committees help local people participate in decision making. For the Albuquerque, New Mexico, MPO's Urban Area Truck Route Task Group, membership was solicited through more than 300 letters to neighborhood, advocacy, and business groups. Volunteers worked with technical staff from the city and a neighboring county to develop a commercial vehicle network plan processed as though it were an agency-prepared plan.

Decisions have greater legitimacy if residents are involved. Including local people in decision making demonstrates an agency's commitment to participatory planning. At the contaminated U.S. Department of Energy site in Rocky Flats, Colorado, a community committee directed the planning of an off-site hazardous waste sampling program. In essence, such empowerment validates the principle that people want—and should be able—to decide what is best for their community.

Do they have special uses?

Citizen committees oversee specific aspects of complicated programs. For the Hudson River Waterfront Alternatives Analysis/Draft Environmental Impact Statement in New Jersey, local residents directed agency staff in implementing air quality monitoring.

Community representatives work directly with project design consultants. For proposed construction of I-70 through Glenwood Canyon in Colorado, the governor appointed area residents to work with the state's highway planners and the principal design consultants to address public concerns from the beginning of preliminary engineering and highway design. Along with frequent public hearings, local representation served to satisfy public demand for a greater voice in the project.

Local people facilitate communication between decision-making bodies. The Airport Policy Committee of the San Diego, California, MPO worked with officials to forge consensus on several controversial issues. These people provided a free flow of ideas, unconstrained by concerns for existing policies, and were able to help overcome political deadlock.

Community representatives serve as informed spokespersons for an agency's programs. Individuals from the Boise, Idaho, MPO citizen committee host public meetings, speak to other organizations, and attend neighborhood events. They use nontechnical language to make citizens more comfortable and willing to participate in discussion.

Residents help achieve an agency's goals. For the Dade County, Florida, rail system, a decision-making committee was appointed, composed of elected officials and neighborhood representatives. These citizens subsequently provided leadership on two referenda supporting funding for the new rail system.

Civic outreach committees assist with public involvement programs and provide advice based on what they hear in their own discussions with the public. Seattle's Central Puget Sound Regional Transit Authority (RTA) appointed a group of people to assist in developing a ballot proposal for regional transit.

Who participates on these boards?

People who serve on policy boards are drawn from many sources. They include community and business leaders, leaders from special interest groups, and interested individuals. Length of tenure varies, depending on tasks, but is generally one to five years. It is important to recognize special interests. The Hartford, Connecticut, MPO agency-wide technical committee includes representatives of four private groups: the American Lung Association, the Chamber of Commerce, a construction industry association, and a ridesharing corporation. The board of the Port Authority of Allegheny County, Pennsylvania, has long included representatives from the Sierra Club and the League of Women Voters.

What are the costs?

Monetary costs are usually nominal. Local people appointed to policy boards are seldom paid. Costs to support their participation include agency staff time, postage, transportation, and occasional meals. Many agencies economize by sending the same information packages to both elected officials and boards that include citizens. Costs of including community people on existing boards are likely to be lower than those of forming an entirely new board or committee such as a collaborative task force.

(continued)

(continued)

Staffing requirements may be very small. A 1995 nationwide survey of transit agency policy committees showed that staff support to the committees averaged 12.4 hours per month. Full-time staff members with assignments including support to these committees averaged 1.2 people. However, even modest requirements of staff time may pose a challenge to small MPOs.

How is this organized?

The first step is to determine the need for local representation. Agencies may be aware of the need because of comment or criticism from local people. The media sometimes call for local representation when an agency undertakes a specific task. An agency also becomes aware through discussions with peers in other areas.

Another step is to research legal requirements. State laws may specify whether individuals may sit on MPO boards. Participation may be limited by an organization's by-laws.

An agency devises a strategy for local representation, designing community positions to suit the board's functions and objectives. The Albany, New York, Capital District Transportation Committee (CDTC)—all elected officials—puts local people on many task forces, along with local agency representatives and institutional and business leaders.

An agency solicits local interests in a variety of ways. The media help by opening the issue to public discussion. A letter soliciting interest in participation on boards or committees might be sent in a general mailing. For a long-range planning effort, the Albany CDTC took a sample survey of local people to determine potential interest in participating on planning and policy committees.

An agency seeks a balance of various viewpoints. The nature of a task may draw volunteers who represent only one side of an issue, yet a board should encompass many stances.

A formal appointment process is established. A simple letter or a more formal event lends legitimacy to the process and gives satisfaction and encouragement to an appointee. A written document formalizes the time frame, responsibilities, and the expected products. It is also important to point out the extent of the powers that accompany the appointment and how the results of the task will affect further agency actions. Agencies involve elected officials and keep them informed. Officials are often able to provide helpful insight. They may also want to be apprised of the board's progress.

Agencies determine the nature of their involvement on boards. It may take the form of representation, usually in an ad hoc and non-voting capacity. It may involve board support, in the form of staff services, meeting space, and use of equipment for presentations and recording of proceedings. In some instances, agencies supply meals, especially if participants travel long distances or a meeting is held during a conventional meal hour.

A method of selecting a committee chair is determined. Often a board selects its own chair, or the chair is appointed. If elections are to take place, introductions of board member candidates are appropriate, so that an informed selection is made. Introductions can be informal or take a more formal approach, such as written position papers that define an individual's expectations and goals for the processes and products.

Meeting frequency is derived from the size of the task and its deadlines. In order to accomplish an assignment, a board may need to meet frequently. Many citizen committees meet monthly, but specific projects or responsibilities may dictate different schedules. Board members should play a major role in determining meeting frequency.

Communication is maintained between meetings. Minutes of each meeting are kept for the record and distributed to remind participants of past events and decisions. Issue papers are distributed prior to meetings to help people prepare and to aid discussions. Many agencies keep local representatives informed with periodic status reports.

Decision-making bodies need time to adjust to the dynamics of public involvement. In some cases, important informal communication occurs during breaks or outside formal meeting hours. For effective communication among policy board members, the sponsoring agency may take time to foster a positive atmosphere or use familiar procedures. For guidance, many MPOs, such as those in Portland, San Diego, and Phoenix, employ the commonly understood meeting procedures outlined in Robert's Rules of Order.

Ethical issues must be considered. Public agencies frequently have established rules of professional ethics, and these rules extend to community participants. For example, potential conflicts of interest need to be identified and addressed immediately.

How is this used with other techniques?

Community representatives are important components of a public involvement program and complement almost any other technique. However, local representation cannot be the sole method an agency uses to involve the public in the planning process. Community representatives are most effective if they relate continuously with their constituent groups and participate in an agency's other public involvement outreach techniques.

(continued)

(continued)

Local representatives are ideal speakers. They are generally well informed and usually have extensive experience and exposure to issues. They are good candidates for a speakers' bureau, but agencies must remain considerate of demands placed on their time.

What are the drawbacks?

The selection and appointment process may be criticized, especially if the appointee's qualifications are questioned or if the process is seen as closed or unfair. To counter such charges, an agency can develop a strategy for the process that is comprehensive and well understood.

Board members may not be fully representative. Selected representatives may not share the prevailing opinions of the communities they represent. An agency sometimes needs to expand the number of representatives to bring in underrepresented interests. Balanced representation of interest groups is crucial in avoiding controversy. Disputes over representation require skillful diplomacy to maintain the legitimacy of the process. Agency culture sometimes presents barriers. Agencies that perceive themselves as empowered with sole decision-making responsibility are reluctant to share authority with non-elected citizens. An agency's traditional organization or decision-making style may block efforts to increase the influence of private citizens on decision or policy bodies.

Source: U.S. Department of Transportation, Federal Highway Administration, "Public Involvement Techniques for Transportation Decision Making," www.fhwa.dot.gov/reports/pittd/citizens.htm.

tion from interest groups run the risk of being swayed into making decisions that serve the interest groups more than the organization itself. This is referred to as "captivity." Captive organizations are more inclined to underemphasize organizational values and goals and overemphasize the values and goals of clientele groups. The participatory model is derived from a school of political-philosophical thought known as pluralism. Contrary to the European oligarchies, the American system of government was founded on the principle of popular sovereignty, the embodiment of which is the right to participate in the electoral process. Participation ensures the stability and prosperity of our political system, and within the context of a pluralistic society, it is a vehicle by which factions compete for political access and policy preferences. The notion of pluralism assumes that voluntary associations or interest groups participate in the interest of persuading key players within the political arena. The outcomes of participation include electoral majorities that support or compete against a group's interests. Pluralism is predicated upon collective behavior and compromise. The ideal democratic system, according to R.A. Dahl (1982), is predicated upon "effective participation," which assumes that all are afforded an equal voice and that cit-

EXERCISE 4.1

The Town of Twin Creeks Considers a New Law (Simulation)

As a member of one of the many constituent groups who will be affected by the town's decision to eliminate motorized vehicles on our 100-acre lake, students will explore the political, personal, and economic issues involved with this pending decision. After completing the simulation, students will be required to summarize the experience by compiling a mini-case study. These case studies will be compared and contrasted with others in the class.

Timothy D. Oliver, Faith Lutheran School, Nevada, "Town Meeting—Direct Representation," Columbia Education Center Lesson Plans http://www.col-ed.org/cur/sst/sst170.txt.

izens share in the decision-making process. Within the context of pluralism, organizations serve to "prevent domination and to create mutual control," notes Dahl in *Dilemmas of Pluralist Democracy: Autonomy vs. Control* (1982, p. 270).

Elite Theory

In contrast to participatory decision making and pluralism, elite theory assumes that a select few are afforded the privilege of making decisions. While the very nature of a democratic system presupposes that a wide range of individuals will have a voice in the decision-making process, elite theory assumes otherwise. A separation exists between the elite members of government and the masses, even though greater public engagement in the policymaking process would allow government to tap wider sources of information, thereby improving the quality of public policy. Nevertheless, according to J.A. Schumpeter in *An Elite Theory of Democracy* (1942/1976), the term "democracy does not mean and cannot mean that the people actually rule in any obvious sense... Democracy means only that the people have the opportunity of accepting or refusing the men who are to rule them" (p. 81). From a decision-making perspective, being one of the elite may center on an individual's knowledge level, education, or status within a public organization.

The Power Elite by C. Wright Mills (1956) contains a widely noted argument for an elitist determination of important decisions. Mills's concept of decision making within the arenas of government is one of executive rather than congressional determinations; decisions by the electorate seem out of the question completely. Within the executive branch, Mills feels that the professional bureaucrats and party politicians are essentially subservient to members of the elite who move in and out of government, pausing for relatively brief stays as opposed to the career orientations of professionals. Elites fill the very top positions of president, vice president, cabinet members, department and bureau heads, agency and commission heads, and the White House staff.

Political Model

The political decision-making model assumes that intra-organizational coalitions compete for influence. This competition establishes which decision-making alternatives are chosen and which are discarded. In other words, the more powerful coalitions win out, as do their decision-making preferences. The political model is thought to be tantamount to office "game playing." Office games are designed to improve an individual's position, while simultaneously hurting and eventually eliminating alternative viewpoints. Game players are skillful at pleasing their superiors, becoming sycophants for the sole purpose of gaining power. They support their superiors' opinions and choices at all costs—even to the point of withholding information that might keep a superior from making a poor decision. Risky and unsafe positions are never taken, and when someone else proffers a good idea, their response is: "I was thinking the same thing." The game player's energy is most concerned with building alliances and consolidating power, which will be use to exert influence over future decisions.

Public Choice Theory

Public choice theory is a school of thought derived from microeconomics, the study of the economic behavior of individuals and organizations. Adherents of the public

FIGURE 4.6 – POLITICAL MODEL OF ORGANIZATIONAL DECISION MAKING

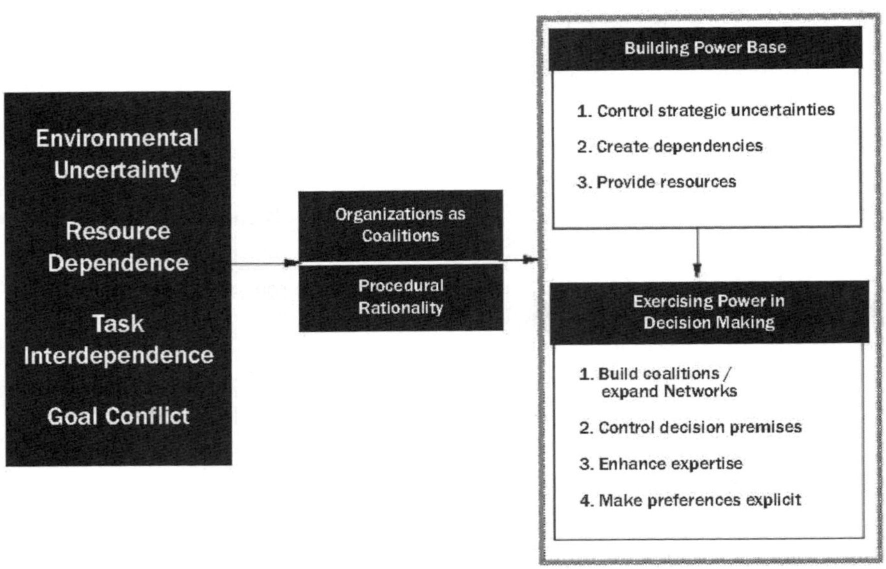

Source: Choo, C.W. 2006. The Knowing Organization: How Organizations Use Information to Construct Meaning, Create Knowledge, and Make Decisions (2d ed.). New York: Oxford University Press.

choice theory argue that self-interest determines how decisions are made. From a public administration perspective, bureaucrats will make decisions that minimize risks and maximize rewards for their department, agency, or organization. This typically involves supporting courses of action that increase the size, area of responsibility, and budget of department, agency, and organization. Public choice theorists underscore the importance of efficiency, and they tend to champion government contracting out and the privatization of government services.

Dysfunctions in Decision Making

Egos can sometimes cause bureaucratic Waterloos; managers can fall victim to the image of the isolated decision maker making difficult choices. While decisions that receive a stamp of approval from yea-saying subordinates may meet the immediate needs of the boss, they often fail to meet the needs of the organization or its clients. In virtually all cases, open and honest discussion of a possibility—branching as far up, down, or sideways as the decision will reach—will result in a different, better choice than instinct might have originally dictated. Clearly, important decisions require input from everyone (not just from top management) affected by the decision. If some midlevel bureaucrat or rank-and-file worker knows why plans "A" and "B" will fail but "C" will succeed, or management styles "X" and "Y" are faulty but can be corrected by "Z," it is only prudent to consider that worker's advice.

> "Bad administration, to be sure, can destroy good policy; but good administration can never save bad policy."
>
> **ADLAI STEVENSON**
> American Politician and Presidential Candidate (1900–1965)

Asking for input may make us feel uncomfortable. But listening to paid employees is more efficient and cost-effective than hiring well-paid consultants (whom those same employees will resist). And failure will deliver a much larger trouncing to the ego than will humility. As any organization caught in a recall has learned, decisions shared could have avoided the prohibitive costs of decisions repaired. The swine flu vaccine is, unfortunately, a good example of a bad decision. In 1976, an Army recruit contracted a rare form of swine flu and died shortly thereafter. Public health experts expressed concern that the swine flu strain closely matched the 1918 influenza strain that killed an estimated 50 to 100 million people worldwide. A swine flu vaccine was developed. However, Dr. Anthony Morris, a government virologist, warned that death and paralysis could result from the use of the vaccine. Under pressure for quick action from the president and Congress, the National Institutes of Health ignored Dr. Morris's findings. Swine flu never materialized, but by the time vaccinations were halted, at least a dozen American had died from the vaccine's effects and hundreds more had been paralyzed. Claims against the government eventually amounted to almost $500 million.

Group Decision-Making Dynamics

The poorest decisions are made when members of the decision-making team are engaged in a power struggle. This leads to accomplishing nothing or arriving at poorly contrived and compromised decisions that fail to meet the organization's goals and objectives. Overconformity is yet another decision-making dysfunction. If some members of the decision-making team are particularly assertive, and the other members are passive to the point of failing to voice their opinions or ideas, there is a greater likelihood that the passive members will conform to the more assertive members. Passive members typically censor their opinions and ideas, given the fear of being derided or criticized by the more assertive members of the decision-making team. This is especially true under circumstances in which a passive member has an innovative idea or an opinion that is considered to be "outside the box." Also, passive members hold back on thinking independently and fail to resist conformity imposed by more assertive members in an effort to stay in the good graces of the group.

Groupthink: When Conformity Kills

According to Irving Janis (1972), *groupthink* is a specialized form of conformity. It occurs only in highly cohesive groups that operate in an environment where there is a feeling of security. The primary goal of this particular decision-making group is to maintain its power and cohesiveness. Groupthink is characterized by extreme conformity that gets in the way of any critical analysis. The circumstances under which groupthink occurs tend to coincide with (1) directive leadership, (2) group homogeneity in terms of ideals and background, and (3) isolation from outside influences. The symptoms of groupthink include:

- Illusion of invulnerability: This refers to the group's overestimation of its worth. Members of the group share the belief that their group is "special," and that they will be successful, regardless of whether they make more conservative or hazardous decisions.
- Stereotyping: Refers to an "us versus them" dichotomy. Those who oppose the group are considered enemies. In more extreme cases, "us versus them" presents itself as "good versus evil."
- Rationalization: Shared rationalizations are used to dismiss warning signs of the potential dangers of groupthink.
- Moral high ground: The belief that the group has a monopoly on what is right or just.
- Self-censorship: If a member of the group has doubts or a dissenting opinion, that individual keeps such thoughts to him or herself.
- Illusion of unanimity: The illusion that everyone within the group agrees 100 percent with a given course of action reinforces self-cen-

What Is a Consensus Process?

A consensus process is an effort in which government agencies and other affected parties seek to reach agreement on a course of action to address an issue or set of related issues. For example, task forces may use consensus to develop recommendations. Stakeholder groups convened by an agency may use consensus to develop legislative recommendations on regulations, or intragovernment work groups involving multiple agencies may use consensus to reach agreement.

In a consensus process, representatives of all the necessary interests with a stake in an issue work together to find a mutually acceptable solution. Each process differs because in each case the parties design it to fit their circumstances. However, successful consensus processes follow several guiding principles:

Consensus decision making—Participants make decisions by agreement rather than by majority vote.

Inclusiveness—All necessary interests are represented or, at a minimum, approve of the discussions.

Accountability—Participants usually represent stakeholder groups or interests. They are accountable both to their constituents and to the process.

Facilitation—An impartial facilitator accountable to all participants manages the process, ensures that ground rules are followed, and helps maintain a productive climate for communication and problem solving.

Flexibility—Participants design a process and address the issues in a manner they determine most suitable to the situation.

Shared control—Participants share responsibility for setting the ground rules for a process and for creating outcomes.

Commitment to implementation—The sponsor and all stakeholder groups commit to carrying out their agreement.

Stages of a consensus process

A consensus process moves through three stages, each with its own set of activities.

Before—Assess whether or not to initiate a consensus process and how to bring diverse interests to the table, then work with the facilitator to plan and organize the process, and write ground rules.

(continued)

(continued)

During—Engage in the problem-solving discussions: exchange information, frame issues, conduct the discussions, generate and evaluate options, develop mutually acceptable solutions, and secure the endorsement of all constituents and authorized decision makers.

After—Implement the agreement: formalize the decision, carry it out, and monitor the results.

How consensus processes differ from consultation

The most significant differences between consultation and consensus processes are how decisions are made and what happens to the product of the discussions. In a consensus process, the parties share decision making about both process and outcome. By contrast, in a consultative process the sponsoring agency decides whether to initiate a process and how it will be organized. In a consensus process, the product of the discussion gets translated into official decisions, while in a consultative process, the agency formulates the decisions. In both approaches, the agency retains final decision-making authority, but in a consensus process, the agency puts the product of a consensus process out for official review as the proposed decision. In consultation, the agency receives input from the participants, and then staff members formulate the proposed decisions.

Sometimes, because of legal requirements, sponsoring agencies refer to a process as "consultative" or "advisory," even when the intent is to agree with stakeholders on an outcome. Federal agencies that sponsor regulatory negotiations must charter the process as an advisory committee under the provisions of the federal Advisory Communications Act. A legislature or administrative policymaking body that authorizes a consensus process may designate the group as advisory in order to make it clear that the formal decision will still be made by government officials.

Again, the most important distinctions among these processes are how decisions are made and what happens to the outcome. If a sponsoring agency treats the committee's final agreement as advice and picks and chooses parts to include in the official decision, the process is consultative. If it participates along with other parties in formulating the agreement, then accepts it as a package consisting of trade-offs that cannot be detached (and if it is committed to implementing the package), then the process is consensual. According to the authors of *Building Consensus for a Sustainable Future*, who first pointed out this distinction, "Consultation is designed to inform decision makers who will ultimately make the decision. Consensus involves the participants as decision makers. . . . In a consensus process, the participants must address and persuade one another and find solutions acceptable to all."

Definition of consensus

A practical definition for consensus in the public policy setting is: the parties have reached a meeting of the minds sufficient to make a decision and carry it out; no one who could block or obstruct the decision or its implementation will exercise that power; everyone needed to support the decision and put it into effect will do so.

This definition does not mean unanimity of thought or abandonment of values. Indeed, one of the characteristics of a well-constructed agreement is that it represents diverse values and interests. Given the mixture of issues and values in public conflict, the resulting agreement often is a package with varying levels of enthusiasm and support for different components, but on balance one that each party or stakeholder can accept. In a consensus process, the parties or stakeholders must define consensus for themselves and include their definition in the ground rules. Most definitions imply acceptance, an acknowledgment that things can move forward, that people support a decision, or at least can live with it. Even if only most participants like the decision, at least all of them are willing to accept it.

Why use consensus and not majority vote?

Because stakeholders and government officials together are the decision makers in a consensus process, participants must try to educate and persuade one another about their needs and interests. They also must listen carefully to determine how the solution can meet the needs of the other parties. Majority voting induces a different kind of interaction than does consensus decision making. When participants know they can revert to a majority vote if they cannot agree, they may focus more on building coalitions for such a possibility rather than trying to meet all the parties' needs.

Source: State of Maine, Public Policy Consensus and Mediation, "What Is a Consensus Process?" www.maine.gov/consensus/ppcm_consensus_home.htm.

sorship. In other words, even if someone has doubts about a decision, that individual will refrain from expressing this doubt so as not to upset the illusion of unanimity.

- Pressure applied to group dissenters: Should the illusion of unanimity fail to reign in any potential dissenters, pressure is applied to any group member who may desire to speak out against the group's decisions.
- Mind guarding: Deals with protecting the group's leader(s) from external dissenters or criticism.

The groupthink atmosphere discourages anyone from conveying a dissenting opinion. If any member argues against any of the group's decisions, direct pressure is placed on this individual by the other members. Group loyalty is paramount, and dissent or criticism undermines loyalty. Even though several group members may have reservations about a decision, each believes that everyone else is in agreement. Great failures are often group failures, as shown by the disaster at Pearl Harbor on December 7, 1941. U.S. intelligence knew Japanese carriers were in the Pacific, but no one dared speak up to question assumptions that Pearl Harbor was impenetrable. The results were disastrous, but the lesson unlearned. Two decades later, no one in the White House dared challenge President John F. Kennedy's decision to invade Cuba's Bay of Pigs—even though the invasion plan hatched out by the Central Intelligence Agency called for using 1,400 Cuban exiles, fewer than 200 of whom had any prior military experience, to overrun Castro and retake control of the island. One White House aide, Arthur Schlesinger, expressed a desire to question the president before the plan was put into action, but he was met by this response from Attorney General Robert Kennedy, "You may be right or you may be wrong, but the President has made up his mind. Don't push it any further. Now is the time for everyone to help him all they can" (quoted by Janis in 2d ed., 1982, p. 40). That same groupthinking group brought about disaster in Vietnam, as the war effort kept growing despite evidence that further escalation would not enable the United States to achieve its military objectives. This mindset is nowhere clearer than in American industry, where groupthinking groups in major competitive corporations arrived at the same wrong conclusions that their Japanese counterparts were not a threat to the market.

In the twenty-first century, we have seen groupthink and its consequences regard-

FIGURE 4.7 – THE GROUPTHINK PROCESS

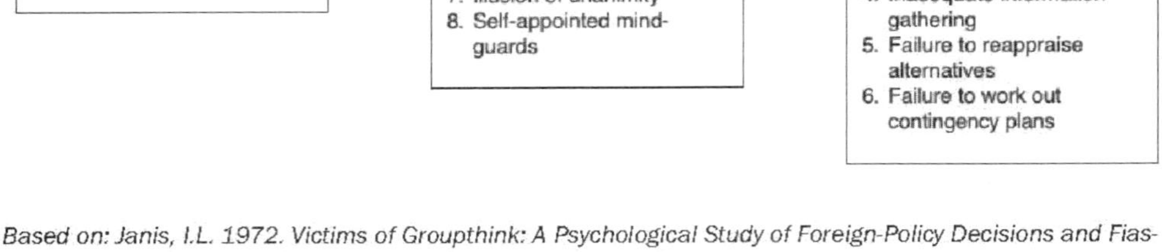

Based on: Janis, I.L. 1972. Victims of Groupthink: A Psychological Study of Foreign-Policy Decisions and Fiascoes. Boston: Houghton Mifflin. 2d ed., 1982.

ing the U.S. occupation of Iraq. When the Iraqi invasion was in the planning stage, there were arguably two identifiable groups: the in-group consisting of Vice President Dick Cheney, Defense Secretary Donald Rumsfeld, Deputy Defense Secretary Paul Wolfowitz, and the former chair of the Defense Policy Board Richard Perle. These four primary members of President George W. Bush's in-group shared similar backgrounds, as both Cheney and Rumsfeld got their starts in politics during the Nixon administration. Wolfowitz and Perle has close working relationships with Cheney and Rumsfeld, and Wolfowitz served as mentor to Cheney's former chief of staff, Lewis "Scooter" Libby, while Libby was a student at Yale and later in his career. These four members of the in-group have been characterized as champions of a foreign policy ethos known as neoconservatism. Neoconservatism embraces notions such as preemptive war and unilateralism. In contrast to President Bush's in-group, former Secretary of State Colin Powell and his deputy, Richard Armitage, arguably represented the out-group within the administration.

"All those in favor say 'Aye.'"
"Aye." "Aye." "Aye." "Aye." "Aye."

Source: The New Yorker Collection.

Some of the classic symptoms of groupthink can be identified easily if we examine the U.S. occupation of Iraq. President Bush and the in-group were reluctant to explore alternative courses of action—even in the context of modifying the occupation strategy following the removal of the Iraqi dictator Saddam Hussein and the Ba'ath Party. For instance, some individuals who were not a part of the president's in-group expressed concerns as to the number of American forces used in the occupation. As it stands, roughly 85,000 American troops have been carrying out the occupation and rebuilding of Iraq. In 1999, four years prior to the Iraq war, a war simulation known as "Desert Crossing" was conducted by the Department of Defense (DoD). The simulation estimated that 400,000 American troops would be needed to successfully control Iraq and respond to security threats that insurgents posed to American forces and Iraqi civilians. General Anthony Zinni, who retired in 2000, oversaw the war simulation. When it became apparent to Zinni that the Bush administration had set its sights on invading and occupying Iraq, he made a call to some of his colleagues in Central Command—the part of the DoD responsible for planning and carrying out military operations throughout the Middle East—and suggested that the Bush administration and military leadership review the findings of Desert Crossing. According to Zinni, Central Command had no idea that this war gaming scenario existed (as quoted in National Security Archive, *Post-Saddam Iraq: The War Game* 2006). Knowing this, it seems possible that the in-group within the Bush administration deliberately avoided the Desert Crossing report for fear that its findings would undermine the current occupation strategy. Another possibility is that the contents of the report were known by some but not conveyed to others for fear of upsetting the cohesiveness and feeling of unanimity within the in-group. Or, perhaps the in-group was well aware of the Desert Crossing findings, yet its findings were rationalized as being "alarmist" or flat out wrong. These classic symptoms of groupthink were most likely present during the planning of the Iraqi occupation.

> "Take time to deliberate; but when the time for action arrives, stop thinking and go."
>
> **ANDREW JACKSON**
> 7th President of the United States

Avoiding Groupthink

The Bay of Pigs, the escalation of the Vietnam War, and the Iraqi occupation demonstrate that groupthink can exist at the highest levels of government, where some of the smartest, most capable people work every day. This being said, can anything be done to reduce the likelihood of groupthink? Yes. There are a number of strategies for avoiding it:

1. The leader of the group should avoid stating his or her preferences. Truth to power is inherently difficult, and even more so if the members of the group believe that the leader prefers one course of action to another.
2. The leader should designate a member of the group to serve as the "devil's

advocate." This person should be given the explicit responsibility of presenting counterarguments and questioning the prudence of the group's ideas.

3. Outside experts can also be used as devil's advocates.
4. Anonymity fosters truthfulness; therefore, the leader needs to give members of the group a means of voicing their opinions anonymously.
5. The leader needs to a create a culture where debate, critical analysis, and creativity are encouraged. Fostering a climate where a range of ideas can flourish is key to avoiding groupthink and its potential consequences.

REACHING CONSENSUS WHEN PEOPLE HAVE DIFFERENT VALUES AND INTERESTS: DOES NATIONAL CULTURE MATTER?

The process of decision making is always complex and leads to conflicts among participants. This is especially true when different participants have different interests and values in a certain policy area. As you learned in the text, governments often suffer from lack of consensus procedures, thereby increasing the level of conflicts among people. Please read the following two newspaper articles and suggest how we reach consensus rather than consultation and majority voting. In particular, please pay attention to the two countries' national cultures. Do you think there could be any different solutions to reach consensus in Korea as opposed to the us?

Case 1: Conflicts escalate over state-run test

By Kang Shin-Who

Conflict between the central government and local education offices is deepening over the state-run standardized tests for elementary and secondary school students.

The Ministry of Education, Science and Technology plans to conduct the academic achievement tests nationwide on July 13 and 14, as part of its efforts to bring fresh competition among schools and boost academic capability.

However, some local education offices, headed by progressive education superintendents, are opposing the tests, claiming they will cause "undue competition" among students.

Amid escalating discord, the ministry has sent an official warning letter to the Jeollabuk-do Office of Education, arguing that the operation of an alternative program aiming to replace or invalidate the test is against the Education Law.

The letter said the heads of education offices have to comply with the standardized assessments, unless they have a valid excuse, under the Primary and Secondary Education Law.

The ministry's move came after Kim Seung-hwa, the education superintendent of the southwestern provincial office, instructed each school in the province to allow students who don't want to take the exam to take part in alternative programs.

Officials from the education office, sandwiched between the central government and their chief educator, are perplexed about the growing discord.

"We never discourage students from taking the standardized exam. We've just requested schools to offer alternative programs for those who don't want the test," an official in charge of the assessment at the provincial education office told *The Korea Times*.

On the education ministry's policy against the alternative programs, the official, who asked to remain anonymous, just said, "I am very troubled."

Complaints from parents

Gangwon-do Office of Education sent out a letter allowing parents and students to choose whether to take the tests or not.

Liberal top educators of the Seoul Metropolitan Office of Education and Gyeonggi Provincial Office of Education also disagree with the state-administered exams, although they have yet to issue any instructions on the tests.

The ministry plans to discipline students regardless of whether they skip the exams intentionally or not. Also, teachers allowing their students to skip the tests will face punishment. A number of teachers who protested the new evaluations were fired last year.

Some schools are also in conflict with parents over the schools' decision to ban students from going abroad for language programs during the test period.

"Some school principals are following the ministry's guidelines too rigidly; they need to adopt them flexibly depending on each student's individual situation. This rigid observation is resulting in clashes between some parents and schools," a school teacher said.

Many members of the progressive teachers' union plan to boycott the test, shrugging off the authorities' demand that they should not allow students to skip the test.

Source: Korea Times, July 7, 2010, accessed at http://www.koreatimes.co.kr/www/news/nation/2010/07/117_68991.html

Case 2: Conflict over Strategic Plan in New Jersey

Conflicting Views Over State's Strategic Growth Plan

Doubts linger over targets for economic growth vs. environmental preservation

Hearing sharply divergent views, the state last night concluded a series of six public hearings on its draft strategic investment plan, ablueprint for targeting where growth should occur in the future in New Jersey and where development should be discouraged.

The plan, unveiled last October by the Christie administration, overhauls and replaces a State Plan and Redevelopment Plan put in place a decade ago, which even its advocates acknowledge failed to achieve its objectives.

The 41-page plan emphasizes economic growth instead of environmental preservation by establishing geographic industry clusters where the state will direct investments and resources to bolster high-growth sectors, such as finance, healthcare, and the ports.

If so, it would reverse a shortcoming of the previous state plan, which most observers said never lived up to its lofty goals because previous administrations failed to force agencies to align state regulations, and more importantly, state aid, to areas designated for growth and away from lands that were designated for preservation.

Much of the comments focused on concerns that the state plan will intrude on local government's tradition of home rule, forcing communities to accept developments and preservation of lands they had not sought or approved. In addition, others worried the plan would strip property-owners of the right to develop their land as they wish.
"The best government is the government that governs the least," said George Gallenthin, an attorney, to a smattering of applause.

Dan Kennedy, deputy director of the Office for Planning Advocacy, tried to allay those concerns by arguing the new plan is not a "land use plan, as it has been in the past." It is not a substitute for local and regional planning, he added.

While about 60 people attended the meeting, most either skeptical of the plan or outright opposed to it, there were some who backed the effort.

Michael Egenton, senior vice president of the New Jersey State Chamber of Commerce, said the plan has great potential to enhance economic opportunities. "The state chamber views the state strategic plan's emphasis on economic prosperity, resource efficiency and realignment of government not only as strengths of the document, but also as necessities for catalyzing the New Jersey comeback," he said.

Peter Kasabach, executive director of New Jersey Future, a smart growth organization, also supported the plan, but urged the staff to do more work in identifying criteria that will be used to target economic growth and preservation.

What worries some environmentalists about the draft plan is the fear that economic growth will trump preservation of open space, a concern voiced at the last hearing held at the Rutgers Eco-Complex in Bordentown.

"It is nothing more than a plan to promote more sprawl in New Jersey under the guise of strategic plan," said Jeff Tittel, executive director of the New Jersey Sierra Club, in his written testimony. "The only thing strategic about this plan how it will turn the state over to developer at the expense of our cities and environment."

Louise Wilson, a Skillman resident, said she fears the new plan will end up resulting in a case-by-case decision basis. She also argued environmental protections should be given the same weight as economic growth objectives.

Mike Pisauro, a lawyer for the New Jersey Environmental Lobby, endorsed that view. He called the plan troubling, saying it "only pays lip service to environmental protections" while repeatedly stressing economic growth.

The plan also includes the establishment of a high-level steering committee chaired by the lieutenant governor to resolve conflicts between state agencies, disputes which prevented the old plan from achieving its objectives, according to dsome smart growth advocates.

Source: http://www.njspotlight.com/stories/12/0302/0116/, accessed on September 26, 2012

KEY TERMS

Balance sheet

Bounded rationality

Cost-benefit analysis (CBA)

Decision-making alternatives

Elite theory

Garbage can model

Groupthink

Incrementalism

Participatory model

Political model

Rational model

Satisficing

REFERENCES

Dahl, R.A. 1982. *Dilemmas of Pluralist Democracy: Autonomy vs. Control.* New Haven, CT: Yale University Press.

Dror, Y. 1964. "Muddling Through—'Science' or Inertia?" *Public Administration Review* 24: 153–57.

Janis, I.L. 1972. *Victims of Groupthink: A Psychological Study of Foreign-Policy Decisions and Fiascoes.* Boston: Houghton Mifflin. 2d ed., 1982.

Kingdon, J.W. 2003. *Agendas, Alternatives, and Public Policies.* 2d ed. New York: Longman.

Lewis, V. 1952. "Toward a Theory of Budgeting." *Public Administration Review* 12 (Winter): 42–54.

Lindblom, C.E. 1959. "The Science of Muddling Through." *Public Administration Review* 19: 79–88.

Mikesell, J.L. 1978. "Government Decisions in Budgeting and Taxing: The Economic Logic." *Public Administration Review* (November/December): 511–13.

Mills, C.W. 1956. *The Power Elite.* New York: Oxford University Press.

National Security Archive. 2006. *Post-Saddam Iraq: The War Game.* National Security Archive Electronic Briefing Book No. 207. Washington, DC: National Security Archive of the George Washington University.

Schumpeter, J.A. 1942/1976. *Capitalism, Socialism, and Democracy.* 5th ed. London: Allen and Unwin.

Simon, H. 1947/1997. *Administrative Behavior.* New York: Simon and Schuster.

SUPPLEMENTARY READINGS

Allison, G., and P. Zelikow. 1999. *Essence of Decision: Explaining the Cuban Missile Crisis.* 2d ed. New York: Longman.

March, J. 1989. *Decisions and Organizations.* Oxford: Blackwell.

ELECTRONIC RESOURCES

The Decision Analysis Society of INFORMS (promotes the development and use of logical methods for the improvement of decision making in public and private enterprise): http://decision-analysis.society.informs.org/

RAND Corporation: http://www.rand.org

The Society for Judgment and Decision Making (an interdisciplinary academic organization dedicated to the study of normative, descriptive, and prescriptive theories of decision making): http://www.sjdm.org/

CHAPTER 5

Politics and Public Administration

This chapter examines the marriage of politics and administration. Upon reading this chapter, students will understand the need for administrative reform following the Jacksonian spoils system, as well as the intersection and reality of politics and administration. Central to this chapter is an examination of bureaucratic discretion and decision making. Further discussion centers on the executive branch's inability to control the bureaucracy, the legislative branch's lack of desire to control the bureaucracy, and the judicial branch's role as a reluctant arbiter of bureaucratic actions.

"A theory of public administration means in our time a theory of politics also."

JOHN GAUS
Political Science;
Public Administration Expert
(1894–1969)

Newark City Hall, Newark, New Jersey

THE INTERSECTION OF POLITICS AND ADMINISTRATION

Reform and Neutrality

Competence versus responsiveness has been a historical struggle in public administration. From George Washington to John Quincy Adams, the small bureaucracies of the federal government valued competence and qualification. In 1828, however, the bureaucracy's focus on competence shifted. The election of Andrew Jackson to the presidency ushered in a new public administration philosophy—the so-called "spoils system." Central to the spoils system was the belief in a more "responsive" bureaucracy. Jackson believed that virtually any individual was capable of executing the "simple" tasks of public management, which were thought to be a matter of "common sense." Disappointingly, a heavy price was paid for more responsive administration under the spoils systems. Inefficiency was widespread, profiteering was common, and scandals were recurrent. The ills associated with the spoils system were pervasive not only at the federal level but also throughout state and municipal bureaucracies. A large, rapidly growing and increasingly industrialized nation could not afford substandard public service administration. Waste and corruption had to be restrained. In the post–Civil War period, reformers made public appeals for efficient and honest government. Reformers, most notably Princeton University academic (and future U.S. president) Woodrow Wilson, insisted on a politics-administration separation. Wilson championed a dichotomy, or firm separation, between the determination and implementation of policy. Policy determination should occur via the political process, while policy implementation should be the realm of apolitical administrators only. In other words, policy stands as an expression of state will through elected officials, and public administrators should execute that expression of state will in a professional, competent, and apolitical fashion.

> "All of us who are concerned for peace and triumph of reason and justice must be keenly aware how small an influence reason and honest good will exert upon events in the political field."
>
> **ALBERT EINSTEIN**
> Physicist;
> Nobel Prize Winner
> (1879–1955)

The Pendleton Civil Service Act of 1883 changed everything by creating a bipartisan Civil Service Commission—the predecessor of the system that is currently responsible for 90 percent of government employees. Critics maintain that a significant price has been paid for this type of merit-based system. By being too shielded from politics, mediocrity and incompetence has again become pervasive, so much so that the system arguably rivals the Jacksonian spoils era. Other critics argue that corruption has yet to be eliminated. Corruption persists in less obvious ways, such as through friendly ties and under-the-table favors, although overt forms of corruption still make headlines from time to time.

The creation of a civil service system provided the basis for more "businesslike" government. The central principle became machinelike efficiency; that is, accomplishing a given task with as little wasted energy as possible. This civil service reform movement influenced governments at all levels to establish ethics codes, which distinguished acceptable from unacceptable public employee behavior. Some of these codes of ethics were incorporated into laws. The idea was that government services must be delivered without passion or prejudice, and that truthfulness and openness were essential to creating a most favorable administrative environment. This reform movement assumed that public administrators would abide by the law and even higher ethical standards. Providing services less efficiently was considered acceptable as long as public servants conducted themselves lawfully and ethically.

Honest, businesslike government became the mantra during this reform movement. Reformers like Woodrow Wilson and Frank Goodnow advocated that greater thought be paid to the "science" of public administration. Wilson believed it was imperative that government not only determine what policies should be enacted but also implement those policies with the highest degree of efficiency and responsiveness to the citizenry. Public administration needed to emerge as a profession,

The attack on the President's life – Scene in the ladies' room of the Baltimore and Ohio Railroad depot.

Source: Berghaus, A., and C. Upham, Frank Leslie's Illustrated Newspaper, 1881 July 16, pp. 332-333. Library of Congress, Prints & Photographs Division, reproduction number LC-USZ62-7622.

and public administrators needed to conduct themselves as such, that is, public administrators must be responsible, professional, and efficient. Theories of "good governance" became widespread, namely from the Bureau of Municipal Research in New York, which was established in 1906. Good governance stresses that efficient service delivery is vital to the public's interest. Additionally, these theories suggest that administration and politics should remain separated. Ideally, public administrators operate in an apolitical environment, removed from the sphere of elected boards and political officials. Furthermore, expertise should be a trademark of reform. The essence of the good governance reform movement is encapsulated in the proverb: "There is neither a Democratic nor a Republican way to build a road, just the right way." As satisfying as this may sound, contemporary public administration has witnessed the movement away from the naive belief that politics and administration can be separated and toward the recognition that the practice of public administration cannot realistically occur in a neutral, apolitical environment.

The Reality of Bureaucratic Politics

In contrast to the notions of nineteenth-century reformers like Wilson and Goodnow, twentieth-century analysts acknowledged the reality that appointed administrative officials often take the lead in making policy, while lower-level public officials often interpret policies. Nineteenth-century policies were largely distributive—meaning the government provided specific services that the free market would not (for example, education, a national defense, and other services that did not require significant interpretation on the part of public administrators). This all changed, however, with the creation of the welfare state that began with President Franklin Roosevelt's policies during the Great Depression and continued with Lyndon Johnson's Great Society, a reform package rooted in the twin concepts of social justice and public improvement. To be clear, the welfare state refers to policies that provide for the general welfare of it citizenry. These policies are, by and large, "redistributive" in nature, meaning that taxes collected from higher-income, wealthier citizens are redistributed to lower-income, poorer citizens in the form of services and benefits. Examples of redistributive policies include welfare benefits, food stamps, and Medicaid (health insurance for the poor, which is not to be confused with Medicare, health insurance for retirees under Social Security). With the arrival of depression-era "big government" and the growing implementation of redistributive policies during Johnson's Great Society, it became clear that any dichotomy between politics and administration was not realistic. Wilson's call for politics-administration separation is now seen as rather naive. Clearly, politics and values encroach on administration from numerous external sources. Public administrators are policymakers, as public administration is ultimately the sum of politics plus management (Holzer and Gabrielian 1998).

Many scholars have spoken against the utopian view of public administrators as neutral and apolitical. This attack on the oversimplistic nature of the politics-administration dichotomy began in earnest in the 1940s, having gained momentum by the end of World War II. Scholars such as P. Appleby (1949) pointed out that "arguments about application of policy are essentially arguments about policy." D. Waldo (1984) maintained that public administration research was grounded in political theory, while N.E. Long (1949) contended that "the lifeblood of administration is power." This underscored public agencies' need to cultivate a clientele in order to ensure political survival. P.A. Selznick (1949) demonstrated how the Tennessee Valley Authority (TVA), a New Deal–era agency providing electricity and resource management for the southeastern United States, survived and accomplished its mission by taking into account the needs of the local citizenry. In his landmark book *Administrative Behavior*, Herbert Simon (1947/1997) demonstrated that facts and administrative realities drive not only how decisions are made but also how values are formed. Simon (1967) disputed Wilson's notion that "the field of administration is a field of business. It is removed from the hurry and strife of politics." Simon stressed that Wilson's notion is normative, and thus "the field of administration ought to be a field of business."

> "There is no doubt that the development of the administrative agency in response to modern legislative and administrative need has placed severe strain on the separation-of-powers principle in its pristine formulation."
>
> **BYRON WHITE**
> Football Player;
> Supreme Court Justice
> (1917–2002)

The assumption that politics and administration could be separated was ultimately disregarded as utopian. Wilson and Goodnow's idea of apolitical public administration proved unrealistic. A more realistic view—the so-called "politics" school—is that politics is very much a part of administration. The politics school maintains that in a pluralistic political system in which many diverse groups have a voice, public administrators with considerable knowledge play key roles. Legislation, for instance, is written by public administrators as much as by legislators. The public bureaucracy is as capable of engendering support for its interests as any other participant in the political process, and public administrators are as likely as any to be part of a policymaking partnership. Furthermore, laws are interpreted by public administrators in their execution, which includes many and often unforeseen scenarios. Policy implementation is the final step in the policy process, and it serves as the last chance for outside interests to influence policy.

Given that laws must be interpreted in the context of unanticipated circumstances, administrative discretion becomes necessary. Administrative organizations are often subject to external pressures by special interest groups and elected officials. This stems from the fact that when public administrators draft policies and interpret those policies, they are making value-based judgments. Even the most "technical" decisions are somewhat value-laden. With such discretion, public administrators fall victim to policy preferences from all sorts of stakeholders, most notably interest groups, legislators, media groups, and rank-and-file citizens. Pressure is also found within public organizations.

The manner in which a policy is interpreted and implemented is as important as the writing stage of the policymaking process. As a result, public administrators are consistently pressured by interest groups and elected officials. Within a public organization, bureaucrats often emerge as advocates for one special interest over another—advocating for one certain position and interpretation of a newly drafted policy. Making the "process" more objective is imperative, and one way of doing this is to make the process more logical. According to the rational-comprehensive school of decision making, the best decisions are logical; that is, decision makers try to meticulously account for every possible consequence involved in choosing one course of action over another. On the other hand, the incrementalist school argues that pressures resulting from crises and deadlines limit the amount of time available for such a detailed analysis. The incremental approach defends the process of making decisions based on choosing a course of action that is both satisfactory and sufficient. In other words, incrementalists advocate finding a "good enough" alternative until a better one presents itself. This is called "muddling through."

The intermingling of politics and administration is fairly obvious when one looks at the budget process. Every government, regardless of the level (municipal, county, state, or federal), operates under the direction of an official spending plan—more simply, a budget. Budgets are massively dense documents filled with calculations and figures. Thus, to most laypeople, budgets are overly dry. While true to some extent, the battle for resources by public organizations is not as dry a process as

EXERCISE 5.1

Tobacco Settlement Distribution Simulation

A $2.5 billion settlement from a tobacco company is awarded to the State. A network of taxpayers, elected officials, and public administrators must distribute the award. This simulation challenges students to balance constituency needs, political forces, and public administrative goals in achieving an equitable distribution plan. What are the guiding principles that should be considered by the group and why? Create a list of the principles with a brief summary justifying each based upon the need to balance both political and equity priorities.

Linda Blessing and Bette F. DeGraw, E-PARCC. Program for the Advancement of Research on Conflict and Collaboration, The Maxwell School, Syracuse University http://sites.maxwell.syr.edu/parc/eparc/simulations/tobacco-settlement-distribution-simulation.asp.

one might think. Money is the lifeblood of any organization. An agency or department's budget affects the number of people it employs and the resources available to them. The struggle for money becomes a struggle over values, prompting questions such as, Should money be spent on more police officers, for emergency medical technicians, or for a remedial mathematics program? Eminent political scientist V.O. Key (1940, p. 1138) recognized this struggle when he asked, "On what basis shall it be decided to allocate x dollars to activity A instead of activity B?" Key believed that personal values and priorities ultimately determine where money is spent. Developing "criteria" to decide how public resources should be spent is nearly impossible, given that people's values and priorities differ. These diverse values and priorities are reflected in budgetary choices. The budget, therefore, is an interest-oriented process defined by constant struggle—struggle to determine whose interests and preferences will be given consideration. Politics ends up being very much a part of this struggle (Wildavsky 1992).

> "Bureaucracies are inherently antidemocratic. Bureaucrats derive their power from their position in the structure, not from their relations with the people they are supposed to serve. The people are not masters of the bureaucracy, but its clients."
>
> **ALAN KEYES**
> Political Activist

Most public administrators will admit that bureaucratic decisions are, to some measure, influenced by politics. Employees are sometimes hired to placate the powerful. Government contracts are sometimes given to friends of powerful officials. Former public officials are given profitable private-sector consulting jobs. Typically, a public administrator's involvement in such situations is not tied to personal gain; rather, involvement is a means of maintaining close ties with important and influential people. The golden rule of public administrators is not to make enemies, which is accomplished, at times, by dodging hard decisions. Sometimes when bureaucrats' interests are severely threatened, they become excessively political. For instance, when stuck in the middle of a financial crisis with significant budget cuts looming, bureaucrats will often underscore the political costs of budget cuts by summoning important "allies" to advocate on their behalf. These allies include employee unions and interest groups. Special interest group representatives can and will lobby forcefully—often with the active cooperation of the bureaucracy—to do away with proposed budget cuts that a chief executive or legislative committee has advocated. The budget reflects the successes and failures of the various contenders—agencies and departments fighting to avoid budget cuts (or increase their budgets) through their relationships with powerful people and the influence they exert among high-ranking political appointees or elected officials. These dynamics are present at the federal, state, and local levels.

Scholar Theodore Lowi (1979) argues against giving public administrators too much discretion. Lowi contends that until the emergence of the administrative state, the

United States was dominated by Congress. He is critical of government programs that grant bureaucrats discretionary powers, given the inherent difficulty of controlling such discretion. Lowi's criticism has added credibility when considering the discretionary power of "street-level bureaucrats." According to Lipsky (1980), street-level bureaucrats are those that provide public benefits and maintain public

order—namely, police officers, social service providers, public school teachers, and judges. Street-level bureaucrats tend to be at the center of political controversies for two reasons: (1) controversies regarding the appropriate scope of government are essentially controversies regarding the functions of that level of bureaucracy, and (2) street-level bureaucrats have extensive power over the lives of ordinary citizens. These public employees play a vital role in citizen entitlements. Also, poorer individuals such as welfare recipients are typically more reliant on the services provided by street-level bureaucrats, and the services delivered by these bureaucrats tend to be immediate and very personal.

Through their exercise of wide discretion, street-level bureaucrats essentially make policy. For instance, police officers make decisions about whom to arrest, and judges impose sentences every day. There are, of course, rules and regulations that guide discretion. In some cases, however, the sheer number and constantly changing nature of these rules and regulations make it extremely difficult to hold street-level bureaucrats accountable for their decisions. Lower-level workers are unlikely to see eye-to-eye with management, as there is often an incentive for managers to curb a worker's discretion in the interest of achieving organization-wide goals. The worker will likely view this exercise of power as illegitimate and resist it. For lower-level street-level bureaucrats, there is a desire to maintain discretionary power. For example, if a prosecutor did not believe in mandatory minimum drug sentences, then he or she might charge a criminal with a less serious crime.

The responsibility of street-level bureaucrats is linked to "client processing goals" and maintaining self-autonomy. Management, however, is more focused on achieving collective goals. Management also works to lessen the autonomy of the lower-level bureaucrats. The relationship between managers and street-level bureaucrats is characterized by mutual dependence. In other words, managers will honor workers' desires as long as managers are rewarded in terms of collective job performance—an example of which is a police chief giving his or her officers what they want, provided crime in their jurisdiction remains low.

Checking Bureaucratic Discretion

Despite the criticisms of Lowi and others, giving bureaucrats discretionary powers is a real necessity. Some argue that the public bureaucracy is more representative than elected institutions. John Rohr (1986) justifies bureaucratic discretion, given the assumption that bureaucracies are microcosms of the American people. Warren (1993) believes it is pointless to argue the legitimacy of bureaucratic discretion; rather, he views bureaucratic discretion as legitimate because it is a response to an increasing demand for services. The delegation of power to bureaucrats who implement and interpret legislation is guided by the principles of *administrative law*, which ultimately dictates what agencies, departments, or other public organizations can do.

The Executive Branch's Futile Efforts

The executive branch attempts to steer the bureaucracy through the president's appointment powers. The president appoints more than 1,300 officials, all of whom require senatorial approval. Presidential appointees, however, are often unfamiliar with their respective agencies or departments, and therefore they depend on the expertise and advice of well-connected midlevel career bureaucrats. Moreover, assuming top-level appointees can influence agency policymaking, their influence is not automatically an extension of presidential priorities. Cabinet and subcabinet officials are usually sympathetic and loyal to the bureaus, agencies, and clientele groups that comprise a given department; for example, agriculture secretaries typically represent midwestern states and therefore identify with farmers (Cann 1998).

In the 1970s and 1980s, respectively, presidents Nixon and Reagan used ideology to counter captivity and loyalty issues; that is, appointments were based on ideological beliefs, as opposed to skill, expertise, or experience. During Reagan's tenure, few individuals were appointed to the cabinet or subcabinet level unless they championed scaling back the bureaucracy and limiting government. Reagan appointees were less concerned about cooperating with career bureaucrats and gave little attention to the day-to-day business. This allowed the Reagan administration to effectively manage loyalty and captivity issues that had so plagued previous administrations (Maranto 1993). In addition to appointments, the reorganization of the executive branch is a powerful tool of presidential control. Consistent with power vested in the Reorganization Act of 1939, Nixon reorganized staff agencies within the Executive Office of the President (EOP) in the interest of gaining leverage over the bureaucracy. Specifically, Nixon created the Office of Management and Budget (OMB), which replaced the Bureau of the Budget (BOB). Political appointees currently head the OMB, while career civil service bureaucrats headed the BOB. The OMB plays an active role in setting agency budgets, and the ability to appoint its members gives the president some control over agency spending limits. In an ideal world, this keeps the bureaucracy in step with the president's wishes (Nathan 1975; Seidman 1980; Arnold 1986).

In contrast to Nixon and Reagan, President Carter tried to control the bureaucracy through civil service reform, namely the Civil Service Reform Act of 1978. Central to this act was the creation of what is known as the Senior Executive Services (SES). Still in existence today, the SES gives high-level bureaucrats the option of forfeiting civil service job protections in exchange for a higher salary, one that is more competitive with the private sector. This measure sought to address captivity and loyalty issues, and roughly 95 percent of those eligible for the SES have accepted it (Cann 1998).

Despite these efforts, the federal bureaucracy is not easily tamed by the Executive Office of the President. The bureaucracy is afforded the upper hand for a number of reasons. First, the EOP exhibits not more than a passing interest in what the bureaucracy does and lacks specialized knowledge needed to effectively monitor the bureaucracy. Second, the EOP lacks the resources to overcome bureaucratic resistance. Bureaucrats resist because of their technocratic nature. Contrary to popular belief, bureaucrats are policy experts, and therefore executive branch intervention is, by and large, perceived to be ill timed and politically motivated (Riley 1987). Third, clientelism and captivity issues still loom in spite of previous presidential efforts.

Congressional Power Unused

Unlike the EOP, Congress is given considerable power over the bureaucracy by the U.S. Constitution. Congress not only funds the bureaucracy but also determines how much power an agency can exert. In terms of power, we are referring to whether an agency will have the authority to make rules or issue orders. While both possess the effect of law, rules are quasi-legislative in nature (meaning they are applied uniformly), while orders are quasi-judicial in nature (meaning they are applied narrowly) (Kerwin 1994). Nevertheless, the intimate relationship between

FIGURE 5.1 – SENIOR EXECUTIVE SERVICE PROGRAM DESIGN LOGIC

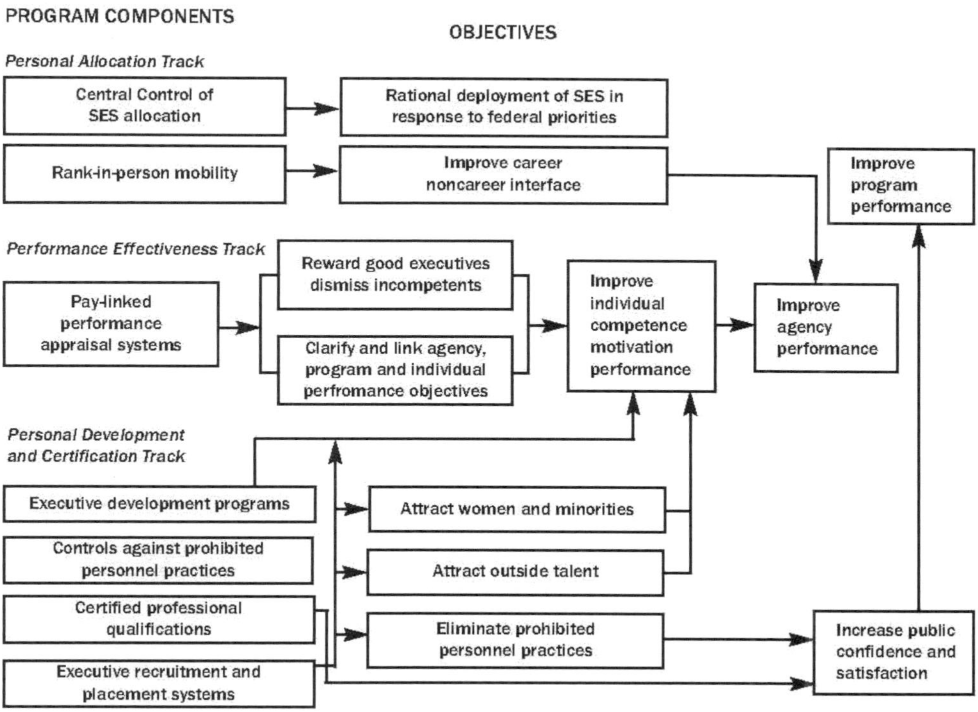

Source: Buchanan, B. 1981. "The Senior Executive Service: How We Can Tell If It Works." Public Administration Review 41 (3): 349–58.

Congress and the bureaucracy arguably precludes meaningful oversight. The quintessential iron triangle exists among congressional subcommittees, bureaucrats, and interest groups.

> The relationship within them [iron triangles] is symbiotic; that is, each member of the triangle gets something that it needs from other members. The agency gets appropriations and new programs from the subcommittee, and the subcommittee gets support and information from the agency. The interest groups get policies and benefits from both the subcommittee and the agency, and the subcommittee gets support, information, and campaign contributions... from the interest groups. (Cann 1998, p. 57)

Cann (1998) maintains that while presidents have demonstrated the will to control the bureaucracy, they have lacked the means. In contrast, Congress is afforded the power to control the bureaucracy but lacks the desire, given its cozy relationship with and dependence on the bureaucracy.

Then, of course, there is the judicial branch of American government. The judicial branch has been forced to play the role of reluctant arbiter when it comes to settling controversies regarding bureaucratic discretion and the implementation of policy. In instances where the politics in administration (or value-based judgments) go too far, the courts must settle the issue. The Supreme Court's rulings determine what bureaucratic actions are appropriate—appropriate in the sense that these actions do not violate the spirit of the U.S. Constitution.

FIGURE 5.2 – CLASSIC IRON TRIANGLE

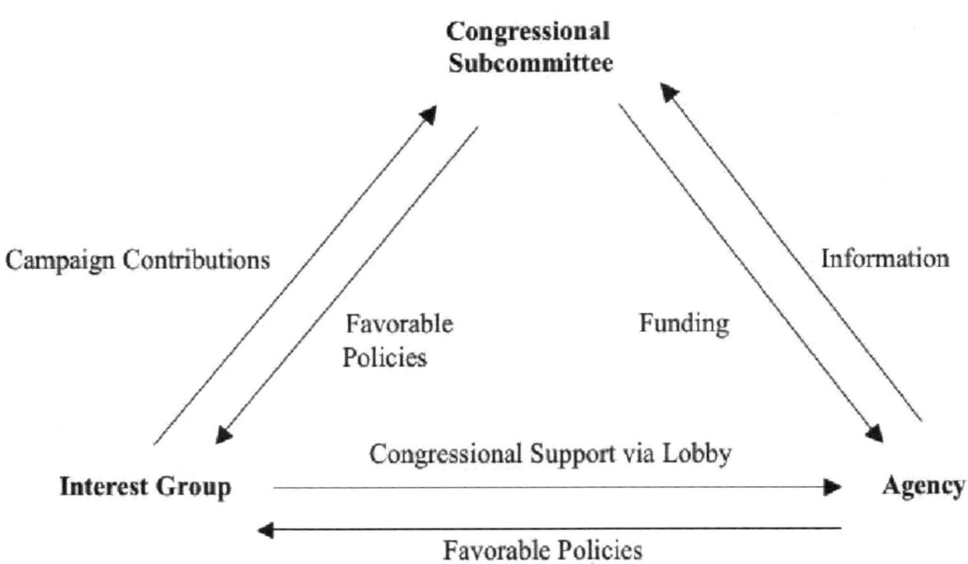

The Court as the Ultimate Arbiter: Federal Administrative Case Law

Congressional Delegation

Given tremendous responsibilities, it is impossible for Congress to carry out all of its duties. According to the Constitution, Congress is allowed to delegate some of its powers to the bureaucracy. In the Supreme Court case of *Hampton v. United States* (1928), the Hampton Company imported barium dioxide assessed at a duty rate of $.06 per pound ($.02 higher than what was mandated by legislation). President Coolidge had raised the duty in accordance with the Tariff Act of 1922, which allowed the president to alter duties in the interest of equalizing costs among foreign and domestic products. The issue before the Court was whether Congress had the authority to delegate its constitutionally enumerated powers to the chief executive (or the bureaucracy, for that matter). The Supreme Court affirmed the constitutionality of congressional delegation, contending that if Congress were required to alter every duty, it would be impossible to exercise any of its powers. This case essentially made it acceptable for Congress to pass on some of its responsibilities to the bureaucrats.

Congress delegates many of its responsibilities to the bureaucracy in the interest of making its workload manageable. Additionally, congressional representatives often lack the technical acumen to address a particular issue, thereby making delegation to an agency of expertise necessary. However, limits are placed on congressional delegation so as to ensure that administrative actions are consistent with constitutional standards. These limits are readily apparent when one examines the case *Industrial Union Department AFL-CIO v. American Petroleum* (1980), which dealt with a regulatory standard issued by the secretary of the U.S. Department of Labor regarding workplace exposure limits to benzene, a potentially carcinogenic agent. In accordance with delegated congressional powers vested in the Occupational Safety and Health Act (OSHA) of 1970, the secretary imposed an exposure limit of

EXERCISE 5.2

The Iron Triangle Simulation

In this role-play exercise, students will take on contemporary public policy issues and experience the challenges of balancing the needs and wants of public administrators, public opinion, lobbyists, legislatures, and presidential pressure when attempting to address the issues. With each of the issues identified in this simulation, create a list of the conflicting values anticipated from each force within the triangle and identify the reasons why.

Gruebs Education Technology
http://gruebs.com/vscentral/irontrianglesimulation.

1 part per million (ppm) and required medical testing for work areas having levels at .05 ppm.

In this case, the issue before the Supreme Court was whether the secretary of Labor, in accordance with OSHA, exceeded his authority by imposing the most rigid regulatory standard without first determining the health risks associated with benzene exposure, and without determining corporate impacts resulting from the regulation. According to the Court, the regulatory standard imposed was deemed invalid, as the secretary failed to comply with explicit and uniform congressional standards. That is, to guarantee the constitutionality of the imposed regulation of benzene, the secretary needed to (1) determine at what levels benzene exposure presents a significant health risk, and (2) account for the economic impacts of the imposed regulation upon industry viability. He failed to make these determinations, and so the imposed regulation of benzene could not be considered constitutionally valid.

> "Politics, it seems to me, for years or all too long, has been concerned with right or left instead of right or wrong."
>
> **RICHARD ARMOUR**
> American Poet; Writer
> (1906–1989)

Consistent with case law, congressional delegation of power to the bureaucracy is constitutionally sound as long as there are sufficient standards to guide bureaucratic actions. Standards are imperative, because they prevent agencies from both promulgating arbitrary regulations and, essentially, making policy, which was highlighted in then-Justice William Rehnquist's concurring opinion in *Industrial Union Department AFL-CIO v. American Petroleum* (1980), the so-called "Benzene Case." Specifically, Rehnquist wrote: "To the extent Congress finds it necessary to delegate authority, it provides the recipient of that authority with an 'intelligible principle' to guide the exercise of delegated discretion" (quoted in Cann 1998, p. 75). According to Rehnquist, the statute used by the secretary of Labor in this case was standardless.

Due Process and Bureaucratic Discretion

The Fifth (federal applicability) and Fourteenth (state applicability) amendments to the Constitution prohibit the government from depriving life, liberty, or property without due process. The notion of due process coincides with a guarantee of fair procedures. Due process is an elastic concept, and it is shaped, in large part, by the prevailing political climate and the ideological makeup of the Supreme Court. Individuals claiming an infringement of due process must demonstrate a property or liberty interest. A property interest coincides with an economic stake. In the context of this discussion, a liberty interest refers to an individual's future employment.

The high mark of administrative due process is embodied in *Goldberg v. Kelly* (1970). The issue before the Court in this case was whether an agency may terminate welfare benefits without providing the recipient with a pre-termination evidentiary hearing. The majority held that a pre-termination evidentiary hearing was warranted in accordance with the due process clause of the Fourteenth Amendment. The basis for this decision lies in the nature of the property interest at stake. That is, welfare benefits are means-tested, meaning their termination would leave recipients without financial support. It is imperative, therefore, that welfare recip-

Uncle Sam's Christmas Dream

Source: Rogers, William Allen, Harper's Weekly, 49:1851 (December 23, 1905). Library of Congress, Prints & Photographs Division, reproduction number LC-USZ62-10352, http://hdl.loc.gov/loc.pnp/cai.2a14425.

ients are given timely and adequate notice of termination, and the reasons for such termination must be clearly stipulated so as to provide recipients with the opportunity to present evidence on their behalf. In this particular case, bureaucratic interests are thought to be secondary, as the erroneous allocation of welfare benefits would prove nominal to the state. The erroneous termination of welfare benefits, however, would have a profoundly negative impact upon one's livelihood.

On the other hand, in *Matthews v. Eldridge* (1976), the issue before the Supreme Court was whether a Social Security recipient is, in accordance with the due process clause of the Fifth Amendment, entitled to a hearing prior to the termination of disability benefits. Unlike the Goldberg case, the Court held that a pre-termination hearing was not due. The basis of this decision rests upon the following assumptions: First, disability benefits are not means-tested, and therefore the termination of such benefits would not leave one destitute. Second, given that disability benefits are allocated on the basis of medical records, the risk of an erroneous decision is thought to be lower than in welfare cases. Finally, in weighing the interests of the state versus the individual, a post-termination hearing more than adequately satisfies due process.

Goss v. Lopez (1975) concerns a due process case in the educational arena. It stemmed from a challenge to an Ohio public school policy that gave principals the authority to suspend students from school for a maximum period of 10 days. The challenge in *Goss v. Lopez* followed the assumption that, consistent with the due process clause of the Fourteenth Amendment, one's right to education cannot be deprived without a hearing. The Supreme Court held that the failure to provide a hearing prior to or within a reasonable time subsequent to a student's suspension violates due process protections. The decision acknowledged the need for a limited hearing (a guarantee of nominal due process) given a student's entitlement to public education as a property interest. A limited hearing may include notifying a student (and parents) of the reasons for the suspension, providing an explanation of the evidence that school officials have against the student, and giving the student in question the opportunity to explain his or her side and present counterevidence.

Property interests are not limited means-tested and entitlement benefits. Taxes represent bona fide property interests, and under specific circumstances, taxes cannot be levied without a measure of due process. For instance, in *Londoner v. Denver* (1908), a nonlegislative body (a local board) established a special tax district for the purpose of financing road improvements. The issue before the Supreme Court was whether a nonlegislative body may levy a special tax assessment without a hearing. According to the majority opinion, no individual should be compelled to pay a specialized tax assessment without having an opportunity to be heard. Specifically, the Court ruled that when a legislative body gives lower units of government the power to determine "upon whom" to impose a tax, an adjudicatory hearing must be provided (Cann 1998, p. 221).

Adjudicatory hearings are most appropriate if a limited number of people claim a property interest, and if a decision is based upon evidence that can be rebutted, which was the case in Londoner. However, an adjudicatory hearing was not considered necessary in *Bi-Metallic Investment Company v. State Board of Equalization* (1915). In this instance, the State Board of Equalization and the Colorado Tax Commission increased property taxes by 40 percent. Claiming a property interest, the petitioner filed suit contending that property cannot be taken without due process, thereby meriting an adjudicatory hearing. According to the Supreme Court, since the tax increase was applicable to all taxable property, it impacted more than a limited number of individuals. Given this fact, individualized hearings are not necessary in accordance with due process protections.

> "Politicians are the same all over. They promise to build a bridge even where there is no river."
>
> **NIKITA KHRUSHCHEV**
> Former Soviet Leader
> (1894–1971)

Due process protections apply to public sector employees, as well. Public employees wrongly terminated may file suit in accordance with the due process clauses of the Fifth and Fourteenth amendments provided they are able to establish a liberty or property interest. In this context, a property interest coincides with the expectation of future employment (for example, a contract or tenure). A liberty interest can be established under the following conditions: (1) A public employee's superior has openly discussed the reasons for that employee's firing, thereby damaging that individual's reputation and compromising his or her ability to gain future employment. This is precisely why public university professors not receiving tenure are rarely, if ever, told why. (2) The reason for a public employee's termination was the exercise of a constitutionally protected right (notably, First Amendment protections of free speech, assembly, and exercise of religion).

In *Hale v. Walsh* (1987), Hale was the untenured chair of the Department of History at Idaho State University. He was threatened with termination given his refusal to change the grade of a student related to a former dean at the university. Aware of his inability to establish a property interest because of his untenured position (and therefore having no expectation of continued employment), Hale attempted to establish a liberty interest by becoming involved in union activities. As a union leader, he made a speech critical of the university president. When subsequently dismissed, Hale argued that he was fired for exercising his constitutionally protected right to free speech, which would theoretically constitute a liberty in accordance with the due process clause. However, he was ultimately unsuccessful in establishing a liberty interest.

Unlike Hale, the petitioner in *Pickering v. Board of Education* (1968) was able to establish a liberty interest. Specifically, *Pickering* was a public school teacher who was terminated for writing a letter to the editor criticizing the board of education and the superintendent of schools for their support of a local bond issue. The issue before the Supreme Court was whether public school teachers may be penalized for First Amendment acts that do not impair their job or the institution. The Court held that an individual's First Amendment rights may be restricted in instances when they interfere with the operation and administration of schools within the district. According to the justices, however, Pickering's letter to the editor failed to interfere in this regard. His termination resulted from the exercise of a constitutionally protected right, thereby establishing a liberty interest in accordance with due process protections.

Administrative Expediency v. Search and Seizure Protections

Consistent with the letter of the Fourth Amendment, individuals have the right to be "secure in their persons, houses, papers, and effects against unreasonable searches and seizures, and no warrants shall issue, but upon probable cause...particularly describing the place to be searched and the person or things to be seized."

The Pendleton Act Provides Civil Service Reform: 1883.

Image Source: Smith, Carter, ed. American Historical Images on File: Key Issues in Constitutional History. New York: Facts on File, 1988.

Accordingly, warrantless searches and seizures are deemed "unreasonable" (Cann 1998, p. 142). The intent of the Fourth Amendment has since served as a means of controlling bureaucratic discretion within the context of information gathering pursuant to the implementation of redistributive or regulatory policies. For example, in *Marshall v. Barlow's, Inc.* (1979), the issue before the Supreme Court was whether a warrant is necessary for administrative searches of industries, assuming there is an absence of criminal charges. The majority held that agencies conducting inspections must obtain a warrant. The rationale for the majority opinion rests on the contention that a warrant, in accordance with the protections vested in the Fourth Amendment, offers proprietors assurances that agency inspections are reasonable. According to the majority opinion, "the authority to make warrantless searches devolves almost unbridled discretion upon executive and administrative officers, particularly those in the field, as to when to search and whom to search" (*Marshall v. Barlow's, Inc.*, as cited in Cann 1998, p. 155). The warrant requirement ultimately protects against the arbitrary exercise of bureaucratic discretion.

> "Bureaucracy is not an obstacle to democracy but an inevitable complement to it."
>
> **JOSEPH A. SCHUMPETER**
> Austrian Economist; Political Scientist (1883–1950)

In *Wyman v. James* (1971), an Aid to Families with Dependent Children (AFDC, a form of welfare) recipient was informed that her home would be visited by a caseworker. While the petitioner offered to provide all relevant information, she refused to allow the caseworker to visit. Subsequently, the petitioner's AFDC benefits were terminated. The petitioner sought injunctive relief, claiming that the caseworker's visit violated the Fourth Amendment, and therefore there was no justification for the termination of her benefits. The Supreme Court needed to decide whether a state agency violates the Fourth Amendment by preconditioning AFDC benefits to home visits. According to the majority, the caseworker's visit was not thought to be a "search" within the context of the Fourth Amendment. Furthermore, even if the visit could be considered a search, it was not unreasonable as it served a valid administrative purpose regarding the dispensation of AFDC benefits (verifying the care of children).

In addition to conducting physical inspections, agencies sometimes use subpoenas to obtain information. The case of the *Federal Trade Commission (FTC) v. American Tobacco Company* (1924) addresses administrative subpoena powers. In this instance, the issue was whether Congress intended to afford the FTC the power to subpoena any information it deemed useful. The Supreme Court held that while the FTC has the authority to subpoena documentary evidence related to a matter under investigation, so-called fishing expeditions remain unjustified. In *Oklahoma Press Publishing v. Walling* (1946), the petitioners claimed that a subpoena issued in accordance with the Fair Labor Practices Act (FLPA) violated the Fourth Amendment. The issue was whether Congress authorized an agency to subpoena nonevidentiary subject matter pursuant to an investigation. According to the majority opinion, the subpoena was thought to be reasonable and germane to the Labor Department's mission, and therefore there was no constitutional breach. That is, employee records were subpoenaed, and consistent with the FLPA, the secretary of Labor has the authority to investigate wage and hour violations.

The Supreme Court attempts to balance the bureaucracy's need to obtain information against the rights of the citizenry. Specifically, within the context of an administrative inspection, a warrant is required where there is a "reasonable expectation of privacy," which coincides with the case of *Barlow's, Inc.* (Cann 1998, p. 162). In *Wyman*, however, an individual receiving AFDC benefits is subjected to warrantless home inspections pursuant to an administrative purpose (verifying the care of children). With respect to administrative subpoena powers, subpoenas can be used to obtain information relevant to an agency's mission and scope of authority, which was the Court's rationale in *Walling*. However, administrative subpoena powers cannot be used to justify fishing expeditions, which was the basis for Court's ruling in *FTC v. American Tobacco*.

Torts as a Bureaucratic Check

In accordance with the notion of sovereign immunity, the government cannot be sued unless it allows itself to be sued. While seemingly monarchical and antithetical to fundamental democratic tenets, sovereign immunity is justified given the assumption that if the government suffers through litigation, then the citizenry will ultimately suffer. However, the Federal Tort Claims Act has altered the dynamic regarding sovereign immunity, as it allows the federal government to be sued under similar circumstances as private citizens. The act, however, contains a number of notable exceptions.

Despite the statutory provisions of the Federal Tort Claims Act, government functions that are discretionary in nature are exempt from tort litigation. The rationale for this exemption is based on the notion that without sovereign immunity coinciding with discretionary actions, the government may discharge its duties in an overly cautious and timid manner. The mere prospect of litigation could have a chilling effect. For example, without discretionary immunity, law enforcement officers may not aggressively pursue suspected criminals for fear of civil liability resulting from, say, a car accident.

While discretionary governmental functions are immune from liability, there are exceptions. In *Bivens v. Six Unknown Named Agents* (1971), Bivens claimed that agents of the Federal Bureau of Narcotics entered his home, placed him in hand shackles, and searched his apartment without a warrant or probable cause. Bivens sought damages, and the Supreme Court held that an individual is entitled to sue federal law enforcement agents (as opposed to the agency) for damages given Fourth

Amendment violations. According to some constitutional scholars, *Bivens* created what has become known as "qualified immunity." That is, while certain officials—judges, prosecutors, the president—are afforded total immunity, the majority of government officials and street-level bureaucrats may be sued for egregious constitutional infringements (Cann 1998; Barry and Whitcomb 1987). The precedent set forth in *Bivens* was taken further in *Butz v. Economou* (1978), whereby the Court held that citizens have grounds to file suit against federal officials in instances when "the officials knew or should have known that the official's action would violate a citizen's constitutional rights" (Cann 1998, p. 394). The *Butz* ruling essentially made it easier for citizens to sue federal bureaucrats, thereby serving as a check against potential abuses of bureaucratic discretion.

> "To the victor belongs the spoils."
>
> **WILLIAM L. MARCY**
> New York Senator

Given the aforementioned discussion, one may assume that the U.S. Supreme Court takes an activist role in checking the power of the bureaucracy. While this assumption is debatable, potential litigants must overcome a number of barriers before a case or controversy is given consideration. Standing proves to be a noteworthy barrier. According to Barry and Whitcomb (1987), standing "involves the question of whether a party has sufficient interest in a controversy to bring an action in court" (p. 90). Establishing standing requires the following conditions: (1) injury or the imminent likelihood of injury, (2) the violation of a constitutional principle, and (3) the presence of redressability. For example, in *Allen v. Wright et al.* (1984), the Wrights sued the Internal Revenue Service for providing tax-exempt status to racially segregated private academies, which is a violation of the Internal Revenue Code. Since the Wrights made no attempt to enroll their children at one of these academies, there was no injury, and therefore the Wrights had no standing.

The doctrine of primary jurisdiction serves as another potential barrier to litigation. Primary jurisdiction involves the question of whether a case or controversy would be better settled in a court or by a bureaucracy. The courts will typically defer to agencies in instances where agency expertise overrides the courts or in the interest of regulatory uniformity (Barry and Whitcomb 1987; Cann 1998). *Nader v. Allegheny Airlines* (1976) is a notable primary jurisdiction case. Specifically, consumer activist Ralph Nader filed suit against the Allegheny Airlines claiming its overbooking practices constituted fraudulent misrepresentation in accordance with the Federal Aviation Act of 1958. The issue before the Supreme Court was whether the Civil Aeronautics Board (CAB) has primary jurisdiction to determine if overbooking practices constitute fraudulent misrepresentation. The Court declared that the CAB does not have primary jurisdiction, as the courts are more than capable of rendering a decision related to statutory interpretations. Hypothetically speaking, had *Allegheny* dealt with issues of regulatory uniformity or expertise, the Court would have deferred to the CAB.

Additionally, a petitioner's claim is unlikely to be given consideration until all administrative appeals have been exhausted. That is, one must exhaust "all legal remedies within an agency" before the Supreme Court will hear a case or controversy regarding agency action (Cann 1998, p. 117). Exhaustion affords agencies the first opportunity to address a dispute, thereby decreasing the likelihood of litigation. Other barriers that litigants must overcome include ripeness and jurisdiction, which is not to be confused with primary jurisdiction. Ripeness simply refers to whether a case or controversy is ready to be heard, and it is highly subjective. Regarding jurisdiction, an individual adversely affected by an agency's action must demonstrate that the courts have the "power to resolve" the controversy. In accordance with Article III of the U.S. Constitution, federal courts have the jurisdiction to hear controversies pertaining to constitutional and federal statutory interpretations, in addition to disputes regarding federal agency action, given Congress's constitutional authority to delegate power to agencies. Barriers to litigation are often used to justify judicial inaction. In many instances, the courts use these barriers to avoid addressing cases or controversies that are overly political in nature. Such barriers reduce the frequency of frivolous lawsuits, thereby preventing the courts from becoming overburdened. This ideally gives the courts the latitude to hear more exigent disputes.

The inherent value conflict between administrative bureaucracy and democratic governance exists on several levels. Bureaucracies are synonymous with a managerial approach, which is predicated on a hierarchical structure, formalization, and uniform procedures that are carried out impersonally. Representative bodies are political in nature, which suggests a certain measure of transparency and accountability. Expertise is the hallmark of a bureaucracy, which affords bureaucrats a monopoly of power. Bureaucracies are closed systems that execute policies in a technical, rationalist manner. This is arguably antithetical to the nature of democratic institutions, which ideally emphasize openness and citizen participation. The president's inability to control the bureaucracy effectively, coupled with Congress's symbiotic relationship with the bureaucracy, necessitates judicial vigilance. And while the nation's High Court serves as a reactive and often reluctant arbiter, its holdings guide the bureaucracy so as to ensure that bureaucratic actions do not run counter to the letter and spirit of the Constitution.

CHECKS AND BALANCES: ARE THEY GOOD INTENTIONS TO SUPPORT GOVERNMENT? OR DO THEY HAMPER GOVERNMENT PERFORMANCE?

As mentioned in chapter 5, it is impossible to imagine government operations outside of the political environment. Although scholars and practitioners following the Wilsonian tradition have tried to argue that government can be efficient and effective in the areas where politics can be excluded, it is difficult to identify the areas where government activities are free from politics. Please read the two articles and discuss how the political environment can contribute to increasing government performance. Although it does seem that the two countries are not so different from each other in terms of the relationship between government and political parties, there might be some differences in the government–politics relationship based on each country's different history. Try to identify these differences and explain what caused the worst situation in each case.

Do you believe political environments are barriers to government performance? Do you think a democratic system where checks and balances are regarded as an important principle ironically prevents governments from serving their citizens?

Case 1: Conflict over school free meal program deepens

By Kwon Mee–yoo

The conflict is deepening between Seoul Mayor Oh Se–hoon and district council chiefs, mostly belonging to the opposition Democratic Party, over providing free meals to primary and secondary school students.

Goh Jae–deuk, the Seongdong District head and chairman of the ward chiefs association, held a press conference denouncing Seoul City's decision not to allocate a budget for the provision of free meals.

His condemnation came days after the city government distributed some 145 billion won for next year's educational budget, but did not allocate any money needed to extend the free meal program pushed by the Seoul Metropolitan Office of Education and district offices.

(continued)

(continued)

"This is obviously a rejection of the free school meal program, not that the city government is short of money," Goh said.

The Seoul education office, led by liberal superintendent Kwak No-hyun, compiled a budget of 116 billion won, half of the amount needed for providing free school lunches to all primary school students in Seoul. The education office asked for the municipal government to share 30 percent, while district offices are responsible for the remaining 20 percent.

"However, the city refused to pay their share for free meal services," Goh said. Seoul City explained Friday that it is continuing the discussion about the free school meal program with the metropolitan council and education office.

It also said the claim of no budget for the free meal plan by some media outlets is not true. "We drew up the 27.8 billion won budget for free school lunches for 62,000 students, which accounts for some 5 percent of the total number of students. We also allotted a 46.3 billion won budget to raise the quality of the school meal service including 15 billion won for better ingredients and 3.3 billion won for ovens," a city official said.

Source: the Korea Times, Nov 12, 2010, accessed at http://www.koreatimes.co.kr/www/news/nation/2010/11/113_76241.html

Case 2: Government Shutdown

The 2006 New Jersey state government shutdown was the first shutdown in the history of the U.S. state of New Jersey. The shutdown occurred after the New Jersey Legislature and Governor Jon Corzine failed to agree on a state budget by the constitutional deadline. Furthermore, Corzine and the Legislature clashed on the issue of raising the state sales tax to help balance budget. Exercising his constitutional powers as governor, Corzine ordered the shutdown as a means of pressuring the Legislature to pass a budget. The shutdown beganat midnight on July 1, 2006, when Corzine called for an orderly shutdown of non-essential government services, which was followed by a second round of shutdowns three days later on July 4.

The shutdown officially concluded after the legislature adopted a budget on July 8, 2006. All government services were restored by 8:30 am on July 10, 2006.

Source: http://en.wikipedia.org/wiki/2006_New_Jersey_state_government_shutdown

KEY TERMS

Administrative discretion

Administrative law

Distributive policies

Due process

Iron triangle

Redistributive policies

Search and seizure protection

Street-level bureaucrats

Tort

Welfare state

REFERENCES

Appleby, P. 1949. *Policy and Administration*. Tuscaloosa: University of Alabama Press.

Arnold, P.E. 1986. *Making the Administrative Presidency: Comprehensive Reorganization Planning, 1905–1980*. Princeton, NJ: Princeton University Press.

Barry, D.D., and H.R. Whitcomb. 1987. *The Legal Foundations of Public Administration*. St. Paul, MN: West Publishing Company.

Cann, Steven J. 1998. *Administrative Law*. Thousands Oaks, CA: Sage Publications.

Holzer, M., and V. Gabrielian. 1998. "Five Great Ideas in American Public Administration." In *Handbook of Public Administration*, ed. J. Rabin, W.B. Hildreth, and G.J. Miller. New York: Marcel Dekker.

Kerwin, C.M. 1994. *Rulemaking: How Government Agencies Write Law and Make Policy*. Washington, DC: CQ Press.

Key, V.O. 1940. "The Lack of a Budgetary Theory." *American Political Science Review* 34 (December).

Lipsky, M. 1980. *Street-Level Bureaucracy*. New York: Russell Sage Foundation.

Long, N.E. 1949. "Power and Administration." *Public Administration Review* 9: 257–64.

Lowi, T.J. 1979. *The End of Liberalism: The Second Republic of United States*. 2d ed. New York: W.W. Norton.

Maranto, R. 1993. *Politics and Bureaucracy in the Modern Presidency: Careerists and Appointees in the Reagan Administration*. Westport, CT: Greenwood Press.

Nathan, R. 1975. *The Plot That Failed: Nixon and the Administrative Presidency*. New York: John Wiley and Sons.

Riley, D.D. 1987. *Controlling the Federal Bureaucracy*. Philadelphia, PA: Temple University Press.

Rohr, J. 1986. *To Run a Constitution: The Legitimacy of the Administrative State*. Lawrence, KS: University Press of Kansas.

Seidman, H. 1980. *Politics, Position, and Power: The Dynamics of Federal Organization*. Oxford, U.K.: Oxford University Press.

Selznick, P.A. 1949. *TVA and the Grass Roots*. New York: Harper and Row.

Simon, H.A. 1947/1997. *Administrative Behavior*. New York: Simon and Schuster.

———. 1967. "The Changing Theory and Changing Practice of Public Administration." In *Contemporary Political Science: Towards Empirical Theory*, ed. I. de Sola Pool. New York: McGraw-Hill.

Waldo, D. 1984. *The Administrative State*. 2d ed. New York: Holmes and Meier.

Warren, K. 1993. "We Have Debated Ad Nauseam the Legitimacy of the Administrative State—But Why?" *Public Administration Review* 53, no. 3: 249–253.

Wildavsky, A. 1992. "Political Implications of Budget Reform: A Retrospective." *Public Administration Review* 52 (November): 594–99.

SUPPLEMENTARY READINGS

Riccucci, N. 1995. *Unsung Heroes: Federal Execucrats Making a Difference*. Washington, DC: Georgetown University Press.

Rosenbloom, D.H. 1987. "Public Administrators and the Judiciary: The 'New Partnership.'" *Public Administration Review* 47, no. 1: 75–83.

ELECTRONIC RESOURCES

OMB Watch (a nonprofit research and advocacy organization): http://www.ombwatch.org/

American Civil Liberties Union (an interest group agency): http://www.aclu.org

Guide to Administrative Law—HG.org, Worldwide Legal Directories: http://www.hg.org/adm.html

CASE CITATIONS

Allen v. Wright et al. (1984). 468 U.S. 737.

Bi-Metallic Investment Company v. State Board of Equalization (1915). 239 U.S. 441.

Bivens v. Six Unknown Named Agents (1971). 403 U.S. 388.

Butz v. Economou (1978). 438 U.S. 478.

Federal Trade Commission (FTC) v. American Tobacco Company (1924). 264 U.S. 298.

Goldberg v. Kelly (1970). 397 U.S. 254.

Goss v. Lopez (1975). 419 U.S. 565.

Hale v. Walsh (1987). 747 P.2D 1288.

Hampton v. United States (1928). 276 U.S. 394.

Industrial Union Department AFL-CIO v. American Petroleum (1980). 488 U.S. 607.

Londoner v. Denver (1908). 210 U.S. 373.

Marshall v. Barlow's, Inc. (1979). 436 U.S. 307.

Matthews v. Eldridge (1976). 424 U.S. 319.

Nader v. Allegheny Airlines (1976). 426 U.S. 290.

Oklahoma Press Publishing v. Walling (1946). 327 U.S. 186.

Pickering v. Board of Education (1968). 391 U.S. 563.

Wyman v. James (1971). 400 U.S. 309.

CHAPTER 6

Intergovernmental Relations

The term intergovernmental relations refers to the collaborative dynamic, or working relationships, that exist among all levels of government—national, state, and local. The U.S. Constitution created what is called a Federalist system of government. A Federalist system consists of a centralized national government that has jurisdiction over the nation as a whole, while at the same time sharing power and responsibility and working in concert with smaller subnational governmental units at the state, county, and municipal levels. This chapter delves into the complex workings of the American Federalist system and examines a growing aspect of intergovernmental relations at the local level—that being interlocal shared services. The chapter concludes with a discussion of intragovernmental and intergovernmental competition as a means of improving performance.

"We're hearing how Pennsylvania municipalities are furloughing employees, cutting services or taking other drastic measures to pay their bills...If they shared services, the financial pain would not be so great."

KEN KLOTHEN
Pennsylvania Department of Community and Economic Development

Source: www.cartoonstock.com

THE LAYERS OF GOVERNMENT

The Idea of Federalism

The U.S. Federalist system created several layers of government. A number of models are used to explain how the Federalist system works; among them are the layer cake, the marble cake, and the picket fence models. The *layer cake model* envisions separate and distinct areas of authority between the national, state, and local governments. For example, this model assumes that the national government (that is, U.S. Congress and the president) is primarily responsible for defending the nation, engaging in international diplomacy, and regulating interstate commerce. State governments are primarily responsible for overseeing education and infrastructure such as building bridges and roads. Local governments, which include county and municipal governments, are responsible for public safety, emergency services, and waste removal.

The *marble cake model* assumes that there are few hard-and-fast lines of distinction as to what constitutes national, state, or local responsibilities. Like a marble cake, governmental responsibilities are, at times, swirled or mixed. For example, while defense would still fall under the domain of the national government, education could potentially involve all three layers of government.

The *picket fence model* of the Federalist system is characterized by close fiscal relationships among the national, state, and local governments. These fiscal relationships emerged given the national government's strong tax base, one that is less affected by the hills and valleys of a fluctuating economy, coupled with the presumption that state and local officials are in a better position to spend money in a manner that is responsive to their citizens. The picket fence model relies on grants-in-aid programs: the national government provides grants (that is, transfers of tax money collected by the Internal Revenue Service) to the states, a portion of which is further filtered down to the county and municipal governments. In some cases, the national government provides grants directly to local governments. These grants not only help the state and local governments to finance necessary activities and programs but also create working relationships among national, state, and local public servants who share common policy concerns. In the picket fence model, the pickets (or vertical slats) represent policy or functional areas that tie together bureaucratic specialists throughout the various levels of government (represented by the three horizontal slats).

There are two types of federal grants: categorical and block grants. Federal *categorical grants* are funds that must be used for very specific purposes. For example, if the national government gives a categorical grant to a state for highway construction, then that state is required to use that money in a way deemed appropriate by the agency that granted it—in this case, the U.S. Department of Transportation. With categorical grants, clearly defined rules and regulations dic-

FIGURE 6.1 – MODELS OF FEDERALISM

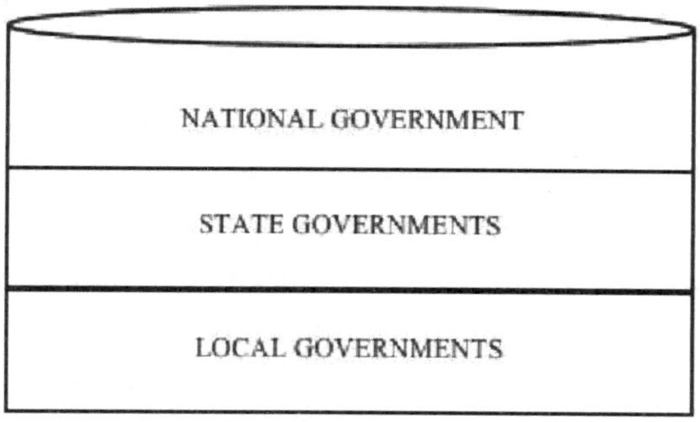

Layer Cake Model: This model envisions separate and distinct areas of authority between the levels of government; no level intrudes upon the others.

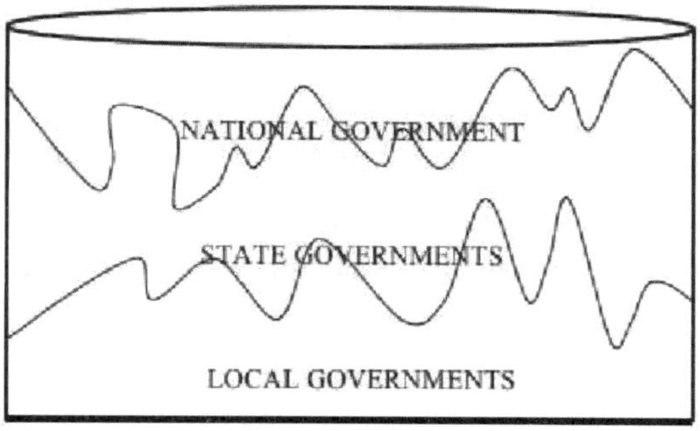

Marble Cake Model: This model assumes that there are few distinct areas that are strictly national, state, or local per se. Education, for example, is one policy area where all levels of government have concerns.

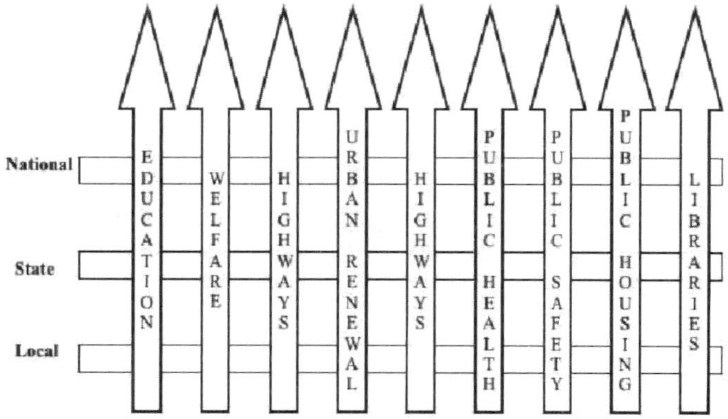

Picket Fence Model: This model is characterized by close fiscal relationships among the various levels of government, as well as the recognition that public servants from all levels of government have similar policy concerns regardless of the level of government.

tate how the money may be spent; there are strings attached and hoops to jump through, and for these reasons, state and local governments tend to prefer *block grants*. Block grants gained popularity in the Nixon era (1969–1974). They afford the states much more freedom in determining how grant money will be spent. Most notably, the Personal Responsibility and Work Opportunity Reconciliation Act (PRWORA) of 1996 implemented a block grant approach to reforming welfare. PRWORA replaced Aid to Families with Dependent Children (AFDC) with Temporary Assistance to Needy Families (TANF). Through TANF, the national government provides a lump sum of money to the states, and from there, each state determines its own eligibility requirements and regulations. Through the TANF block grant system, welfare became much more decentralized than under the old system, meaning that power has shifted away from the national government and to the states. Some observers have criticized this particular approach to welfare, arguing that the block grant system creates a "race to the bottom" as states seek to lower their TANF benefits to avoid becoming "welfare magnets." In other words, by having better benefits, states are fearful that they will attract more welfare recipients.

Interlocal Shared Government

Pubic demands for doing more with less, promoting public organizations that are efficient and effective, and bolstering citizen trust through improved governmental responsiveness have engendered interest in interlocal *shared service agreements*. State governments are exploring interlocal shared service agreements in order to re-

FIGURE 6.2 – POTENTIAL SHARED SERVICE OUTCOMES

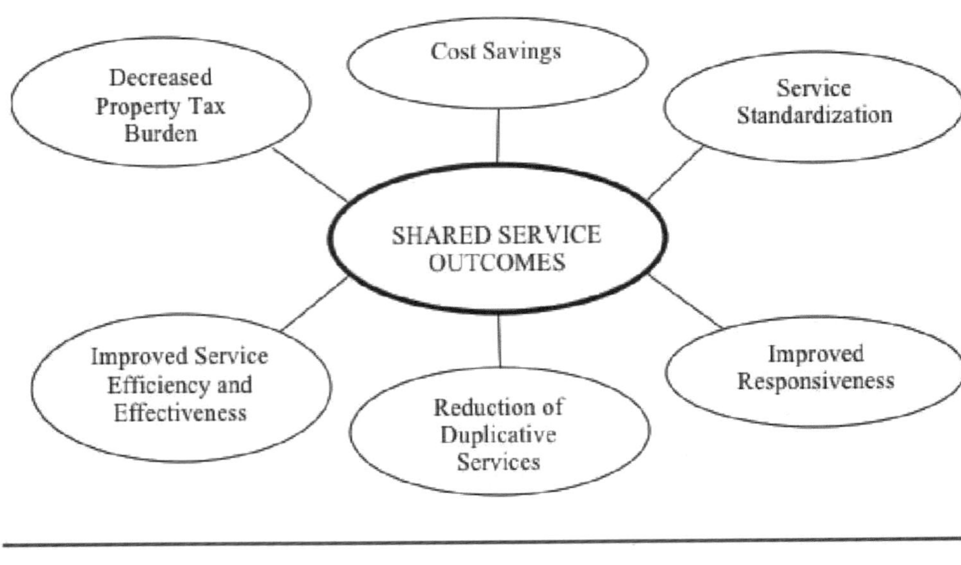

duce service delivery costs and ease the tax burden on their citizens while simultaneously streamlining local services, doing away with duplicative services, and enhancing governmental responsiveness.

Types of Shared Services

Sharing Personnel

Sharing personnel is a straightforward concept. Smaller governmental units such as municipalities and small cities recognize that while specific governmental functions must be performed, sometimes there is simply not "enough work" to require a full-time employee. While this dilemma may be resolved by having one worker handle multiple functions, such a solution is not sensible when the functions require specific technical or professional skills. Part-time workers commonly fill these positions, which include posts like certified assessor, certified municipal finance officer, or zoning officer. Cost is one advantage of the part-time employee option, but other problems come to pass, namely management control, pubic availability, and accountability. Sharing personnel with other jurisdictions may provide a better solution, but it requires planning and cooperation among the jurisdictions involved. Shared staff is preferable to the use of part-time staff due largely to increased accountability over an individual managed by more than one municipality.

> "Government compares favorably to the private sector in characteristics and performance, particularly when it is called upon to achieve what other sectors of the society could not achieve. Government works."
>
> **CHARLES GOODSELL**
> Virginia Polytechnic Institute and State University

Sharing Equipment

Sharing equipment represents a partner model in which ownership is shared by each community owning an individual part of the entire piece of equipment. For example, a piece of equipment known as the "Ditch Master" is owned jointly by the townships of Franklin, Bridgewater, and Montgomery in New Jersey. Each township has one-third ownership of the device, which is used to remove debris from roadside drain ditches. Franklin Township provides for upkeep and stores the Ditch Master, given that it has large garage and a number of trained mechanics. Bridgewater Township holds the escrow account of rental fees when neighboring municipalities contract to use the Ditch Master. Fees collected are used to offset maintenance costs (Hester 2000).

Sharing Internal Services

Sharing internal services is ideal when the service function requires little interaction with the public. A prime example is the shared animal shelter in Maplewood and South Orange, two municipalities in New Jersey. To the individual municipality, this is similar to a relationship with a private vendor. The difference, however, is that all communities have a vested interest in making the relationship succeed. The shared service agreement benefits all participants who are acting collectively.

Sharing External Services

External services refer to agreements in which one governmental unit consents to provide essential services to another that no longer provides such services. An alternative arrangement entails two or more governmental units consolidating services into a single regional service delivery system. These shared service arrangements may involve regional fire and police, public works departments, and waste disposal. External shared service models are pursued in the interest of saving money and improving service quality. It is believed that cost savings are the result of economies of scale (Staley et al. 2005), which is a principle that assumes larger organizational units are able to provide comparable service quality but at a lower cost. That is, a larger, shared sanitation department will keep the streets just as clean as a smaller, independent sanitation department—but at a lower public cost.

Shared Service Examples

Shared service efforts are being explored in the hopes of cutting service delivery costs, reducing tax burdens, and improving governmental responsiveness through better services. For example, in California, the cities of Moreno Valley and Riverside reached an agreement in 1996 to jointly construct a shared fire station instead of constructing separate, independent stations separated by only one mile. Sharing a fire station saves an estimated $750, 000 in capital and operating costs annually. Serving the western part of the Moreno Valley and the Canyon Crest and Canyon Springs areas of Riverside, the shared station has been responsible for significantly reducing response times; for example, the response time to the Canyon Springs area of Riverside has decreased from fifteen minutes to five (U.S. Conference of Mayors 1997).

The North Hudson Regional Fire and Rescue Department, a shared service initiative created in 1999, serves 200,000 residents throughout five New Jersey municipalities—Guttenberg, North Bergen, Union City, Weehawken, and West New York. This regional department has saved each municipality about $5 million in service costs annually. It has also created a more responsive and efficient fire department. Not long after its creation, firefighters rushed to a house fire in a neighborhood of West New York. Fire stations in the municipalities of Weehawken and North Bergen were actually closer to this house fire than stations in West New York. In this case, removing municipal boundaries allowed firefighters to respond faster and therefore better ensure the safety of West New York residents (Smothers 1999).

The Pine-Marshall-Bradford Woods joint police force represents another groundbreaking shared service model. The small Pennsylvania communities of Pine, Marshall, and Bradford Woods merged their police forces in 1969. Consolidation has enabled these communities to support an 18-member police force. This includes a detective—a resource not afforded to most small communities (Barcousky 2005). Several communities in the United States have since emulated the Pine-Marshall-Bradford Woods model to capture improvements in safety and service quality, most specifically: an improved police presence and officer coverage; improved training; and more opportunities for officers to specialize.

Sanitation and public works departments have become opportunities for shared

– WE'VE GOT PLURALISM! ONE TRAFFIC LIGHT IS RUN BY THE CITY, ANOTHER BY THE REGION, AND A THIRD ONE BY THE DISTRICT
Artist: V. Uborevich-Borovsky (caption: A. Gostiushin)
Cover of *Krokodil* [*Crocodile*] satirical magazine, 1991, No. 23.

services, as well. Most notably, the Wisconsin counties of Outagamie, Winnebago, and Brown merged their waste disposal and recycling departments in 2003. This multicounty agreement projects cost savings of $35 million over 25 years for waste disposal, and $8 million over 12 years for recycling (Tom 2003). The bridge maintenance program in Chautauqua County, New York, is a collaborative effort between the County Department of Public Facilities and the municipalities within the county. The bridge maintenance program was established to ensure bridge and roadway safety. When established, 62 percent of the county's 488 bridges were in need of significant repair and 69 bridges were impassable or weight restricted by the State Department of Transportation. By pooling municipal and county resources, bridge conditions within the county improved significantly. For example, when the bridge program was introduced in 1988, 55 percent of the county's bridges were considered "deficient," compared to 34 percent eight years later (Hattery 1996).

> "Doing more with less is an impressive sound bite... Politicians looking for a quick fix and corporations looking to make quick profits are promoting privatization as the magic answer to government deficit problems... Privatization is undermining the public services that bind us together and underpin the foundations or our democracy."
>
> **JUDY DARCY**
> President, Canadian Union Public Employees

Communities are seeking better parks and recreational opportunities through shared service agreements. Due to limited resources, the village of Pewaukee, Wisconsin could provide recreational services only during the summer months. The neighboring city of Pewaukee provided recreational services year-round, yet its director of recreation was employed only part-time. The village and city ultimately combined their recreation departments, forming the Pewaukee Joint Parks and Recreation Department. Village residents were provided year-round recreational services, while the city gained a full-time director of recreation. This agreement has been credited with enhancing parks and recreational services for both municipalities, in addition to reducing operating costs (Johnson 2006).

In the interest of enhanced library services, the municipality of Chula Vista, California, cooperated with the Sweetwater Union High School District. The jointly supported East Lake Branch Library was established in 1993. For the students and residents of Chula Vista, the shared municipal and school district resources afford library users a more comprehensive and up-to-date book collection than could otherwise be provided without this agreement (Repard 1993).

State Financial Support to Encourage Shared Services

The prospects of cost savings and improved services have prompted many states to establish funding streams that encourage intergovernmental shared service initiatives. For instance, the New Jersey Department of Community Affairs created a program known as Sharing Available Resources Efficiently (SHARE). The SHARE program provides municipal and county governments with feasibility or implementation grants. Typically in the range of $20,000, feasibility grants help governments with the planning and developing stages of shared service initiatives. Implementation grants of up to $200,000 help governments cover costs associated with putting a shared service arrangement into action (SHARE 2006).

New York established a program called the Shared Municipal Service Incentive program (SMSI), which is a $25 million program designed to help municipalities consolidate local government services. For municipalities that want to consolidate into one government unit, grants of up to $1 million are offered to offset the upfront costs of consolidation. Grants of up to $300,000 are available for countywide-shared service programs (NYSAC 2006).

The Department of Community and Economic Development for the State of Pennsylvania created the *Shared Municipal Services Program* (SMSP). Grants are provided ranging from $10,000 to $25,000 for intermunicipal agreements that promote cooperation (SMSP 2005), including but not limited to:

- Sharing technology
- Municipal insurance cooperatives
- Sharing public works departments
- Sharing recreation services
- Sharing code enforcement operations
- Sharing equipment

EXERCISE 6.1

Emergency Management and Homeland Security Plan (Simulation)

Collaboration is a key learning objective in this role-play simulation. Students become members of an intergovernmental agency task force commissioned to create an emergency response plan for their city. After reviewing the task, groups of six students will draft a plan for emergency response, including a public relations effort strategy that involves local citizens. After completing this simulation, teams will present their plans to the class.

David E. Booher and Adam Sutkus, E-PARCC, Program for the Advancement of Research on Conflict and Collaboration, The Maxwell School, Syracuse University http://sites.maxwell.syr.edu/parc/eparc/simulations/booher-sutkus.asp

There are three main obstacles that impede the implementation of shared service initiatives: (1) shared service proposals are typically opposed by union, civil service, and tenured government employees; (2) local residents may oppose shared service proposals given insufficient information regarding the potential benefits; and (3) local community officials may fear losing total control over specific service areas. The loss of "home rule" is a significant psychological obstacle, making the shared service model particularly difficult for states having large numbers of independent governmental units. New Jersey is a prime example, with 566 municipalities, 611 school districts, 212 fire service districts, and 21 counties packed within a relatively small geographic area. In overcoming these obstacles, states must take the lead in encouraging interlocal and regional service, perhaps through grant programs that support feasibility studies and help to offset implementation costs. Accurately and routinely measuring and disseminating cost savings and service delivery improvements of shared service initiatives is important as well.

Improving Performance via Intragovernmental and Intergovernmental Competition

Government should not be cast aside. Government must learn to compete with the private sector. Public organizations might compete for government contracts against one another and against private-sector organizations as well. The debate regarding *privatization*—employing the private sector or nonprofit sectors to do the work of government—is based on the following premise: what the citizenry, private businesses, and policymakers truly desire is productivity. Those who embrace privatization have underscored the importance of high performance, defined in the context of efficiency and effectiveness. Champions of government underscore less tangible and more value-oriented impacts. However, advocates of both privatization and government must address each other's concerns. In other words, government services that are privatized must be responsive to the public, and services delivered by government must be done so efficiently and effectively. Competition has been promoted to the citizenry and to policymakers as the best way of achieving efficiency and effectiveness. Privatization is the type of competition that is talked about most. A main argument advanced by the so-called "guru" of privatization, E.S. Savas, is that "competition, achieved by prudent privatization, is the key to improving the productivity of public agencies and, more broadly, of public programs and public services. . . . Competition must be introduced and institutionalized, and privatization is the technique of choice for accomplishing this" (Savas 1992).

Undoubtedly, competition can improve organizational efficiency and effectiveness. However, linking competition to privatization assumes an overly narrow view of competition. It is important to consider "government as competitor." This idea offers an expanded set of approaches to solving the problem of government performance. The notion of "government as competitor" allows for intragovernmental competition in the delivery of public services as a substitute for private-sector delivery. There are at least three approaches to competitive government:

1. *Dye's Competitive Federalism.* T.R. Dye's approach (1990) deals with competition among units of government. Individuals are capable of "voting with their feet." This simply means that, when economically feasible, individuals have the freedom to live where specific services are provided or where a certain degree of service quality is provided. People can choose a specific town, state, or even country in which to live. The dynamics of competitive federalism can be seen quite often in debates about public school quality. Families with school-age children will often move to municipalities that have high-performing schools. On the other hand, empty nesters or singles may want to live where school taxes are relatively low. Although Dye's model of intragovernmental competition is valid, whether between states or localities, it has done little to create the image of government as competitor. Thus, it fails to establish government's claim to manage scarce resources better than other providers.

> "One of the major changes taking place today in government management (federal, state, and local) is the shift from the government as the historic 'provider' of public services to the government as the 'manager of providers' of services to the public."
>
> **JACQUES S. GANSLER**
> Educator; Corporate Director; Political Appointee

2. *Public v. Private Competition.* Under this longstanding but less familiar concept, services are "contracted in" to government rather than "contracted out" to private or nonprofit organizations. In Phoenix, Arizona (Holzer 1991), the Department of Public Works "won back" services it had contracted out by lowering service costs. The department's Competition with Privatization program utilized nontraditional approaches to competing with private-sector organizations. Other jurisdictions—New Orleans, Kansas City (MO), Newark (NJ), Oklahoma City, and Minneapolis—have competed with the private sector for sanitation services (Savas 1992). Although Savas contends that government "should be given an opportunity to compete with the private firms in an even-handed bidding process" (1992), he is rather cynical about the impact of contracting in within the United States. However, he does describe effective competitive bidding by government agencies throughout the United Kingdom .

3. *Public vs. Public Competition.* Governmental units compete to provide services appropriate only to the public sector. The model described next is developed according to the public-private and public-public concepts.

An Expanded Model of Governmental Competition

Public administration scholars accept privatization given the assumption that governments are altogether ill equipped to provide certain services in any capacity, much less high-quality services. Even more accept the premise that government monopolies are intrinsically inefficient. According to Savas (1992):

> A government agency that enjoys a monopoly or is otherwise shielded from competition can be expected to behave no differently than a private monopoly: Without the spur of competition, managers and workers alike generally lack the motivation to innovate, to seek better ways, to make changes, to work smarter or harder, or to increase productivity.

There are inherent weaknesses in the argument that privatization is the only solution to government inefficiency and ineffectiveness, in addition to being the only source of competition for government. First, using private providers does not ensure meaningful competition. Second, in a growing number of cases, private contractors have failed to provide public-sector services at a level promised. Third, there is a growing database of innovative and successful state and local performance improvement projects. The Exemplary State and Local (EXSL) Awards program database, for example, demonstrates that many public organizations are "businesslike"—in other words, they are competitive. These award winners undermine the stereotypical view that government is inherently inept.

Drawing on government's capacity for innovation, the open competition model of government service delivery is discussed.

1. *Open Competition.* Many services are suitable for contracting out to private or nonprofit organizations. In cases where private organizations are reluctant to bid on a government project, or in cases where collusion is suspected, public-sector bidders represent an important competitive force. In the spirit of maximizing competition, all public organizations—regardless of their place within the government, their jurisdiction, or their mission—should be encouraged to bid on government contracts. A school district, for example, could very well provide maintenance services to a police department. A state highway department could bid on a management services project for a municipal parks department. Many public organizations have the know-how and surplus capacities that cannot be reduced because of technical, financial, or legal reasons. At the same time, if the private sector or nonprofit organizations can do these jobs better, then so be it. Consider that in some European countries, government-owned and private airlines compete for government contracts. In another case, the vehicle maintenance division of the New York City Department of Sanitation won contracts to service city emergency service and police vehicles over private organizations (Holzer 1988).

2. *Open Competition Within Government Only.* Sanitation, training, and maintenance are typical target areas for privatization. Some public-sector functions, however, are relatively intangible and complex, and thus these services are best delivered by public organizations. For public accountability purposes, services such as public safety and law enforcement, public education, social services, public health, air traffic control, and environmental regulation should be under the direction of government-owned contractors without bids from private or nonprofit contractors. To protect democratic and service-delivery capacities, intragovernmental competition may prove ideal. Those bidders might include departments within the contracting organization, other organizations within the same jurisdiction, or organizations at other levels (federal, state, county, or local) of government. In many cases, legislation would be needed to allow public organizations to bid on projects outside the realm of their stated missions. Shared services represent an informal application of this model.

3. *Expanded Capacity for Competition.* To strengthen the competitive forces suggested above, one might hypothesize that government's competitiveness will increase given the introduction of new government-based competitors. The collection of public-sector bidders should be expanded to include more generic agencies or units, the mission of which is improved productivity. "Generic" agencies would be similar to government-based conglomerates or internal consulting firms that would serve a host of functions, ranging from internal capacities (such as maintenance, information services, duplicating, and training) to external capacities (such as housing, education, transportation, or perhaps even defense). These generic government agencies would include public authorities or corporations and ad-hocracy with the ability to incorporate facets of several models, thereby allowing for the flexibility necessary to sustain competition.

"A proponent of aggressive contracting out declares that 'the purpose of local government is not to provide jobs; it is to deliver services to people.' A critic insists upon government's 'socially important role of providing good jobs to people who might otherwise not get them.' Is local service privatization a good thing, or not? The question is as political as a question can be."

JOHN D. DONAHUE
The Privatization Decision, 1989

Public Authorities or Corporations

Construction, transportation, highway, or port authorities and corporations are often created as quasi-independent organizations that have their own revenue sources; therefore, they have greater flexibility in raising the resources needed to accomplish specific tasks. Public authorities and corporations have fewer constraints than regular government organizations, which makes achieving private sector–like efficiency easier. In some cases, authorities and corporations have been asked to expand their missions to contract for other government services.

Ad-hocracy

Regardless of the competitive vehicle—whether it is a new agency, agency sub-unit, authority, or corporation—the nature and resources of this vehicle must be flexible. Using "matrix organizations" and "project management practices" (Halachmi 1989) facilitates the creation of ad hoc—or temporary—work groups to complete tasks typically reserved to public organizations. These work groups have the skills to perform specific tasks for a certain period of time. A work group's size, skills, and other aspects of its performance can be altered to achieve a specific goal. This affords flexibility—the level of which will be comparable to that of similar private-sector groups—and this flexibility will likely foster comparable levels of performance. Adhocracy substitutes an agency-specific civil service career model with a more flexible career option, the latter stemming from an employee's successful completion of other ad hoc assignments in task-specific working groups. More often than not, the assignment of successive ad hoc duties to an employee is based on the past performances of the individual and the working group.

There are a number of advantages to public-sector responses to bid notifications by public organizations. A competitive governmental environment should:

1. Encourage greater managerial innovation, thereby making the jobs of managers and workers more appealing.
2. Improve the use of available information resources. Far too many public

EXERCISE 6.2

Electronic Hallway—Keep Your Eye on the Ball: The Road to the Real Salt Lake Stadium Deal (Case Study)

This case study examines intergovernmental conflict. Tension erupts between city and state officials when Salt Lake City decides to use state funds to build a new stadium. The impact of this intergovernmental conflict on the sports team seeking to relocate to Salt Lake City is also examined. Students will read the case study and critique it with the goal of creating an alternative strategy that would result in more of a win-win situation for all four parties involved: city, state, team, and citizens.

http://hallway.evans.washington.edu/cases/details/keep-your-eye-ball-road-real-salt-lake-stadium-deal

managers are lethargic readers, meaning they are not likely to mine information from dense reports, professional conferences, electronic databases, and tedious academic journals. Information needs to be a valued resource that is critical to competitive survival, and thus it needs to be sought out with greater frequency.

3. Improve the public sector's competitive image. The popular image, which is reinforced by politicians and media outlets on a daily basis, is one of waste and ineptitude (Holzer and Rabin 1987).

The previous discussion engenders a range of questions:

Q: *What if a public organization is too successful, becoming a monopoly?*

A: Success should never be a deterrent to innovation. For example, if an agency that is intended to increase competition becomes too dominant, then policymakers should limit its size by splitting the agency into smaller units. Much like Darwin's theory of survival of the fittest, an agency's "offspring" could replace unsuccessful government bidding units.

Q: *What will public organizations do with additional resources—or profits—generated by contracts?*

A: Profits can be reinvested in the public contractor. In the private sector, large portions of profits are dispersed among individual managers as bonuses; in the public sector, profits can be reinvested with ease. For one, improving the quality of work life and enhancing worker recognition is paramount to public managers. Additionally, legislators and citizenry are unlikely to approve of the large bonuses being doled out to public employees.

> "It is federal, because it is the government of States united in a political union, in contradistinction to a government of individuals, that is, by what is usually called, a social compact. To express it more concisely, it is federal and not national because it is the government of a community of States, and not the government of a single State or Nation."
>
> **JOHN C. CALHOUN**
> Seventh Vice President of the United States (1782–1850)

Q: *Are public organizations capable of making decisions as quickly or flexibly as their private-sector counterparts?*

A: Quite possibly, especially if generic agencies or agency units are expected to operate nonbureaucratically. However, this may call for rewriting existing regulations or legislation.

Q: *Are public agencies prepared to compete with the private sector?*

A: Not necessarily. A significant proportion of public agencies have experienced a loss of talent and capital equipment. Historically, some public agencies have never been funded adequately. One distinct advantage of privatization is that private organizations have greater access to investment resources, which is not characteristically the case for their public-sector counterparts.

Q: *Will internal government competition have consequences that may be dysfunctional?*

A: Of course. But these dysfunctions can be minimized if they are anticipated and monitored. Such dysfunctions may include:

- Pirating information: Will managers attempt to dig for private information to gain unfair advantages?
- Corruption: Will government managers attempt to influence each other through bribery and other unethical or illegal means?
- Undue political influence: Will elected officials direct contracts to organizations where they have more influence?

Q: *Will public agencies be able to endure "slack" in order to invest in public bidding—in other words, will public agencies be afforded a long-term view that, in time, success will emerge?*

A: Possibly yes, given the argument that there is underutilized capacity in government. Internal bidding units may be criticized as redundant resources that compete unfairly with the private sector. A related problem is expectations: The expectations for bidding units may be unreasonably high, exerting pressure for quick successes.

Q: *Are public agencies less willing to transfer functions to other public agencies and more willing to contract out to private organizations?*

A: Perhaps. Contracting to the private sector does not mean that an agency is giving up its territory per se; permitting another public agency to provide a service, however, may be perceived as such.

Improved competitive capacities may help convince cynics that government does—or at least can—perform at a high level. Under a model of "government as competitor," the change in public opinion is not likely to be remarkable, but the direction is likely to be more positive as governments' reassert their missions and highlight their competency.

SHARED SERVICE AMONG LOCAL ENTITIES: WOULD BOTH COUNTRIES SUFFER FROM THE SAME PROBLEMS?

As mentioned in the text, the idea of shared service among local governments is based on the fact that it can reduce service delivery costs and tax burdens as well as improve governmental responsiveness through better service. It should be mentioned, however, that a local government might not be willing to share services simply because it can cut costs and tax burdens. From such a point of view, we need to think about the barriers that might prevent local governments from sharing services. They often like to control their own services and to be the provider for other local entities. Please read the following article and discuss barriers and strategies to overcome this problem among local governments in Korea. Comparing the US case (for example, cities of Moreno Valley and Riverside in California), do you find any possible difference in terms of background and settings?

Science belt to be built in Daejeon

By Na Jeong-ju

The government has chosen Daejeon as the site of an international science-business belt over other candidate cities from the Gyeongsang and Jeolla provinces, sources said Sunday.

Education, Science and Technology Minister Lee Ju-ho will announce the decision today. Prime Minister Kim Hwang-sik will also issue a statement to seek public understanding of the conclusion as well as address complaints from other candidate cities, the sources said.

"We've chosen Daejeon because it is located close to existing R&D facilities and state science-related agencies," a government source said.

"The decision was solely based on opinions from scientists and businesses and the principle of balanced regional development. There have been no political considerations in selecting the site."

The issue of where the complex should be set up has remained controversial amid stiff competition among cities to attract it.

(continued)

(continued)

During the 2007 campaign, then-presidential candidate for the Grand National Party Lee Myung-bak pledged to set up the science complex in the Chungcheong region. Broad support from the area helped him win the election in December that year in a landslide victory.

However, Lee said in a nationally-televised address in February that he would reconsider the plan, triggering a furious reaction from residents and politicians there.

Since then at least 10 cities, including Daegu, Busan, Changwon and Gwangju, have vied for the lucrative project.

Reports said Daejeon will house basic science and R&D facilities, while other functions could be shared by the Gyeongsang and Jeolla provinces.

The decision is expected to spark a fierce backlash.

Criticizing the government's decision, North Gyeongsang Province Governor Kim Kwan-yong said he would go on a hunger strike for an indefinite period. Daegu Mayor Kim Bum-il also warned of a wave of protests by Daegu residents unless the government changes the plan.

Lee's aides are concerned that the selection of Daejeon will add fuel to bad public sentiment in the Gyeongsang provinces over the government's recent abolishment of an airport construction project.

In early April, the government scrapped the plan to build an international airport in the Gyeongsang region after a government panel concluded that building and operating the airport was not economically feasible. The construction of the airport was also one of President Lee's campaign pledges.

Source: http://www.koreatimes.co.kr/www/news/nation/2011/05/116_87042.html

KEY TERMS

Ad-hocracy

Block grants

Categorical grants

Economies of scale

Federalist system

Layer cake model

Marble cake model

Picket fence model

Privatization

Public authority or corporation

Shared service agreements

REFERENCES

Abramovitz, M. 1986. "The Privatization of the Welfare State: A Review." *Social Work* 31 (July-August): 257–64.

Bailey, R.W. 1987. "Uses and Misuses of Privatization." In *Prospects for Privatization*, ed. S.H. Hanke. New York: Academy of Political Science.

Bamekov, T.K., and J.A. Raffel. 1992. "Public Management of Privatization." In *Public Productivity Handbook*, ed. Marc Holzer. New York: Marcel Dekker.

Barcousky, L. 2005. "One Chief, Two Departments: Police Chief for Pine-Marshall-Bradford Woods Force Also Will Lead Richland Department Under One-Year Agreement." *Pittsburgh Post-Gazette*, January 2, N6.

Dye, T.R. 1990. *American Federalism: Competition Among Governments*. Lexington, MA: Lexington Books.

Ferris, J., and E. Graddy. 1986. "Contracting Out: For What? With Whom?" *Public Administration Review* 46, no. 4: 332–44.

Halachmi, A. 1989. "Ad-Hocracy and the Future of the Civil Service." *International Journal of Public Administration* 12, no. 4: 617–50.

Hanke, S.H., ed. 1987. *Prospects for Privatization*. New York: Academy of Political Science.

Hatry, H.P. 1983. *A Review of Private Approaches for Delivery of Public Services*. Washington, DC: Urban Institute Press.

Hattery, M. 1996. "Chautauqua County Bridge Program." *Cooperative Highway Services Case Study Report Number 2*. Local Government Program, Department of Agricultural, Resource, and Managerial Economics, College of Agriculture and Life Sciences, Cornell University, December.

Hester, T. 2000. "More Towns Reap What They Sow Through Pooling of Vital Services." Newark, NJ: *Star-Ledger*, August 8, 21.

Holzer, Marc. 1988. "Productivity In, Garbage Out: Sanitation Gain in New York." *Public Productivity Review* 11, no. 3 (Spring): 37–50.

———. 1991. "Exemplary State and Local (EXSL) Awards Program." Newark, NJ: National Center for Public Productivity, Rutgers University, January.

Holzer, M., and J. Rabin. 1987. "Public Service: Problems, Professionalism, and Policy Recommendations." *Public Productivity Review* 43 (Fall): 3–14.

Holzer, M., L. Sadeghi, and R. Schwester. 2007. "Exploring State Shared Services and Regional Consolidation Efforts." In *The Book of the States*, ed. Keon S. Chi, 451–56. Lexington, KY: Council of State Governments.

Jennings, E.T. 1986/1991. "Public Choice and the Privatization of Government: Implications for Public Administration." In *Public Management: The Essential Readings*, ed. J. Steven Ott et al., 113–29. Chicago: Lyceum Books, 1991.

Johnson, M. 2006. "Village Open to Merger, Officials Say Committee May Form on Consolidation Issues for Two Pewaukees." *Milwaukee Journal Sentinel*, July 20, B3.

Katz, J.I. 1991. "Privatizing Without Tears." *Governing*, (June): 38–42.

Kettl, D.F. 1991. "Privatization: Implications for the Public Work Force." In *Public Personnel Management*, ed. C. Ban and N.M. Riccucci. New York: Longman.

McManus, S.A. 1991. "Why Businesses Are Reluctant to Sell to Governments." *Public Administration Review* 51, no. 4 (July-August): 328–44.

Morgan, D.R., and R.E. England. 1988. "The Two Faces of Privatization." *Public Administration Review* 48, no. 6 (November-December): 979–87.

New York State Association of Counties (NYSAC). 2006. "The Shared Municipal Service Incentive Program: A Policy Primer." NYSAC Policy Brief. http://www.fredonia.edu/crrdg/docs/NYSACguide.pdf.

Osborne, D. 1990. "Ten Ways to Turn D.C. Around." *Washington Post Magazine*, December 9, 19–43.

Repard, P. 1993. "City-School Library Is One for the Books." *San Diego Union-Tribune*, August 3, B2.

Savas, E.S. 1992. "Privatization and Productivity." In *Public Productivity Handbook*, ed. M. Holzer. New York: Marcel Dekker.

Schneider, M. 1989. "Intermunicipal Competition, Budget-Maximizing Bureaucrats, and the Level of Suburban Competition." *American Journal of Political Science* 33, no. 3 (August): 612–28.

Shared Municipal Services Program (SMSP). 2005. *SMSP Program Guidelines*. Harrisburg: Pennsylvania Department of Community and Economic Development.

Sharing Available Resources Efficiently (SHARE). 2006. *SHARE Best Practices Handbook*. Trenton: New Jersey Department of Community Affairs. http://www.nj.gov/dca/lgs/share/share_handbook.pdf.

Smothers, R. 1999. "Regional Fire Service Succeeds in Its First Test." *New York Times*, January 12, B5.

Staley, S.R., Faulk, D., Leland, S.M., & Schansberg, D.E. 2005. "The Effect of City-County Consolidation: A Review of the Recent Academic Literature." Prepared by the Indiana Policy Review Foundation, http://www.in.gov/legislative/interim/committee/2005/committees/prelim/MCCC02.pdf; accessed on 19 September 2009.

Tom, P.A. 2003. "It Takes Three." *Waste Age* 34, no. 10.

U.S. Conference of Mayors. 1997. "Shared Fire Station Saves Money, Improves Service for Moreno Valley, Riverside Residents." November 24. http://usmayors.org/usmayornewspaper/documents/12_22_97/documents/Best_Practices__97___Moreno_Valley__CA_and_Riverside__CA__11_24_97__012098.html.

SUPPLEMENTARY READINGS

Agranoff, Robert. 2007. "Managing within Networks: Adding Value to Public Organizations." Washington, DC: Georgetown University Press.

Gazley, Beth.2008. "Beyond the Contract: The Scope and Nature of Informal Government–Nonprofit Partnership." *Public Administration Review* 68(1): 141-154.

ELECTRONIC RESOURCES

Advisory Commission on Intergovernmental Relations (ACIR was an independent, bipartisan intergovernmental agency established in 1959 and disbanded in 1996; the ACIR Digital Library is composed of publications that study the interactions between different levels of government), http://digital.library.unt.edu/browse/department/govdocs/acir/

The Share Program—New Jersey Division of Local Government Services, http://www.nj.gov/dca/lgs/share/

CHAPTER 7

Public Performance

This chapter examines strategies for improving the performance of public organizations. Upon reading this chapter, students will understand the concepts of total quality management (TQM) and performance measurement, specifically the different types of performance indicators, how to create a performance measurement system, and the role of citizens in this process. This chapter transitions into a discussion of the many social factors that influence organizational performance and concludes with a discussion of the privatization of government services.

"An acre of performance is worth a whole world of promise."

WILLIAM DEAN HOWELLS
American Author
(1837–1920)

– YOUR APPLICATIONS ARE BEING LOOKED INTO...
Artist: V. Travin; Poet: A. Shkliarinsky; "The Fighting Pencil" group, 1976.

The promise is given only as a blind.
They will have to come back not once, not twice...
But many, many times.

IMPROVING GOVERNMENT PERFORMANCE

The Importance of Knowledge Sharing and Training

There is undoubtedly a relationship between knowledge and performance. All "professionals" are expected to be current: Doctors must read the latest medical journals and attend professional seminars and conferences. Lawyers must understand changes in the legal field. Professionals must be innovative. There is significant innovation in government, yet there is also a significant amount of ignorance of innovation. Too few of the truly successful projects have been replicated widely throughout the public sector. The fault lies somewhat with small-minded professionals who resist going beyond the borders of their own disciplines. Maybe they are lazy or arrogant or simply lack the foundational knowledge necessary for improving their performance. The fault also lies with a budget process that is overly political and shortsighted in terms of knowledge investments. Luxuries like conferences, academic journals, and professional association memberships are thought to be needless or gratuitous and offer no clear payoffs. Knowledge investments have a difficult time surviving the budget process, losing out to more immediate needs. Professional knowledge, under the best of circumstances, is treated as a discretionary expenditure as opposed to a necessary investment. However, if public managers are not afforded access to timely and adequate information, we can expect that same mistakes will be repeated in the future.

> "Measurement is the first step that leads to control and eventually to improvement. If you can't measure something, you can't understand it. If you can't understand it, you can't control it. If you can't control it, you can't improve it."
>
> **H. JAMES HARRINGTON**
> Quality and Performance Improvement Consultant

Public organizations need to learn from their successes and failures—but perhaps more important, they need to learn from the successes and failures of other public organizations. Strategies for government performance improvement are being reported in hundreds of publications and conferences. Public organizations need to unearth the mountains of available information by sharing experiences, participating in conferences, and joining Internet-based networks such as the Public Performance Measurement and Reporting Network (http://www.ppmrn.net), a key information-sharing tool in the field. Launched in 2006 by the National Center for Public Performance at Rutgers University's School of Public Affairs and Administration, the Public Performance Measurement and Reporting Network was created to support networks that include government officials, public and non-profit managers, professors and researchers, citizens, and other stakeholders that are looking to improve public-sector performance through the use and sharing of valid and reliable information. In supporting this network, the National Center for Public Performance has launched several initiatives: an all-inclusive and up-to-date database of publications and case studies; academic conferences; professional workshops; books and articles dealing with measurement; an Online Public Performance Measurement Certificate; and a monthly electronic newsletter.

In addition to knowledge and information sharing, a trained workforce is indispensable. In many public organizations, however, on-the-job training is thought to be "good enough." Many public organizations suffer from the mistaken belief that government work is simple—that it can be learned rather quickly by virtually anyone. In a postindustrial society, however, on-the-job training is insufficient preparation for a public sector with increasingly complex responsibilities. Still, public managers with only modest professional management training are often given the responsibility of running public organizations.

Total Quality Management: Customer Focus and Responsive Public Organizations

The adoption of total quality management (TQM) as a management philosophy has been debated among public administration scholars and practitioners. TQM, originally intended to change American private-sector work environments, has been implemented by numerous public agencies. TQM is defined as "an enterprise lifestyle that emphasizes customer satisfaction, excellent service and rapid adjustment to address ever-changing customer needs" (McCloskey and Collett 1993, quoted in Flynn, Sakakibara, and Schroeder 1995, p. 1325). TQM is a strategy for improving processes and services on a continual basis. Customer focus, upper-management commitment, continuous improvement, participative management, labor-management cooperation, and organized analysis are essential functions in a TQM environment (Shea and Howell 1998).

The difference between the public and private sectors has raised discussions about what prevents TQM from being used within public organizations (Swiss 1992). Experience with TQM in the public sector has produced mixed results. Some public organizations have reported success in using TQM, while others believe it has not contributed to improvements in performance. Perhaps this is somewhat attributable to a major misunderstanding associated with TQM (White and Wolfe 1995). TQM's central emphasis is *customer focus*—improving public agencies' responsiveness to the people they serve (Swiss 1992).

Assumptions of Total Quality Management

W. Edwards Deming (1986) is the father of TQM, and he notes that it requires transformation of the American business management style. It is also applicable to governmental transformation. According to Milakovich (1992, pp. 584–86), the key elements of TQM include the following:

1. Leaders must develop and disseminate the aims and purposes of the organization. Management must commit to these aims and purposes.
2. All must learn the new philosophy—including upper management.
3. In the interest of processes improvement and cost reductions, all must understand the purpose of inspection.
4. Eliminate the practice of using cost as the basis for awarding business.
5. Continuously improve systems of production and service.
6. Implement modern training methods.
7. Teach leadership.
8. Eliminate fear, build trust, and create an environment conducive to innovation.
9. Staff and work groups must be optimized toward the aims of the organization.
10. Eliminate pleas to the workforce.
11. Eliminate numerical quotas for work—rather, learn and implement methods for improvement.
12. Eliminate obstacles that deprive people of pride in their work.
13. Encourage worker education and self-amelioration.
14. Act to bring about the transformation.

Based on Deming's 14 points, several assumptions can be drawn.

Customer Focus

Without question, TQM assumes that the customer is paramount. This is because the customer is the ultimate judge of quality. Performance improvement cannot really exist without customer satisfaction. The customer base is composed of both internal (employees) and external customers (citizens). *Internal customers* receive "any work output in the service or production process," while *external customers* purchase the product (McGowan and Wittmer 1997). Customer satisfaction, therefore, must be the supreme priority of any organization. Both employee and citizen satisfaction are important elements in measuring performance.

Continuous Improvement

Another important assumption of TQM is *continuous improvement*. Any performance improvement program is dependent on feedback from employees and citizens on a continuous basis. Continuous improvement includes: "(1) enhanced value to the customer through new and improved products and services, (2) reduced errors, defects, and waste, (3) improved responsiveness and cycle-time performance, and (4) improved productivity and effectiveness in the use of all resources" (McGowan and Wittmer 1998, p. 313). As Swiss (1992) points out, "Quality is not a static attribute; it is a constantly changing target because it represents a delighted customer" (p. 358).

Top Management Commitment and Leadership

Upper-management commitment is essential to TQM's success. TQM is unlikely to work unless implemented through strong leadership. Like other performance improvement strategies, TQM requires a long-term commitment from upper management (Lee 2000a). Berman and West (1995) argue that too many organizations are inclined to implement strategies such as TQM at "a token level rather than fully committing themselves to success." In this regard, Rago (1996) points out that "agency vision and goals need to be clearly communicated throughout all levels of the agency and leadership needs to be actively involved in this effort" (p. 234).

> "In God we trust, all others bring data."
>
> **W. EDWARDS DEMING**
> American Statistician; Quality Consultant (1900–1993)

Upper management needs to assume a significant role in changing an organization's culture so that TQM initiatives can be fully embraced by employees at all levels. It is necessary to change "bureaucratic" organizational culture—which can be excessively hierarchical, centralized, and firmly structured—to a more innovative and supportive type of culture. Innovative culture has a collaborative and people-oriented focus. Supportive culture embraces creativity and getting results (Wallach 1983). White and Wolf (1995) note that "the culture of public sector organizations must be shifted away from blame and control to one of support for positive action" (p. 224). This culture change cannot occur in the short run. It requires time and perseverance.

Empowerment and Teamwork

Empowerment and *teamwork* assume that performance improvement cannot occur because of one person's effort. Furthermore, no single managerial action can foster employee loyalty and full support (Pollock 2001). There are several ways of defining empowerment, but for our purposes empowerment involves a leadership approach whereby decision-making authority is given to lower-level employees. In doing so, employees are more likely to take ownership of their jobs and embrace more responsibility (Holt, Love and Jawahar-Nesan 2000). Since empowered teams are seen as central to correcting organizational problems, TQM suggests that employees work as a team to overcome existing management problems rather than ask for external help. The reason for this is straightforward: employees are the people who really know what is going on in their organization; therefore, no one can do a better job of correcting existing work problems than they can.

There are three levels of teamwork (McGowan and Wittmer 1997). With *vertical teamwork*, upper management gives lower-level employees authority to make decisions that would meet customers' demands. In the interim, *horizontal teamwork* enables different functional groups within an organization to deal with external de-

FIGURE 7.1 – FEDERAL QUALITY INSTITUTE APPROACH TO TQM

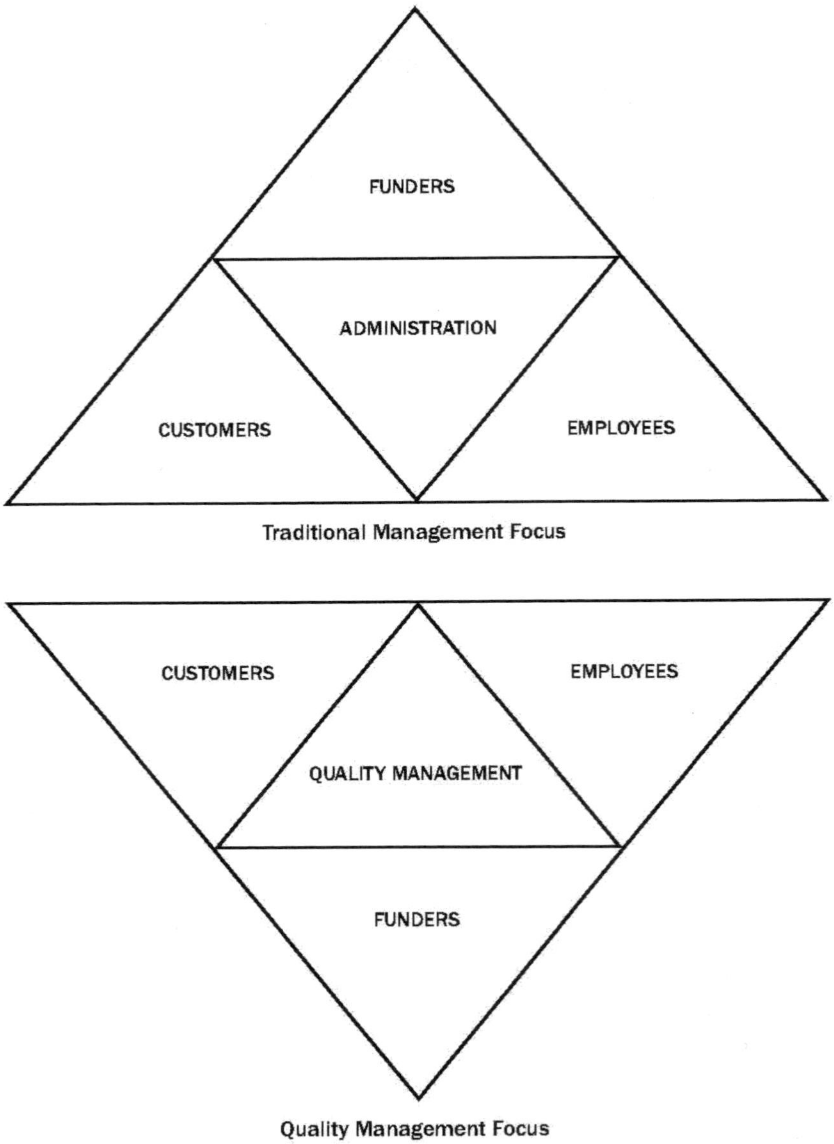

Source: Federal Quality Institute. 1991. Introduction to Total Quality Management in the Federal Government. Washington, D.C.: U.S. Office of Personnel Management.

mands. *Interorganizational teamwork* includes establishing work teams of suppliers, customers, and other external groups. In the public sector, this level of teamwork might be used to involve interest groups, agency representatives, citizen representatives, subcontractors, and elected officials in the decision-making process.

Issues in Organizational Responsiveness

Responsiveness is an important value of public organizations. Rourke (1984) defines responsiveness as "the extent to which [an organization] promotes correspondence between the decisions of bureaucrats and the preferences of the community or the officeholders who are authorized to speak for the public" (p. 4). Such responsiveness can be attained in an "organizational arrangement under which a great deal of authority is delegated to lower levels of administration" (p. 8). Responsiveness coincides with bringing government closer to its people. In this context, Kaufman (1987) argues that *representativeness*, politically neutral competency, and executive leadership are important values in government. In particular, regarding representativeness, "there is a need to improve public representation within organizations because 'many unorganized interests' are excluded from formulation of decisions" (p. 394).

Barriers to Responsiveness and Solutions: Linking TQM's Philosophy

Situation 1

Problem 1: Interest Group Politics and Captive Bureaucracy. Sometimes, public organizations adhere to the desires of political parties and interest groups even if these desires clash with what the public wants. This leads to unbalanced political influences. Regarding interest group politics, the concept of a captive agency should be noted. Rourke (1984) describes a captive agency as one that becomes overly dependent on "the political support of an outside group." This dependence is so great that it ultimately ascribes the outside group with "veto power over many of the agency's major decisions. In [an] extreme case, the agency becomes in effect a captive organization, unable to move in any direction except those permitted it by the group upon which it is politically dependent" (p. 58). As a result, the organization loses its capacity to respond to the demands of the public.

According to Lee (2001), unbalanced participation led by organized interest groups makes it difficult for public organizations to reflect citizen desires. A common dilemma with citizen participation is that citizens tend to keep their opinions to themselves. Organized interest groups, however, participate in and try to influence political agendas by making their opinions known. In this situation, policy outcomes are likely to favor interest groups and not individual citizens. Lee argues that this effect stems not from citizens' indifference about policy issues but from the fact that most citizens do not have the time, money, civic skills, and degree of organization necessary to participate in political life.

TQM Solution 1: Establishing Interorganizational Teamwork and Training for External Customers. In most cases, becoming a captive agency is a consequence of not having institutionalized mechanisms for involving a wide range of citizen groups in the political process. As mentioned earlier, the concept of interorganizational teamwork can assist in evening out this unbalanced political participation. That is, it may be possible to involve various citizen groups, voluntary associations, and citizen representatives in making major decisions within a local community.

Furthermore, given that individual citizens are less inclined to participate in the political process because of time and money constraints, Internet-based participation may serve as an equalizing alternative. Washington State's Internet-based participation initiative explains how interorganizational teams composed of numerous state agencies, boards, and commissions have established a digital government to improve citizen participation. An interorganizational team called Access Washington in the Department of Information Services has developed web-based participation tools. As its progress report from 2000 states:

> The *Access Washington* state Internal Portal was launched in 1998 to replace a static, billboard-style state website called *Homepage Washington* that averaged only 170,000 monthly visitors. Within one year, page views on *Access Washington* increased 488 percent to an average of one million per month, and the numbers keep climbing. Today's *Access Washington* turns government to face the people, organizing hundreds of government information programs and dozens of transactional services in citizen-centric navigation paths. *Access Washington* at access.wa.gov is the gateway to the digital government community: on-line storefronts and service centers filled with the government information and tools that citizens want, when they want them. (Washington State Governor's Office)

Chapter 12 of this book, Technology and Public Administration, provides numerous other examples of how the Internet and other information and communications technologies are changing citizens' interactions and communication with bureaucratic and political institutions.

Situation 2

Problem 2: Expertise and Information Distortion. Bureaucratic expertise is a function of a public organization's characteristics and the capabilities of its members. The operation of public organizations requires employment of a complex range of people with specialized skills. Rourke (1984) asserts that bureaucratic expertise influences public policy development via three primary channels: "(1) the ability of bureaucrats to gather information and to give advice that often shapes the decisions of political officials; (2) the capacity of bureaucratic organizations to carry on the tasks that must be performed once policy goals are decided upon—the power of implementation; and (3) as a critical dimension of this power to implement policies, the discretion with which bureaucracies are commonly vested as they carry on the work of government" (p. 20).

These three factors can cause negative results, most notably information distortion in an organization. O'Reilly (1978) defines information distortion as "the incorrect reproduction of objectively correct information," resulting "from either conscious or deliberate alteration or unconscious manipulation" (p. 329). That is, supposedly objective information is knowingly or unknowingly biased—usually in the interest of self-preservation. Negative but vital information is sometimes not delivered to upper-level decision makers, who are reliant upon top-down communication. In 1967, Downs contended that officials tend to distort the information they pass upward in the organizational hierarchy—overemphasizing (or at times even exaggerating) information that looks good personally and deemphasizing information that could be personally detrimental. This type of information distortion can make it complicated for public organizations to adapt.

> "When you can measure what you are speaking about, and express it in numbers, you know something about it: but... when you cannot express it in numbers, your knowledge is of a meager and unsatisfactory kind."
>
> **LORD KELVIN**
> Nineteenth-Century Mathematical Physicist

TQM Solution 2: Utilizing Vertical Teamwork and Empowerment. Information distortion is likely to occur within vertical hierarchical structures, where authorized communication is limited to the channels between upper managers, middle managers, and rank-and-file employees. Central to avoiding this distortion is the building of multiple communication paths so that important information is available to upper management at all times. As Gortner and colleagues (1987) put it, "Information tends to be transmitted upward in the organization only if (1) its transmission will not have unpleasant consequences for the transmitter, or (2) the superior will hear of it anyway from other channels, and it is better to tell him first, or (3) it is information that the superior needs in his dealings with his own superiors, and he will be displeased if he is caught without it" (p. 203).

The use of "vertical teams" makes it possible for all employees to share important information and to facilitate information flows within the organization. Vertical teams enable upper-level management to receive information from lower-level management and afford lower-level employees the power to make decisions. Empowered employees are more inclined to accept responsibility and risk for their actions, and they are less likely to hold onto unfavorable yet important information. Additionally, they are more inclined to solve the problems with their superiors and colleagues in a cooperative manner.

Situation 3

Problem 3: Specialized Structure and Parochialism. As specialization increases, so too will administrative efficiency. According to Nobel laureate Herbert Simon (1997, p. 292), "a major problem in an effective organization is to specialize and subdivide activities in such a manner that the psychological forces of identification will contribute to, rather than hinder, correct decision making." Organizational structures are centered on *functional differentiation*. This means that there are cognitive and emotional differences between specialists and separate organizational departments. To effectively tie an organization's different functions to its broader goals, it is essential to integrate and coordinate these separate and specialized functions. Therefore, integration is related to cooperation problems among departments in an organization. Significant functional specialization can foster parochialism among public organizations—that is, organizations become too narrowly focused. This makes it very difficult for public organizations to respond to the various demands of citizens and ensure the appropriate delivery of services.

TQM Solution 3: Utilizing Horizontal Teamwork and Preventing Variation in the Product and Process. While functional specialties are sometimes necessary for achieving efficiency and high organizational performance—especially if that organization is operating within a turbulent environment—excessive specialization may serve as an impediment to the delivery of public services in a timely or appropriate manner. As mentioned earlier, central to TQM is the removal of barriers between organizational departments. The use of "horizontal teams" minimizes conflict and reduces tension between departments. In a horizontal team, members representing various organizational departments learn how to cooperate beyond their departmental boundaries. Formation of these "cross-functional teams" helps to reduce costs and time in producing and delivering citizen services.

Sometimes, becoming a high-performing organization is a function of minimizing variations in the way things are done. Swiss (1992) points out that "slippages in quality arise from too much variation in the product or service" (p. 357). Using multi-unit teams also enables public agencies to rectify process variation problems. The Department of Labor and Industries in Washington State serves as a good example: In July 2000, the department created a multi-unit team called the "Factory Assembled Structures (FAS) Process Improvement Team" to solve process problems:

> Labor and Industries approved plans for modular building construction. Manufacturers complained about the process, citing a low 30 percent acceptance rate for first time plans, poor communications and a lack of consistency and professionalism. In collaboration with manufacturers, the team improved communications, developed training and computerized processes. They raised approval rates and enhanced customer service without lowering standards or sacrificing public safety. The plan approval rate went from 30 to 72 percent for the following 19-month period, an increase of 140 percent. Training is provided on-site and online, and issues are cor-

rected over the phone, saving time and money for the manufacturers. (Washington State Governor's Office, 2000)

Situation 4

Problem 4: Attribution Error and Management Failure. Under some conditions, the cultivation of stereotypical beliefs may stem from cognitive and information-processing biases. In typical usage, "attribution refers to judgments about one's perceptions rather than causal perception" (Hamilton 1980, p. 767). Attribution theory is concerned with how ordinary people attempt to understand the causes and consequences of events they witness. Potential causal factors are thought to be internal to the actor (for example, ability, effort, and intention) or external to the actor (for example, task-related factors and luck). According to Heider (1958), people searching for the causes of events rely either on environmental attributes (external attribution) or on attributes of the person involved in the event (internal attribution). In reality, most leaders are inclined to believe that organizational success stems from their own actions and that organizational failure stems from the actions of others externally. The same situation in reverse is usually seen by groups in opposition (Miller and Ross 1975).

> "The only man I know who behaves sensibly is my tailor; he takes my measurements anew each time he sees me. The rest go on with their old measurements and expect me to fit them."
>
> **GEORGE BERNARD SHAW**
> Playwright; Critic; Nobel Prize Winner (1856–1950)

The same principle may characterize the relationship between managers and subordinates as it relates to performance evaluations. In this situation, people avoid finding out the causes of policy or management failures, and they most likely fail to admit that "it was our fault," even if it was. This makes it hard for public organizations to find out what went wrong, which likely reduces responsiveness to the demands of citizens.

TQM Solution 4: Admitting Variations in Employees' Performance and Eliminating Numerical Quota. One underlying assumption of TQM is that "it is the management, not the worker, that is a problem in many cases." As White and Wolf (1995) explain,

> Typically, when a manager sees a performance distribution in which one or some workers are low and others are high, the response is to evaluate the low workers as bad, the high workers as good, and then set out to make the bad workers like the good ones... In contrast, the TQM managers simply consider that the workers at the good end of the distribution have been lucky and the ones at the bad end have been unlucky. (pp. 210–11)

TQM presupposes that any public organization is comprised of good and poor performers. Being a good performer today does not necessarily mean that a worker will be a good performer tomorrow. Similarly, it is not known whether a poor performer today will become a good performer tomorrow. As a result, TQM managers do not hold employees directly responsible for low performance. Instead, they try to determine the reasons for the decline in performance. One of Deming's 14 points, "eliminate numerical quotas for work," has been recommended in this context. In instances where numerical quotas serve as major performance indicators, the relationship between labor and management is likely to be adversarial. While managers attribute the cause of poor performance to employees—arguing, for example, that employees use official work time for union activities—employees contend that poor performance is not their fault (Holzer and Lee 1999). The following statement by Bobby Harnage, past president of the American Federation of Government Employees, shows how management and workers see the causes of poor performance quite differently:

> There is no such thing as one poor performer. That individual has a supervisor. If he or she is staying on the rolls, then we have two poor performers. Performance management rules, which were established by the Civil Service Reform Act, do not need to be changed. Instead, managers need to have the courage to deal with poor performance. (*Government Executive Magazine,* January 12, 1999)

Harry Singletary, former secretary of the Florida Department of Corrections, emphasizes that people are key to successful TQM application: "We, the members of the Florida Department of Corrections, believe in the worth of the individuals," he stated, adding, "Our most valuable asset is a well-trained dedicated staff working as a team to meet a challenge" (Florida Department of Corrections, 1997). Every aspect of TQM is directed toward customer focus. Accepting employee performance variations and removing numerical goals and quotas will enable public organizations to respond more effectively to the customers' demands.

Situation 5

Problem 5: Organizational Entrapment and Trained Incapacity. Organizations often suffer from past resource allocation mistakes. Entrapment refers to "the tendency to persist in a failing course of action in order to justify the allocation of prior resources to that course of action" (Brocker and Rubin 1985, p. 242). Entrapment is much more likely to occur in a public organization than in a private organization. In addition, it should be noted that *trained incapacity* (Merton 1987) also hinders responsiveness to customers' demands. Merton asserts that "actions based upon training and skills which have been successfully applied in the past may result in inappropriate responses under changed conditions" (1987, p. 109).

TQM Solution 5: Driving Out Fear, and Training on a Continuing Basis. A critical element of TQM is eliminating fear. This means that employees—regardless of their level within an organization—should feel comfortable suggesting new ideas and innovative behaviors to their superiors and colleagues. Managerial innovation often necessitates risk taking. It then becomes crucial that employees feel it is acceptable—and at times even expected—that they will make mistakes. Creating an innovative culture of "it is okay if you make a mistake" is imperative for *productivity improvement.* Employees must be encouraged to abandon a failing course of action without fear. This is possible only if employees are encouraged to suggest ideas at any time. Therefore, "driving out the fear" ensures that the possibility of entrapment is minimized.

> "What gets measured gets done, what gets measured and fed back gets done well, what gets rewarded gets repeated."
>
> **JOHN E. JONES**
> American Attorney

Well known for its successful implementation of TQM, the Florida Department of Corrections places considerable emphasis on driving out fear among its employees. As Secretary Singletary noted, "Thomas Edison once said: Genius is one percent inspiration and 99 percent perspiration. I am challenging each of you to perspire often and regularly. Go forth and sweat" (Florida Department of Corrections, 1997). Moreover, Pennsylvania State has emphasized employee innovation, assuming that frontline employees are central installers of change. With the support of Pennsylvania's former governor Mark Schweiker (2001–2003), innovation teams have played an important role in state policymaking. The teams have found groundbreaking ways of recognizing change ideas proposed by employees, as well as recognizing individual or group creativity. As a result, numerous innovative ideas have originating from within the agency, among them environmental site assessments in the Pennsylvania Department of Transportation.

> The Pollution Prevention Division within PennDOT reexamined the process used to perform site investigations on underground fuel tanks. This involved obtaining soil samples by drilling into the ground around the tank and testing the samples for contaminants from possible leakage or spillage from the tanks. The testing and analysis of these sites were at the time being contracted to a private firm. The staff analysis showed that the testing and analysis could be accomplished more cost-effectively if they undertook the task themselves. Contracted testing was determined to cost $28,000 per site. PennDOT staff could perform the same investigation for $5,600 per site—saving $22,400 per site investigation. Consequently, the Pollution Prevention Division staff reaped a savings award of $26,000. (Pennsylvania State Governor's Office 2001)

At the same time, supporting various training programs on a continuing basis is critical to avoiding trained incapacity. Many observers agree that training is integral to managerial and organizational changes (Paddock 1997; Hannah 1995). Despite the importance of management training, though, training budgets are most likely to suffer in this period of cutback management (Paddock 1997). Training is critical to cultivating and enhancing employee *knowledge, skills*, and *abilities* (typically referred to as KSAs) and reduces the likelihood that employees will become obsolete over time (Klingner and Nalbandian 1998). Continuous training requires upper-management support, constant program evaluation, financial support, and full backing from participants. It is expected to decrease the possibility of trained incapacity in an ever-changing environment.

According to some public administration scholars and practitioners, short-sighted goals, regular turnover among upper-level managers, and individualistic organizational cultures may prevent TQM from being successfully implemented (Swiss 1992; White and Wolf 1995). However, many public organizations find TQM is feasible and compatible with their goals. In a study examining managerial public employees' attitudes in New Jersey State, Lee (2000b) found that of 19 various productivity and performance enhancement strategies, managerial employees reported "Total Quality Management" as the most favored strategy. TQM is a way of transforming organizational cultures and structures to improve performance. Central to this is creating organizations that are customer-focused, cost-efficient, and competitive. Correctly understanding and implementing TQM strategies will foster responsive, customer-centered public agencies, even in turbulent environments.

Measuring Performance to Improve Performance

Measuring government performance is a requisite tool for accountability and, consequently, for improvement. Generally speaking, *performance measurement* entails trying to answer questions such as:

- Is the organization fulfilling its mission and accomplishing stated goals and objectives?
- Is the organization producing unintended impacts?
- Is the organization responsive to the people?
- Does the organization keep within its scope of authority?
- Is the organization productive?
- Does it perform well?

Performance measurement is implied when we ask questions that deal with the quality of government services: "Is the neighborhood dangerous?" "Are the streets dirty?" "Are the schools succeeding?" Citizens often answer these questions with tales told by friends and acquaintances, rumors, and personal experiences.

Public organizations need to know how well they are performing, and in doing so they must rely on hard data: "Crime is down 10 percent." "The streets are 25 percent cleaner." "Standardized test scores have increased by an average of five points in the last year." Public organizations often possess the hard data to develop objective performance measures. As award-winning and innovative cases suggest, measuring public service quality is indeed feasible. Data are available, and the results need not be too complicated to use (EXSL 1989–1995). Performance measurement provides an opportunity to present "hard" feedback in place of "perceptions" that are often fueled by incorrect information, gossip, and conjecture. According to the U.S. General Accounting Office (GAO 1992):

> "When dealing with numerical data, approximately right is better than precisely wrong."
>
> **CARL G. THOR**
> Performance Improvement Expert

> Managers can use the data that performance measures provide to help them manage in three basic ways: to account for past activities, to manage current operations, or to assess progress toward planned objectives. When used to look at past activities, performance measures can show the accountability of processes and procedures used to complete a task, as well as program results. When used to manage current operations, performance measures can show how efficiently resources, such as dollars and staff, are being used. Finally, when tied to planned objectives, performance measures can be used to assess how effectively an agency is achieving the goals stated in its long-range strategic plan. Having well-designed measures that are timely, relevant, and accurate is important, but it is also important that the measures be used by decision makers.

Performance measures serve several purposes. To successfully operate their organizations, public managers need specific information. This applies to all management levels within all organizations. Performance measurement must be considered a requisite and critical part of the management process. Performance management is thought to contribute to the following:

- Improved decision making: Performance measures afford managers needed information to execute their control functions.
- Performance assessment: The measures connect individual and organizational performance to the management of employees, serving as a means of motivation.
- Accountability: The process engenders managerial responsibility.
- Service delivery: The process fosters service performance improvements.
- Public participation: Performance reporting can influence the citi-

zenry to care more about public workers' efforts to improve service delivery.

- Improvement of civic discourse: This makes public discussions about public service delivery more factual.

While valuable to the full range of organizational personnel, performance measurement is especially valuable to staff analysts and auditors. Measures can be useful for both internal decision makers (i.e., public managers and policymaking appointees) and external groups in improving their assessments of government. This is because such assessments are based on real performance data as opposed to anecdotal and unreliable information. Harry Hatry, an expert on performance management at the Washington, D.C.–based Urban Institute, was instrumental in cultivating and spreading public-sector performance measurement (Hatry et al. 1977, 1979, 1990; Urban Institute 1974, 1980). Public agencies, professional associations, research centers like the Urban Institute, and academics have developed many performance measurement standards. In particular, the Government Accounting Standards Board (GASB) has published several volumes that recommend standards for Service Efforts and Accomplishments (SEA). "Doing more with less" has emerged as an enduring maxim directed toward all levels of government, and as such, performance measurement has become a vital tool for organizational improvement in the contexts of efficiency, effectiveness, and accountability.

Types of Performance Indicators

Several different *performance indicators* are featured in a performance measure-

TABLE 7.1 – TYPES OF PERFORMANCE MEASUREMENT INDICATORS

Government function	Input indicators	Output indicators	Outcome indicators	Efficiency indicators
Department of Sanitation	• The number of labor-hours worked by employees of the Sanitation Department • The department's budget • The number of vehicles used by the department	• Tons of garbage collected • Miles of roads cleaned • Number of customers served	• Percentage of clean streets (as measured by periodic visual inspection, citizen surveys, and so on)	• Employee-hours per ton of garbage collected • Dollars spent for one mile of snow removal

ment system. The most common are: (1) inputs, (2) outputs, (3) outcomes, and (4) efficiency indicators.

Input Indicators. Inputs reflect the quantity of resources appropriated to a government organization, service, or program. Input indicators are typically contained within the budget, representing financial or personnel resources.

Output Indicators. Outputs are workload indicators. They reflect the amount of work done or the number of services provided by a government program.

Outcome Indicators. These indicators capture the results (or quality) of the services provided. Outcome indicators are essential to establishing whether an organization or program has met predetermined goals and objectives. They help answer questions about service quality and the impacts of service delivery. A measurable change in students' test scores resulting from a government-funded tutoring program is an example of an outcome indicator.

Efficiency Indicators. These indicators examine the extent to which a public organization or program is performing in relation to service delivery costs. Efficiency indicators refer to the ratio of the service provided (for example, tons of trash collected) to the cost required to deliver that service (wages for workers, gasoline for trucks, and the like).

Robert Behn (2003) argues that performance measurement systems serve seven fundamental purposes that go beyond simply evaluating how well a public organization is performing. These include:

- Control: Performance measures serve as a means of maintaining managerial control, ensuring that workers are doing what is required of them.
- Budget: Performance-based budgeting (or results-based budgeting) links performance measures with how much money a public agency or department receives. In other words, agencies and departments that perform well may receive more money, while those that do not may find their budgets cut. Critics argue that using performance measurement as a basis for determining budgets is crude and counterintuitive; that is, are we to believe that actually taking money away from a public organization will help its situation? Perhaps this is not a good idea.
- Motivate: By setting performance goals, public managers give their staff something to work toward. Performance goals serve to focus workers.
- Promote: Unlike the private sector, public organizations are dreadful when it comes to self-promotion. The media effectively points out every

flaw and misstep that government encounters, making it ever more important for public organizations to convey their accomplishments. Performance measures can be very helpful in this regard. The New Jersey Motor Vehicle Commission (NJMVC) serves as a vivid example. Perhaps no public organization has been ridiculed as much as the NJMVC (2006), where nightmarish stories of DMV ineptitude and inefficiency are legendary. The NJMVC went through a massive reorganization, reformed itself, and is now doing a better job. How do we know this? Service assessment results indicate that wait times have decreased dramatically and customer satisfaction has increased (NJMVC 2006).

- Celebrate: Taking a moment to smell the roses is important. It is important from a morale standpoint that public managers use performance measures to celebrate organizational accomplishments with their staff. This not only reaffirms the importance of measuring performance, but also serves as motivation for future projects, endeavors, etc.
- Learn and Improve: Collecting performance data is not an end in itself. Rather, it is a tool by which public managers can learn about what is working and what is not, and make appropriate changes to improve an organization. The City of Baltimore's CitiStat program is an example of using performance measurement data to learn about and improve an organization's operations. Developed by the former mayor of Baltimore, Martin O'Malley (1999–2007; elected governor of Maryland, 2006), CitiStat is a performance measurement–based management system that uses computer pin mapping. CitiStat evolved from New York City's CompStat program, which was used by the NYPD to pinpoint crime hotspots. CitiStat built upon CompStat's model by including all areas of government. Cooperation and communication make CitiStat work. City agency and bureau heads develop strategies and set goals, collect performance data that coincide with these strategies and goals, and then present the data every two weeks at CitiStat meetings, where the mayor, deputy mayors, and other key officials are present. For instance, Baltimore's Solid Waste Bureau would present performance data ranging from the number of complaints about dirty alleys or missed trash pick-ups to the number of sick days taken and the amount of overtime paid in a given two-week period. With this information, both the mayor and the head of the Solid Waste Bureau can devise a plan to ensure that missed trash pick-ups happen less frequently or that those dirty alleys are cleaned up. CitiStat has proven to be a very powerful management and accountability tool, allowing the mayor to hear how the various functions of the city's government are performing.

FIGURE 7.2 – SAMPLE PERFORMANCE MEASUREMENT ARCHITECTURE FOR A HUMAN RESOURCE (HR) ORGANIZATION

Mission

To be recognized as an innovative and efficient business partner in the provision of high quality human resource services across the organization

Objectives

Finances	Quality of Service	Client Satisfaction	Employee Satisfaction	Continuous Improvement
To ensure cost effective HR services	On time delivery of high-quality HR services across the organization	To achieve a high level of customer satisfaction with HR services	To develop and maintain an organization of highly professional and dedicated staff	To establish a culture dedicated to innovation and learning

Strategies

Resource Review HR Framework	Best-in-Class Service Regional Leadership Quality Control IT Strategy	Client Communication and Education Client Partnership	Recruit/ Retain Staff Staff Development & Communication Reward/ Recognition Program	Best Practices

Performance Measures

Revenues Expenditures Capital Financial Ratios	HR Management Index Project Management Index	Client Satisfaction Index	Employee Satisfaction Index Human Resource Management Index	Continuous Improvement Index

Source: Shane, Bryan. 2003. "Performance Measurement System: A Leadership-Driven Methodology." Optimum online. The Journal of Public Sector Management. Vol. 33, Issue 3, Sep 2003. http://www.bpc-gallery.com/leadership_driven.html.

Designing a Performance Measurement System

Developing a *performance measurement system* need not be complex. It is likely, however, to be trying for those unaccustomed to measuring and establishing *performance targets*. A system of measuring performance requires that one understand what an organization or program is trying to achieve, who its clients are, and what level of service is being delivered at the time. The seven specific steps are:

1. Identifying a program to measure
2. Designing a purpose statement
3. Classifying program inputs, outputs, outcomes, and efficiency indicators
4. Setting performance targets
5. Monitoring performance
6. Reporting performance results
7. Concluding with analysis and action

Step 1. Identifying a Program to Measure. Governmental activities need to be identified clearly and separated into distinct programs. Programs are collections of activities that provide a specific public service. For example, street resurfacing, pot hole filling, and curb repairing are three activities that could collectively comprise a program called "street maintenance." Selecting what programs to measure is somewhat subjective. Regardless of the programs selected, though, performance measurement systems typically are most effective when they collect a limited amount of essential information about a program's performance.

> "You get what you measure. Measure the wrong thing and you get the wrong behaviors."
>
> **JOHN H. LINGLE**
> Target Measurement Pioneer

Step 2. Designing a Purpose Statement. Preparing a statement of purpose is a vital step in the development of a performance system. Measuring a program's performance is not feasible without an initial understanding of what the program should accomplish. A cogent mission statement is highly desirable. If the program does not have mission statement, then a detailed program description may suffice. For example, the Government Accounting Standards Board (GASB) provides the following purpose statement for government transportation services: "The basic purpose is to provide safe, dependable, convenient, and comfortable transportation services at minimum cost to the citizens, including special client groups such as the handicapped and elderly" (Hatry et al. 1990).

Step 3. Classifying Program Inputs, Outputs, Outcomes, and Efficiency Indica-

tors. Inputs represent resources; they are expressed within a given program's operating budget, in addition to the number of employee hours allotted over a specified period of time. Outputs are workload measures such as the amount of work completed or the quantity of services a program provides. Outcome indicators reflect the results of a program's efforts. Efficiency indicators measure the relationship of cost (whether in dollars or employee hours) to either outputs or outcomes.

Step 4. Setting Performance Targets. Managers need to know when program goals and objectives have been met. A program's effectiveness and quality is best determined by establishing measurable objectives in the context of time periods, quantities, and percentages. For example, for a street cleanliness program, this may mean having a citizen cleanliness rating of at least 70 percent each year, and a trained observer cleanliness rating of at least 80 percent each year. Note, however, that performance targets are not restricted to outcome indicators. Organizations

FIGURE 7.3 – STRATEGIES FOR PERFORMANCE MEASUREMENT SUCCESS

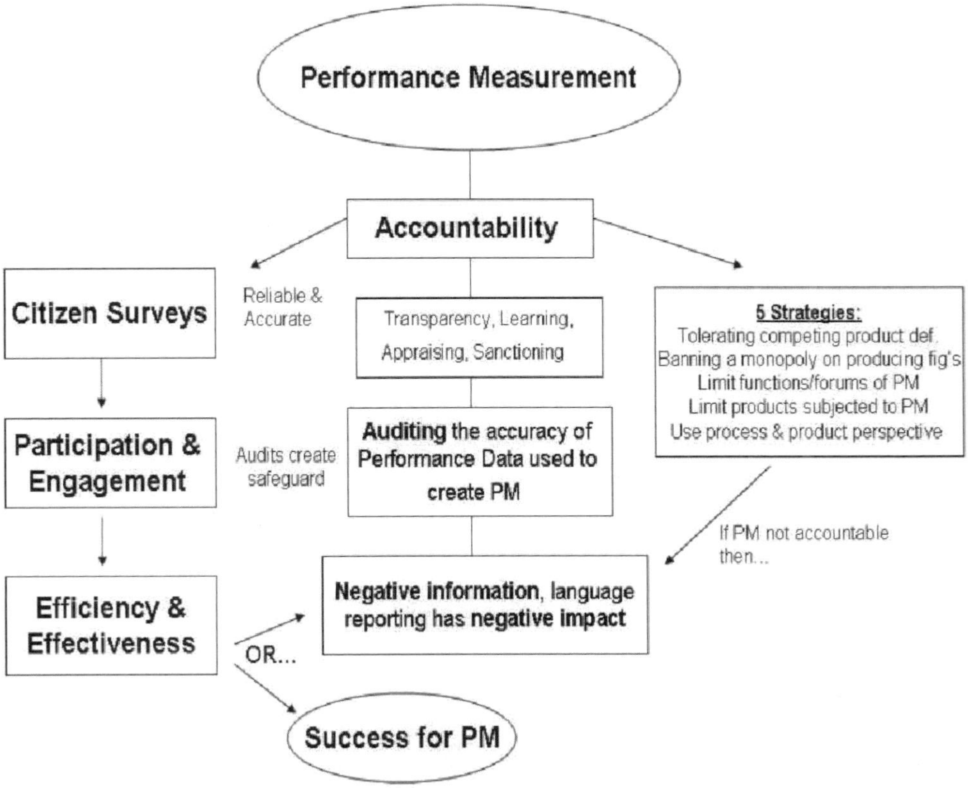

Source: M.B. Vergara. 2006. School of Public Affairs and Administration, Rutgers University–Newark.

can set similar targets for input, output, or efficiency indicators (for example, when budgets are experiencing shortfalls, setting input targets may prove worthwhile).

Step 5. Monitoring Performance. Each performance target needs to be monitored. Public managers can then make corrective changes if the performance data indicate a potential problem. Systematic and regular monitoring is essential. For instance, if a performance target is that 95 percent of park visitors are "satisfied" with a park's cleanliness and general maintenance from year-to-year, it does not mean that performance data should be collected and examined only once a year. Smaller-scale data collection efforts should be completed on a quarterly or even monthly basis. Doing so affords managers a more complete understanding of what is going on in terms of performance. Using the parks example, it would be easy to miss seasonal (or cyclical) patterns in customer satisfaction if data were collected at only one point in time during the year. An equally important point is the performance data collection should be practical and not overburden an organization's resource and personnel capacities.

Step 6. Reporting Performance Results. Performance reporting entails summarizing all the indicators and comparing the collected data to the performance targets

FIGURE 7.4 – DOWNSIDE OF PERFORMANCE MEASUREMENT

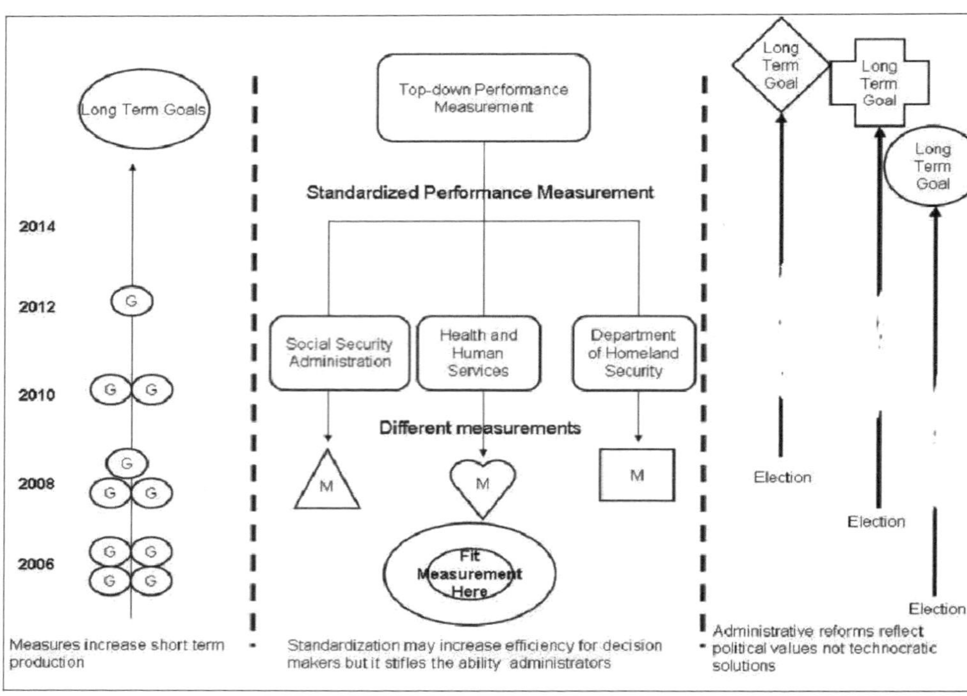

Source: D. Bromberg. 2006. School of Public Affairs and Administration, Rutgers University–Newark.

discussed previously. Besides performance target comparisons, performance reporting can include comparisons with: (1) past years, (2) similar jurisdictions, or (3) professionally developed standards or norms. Performance reporting formats vary somewhat, but, at a minimum, they should be presented in a convenient arrangement that includes: (1) program name, organization, and statement of purpose; (2) inputs, outputs, outcomes, and efficiency indicators; (3) performance targets; and (4) presentation of performance data in a way that facilitates clear comparisons.

FIGURE 7.5 – THE CONCEPTUAL FRAMEWORK OF CITIZEN-INITIATED PERFORMANCE ASSESSMENT

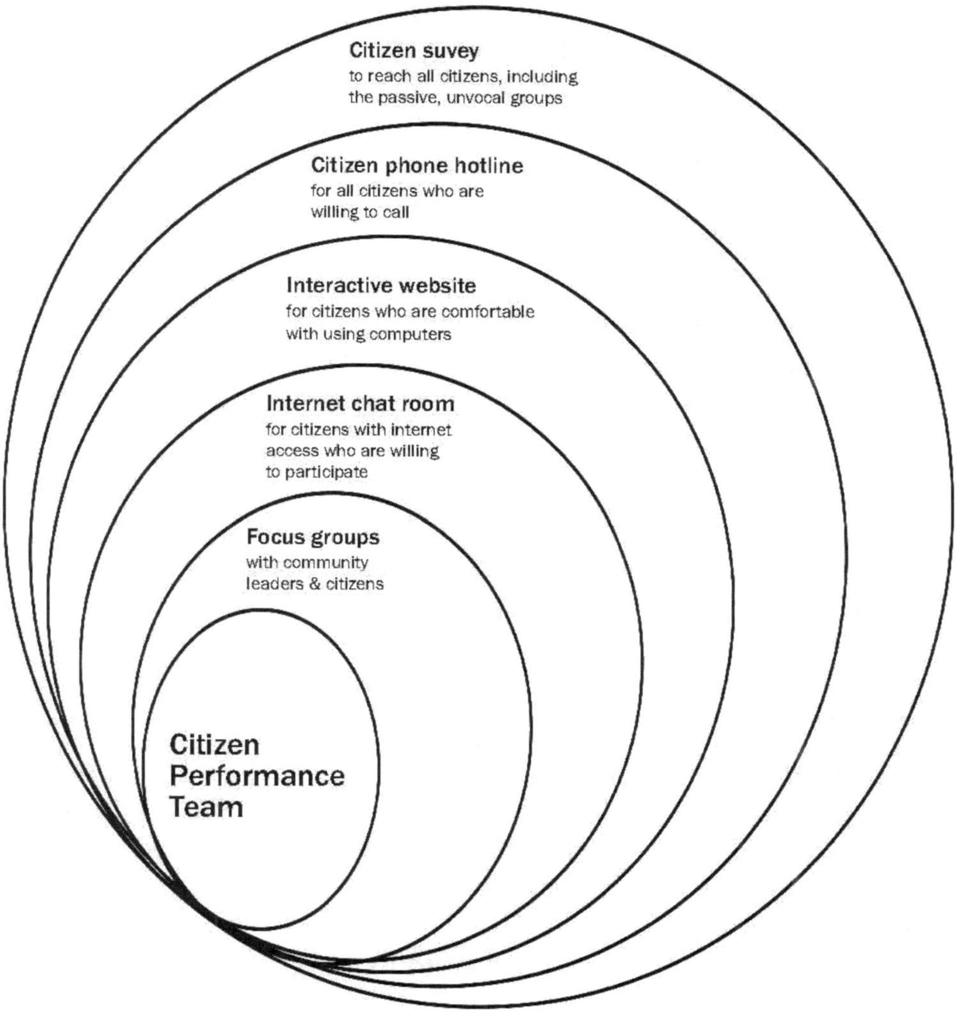

Source: A. Ho and P. Coates. 2004. "Citizen-Initiated Performance Assessment: The Initial Iowa Experience," Public Productivity & Management Review 27, no. 3: 34. Used by permission of M.E. Sharpe, Inc.

Straphangers Campaign

The Straphangers Campaign represents a bold attempt to influence the accountability, accessibility and performance of local government on behalf of its citizens.

Through the New York Public Interest Research Group (NYPIRG), the Straphangers Campaign received a grant from the Alfred P. Sloan Foundation to "launch a new in-depth effort to measure the quality of the transit service." The goal was to accurately report on the condition of the New York City's transit system and to draw media, public and governmental attention to the need to continue to invest in transit.

By the mid 1990s, ridership had plummeted to its lowest level since 1917. Many businesses cited poor transportation as the main reason for relocating from New York City. An editorial in the *New York Times* on October 5, 1995 seemed to summarize the sentiment at the time: "Then the near-ruin of local mass transit was taken as a metaphor for the decline and fall of the City itself. But New York did not fall, and thanks to a $20 billion rebuilding plan, the subways got better. Now, it seems the battle must be fought all over again."

In their application to the Alfred P. Sloan Foundation, the NYPRIG wrote, "It is to hold the Transit Authority accountable by a sophisticated range of measures – and to communicate that information to the public in lively and meaningful ways."

The Straphangers Campaign has developed a measure of how riders rate their subway lines. The Straphangers Campaign has also collected data from transit officials and all data is presented in a clear and accessible format. A panel of thirty-eight transit experts also completed questionnaires by prioritizing certain aspects of the subway and bus service. This information was compiled for use in two sets of reports: one based on a review of official transit statistics and the other, based on NYPIRG's own field studies.

The first report under this Sloan project was released in 1997, profiling New York City's twenty major subway lines on six key official measures of service, including the amount of scheduled service, the chance of getting a seat during the most congested periods, the cleanliness of the cars and the adequacy of the announcements. Another twenty-one page report highlighted the state of the bus system. These two sets of reports represented the most comprehensive review by any non-governmental organization of the performance of a major public transportation system. They achieved two goals. First, they provided a solid baseline for comparing subway service in the future. And, second, they gave riders, communities and officials information they would need to press the transit authority for better service.

The Straphangers Campaign's work generated substantial media coverage. In particular, the comparative value assigned to each of the twenty subway lines evaluated enabled riders to make decisions about those lines that they frequented, i.e, what percentage of the full value of a token had been achieved. According to the 1998 report, riders just wanted to know how their lines performed. Do their trains break down more or less often than the average for New York City subways? Is there a better or worse chance of getting a seat? How clean are the subway cars? Do the trains come more or less often? Do the trains arrive irregularly or with few gaps in service? How good or bad are the announcements?

Recently, the Straphangers Campaign concluded the following about the subway system:

- Subway cars grew dirtier and announcements poorer. The findings on announcements and dirt mirror independent surveys by the Straphangers Campaign
- There was a slightly greater chance of getting a seat during rush hour. However, the report probably underestimated the impact of recent increases in ridership.
- Car breakdowns occurred less often. However, on a majority of lines, car breakdowns increased, although any improvement to the system was due to large improvements on several lines.
- There were great disparities in how subway lines performed as measured in response to questions posed by riders.

Overall, the Straphangers Campaign has found that riders simply want short waits, regular and reliable service, a chance for a seat, a clean subway car and clear announcements.

Although the Straphangers Campaign encountered a number of obstacles, including limited access to transit officials, they stepped up efforts to bring "real time" information to the public. An interactive website has also been established.

Source: Written by G.L.A. Harris and Marc Holzer. For more information, visit the Straphangers website at www.straphangers.org. Reprinted with permission from the PA TIMES, monthly newspaper of the American Society for Public Administration (ASPA), www.aspanet.org.

Step 7. Concluding with Analysis and Action. A well designed system of measuring performance will enable decision makers to identify organizational or program strengths, weaknesses, opportunities, and threats. An enhanced understanding of strengths and weaknesses assists managers in diagnosing problems and taking relevant actions to remedy those problems.

Citizen-Driven Performance Measurement

The public sector offers an ideal venue for implementing a formal performance measurement system. Based on the information collected, public managers identify weak areas within an organization and make corrective changes. A supplementary approach to performance measurement entails bringing average citizens into the process. Weeks (2000) maintains that including citizens in the performance measurement process can potentially reduce participatory lethargy, skepticism toward government, and the rift between the citizenry and public decision makers—and these important benefits accrue as on outgrowth of reaching the primary goal, which is enhancing performance measures.

While there are benefits to including citizens in public-sector performance measurement, there are a number of noteworthy challenges, as well. A citizen's role in

FIGURE 7.6 – CITIZEN INVOLVEMENT: THE CASE OF DES MOINES, IOWA

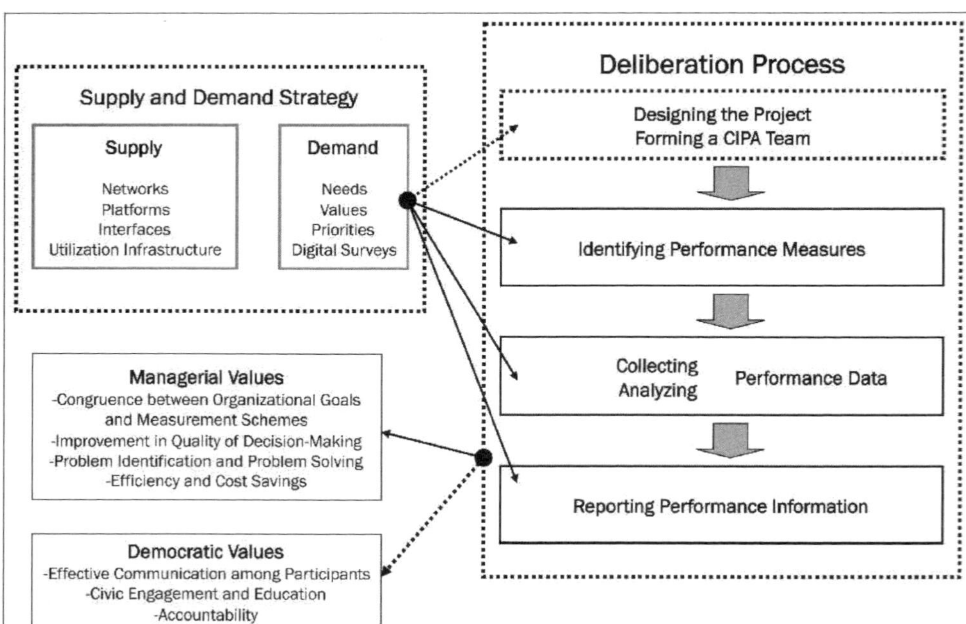

Source: S. Kwak. 2006. School of Public Affairs and Administration, Rutgers University–Newark.

government is typically distant and passive, rarely going beyond writing letters or signing petitions (King 2002). Many citizens prefer passivity, and many officials welcome it. Public managers would need additional training to engage citizens in processes of decision-making, and doing so would require commitments of time and resources (Roberts 1997; Weeks 2000). Regardless of such challenges, the inclusion of citizens in performance measurement has become central to public administrators (Nalbandian 1999; Vigoda 2002).

The Balanced Scorecard

The balanced scorecard concept as a management tool was first developed in 1992 by David Norton and Robert Kaplan. Adopted in the private sector first, it allowed for significant improvements in organizational performance. The balanced scorecard (BSC) goes beyond traditional measures—measures that are chiefly financial in nature—by offering a "balanced" methodology for assessing the effectiveness with which the organization fulfills its vision and strategy. It aligns performance measures in four categories: financial management, customer focus, internal business processes, and learning and growth. BSC translates strategies into clearly de-

FIGURE 7.7 - PERFORMANCE MANAGEMENT DASHBOARD WITH THE BALANCED SCORECARD OF THE WASHINGTON STATE TRANSPORTATION IMPROVEMENT BOARD

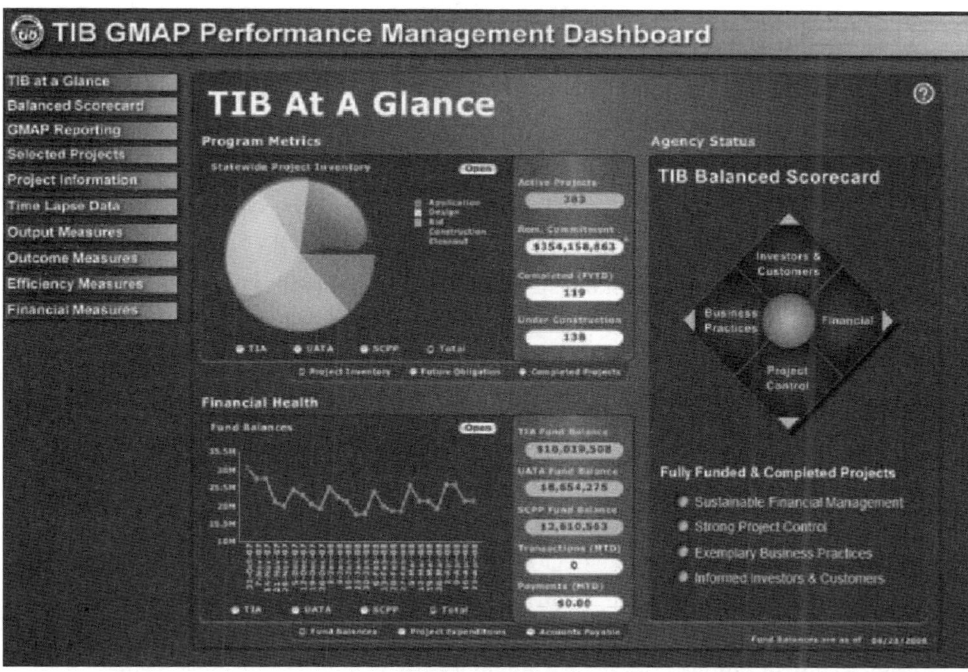

Source: S. Kwak. 2006. School of Public Affairs and Administration, Rutgers University-Newark.

Citizen-Initiated Performance Assessment: The Case of Iowa

In 2001, the Alfred P. Sloan Foundation funded a three-year project in Iowa called Citizen-Initiated Performance Assessment, which engages citizens, city council members, and departmental staff in the development and use of performance measures to evaluate public services. Thirty-two Iowa cities with populations above 10,000 were contacted initially. Eventually, the city councils, departmental staff, and citizen representatives of nine cities (Burlington, Carroll, Clive, Des Moines, Indianola, Johnston, Marion, Marshalltown, and Urbandale) made the commitment to the project.

The Iowa CIPA project differs from traditional performance measurement in three major respects. First, it emphasizes collaboration among citizens, elected officials, and managers in developing performance measures to ensure political credibility and receptivity of the measures. Second, it emphasizes the citizen perspective in performance measurement, rather than the managerial perspective that often emphasizes input and cost-efficiency. Third, it emphasizes public dissemination of performance measurement results to hold government accountable.

In the first year of the CIPA project, each participating city formed a "citizen performance team." Citizens from diverse backgrounds make up the majority of the team. For example, the city of Des Moines asked representatives from neighborhood associations to participate. Some cities pursued public recruitment of citizens through newspaper announcements, city newsletters, and the city cable TV. Many also recruited members from other citizen committees and community organizations. In addition to citizens, each performance team had one or two staff representatives and a city council member.

In the initial meetings, the performance team had a brief review of city government operations. Some cities also asked citizens to develop strategies to recruit additional members based on a city's demography. Then the team selected one or two public services for performance measurement, usually based on fiscal significance, direct impact on citizens, and current citizen concerns. The Iowa CIPA project currently covers police, fire and EMS, library, recreational center, street repair, snow removal, public transportation, solid waste management, nuisance control, and park and recreation services.

While each of the nine cities can decide its project progress, all of them generally adhere to the following model: In the first stage of the project, the citizen performance team identifies the "critical elements" of a selected public service. For example, for nuisance control, some of the critical elements are response time, effectiveness in resolving service requests, and effectiveness in public reporting of departmental actions. For the police, the critical elements include response time, professionalism in interaction with citizens, competency and effectiveness in investigation, sufficiency of patrol, and legal compliance of officers.

Based on the critical elements, the performance team develops measures and evaluates them. Among evaluation criteria, understandability and usefulness to the public are the most important measures developed for public reporting.

In the second stage of CIPA, city departments develop necessary instruments, such as citizen or user surveys, to collect performance data. At the same time, citizens help collect some performance data, report the project progress to the city council, and develop strategies to better engage the general public in the project.

Finally, the performance measurement results are reported to the performance team, the city council, and the general public. Public input is solicited to improve performance. City departments then integrate the results in strategic planning, performance-based budgeting, and activity-based management of service operations.

The Iowa CIPA project is currently in its second stage. While it may be premature to conclude any long-term impact of the project, several lessons have been learned. First, CIPA helps officials focus on outcome measures and citizen concerns. This enhances public accountability and the result orientation of public services. Second, CIPA shows the importance of public communication. For example, a department should not ignore notification of citizens about the progress or results of departmental actions after a service request is filed. Third, managers should prepare for comparative performance measurement, as many citizens are interested in knowing how well their city performs relative to others in the neighboring area. Fourth, many performance measures should be reported at the neighborhood level to enhance their relevancy to citizens. Finally, public reporting of performance measurement is important. Cities should consider the usage of technologies, such as the Internet, to do this cost-effectively. Many cities have been collecting performance data for decades. CIPA simply changes the perspective of managers and elected officials by engaging citizens so that the public can influence the bases on which government services are evaluated.

Source: National Center for Public Performance. 2004. "Iowa. Citizen Initiated Performance Assessment (CIPA)." Teaching Case. Citizen-Driven Government Performance. Written by Paul Coates and Alfred Tat-Kei Ho. ASPA members Paul Coates and Alfred Ho co-lead the Iowa project. Reprinted with permission from the PA TIMES, monthly newspaper of the American Society for Public Administration (ASPA), www.aspanet.org.

fined objectives, measures, performance targets, and initiatives that address achievement in those four categories.

- Financial: "To succeed financially, how should we appear to our shareholders?"
- Customer: "To achieve our vision, how should we appear to our customers?"
- Internal processes: "To satisfy our shareholders and customers, at what business processes must we excel?"
- Learning: "To achieve our vision, how will we sustain our ability to change and improve?" (Mathys and Thompson 2005)

The Social Aspects of Performance

Bureau-pathology

Public organizations are facing increasing pressures to perform at a high level, but several sources of tension may undermine efforts to improve performance. In particular, most organizations suffer from bureaucratic stagnation, which can have unanticipated pathological consequences. Whether justified or not, bureaucracy carries with it a reputation for mediocrity, which is captured in sayings like "don't rock the boat" or "go along to get along." Other negative consequences of bureaucracy include a loss of personal autonomy, directing one's energies toward resolving personal problems rather than organizational problems, engaging in office politics, and abusing fellow employees. Bureaucracies—sometimes too often—transform their workers into impersonal machines, the consequence of which is less productive responses to citizen demands and needs.

Management-Workforce Cooperation

The contention that too much bureaucracy suppresses public performance has given rise to alternative theories. Osborne and Gaebler (1992) champion an en-

EXERCISE 7.1

City of Deficitprone—Improving Public Performance (Simulation)

After completing the simulation, students will identify the unrealized opportunities for productivity improvements and the obstacles to them. What are the conflicts and how would you address them?

Canfield, Roger and Marc Holzer. 1977. Management-Labor Productivity Simulation: City of Deficitprone. *Public Productivity Review* 2 (4) (Fall): 38–47.

trepreneurial approach to public administration as opposed to the traditional bureaucratic approach. Central to overcoming bureaucratic pathologies is management-workforce collaboration. Many public administrators agree that cooperation between rank-and-file workers and upper-level decision makers—that is, labor and middle management—is essential to improving organizational performance. However, the notion of cooperation goes well beyond contributions to the office suggestion box; rather, it involves the formation and use of performance committees and quality circles. These provide a means of discussing and disseminating innovative and productive ideas throughout an organization. The hierarchical and centralized bureaucratic model is replaced by an egalitarian partnership comprised of upper- and lower-level employees, which increases the possibility of innovation and risk taking, given that everyone within the organization possesses a psychological stake in its improvement (Grace and Holzer 1992).

– I'VE BEEN WHATCHING THEM ALL DAY: NOT A SINGLE PERSON IS WORKING...
Artist: Z. Yefimovsky; "The Fighting Pencil" group, 1980.

Workforce Motivation and Incentives

Often overlooked are the social and psychological aspects that affect organizational performance. Classical performance improvement models were borrowed from the private sector, an example being Frederick Taylor's scientific management model. Rooted in the assumption that workers are motivated primarily by money, Taylorism provides a limited perspective of productivity and performance. Classical management principles maintain that individuals are motivated by fear—the fear of losing their jobs. As a result of this fear, workers will follow orders. The intricacies of worker motivation are underscored in the Hawthorne experiments, Maslow's hierarchy of needs, and in particular McGregor's Theory X and Theory Y assumptions about workers (all of which have been discussed in earlier chapters).

At times, the authority vested in supervisory, management, and upper-management positions may lead some "higher ups" to make erroneous assumptions about lower-level workers. Such individuals embrace Theory X assumptions that:

- Supervisors and managers are given the lead roles.
- Workers are the supporting cast for supervisors and managers.
- The cast must be micromanaged.
- Employees require comprehensive training because they inherently resist change.
- Fear is the chief motivator.

> "Without a standard there is no logical basis for making a decision or taking action."
>
> **JOSEPH M. JURAN**
> "Father" of Quality Management
> (1904–2008)

Most people in positions of authority are inclined to take the Theory X view of workers, while those in subordinate positions are more likely to view themselves as "Y" workers. The Y scenario assumes:

- All workers are important.
- Workers are professionals who are willing to learn and prefer being self-directed.
- There are many sources of motivation that go beyond fear and money, such as praise and feeling good about one's work.

The differences between Theories X and Y is the difference between a success and a flop, between an underachiever and an overachiever, between loss and profit, between employee conflict and cooperation, between success and organizational failure. Rigid "X" assumptions can be broken. Transitioning from X to Y is possible when status, dominance, distance, decision-making power, praise, and information are available to employees at all levels in an organization.

The Role of Privatization in Government Performance

Under increasing scrutiny regarding their efficiency and effectiveness, public organizations risk losing some of their essential functions to the private sector. Privatization and contracting out are two frequently used and often expensive alternatives to underachieving public organizations. Even though these terms are often used interchangeably, privatization and contracting out are slightly different. *Privatization* refers to the complete transfer of a government function to the private sector. It sometimes entails the sale of government enterprises and assets or the demonopolization of government functions—which will allow private-sector alternatives to emerge (Savas 1992). With privatization, government is removed, and what remains is a relationship between a private entity and its customers. This relationship is a financial one. With *contracting out*, a private organization works on behalf of the government. The relationship essentially involves three parties—the private organization provides the service, the customers receive the service, and the entire process is overseen by the government. Contracting out differs from privatization given that government still has some measure of control over the private organization delivering the services.

Champions of privatization and contracting out argue that the private sector does things better. Private organizations are more innovative and more fiscally responsible than government. They have greater motivation and fewer impediments to delivering services. A recurring argument for privatization and contracting out is that market competition makes all the difference: because private organizations are competing with each other, they will work to provide the best service at the lowest cost (Donahue 1989).

UOFO (UNREASONABLE OBJECTIVES–FOCUSED ORGANIZATION): WORKING BEYOND BOUNDARIES ON THE ORGANIZATIONAL CHART

Performance measurement and management is a critical action for enhancing the level of performance as well as increasing accountability to citizens. It is important, therefore, to design a correct performance measurement and management system for any type of organization. Perhaps, most important, a performance measurement system should induce employees to work together for an upper level goal beyond departmental boundaries. This means that performance measurement system should deal with "white space" (or missing capacities) on the organizational chart. Every organization might have long term plans and strategies, but very few organizations fully and effectively implement those strategies. This does not mean that organizations are not willing to implement strategies, but that they do not know how to allocate resources for an upper level goal beyond an organizational unit boundary. To do this, cooperation among different organizational units is critical and a performance measurement system should encourage employees to work together for an organizational goal outside the confines of the formal organizational chart.

We call this an Unreasonable Objectives–focused Organization (UOFO). These objectives are unreasonable to those who believe achieving their unit's/department's established goals is their duty and there is no need to look at upper level goals. These people believe that forcing them to take care of upper level goals is beyond their responsibilities. They are likely to assume that summation of parts will automatically be the whole. It should be mentioned, however, that the whole is not always the summation of the parts.

From this perspective, UOFO pushes employees to cooperate beyond boundaries in order to achieve upper level goals at those organizational levels. The following figure shows how different units can work together to reach organizational goal.

For this organization to work, an organization must designate the–so–called performance owner whose power and responsibility are sufficiently substantial to control or influence employees from other units/departments.

In Korea, the city of Nonsan (local government) and Mine Reclamation Corporation (public enterprise) have recently adopted the UOFO model. Under this model, different units work together on a number of jobs created at the organizational level. Before the UOFO was introduced, each department was trying to fulfill jobs for different customers and citizens in its own area. Now, the Department

FIGURE 7.8 – UOFO APPLICATION EXAMPLE

of Social Welfare (creating jobs for the handicapped and senior citizens) works together with the Department of Enterprise Support (inducing enterprises and supporting small businesses) in Nonsan city.

Considering the traditional hierarchical structure wherein the unit of command principle has dominated, applying UOFO might be expected to lead to resistance from organizational members to the extent they have two bosses at the same time (Performance Owner and Chief of Business Unit). Please discuss barriers and strategies to successfully implement the UOFO model in the public sector. Can you also identify different strategies and barriers given that the two countries' organizational cultures are different?

KEY TERMS

Attribution
Captive agency
Continuous improvement
Contracting out
Customer focus
Decentralization
Efficiency indicators
Empowerment
Entrapment
External customer
Functional differentiation
Horizontal teamwork
Information distortion
Input indicators
Integration
Internal customer
Interorganizational teamwork
KSAs (knowledge, skills and abilities)
Output indicators
Outcome indicators
Parochialism
Performance measurement
Performance measurement system
Performance targets
Privatization
Productivity improvement
Programs
Public performance
Representativeness
Responsiveness
Teamwork
Total Quality Management (TQM)
Trained incapacity
Vertical teamwork

REFERENCES

Behn, R.D. 2003. "Why Measure Performance? Different Purposes Require Different Measures." *Public Administration Review* 63, no. 5: 586–606.

Berman and West. 1995. "Municipal Commitment to Total Quality Management: A Survey of Recent Progress." *Public Administration Review* 55, no. 1: 57–66.

Brocker, J and Rubin J.Z. 1985. *Entrapment in Escalating Conflicts: A Social Psychological Analysis*. New York: Springer-Verlag.

Deming, W.E. 1986. *Out of the Crisis*. Cambridge, MA: MIT Center for Advanced Engineering Study.

Donahue, J.D. 1989. *The Privatization Decision: Public Ends, Private Means*. New York: Basic Books.

Downs. 1967. *Inside Bureaucracy*. Boston: Little, Brown and Company.

Exemplary State and Local Awards Program (EXSL). 1989–1995. National Center for Public Productivity, Rutgers University, Newark, NJ.

Florida Department of Corrections. 1997. "Secretary's Message, 1996–97 Annual Report." http://www.dc.state.fl.us/pub/annual/9697/sec.html.

Flynn, B.B., S. Sakakibara, and R.G. Schroeder. 1995. "Relationship Between JIT and TQM: Practices and Performance." *Academy of Management Journal*. 38, no. 5: 1325–60.

General Accounting Office (GAO). 1992. "Program Performance Measures: Federal Agency Collection and Use of Performance Data." Report to the Chairman and Ranking Minority Member, Committee on Governmental Affairs, U.S. Senate. Washington, DC: GAO.

Gortner, H., J. Mahler, and B.J. Nicholson (eds.). 1987. *Organization Theory: A Public Perspective*. Pacific Grove, CA: Brooks/Cole.

Government Executive Magazine, January 12, 1995.

Grace, S.L., and M. Holzer. 1992. "Labor-Management Cooperation: An Opportunity for Change." In *Public Productivity Handbook*, ed. M. Holzer, 487–98. New York: Marcel Dekker.

Hamilton, Lee V. 1980. "Intuitive Psychologist or Intuitive Lawyer? Alternative Models of the Attribution Process." *Journal of Personality and Social Psychology*. 39, no. 5: 767–72.

Hatry, H.P. 1977. *How Effective Are Your Community Services?* Washington, DC: Urban Institute.

———. 1979. *Efficiency Measurement for Local Government Services*. Washington, DC: Urban Institute.

Hatry, H.P., Fountain, J.R. Jr., Sullivan, J.M., and Kremer, L. 1990. "Service Efforts and Accomplishments Reporting: Its Time Has Come." Government Accounting Standards Board (GASB): Library of Congress Catalog Card Number: 90–80879.

Heider, F. 1958. *The Psychology of Interpersonal Relations*. New York: Wiley.

Holt, G.D., P.E.D., Love, and L. Jawahar-Nesan. 2000. "Employee Empowerment in Construction: An Implementation Model for Process Improvement." *Team Performance Management*. 6 (3/4): 47–51.

Holzer, M. and S. H. Lee. 1999. "Labor Management Tension and Partnership: Where Are We? What Should We Do?" *International Review of Public Administration*. 4, no. 2: 33–44.

Kaufman, H. 1987. Administrative Decentralization and Political Power. In *Classics of Public Administration,* 1969, ed. J.M. Shafritz and A. C. Hyde, pp. 389–404. 2d.ed. Chicago: Dorsey.

King, C.S. 2002. "Is Performance-oriented Government Democratic?" In *Meeting the Challenges of Performance-oriented Government.* ed. K. Newcomer, E.T. Jennings, Jr., C. Broom, and A. Lomax. Washington, DC: ASPA.

Klingner, Donald E. . and John Nalbandian. 1998. *Public Personnel Management: Contexts and Strategies*. Upper Saddle River, NJ: Prentice Hall/Simon & Schuster.

Lee, S.H. 2000a. "Understanding Productivity Improvement in a Turbulent Environment: A Symposium Introduction." *Public Productivity and Management Review* 23: 423–27.

Lee, S.H. 2000b. "A Multidimensional View of Public Sector Employee Commitment and Willingness to Support Productivity Improvement Strategies: A Comparative Study of Public Employees at Managerial Level between the United States and South Korea." Unpublished dissertation, Rutgers University, Newark, NJ.

Lee, S.H. 2001. "Barriers to Active Citizen Participation in the Public Sector: Lessons Learned from South Korea." In *Current Topics in Management,* ed. M.A. Rahim, R.T. Golembievski, K.D. Mackenzie, vol.6, 309–30. New York: JAI.

Mathys, N.J., and K.R. Thompson. 2005. *Using the Balanced Scorecard: Lessons Learned from the U.S. Postal Service and the Defense Finance and Accounting Service.* Washington, DC: IBM Center for the Business in Government.

McGowan, R.P., and Wittmer, D.P. 1997. "Five Great Issues in Decision Making." In *Handbook of Public Adminsitration,* ed. J. Hildreth, W.B. Miller, 2d ed, 293–320. New York: Marcel Dekker.

———. 1998. "Gaining a Competitive Edge: Economic Development Strategies for State and Local Governments," *Public Administration Quarterly* 22, no. 3: 301–14.

Merton, R. K. 1987. "Bureaucratic Structure and Personality (1940)." In *Classics of Public Administration,* ed. J.M. Shafritz, A.C. Hyde, 2d ed., 107–16. Chicago: Dorsey.

Milakovich, M. 1992. "Total Quality Management for Public Service Productivity Improvement." In *Public Productivity Handbook,* ed. M. Holzer, 577–602. New York: Marcel Dekker.

Miller, D.T. and Ross, M. 1975. "Self-Serving Biases in the Attribution of Causality." *Psychological Bulletin* 82: 213–25.

Nalbandian, J. 1999. "Facilitating Community, Enabling Democracy: New Roles for Local Government Managers." *Public Administration Review* 59, no. 3: 187–97.

New Jersey Motor Vehicle Commission (NJMVC). 2006. "Toward a Serviced Model of Efficiency: New Jersey Motor Vehicle Commission Service Assessment." www.state.nj.us/mvc/pdf/About/assess_2006_0330.pdf.

Norton, D. and R. Kaplan. 1992. "The Balanced Scorecard—Measures that Drive Performance." *Harvard Business Review* January/February: 71–79.

O'Reilly, C. A. 1978. "The Intentional Distortion of Information in Organizational Communication: A Laboratory and Field Investigation." *Human Relations* 31, no. 2: 173–93.

Osborne, D., and T. Gaebler. 1992. *Reinventing Government: How the Entrepreneurial Spirit Is Transforming the Public Sector*. Reading, MA: Addison-Wesley.

Paddock, S. C. 1997. "Administrative Benchmarks in Management Training." *Public Productivity and Management Review* 21, no. 2: 192–202.

Pennsylvania State Governor's Office. 2001. http://www.governor.state.pa.us/portal/server.pt/community/governor%27s_web_site/2985.

Pollock, T. 2001. "For Improved Teamwork, Keep Them Informed." *Automotive Design and Production* 10: 10.

Public Performance Measurement and Reporting Network. http://www.ppmrn.net.

Rago, W. V. 1994. "Adapting Total Quality Management (TQM) to Government: Another Point of View." *Public Administration Review* 54: 61–64.

——. 1996. "Struggles in Transformation: A Study in TQM, Leadership Organizational Culture in a Government Agency." *Public Administration Review* 56: 227–34.

Roberts, N. 1997. "Public Deliberation: An Alternative Approach to Crafting Policy and Setting Direction." *Public Administration Review* 57, no. 2: 124–32.

Rourke, F. E. 1984. *Bureaucracy, Politics, and Public Policy*. 3d ed. Boston: Little, Brown.

Savas, E.S. 1992. "Privatization and Productivity." In *Public Productivity Handbook*, ed. M. Holzer, 79–98. New York: Marcel Dekker.

Shea, C.M. and Howell, J.M. 1998. "Organizational Antecedents to the Successful Implementation of Total Quality Management." *Journal of Qualitative Management* 3: 3–24.

Simon, H. A. 1997. *Administrative Behavior. A Study of Decision Making Processes in Administrative Oraanizations*. 4th ed. New York: Free Press.

Swiss, J. E. 1992. "Adapting Total Quality Management (TQM) to Government." *Public Administration Review* 52: 356–62.

Urban Institute and International City Management Association. 1974. *Measuring the Effectiveness of Basic Municipal Services*. Washington, DC: Urban Institute.

Urban Institute. 1980. *Performance Measurement: A Guide for Local Elected Officials*. The Urban Institute in cooperation with The National League of Cities and National Association of Counties. Washington, DC: The Urban Institute Press.

Vigoda, E. 2002. "Administrative Agents of Democracy? A Structural Equation Modeling of the Relationship Between Public-Sector Performance and Citizenship Involvement." *Journal of Public Administration Research and Theory* 12, no. 2: 241.

Wallach. 1983. "Individuals and Organizations: The Cultural Match." *Training and Development Journal* 37: 29–36.

Washington State Governor's Office. 2000. http://access.wa.gov/.

Weeks, E.C. 2000. "The Practice of Deliberative Democracy: Results from Four Large-Scale Trials." *Public Administration Review* 60, no. 4: 360–72.

White, O. E. and J. E. Wolf. 1995a. "Deming's Total Quality Management Movement and the Baskin Robbins Problem. Part One: Is It Time to Go Back to Vanilla?" *Administration & Society*. 27, no. 2: 203–25.

——1995b. "Part Two: Is This Ice Cream American?" *Administration & Society* 27, no. 3: 307–21.

SUPPLEMENTARY READINGS

Gore, A. 1993. *From Red Tape to Results: Creating a Government That Works Better and Costs Less: The Report of the National Performance Review*. Washington, DC: U.S. Government Printing Office.

ELECTRONIC RESOURCES

APQC (formerly known as the American Productivity and Quality Center; a non-profit agency that provides benchmarking and best-practice research to organizations worldwide): http://www.apqc.org

ExpectMore.gov (a site developed by the U.S. Office of Management and Budget devoted to ranking the performance of federal agencies): www.expectmore.gov

Government Accounting Standards Board (GASB), Service Efforts and Accomplishments Reporting for Governments: http://www.seagov.org/index.shtml

Government Finance Officer's Association (GFOA) of the United States and Canada, Performance Measurement Website:
http://www.gfoa.org/index.php?option=com_content&task=view&id=479&Itemid=250

National Institute of Standards and Technology, Baldrige National Quality Program: http://www.quality.nist.gov

Office of Management and Budget: Performance Measurement Challenges and Strategies http://www.whitehouse.gov/omb/challenges_strategies

Office of Management and Budget: Best Practices for Collecting and Using Current and Past Performance Information

http://www.whitehouse.gov/omb/best_practice_re_past_perf

The W. Edwards Deming Institute: www.deming.org

CHAPTER 8

Program Evaluation

In Chapter 8, students are presented with the fundamentals of program evaluation. Upon reading this chapter, students will understand what program evaluation is and how one goes about completing an evaluation. This chapter discusses the various techniques for collecting information (or data) and the importance of stakeholders in this process. It also examines the types of program evaluations and concludes with a discussion of ethical conduct for program evaluators.

"Evaluation is the process of determining the merit, worth, and value of things."

MICHAEL SCRIVEN
Evaluation Theorist

A focus group can provide valuable feedback.

WHAT IS PROGRAM EVALUATION?

Throughout the late 1950s and early 1960s, the *policy sciences* emerged as a means of studying and addressing some of the most pressing societal problems through the use of highly quantitative and *quasi-scientific* approaches to social problem solving. Examples of these approaches include *operations research* and *planning programming budgeting systems (PPBS)*. Operations research entails the use of statistics and mathematical modeling in decision making, while PPBS is the systematic comparison of different programs with regard to costs and effectiveness. With the advent of the antipoverty movement during the administrations of President John F. Kennedy and President Lyndon Baines Johnson, the policy science community saw an opportunity to contribute in the area of policy formulation. Policy science contributions culminated with the Economic Opportunity Act of 1964, which was the centerpiece of Johnson's Great Society agenda. In spite of a comprehensive legislative effort to combat poverty, there was little improvement in the lives of the nation's poor. Johnson's antipoverty programs were, by and large, unsuccessful, and this consequently altered the focus of the policy science community, whereby *program evaluation* research moved to the forefront (deLeon 1988).

> "Everything that can be counted does not necessarily count; everything that counts cannot necessarily be counted."
>
> **ALBERT EINSTEIN**
> Physicist;
> Nobel Prize Winner
> (1879–1955)

Program evaluation is the use of social science research methods in an effort to determine whether a public program is worthwhile. Program evaluation is systematic—which is to say that it is a quasi-scientific process. Unlike more traditional academic research, program evaluation is more client-centered. Evaluation research is often referred to as applied research. There are two schools of thought regarding how program evaluations should be conducted. On the one hand, some would argue that program evaluations should follow social science research principles to the letter, whereby very few, if any, concessions are made regarding the needs of the client. In other words, program evaluations should differ very little from purely academic research that appears in scholarly publications. On the other hand, while program evaluations must be grounded in social science research principles, it is necessary to take into account the individual needs of the client (Rossi, Lipsey, and Freeman 2004).

There are several reasons why program directors initiate an outside evaluation. For most program directors, the motivation for an evaluation is to gain knowledge and improve some aspect of their program. For some others, however, political or public relations considerations serve as motivation. At times, program evaluations are ritualistic endeavors that are meant to appease policymakers and/or advocacy groups that are pressuring a government department or agency for more accountability or better results.

For an evaluator, it is important to have an understanding as to what is motivating an evaluation. Evaluations motivated by veiled agendas or politics raise the possibility that a program's director may apply pressure on an evaluator to conduct an evaluation that lacks necessary objectivity (that is, the absence of personal bias). If the motivation of an evaluation is unclear, the evaluator may ask:

- Why is there a need for this program to be evaluated?
- What questions will this evaluation try to answer?
- How will the research results and data be used?

How to Collect Empirical Data

Program evaluations are based on the collection of empirical data. Empirical means observable through one's senses. In other words, empirical data are seen or heard, and they are typically collected by surveys, *in-depth interviews, focus groups, field observations, experimentation*, and *existing data* (Singleton and Straits 2004). Surveys involve asking a significant number of individuals a set of structured questions. These questions are usually *close-ended*, which means that the survey respondent is presented with a question and a specific number of corresponding answer choices. Some surveys use *open-ended* questions, whereby the respondents provide their own answers. Examples of closed and open-ended survey questions might include:

Close-ended example:
How would you rate the quality of the after-school mathematics tutoring program?

A. Excellent

B. Above average

C. Average

D. Below average

E. Poor

F. Unsure

Open-ended example:
How would you rate the quality of the after-school mathematics tutoring program?

Close-ended survey questions are preferable for several reasons. First, the data collection process can be completed more quickly and efficiently, as survey respondents are not compelled to search for answers. Second, it is easier for an evaluator to organize, summarize, and analyze data obtained via close-ended survey questions. Third, close-ended questions are easier for respondents, which reduces what is known as *survey response fatigue*. Completing a survey requires you to think, and as such, you will begin to tire at some point during the survey. Response fatigue

The Pros and Cons of Using Surveys to Measure

Accurate measurement requires valid data. This requires reliable data collection procedures. Several methods of data collection are available, including written surveys, telephone surveys, focus groups, interviews, intercepts, experiments and systematic observation. Of these, written surveys are probably the most widely used and abused. Because they can be written fairly easily, printed surveys are often used rather than more in-depth, difficult and expensive techniques. However, surveys should only be used when information from other methods is not available or to verify the results of other methods. If questionnaires are written, tested and administered correctly, the results can be most informative. If they are not, the results can be misleading and, if used for policy decisions, potentially disastrous.

When Should I Use a Survey?

- *Physical Limitations.* Sometimes it is physically impossible to interview members of a population. For example, the population of air travelers is large, ill-defined and in constant motion. They are not predisposed to stop and submit to interviews or intercepts. However, they might complete a survey after being boarded if one is included with a boarding pass or with a complimentary beverage after being seated.

- *Cost Limitations.* The cost of interviewing a representative sample of a population is often prohibitive. Staff and training costs are major considerations.

- *Time Limitations.* Even if a large staff of interviewers could be funded, assembled and trained, the time necessary to do this and then to interview a selection of a population is significant. If timeliness is critical, this can be a determining factor.

- *Confirmation.* Surveys are well suited to confirm the findings of other types of data collection. They can be used as follow-up inquiries after interviews and focus groups to concentrate narrowly on specific issues uncovered by these prior methods.

Advantages of Written Surveys

- *Inexpensive.* They are not as labor-intensive as interviews or focus groups. A well-designed survey can generate a substantial amount of data without requiring a significant investment of staff time.

- *Easy to Administer*. Since the questions are written, staff members do not need to be trained in techniques of interviewing, systematic observation or focus group facilitation.
- *Anonymous*. Respondents tend to be more frank and honest if they can be assured that their answers are anonymous. Anonymity is more difficult to maintain in face-to-face encounters.
- *Easy to Process*. Survey responses are quantitative and easily analyzed via any number of computer-based statistical analysis packages. Other forms of data collection tend to use open-ended questions requiring more complex qualitative analysis procedures.
- *Reduced Time Pressure*. Respondents can answer questionnaires at their leisure and consider their responses. This is not the case in interview situations.

Disadvantages of Written Surveys

- *Impersonal and Structured*. Written questions generally do not allow respondents to clarify their answers. This makes data analysis relatively easy, but does not necessarily allow for a full range of responses.
- *Over-interpretation*. Sometimes, respondents read meaning into a question that is not there. They also occasionally try to guess how the questioner would like them to answer.
- *Time-consuming*. This is particularly true if the survey is sent through the mail. Time must be allocated both for delivery and response.
- *Low Response Rates*. This is common with mail surveys. Many people simply throw away all mail surveys.
- *Distortion*. Respondents who either strongly agree or strongly disagree tend to respond to surveys in greater numbers than do those who have moderate feelings.

Overcoming Disadvantages

- The impersonal, structured nature of surveys can be tempered by giving clear oral instructions when possible and by using a friendly conversational tone in written instructions. The second person is preferred in writing (e.g., "If you have any questions, please call me—."). Over-interpretation can be reduced by instructing respondents to give their

(continued)

(continued)

first impressions and not to attempt to analyze the question.

- A lack of timeliness can be addressed by administering the survey to larger groups of people in one place (auditorium, gymnasium, etc.) and by budgeting enough time to compensate for possible mail delays.
- Low response rates can be improved by offering respondents a small token of appreciation for their participation. One must be careful, however, not to bias the responses by "paying" people to complete the surveys. People who are in financial difficulties tend to be over-represented in surveys that make this error.
- Distortion can be overcome by conducting follow-up contacts with nonrespondents, thanking them for their participation and encouraging them to return the survey if they have not yet done so. This may take the form of postcards or telephone calls.

Conclusion

Surveys are "lagging indicators." They measure what is in the past. Many things can happen to change situations between the time respondents complete a survey and the time the survey is fully analyzed and reported. To be truly proactive, we should use "leading indicators" to measure what is occurring now and how well we are achieving what we want in the future.

Source: H.L. Merritt. 2001. "On Measurement II." Impact: The Official Newsletter of the South Carolina State Government Improvement Network 10 (2).

increases the likelihood of *satisficing*, which occurs when a respondent manages to answer survey questions without expending substantial effort. In other words, respondents that are satisficing do not think very much about the questions—they simply complete the task quickly and mechanically. In more extreme cases, satisficing emerges in the form of random guessing and an inordinate number of "I don't know" responses. Response fatigue and satisficing can have a significant impact on the quality of an evaluator's data. Close-ended questions are much less prone to response fatigue and satisficing compared to open-ended questions. Close-ended questions, however, are disadvantageous because they limit the amount of information that can be collected from the respondent; open-ended questions do not confine the respondent to a few answer choices, which allows an evaluator to collect richer data.

In addition to surveys, in-depth interviews and focus groups are an effective means of collecting empirical data. In-depth interviews involve asking broad, open-ended questions that elicit lengthy and detailed responses. They differ fundamentally from surveys in that they are less structured, include far fewer respondents, and produce a tremendous amount of qualitative data. Focus groups are small groups, usually consisting of six to ten participants, the purpose of which is to establish a dialogue about a specific aspect of a program. Much like in-depth interviews, focus groups use broad themes and open-ended questions to drive the dialogue. In-depth interviews and focus groups often rely on the use of follow-up (or probing) questions, the purpose of which is to address inadequate answers, gain additional information, or clarify statements made by interviewees or focus group participants (Camino, Zeldin, and Payne-Jackson 1995). General follow-up questions may include:

- Could you tell me more about that?
- Could you give me some examples?
- I am not quite sure I understand. Could you elaborate some more?
- What are some of the reasons you feel that way?

> "What gets measured gets done.
>
> If you don't measure results, you can't tell success from failure.
>
> If you can't see success, you can't reward it.
>
> If you can't reward success, you're probably rewarding failure.
>
> If you can't see success, you can't learn from it.
>
> If you can't recognize failure, you can't correct it.
>
> If you can demonstrate results, you can win public support."
>
> **DAVID OSBORNE**
> and
> **TED GAEBLER**
> Architects of *Reinventing Government*

Field observation is another tool of the program evaluator. There are two primary types of field observations: *participant observations* and *nonparticipant observations*. With participant observations, evaluators immerse themselves into the program that is being evaluated, documenting what they see or hear. Central to this is establishing and maintaining relationships with program managers and practitioners, as well as participating in some aspect of a program's operations. Conversely, nonparticipant observations assume complete detachment. The evaluator has no participatory role. For participant observers, the relationships that are cultivated and experiences that occur as an "insider" serve as sources of intimate knowledge about a program's structure and processes. It is possible, however, for a participant observer to become too close. In other words, the relationships and experiences cloud the evaluator's judgment and introduce subjective bias. From an anthropological perspective, this is referred to as having gone native. So, while more intimate data can be collected via participant observations compared to nonparticipant observations, there is the risk of biasing one's research by becoming too immersed in the group. Which, then, is ultimately better—participant observations or nonparticipant observations? Unfortunately, there is no clear answer here, as this boils down to a judgment call. Participant observers have the luxury of getting intimately connected with the group, which may yield a rich amount of data and tremendous insight—although some of this insight may be biased due to personal interactions and actually becoming part of the group. Nonparticipant observations are safer in terms of limiting bias, but do not yield as much data as to the personal dynamics of a group.

Social science methods of experimentation are quasi-scientific, as they follow the logic of natural science experiments. Experimentation (whether scientific or social) involves manipulation and control in an effort to test causal relationships. In the medical sciences, the most recognizable example is the drug experiment, whereby there are two groups: the first group receives the drug (treatment group), while the second group receives a placebo (control group). The results of the treatment and control groups are ultimately compared in order to determine the effect of the drug. In the context of evaluation research, experiments are the primary way of assessing the impact of a program. Consider that we are interested in determining the effect of a peer-tutoring program on student performance in mathematics. As in the case of the drug experiment, some students would partake in the peer-tutoring program (the treatment group), while other students would not (the control group). Any differences between the treatment and control groups are considered to be a function of the peer-tutoring program. A more detailed discussion of experimentation is forthcoming, when we address program impact assessment.

Often overlooked is the fact that evaluative data may already exist. Existing data includes any information that the program formally collects, or any information that can be obtained through internal program documents such as reports or memoranda. Before collecting any new data via surveys, interviews, focus groups, observations, or experiments, an evaluator should first determine what data a program already possesses and review internal documents relevant to the scope of the evaluation.

Conducting Evaluations and the Importance of Stakeholders

Key to the entire program evaluation process is the relationship and interactions that the evaluator (or evaluation team) has with a program's *stakeholders*. Stakeholders are individuals or groups that have an interest in how a program is performing. In simplest terms, these are people who, in one way or another, care about a program. The process of identifying stakeholders is sometimes referred to as an environmental scan. According to Rossi, Lipsey, and Freeman (2004) there are six primary stakeholders. They include:

- Policymakers
- Program Sponsors

TABLE 8.1 – OVERVIEW OF METHODS TO COLLECT INFORMATION

Method	Overall purpose	Advantages	Challenges
Questionnaires, surveys, checklists	When need to quickly and/or easily get lots of information from people in a nonthreatening way	• Can complete anonymously • Inexpensive to administer • Easy to compare and analyze • Administer to many people • Can get lots of data • Many sample questionnaires already exist	• Might not get careful feedback • Wording can bias client's responses • Are impersonal • In surveys, may need sampling expert • Doesn't get full story
Interviews	When want to fully understand someone's impressions or experiences, or learn more about their answers to questionnaires	• Get full range and depth of information • Develops relationship with client • Can be flexible with client	• Can take much time • Can be hard to analyze and compare • Can be costly • Interviewer can bias client's responses
Documentation review (existing data)	When want impression of how program operates without interrupting the program; is from review of applications, finances, memos, minutes, etc.	• Get comprehensive and historical information • Doesn't interrupt program or client's routine in program • Information already exists • Few biases about information	• Often takes much time • Info may be incomplete • Need to be quite clear about what is being looked for • Not flexible means to get data; data restricted to what already exists
Observation	To gather accurate information about how a program actually operates, particularly about processes	• View operations of a program as they are actually occurring • Can adapt to events as they occur	• Can be difficult to interpret seen behaviors • Can be complex to categorize observations • Can influence behaviors of program participants • Can be expensive
Focus groups	Explore a topic in depth through group discussion, e.g., about reactions to an experience or suggestion, understanding common complaints, etc.; useful in evaluation and marketing	• Quickly and reliably get common impressions • Can be efficient way to get much range and depth of information in short time • Can convey key information about programs	• Can be hard to analyze responses • Need good facilitator for safety and closure • Difficult to schedule 6–8 people together
Case studies	To fully understand or depict client's experiences in a program, and conduct comprehensive examination through cross comparison of cases	• Fully depicts client's experience in program input, process and results • Powerful means to portray program to outsiders	• Usually quite time consuming to collect, organize and describe • Represents depth of information, rather than breadth

Source: Carter McNamara, Authenticity Consulting, LLC.

- Evaluation Sponsor
- Program Managers and Practitioners
- Program Targets
- Other Related Stakeholders

Policymakers usually represent elected officials or high-level governmental appointees who determine whether a program is created. Program sponsors are responsible for a program's funding. From a public-sector point of view, there is significant overlap between policymakers and program sponsors. From a nonprofit point of view, policymakers would represent those who initiate or develop the program, while the program sponsors would likely represent a philanthropic foundation (or individual) that financially supports the nonprofit program.

> "However good our futures research may be, we shall never be able to escape from the ultimate dilemma that all our knowledge is about the past, and all our decisions are about the future."
>
> **IAN WILSON**
> Scenario Planning Expert; Strategy Consultant

The evaluation sponsor initiates and/or authorizes the evaluation. The sponsor serves as the conduit between the evaluator and the program itself. When conducting a program evaluation, the evaluator will likely need access to managers, key personnel, rank-and-file personnel, internal records and data, and so on. The evaluation sponsor is responsible for getting the "things" that the evaluator needs to conduct the evaluation. Therefore, it is important that the evaluator maintain a good working relationship with the evaluation sponsor. In some instances, the sponsor may guide or shape the direction of the evaluation.

Program managers are responsible for directing or supervising some aspect of the program's day-to-day operations, while practitioners implement policies and administer a program's services.

Program targets are the direct recipients of a program's services. For example, if we were evaluating an after-school tutoring program for secondary school students failing algebra, then the program targets would be high school students failing algebra.

Finally, related stakeholders refer to all other stakeholders who have an "interest" in how well a program performs. Returning to our high school tutoring program, some related stakeholders may include parents, the board of education, the superintendent of schools, and so on. In terms of identifying related stakeholders, an evaluator should start by asking the evaluation sponsor, program managers, and practitioners to identify key outside parties that have an interest in the program's performance. This will enable the evaluator to generate a list of related stakeholders. The problem here, however, is that a list generated solely by individuals within the program is likely to be biased, given the tendency to identify related stakeholders that have a good working relationship with the program. As a result, the information that these stakeholders provide may be biased in positive way. The evaluator must minimize bias by ensuring a wide representation of related stakeholders. This can be accomplished through *snowball sampling*, which is predicated on one stakeholder referring the evaluator to another stakeholder, who, in turn, refers the evaluator to yet another stakeholder, and so on and so forth. Thus, the original related stakeholder list "snowballs" into a larger, more representative list.

Obtaining Stakeholder Input

Stakeholder input is obtained, by and large, through in-depth interviews or through focus group sessions. Key to this process is getting stakeholders to talk candidly about the program. A good starting point is asking stakeholders: *Why do you think that program x is conducting an evaluation?* Other questions include: *What is your perception of program x? What do you feel are the broader goals and objectives of the program? To what extent do you agree or disagree with these goals and objectives?*

Another approach is to design open-ended questions around a concept known as *SWOT analysis*. SWOT stands for strengths, weaknesses, opportunities, and threats. The evaluator essentially wants to ask: What does the program do well

FIGURE 8.1 – GENERAL LOGIC MODEL

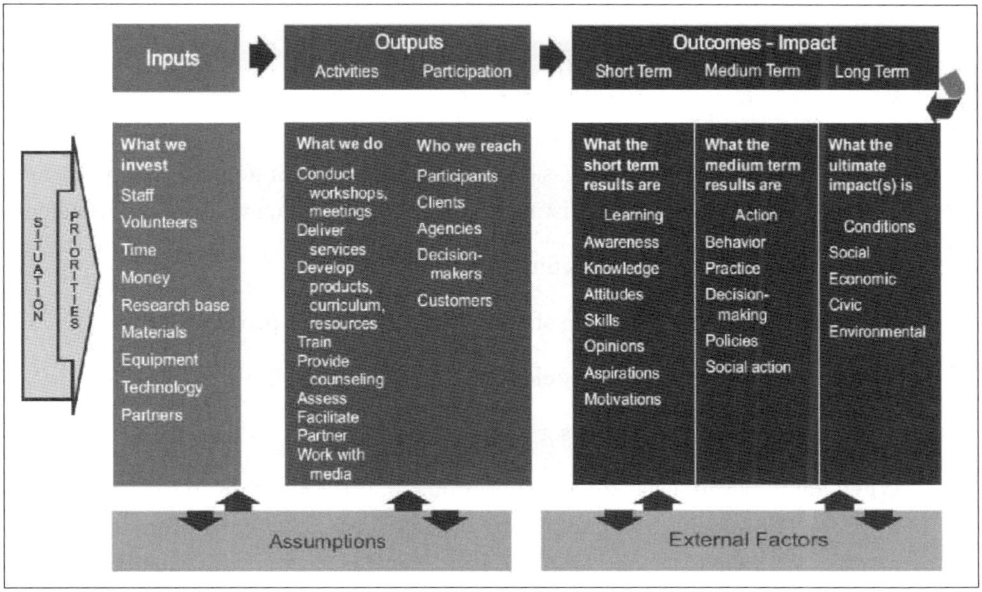

Source: University of Wisconsin-Extension, Program Development and Evaluation. 2002. http://www.uwex.edu/ces/pdande/evaluation/evallogicmodel.html.

(strengths)? What does the program need to improve upon (weaknesses)? Is there anything that the program does not do that it should (opportunities)? Is there anything that could potentially be damaging to the program's future (threats)? The idea with these broad questions is to get the stakeholders thinking and talking about the program. As the evaluator, your job is to document what is conveyed and try to "make sense" of the information that you have gathered.

"Making sense" of interview and focus group data can be daunting because of the large amount of information one can gather through just a few interviews and focus group sessions. Interview and focus group transcripts can be dozens or even hundreds of pages long. A general rule of thumb is to look for recurring themes and stories. When similar patterns or stories begin repeating, an evaluator knows that he or she has uncovered important information.

Types of Program Evaluations

There are primarily five distinct but interrelated types of program evaluations (Rossi, Lipsey, and Freeman 2004; Posavac and Carey 2007). They include:

- Needs Assessment
- Assessment of Program Theory
- Assessment of Program Process
- Program Impact Assessment
- Program Efficiency Assessment

Needs Assessment

When conducting a *needs assessment*, an evaluator tries to determine if, and to what extent, a social condition or problem exists. In other words, is there a "need" for a program? Conducting a needs assessment is a fundamental step in developing a new program or restructuring an existing one. A needs assessment consists of four steps:

1. Defining the social condition or problem.
2. Determining the scope of the social condition or problem.
3. Defining the target population.
4. Briefly describing the services that are needed.

When defining the social condition or problem, it is important to be as specific as possible. For instance, it is not enough to say simply that student underachievement in mathematics is the problem. It is important to stipulate what is meant by underachievement. A clearer definition would be: Underachievement in mathematics exists when students receive a grade of "D" or lower on two consecutive quarterly grade reports.

Program Evaluation Questions

Needs Assessment

- What is the problem?
- What is the scope of the problem?
- Where is the problem localized?
- Who are the targets (those in need)?
- What are the characteristics of the targets?
- What are the target boundaries?
- What services are needed?

Program Theory

- What services will be provided?
- What are the program's goals and objectives?
- How will services be delivered?
- How will the program identify and sustain target participation?
- What resources are needed, and how will they be organized?
- What will the program look like in terms of organizational structure?

Program Process

- How well are program services being delivered?
- How many targets have been served in a given time period?
- What proportion of the total number of eligible targets has been served in a given time period?
- Do "enough" targets participate?
- To what extent are the targets satisfied with the program's services and/or staff?
- How effectively do the program's personnel work with one another or with inter-related government programs, departments, and/or agencies?

Impact Assessment

- Are program goals and objectives being achieved?
- How do the services benefit the targets?
- Are there any adverse or unintended consequences of the program's services?
- Has the social problem improved?

Efficiency Assessment

- Do program benefits outweigh program costs?
- Are the costs to achieve program goals and objectives reasonable compared to similar programs?

Shifting gears to a more difficult population to identify, consider that the social condition or problem under investigation is homelessness, which is defined as "individuals who lack a fixed, regular, and adequate nighttime residence" (42 USC [United States Code] 119). In trying to determine the scope of homelessness in a particular neighborhood, an evaluator may: (1) Survey and/or interview neighborhood residents and business owners, asking these individuals their perceptions regarding the scope of homelessness; (2) interview key informants, such as social workers, church leaders, advocacy groups, and law enforcement officers; (3) conduct a street-by-street count of homeless individuals throughout a census (or sample) of neighborhood blocks. There are a couple of ways in which a street-by-street count can be done: there are simple street counts and street counts with a short interview component. The nomadic nature of homeless individuals increases the likelihood of double counting. In other words, a homeless person counted on *Block A* on Monday may be on *Block B* on Tuesday and thus could be counted twice. This makes the street count with an interview component the method of choice, assuming the researcher has the resources and time, as this helps guard against double counting. Also, counting estimates are further complicated given that homeless individuals may not necessarily be easy to find—or our stereotypical impressions of what a homeless person "looks like" will cause us to undercount people who do not fit the "profile." Determining the scope of a homeless problem is particularly difficult, and in instances such as these, it is important to rely on multiple methods to empirically evaluate whether there is need (or how large the need is).

> "Evaluation... [is] careful retrospective assessment of the merit, worth, and value of administration, output, and outcome of government interventions, which is intended to play a role in future, practical action situations."
>
> **EVERT VEDUNG**
> Author, *Public Policy and Program Evaluation*

In determining the scope of a social condition or problem, we want to understand where the problem is and how large it is. These determinations can be made by collecting either existing data or by collecting new data through interviews, surveys, and/or focus group sessions that show that there is "need" for a program to address a specific problem. Consider, for instance, that there are anecdotal reports that the high school students in your locality are "falling behind" their peers at neighboring schools in terms of mathematics and science achievement. An evaluator conducting a needs assessment would likely collect data regarding student achievement on state standardized tests, which are typically administered each academic year, in addition to interviewing and/or surveying *key informants*. Key informants are individuals who have an intimate knowledge regarding the needs of the targets. In this case, the school's mathematics and science teachers and students' parents would serve as key informants—as they could attest to how students or children are faring in school.

EXERCISE 8.1

Which Are Outcomes?

Nutrition Education Programs

____ 1. Older adults increased the amount of calcium-rich foods they eat.
____ 2. A series of lessons on healthy eating was taught in collaboration with a drug treatment program.
____ 3. Participants serve more than one kind of vegetable to their families every day after participating.
____ 4. Participants report savings as a result of wiser spending at the grocery store.
____ 5. 75 adults have consistently attended all the nutrition workshops.

Food Safety Programs

____ 1. The ServSafe education program is working with 80 percent of all food service managers in the state.
____ 2. Food poisonings dropped from 677 incidents in 1996 to 225 in 1997.
____ 3. Food service workers reported increased knowledge of safe handling practices.
____ 4. Food safety skills were taught to state fair food vendors and restaurant workers.
____ 5. Food safety information in English and Spanish is available on the University web site.

Small Business Development Programs

____ 1. The small business development network grew from 10 to 13 offices in two years.
____ 2. Clients generated nearly $40 million in sales.
____ 3. Clients received 12,138 hours of counseling in 1999.
____ 4. 6,349 participants attended 380 seminars and workshops.
____ 5. Clients created and retained 681 jobs.

Youth Citizenship Programs

____ 1. 4-H groups in 45 counties participated in community service projects.
____ 2. Teens volunteered in community service an average of 10 hours over the year.
____ 3. Teens reported increased ability to identify and help solve a community need.
____ 4. Teens feel more engaged in and responsible for their community.
____ 5. A local industry contributed $1,500 to the 4-H community service project.

(continued)

EXERCISE 8.1

(continued)

Quality Assurance

____ 1. Producers decreased their use of medications and made biosecurity improvements to prevent health problems.

____ 2. 724 adults and 1026 youth participated in training sessions.

____ 3. Producers changed management practices because of what they learned.

____ 4. Veterinarians co-taught the sessions.

____ 5. Overall herd health helped to reduce production costs.

Answer key at the end of chapter.

Source: Developing a Logic Model: Teaching and Training Guide, February 29, 2008.

Defining the target population entails developing criteria that determine who is eligible to receive a program's services. Therefore, if we have determined that there is an empirically based need for a mathematics and science tutoring program, then it is important to be clear as to which students will be offered such services. In other words, benchmarks must be set, which in this context may be based on a student's grades, performance on standardized tests, and/or some other criterion.

After clearly defining the problem, determining empirically that there is a need, and setting target boundaries, the final step of a needs assessment entails describing the services that are needed; that is, what will the program do to improve the problem?

Assessment of Program Theory

Program theory refers to the conceptual design of a program. It centers on the way in which a program is supposed to operate in a perfect world. There are three essential elements that comprise a program theory. They include: the program's *impact theory, organizational plan*, and *service delivery plan*. Program impact theory outlines assumptions regarding the impact of program "x" on social condition "y." Consider a high school tutoring program for students failing high school mathematics. In simplest terms, the impact theory for this program would be: students that attend the tutoring program will improve their mathematics skills. An organizational plan involves resources and personnel, while a service delivery plan underscores how a program's services will be delivered to its targets. A program's impact theory and service utilization plan coincide with a number of program goals and objectives. Goals and objectives differ somewhat, even though the terms tend to be used interchangeably. Goals signify a general direction. They are broadly based. Objectives are narrow, specific, and measurable. Again, consider our high school mathematics tutoring program. The goal of this program may be to improve

FIGURE 8.2 – LOGIC MODEL FOR A HIGH SCHOOL MATHEMATICS TUTORING PROGRAM

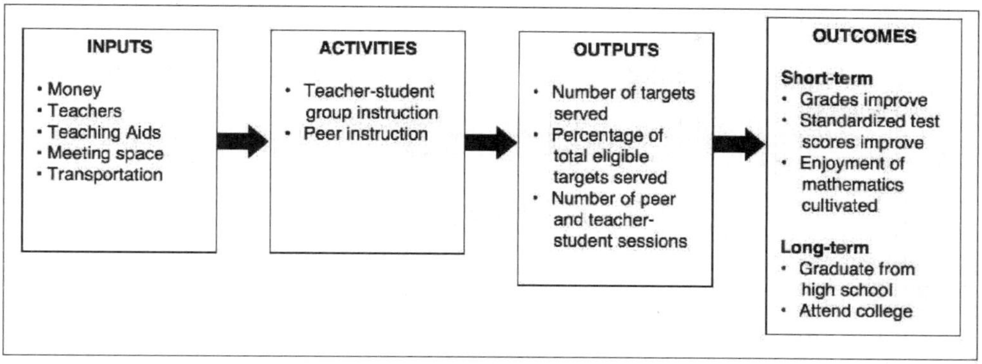

the mathematics skills of failing students. Objectives may include: increasing standardized test scores x percent in y time period; or improving mathematics course grades so that a student attains a "C" or better. These objectives are specific and can be measured simply by gathering data that are routinely collected by schools.

In order to effectively assess a program's theory, the evaluator must have clear understanding of a program's impact theory, organizational plan, and service delivery plan. In terms of theory assessment, an evaluator relies on information provided from stakeholders, key informants, and research on comparative program theories.

Logic Model

A *logic model* is a conceptual representation of a program's theory that includes information regarding a program's resources, the services it provides, and the outcomes it hopes to produce. A logic model is organized in terms of program inputs, activities, outputs, and outcomes. *Inputs* refer to a program's resources (such as money, staff, supplies, buildings, and the like). *Activities* refer to the services that a program provides. *Outputs* refer to the "amount" of services delivered. Outputs are workload measures. *Outcomes* refer to the anticipated short-term and long-term impacts of a program.

Assessment of Program Process

Program process assessment centers on the extent to which a program's services are reaching its targets. This is typically thought of in terms of coverage and bias. *Coverage* refers to the level of participation by eligible targets. Undercoverage is a significant concern, and it is typically the result of recruitment and retention problems or inadequate awareness of a program and its services. *Bias* assumes that certain subgroups of the target population are participating with either greater or less frequency.

Program process analyses, by and large, focus on the number of targets served during a specific time period, the proportion of the total number of eligible targets served in

EXERCISE 8.2

Logic Model Lingo

Place the appropriate number or letter code on each line. Be prepared to explain your choices.

1 - Input	a - Short-Learning
2 - Activity	b - Medium-Action
3 - Output	c - Long-term–Ultimate benefit
4 - Outcome	0 - Cannot identify

____ a. Teens learned leadership skills.
____ b. A new curriculum was developed.
____ c. Students reported increased confidence in negotiation skills.
____ d. Training programs included seminars and workshops.
____ e. Parents from around the state attended.
____ f. Operators applied their new skills on the job.
____ g. Two agencies partnered to design the program.
____ h. Volunteers provided over 300 hours of support to the project.
____ i. 25 teen mentors were trained.
____ j. Owners learned how to develop a woodland management plan.
____ k. Sessions were held in 10 locations.
____ l. Reported cases of abuse declined.
____ m. Food safety skills were taught to food vendors and restaurant workers.
____ n. Books were distributed to children.
____ o. Parents increased their employment skills.
____ p. Increased numbers of high school students graduate.
____ q. We helped the community assess the needs of families.
____ r. Specialists educated owners about effective production methods.
____ s. Youth serving agencies increased their collaboration.
____ t. Teens established a teen court and hear cases monthly.
____ u. 3 two-day workshops were conducted in each region.
____ v. Newsletters are distributed in three languages.
____ w. 30 listeners per week tune into the radio broadcast.
____ x. Teens learned to counsel other teens on tobacco prevention.
____ y. Town enacted a policy for youth curfew.
____ z. More kids walk to school.

Answer key at the end of chapter.

Source: Adapted from Taylor-Powell, Ellen and Ellen Henert. 2008. Developing a Logic Model: Teaching and Training Guide, February 29, Handout no. 22. Copyright © 2008 by the Board of Regents of the University of Wisconsin System, http://www.uwex.edu/ces/pdande/evaluation/pdf/lmguidecomplete.pdf.

a specific time period, and/or the degree in which the targets are satisfied or dissatisfied with the program's services and/or staff. It is necessary to establish achievement levels or benchmarks, and in doing so, it is best to examine comparable programs and use the professional judgment of the program's personnel and related stakeholders. Moreover, through the use of *management information systems,* organizations are collecting program process data at regular intervals, which allows managers and evaluators to continuously monitor program service delivery effectiveness.

Program Impact Assessment

The first step to assessing a *program's impact* is to identify measurable outcomes. An outcome is an observable characteristic relating to the potential benefits of a program. In terms of identifying outcomes, examining a program's logic model will prove useful. It is important that one not confuse program outcome and program impact. A program outcome refers to change in a characteristic of the target population, while impact assumes that a change in a characteristic of the targets is a result of the program and its services. Outcomes must be made measurable, either though existing data or records, or by collecting new data through surveys, interviews, or observations. If we revisit the logic model presented in Figure 8.1, we see that the short-term outcomes for a remedial high school mathematics program include improving a student's mathematical skills and course grades. Each of these outcomes is measurable through quarterly grade reports and standardized proficiency tests.

FIGURE 8.3 – PROGRAM EVALUATION (ASSESSMENT AND MONITORING) IN RELATION TO PROGRAM ELEMENTS

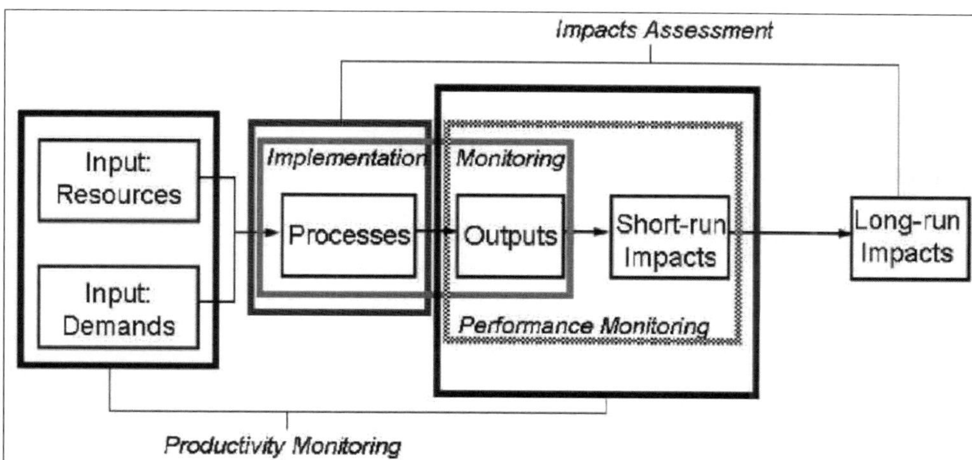

Source: R. Hendrick. 1994. "An Information Infrastructure for Innovative Management of Government." Public Administration Review 54 (6): 543–50. Reprinted in Holzer, M., and E. Charbonneau. 2008. Public Management & Administration Illustrated. Available online at http://unpan1.un.org/intradoc/groups/public/documents/aspa/unpan029896.pdf.

The simplicity of the *before and after* method of impact assessment makes this approach popular among stakeholders. With this method, target outcomes are measured at two points in time: before and after a program's delivery of services. Consider, for example, that there are 100 students who participated in the remedial mathematics program as outlined in Figure 8.1. Of those 100 students, 50 percent showed improvement in terms of their mathematics course grades, and 35 percent showed improvement on their standardized tests. The important questions here are whether these observable outcomes are a result of the program itself, or are they merely the result of some other external factor. In other words, how does the evaluator know that the program, and not something else, is producing the desired results? When using the before and after method, there is no way of really knowing. It is through experimentation that we are able to better determine a program's impact.

Experimentation

There are two distinct *experimentation* methods. The first is the *randomized field experiment*—the gold standard of experimental methods because it follows most closely the classic scientific laboratory experiment featuring two groups: the *treatment* group and the *control* group. The treatment group, in the context of this discussion, would receive a program's services, while the control group would not. The key to this experimental technique is the random assignment of individuals into either the treatment or control group. Consider hypothetically that there are 200 students in high school x that are, based upon a needs assessment, eligible for remedial mathematics instruction. Then, if we were going to conduct a randomized field experiment, 100 randomly chosen students would be assigned to the treatment group and receive tutoring, while the remaining 100 would receive no tutoring.

The idea of random assignment needs clarification. Random does not mean hap-

EXERCISE 8.3

The Grantmaker: Inner City Youth Organizations Compete for Funds (Simulation)

Students will read the case study and assume the role of the foundation program director. As the program director, students will prepare a report for the foundation's board, recommending the funding allocations to the selected organizations. Students will compile this board report with concise and specific reasons as to why they are recommending the funding allocation. All students will present their recommendations to the class (role-playing the board). The class will determine which recommendation to support.

Wood, Miriam, M. 1996. Nonprofit Boards and Leadership—Cases on Governance, Change, and Board-Staff Dynamics. San Francisco, CA: Jossey-Bass, 62–82.

hazard or chaotic. In fact, from a social science perspective, randomness is a mathematical distinction whereby each eligible unit has the same mathematical chance of selection. In other words, we hypothetically have 200 total students eligible to participate, and a truly random assignment means that each student has the same 50 percent chance of being selected into either the treatment or control group. Why does randomness matter? By randomly assigning individuals, the evaluator can be reasonably certain that individual characteristics, experiences, and biases will be equally distributed among the two groups. This is referred to as *equivalence*.

> "Reform is always a work in progress. Since the world is a dynamic place and conditions within schools and communities change over time, there is no guarantee that a strategy that works today will work equally well tomorrow... Evaluation can help schools determine how to adjust the reform process to meet selected objectives."
>
> **U.S. DEPARTMENT OF EDUCATION**
> *Fitting the Pieces: Education Reform That Works*, October 1996

The second experimental technique is the *quasi-experiment*. The quasi-experiment differs from the randomized field experiment in that the assignment of individuals into the treatment and control groups is not done randomly, resulting in a lack of mathematical equivalence. In trying to achieve *near equivalence*, it is important to minimize the differences between the treatment and control groups. This is done through *matching* on either an individual or an aggregate basis. Individual matching entails partnering; that is, two individuals with similar demographic and experiential characteristics (characteristics that are most relevant to the program's outcomes) take part in the experiment, with one participating in the treatment group and the other in the control group. With aggregate matching, however, there is no element of partnering. The evaluator tries to ensure that the treatment and control groups are aggregately similar based upon relevant characteristics. Individual matching is preferable.

After selecting and employing an experimental method, the evaluator compares the observed outcomes of the treatment group with the observed outcomes of the control group. If there is a *statistically significant* outcome difference, then the evaluator can be reasonably sure that the program has had some measure of impact. Statistical significance means that the results (or outcome differences of the two groups) are not likely to have occurred because of chance and/or because of some other external factor.

Program Efficiency Assessment

The final type of program evaluation, *efficiency assessment*, centers on whether the money and resources put toward a program are "well spent." The two primary approaches to determining whether money and resources are well spent include cost-benefit analysis and cost-effectiveness analysis. With cost-benefit analysis, program costs are compared to tangible and intangible program benefits, which are expressed in monetary terms. Results are typically expressed in terms of a benefit-cost ratio, which is equal to the benefits of the program divided by its costs. If the benefit-cost ratio is greater than one, it can be said that the benefits of a program outweigh its costs. The challenging and sometimes controversial nature of cost-benefit analysis stems from trying to place a monetary value on the "intangible" or "public good" benefits of specific programs. A common way of determining the value of an intangible or public good benefit is through a technique known as contingent valuation. Contingent valuation entails using surveys to ask people how much they would be "willing to pay" for an intangible public good (Mitchell and Carson 1989).

From a practical perspective, Small and O'Connor (2006) provide a cogent illustration of a cost-benefit analysis of a Chicago preschool program known as the Child Parent Center. In determining the costs and benefits of the Child Parent Center, 989 Center participants and 550 nonparticipants were tracked longitudinally from preschool to the age of 21. Small and O'Connor underscore the outcome differences of "Johnny" and "Ricky." Johnny and Ricky are similar in that both come from impoverished, single-parent family households where the mother has little education. There is also a history of neglect and criminal activity. At age three, Johnny is cared for at home, while Ricky is enrolled at the Child Parent Center. At the Center, Ricky is nurtured and stimulated educationally, while parental education is provided for

FIGURE 8.4 – PROGRAM EVALUATION LADDER

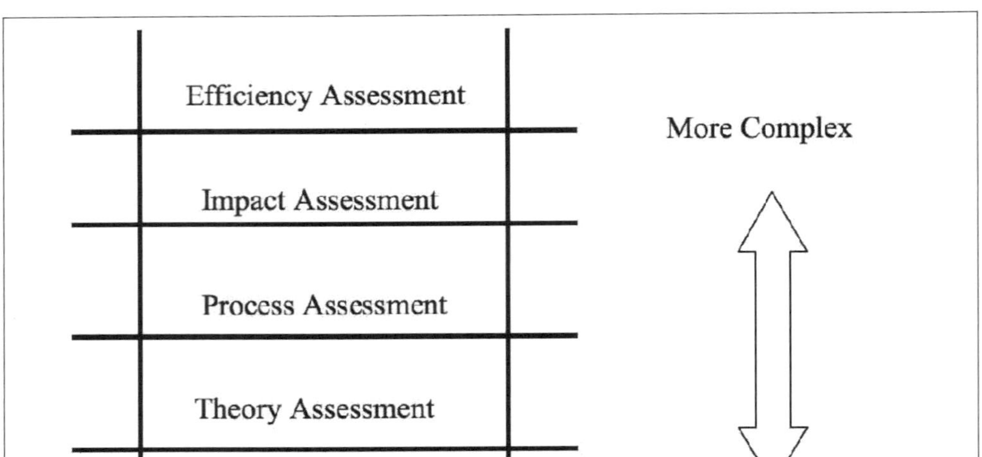

Ricky's mother. In addition, the Center provides home visits and other family services. Johnny is not afforded these services. The costs and benefits relevant to Ricky's participation in the Child Parent Center versus Johnny's nonparticipation are summarized below.

> "What explains this paradox of successful programs and failing students?... Despite many reports of success, we find few objective evaluations conducted by independent investigators."
>
> **HERBERT J. WALBERG** and **REBECCA C. GREENBERG**
> *"The Diogenes Factor,"* Education Week, April 8, 1998

- At age three, Ricky is enrolled in the Child Parent Center for two years at a total cost of $10,728.
- At age nine, Johnny is enrolled in special education classes for four years, the cost of which is $9,497 per year ($37,988 total).
- At age 10, Johnny is abused. The costs of child protective services filing a report and conducting an investigation amount to $10,861.
- At age 14, Johnny gets into trouble with the police. Juvenile justice costs amount to $16,690.
- At age 18, Ricky graduates high school and enrolls in Chicago City College, of which the average taxpayer costs amount to $4,039 per year ($16,156).
- At adulthood, Johnny is consistently in trouble with the law, the costs of which are $40,195 (the average criminal justice system costs for career adult criminals). Ricky graduates from college and gains employment. Small and O'Connor estimate that a college graduate's lifetime earnings exceed a high school graduate by $223,303. This translates into $73,838 in additional tax revenues.

So, here is the bottom line:

Johnny

- Special education costs = $37,988
- Child protective service costs = $10,861
- Juvenile justice costs = $16,690
- Adult criminal justice costs = $40,195
- Public benefits = $0 vs. public costs = $105,734

Ricky

- Child Parent Center costs = $10,728
- City College taxpayer costs = $16,156

- Tax revenue benefits = $78,838
- Public benefits = $78,838 vs. public costs = $26,488

The difficulty of accurately placing a monetary value on the intangible, public good benefits of programs is why evaluation studies tend to rely more on cost-effectiveness rather than on cost-benefit analyses. Cost-effectiveness analysis entails estimating the costs of achieving a specific outcome. Consider, for instance, that three mathematics teachers are hired to administer an after-school mathematics tutoring program at your local high school. Let us assume that the per-pupil cost is $100 per tutoring session. Let us also assume that the program has resulted in a 20 percent increase in standardized test scores. Consider, however, that a similar program at a neighboring high school achieves the same result at a cost of only $75 per pupil. This program would be considered more cost-effective because it achieves a similar result for less money.

Each of the five program evaluations discussed here is interrelated hierarchically and ordered with regard to complexity. A needs assessment represents the foundation, or the bottom rung of the evaluation ladder. As noted, this is the first step in either developing a new program or restructuring an existing one. There is no point in moving forward with a program theory assessment without first establishing that there is a need for a program. Similarly, one would not assess a program's processes or service delivery aspects without first establishing that the program's theory is sound. Moreover, an impact assessment cannot proceed until we establish that the program is reaching "enough" targets. Finally, one would not embark on an efficiency assessment unless it was clear that the program has had some positive impact upon the target population.

Ethical Concerns

Primary ethical concerns deal with the treatment of human subjects. First and foremost, an evaluator must take all necessary measures to protect his or her subjects from harm. Second, obtaining *informed consent* is a way of protecting human subjects. When obtaining informed consent, an evaluator must: (1) Explain the nature of the program evaluation, what it entails, and what the potential implications may be. (2) Inform human subjects that their participation is completely voluntary. It is important to stress that human subjects may decline to participate at any time during the evaluation. Subjects may decline to answer any questions or refuse to engage in any activities that they feel may prove harmful either physically or emotionally. (3) Inform human subjects that ever effort will be made to maintain the confidentiality of all information collected. In maintaining confidentiality, subjects are typically referred to by number rather than name, and their responses are kept in a password-protected computer.

In addition to the treatment of human subjects, evaluators must be concerned about potential bias regarding the presentation of their data and findings. In order to conduct an evaluation properly, relationships must be cultivated with a program's stakeholders. Given the fact that evaluation research is dependent upon interpersonal relationships, there is always the potential for bias. Consider that evaluator x encounters program managers and practitioners who are approachable, flexible, and willing to work with the evaluation team. On the other hand, consider that evaluator y encounters managers and practitioners who are resistant, inflexible, and suspicious of the entire process. Is it reasonable to assume the potential for bias given that evaluator x has good working relationship with program stakeholders while evaluator y does not? Is it fair to assume that evaluators having good working relationships with program stakeholders may be influenced to present their data and findings in, let us say, a more positive light? This possibility alone underscores the importance of making every effort to keep personal feelings from clouding one's objectivity.

The program evaluation process is client centered. External evaluators are compensated for providing a service to their clients. There is a financial relationship between the evaluator and the program, which presupposes the potential for bias. Given that money can be a tremendous source of influence, it is important that an evaluator have a clear understanding of what is motivating an evaluation. Evaluation projects that are motivated by personal interest or politics, as opposed to more sincere reasons, increase the likelihood that money could be used either explicitly or implicitly as a means of pressuring an evaluator.

COMPLEXITY OF PROGRAM EVALUATION: CAN WE CONTROL EXOGENOUS VARIABLES?

Assessing public policies and programs is not easy as each policy/program is surrounded by a number of variables that are uncontrollable in the broader environment. It should be mentioned, however, that wise selection of indicators and detailed evaluation models will ensure the real impact of a specific policy or program. Please read the following article. Following the logic model identified in the text, please construct possible indicators for the real estate market stability program in Korea.

[NEWS IN FOCUS] Families don't want to buy apartments in flat market, so rental units are hot

People renting houses or apartments in southern Seoul are being hit with ever-increasing demands for key money deposits because of a severe shortage in the number of places available for lease.

Tenants renewing two-year leases are being asked to pony up an extra 50 million won ($46,772) to 100 million won in deposits.

The spiraling deposits show no sign of abating with a substantial jump last month. Jeonse, or key money deposits, rose 1.3 percent in Seoul in August from a month ago, according to Kookmin Bank.

The increases subsided a little in April, giving hope that the market was stabilizing, but it started soaring again in July and then advanced sharply in August as the fall moving season approached.

According to Kiwooml.com, a real estate information Web site, jeonse for a Woosung apartment covering 95 square meters (1,022 square feet) was between 320 million won and 360 million won a year ago, but it jumped to between 380 million won and 420 million won recently.

The increase was most visible in southern Seoul. Deposits in Gangnam District rose by the biggest margin, 2 percent, among all districts in Seoul. Next were Songpa with 1.8 percent and Gangdong with 1.7 percent.

The rise in jeonse is expected to accelerate further in Gangnam as urban renewal is on the way.

The Chungsil and Woosung apartments in Daechi-dong, Gangnam, are scheduled to be demolished to give way to new high-rise apartments, and families there have started clearing out of their homes.

"There are few houses available for lease because of urban renewal," said a real estate agent in Gangnam.

Surrounding districts including Gwangjin and Seongdong are also affected due to a spillover effect as families from Songpa and Gangnam look for places nearby.

There are multiple reasons cited for the soaring jeonse. Most of all, a shortage of small to midsize apartments available for lease and a stagnant real estate market have contributed to the hike.

People are reluctant to buy apartments as they do not expect apartment prices to rise.

In Gwacheon, Gyeonggi Province, the government complex in the area is scheduled to relocate to Sejong City at the end of 2012, which is expected to draw a lot of residents out of the city.

As residents anticipate a decline in apartment prices, there are few home buyers and people want to lease instead.

As a result, jeonse climbed as much as 3.1 percent in August.

"The demand for rental housing is not as high as in the beginning of the year but the problem is a lack of supply," said Kim Gyu-jeong, a senior analyst at Real Estate 114. "Landlords increasingly opt for monthly rents instead of lump sum jeonse and lessees are likely to feel a bigger burden."

Source: By Limb Jae-un, "Key Money Just Keeps on Growing," Korea JoongAng Daily, Opinion, Sep. 06 2010, accessed Dec 26, 2011, http://koreajoongangdaily.joinsmsn.com/news/article/html/172/2941172.html

KEY TERMS

Activities

Before and after method

Bias

Close-ended

Contingent valuation

Control group

Cost-benefit analysis

Cost-effectiveness

Coverage

Efficiency assessment

Empirical

Equivalence

Existing data

Experimentation

Field observation

Focus groups

Impact assessment

Impact theory

In-depth interview

Informed consent

Inputs

Key informants

Logic model

Management information systems

Matching

Near equivalence

Needs assessment

Nonparticipant observations

Open-ended

Operations research

Organizational plan

Outputs

Participant observations

Planning programming budgeting systems (PPBS)

Program evaluation

Program process assessment

Program targets

Program theory assessment

Quasi-experiment

Quasi-scientific

Random assignment

Randomized field experiment

Satisficing

Service delivery plan

Snowball sampling

Stakeholders

Statistically significant

Survey

Survey response fatigue

SWOT analysis

Treatment group

REFERENCES

Berk, R.A., and P.H. Rossi. 1998. *Thinking About Program Evaluation*. Thousand Oaks, CA: Sage Publications.

Camino, L., S. Zeldin, and A. Payne-Jackson. 1995. *Basics of Qualitative Interviews and Focus Groups*. Washington, DC: Center for Youth Development and Policy Research, Academy for Educational Development.

Chelimsky, E., and W.R. Shadish. 1997. *Evaluation for the 21st Century: A Handbook*. Thousand Oaks, CA: Sage Publications.

deLeon, P. 1989. *Advice and Consent: The Development of the Policy Sciences*. Russell Sage Foundation.

Hatry, H.P., R.E. Winnie, and D.M. Fisk. 1973. *Practical Program Evaluation for State and Local Government Officials*. Washington, DC: The Urban Institute.

Mitchell, R. C. and R. T. Carson 1989. *Using Surveys to Value Public Goods. The Contingent Valuation Method.* Washington DC: Resources for the Future.

Posavac, E.J. and R.G. Carey. 2007. *Program Evaluations: Methods and Case Studies*, 7th ed. New Jersey: Prentice Hall.

Preskill, H., and R.T. Torres. 1998. *Evaluative Inquiry for Learning in Organizations*. Thousand Oaks, CA: Sage Publications.

Rossi, P.H., W.M. Lipsey, and H.E. Freeman. 2004. *Evaluation: A Systematic Approach*, 7th ed. Thousand Oaks, CA: Sage Publications.

Scriven, M. 1991. *Evaluation Thesaurus*, 4th ed. Newbury Park, CA: Sage Publications.

Shadish, W.R., T.D. Cook, and L.C. Leviton. 1991. *Foundations of Program Evaluation: Theories of Practice*. Newbury Park, CA: Sage Publications.

Singleton, R., and B.C. Straits. 2004. *Approaches to Social Research*, 4th ed. Oxford, UK: Oxford University Press.

Small, S., and C. O'Connor. 2006. "Cost-Benefit Analysis." University of Wisconsin–Extension EvalEXchange. http://whatworks.uwex.edu/attachment/whatworks_cost_benefit.pdf.

Taylor-Powell, E., and E. Henert. 2008. *Developing a Logic Model: Teaching and Training Guide.* Madison: University of Wisconsin–Extension.

U.S. Code, Title 42, Chapter 119, Subchapter 1, § 11302. General definition of homeless individual.

U.S. General Accounting Office (GAO), General Government Division. 1998. *Program Evaluation: Agencies Challenged by New Demand for Information on Program Results.* Report to the U.S. Committee on Government Affairs, U.S. Senate. April.

Wholey, J.S., H.A. Hatry, and K.E. Newcomer. 2004. *Handbook of Practical Program Evaluation,* 2d ed. Hoboken, NJ: Jossey-Bass.

SUPPLEMENTARY READINGS

Taylor-Powell, E., and C. Hermann. 2000. *Collecting Evaluation Data: Surveys.* University of Wisconsin–Extension Cooperative Extension.

Taylor-Powell, E., and S. Steel. 1996. *Collecting Evaluation Data: An Overview of Sources and Methods.* University of Wisconsin–Extension Cooperative Extension, Program Development and Evaluation Unit. http://learningstore.uwex.edu/assets/pdfs/G3658–4.pdf

W.K. Kellogg Foundation. 1998. *W.K. Kellogg Foundation Evaluation Handbook.* Battle Creek, MI.

ELECTRONIC RESOURCES

American Evaluation Association: http://www.eval.org/

Australasian Evaluation Society: http://www.aes.asn.au/

Canadian Evaluation Society: http://www.evaluationcanada.ca/

Centers for Disease Control (CDC) Evaluation Working Group: http://www.cdc.gov/eval/

The Centre for Program Evaluation (CPE) at the University of Melbourne Graduate School of Education, Melbourne, Australia: http://www.edfac.unimelb.edu.au/cpe/

The Evaluation Center at Western Michigan University: http://www.wmich.edu/evalctr/

The Evaluation Exchange at Harvard University: http://www.hfrp.org/evaluation/the-evaluation-exchange

Evaluation Handbook, Evaluation Assistance Center–Western Region, New Mexico Highlands University: http://www.ncela.gwu.edu/files/rcd/BE020502/Evaluation_Handbook.pdf

Free Management Library, Basic Guide to Program Evaluation:

http://www.managementhelp.org/evaluatn/fnl_eval.htm

Online Evaluation Resource Library (supported by the National Science Foundation [NSF]): http://oerl.sri.com/

Oregon Program Evaluators Network (OPEN): http://www.oregoneval.org/

Program Development and Evaluation, University of Wisconsin–Extension: http://www.uwex.edu/ces/pdande/

U.S. Department of Justice, Office of Justice Programs, Bureau of Justice Assistance, Center for Program Evaluation and Performance Measurement: http://www.ojp.usdoj.gov/BJA/evaluation/

U.S. Environmental Protection Agency, Program Evaluation Glossary: http://www.epa.gov/evaluate/glossary.htm

The World Wide Evaluation Information Gateway: http://www.policy-evaluation.org/

EXERCISES ANSWER KEY

Exercise 8.1

Nutrition: 1, 3, 4
Food safety: 2, 3
Small business: 2, 5
Youth Citizenship: 3, 4
Quality Assurance: 1, 3, 5

Exercise 8.2

4a a.
2 b.
4a c.
2 d.
2 e.
4b f.
1 g.
1 h.
3 i.
4a j.
2 k.
4c l.
2 m.
2 n.
4a o.
4c p.
2 q.
2 r.
4b s.
4b t.
3 u.
2 v.
3 w.
4a x.
4b y.
4c z.

Note: Several of the above are debatable given the program goal that is assumed. Participants should be able to explain and defend their choices. To test outcomes, ask "so what?"

CHAPTER 9

Public Budgeting

In this chapter, students are acquainted with a most fundamental yet vital aspect of the public organization: the budget. Upon reading this chapter, students will understand the federal budget process and the different types of budgets—namely, operating, capital, line-item, performance, and zero-based budgets. The ways in which governments raise revenues is also discussed. The chapter concludes by examining competing theories as to how scarce government resources should be allocated.

"A budget tells us what we can't afford, but it doesn't keep us from buying it."

WILLIAM FEATHER
American Publisher; Author
(1889–1981)

New York Mayor Michael Bloomberg presents a Fiscal Year 2011 Executive Budget and an updated four-year financial plan in May 2010. Photo by Edward Reed.

BUDGETING PROCESSES

The Federal Budget Process

The idea of having a government budget is a twentieth-century phenomenon. Prior to 1921, the federal budget process was fragmented and disorganized. The American budget process was dominated by Congress: If an agency wanted money to do something, an agency's leaders were forced to petition Congress directly. The executive branch, more specifically the U.S. president, had no formal role in federal budgetary decisions until the passage of the Budget and Accounting Act of 1921. Momentum to alter the federal budget process began to build as the nation moved into the twentieth century. The United States was growing quite rapidly, and society's problems were becoming increasingly complex. As a result, the Commission on Economy and Efficiency, chaired by then-President William Howard Taft (thus referred to as the Taft Commission) made a number of recommendations in 1912 that would permanently alter the federal budget-making process. The Taft Commission's proposals were embodied in the Budget and Accounting Act, which specifically called for the creation of the Bureau of the Budget (BOB) and the Government Accountability Office (GAO). The BOB was the federal agency through which the president would prepare a formal budget for presentation to Congress; it was replaced by the Office of Management and Budget (OMB) in 1970 during the Nixon administration. The GAO still exists in its original form and is responsible for auditing (or reviewing) the federal budget. The Budget and Accounting Act created a formal process for shaping a federal budget, and it also thrust the president into the dominant budgetary role.

> "A billion here, a billion there, pretty soon it adds up to real money."
>
> **EVERETT DIRKSEN**
> Congressional Representative; Illinois Senator (1896–1969)

Each February, the president presents the U.S. Congress with a budget request, which details the amounts of money needed by the cabinet-level agencies for the upcoming fiscal year. The federal government's fiscal year begins October 1. This budget request is prepared by the OMB—part of the Executive Office of the President (EOP)—after the OMB receives funding estimates from the federal agencies. The OMB then dispatches budget examiners to each of the agencies in order to ensure that the agency funding estimates are reasonable. Specifically, the budget examiners for the OMB meet with agency representatives and hold hearings with agency heads to examine what the agency does and whether the amount of money requested is necessary. The budget examiners then make their final recommendations to the OMB.

The OMB provides the following financial information to Congress: (1) how much money the president is requesting for the various federal agencies; (2) how much money in taxes the federal government will collect in a fiscal year; (3) whether the federal government will have a *budget surplus* (that is, money left over) or a *budget shortfall* (that is, a *budget deficit*); and (4) how much either the budget surplus or shortfall will amount to. The budget crafted by the OMB reflects the spending priorities of the president—priorities that relate to both *discretionary* and *entitlement* program spending. Programs that are deemed discretionary must have their funding approved each year. Defense, education, and housing are examples of discretionary programs. Unlike discretionary programs, the funding for entitlement programs such as Social Security and Medicare are mandated by law; therefore, the president does not have to request funds for these programs on an annual basis. The president can make recommendations for programmatic changes to these programs—one example being when President George W. Bush used the budget request to initiate changes to Medicare by introducing prescription drug benefits.

After receiving the president's budget request, Congress holds meetings to question EOP officials about their funding requests. Then, both chambers of Congress develop separate versions of a *budget resolution*. The separate budget resolutions

TABLE 9.1 – THE 20 BUDGET FUNCTIONS

Function number	Budget function
050	National defense
150	International affairs
250	General science, space, and technology
270	Energy
300	Natural resources and environment
350	Agriculture
370	Commerce and housing credit
400	Transportation
450	Community and regional development
500	Education, training, employment, and social services
550	Health
570	Medicare
600	Income security
650	Social Security
700	Veterans benefits and services
750	Administration of justice
800	General government
900	Net interest
920	Allowances
950	Undistributed offsetting receipts

Source: House Committee on the Budget, "Basics of the Budget Process: A Briefing Paper," February 2001.

crafted by the House and Senate Budget Committees are sent to the House and Senate floors for debate, which allows for changes to be made to each version by a majority vote. At this point, small differences usually exist between the House and Senate versions of the budget resolutions. These differences are ironed out, so to speak, in what is called a conference, and a single agreed-upon version of the budget resolution is produced and then presented to both congressional chambers for passage by a majority vote. This resolution is *not* presented to the president for his signature, because it is not a typical bill possessing the effect of law. What this joint House and Senate budget resolution does is set forth a blueprint for future *appropriations* (or spending) legislation. This blueprint highlights spending totals, which are divided into 20 specific functional spending categories. The congressional budget resolution typically is passed on April 15. Within this budget resolution, "spending" is defined in two ways: (1) as *budget authority* and (2) as *outlays*. Budget authority represents the amount of money that Congress permits the federal government to spend. Outlays refer to actual amounts that are spent by the federal government each year. For example, the budget authority may appropriate $100 million for new school construction in a given year, but that may not necessarily result in $100 million in outlays until the next fiscal year. Budget authority is typically the spending measure that Congress uses to make budget decisions.

> "Collecting more taxes than is absolutely necessary is legalized robbery."
>
> **CALVIN COOLIDGE**
> 30th President of the United States (1872–1933)

After the joint House-Senate budget resolution is approved by Congress, it is sent to both the House and Senate Appropriations Committees, which divide the "discretionary" spending totals into 13 categories or government functions. These 13 categories represent 13 individual *appropriations bills* (or spending legislation). The appropriations bills are debated and amended in both the House and Senate, and as with the original versions of the budget resolution, the differences in the

FIGURE 9.1 – THE SPENDING PIPELINE

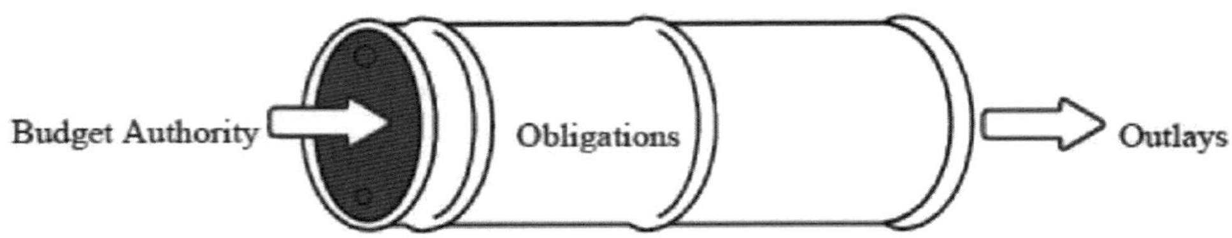

Source: CRS Report for Congress. "The Spending Pipeline: Stages of Federal Spending," June 17, 2008.

House and Senate versions are settled in a conference. Once the differences are ironed out, the House and Senate vote to approve the 13 agreed-upon appropriations bills, a process that is usually completed by June 30. The appropriations are finally presented to the president for approval or veto.

The federal budget process includes what is called an audit. The purpose of a *budget audit* is to certify that the funds appropriated by Congress are spent lawfully, efficiently, or in a way that contributes to achieving an agency's mission and goals. The GAO—the investigative or watchdog organization within Congress—has primary budget auditing responsibilities. The GAO is directed by the comptroller general of the United States, an apolitical, nonpartisan position that is appointed by the president with the advice and consent of the Senate. The comptroller general of the United States serves one 15-year term.

Types of Budgets

In simplest terms, a budget is a plan regarding how revenues (or, in the case of public organizations, tax dollars) will be spent on a year-to-year basis. Each year, the budget follows a predetermined cycle that includes: (1) the preparation of the budget—which entails deciding where tax dollars will be spent; (2) budget approval;

FIGURE 9.2 – RELATIONSHIP OF BUDGET AUTHORITY TO OUTLAYS FOR FY2009 (BILLIONS OF DOLLARS)

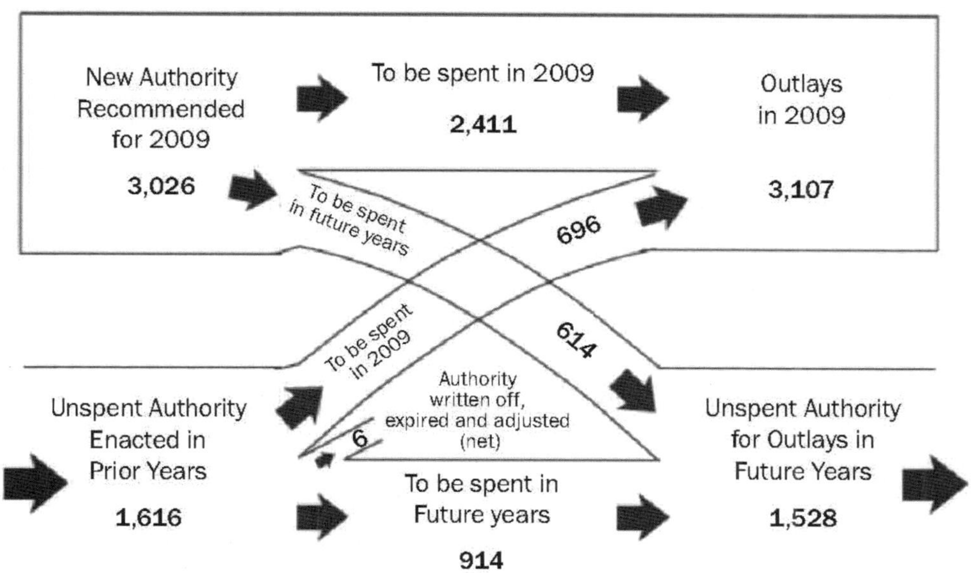

Source: Office of Management and Budget. "Analytical Perspectives, Budget of the U.S. Government, Fiscal Year 2009," Washington, DC: GPO, 2008. Chart 26-1, p. 402.

FIGURE 9.3 – WHO PUTS THE BUDGET TOGETHER AND HOW?

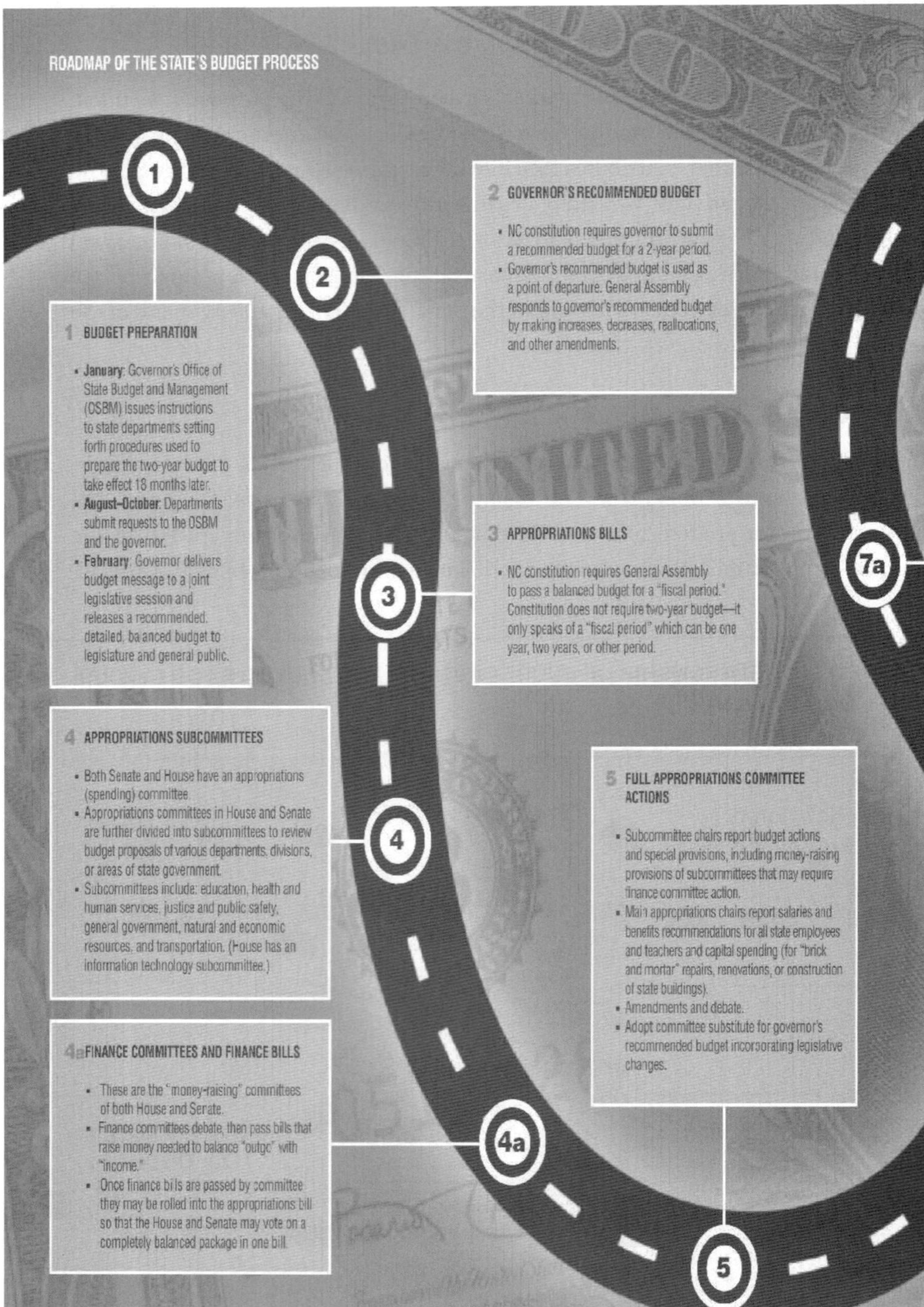

Source: North Carolina Progress Board. Our State, Our Money: A Citizens' Guide to the North Carolina Budget,

(ROADMAP OF NORTH CAROLINA'S STATE BUDGET PROCESS)

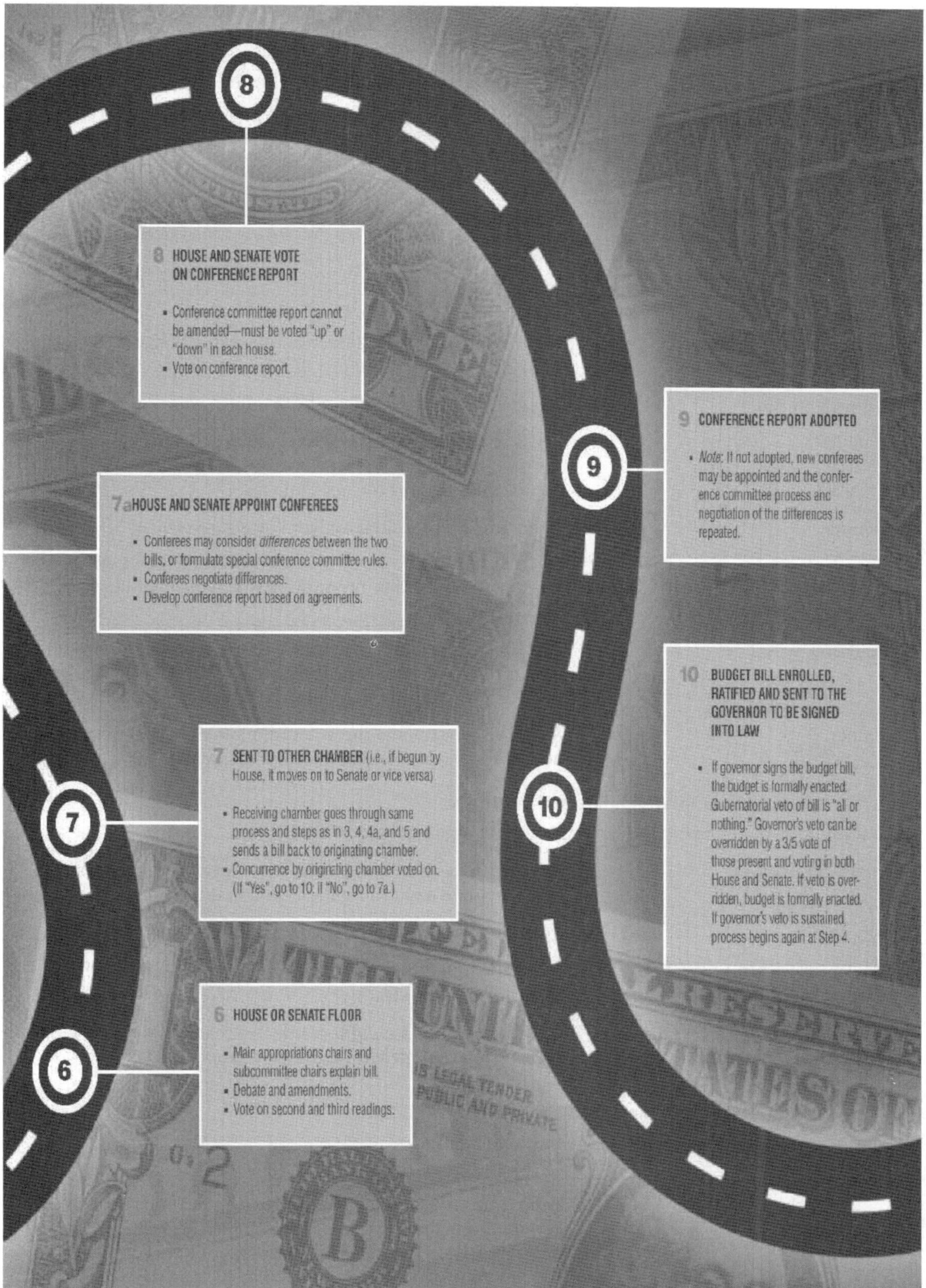

September 2003. http://fsv.uncg.edu/budgets/Citizens_Guide.pdf.

(3) budget implementation; and finally (4) budget auditing—which is intended to make sure that tax money allocated to various government organizations is spent appropriately. An obvious question at this point is, Who actually prepares the budget? There are essentially two answers. *Executive budgets* are prepared by chief executives within a government's executive branch. At the federal level, this would be the president; at the state level, it would be the governor; at the county level, it

TABLE 9.2 – THE EXECUTIVE BUDGET PROCESS TIMETABLE

Date	Activities
Calendar Year Prior to the Year in Which Fiscal Year Begins	
Spring	OMB issues planning guidance to executive agencies for the budget beginning October 1 of the following year.
Spring and Summer	Agencies begin development of budget requests.
July	OMB issues annual update to Circular A-11, providing detailed instructions for submitting budget data and material for agency budget requests.
September	Agencies submit initial budget requests to OMB.
October-November	OMB Staff review agency budget requests in relation to President's priorities, program performance, and budget constraints
November-December	President, based on recommendations by the OMB director, makes decisions on agency requests. OMB informs agencies of decisions, commonly referred to OMB "passback."
December	Agencies may appeal these decisions to the OMB director and in some cases directly to the President.
Calendar Year in Which Fiscal Year Begins	
By first Monday in February	President submits budget to congress.
February-September	Congressional phase. Agencies interact with Congress, justifying and explaining President's budget.
By July 15	President submits mid-session review to Congress.
August 21 (or within 10 days after approval of a spending bill)	Agencies submit appointment requests to OMB for each budget account.
September 10 (or within 30 days after approval of a spending bill)	OMB apportions available funds to agency by time period, approval period, program, project, or activity.
Calendar Year in Which Fiscal Year Begins and Ends	
October 1	Fiscal year begins.
October-September	Agencies make allotments, obligate funds, conduct activities, and request supplemental appropriations, if necessary. President may propose supplemental appropriations and impoundments (i.e. deferrals or recissions) to congress.
September 30	Fiscal year ends.

Source: Office of Management and Budget, Circular No. A-11 (Washington, DC: July 2007), Section 10.5.

would be the county executive; and at the municipal level, it would be the mayor. With an executive budget, the chief executive (along with budget personnel) develops a budget after receiving "requests" from various government agencies and departments. The budget is then submitted for approval by a legislative body—which may be the U.S. Congress, the state legislature, or the city/town council at the municipal level. An executive budget is used more widely than the alternative, which is a *legislative budget*. A legislative budget is prepared by a body of elected representatives (for example, the state legislature or city council). Executive budgets are more prevalent simply because they can be developed with far greater efficiency.

Operating Versus Capital Budget

There are two types of public budgets—*operating budgets* and *capital budgets*. An operating budget is a short-term, year-to-year budget that plans how resources will be allocated for government agencies and programs. A capital budget is a long-term plan that deals with the financing of capital projects—long-term investments that include buildings, bridges, and even quality of life projects such as parks. Capital budgets are financed through borrowing, usually in the form of bonds. States, coun-

TABLE 9.3 – CONGRESSIONAL BUDGET PROCESS TIMETABLE

Date	Action
First Monday in February	President submits budget to Congress.
February 15	Congressional Budget Office submits economic and budget outlook report to Budget Committees.
Six weeks after President submits budget	Committees submit views and estimates to Budget Committees.
April 1	Senate Budget Committee reports budget resolution.
April 15	Congress completes action on budget resolution.
May 15	Annual appropriation bills may be considered in the House, even if action on budget resolution has not been completed.
June 10	House Appropriations Committee reports last annual appropriations bill.
June 15	Congress completes action on reconciliation legislation (if required by budget resolution).
June 30	House completes action on annual appropriations bills.
July 15	President submits mid-season review of budget to Congress.
October 1	Fiscal year begins.

Source: Section 300 of the Congressional Budget Act of 1974, as amended (P.L. 93-344, 2 U.S.C. 631).

ties, or municipalities issue bonds to raise revenue for these capital projects. Investors (which could include you) buy the bonds and earn interest on them. In most instances, the interest made on government bonds is tax exempt, thus increasing their appeal from an investment perspective. Note that there is no capital budget at the federal level.

Line-Item Budget

A *line-item budget* illustrates where public money will be spent item by item. Line-item budgeting is most popular among local governments, given its relative simplicity. In other words, you do not need to be a financial wizard to create a line-item budget. Personnel costs, office supplies, and the like are projected each year and are "lined up," so to speak, beneath one another. This type of budget is advantageous from an accountability perspective; that is, the amount that will be spent on x, y, and z is clearly delineated to keep spending under control. It is a simple tool for keeping tabs on where money goes, ensuring that funds are spent appropriately. A major disadvantage of the line-item budget is that it is not tied to performance. Year-to-year allocations in line-item budgets differ very little, so there is a degree of sluggishness when it comes to assessing how much "should" be spent on x, y, and z.

> "Whatever else they may be, budgets are manifestly political documents. They engage the intense concern of administrators, politicians, leaders of interest groups and citizens interested in the 'who gets what and how much' of governmental allocations."
>
> **AARON WILDAVSKY** and **ARTHUR HAMMOND**
> Authors

Performance Budget

The idea behind *performance budgeting* is that how much you spend on department x is tied directly to how well department x is performing. Performance budgeting requires the establishment of performance levels and the collection of information (or data) that tells whether those performance levels have been met. The most common types of performance indicators are outputs and outcomes. Output indicators report units produced or the quantity of services provided by a department, an agency, or a program. Outcome indicators reflect how well a government entity is meeting its goals and objectives. These indicators are designed to answer questions that deal with the quality and impacts of government service delivery. Consider outputs and outcomes in the context of the Department of Public Works and their street-sweeping responsibilities. An output indicator may be miles of roads swept monthly—which is a clear indicator of the amount of work that is done. If it is predetermined that 1,000 miles of streets should be swept per month, but the street sweepers clean only 980 miles in the month of February, then they have underperformed. On the other hand, if they cleaned 1,200 miles, then they have overperformed when it comes to this specific output indicator. "Street

TABLE 9.4 – LINE-ITEM BUDGET EXAMPLE: LONGMONT, COLORADO, FIRE DEPARTMENT

	Personal Services	2009 Actual	2010 Budget	2011 Budget
111	Salaries and Wages	5,000,842	5,161,371	5,066,131
114	Skill Based Pay	1,124	900	2,700
121	Wages - Overtime	491,006	380,492	390,003
122	Longevity Compensation	33,435	34,080	29,040
123	Leave Expense	142,182	-	-
124	Skill Based Overtime Pay	197	-	-
126	Retirement Health Savings Plan	39,328	47,521	47,653
127	FPPA Death and Disability	36,126	35,591	32,681
129	Medicare	58,325	58,458	60,383
132	Employee Insurance	671,205	661,358	673,808
134	Police and Fire Retirement	690,678	640,890	641,892
135	Compensation Insurance	90,871	91,193	89,945
136	Unemployment Insurance	4,508	10,114	12,483
137	Staff Training and Conferences	28,446	-	-
139	Dental Insurance	-	-	24,958
141	Uniforms and Protective Clothing	41,664	96,043	95,568
142	Food Allowance	12,872	500	-
	Subtotal	*7,342,809*	*7,218,511*	*7,167,245*
	Operating and Maintenance			
210	Office Supplies	225	-	-
216	Reference Books and Materials	3,544	390	390
217	Dues and Subscriptions	658	-	-
218	Non-Capital Equipment and Furniture	28,243	30,102	29,102
228	Janitorial Supplies	14,409	10,000	10,000

(continued)

(continued)

229	Materials and Supplies	25,497	28,000	27,000
232	Building Repair and Maintenance	42,393	39,000	39,000
233	Facility Repair and Maintenance	-	2,000	2,000
240	Equipment Repair and Maintenance	22,692	42,000	32,000
241	Grounds Maintenance	1,328	2,000	2,000
243	Non-Capital Computer Equipment and Supplies	505	392	-
245	Mileage Allowance	485	1,000	1,000
246	Liability Insurance	59,390	65,518	76,372
247	Safety Expenses	6,488	20,000	12,000
250	Professional and Contracted Services	30,398	30,000	-
261	Telephone Charges	655	13,800	13,800
262	Radio Repair and Maintenance	1,652	-	-
263	Postage	6	-	-
273	Fleet Lease - Operating and Maintenance	4,617	9,000	9,000
274	Fleet Lease - Replacement	263,448	223,262	264,281
	Subtotal	*348,357*	*373,014*	*433,457*
	Capital Outlay			
440	Machinery and Equipment	-	-	69,000
	Subtotal	-	-	*69,000*
	SERVICE TOTAL	$ 8,197,798	$ 8,107,989	$ 8,187,647

Source: City of Longmont, Colorado. "2009 Operating Budget. Fire Department."

cleanliness"—as measured through visual inspections of streets and the degree of citizen satisfaction or the number of citizen complaints—would serve as an outcome indicator. A stipulated performance level could be 90 percent of streets are rated as "clean," and fewer than 20 complaints for dirty streets are filed per month.

The central points of performance budgeting are: (1) the amount of work that is done is measured; (2) the quality (or the results) of that work is measured; and (3) this impacts how much money a department will receive in the future. Departments that overperform may receive more money, while those that underperform may receive less. Critics argue that using performance measurement as a basis for deter-

TABLE 9.5 – PERFORMANCE BUDGET: MUNICIPAL DEPARTMENT OF HEALTH

Goal 1: To control the spread of influenza by increasing vaccination rates among children 5 years and younger and among senior citizens, age 65 and over.

Objective 1.1: Increase yearly influenza vaccination rates from 50 percent in 2008 among children 5 years and younger to 70 percent by 2010.

Objective 1.2: Increase yearly influenza vaccination rates from 70 percent in 2008 among senior citizens age 65 and over to 90 percent by 2010.

Outcome measures	2008 actual	2008 expenditure	2009 estimate	2009 budget
Percent of children (5 years or younger) vaccinated each year	50%	53,050	60%	65,542
Percent of senior citizens (65 years and over) vaccinated each year	70%	71,336	80%	81,995

mining budgets is counterintuitive, because taking money away from a struggling department is likely to make matters worse. Also, some might argue that measuring performance is inherently problematic; that is, designing performance indicators is subjective, and collecting data can be time-consuming and expensive.

Zero-Based Budget (ZBB)

The key to *zero-based budgeting (ZBB)* is that all departments must defend their programs and consequently their level of funding each year. Rather than earmarking additional funds that are needed annually, the department head must demonstrate how different levels of funding would impact the delivery of a given program's services. In other words, the head of the Department of Public Works (DPW) would be required to show what would happen to the department's street-sweeping outputs if the amount budgeted for this operation were maintained at its current level, reduced by a certain percentage, increased, or even if the funding for the street-sweeping program were eliminated altogether. These are referred to as decision packages, and one would be prepared for each program within the DPW. The department head is required to rank the importance of each decision package; if budget cuts become necessary, higher ranked decision packages are spared, while lower ranked packages are cut.

> "Never base your budget requests on realistic assumptions, as this could lead to a decrease in your funding."
>
> **SCOTT ADAMS**
> Cartoonist, in his *Dilbert* comic

ZBB is advantageous in that it allows department heads to set priorities, letting

TABLE 9.6A – ZERO-BASED BUDGETING: MUNICIPAL DEPARTMENT OF PUBLIC WORKS

	FY 2007 2,984,285	FY 2008 = + 3% 3,073,814			
Solid Waste	709,626	730,915	1 Minimum 2 Current 3 Enhanced	90% 10% 10%	657,823 73,091 73,091
Recycling	211,665	218,015	1 Minimum 2 Current 3 Enhanced	90% 10% 10%	196,213 21,801 21,801
Street Repair and Cleaning	1,039,048	1,070,219	1 Minimum 2 Current 3 Enhanced	90% 10% 10%	963,197 107,022 107,022
Snow and Leaf Removal	694,736	715,578	1 Minimum 2 Current 3 Enhanced	90% 10% 10%	644,020 71,558 71,558
Special Projects	329,210	339,086	1 Minimum 2 Current 3 Enhanced	90% 10% 10%	305,178 33,909 33,909
			Total		**3,381,195**

TABLE 9.6B – HYPOTHETICAL RANKING

Rank	Package	Rank	Package
1	Solid Waste 1	9	Recycling 2
2	Solid Waste 2	10	Solid Waste 3
3	Street Repair and Cleaning 1	11	Street Repair and Cleaning 3
4	Snow and Leaf Removal 1	12	Snow and Leaf Removal 3
5	Street Repair and Cleaning 2	13	Recycling 3
6	Recycling 1	14	Special Projects 2
7	Special Projects 1	15	Special Projects 3
8	Snow and Leaf Removal 2		

The "minimum" package represents a 10 percent cut. The "current" package represents 100 percent funding, and the "enhanced" represents a 10 percent increase. The ranked decision packages in Table 9.6b represent funding priorities. In times of revenue scarcity, the decision packages ranked toward the bottom will not be funded.

the budget makers know where cuts are more acceptable and where increases would be desirable. It makes sense to allow department heads to set these priorities, given that they are in a position to know how best to carry out a department's programs. A disadvantage of ZBB deals with its labor intensiveness. Preparing and ranking the decision packages can be overwhelming. Additionally, the way in which the decision packages are ranked can be highly subjective.

> "Taxes, after all, are dues that we pay for the privileges of membership in an organized society."
>
> **FRANKLIN D. ROOSEVELT**
> 32nd President of the United States (1882–1945)

PBBS

First implemented by the U.S. Department of Defense secretary Robert McNamara during the administration of President Lyndon B. Johnson, *PPBS* (or *planning program budgeting systems*) is based on the principles of rational decision making. Rational decision making mirrors the aim of cost-benefit principles. When using cost-benefit analysis, program costs are compared to program benefits, both of which are expressed in monetary terms. Results are presented as a benefit-cost ratio, which equals the benefits of a program divided by its costs. If the benefit-cost ratio is greater than 1.0, the benefits of the program are greater than its costs. The difficulty of cost-benefit analysis stems from trying to place a monetary value on the "intangible" benefits of specific programs. With PPBS, a particular program's cost and benefits are weighed against the potential costs and benefits of possible alternative programs.

TABLE 9.7 –TRADITIONAL VS. ZERO-BASED BUDGETING

	Traditional budgeting	Zero-Based budgeting
Period of expenditure	References are given to previous year estimates. Factors like inflation, etc., are adjusted to previous estimates to arrive at the figures of the current year's budget.	The budgeting process starts from scratch. Previous year prices are not used for calculation.
Overinflation of budget	Managers in traditional method were able to manipulate their budget estimates.	In ZBB, overestimation is not possible, as managers have to justify their budget estimates.
Responsibility	Top management decides on the allocation of funds.	Managers of each unit decide on their division's expenditure.
Orientation	Accounting.	Decisions.
Approach	Routine.	Priority based.

Source: C&K Management Limited, TheManageMentor (TMM). Copyright © 2003 by C&K Management Limited. www.themanagementor.com/enlightenmentorareas/finance/CFA/ZeroBasedBudge.htm.

Budget Auditing

The auditing part of the budget process is designed to ensure that public money is spent appropriately. In short, audits are independent budgetary investigations that look to see if government agencies, organizations, or programs are spending their money lawfully and efficiently. As noted previously, the Government Accountability Office is responsible for audits at the federal level. At the state level, the Office of the Comptroller is responsible for budget audits. Most local governments rely on private auditing firms. Larger cities, however, tend to have a comptroller. Common types of

FIGURE 9.4 – COMPARISON OF TWO APPROACHES TO BUDGETING

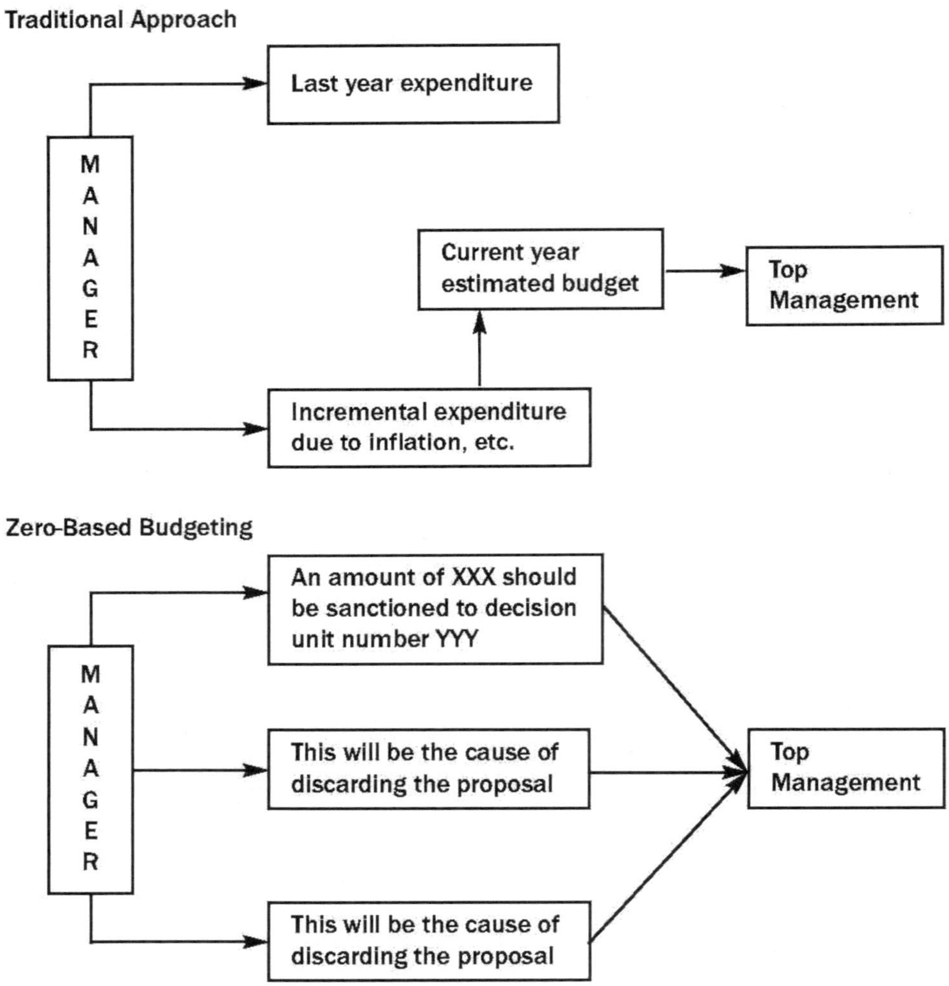

Source: C&K Management Limited, TheManageMentor (TMM). Copyright © 2003 by C&K Management Limited. www.themanagementor.com/enlightenmentorareas/finance/CFA/ZeroBasedBudge.htm.

audits include what are called compliance and performance audits. Compliance audits ensure that a government organization spends its money in accordance with the law. Performance audits examine organizational effectiveness and efficiency; that is, a performance audit looks at whether a public organization is accomplishing its stated goals and objectives, and whether this is being done at a reasonable cost.

Where Do Governments Get This Money?

Now that we have a better understanding of what budgets are and how the process works, a logical question is, How do governments at various levels collect the money that makes up these budgets? Anthony Downs (1959) argued that the federal budget is smaller than it ought to be. This coincides with the belief that governmental ben-

Advantages of Zero-Based Budgeting

1. Results in efficient allocation of resources, as it is based on needs and benefits.
2. Drives managers to find out cost effective ways to improve operations.
3. Detects inflated budgets.
4. Useful for service department where the output is difficult to identify.
5. Increases staff motivation by providing greater initiative and responsibility in decision making.
6. Increases communication and coordination within the organization.
7. Identifies and eliminates wastage and obsolete operations.

Disadvantages of Zero-Based Budgeting

1. Difficult to define decision units and decision packages, as it is very time-consuming and exhaustive.
2. Forced to justify every detail related to expenditure. The R&D department is threatened whereas the production department benefits.
3. Necessary to train managers. ZBB should be clearly understood by managers at various levels, otherwise they cannot be successfully implemented. Difficult to administer and communicate the budgeting because more managers are involved in the process.

Source: C&K Management Limited, TheManageMentor (TMM). Copyright © 2003 by C&K Management Limited. www.themanagementor.com/enlightenmentorareas/finance/CFA/ZeroBasedBudge.htm.

efits tend to be remote, while taxes tend to be immediate and evident. In other words, people notice that income and payroll taxes are taken from their checks biweekly. Seemingly rational voters are ignorant, though, when it comes to assessing benefits as a function of taxation. In spite of recent tax revolts, if governments at all levels stopped doing what they do, we would surely notice. Roads need to be fixed, schools need to be built, fires need to be put out, health care needs to be provided to the poor and elderly, food and drugs need to be inspected, and the list goes on and on. Necessary public services must be delivered, and these services are provided and paid for with tax money.

> "It's clearly a budget. It's got a lot of numbers in it."
>
> **GEORGE W. BUSH**
> 43rd President of the United States

Governments raise revenues, by and large, through the taxation of income, wealth, and consumption. The federal government's major source of revenue is the personal income tax, which is a certain percentage of an individual's wages or salary. This percentage is based upon the

FIGURE 9.5 – GOVERNMENT NET COST, 2007

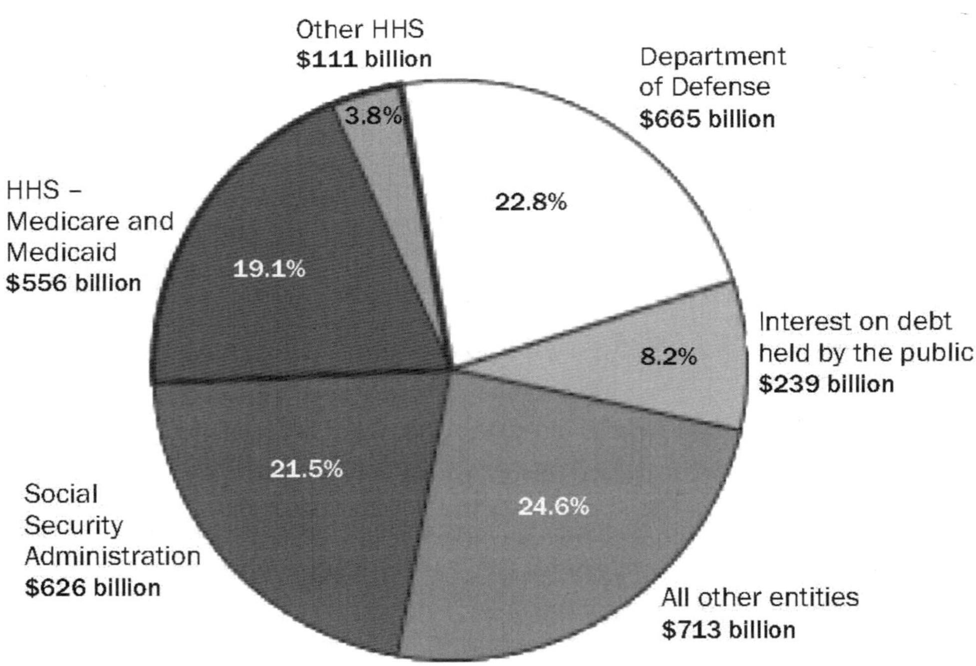

Source: "The Federal Government's Financial Health: A Citizen's Guide to the 2007 Financial Report of the United States Government." Washington, DC: U.S. Government Accountability Office (GAO). http://www.gao.gov/financial/fy2007financialreport.html.

amount an individual earns: Those who earn more pay a higher rate than those who earn less. This is referred to as a progressive tax system. Currently, as of 2010, the highest personal income tax rate is 35 percent. In addition to personal income, the federal government relies on corporate income taxes and payroll taxes. Corporate income taxes are similar to personal income taxes, as the revenues generated by for-profit businesses are taxed at varying rates depending upon the profitability of the business. Payroll taxes are taxes that both employees and employers pay jointly. Money withheld from a person's paycheck for Social Security and Medicare represent payroll taxes. As of 2010 employers withheld 6.2 percent of an individual's wages/salary for Social Security and matched that amount until the employee reached $106,800 of gross earned income for the year (gross meaning earned income before taxes are taken out). Beyond the $106,800 mark, the individual and employer were no longer required to withhold any additional payroll taxes. The withholding rate and employee match for Medicare is currently 1.45 percent. There is no income ceiling for

FIGURE 9.6 – GOVERNMENT REVENUE, 2003–2007 (IN TRILLIONS OF DOLLARS)

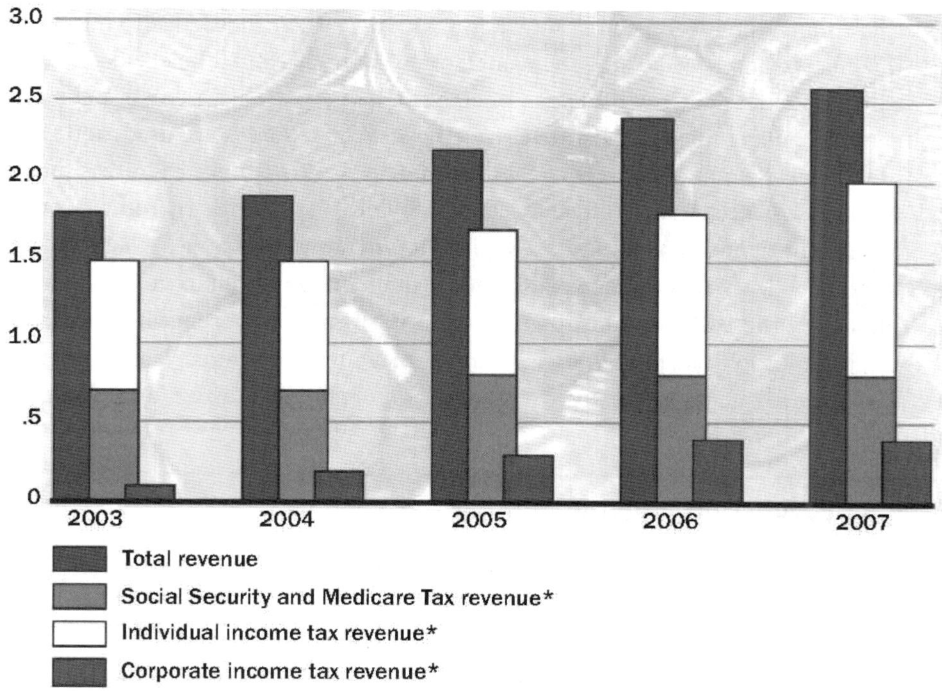

* In the *Financial Report*, Social Security and Medicare tax revenue are combined with individual tax revenue.

Source: "The Federal Government's Financial Health: A Citizen's Guide to the 2007 Financial Report of the United States Government." Washington, DC: U.S. Government Accountability Office (GAO). http://www.gao.gov/financial/fy2007financialreport.html.

Medicare withholdings. The federal government also taxes wealth, examples of which include profits from the sale of stocks, bonds, precious metals, and real estate. This is referred to as the capital gains tax, and the highest capital gains tax rate sits at 15 percent. Estates that are passed on after an individual's death may also be subjected to federal taxation, depending upon the value of the estate.

Like the federal government, state governments typically rely on personal and corporate income taxes—in addition to consumption or sales taxes. With consumption taxes, x number of cents will be added to every dollar you spend on goods and certain services. Income, corporate, and sales tax rates differ from state to state. Local governments principally rely on property taxes to finance government services and projects. With property taxes, an assessor within a municipality will physically go to a person's home or privately owned building and place what is known as an assessed value on it. When the assessed value is multiplied by a set tax rate, the result is one's property tax bill for the year. Property tax rates differ from municipality to municipality. Some municipalities do have income taxes, but these are typically very large cities—a good example being New York City.

Theories of Budgeting

The eminent political scientist V.O. Key (1940, p. 1138) acknowledged a budgeting quandary when he asked the following: "On what basis shall it be decided to allocate x dollars to activity A instead of activity B?" Given the scarcity of public resources, budget makers must determine how such resources are used, and there are various schools of thought or theories that dictate how public resources should be allocated. Miller (1976) offers three philosophical viewpoints regarding resource allocation: rights, deserts, and needs. The notion of rights assumes a legal or contractual obligation; deserts is synonymous with merit and utilitarianism, as championed by the British philosophers John Stuart Mill and Jeremy Bentham; the needs philosophy is redistributive in nature, meaning public money taken from the wealthier segments of society are used to support the less fortunate. These indi-

TABLE 9.8 – FEDERAL PERSONAL INCOME TAX RATES (2008)

Married Filing Jointly			Married Filing Separately			Single			Head of Household		
Marginal Tax Rate	Tax Brackets Over	But Not Over	Marginal Tax Rate	Tax Brackets Over	But Not Over	Marginal Tax Rate	Tax Brackets Over	But Not Over	Marginal Tax Rate	Tax Brackets Over	But Not Over
10.0%	$0	$16,050	10.0%	$0	$8,025	10.0%	$0	$8,025	10.0%	$0	$11,450
15.0%	$16,050	$65,100	15.0%	$8,025	$32,550	15.0%	$8,025	$32,550	15.0%	$11,450	$43,650
25.0%	$65,100	$131,450	25.0%	$32,550	$65,725	25.0%	$32,550	$78,850	25.0%	$43,650	$112,650
28.0%	$131,450	$200,300	28.0%	$65,725	$100,150	28.0%	$78,850	$164,550	28.0%	$112,650	$182,400
33.0%	$200,300	$357,700	33.0%	$100,150	$178,850	33.0%	$164,550	$357,700	33.0%	$182,400	$357,700
35.0%	$357,700	-	35.0%	$178,850	-	35.0%	$357,700	-	35.0%	$357,700	-

Source: Congressional Budget Office.

vidual-centered philosophies represent three ways of dealing with equity, which Frederickson (1990) envisions as the third pillar of public administration (economy and efficiency being the initial two pillars). And so the question remains, Should government allocate resources based upon need, which is the case with means-tested programs such as Temporary Assistance for Needy Families (TANF)? Or, should entitlement or contract be the basis of budgetary theory, which is the rationale for social insurance programs like Social Security and Medicare? The answers reflect different social philosophies and have a profound impact on how public resources are budgeted.

When assessing V.O. Key's question, one must consider budgetary theory from the perspective of the economist, the political scientist, and the public administrator. The economic perspective is best captured by V. Lewis (1952), who adds a measure of rationality with regard to cultivating a normative theory of budgeting. According to Lewis, philosophy should determine organizational goals, but economy and efficiency in terms of relative value, effectiveness, and incremental comparisons should serve as the means of goal attainment. Relative value refers to the opportunity cost of a particular policy decision, and it reflects the real consequences one expects will follow from making a particular decision. This cost is typically the difference between one's first and second choices. Relative effectiveness refers to evaluating a policy or budgetary preference in terms of achieving a common purpose. The notion of incremental comparisons refers to comparing value or cost at the margin, assuming that value diminishes with quantity (that is, as we acquire additional units of anything, an added unit has decreasing value). Regardless of individual policy preferences as dictated by philosophy, economic principles must remain paramount, and the closest application of this concept is zero-based budgeting (ZBB). Much like Lewis, Mikesell (1978) argues that the objective of the

TABLE 9.9 – WHICH TAX SYSTEM IS MOST FAIR?

Taxpayer income $	Regressive system		Proportional system		Progressive system	
	Tax rate %	Tax paid $	Tax rate %	Tax paid $	Tax rate %	Tax paid $
20,000	15.0%	3,000	10.0%	2,000	5.0%	1,000
40,000	7.5%	3,000	10.0%	4,000	7.5%	3,000
60,000	5.0%	3,000	10.0%	6,000	15.0%	9,000

Ability to pay dictates the type of tax system governments impose. Income taxes are progressive, in that those who make more pay a higher rate. Consumption taxes are proportional, as everyone pays the same rate on the sale of goods and services. Billionaire and former Republican presidential candidate Steve Forbes is a proponent of changing the income tax to reflect a proportional system, whereby everyone would pay the same rate—this is the so-called flat tax.

budget process is to support public policies and projects where the value exceeds the costs. The budget process should strive to identify and sustain worthwhile government activities, while minimizing the wasteful misallocation of scarce resources.

According to Brubaker (1997), the budgetary process engenders a "common pool" of resources. Private income becomes common property, and this consequently fosters what Brubaker terms the "tragedy of the budgetary commons," whereby the transfer of private income into a finite common pool creates incentives for exploitation. While the common pool should be used for purely public goods and services, this pool represents a depletable pie that is "up for grabs" among competing interests. As such, incentives are created to avoid contributing to the common pool, but a simultaneous struggle to obtain a share of it (i.e. budgetary rent seeking) exists as well. The struggle to obtain appropriations from the common pool creates tension and conflicting priorities, and such conditions prove counterproductive in terms of fostering careful and detached budgetary decisions. Brubaker (1997) embraces a budgetary process that provides a clear expression of public preference, produces net benefits for all, decreases opportunities for rent seeking, and allows people to participate directly. Brubaker advocates public choice measures that would reduce the magnitude of the budgetary commons. For instance,

- Tax credits could be offered for contributions made to providers of quasi-public services.
- Taxpayers could choose to no longer participate in programs that provide dividable goods or services.
- Citizens could participate in determining their tax share; however, this idea is prone to so-called free rider problems and lack of knowledge. (Brubaker 1997)

EXERCISE 9.1

Urban Institute—Catastrophic Budget Failure November 25, 2009 (Video)

Len Burman, former director of the Urban-Brookings Tax Policy Center, explains why our spending and borrowing policies are leading the country toward catastrophic budget failure. Burman argues that the Congressional Budget Office's bleak economic forecasts are too optimistic, so we must act quickly to reduce our deficits. After viewing this video, students will critique the Burman plan, identifying strengths, weakness, and omissions. An alternative plan will be created based upon this analysis.

http://www.urban.org/publications/500137.html

Political scientists maintain that the budget is an interest-oriented process in which decisions are made in the context of who pays and who receives. The budget represents individual preferences and conflicts over whose preferences should prevail. As such, the process for dealing with differing budgetary preferences is not economic but political, according to Wildavsky (1992). Wildavsky underscores the inevitability of budgetary incrementalism as a function of politics (1961; 1992), suggesting that only a small number of politically feasible alternatives are considered at any one time, and in a democracy, these policies typically differ only in small increments from previous policies.

Whicker (1992) offers a "grander budget theory" that has a redistributive aspect—that is, tax dollars collected from wealthier individuals are spent on agencies and programs that provide services to the less fortunate. According to Whicker, ideology filtered through political parties controls politics and the budget. A grander budget theory would therefore pay greater attention to the redistributive components of the prevailing political ideologies, which would serve as a basis for determining that x ideology equals a y distribution of resources. Whicker's grander budget theory takes into account economic variables and budget actors' perceptions of economic conditions, thereby accounting for the ideological disparities that are manifest in times when government resources are less abundant.

Individuals like B. Swedlow (2002) would argue that cultural theory serves as a basis for understanding budgetary decisions. Culture embodies ideology, philosophies regarding human nature, the economy, and the impact of redistributive policies on individual autonomy and collective relationships. Cultural theory is a basis for predicting which political actors will form coalitions and which budgetary outcomes they will prefer. Swedlow characterizes budgeting as inherently normative insofar as it promotes some values over others. Norms and values permeate the budget process: the question of who gets what is value-laden. A normative theory of budgeting is one that reflects preferences of ways of life proportional to political representation. For example, if an egalitarian culture dominates, then budgeting may be done via referendum. If an individualistic culture dominates, then budgeting may be decentralized and fragmented.

The public administration perspective has, to some extent, evolved from economic and political science logic. Public administration's emphasis on efficiency and effectiveness is analogous to the economic principles set forth by Lewis (1952), Mikesell (1978) and others. Further, Holzer and Gabrielian (1998) stress that budgetary decisions, even from the perspective of public administrators, tend to be political in nature. Public administration has gone further, interjecting the notion of equity into the budgetary decision-making process. Frederickson (1990) embraces social equity as a standard for budgetary preferences and government action in general. Social equity is envisioned as the third pillar of public administration (after economy and efficiency), and it encompasses notions such as equality in governmental

EXERCISE 9.2

American Public Media—Engage 08: Budget Hero (Simulation)

Take the budgeting process for the U.S. government into your own hands and feel the impact of your distribution and taxation decisions in real time. Set tax rates and spending rates to determine the equitable distribution of public services. Experience the impact of balancing policy priorities of security and health care with education and insurance benefits, while maintaining the safety net that government is expected to provide. After completing the simulation, students will summarize the actions they took and the results of those actions.

http://americanpublicmedia.publicradio.org/engage08/budgethero/

services, responsiveness to the needs of the citizenry, and an approach to public administration that has practical applications, is problem oriented, and theoretically sound. Public administrators, according to Frederickson, require a better understanding of fairness and equality in order to balance the needs for economy, efficiency, and social equity. Moreover, Frederickson (1994) advocates policies or budgetary preferences that have intergenerational social equity—policies that do not shift costs or benefits from one generation to another.

V.O. Key questioned the rationale by which x dollars are allocated to one activity at the expense of another. While budgetary preferences are largely a function of philosophy and values, efficiency and cost-benefit principles must guide the budget process. From a political science perspective, bargaining and incrementalism prove central to the budgetary process, which is consistent with pluralist notions. Finally, the notion of social equity is essential to the public administration logic regarding resource allocation. Key (1940) suggests that solving this budgetary dilemma does not entail the establishment of a single paradigm or criteria by which budgetary decisions should be made. Specifically, Key notes: "It is not to be concluded that by excogitation a set of principles may be formulated on the basis of which the harassed budget official may devise an automatic technique for the allocation of financial resources. Yet the problem needs study in several directions" (1940, p. 1140).

PERFORMANCE, BUDGET AND POLITICS RELATIONSHIP: WHAT IS RIGHT?/WHAT IS WRONG?

It is theoretically right that performance has to be measured and that the measurement information has to be utilized for budget-based decision making in an organization. However, in reality, it does not seem that performance measurement is effectively related to budget-based decisions. Furthermore, we sometimes notice that performance measurement information, if any, is wrongly connected to budget-based decision makings. The following article touches on the issue of the performance-budget link. Do you think a poorly performing organization should receive increased budgets in order to improve performance? Or do you think a poorly performing organization must be penalized due to that poor performance? What is right and what is wrong in this case article?

Poor-Performing Public Firms Face Wage Cut

By Lee Hyo-sik

Most state-run companies and quasi-government organizations performed poorly last year, failing to live up to management goals, and will face cuts in employee salaries and budgets this year.

After evaluating the management performance of 24 public firms and 77 quasi-government bodies, the Ministry of Strategy and Finance said Friday that their overall showing deteriorated in 2007 from a year earlier on sluggish business performance and rising inefficiency in organizational management. Also, heads of state-run firms and government-financed institutions posted poorer management results and will face a reduction in year-end bonus.

Twenty-four public companies received 73.2 points out of 100 on average last year, down from 75.7 in 2006. Korea Electric Power Corp. topped the list. The company was highly rated for its effort to reduce power outages by 49 percent in 2007. The electricity generator received high marks on its successful advancement into Azerbaijan and other foreign countries.

Korea District Heating Corp. also got high scores on its effort to promote and use renewable energy for heating generation.

(continued)

(continued)

However, Korea Coal Corp. ranked at the bottom for its poor financial status. Jeju International City Development Center was also rated low because of its failure to implement effective programs to attract investment from outside.

Most heads of 24 state-run firms received lower scores in 2007, compared to the previous year, as they were unable to deliver management promises. The average score stood at 71.4 last year, down from 77.5 a year ago.

Among 77 quasi-government organizations, the story is not much different. Their average score in business performance fell to 71.4 in 2007 from 72.4 a year earlier. Korea Energy Management Corp. topped the list on its effort to build databases on greenhouse gas emissions and promote energy conservation.

But Korea Securities Depository received the lowest points for its inefficient management of budget and business information. Top executives of semi-government bodies received an average of 67.9 points.

The ministry said it will differentiate bonus payments to employees and executives of public institutions in accordance with assessment of their management performance. Employees are entitled to the maximum 500 percent of their annual base salary as a bonus, while presidents and executives can receive up to 200 percent bonus.

"We will also boost the annual budget by 1 percentage point for 16 state-run organizations that posted superior performance. But we will issue an administrative warning to 15 institutions which performed poorly, and slash their annual spending by 1 percentage point. They will also be required to go through a rigorous management consulting program to increase organizational efficiency," he noted.

Source: Lee Hyo-Sik, "Poor-Performing Public Firms Face Wage Cut," The Korea Times, Biz/Finance, June 20, 2008, accessed Dec 25, 2011, http://www.koreatimes.co.kr/www/news/biz/2011/12/%20%20123_26255.html

The budget process is always said to be a political process. Rather than investigating objective performance and results of programs or policies, Congressmen oppose the passage of bills for political reasons. It seems that this political process is common in both countries. Please read the following article. Which budget process system looks more efficient? Do you agree with Mr. Jay Kim that the Korean system looks more efficient than the US system? Please discuss advantages and disadvantages of each budget process in each country.

Difference in budget process

By Jay Kim

The top news in the United States early this month was the nation-straining threat of a government shutdown. The media coverage focused both on the possibility of a shutdown and its negative impact on the economy and the lower classes, which made the nation fear a possible repeat of the nightmare that surrounded the government shutdown during President Bill Clinton's first term 16 years ago.

Fortunately, an agreement was reached at 11 p.m. on April 8, an hour before the imposed deadline, ending the threat of shutdown.

However, now the real fight begins — the debates over the debt ceiling law, a law that prevents the limitless increase of government deficits. Since its passing in 1917, there have been many changes to the debt limit. It is law that the maximum limit of the government's debt cannot be raised without consent from Congress.

The current debt ceiling is $14.3 trillion, which will be reached in the middle of next month, with the debt already at close to $14 trillion. Without raising the debt ceiling, the U.S. would default on its debts and obligation payments, which will have a serious and negative effect on the stock and bond market and cause another financial crisis.

The obvious solution is for the government to stop borrowing money; there are only two ways to do this. One is to reduce government spending, and the other is to raise taxes to increase government revenue. Though it would be optimal to do both, it is not that easy.

On top of that, the Republican strategy for next year appears to be to prevent Obama's re-election in any way possible, which will make the debt ceiling fight even more severe than the one that threatened a government shutdown.

One assumes that a solution will be found after a serious clash between both parties, but not after a nasty political fight. After all, there is no easy way to reduce government spending. Sixty percent of the federal budget is spent on so-called mandatory entitlements such as those payments for Medicare (to those over 65) and Social Security.

Cutting these would anger not only those over 65, but also those over 50 who are near retirement after having contributed to Social Security all throughout their lives. By the way, these generations also have the highest voting rates. However, there is no easy way to raise taxes, either.

The Democrats argue that the tax rate for the upper economic classes should be

(continued)

(continued)

raised, but the Republicans demand that the top tax rate should be reduced from the current 35 percent to only 25 percent. Since their positions are so far apart, an agreement would be really difficult to reach.

The current $14 trillion debt, which equals out to $52,000 of debt for each American, would not make it easy for Obama to call for a debt increase. However, raising taxes would face severe resistance from the Republicans, and cutting spending would open the door for Republicans to nullify the health care reform for which Obama has risked his political life.

Furthermore, there are 87 first-term Republican representatives supported by the far-rightwing Tea Partiers, all of whom strongly oppose raising the debt limit and will be extremely hard to persuade otherwise.

In Korea, there is never a government shutdown. A case like in the U.S., where a temporary budget is put into place without an agreement on the 2011 budget until half of the 2011 fiscal year (from Oct. 1, 2010 to Sept. 30, 2011) has passed seems to me like putting the nation on life support to extend its life for a couple of months at a time.

For example, though the first four temporary budgets were nearly similar to the previous year, the fifth one (passed in early March and lasting two weeks) contained a $40 billion cut and the sixth (passed in mid-March and lasting three weeks) contained a $60 billion cut. That sixth temporary budget ended on midnight on April 8, which would have caused the shutdown. Fortunately, a $38 billion cut was agreed, and the budget that would last until September was passed. How can this be a good thing?

In Korea, if a budget bill fails to pass 30 days before the deadline, the President can automatically use the previous year's budget temporarily. I think it's better for the U.S. to adopt the Korean system to negate the chances of a government shutdown and debt limit issues and to simply reduce the budget process. In this way, the National Assembly of Korea, despite the occasional physical scuffle, actually looks more efficient.

Jay Kim is a former U.S. congressman. He serves as chairman of the Washington Korean-American Forum. For more information, visit Kim's website (www.jayckim.com).

Source: Jay Kim, "Difference in Budget Process," The Korea Times, Opinion, April 25, 2011, accessed Dec 25, 2011, http://www.koreatimes.co.kr/www/news/opinon/2011/12/305_85829.html

KEY TERMS

Appropriations
Appropriations bill
Budget and Accounting Act of 1921
Budget audit
Budget authority
Budget deficit (or shortfall)
Budget resolution
Budget surplus
Capital budget
Discretionary spending
Entitlement spending
Executive budget
Executive Office of the President (EOP)
Fiscal year
Government Accountability Office (GAO)
House Appropriations Committee
House Budget Committee
Legislative budget
Line-item budget
Office of Management and Budget (OMB; formerly Bureau of the Budget [BOB])
Operating budget
Outlays
Performance budgeting
Planning program budgeting systems (PPBS)
President's budget
Senate Appropriations Committee
Senate Budget Committee
U.S. Comptroller General
Zero-based budgeting (ZBB)

REFERENCES

Brubaker, E. 1997. "The Tragedy of the Public Budgetary Commons." *The Independent Review* 1, no. 3: 353–70.

Downs, A. 1959. *An Economic Theory of Democracy*. New York: Harper & Row.

Frederickson, H.G. 1990. "Public Administration and Social Equity." *Public Administration Review* 50, no. 2: 228–37.

———. 1994. "Can Public Officials Correctly Be Said to Have Obligations to Future Generations?" *Public Administration Review* 54, no. 5: 457–64.

Government Accountability Office (GAO). "The Federal Government's Financial Health: A Citizen's Guide to the 2007 Financial Report of the United States Government." Washington, DC: U.S. GAO.

http://www.gao.gov/financial/fy2007financialreport.html.

Heniff, Bill, Jr. 2008. "The Spending Pipeline: Stages of Federal Spending," CRS Report for Congress, Order Code 98–405 GOV, June 17.

Holzer, M., and V. Gabrielian. 1998. "Five Great Ideas in American Public Administration." In *Handbook of Public Administration*, ed. J. Rabin, W.B. Hildreth, and G.J. Miller. New York: Marcel Dekker.

Key, V.O. 1940. "The Lack of a Budgetary Theory." *American Political Science Review* 34 (December): 1137-1144.

Lewis, V. 1952. "Toward a Theory of Budgeting." *Public Administration Review* 12 (Winter): 42–54.

Mikesell, J.L. 1978. "Government Decisions in Budgeting and Taxing: The Economic Logic." *Public Administration Review* (November/December): 511–13.

Miller, D. 1976. *Social Justice*. Oxford: Clarendon Press.

North Carolina Progress Board. 2003. *Our State, Our Money: A Citizens' Guide to the North Carolina Budget*, September. http://fsv.uncg.edu/budgets/Citizens_Guide.pdf.

Office of Management and Budget. 2002. *A Citizen's Guide to the Federal Budget*. http://www.gpoaccess.gov/usbudget/fy02/pdf/guide.pdf.

Ramkumar, V. *Our Money, Our Responsibility: A Citizen's Guide to Monitoring Government Expenditures*. http://www.internationalbudget.org/resources/expenditure/

Swedlow, B. 2002. "Toward Cultural Analysis in Policy Analysis: Picking Up Where Aaron Wildavsky Left Off." *Journal of Comparative Policy Analysis: Research and Practice* 4: 267–85.

Whicker, M.L. 1992. "An Academician's Response: Toward A Grander Budget Theory." *Public Administration Review* 52 (November/December): 601–03.

Wildavsky, A. 1961. "Political Implications of Budget Reform." *Public Administration Review* 21 (January): 183–90.

———. 1992. "Political Implications of Budget Reform: A Retrospective." *Public Administration Review* 52 (November): 594–99.

SUPPLEMENTARY READINGS

California Senate Publications. 2000. *The Budget Process: A Citizen's Guide to Participation*. Sacramento, CA: Senate Publications.

Heniff, Bill, Jr. 2007. "Formulation and Content of the Budget Resolution," CRS Report for Congress, Order Code 98–512 GOV, May 1.

Schick, A. 2000. *The Federal Budget: Politics, Policy, Process.* Washington, DC: Brookings Institution Press.

ELECTRONIC RESOURCES

An Example of a City Budget—"The City of San Diego: A Citizen's Guide to the City's Budget Process," Independent Budget Analyst (IBA), 2008: http://www.sandiego.gov/iba/pdf/bpguide.pdf

An Example of a County Budget—"A Citizen's Guide to the Clallam County Budget," Port Angeles, Washington, 2004: http://www.clallam.net/Board/assets/applets/Citizen_s_Guide1.pdf

An Example of a Municipal Budget—"Citizen's Guide to the Budget," Town of Hamden, Connecticut, 2007: http://www.hamden.com/filestorage/43/79/Citizen's_Guide_to_the_Budget.pdf

An Example of a State Budget—"Our State, Our Money: A Citizens' Guide to the North Carolina Budget," North Carolina Progress Board, 2003: http://fsv.uncg.edu/budgets/Citizens_Guide.pdf

National Budget Simulation: http://www.nathannewman.org/nbs/

Uncle Sam's Budget Balancer: http://www.klhess.com/unclesam/

U.S. Department of the Treasury's Financial Management Service: http://www.fms.treas.gov

U.S. Government Accountability Office: http://www.gao.gov

The White House Office of Management and Budget: http://www.whitehouse.gov/omb

The World Bank Website on Financial Management Budget Preparation: Policy-Based Budgeting (includes international best practices): http://web.worldbank.org/WBSITE/EXTERNAL/PROJECTS/EXTFINANCIALMGMT/0,,contentMDK:21462122~isCURL:Y~menuPK:3914586~pagePK:210058~piPK:210062~theSitePK:313218,00.html

CHAPTER 10

Public-Sector Leadership

Chapter 10 examines leadership within the public organization. In this chapter, students are provided practical leadership examples, with an emphasis on the managerial responsibilities of the leader. The discussion then turns to various and competing theories of "good" leadership. To conclude, students look at leadership and power, as well as the importance of effective communication in coordinating the human elements of the organization.

"You can only govern men by serving them."

VICTOR COUSIN
French Philosopher
(1792–1867)

Ineffective conducting.

Source: www.cartoonstock.com

LEADING PEOPLE

Management Functions

On cable and network television, shows offer prime-time stereotypes of people in command almost hourly—authoritative police commanders on *Law and Order*, a decisive doctor on *House*, and a confident President on the *West Wing*. Commercials on both TV and radio almost invariably present the boss as a figure to be both feared and pleased. The executive's voice is loud and strong, his or her manner is forceful, and subordinates are relegated to inferior positions. In bestselling fiction, the genre of Michael Crichton and colleagues deals primarily in stereotypes of powerful figures. Novels of politics or crime seem to trade in images of strong presidents, CIA directors, admirals and generals, commissioners and commanders. The language is idiomatic; the characterizations are two-dimensional. In sports, the image of the lone, aggressive decision maker is reinforced daily, and especially on the weekends, by stern-faced coaches and managers pacing the sidelines or sitting on the bench: They play the role of chess master, while the players are simply pieces on the game board. In comics, the boss often is portrayed as insensitive, and the power relationship is lopsided. Take *Dilbert*, for example—the staff in this cartoon typically suffers from the wrong-headed behavior of management, but those same incumbent, incompetent managers seem to survive. In *Blondie*, the boss is the productivity figure, while Dagwood is the buffoon. This chapter takes a closer look at the notions of leadership. Students will be presented with theories of leadership and real-world leadership examples, which are tied to a broader discussion of public-sector management.

> "A good leader is a person who takes a little more than his share of the blame and a little less than his share of the credit."
>
> **JOHN C. MAXWELL**
> Pastor; Author; Leadership Expert

Organizational leaders must carry out specific managerial functions. These functions include planning, organizing, directing, coordinating, controlling, and implementing.

- *Planning:* Determining what is to be done to accomplish a specific purpose, objective, or the mission of the department, section, or unit.
- *Organizing:* The formal arranging and balancing of activities, the determination of who will do what, the assigning of authority and responsibility so that that which is being planned will be accomplished.
- *Directing:* Assigning tasks, ordering, instructing, telling subordinates what to do in order to accomplish the objective.
- *Coordinating:* Integrating a schedule of activities so that the plans will be carried out on time.

- *Controlling:* Checking the progress of work against plans or standards to determine if activities are under way and progressing satisfactorily; making corrections and adjustments or even new plans in the light of new developments or unforeseen circumstances.

- *Implementing:* Accomplishing or fulfilling the purposes or ends of the work plan.

According to Leonard Sayles (quoted in Rao, 1999), managers are people who:

1. Work to implement their personal career plans, using the firm as a vehicle for so doing while seeking to meet its requirements.

2. Work to be sensitive to the expressed or more often implied expectations of their immediate superiors. They seek to tune in on new pressures, new developments, and new requirements that may subtly or sharply alter how they go about their work.

Eleanor Roosevelt and Fala, the Roosevelts' dog during the White House years.

3. Negotiate continuously with their peers in other departments on whom they depend and who depend upon them and their work group to get the total job done effectively.

4. Cultivate good relations with staff and service groups whose attitudes and actions can make their jobs easier or harder, for they realize that at times support groups have the ear of the throne.

5. Respond to the requests, demands, and requirements of significant individuals and groups in their occupational life spans to retain their goodwill or at least not alienate them. They must be flexible in adjusting to an astounding variety of personalities, cliques, in-groups, parochial loyalties, expertise, and eccentricities.

6. Oversee the flow of work into, within, and out of their departments to assure that it proceeds with a minimum of interruption or static that may draw unwanted attention from superiors.

7. Are alert to the work output, needs, desires, and morale of their subordinates, interacting with them, yet maintaining their own managerial position.

8. Represent their people and their views in dealings with their superiors and other departments.

9. Try to remain their own person while accommodating themselves to the legitimate demands of the organization. They must establish a valid order of priorities balancing out what is rightly due the firm, their families, and themselves.

10. Attempt to cope adequately with their own tensions to receive a fair share of psychic as well as economic income from their work. (Rao, 1999)

The successful accomplishment of these managerial functions stems from the management of interpersonal relationships—in other words, leadership. Leadership is present at all levels in an organization, whether private or public. A leader must be decisive, yet listen to others. He or she must be firm, yet know when to retreat. He or she must exercise authority, but in a restricted way. In brief, a leader must know when to "zig" and when to "zag." Effective leadership assures success in planning, organizing, and controlling staff.

> "To lead people, walk beside them."
>
> **LAO-TSU**
> Philosopher
> (c. Fourth–Sixth Century B.C.E.)

- The essence of leadership is followship—people's willingness to follow makes for leadership.

- Leadership is generally defined simply as influence—the art of influencing people to work freely toward the achievement of collective goals.

Traditional, simplistic models of leadership pervade our society and condition our public managers from a very early age. Those ingrained top-down models frustrate policy implementers—or public servants—by making the least, rather than the most, of our critical human resources. Models of excellent leadership, on the other hand, can be especially powerful in informing the study and implementation of public administration, offering salient models that can gain and maintain the attention of busy policy implementers. If better leadership "prescriptions" are to be constructed, they will have to rely on lessons of successful leadership as viewed through new lenses. The literature of leadership focuses on partnerships as a means to attain the stated goals of a particular public policy. Programs in public administration and public affairs, as well as in business and management, are expending much effort in undoing the assumptions that students bring to the classroom; as a consequence, they are ignoring the problems and constraints of such deep-seated, albeit simplistic, views. Those simplistic assumptions essentially follow an authoritarian, or Theory X, model.

> "Leaders are visionaries with a poorly developed sense of fear and no concept of the odds against them. They make the impossible happen."
>
> **ROBERT JARVIK**
> Twentieth-century Heart Surgeon

- Leaders must be strong and decisive; under continuous pressure, they must act on the spot, reaching decisions without taking much time to consider the subtleties and implications of their choices.
- Leaders are expected to act as authoritarian, lone decision makers; they may solicit advice, but their operative paradigm is "the buck stops here"—the adage that the decision is on their desk, on their watch. They are expected to act, and they do so as much to serve their egos as to respond to the expectations of their colleagues, superiors, and board members that they present a strong and decisive persona.
- The "team" must back up the leader, right or wrong. Team members do not argue; soldiers carry out their orders, athletes execute their plays, and subordinates follow directions.
- Authority emanates from the top and is to be automatically accepted. Members of an organization, paid or volunteer, rarely talk back or challenge top-down directives. And they are just as rarely ignored in the formulation of decisions and strategies.
- Leaders know best and the workforce must therefore follow. Generals and secretaries of defense view wars as too complex for the average soldier or citizen to understand. Principals view education as too complex for students, parents, and even teachers to comprehend.

Thus, public management is driven by assumptions of leadership that are widely accorded legitimacy by the workforce exposed to Theory X-type role models from birth.

- Young children are socialized to follow the authoritative directions of their parents. This is a necessary pattern of survival and cultural transference that often continues throughout the life cycle of parents' relationships with their children.
- Other authority-oriented role models insert themselves into the lives of children as they grow and gain independence.
- Students are expected to follow the lead of their teachers and later, their professors, who are given immense authority to direct, judge, punish, and reward.
- Student-actors must follow the directions of the drama coach or director of the school play.
- Student-athletes are acculturated never to question the edicts from their coaches.

The aforementioned role models are reinforced throughout adulthood, and the prevailing stereotype of the authoritative leader appears in multiple venues. For instance, in the 1970 award-winning film *Patton*, George C. Scott portrays the revered U.S. army general as a larger-than-life figure, intimidating his troops into courageous actions, accusing slackers of cowardice, and exposing himself to enemy fire as an example to the soldiers under his command. That image, as portrayed by other actors who represent real and fictional characters, is a thread that is woven through movies of wartime action and Cold War deception, of the Wild West, and of police and firefighting heroics.

> "There are always a lot of people so afraid of rocking the boat that they stop rowing. We can never get ahead that way."
>
> **HARRY S. TRUMAN**
> 33rd President of the United States

Although simplistic assumptions are widely discredited in the research-based literature, few people are exposed to such studies or taught about those research findings. In the United States, tens of millions of people staff public and quasi-public organizations (nonprofits, private-sector contractors, and the like). Only a very small percentage (in the range of tens of thousands) are educated in public management at the graduate level, having obtained a master's degree in public administration or public policy, and many of those graduates lack formal leadership training. Most people in positions of public-sector leadership come from fields such as law, medicine, engineering, social work, or education, where little but the stereotypes inform their expectations.

A thorough examination and analysis of case studies in leadership could help reverse the erroneous notions of authority that our society communicates so perva-

The Case of Nancy Hanks

According to Richard Loverd (1997), Nancy Hanks (1927–1983), as the second chairperson of the NEA, is regarded as an especially successful policy implementer. Bringing unusually deep and broad leadership skills to the NEA, she executed a strategy for advancing and adapting the agency to a changing policy environment. During Hanks's tenure from 1969 to 1977, the agency budget increased twelvefold. Its staff increased sixfold. The number of applications for funding increased ten times. The number of grant awards rose by a factor of seven. Overall, Hanks nurtured an arts boom throughout the country. Theater audiences more than tripled. Dance audiences increased by a factor of ten. Other measures of the arts showed similar growth. Just as important, artists and government officials came to feel they were full partners in a set of long-term endeavors. Loverd (1997) characterized the ingredients of Hanks's leadership—the "recipe" for implementation—as a winning combination of environmental context, bureaucratic resources, political tactics, and personal style.

In terms of the context, Hanks was relatively nonpartisan. Although a Republican like Richard Nixon, the U.S. president at the time of her appointment, Hanks came across as a neutral figure—neither a politician nor an artist. She was able to build partnerships (that is, political coalitions) by avoiding any political or artistic labels. She described herself modestly as a budgeting specialist—an arts administrator who could creatively put a program into a political context. Hanks was adept at partnering: building networks, convening panels of experts, coordinating advisory committee decisions, integrating diverse viewpoints, and reformulating information and opinion into an acceptable, practical product. She was also known for her meticulous preparation skills and her keen attention to detail.

Hanks successfully defined a long-term financial growth strategy for the NEA. Her three goals were:

1. Developing cultural resources, targeting nonprofit arts agencies for competitive grants,
2. Making artistic resources available to a much wider audience, and
3. Advancing our cultural legacy by funding new creative opportunities for artists and new artistic experiences for audiences.

Each of these three goals formed the basis for a new coalition of partners: arts agencies, audiences, and artists.

To fund her initiatives, Hanks took advantage of the newly passed Budget and Im-

(continued)

(continued)

poundment Control Act of 1974 to secure more than $10 million in transitional funding. In addition, by developing a new category of funding known as "challenge grants," which required a three-to-one match of private-to-federal dollars, she effectively stretched the NEA's budget. Both actions required substantial coalition building in the arts and political communities, as well as alliance building with other federal agencies such as the U.S. Information Agency and the General Services Administration. To staff the NEA's initiatives, she built a capable, loyal staff, in large part by drawing on her wide networking skills. That staff underscored and reinforced her own capabilities and acted very much as a fourth partner in building momentum for the arts.

Finally, Hanks became known for results-oriented programs. She relied on ideas that had been piloted successfully elsewhere, often at the state level. By paying attention to such innovations, she was able to adapt workable ideas rather than risk implementing something entirely new. Compared to her successors, who were notably less successful, Hanks is viewed as a person with the right qualities and the necessary skills to take advantage of an environment that presented opportunities for the implementation of public policy. She is remembered as a leader who worked effectively with a broad range of allies, including bureaucrats in her own agency and in other federal venues, and politicians in the White House and U.S. Congress.

Overall, then, we can extract the following guidelines from Hanks's case.

1. Build networks resulting in partnerships.
2. Bring technical expertise to the position.
3. Increase resources and disburse them to partners.
4. Integrate diverse viewpoints.
5. Adapt proven ideas.
6. Demonstrate results.
7. Build a capable, loyal staff as internal partners.
8. Take advantage of opportunities in the policy environment.

Source: Loverd, R.A., ed. 1997. Leadership for the Public Service. Upper Saddle River, NJ: Prentice Hall.

sively. Developing alternative models of leadership behavior would likely make much better use of our human resources in the quest for more effective public organizations and programs. We cannot govern in the twenty-first century from first-century models such as the Caesars. As examples of efficiency and power, we examine the leadership style of two federal administrators: Nancy Hanks of the National Endowment for the Arts (NEA) and Colin Powell of the U.S. Department of Defense (DoD). Both offer practical models for leadership, as well as insights on building and maintaining sometimes fragile partnerships.

Prevailing Leadership Theories

Trait Theory

Trait theory embraces the idea that leaders are born; therefore, they must possess certain innate characteristics that make them well suited for leadership. Height—justifiably or not—is thought to be a leadership trait; that is, there is the perception that taller individuals are better leaders. Height is often associated with dominance and power. Other leadership traits include intelligence, self-confidence, sociability, integrity, and diligence. Good reasoning skills and the ability to use language persuasively are positive leadership traits, but there is such a thing as being too smart for one's own good. Off-the-charts intelligence can sometimes be misinterpreted and can actually hinder a leader's ability to connect with his or her subordinates.

The essence of leadership is getting people to follow. People are more inclined to follow someone who exudes confidence. Having confidence in your abilities and conveying this confidence ultimately make people feel that your decisions are the correct ones, and thus following is the "smart" or "right" thing to do. There is, how-

EXERCISE 10.1

What Are the Qualities of a Poor Leader Versus an Excellent Leader?

Think for a moment of a manager you have worked for that you considered to be an excellent leader. List the qualities that made you feel that he or she was an excellent leader.

1. Observed qualities?
2. How did you feel working for this manager?
3. What was your reaction on the job to this treatment?

Now, think of a manager you have worked for who was simply awful. List the qualities that made you feel he or she was a poor leader.

1. Observed qualities?
2. How did you feel working for this manager?
3. What was your reaction on the job to this treatment?

The Case of Colin Powell

Nancy Hanks had a clear mission, one in which she ardently believed: the growth of the arts. U.S. Army General Colin Powell was given the task of implementing an even clearer mission, but one that he may not have championed initially: gaining support for the Persian Gulf War (also known as the First Gulf War, the Iraq War, and Operation Desert Storm, 1990–1991). By all accounts, however, he did so quite effectively. According to Jon Meacham (1997), Powell reportedly had reservations about going to war against Iraq. As an alternative, he favored a strategy of containment. But Powell's responsibility as chairman of the Joint Chiefs of Staff was to implement President George H.W. Bush's decision to go to war. By all accounts, Powell was adroit in his support of the President (Bush the elder), partnering with different players to build a supportive constituency. Meacham characterizes Powell's skills as more than just technical. He was viewed by White House staffers as a politically adept player who knew how to work the levers of power at the departmental and interagency levels. Among members of the press, he was seen as especially cooperative in helping to develop stories—a clear indication of his subtle skillfulness in enlisting the press as a policy implementation partner.

Like Hanks, Powell's attributes include an efficient manner and an ability to get things done. Firmly committed to the principles of merit, he attributes his success to the army's objectivity in assessing the skills and accomplishments of its members. This belief underscores his awareness of the need to build and maintain support within the military bureaucracy over the long haul (i.e., the course of his career).

In terms of policy implementation, Powell has a reputation as a conservative manager. He is described by Meacham (1997) and others as someone who knows how far to take an argument, and was understandably reluctant to antagonize other decision makers who did not share his understanding of facts, strategies, or tactics. But his persuasive abilities and negotiating skills enabled him to fight for federal funds for defense and to prevail. In 1990 he took the initiative, convincing then-President Bush (the elder) and Defense Secretary Dick Cheney to maintain a "base force" of 1.6 million troops and an overall defense spending budget of $290 million. In arguing for those numbers, he used his ties with the press to "float" his own position in advance of that of the White House. Powell preserved Cold War levels of funding without a Cold War enemy. He did this in part by building a coalition of interests within the DoD, a mutually advantageous strategy of multiple, overlapping forces, thus begging the questions of efficiency and redundancy and minimizing opportunities for drastic budget cuts. During the Gulf War, Powell was as adept at being a politician as he was at being a military strategist. According to General Norman Schwarzkopf, he was never sure whether Powell was representing his own views or those of others.

Overall, Powell emerged from the Persian Gulf War as a hero—highly respected and positioned for future leadership. He was perceived as an effective leader by his troops and the public, and as an effective soldier by his civilian superiors. Powell had managed to implement national policy largely by recruiting organizational allies and maintaining coalitions, much as he had done in earlier budgetary and intradepartmental "wars."

We can also extract guidelines for successful policy implementation from the Powell case, according to Meacham (1997).

1. Know how to "partner" in the process of implementing desired policy.
2. Become a reliable source for potential press partners.
3. Project an image of efficiency.
4. Advocate principles of merit, thereby building a positive image for the organization.
5. Build both internal and external coalitions.
6. Be able to represent the views of other partners.
7. Argue preemptively, thereby facilitating partnership opportunities.
8. Be willing to implement orders to be an "inside" partner.

Source: The Washington Monthly, December 1994. Copyright by the Washington Monthly Company, 1611 Connecticut Ave., N.W., Washington, D.C. 2009.

Colin Powell, center, former Chairman of the Joint Chiefs of Staff and Secretary of State. White House photo by Paul Morse.

ever, a thin line between confidence and arrogance—the latter of which may alienate people. Michael Bloomberg, the mayor of New York City, attributes his success in life to interpersonal skills and determination (Bloomberg 1997). A leader must be able to work with people. A leader must be sociable, which is synonymous with being courteous, sympathetic, and cooperative. Trait theory assumes that the best leaders are proactive, persistent, and show a willingness to accomplish the task at hand. Finally, integrity assumes a certain measure of ethical clarity. Leaders with integrity can be counted on to do what they say they will do. Having integrity means being dependable and loyal. It also means that a leader is willing to accept responsibility for his or her actions. Aside from being highly subjective, the main criticism of trait theory is the implication that leadership cannot be learned.

> "Leadership: The art of getting someone else to do something you want done because he wants to do it."
>
> **DWIGHT D. EISENHOWER,**
> 34th President of the United States (1890–1969)

Skills Theory

While trait theory emphasizes personal characteristics, the skills approach to leadership is centered on human capital. In other words, an individual's skills and abilities determine the extent to which he or she is fit for leadership. There are three distinct types of skills: technical, human, and conceptual. Technical skill refers to the abilities and knowledge necessary to complete a particular task. Human skill is analogous to having interpersonal skill or simply being good with people. A leader with interpersonal skills is aware of individuals' needs and tries to motivate subordinates by fulfilling those needs. Conceptual skill refers to the ability to think critically and work with ideas. Long-term visioning, strategic planning, and analyzing hypothetical scenarios are conceptual skill sets. Conceptual skills are thought to be most important among top management, while human and technical skills are most important among middle and line managers.

Style Theory

The style theory of leadership is framed in terms of task-oriented behavior and relationship-oriented behavior. Task behaviors deal exclusively with organizational goal attainment, while relationship behaviors deal with the sociopsychological aspects of managing employees—creating a harmonious and cooperative work environment and making sure that employees get along with each other and their supervisors. Style theorists examine how well leaders balance the need to achieve results (task behavior) versus the needs of the people within the organization (relationship behavior). Leaders who place a high priority on relationships as opposed to tasks are often described as "country club" managers: they do a good job of creating a pleasant work environment and satisfying the needs of their subordinates. Leaders who place a high priority on tasks as opposed to relationships are said to be "authority-compliance" managers: they are good at achieving organizational

EXERCISE 10.2

Skills Inventory

Read each item carefully and decide whether the item describes you as a person. Indicate your response to each item by circling one of the five numbers to the right of each item.

Key: 1 = Not true; 2 = Seldom true; 3 = Occasionally true; 4 = Somewhat true; 5 = Very true

1.	I enjoy getting into the details of how things work.	1 2 3 4 5
2.	As a rule, adapting ideas to people's needs is relatively easy for me.	1 2 3 4 5
3.	I enjoy working with abstract ideas.	1 2 3 4 5
4.	Technical things fascinate me.	1 2 3 4 5
5.	Being able to understand others is the most important part of my work.	1 2 3 4 5
6.	Seeing the "big picture" comes easy for me.	1 2 3 4 5
7.	One of my skills is being good at making things work.	1 2 3 4 5
8.	My main concern is to have a supportive communication climate.	1 2 3 4 5
9.	I am intrigued by complex organizational problems.	1 2 3 4 5
10.	Following directions and filling out forms comes easily for me.	1 2 3 4 5
11.	Understanding the social fabric of the organization is important to me.	1 2 3 4 5
12.	I would enjoy working out strategies for my organization's growth.	1 2 3 4 5
13.	I am good at completing the things I've been assigned to do.	1 2 3 4 5
14.	Getting all parties to work together is a challenge I enjoy.	1 2 3 4 5
15.	Creating a mission statement is rewarding work.	1 2 3 4 5
16.	I understand how to do the basic things required of me.	1 2 3 4 5
17.	Thinking about organizational values and philosophy appeals to me.	1 2 3 4 5

Scoring: The skills inventory is designed to measure three broad types of leadership skills: technical, human, and conceptual. Score the questionnaire as follows:

Technical skill score: Sum the responses on items 1, 4, 7, 10, 13, and 16.

Human skill score: Sum the responses on items 2, 5, 8, 11, 14, and 17.

Conceptual skill score: Sum the responses on items 3, 6, 9, 12, 15, and 18.

Scoring Interpretation: The scores you received on the skills inventory provide information about your leadership skills in three areas. By comparing the differences between your scores, you can determine where you have leadership strengths and where you have leadership weaknesses. Your scores also point toward the level of management for which you might be suited.

Source: Northouse, P.G. 2004. Leadership: Theory and Practice, 3d ed. Thousand Oaks, CA: Sage Publications.

goals in an efficient manner. The needs of the employees are often disregarded, as workers are thought to be cogs within a machinelike operation. This type of leader is overly controlling. Leaders who place a high priority on both tasks and relationships are described as "team" managers: they emphasize results and employee needs by incorporating participatory management. The concept of the quality circle serves as an example. A quality circle consists of a small group of workers that perform similar tasks who meet frequently and willingly to pinpoint, examine, and solve work-related problems. The overriding purpose is to improve the quality of an organization's services or products by systematically involving employees in the decision-making process. This, in turn, creates a team environment. Leaders placing a low priority on both tasks and relationships can be described as "impoverished" managers: they do only the bare minimum. This type of leader simply "goes through motions" (Blake and McCanse 1991, as cited in Northouse 2004).

> "The art of leadership is saying no, not yes. It is very easy to say yes."
>
> **TONY BLAIR**
> Former Prime Minister of Great Britain

Situational Leadership

The idea behind situational leadership is that the leader must alter his or her leadership approaches based upon the circumstances (or the situation, hence the name). Observation of leaders' behaviors in a wide range of situations has revealed that leaders often exhibit one or a combination of these behaviors. Relationship or consideration behavior deals with the extent to which a leader is likely to maintain personal relationships with supervisees through communication, delegation, and offering opportunities for growth and potential. This is characterized by trust and respect, in addition to concern for their feelings. The leader spends time directing group activities: identifying tasks and how they should be accomplished, as well as defining patterns of organization, communication channels, and schedules. Most managers exhibit both styles in combination, to a greater or lesser degree, depending upon the situation. Knowing this, what determines which style a leader uses? The development level of the employee determines whether a leader should be more "relationship"-oriented or "task"-oriented. Development level refers to how competent and dedicated an employee is toward accomplishing an organization's goals. In other words, highly developed employees would be very good at their jobs and show a high degree of interest in what they are doing. Lower developed employees are not very competent and exhibit a low level of job interest. Moderately developed employees fall somewhere in between—either they are more competent and less motivated or vice versa. A motivated but less competent employee would benefit from having a more "task"-oriented leader—while a competent but unmotivated employee would benefit more from a more "relationship"-oriented leader.

Contingency Theory

Some leaders are better suited for certain situations. The idea behind contingency theory is fitting leadership style to a particular situation (Fiedler 1964; 1967). The first step is to determine one's leadership style. Fiedler constructed a survey known as the Least Preferred Coworker (LPC) scale, the purpose of which is to determine whether a leader is more relationship oriented or task orientated. After assessing a leader's orientation type, the next step is to examine the leadership situation from three different vantage points: (1) leader-member relations, (2) task structure, and (3) position power (Northouse 2004). *Leader-member relations* centers on whether the work environment is positive or negative. In other words, are the relationships between the leader and his or her subordinates friendly, or are they confrontational? Do the subordinates trust and exhibit loyalty to their leader, or is the opposite true? *Task structure* deals

> "The manager accepts the status quo; the leader challenges it."
>
> **WARREN BENNIS**
> Leadership Studies Trailblazer

FIGURE 10.1 – SITUATIONAL LEADERSHIP

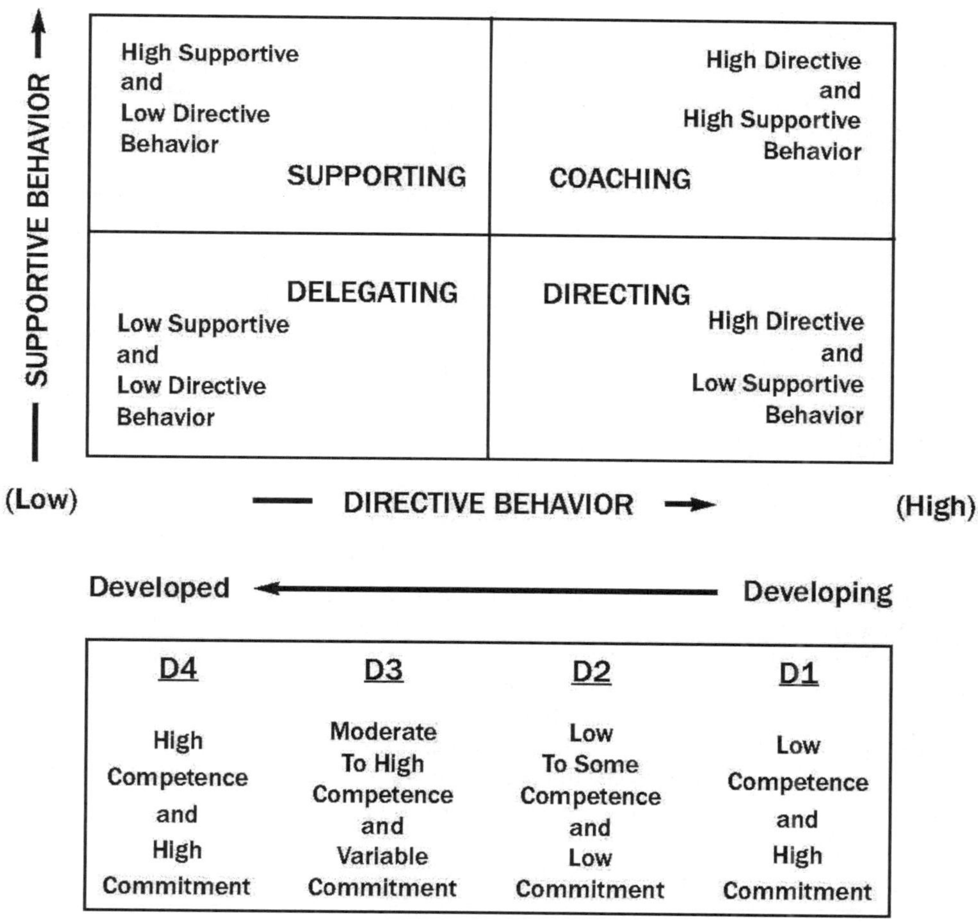

with whether employee tasks and responsibilities are clearly defined. An example of clearly defined tasks might include the assembly-line production of an automobile. These tasks are clearly defined in that there is "standard" way of assembling an automobile, which is taught to assembly-line workers. A loosely defined task might include developing an advertising strategy to sell the car that comes off the assembly line. This task is considered loose because there are many different ways of accom-

EXERCISE 10.3

Least Preferred Coworker Scale (LPC)

Think of a person with whom you have difficulties working. He or she may be someone you work with now or someone you knew in the past. The person need not be someone you like the least but should be someone with whom you had the most difficulty in getting a job done. Describe this person as he or she appears to you.

1. Pleasant	8	7	6	5	4	3	2	1	Unpleasant
2. Friendly	8	7	6	5	4	3	2	1	Unfriendly
3. Rejecting	1	2	3	4	5	6	7	8	Accepting
4. Tense	1	2	3	4	5	6	7	8	Relaxed
5. Distant	1	2	3	4	5	6	7	8	Close
6. Cold	1	2	3	4	5	6	7	8	Warm
7. Supportive	8	7	6	5	4	3	2	1	Hostile
8. Boring	1	2	3	4	5	6	7	8	Interesting
9. Quarrelsome	1	2	3	4	5	6	7	8	Harmonious
10. Gloomy	1	2	3	4	5	6	7	8	Cheerful
11. Open	8	7	6	5	4	3	2	1	Guarded
12. Backbiting	1	2	3	4	5	6	7	8	Loyal
13. Untrustworthy	1	2	3	4	5	6	7	8	Trustworthy
14. Considerate	8	7	6	5	4	3	2	1	Inconsiderate
15. Nasty	1	2	3	4	5	6	7	8	Nice
16. Agreeable	8	7	6	5	4	3	2	1	Disagreeable
17. Insincere	1	2	3	4	5	6	7	8	Sincere
18. Kind	8	7	6	5	4	3	2	1	Unkind

Scoring Interpretation: Your final LPC score is determined by adding up the numbers you circled on all of the 18 scales. If your score is 57 or below, you are a low LPC, which suggests that you are task motivated. If your score is within the range of 58 to 63, you are a middle LPC, which means you are independent. Individuals who score 64 or above are called high LPCs, and they are thought to be more relationship motivated. Because the LPC is a personality measure, the score you get on the LPC scale is believed to be quite stable over time and not easily changed. Low LPCs tend to remain low, moderate LPCs tend to remain moderate, and high LPCs tend to remain high.

Source: Northouse, P.G. 2004. Leadership: Theory and Practice, 3d ed. Thousand Oaks, CA: Sage Publications.

Innovation in Management and Leadership: "Working in the Triangle"

The South Carolina State Park Service has embarked on a journey that will secure that vision while using the very approaches that too often strike fear into an organization. The State Park Service has laid the foundation to build on "results—not just effort." The State Park Service has implemented an innovative approach to managing parks. The "Management Triangle" provides Park Managers with the necessary parameters and tools to manage their parks. Moreover the Triangle allows for creativity, innovation and the ability for field staff to "make decisions." The triangle is simple:

The Management Triangle

The triangle does not close at the bottom for a reason. It's open for staff to create opportunities and procedures at the park level and on the front lines that produce results without bogging down in unnecessary levels of authorization or approval. Park Managers, Park Rangers and State Park "stakeholders" have developed the components of the Triangle. Each level is detailed to provide direction and the necessary parameters to achieve the "long-term desired results" of the Park Service and each particular State Park or Historic Site. The key is for the Park Staff to "work in the Triangle" to achieve those desired results.

Real change and results take place at the park, on the front lines. There must be a mechanism to make this happen while satisfying the realities of government. With this approach, managers manage, and have the freedom to make decisions. The Triangle utilizes many approaches including the principles of Baldrige. More impor-

(continued)

(continued)

tantly it produces results—not just effort. Managers are working in the triangle and focusing on accomplishing the goals of the Park Service.

The five goals are in fact linked to the seven principles of Baldrige. One of the philosophies of Baldrige is the involvement and buy-in from the entire organization top to bottom, bottom to top, involvement from all levels of the organization. In order to achieve this, a new approach was developed – the Annual Park Planning (APP) process was implemented this past year. The APP enables managers to bring not only budget requests, but also issues and opportunities to "the table." Every spring, each park manager meets with decision makers and support personnel for answers and direction for the following fiscal year. The manager and whomever they deem necessary to bring with them state their case, from budget requests to innovative new initiatives and from opportunities to answers for pressing issues. The meeting allows information to flow from the top management of the Park Service but more importantly the field and front line employees now have a forum to express views and initiate new ideas and programs. Did it happen overnight? Absolutely not. Was it difficult? You bet! Are we there yet? No way! We are just now feeling comfortable in the process. We have, however, discovered a few things:

1. First you must determine your mission and vision (get back to basics).
2. You must provide the necessary tools for employees to "make things happen."
3. Remember—results are in the small stuff.
4. Leadership is more important than ever.

The process continues. We can no longer expect the General Assembly or our customers to let us work under the premise of give us funding and revenues, and we will do good stuff. There must be a strategic approach, one that produces results, one that measures performance, and one that gets us closer to the "desired results." Not because it's required or fashionable, but because it's necessary. Not only for this generation but also for the generations to come. What's a Park Ranger to do? Get back to basics, Stewardship and Service, use these new tools that are available, be creative and innovative and remember that the next generation is depending on us.

Source: Gaines, P. 2001. "Working within the Triangle," IMPACT, The Official Newsletter of the South Carolina State Government Improvement Network, volume X, issue III.

plishing it. Tasks that are clearly defined offer a leader more control, while more loosely defined tasks afford the employees more control. *Position power* simply refers to the amount of authority a leader has to either reward or punish. A leader who can hire, fire, give raises, or reprimand can be said to have high position power. Taken together, "very favorable" work situations exist when leader-member relations are positive, tasks are defined, and the leader has a high degree of position power. "Very unfavorable" situations are those in which leader-member relations are negative, tasks are loosely defined, and the leader's position power is low. Contingency theory suggests that task-oriented leaders (low LPC score) are more likely to thrive in *both* very favorable and very unfavorable situations. Relationship-oriented leaders (high LPC score) tend to thrive in moderately favorable situations.

Path-Goal Theory

Employee motivation is central to the path-goal theory of leadership. Leaders must embrace behaviors that deal with the motivational needs of their employees. In the context of path-goal theory, four types of leadership behaviors have been identified:

- Directive leadership: deals with clearly informing subordinates what needs to be accomplished, how it should be accomplished, and what the expected results should be.
- Supportive leadership: deals with "human" needs (e.g., being friendly and approachable).
- Achievement-oriented leadership: deals with challenging subordinates to do their very best.
- Participative leadership: deals with including subordinates in decision making.

> "Leadership is a combination of strategy and character. If you must be without one, be without the strategy."
>
> **H. NORMAN SCHWARZKOPF**
> U.S. Army General

Based on an employee's personality and task, a leader would use one of these approaches. Directive leadership would work well with a more authoritarian worker whose is responsible for overly complex or unclear tasks. Supportive leadership would motivate workers who express dissatisfaction stemming from mundane and repetitive tasks. Achievement-oriented leadership would be appropriate for workers who exhibit a desire to excel and who perform complex tasks. Finally, participative leadership would serve to motivate individuals who have desire for control and are responsible for unclear and loosely structured tasks (Northouse 2004, p. 130).

Transformational Leadership

Like path-goal theory, transformational leadership deals with subordinate motivation. Transformational leadership, however, goes a step further by focusing on the subordinate's values, ethics, long-term aspirations, and general workplace needs. Transformational leaders are charismatic and serve as role models for their

EXERCISE 10.4

Path-Goal Questionnaire

Indicate how often each statement is true of your own behavior using the following key: 1 = Never; 2 = Hardly ever; 3 = Seldom; 4 = Occasionally; 5 = Often; 6 = Usually; 7 = Always

1. I let subordinates know what is expected of them.
2. I maintain a friendly working relationship with subordinates.
3. I consult with subordinates when facing a problem.
4. I listen receptively to subordinates' ideas and suggestions.
5. I inform subordinates about what needs to be done and how it needs to be done.
6. I let subordinates know that I expect them to perform at their highest level.
7. I act without consulting my subordinates.
8. I do little things to make it pleasant to be a member of the group.
9. I ask subordinates to follow standard rules and regulations.
10. I set goals for subordinates' performance that are quite challenging.
11. I say things that hurt subordinates' personal feelings.
12. I ask for suggestions from subordinates concerning how to carry out assignments.
13. I encourage continual improvement in subordinates' performance.
14. I explain the level of performance that is expected of subordinates.
15. I help subordinates overcome problems that stop them from carrying out their tasks.
16. I show that I have doubts about subordinates' ability to meet most objectives.
17. I ask subordinates for suggestions on what assignments should be made.
18. I give vague explanations of what is expected of subordinates on the job.
19. I consistently set challenging goals for subordinates to attain.
20. I behave in a manner that is thoughtful of subordinates' personal needs.

Scoring: Reverse the scores for items 7, 11, 16, and 18.
Directive style: Sum of scores on items 1, 5, 9, 14, and 18.
Supportive style: Sum of scores on items 2, 8, 11, 15, and 20.
Participative style: Sum of scores on items 3, 4, 7, 12, and 17.
Achievement-oriented style: Sum of scores on items 6, 10, 13, 16, and 19.

Scoring Interpretation: Directive style: A common score is 23; scores above 28 are considered high; scores below 18 are considered low. Supportive style: A common score is 28; scores above 33 are considered high; scores below 23 are considered low. Participative style: A common score is 21; scores above 26 are considered high; scores below 16 are considered low. Achievement-oriented style: A common score is 19; scores above 24 are considered high; scores below 14 are considered low. The scores you received on the path-goal questionnaire provide information about which style of leadership you use most often and which you use less frequently.

Source: Northouse, P.G. 2004. Leadership: Theory and Practice, 3d ed. Thousand Oaks, CA: Sage Publications.

subordinates. They inspire by conveying high expectations. The transformational leader inspires intellectually by being creative and innovative and also by encouraging their subordinates to be the same way. This type of leader further emphasizes the importance of communication and listening, which aids in cultivating a workplace environment that addresses one's job-related and personal needs. There is a true sense of employee nurturing among transformational leaders.

> "A good leader inspires others with confidence; a great leader inspires them with confidence in themselves."
>
> **UNKNOWN**

Theory of Life Cycle Leadership

This theory deals with the levels of direction (task behavior) and emotional support (relationship behavior) a leader provides, while taking into consideration the subordinate's maturity level.

In the context of life cycle theory, maturity encompasses the following:

- Motivation to achieve
- Degree to which a subordinate desires and has ability to handle responsibility

FIGURE 10.2 – GAINING THE POWER TO LEAD

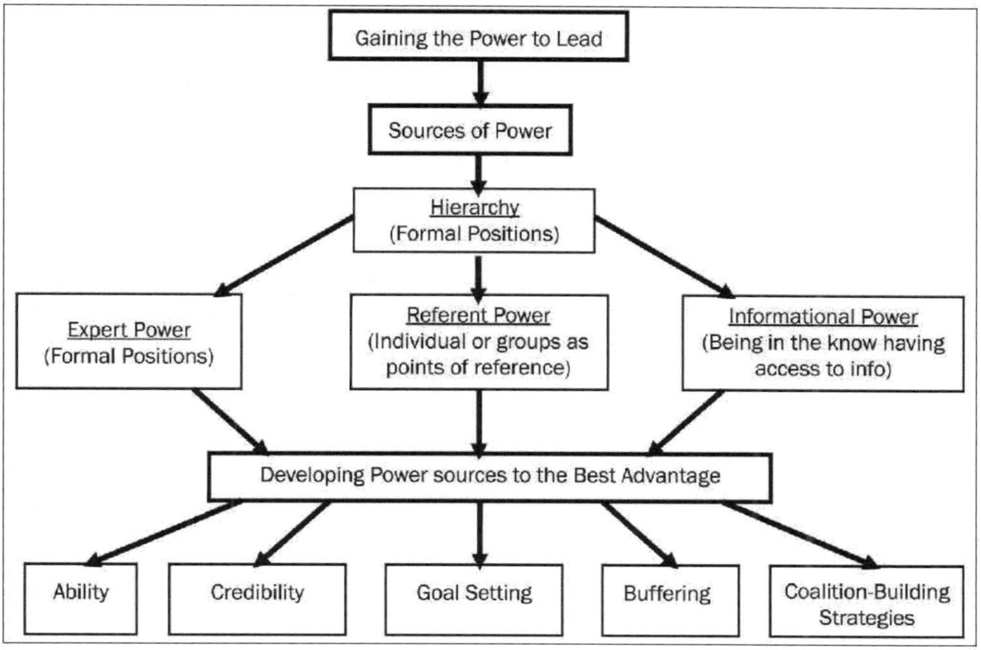

Smith, J. 2000. School of Public Affairs and Administration, Rutgers University–Newark.

EXERCISE 10.5

Your Professional Power

1. In your job, how much control do you usually have over when and how you carry out your tasks?
   a. Just about no control—I do what everybody else wants, and when they want it.
   b. Most of my work is under my control.
   c. Most of my work is not under my control.
   d. Just about 100 percent control—I do what I want, when I want to.

2. If you have ever had to fire an incompetent person who worked for you—employee, housekeeper, tutor, and so forth—which of the following statements is most true?
   a. I've never needed to fire someone, but never had the nerve.
   b. I've wanted to fire someone, but never had the nerve.
   c. I have fired someone, but it took me weeks or months to drum up enough nerve, and then I felt awful.
   d. I have (or would have) no trouble firing incompetents.

3. When you have to tell an employee or coworker to do something she or he doesn't want to do, which of the following are you most likely to say?
   a. "I'll do it myself."
   b. "I feel awful having to impose on you, but would you consider writing this report in the next few days?"
   c. "I hope this is okay with you, but I'd sure like to have this report ready by tomorrow at five o'clock."
   d. "Please have this report ready by tomorrow at five o'clock."

4. To what extent do other people at your place of work depend on your decisions?
   a. No at all; I'm a cog in a big machine.
   b. Rarely.
   c. Occasionally.
   d. All the time; I am the machine.

5. If you had to single out one factor, what do you like most about your work?
   a. The social life; the friends I work with.
   b. The steady income.
   c. The intellectual challenge.
   d. Having the power to make decisions that affect others.

EXERCISE 10.5

6. How often have you sabotaged your employer's requests or needs, by purposely "forgetting" to do them, or delaying, or carrying out your assignments badly?
   a. All the time; it's a way of life.
   b. Occasionally; it's the only way I can question my employer's judgment.
   c. Rarely; only when I'm angry with her or him.
   d. Never; I'm my own boss.

7. Suppose you were offered a promotion to a position of greater authority and responsibility than you have now. How would you feel and what would you do?
   a. Scared to death; I'd turn it down because I'm not confident of my abilities.
   b. Nervous and worried, but I'd take it.
   c. I'd be flattered, but I'd say no; I have as much responsibility as I want.
   d. I'd be delighted—I'd jump at the chance.

8. How important is it to your career plans to have a powerful job—one in which you have authority to make decisions and to control the activities of others?
   a. Totally unimportant—I'd never want any such authority.
   b. I want only enough power to do my present job as well as I can.
   c. Very important
   d. Essential—I'm going for it.

Scoring: Give yourself three points for every d, down to no points for every a. Questions 1 and 4 tap the literal amount of power you have over the work you do and the people with whom you work. The others measure your feelings about having power. Power and feelings of power may be quite different; that is, power is an action, and powerful people may or may not feel guilty or ambivalent about what they do, but they do it. But powerless people often worry so much about making decisions that they do nothing at all. Denied real authority, they may take it out on the employer, sabotaging the employer's needs (question 6) or sabotaging their chances for advancement in fears and low self-confidence (question 7), or by playing up the social aspects of the job over the issues of advancement. As sociologist Rosabeth Moss Kanter (1977) showed, men and women who are denied real channels of power tend to deemphasize goals of achievement and emphasize the aspects of the job that are within their reach—such as friends. In fact, as Kanter's work demonstrates, supposed motives of "fear of power" tend to vanish pretty quickly when women, and men, are actually freed to exercise power.

Source: Management Skills. 1980. New York: National Center for Public Productivity, John Jay College.

- Education or formal training related to tasks
- Experience

While age may affect maturity level, it is not directly related to this type of maturity. As a subordinate's maturity increases, a leader's task behaviors should decrease and their relationship behaviors should increase to the point where the individual is sufficiently mature that the leader can decrease relationship behavior (emotional support) as well.

> "If your actions inspire others to dream more, learn more, do more and become more, you are a leader."
>
> **JOHN QUINCY ADAMS**
> Sixth President of the United States (1767–1848)

Life cycle theory deals with the application of certain leadership styles in the context of an individual's (or group's) maturity level.

Style Adaptability

Style adaptability is the degree to which leader behavior is appropriate to the demands of their situations and followers. A person with a narrow style range can be effective over a long period of time if the leader remains in situations in which his or her style has a high probability of success.

Types of Leadership Power

Many managers believe that their effectiveness as a leader is determined by how much and what kind of power they have. The five types of power are discussed below.

1. Reward power: The ability to meet the needs of another, or control him or her, by giving rewards for desired behavior. Pay, promotions, or bonuses may be ways that organizations exert reward power over their employees.
2. Punishment power: Coercive power, or the ability to deliver a painful or punishing outcome to another, and hence control him by his desire to escape the punishment. Firing, ridiculing, or disciplining an individual are common techniques of coercive power.

EXERCISE 10.6

Small Group Discussion

Questions to be discussed, then shared with entire group:

1. Are you comfortable with power (your own and others)? Why or why not?
2. What use of power would you expect from an effective worker? Does it differ from your own use? How?
3. How might you be sabotaging your goals by the ineffective/inappropriate use of power?

3. Expert power: Power based on the ability to understand, use, and deliver information that others need.

4. Legitimate power: Control or influence that is exerted by virtue of the person's holding a particular position in the organizational structure. The power is vested in the rights and responsibilities of the position, not the person. Compliance with that power occurs because other individuals in the organization respect the organizational structure and the rights and responsibilities that accompany particular positions.

5. Referent power: Having the desire to comply with a leader's wishes because of your attraction to him/her describes referent power (French and Raven, 1959). Control based on referent power will be dependent upon the leader's ability to persuade others to follow based on attraction or charisma.

Leader as Communicator

When you take a moment and think about what managers and leaders do, you will inevitably come to the conclusion that the vast majority of their time is spent communicating—communicating in an effort to coordinate the human elements of the organization. Thus, when communication is broken, the organization is usually broken as well. There are several human barriers to communication, which are often referred to collectively as "noise." Noise can be external or internal, and it includes:

- Attitudes and values;
- Lack of listening and attention;
- Sound level and environment;
- Poor message construction and semantics;
- Perception difficulty;
- Faulty transmission;
- Unclarified assumptions;
- Absence of feedback.

Effective communication involves a two-way flow of information. As managers, we must know whether our intended messages are the ones our coworkers and supervisees receive. We learn this through feedback—verbal and nonverbal cues that tell us how others interpret our messages. We should be open and alert to these cues. Feedback permits us to adjust our message as needed. It also reinforces us by indicating whether we are being clear, accepted, or understood. We need to give as well as get feedback. By requesting clarification, we understand other people bet-

"An effective public works leader..."

Possesses Integrity—acts forthrightly and honestly, demonstrating through his or her actions how high moral character may be reflected in both the delivery of public works services and the operations of the public works organization.

Is Accountable—takes responsibility for his or her individual actions as well as those of the organization and its members, using explicit explanations of expectations and objective measures to monitor progress.

Is Decisive—draws conclusions, resolves disputes, and exercises judgment forthrightly, unambiguously, and with firmness.

Is Public Service Oriented—acts in the public interest and demonstrates through his or her actions belief in the value of public service.

Empowers Others—grants authority and acts to allow subordinates to make decisions and act independently, providing support as necessary to encourage responsible independent action.

Is Deliberate—makes decisions with careful consideration of the merits of alternative choices or courses of action available in a situation.

Is a Communicator—listens to what others have to say about a situation and explains forthrightly his or her own views.

Shows Respect for Others—demonstrates through his or her actions consideration for colleagues, subordinates, and members of the public, and an appreciation of concerns and contributions of each.

Is Technically Knowledgeable—understands how the operations and facilities for which he or she is responsible work and maintains that understanding as these operations and facilities evolve.

Manages Resources—recognizes the value of the organization's personnel, equipment, materials, facilities, funds, and reputation and allocates these to accomplish the organization's objectives.

Is Resilient—is able to recover and bounce back from frustrations, disappointments, and setback without undue loss of confidence in his or her own capabilities or those of associates or the organization.

Delegates—willingly assigns responsibility and authority to others capable of acting in his or her place to enhance the quality of the organization.

Maintains Balance—recognizes that an individual's work is only a part of life and demonstrates through his or her actions all aspects of one's life merit time and energy.

Source: Public Works Leaders – Core Competencies. Brochure developed by American Public Works Association – Leadership and Management Committee. http://www.apwa.net/Documents/About/TechSvcs/Leadership/CoreCompBrochure.pdf

ter. Giving feedback is a form of active listening. It not only makes people feel unique and worthwhile but heightens their sense of well being. In terms of feedback skills, some specific recommendations include the following:

1. Be prepared to give feedback, verbally and nonverbally.
2. Make feedback prompt. The longer the delay between message and feedback, the more likely we are to confuse the other person.
3. Feedback should be specific and not general:
   - Wrong: "Your description of the place just didn't sound right."
   - Right: "It was not complete enough, not enough description."
4. Feedback should be given in a way that is descriptive and not evaluating or judgmental.
   - Wrong: "Joe, you talk too fast."
   - Right: "Joe, when you get into a group meeting, you speak so quickly that I have a hard time understanding you."
5. Monitor your own feedback. If your feedback is not interpreted by the other person as you meant it, it serves no purpose.

> "Management is doing things right; leadership is doing the right things."
>
> **PETER DRUCKER**
> Economist; Author

When we think of ourselves in communication situations, we usually think more about getting our ideas across to someone else than about receiving ideas from them. This is normal. We have come to think the word "communication" means a process that flows out from us rather than one in which we are the receiver. But communicating orally involves far more than just speaking to a person: It involves

EXERCISE 10.7

Cyber Nations (Simulation)

Individually or as a class, students create an ideal nation. Select the governing structure, services, and income generation/cost-sharing policies which you and/or your class determine together. Create a summary of the new government. Include in this summary the public service principles discussed in all of the earlier chapters and how they are represented in the new nation. Specifically address the transformational leadership and the distribution of power strategies utilized in creating this new nation.

http://www.cybernations.net/default.asp

sharing ideas and trying to exchange meaning with each other as perfectly as possible. In most interpersonal and group situations, including supervisory communication, we spend nearly the same amount of time listening and responding to the other people as we do speaking. During a typical day, a manager likely spends more time listening, on average, than speaking, reading, or writing.

Do I listen well? Chances are this is a question you have never answered. After all, listening is something we have done all our lives with no special training. We take it for granted. Listening is an essential part of the circular give-and-take communication process. But true listening involves more than just putting on our "listening" expression and nodding in agreement now and then while mentally planning our evening; it involves listening with our full and active attention—listening empathically, as though we are in the other person's place. We can never take this kind of listening for granted. It takes skill and constant practice. The rewards, however, are improved communication and a more productive work climate. Listening is a skill, like any other, and it needs to be cultivated. Active listening skills include:

1. Encouraging nonverbal signals: Good eye contact; supportive, interested facial expression; nods.
2. Encouraging verbal signals: For example, "Tell me more"; and "Then what happened?"
3. Restatement or paraphrasing: Repeating the idea or content serves as an understanding and accuracy check. It lets the speaker know that you understand what he or she is saying and, consequently, elicits more from speaker.
4. Silence: This lets the speaker know that you are interested in what he or she is saying. Silence can be used to organize one's thoughts.

(Source: Management Skills. 1980. New York: National Center for Public Productivity, John Jay College.)

ORGANIZATIONAL CULTURE AND DIFFERENT LEADERSHIP STYLES

As the text argues, leadership is the art of getting someone else to do something you want done because he or she wants to do it. Given the different organizational cultures between the two countries, do you think the Korean leadership style is different from the US leadership style? Do you think the Confucian custom deeply rooted in Korean society had an impact on vertical leadership style as opposed to the US leadership style? Please read the following article. Do you think an authoritarian style of leadership was effective because Korea was at the earlier stage of nation building? Or do you think this authoritarian style was effective due to the Confucian value rooted in Korean society? Could the American President, using an authoritarian style of leadership, also be successful in the same situation? Please discuss.

By Kim Choong-nam

Contributing Writer

Hawaii–Koreans will have to choose their next president on December 19. When a company hires its president, it adopts very rigorous criteria of selection. Selecting a president of a nation is much more important than that of a company head.

But the responsibility of choosing a president is shared by tens of millions and voters tends to slight the heavy duty of vote choice. If people are not well prepared, they may end up with selecting an unqualified president.

In order to choose a qualified president, understanding the leaderships of former presidents is essential. We could learn lessons from the experience of former presidents and see what worked and what didn't.

Unfortunately, Korean presidents have been criticized yet never properly evaluated by the blind application of Western liberal democratic criteria.

They are judged in a biased way and underestimated without due consideration to the historical, economic, social and security realities in which they operated.

Different circumstances demand different demands on leaders. Leadership tasks in developing nations are quite different from those encountered in Western democracies.

(continued)

(continued)

Leadership effectiveness is the result of leadership style and the characteristics of the environment in which the leader works. A leader is more likely to be successful if he can meet the challenges his nation faces.

A leader in a developing nation has to promote formidable tasks of nation building with limited resources and ineffective institutions under challenging circumstances.

An ordinary approach is usually inappropriate under such extraordinary conditions: a task-oriented and authoritarian style of leadership is more likely effective. Can an American president become an effective democratic leader in Afghanistan or Iraq?

Korea has become an economic powerhouse and a dynamic democracy in a single generation under the most trying circumstances—the legacy of colonial rule, national division, the 1950–53 Korean War and continual confrontation with the Communist North.

Korean presidents, especially Syngman Rhee and Park Chung-hee, played central roles in the process of the successful nation building.

We may learn some lessons from the leaderships of Korean presidents.

First of all, a great leader possesses a keen sense of history and a good vision for the future of his country.

Syngman Rhee possessed a compelling vision of Korean nationalism—an independent nation from Japanese and Communist threats.

He played a pivotal role in the founding of the republic based on democracy and market economy. Without his vision and determined leadership, the establishment of the republic might have remained a dream rather than becoming a reality.

Park Chung-hee possessed an unusually strong sense of history. He had a great vision called "modernization of the fatherland" and promoted export-oriented industrialization. Kim Young-sam and Kim Dae-jung had long struggled for a vision of a democratic Korea.

Based on his diplomatic vision, President Rhee persistently demanded and signed a security treaty with the United States.

Under the slogan of "the northern policy," Roh Tae-woo normalized relations with most of the socialist countries. Kim Dae-jung's "sunshine policy" is also regarded as a courageous initiative toward North Korea.

Second, with limited capabilities under unusual challenges, agenda setting is more important for leaders in developing nations. If a leader tries to solve all the problems, he could end up achieving nothing. To be effective and successful, the leader needs to choose a primary agenda and focus on achieving it.

Rhee has been criticized for his authoritarian rule. Under the acute security crisis during and after the Korean War, his security first policy was inevitable. Without his uncompromising anti-Communist policy, the nation's survival would have been questionable.

Park was committed to what was possible (economic development) rather than what was desirable (democratic development). On the other hand, Kim Young-sam focused on democratic reform and neglected economic policy, resulting in 1997 financial crisis.

Both Kim Dae-jung and Roh Moo-hyun were preoccupied with North Korea policy, compromising national security and bringing ideological conflicts.

Third, a managerially capable leader is more likely to be effective. Both Park Chung-hee and Chun Doo-hwan were strong in organizational leadership. They made the best use of governmental institutions with emphasis on delegation, teamwork and coordination.

On the other hand, recent presidents who lacked experience in government or a large organization and managerial skills ran the government largely by personal whim, resulting in relatively poor performance.

Fourth, an effective leader is one who surrounds himself with capable advisers. Both Park and Chun were very cautious in selecting his ministers and advisers.

One of Park's merits was his ability to appoint the right people to the right positions at the right time. His appointment policy was characterized not only in the selection of well-qualified persons but also by the long duration of their tenures.

On the other hand, although they lacked administrative experience and needed experienced advisers, recent presidents appointed to key government posts a hodgepodge of their coteries, who were loyal to them but seriously unqualified to advise their president.

They thus reshuffled the Blue House staff and the cabinet frequently, leading to administrative instability and inconsistent policies. For example, the United States had only 60 secretaries of education during its 230-year history while Korea has similar number of education ministers during its 59-year history. This last sentence is inaccurate as the US Department of Education was only created a few decades ago···

Fifth, a president who focused on the pressing needs of the people was more likely successful. In earlier decades, Korean people were preoccupied with the basic

(continued)

(continued)

needs of everyday life.

Both Park and Chun succeeded in promoting continuous economic growth. A pragmatic agenda is also easier to plan and implement than an abstract one.

On the other hand, both Kim Young-sam and Roh Moo-hyun promoted what they thought important and neglected what was important to the people.

The former focused on anti-corruption drive and historical rectification, while the latter was preoccupied with North Korea policy and the campaign for dismantling the old establishment.

They were arrogant and selfassertive and wielded the sword of morality against the establishment of Korea as well as political enemies that they considered immoral and corrupt.

They wasted their precious political capital to correct past wrongdoings. A leader who does not pay enough attention to the pressing needs of his people cannot be successful.

Finally, a man of conviction with a strong sense of mission is more likely to be successful. Rhee's determination led to the signing of U.S.-Korea security treaty, which has become the backbone of Korean security and stability. Park's strong conviction was a source of his success.

Despite strong protest, he normalized diplomatic relations with Japan, built the Seoul-Busan expressway and heavy industries, and sent troops to Vietnam. Chun also succeeded in controlling inflation by overcoming strong opposition.

Meanwhile, a passive and indecisive leader will be more likely ineffective in achieving his goals. Such a leader will be push aside by aggressive political enemies and hostile pressure groups.

Both short-term Prime Minister Chang Myon and interim President Choi Kyu-ha were regarded as such leaders.

The writer is a Korea expert at the East-West Center in Honolulu and the author of a new book, "The Korean Presidents: Leadership for Nation Building." -ED.

Source: http://www.koreatimes.co.kr/www/news/special/2008/04/180_13602.html

KEY TERMS

Achievement-oriented leadership
Contingency theory
Development level
Directive leadership
Expert power
Feedback
Leader-member relations
Leadership trait
Legitimate power
Life cycle theory
Maturity
Noise
Participative leadership
Participatory management
Path-goal theory
Position power
Punishment power
Quality circle
Referent power
Relationship-oriented behavior
Reward power
Servant leadership
Situational leadership
Style adaptability
Supportive leadership
Task-oriented behavior
Task structure
Transformational leadership

REFERENCES

Text for this chapter is based in part by M. Holzer, School of Public Affairs and Administration, Rutgers University, Newark Campus, Newark, NJ. "Culture and Leadership." Paper presented at "Workshop 1: Leading for the Future," Leading the Future of the Public Sector: The Third Transatlantic Dialogue. University of Delaware, Newark, Delaware, USA. May 31–June 2, 2007.

Blake, R.R., and McCanse, D. 1991. *Leadership and Dilemmas—Grid Solutions*. Houston: Gulf Publishing Company.

Bloomberg, M.R. 1997. *Bloomberg by Bloomberg*. New York: John Wiley and Sons.

Fiedler, F.E. 1964. "A Contingency Model of Leadership Effectiveness." In *Advances in Experimental Social Psychology*. Vol 1, ed. L. Berkowitz, 149–190. New York: Academic Press.

Fiedler, F.E. 1967. *A Theory of Leadership Effectiveness*. New York: McGraw-Hill.

French, J.R.P., and B.H. Raven. 1959. "The Bases of Social Power" In *Studies in Social Power*, ed. D. Cartwright. Ann Arbor, MI: Institute for Social Research.

Kanter, R. M. 1977. *Men and Women of the Corporation*. New York: Basic Books.

Loverd, R.A., ed. 1997. *Leadership for the Public Service*. Upper Saddle River, NJ: Prentice Hall.

Management Skills. 1980. New York: National Center for Public Productivity, John Jay College.

Meacham, J. 1997. "Colin Powell: How Colin Powell Plays the Game." In *Leadership for the Public Service*, ed. R.A. Loverd, 159–70. Upper Saddle River, NJ: Prentice Hall.

Northouse, P.G. 2004. *Leadership: Theory and Practice*. 3d ed. Thousand Oaks, CA: Sage Publications.

Rao, V.S.P. 1999. *Bank Management*. New Delhi: Discovery Publishing House Pvt Ltd.

Van Wart, M. 2005. *Dynamics of Leadership in Public Service: Theory and Practice*. Armonk, NY: M.E. Sharpe.

SUPPLEMENTARY READINGS

Public Voices Symposium: Servant Leadership. 2002. Vol. 5 (1–2), pp. 1–76. http://andromeda.rutgers.edu/~ncpp/pv/issues/5–1&2.pdf

ELECTRONIC RESOURCES

U.S. Government Simulation: http://www.usgovsim.net/USG/index.php

Virtual U is designed to foster better understanding of management practices in American colleges and universities. It provides students, teachers, and parents the unique opportunity to step into the decision-making shoes of a university president. Players are responsible for establishing and monitoring all the major components of an institution, including everything from faculty salaries to campus parking. As players move around the Virtual U campus, they gather information needed to make decisions such as decreasing faculty teaching time or increasing athletic scholarships. However, as in a real college or university, the complexity and potential effects of each decision must be carefully considered. And the Virtual U Board of Trustees is monitoring every move. New Virtual U homepage: http://www.virtual-u.org/index.asp

CHAPTER 11

Ethics and Public Administration

In Chapter 11, students are introduced to ethics in public administration. The chapter begins with a theoretical discussion of administrative ethics, transitioning into a more practical and real-world discussion of bureaucratic discretion and the formal rules guiding such discretion. This chapter also covers codes of ethics; the ways in which public administrators can combat corruption and unethical practices; and various self-correcting mechanisms for shady tactics, including whistleblowing.

"Always do right. This will gratify some people and astonish the rest."

MARK TWAIN
Author; Satirist
(1835-1910)

– YOUNG MAN, WHY DID YOU CHOOSE THIS PARTICULAR COLLEGE?
– DAD, DON'T ASK STUPID QUESTIONS!
Artist: Y. Shcheglov; Cover of *Krokodil [Crocodile]* satirical magazine, 1983, No. 19.

ADMINISTRATIVE ETHICS

What Are Ethics?

Ethics are grounded in Greek tradition, represented by *teleological* and *deontological* theories. According to teleological theories, the consequences of actions are the most critical factor in determining whether an action should be pursued. Derived from the Greek *telos,* meaning "result," teleological theories stress the importance of maximizing what is "good." Deontological theories—derived from the Greek *deon,* meaning "that which is binding"—stress motives and intentions, as opposed to the consequences, as the critical factor in making decisions. Frederickson and Walling (1999, p. 501) note that distinctions "between teleological and deontological ethics might be dismissed as useless academic differentiation. But, it matters a great deal whether a human resources manager bases actions on teleological reasoning, in which the ends justify the means, as opposed to deontological reasoning, in which decisions are based upon principle."

> "[Because power corrupts,] society's demands for moral authority and character increase as the importance of the position increases."
>
> **JOHN ADAMS**
> 2nd President of the United States (1735–1826)

Ethics, according to French and Granrose (1995), "is a set of normative guidelines directed at resolving conflicts of interest so as to enhance societal well-being" (cited in Zinkhan et al. 2007, p. 363). Thompson (1985) provides a good definition of what constitutes *administrative ethics.* Administrative ethics emphasize "(a) the rights and duties that individuals should respect when they act in ways that seriously affect the well-being of other individuals and society; and (b) the conditions that collective practices and policies should satisfy when they similarly affect the well-being of individuals and society." Pinpointing all the factors that bring about and reinforce unethical conduct at the individual and organizational levels is inherently difficult. Understanding the theoretical and social bases of ethics may shed light on what motivates unethical behavior. Bottorff (1997) describes ethics as "a body of principles or standards of human conduct that govern the behavior of individuals and groups. Ethics is a branch of philosophy and is considered a normative science because it is concerned with the norms of human conduct, as distinguished from formal sciences (such as mathematics and logic) and empirical sciences (such as chemistry and physics). The study of ethics has been at the heart of intellectual thought since the earliest writings by the ancient Greeks, and its ongoing contribution to the advancement of knowledge and science continues to make ethics a relevant, if not vital, aspect of management theory" (p. 57).

Unethical behaviors may result from individual and organizational factors. That is, unethical behavior may be the result of personal values or personality traits. Organizational characteristics may be contributing factors as well. Some organizational cultures place no importance on whether goals and objectives are accomplished ethically. Without clear ethical standards within an organizational structure, unethical conduct may actually be encouraged. The "end justifies the means" philosophy—one that rewards "getting the job done" regardless of the potential

– A BRIBE?!.. NEVER!..
– A PRESENT? QUITE ANOTHER MATTER...
Artist: V. Travin; "The Fighting Pencil" group, 1969.

consequences—is often referred to as Machiavellianism. The Machiavellian philosophy was set forth by the Italian diplomat Niccolo Machiavelli in his treatise *The Prince*, which was written around 1513 and published posthumously in 1532. The Prince provides recommendations on how rulers can gain and maintain power. The following excerpt centers on Machiavelli's "means to ends" philosophy:

> Upon this a question arises: whether it be better to be loved than feared or feared than loved? It may be answered that one should wish to be both, but, because it is difficult to unite them in one person, it is much safer to be feared than loved, when, of the two, either must be dispensed with. Because this is to be asserted in general of men, that they are ungrateful, fickle, false, cowardly, covetous, and as long as you succeed they are yours entirely; they will offer you their blood, property, life and children . . . when the need is far distant; but when it approaches they turn against you. And that prince who, relying entirely on their promises, has neglected other precautions, is ruined; because friendships that are obtained by payments, and not by greatness or nobility of mind, may indeed be earned, but they are not secured, and in time of need cannot be relied upon; and men have less scruple in offending one who is beloved than one who is feared, for love is preserved by the link of obligation which, owing to the baseness of men, is broken at every opportunity for their advantage; but fear preserves you by a dread of punishment which never fails.
>
> Nevertheless a prince ought to inspire fear in such a way that, if he does not win love, he avoids hatred; because he can endure very well being feared whilst he is not hated, which will always be as long as he abstains from the property of his citizens and subjects and from their women. But when it is necessary for him to proceed against the life of someone, he must do it on proper justification and for manifest cause, but above all things he must keep his hands off the property of others, because men more quickly forget the death of their father than the loss of their patrimony. Besides, pretexts for taking away the property are never wanting; for he who has once begun to live by robbery will always find pretexts for seizing what belongs to others; but reasons for taking life, on the contrary, are more difficult to find and sooner lapse. But when a prince is with his army, and has under control a multitude of soldiers, then it is quite necessary for him to disregard the reputation of cruelty, for without it he would never hold his army united or disposed to its duties. (Machiavelli 1532/1984)

"The time is always right to do what is right."

MARTIN LUTHER KING, JR.
Civil Rights Leader (1929–1968)

Machiavelli's recommendations from nearly five centuries ago reinforce what we observe all too often—instances of corruption and misdeeds in government. There are countless examples of unethical behaviors perpetuated by agents of governmental and nongovernmental organizations. The list of unethical conduct by public administrators and officials is too long—the 1972 Watergate Hotel break-in and burglary of the offices of the Democratic National Committee, which led to the eventual resignation of President Richard M. Nixon; racial profiling within the ranks of the New Jersey State Police; incidents of detainee abuse and torture at the Abu Ghraib Prison in Baghdad, Iraq; South Carolina governor Mark Sanford's personal transgressions; the "CIA leak" that brought about Lewis "Scooter" Libby's obstruction of justice and perjury convictions; claims that former Illinois governor Rod Blagojevich peddled Barack Obama's U.S. Senate seat after Obama was elected president, and list goes on.

One particular "official act of misconduct" deals with a notorious clinical study known as the Tuskegee Experiment. In this 40-year-long experiment, medical treatment was deliberately withheld from 399 poor, African American sharecroppers from Alabama who had tested positive for syphilis, a highly contagious bacterial STD. Deceived by doctors from 1932 to 1972, the patients were never told that they suffered from syphilis. Officials from the U.S. Public Health Service went "to extreme lengths to insure that they received no therapy from any source," making this "the longest non-therapeutic experiment on human beings in medical history,"

Tuskegee Study Images from the Records of the Centers for Disease Control and Prevention.

Source: Inside the National Archives Southeast Region. "6. The Tuskegee Study (1930s-1972)" http://www.archives.gov/southeast/exhibit/6.php.

according to an article in the *New York Times* (Heller 1972). In 1997 President Bill Clinton offered a formal apology to the eight living survivors for what its government had done.

> The United States government did something that was wrong—deeply, profoundly, morally wrong. It was an outrage to our commitment to integrity and equality for all our citizens. To our African American citizens, I am sorry that your federal government orchestrated a study so clearly racist. That can never be allowed to happen again. It is against everything our country stands for and what we must stand against is what it was. The people who ran the study at Tuskegee diminished the stature of man by abandoning the most basic ethical precepts. (Clinton 1997)

Bureaucracy and Ethics

The mere mention of "bureaucracy" invokes images ranging from gross ineptitude and the inability to complete simple tasks to elitist public officials abusing their power. Even though bureaucracy is an essential part of any organization, none wants to be thought of as bureaucratic (Healy 1996). Conversations about bureaucracy often begin and end with comments from the writings of the eminent sociologist Max Weber. Weber created the bureaucratic model, a model characterized by formal rules and regulations, specialized roles, a hierarchical structure, and a clear chain of command. Central to bureaucracy is consistency in terms of actions and behaviors. According to Eugene Litwak (1961), within a bureaucracy an individual's job position is based on merit (as opposed to nepotism); individual authority and responsibility is dictated by an individual's job description; and there is clear separation between one's personal life and one's work life.

> "Nothing is so contagious as example; and we never do any great good or evil which does not produce its like."
>
> **FRANCOIS DE LA ROCHEFOUCAULD**
> Writer

Weber failed to realize that the dynamics of bureaucracy itself brought about unintended consequences resulting from personal interests. There are countless examples of bureaucracies acting without regard for human costs. According to J. Krohe, "The fit between business bureaucracies and conscience is particularly poor. Bureaucracies insulate individuals from the ultimate victims of misconduct, be they babies drinking doctored apple juice, drivers in unsafe cars, or little old ladies who lose their savings; people are thus also insulated from the empathetic impulse that so often sparks conscience" (1997, p. 17). Ferrell and Skinner (1988) argue that bureaucracy's centralized and hierarchical power base actually helps create opportunities for unethical behavior. That is, with power held in the hands of so few, the discretion of rank-and-file and middle-level bureaucrats is severely limited. The result is that these bureaucrats tend to follow authority blindly, regardless of any ethical dilem-

"No Surrender"

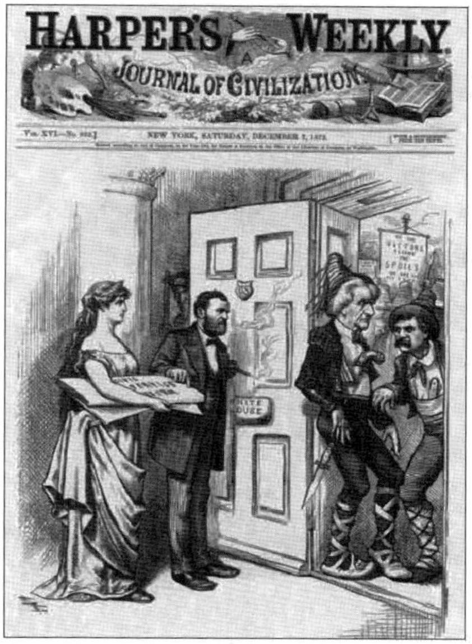

U.S.G. (Ulysses Grant): ***"I am determined to enforce those regulations."***

With the expansion of the federal government during the Civil War, and the postwar struggle between Democratic President Andrew Johnson and Congressional Republicans over control of Reconstruction, the civil service reform movement began in earnest in the late 1860s. Reformers, such as cartoonist Thomas Nast, considered the patronage system of government appointments based on partisan loyalty to be corrupt and inefficient. They wanted to replace it with a system of government service based on merit appointments (through standardized examinations), promotion, and tenure. In 1867, the U.S. House of Representatives narrowly voted to table a civil service reform bill, and with the election of Republican Ulysses S. Grant as president in 1868, some Republican supporters of the reform during the Johnson years suddenly decided that the patronage system worked quite well. In 1871, however, President Grant created the nation's first Civil Service Commission, naming as its chairman George William Curtis, the editor of *Harper's Weekly* and president of the National Civil Service Reform Association.

The cartoon presents a scene following Grant's reelection in November 1872. In the glow of Republican victory, Senator Simon Cameron and Governor John Hartranft, both of Pennsylvania, pressured the president to suspend the civil service rules for the Philadelphia post office, an important source of patronage for the Republican Party in that state. Grant steadfastly refused, reaffirming his commitment to civil service reform. Here, Cameron (left) and Hartranft (right) are dressed as Italian bandits, while their supporters in the background carry aloft a banner inscribed with the battle cry of the patronage ("spoils") system: "To the Victors, Belong the Spoils." Grant expresses his determination to implement the new civil service regulations, which are held by Columbia, and Uncle Sam appears (behind the door) as a policeman ready to enforce the law. The cartoon's title—"No Surrender"—alludes to Grant's commitment as Union commander during the Civil War to full Union victory and the "Unconditional Surrender" (his nickname) of the Confederacy.

Source: Thomas Nast, Harper's Weekly, December 7, 1872. http://www.harpweek.com.

mas. This tendency clearly underscores the importance of establishing and adhering to administrative ethical standards.

The Need for Administrative Ethics

Decisions based on convenience and efficiency—"means to ends"—or on the basis of economics may be at the heart of unethical behavior.

> One of the most commonly agreed-upon notions in the field of public administration is that administrators have numerous roles, or value sets, which are sources for the decisions they make. For example, an administrator may concentrate quite appropriately on legal issues at one point, organizational issues at another, and personal interests at still another. Although there is widespread agreement that these roles and their concomitant value sets exist, that agreement quickly dissipates when one tries to identify and name which roles or value sets are crucial for public administrators. (Van Wart 1996, p. 526)

An inherent challenge for public employees is balancing diverse and competing demands. P.B. Strait (1998, p. 12) contends that public employees "must be able to work within the framework of three goals: loyalty to the organization, responsiveness to the needs of the public, and consideration for the employees' own objectives and desires. These goals provide an environment that is rich in ethical dilemmas." The organizational structure in which public employees currently operate engenders ethical dilemmas.

> "Glass, china, and reputation are easily cracked, and never well mended."
>
> **BENJAMIN FRANKLIN**
> American Statesman; Ambassador; Patriot

> Public employees are often forced to choose between obeying policy and serving the needs of clients. For example, public health clinics exist to serve those who cannot otherwise afford care. Patients pay according to their income. The working poor are caught in between: not qualifying for assistance and not able to afford to purchase health care. This same irony also exists in higher education for students who come from working families who cannot afford the steep tuition prices and yet do not qualify for tuition aid. Law enforcement officers face a similar dilemma when they are required to spend half of their shifts doing paperwork at the expense of providing a rapid response to citizens. Employees who work for agencies with such incongruent policies are often placed in the uncomfortable position of trying to uphold policy to the detriment of the very people the agencies are attempting to serve. In choosing to serve the needs of their clients, employees violate organizational policies and put themselves at risk. Policies of this nature need to be reviewed to eliminate this unnecessary ethical dilemma. Until then, choosing the client's interests over the interests of oneself or the organization may be the most ethical action of all. (Strait 1998, p. 18)

There are several examples where the actions (or inactions) of bureaucrats, who by virtue of their position are trusted with upholding the public interest, have dishonored this responsibility. A potential cure for corruption may lie in organizational codes of ethics.

"Every Public Question with an Eye Only to the Public Good"

"Well, the wickedness of all of it is, not that these men were bribed or corruptly influenced, but that they betrayed the trust of the people, deceived their constituents, and by their evasions and falsehoods confessed the transaction to be disgraceful." —New York Tribune, February 19, 1873.

Justice (to the Saints of the Press):
"Let him that has not betrayed the trust of the People, and is without stain, cast the first stone."

This Harper's Weekly cartoon by Thomas Nast indicts the congressmen involved in the Credit Mobilier scandal as well as an irresponsible press corps for violating the public trust. Credit Mobilier was the holding and construction company of the federally subsidized Union Pacific Railroad. Its managers were accused of siphoning off huge amounts of public money for personal gain, and of attempting to cover up their misdeeds by bribing congressmen with discounted stock and bonds.

Source: Thomas Nast, Harper's Weekly, March 15, 1873. http://www.harpweek.com.

EXERCISE 11.1

Misuse of Position Employee Crossword Puzzle

Across

2. You can't use ___ information to further your own private interest or that of another.

5. Generally, you can't use your government title or position to ___ any product, enterprise, or service.

7. Generally, you can't use your position, title, or ___ associated with your public office to imply that your agency sanctions your outside activities.

9. You can't use government property, including the services of ___, for unauthorized purposes.

11. Unless authorized, playing games on your office computer is a misuse of official ___ and government property.

12. Widely used and misused piece of government equipment.

Down

1. You are to protect and ___ government property.

3. Your ___ can't ask you to shop for his wife's birthday present during duty hours.

4. Recommending your neighbor for a federal job on agency ___ is ok if you have personal knowledge of his abilities or character.

6. You can't use your public office for private ___.

8. Don't use your public office to ___ yourself or others.

10. You learn on the job that Company X found the cure for a major disease. You may not buy ___ in Company X before your agency announces the company found the cure.

Answer key at the end of chapter.

Source: U.S. Office of Government Ethics, "Crossword Puzzles," 2007. www.oge.gov/training/crossword_puzzles.aspx.

Countless oaths, pledges, and codes champion the tenets of ethical conduct. They typically underscore the importance of duty, service, honor, and fairness. One such noteworthy call for ethical behavior is embodied in Greek tradition—that being the Athenian Oath:

> We will never bring disgrace on this our City by an act of dishonesty or cowardice. We will fight for the ideals and Sacred Things of the City both alone and with many. We will revere and obey the City's laws, and will do our best to incite a like reverence and respect in those above us who are prone to annul them or set them at naught. We will strive increasingly to quicken the public's sense of civic duty. Thus in all these ways we will transmit this City, not only not less, but greater and more beautiful than it was transmitted to us.

Declarations of loyalty and commitment to ethical conduct are common throughout several occupational fields and disciplines. Almost routinely, elected and public officials are sworn into service by taking an oath. Physicians must take an oath to "do no harm," while attorneys must swear to uphold the U.S. Constitution and the constitution of the state in which they are admitted to the bar. Like an oath of office, organizational *codes of ethics* affirm the importance of ethical standards of conduct. The American Society for Public Administration's (ASPA) Code of Ethics includes five principles that public administration should champion.

> "Relativity applies to physics, not ethics."
>
> **ALBERT EINSTEIN**
> Physicist;
> Nobel Prize Winner
> (1879–1955)

Unethical behavior will occur despite clearly defined codes of ethics. A multitude of factors influence unethical decision making and behaviors. In some cases, employment conditions, such as dissatisfaction with wages and benefits, may influence individuals to take what they feel is owed to them. Other factors may concern organizational culture, whereby a culture of "getting the job done at any cost" encourages disregard for ethical considerations in the interest of achieving outcomes. Nevertheless, codes of conduct are a necessary first step toward ensuring ethical conduct.

Condoning Corruption

Citizens frustrated with public bureaucracies are inclined, at times, to take out these frustrations by using subtle, but nevertheless illicit, strategies. As customers of government, citizens often savor mistakes in their favor, such as a failure to bill for goods or to stop checks to deceased relatives. Some citizens try to punish public bureaucracies—which they feel punish them by misrepresenting their eligibility for assistance when they cannot find a decent job, their personal tax liability when rates go up, or their own negligence in a product's failure. Even those bureaucrats who anger clients can become so turned off that they rip-off their own organizations. As so-called "time bandits," they arrive late to work, leave early, take long

EXERCISE 11.2

Employee Conduct: Ethical or Unethical?

Scenario: Catherine is an official at the Small Business Administration. From time to time, she looks in on an elderly neighbor to see if she needs anything. On a recent visit, Catherine learned that her neighbor was upset over the Internal Revenue Service's assessment of a penalty against her because of a claimed overdue payment. The neighbor is apprehensive about calling the IRS to explain the error, so Catherine would like to call for her. She does not intend to take any compensation.

Is the representational service Catherine proposes to provide permissible?

Answer: No.

Explanation: Two overlapping federal statutes, 18 U.S.C. §§ 203 and 205, prohibit an employee from making representations—whether for compensation or not—before any department, agency, or court if the matter is one in which the United States has a substantial interest. The statutes also prohibit an employee from—

- Taking compensation for such representational services provided by another; and
- Receiving consideration for assisting in the prosecution of a claim against the United States.

There are a number of exceptions to sections 203 and 205. An important one allows an employee, under certain circumstances, to represent himself, his parents, his spouse, his children, and certain others for whom the employee serves in a specific fiduciary capacity such as a guardian.

Scenario: Paula works in the public information office of the Internal Revenue Service. A private trade association offers to pay her to teach a short course on a new taxpayer assistance program being implemented by the IRS.

May Paula accept the offer?

Answer: No.

Explanation: An employee may not receive compensation—including travel expenses for transportation and lodging—from any source other than the government for teaching, speaking, or writing that relates to the employee's official duties. For most employees, teaching, speaking, or writing is considered "related to official duties" if—

- The activity is part of the employee's official duties;
- The invitation to teach, speak, or write is extended primarily because of the employee's official position;
- The invitation or the offer of compensation is extended by a person whose interests may be affected substantially by the employee's performance of his official duties;
- The activity draws substantially on nonpublic information; or
- The subject of the activity deals in significant part with agency programs, operations, or policies or with the employee's current or recent assignments.

Scenario: Sylvia, an employee of the Securities and Exchange Commission, offers to help a friend with a consumer complaint by calling the manufacturer of a household appliance. In the course of the conversation with the manufacturer, Sylvia states that she works for the SEC and is responsible for reviewing the manufacturer's SEC filings.

EXERCISE 11.2

Has Sylvia misused her public office?

Answer: Yes.

Explanation: Employees may not use their public offices for private gain, either their own gain or that of others. Sylvia used her office to induce a benefit for private purposes.

Scenario: Joe is delighted with his new boss, Dan. In a few short months, Dan has brought about creative changes in the division's work product while, at the same time, improving efficiency and boosting office morale. The two workers have also developed a friendship based on mutual respect and shared outside interests. Because of a conflicting family commitment, Joe and his daughter will be unable to use their season tickets for the next Orioles home game, so Joe thinks he'd like to give them to Dan.

May he do so?

Answer: No.

Explanation: And it would be impermissible for Dan to accept the tickets if offered.

An employee may not—

- Give or solicit for a gift to an official superior; or
- Accept a gift from a lower-paid employee, unless the two employees are personal friends who are not in a superior-subordinate relationship.

In this context, the words "superior" and "subordinate" refer to people in the employee's chain of command.

Scenario: Jenny is employed as a researcher by the Veterans Administration. Her cousin and close friend, Zach, works for a pharmaceutical company that does business with the VA. Jenny's 40th birthday is approaching, and Zach and his wife have invited Jenny and her husband out to dinner to celebrate the occasion.

May Jenny accept?

Answer: Yes.

Explanation: Gifts are permitted where the circumstances make it clear that the gift is motivated by a family relationship or personal friendship rather than the position of the employee. It would be improper, however, for Jenny to accept the dinner if Zach charged the meal to his employer because then it would no longer be a gift from Zach.

Exceptions to the rule against acceptance of gifts allow employees to accept—

- Unsolicited gifts with a value of $20 or less;
- Gifts clearly given because of a family relationship or personal friendship;
- Free attendance at an event on the day an employee is speaking or presenting information on behalf of the agency;
- Free attendance at certain widely attended gatherings;
- Certain discounts and similar opportunities and benefits;
- Certain awards and honorary degrees; and
- Certain gifts based on outside business or employment relationships.

Source: U.S. Office of Government Ethics. Do It Right: An Ethics Handbook for Executive Branch Employees. Washington, DC: OGE, January 2005. http://www.usoge.gov/training/training_materials/booklets/bkdoitright_95.pdf.

lunch breaks, and manipulate leave records. When they are at work, it is often with a smirk: photocopying personal papers, pilfering office supplies, making personal or long-distance calls, shopping on the Internet, stealing computer supplies, using office postage, or perhaps even abusing expense accounts. A particularly blatant form of such thievery is running a small personal business from a bureaucracy's big base: law or accounting, repairs or typing, sales or printing. As Roberts (2007) indicates, condoning corruption is the result of lowering ethical expectations. As a consequence of lowered ethical expectations, many ethical misdeeds are viewed as acceptable, as long as they are not egregious or newsworthy.

Combating Corruption

Petty theft is a by-product of petty bureaucrats. Almost everyone is "guilty" of taking home a few folders or making a few personal calls. Public bureaucracies would be depopulated if that were cause for dismissal. Some might argue that corruption worth countering is corruption worth counting. By regularly take petty cash and office stamps, for instance, petty thieves provide a foundation for building criminal momentum—in other words, they create a slippery slope. Falsifying expense vouchers can amount to thousands. Rocketing payments to fictitious vendors or clients is an example of white-collar crime. Clerks are often in the uncomfortable position of observing such corruption but have no apparent means to stop it.

> "It is naïve to believe that ethic rules will prevent an administration from using its bureaucratic power to favor special interests that support its public policy and political agendas."
>
> **ROBERT ROBERTS**
> Professor; Author

Although petty corruption is too widely tolerated, it can be toned down if logged in. Logs are like God, country, and apple pie—few people object to them openly. For those individuals in charge of a public organization, logging (or listing) is a psychological deterrent for long-distance calls or personal Internet surfing, for making non-work-related copies and taking supplies—even if the logs are never checked against the meters, the bills, or the inventories. While organizations are reluctant to act on seemingly modest (but ultimately expensive) abuses of expense accounts, conveying that "we have heard" the business office is cracking down on undocumented expenses, or that the auditors are stepping up their scrutiny of certain vouchers, may indeed deter temptation. Of course, those white lies must be carefully timed to precede, rather than coincide with, submission of forms an individual may be asked to type, photocopy, or initial.

Countering large-scale corruption is difficult, to say the least. If it continues, rather than quietly ignoring it, public servants can try quietly deploring it. Public servants can help to establish an anticorruption culture by expressing disgust with a rip-off that one has heard about in another department or requesting an explanation of questionable financial decisions. As diplomats daily demonstrate, tactfully pointing out an uncorrected wrong or broken rule gives a superior or colleague a chance to correct it without consequence—to stop taking bribes, passing faulty parts, permitting physically unsafe procedures, and so on. Since they have signaled that someone is now noticing the situation—and might well bring it to the attention of higher-ups—there is a good chance that the improprieties will end without the need for further action.

Formal Rules and Bureaucratic Discretion

An understanding among public employees is that the so-called "inner face" (or the informal rules) supports the "outer face" (which represents the bureaucratic rules, or the "rulebook"). Productive executives understand that organizations operating completely by the "rulebook" will have difficulty serving the public interest precisely because rules are not always realistic. The inner face helps determine when it is acceptable to take shortcuts in the interests of both the organization and client. At times, however, a bureaucrat with a pet project or pet position inflexibly places paper over products, procedures over profits, or pettiness over people. Some bureaucrats agree informally to be formal. Initiative becomes a dirty word. All orders are followed explicitly, without any shortcuts. All procedures are carried out meticulously, no matter how ridiculously. Without the informal rules to "grease the wheels," the organizational gears lock. Traffic backs up, orders back up, and lines back up. The output of public organizations drops and clients naturally become irate, but the untrustworthy bureaucrat capitulates and goes along.

> "To educate a person in mind and not in morals is to educate a menace to society."
>
> **THEODORE ROOSEVELT**
> 26th President of the United States (1858–1919)

Bureaucrats determined to serve the public good will disregard orders that are likely to result in their customers and citizens being taken down the paths of danger. Many unethical orders—to pass diseased food, to approve faulty products, or to certify dangerous drugs—are verbal commands without a prosecutable paper trail. Therefore, unethical bureaucrats typically will not be able to make an issue of ethical public servants who choose to blatantly disregard such orders. However, if unethical bureaucrats persist in their demands, it may be possible to stop them by insisting that they put their orders in writing. If not, then probably the best defense is reference to the agency-specific "rulebook," as well as the broader rules covered by codes of ethics, the protocols of the Geneva Conventions, government regulations, and industry standards.

Using good judgment and discretion is probably the most effective means for changing organizational behavior. By working through established channels, an individual can make good use of a largely underutilized asset—discretion. Discretion

Fourteen Principles of Ethical Conduct for Federal Employees

(1) Public service is a public trust, requiring employees to place loyalty to the Constitution, the laws and ethical principles above private gain.

(2) Employees shall not hold financial interests that conflict with the conscientious performance of duty.

(3) Employees shall not engage in financial transactions using nonpublic Government information or allow the improper use of such information to further any private interest.

(4) An employee shall not, except as permitted by the Standards of Ethical Conduct, solicit or accept any gift or other item of monetary value from any person or entity seeking official action from, doing business with, or conducting activities regulated by the employee's agency, or whose interests may be substantially affected by the performance or nonperformance of the employee's duties.

(5) Employees shall put forth honest effort in the performance of their duties.

(6) Employees shall not knowingly make unauthorized commitments or promises of any kind purporting to bind the Government.

(7) Employees shall not use public office for private gain.

(8) Employees shall act impartially and not give preferential treatment to any private organization or individual.

(9) Employees shall protect and conserve Federal property and shall not use it for other than authorized activities.

(10) Employees shall not engage in outside employment or activities, including seeking or negotiating for employment, that conflict with official Government duties and responsibilities.

(11) Employees shall disclose waste, fraud, abuse, and corruption to appropriate authorities.

(12) Employees shall satisfy in good faith their obligations as citizens, including all financial obligations, especially those—such as Federal, State, or local taxes—that are imposed by law.

(13) Employees shall adhere to all laws and regulations that provide equal opportu-

nity for all Americans regardless of race, color, religion, sex, national origin, age, or handicap.

(14) Employees shall endeavor to avoid any actions creating the appearance that they are violating the law or the ethical standards set forth in the Standards of Ethical Conduct. Whether particular circumstances create an appearance that the law or these standards have been violated shall be determined from the perspective of a reasonable person with knowledge of the relevant facts.

Source: U.S. Office of Government Ethics. Do It Right: An Ethics Handbook for Executive Branch Employees. Washington, DC, January 2005. www.usoge.gov/training/training_materials/booklets/bkdoitright_95.pdf.

is a powerful but silent tool for righting organizational wrongs. Because orders from generals high above must be carried out by troops far below, almost every bureaucrat has a little leeway in making some decisions. No rulebook can anticipate every possible scenario, so bureaucrats must develop substantial decision-making skills. Often their most effective tactics is not to act: They can pretend they never received a change in orders and wait to see if anyone notices their inaction, or they can simply delay, holding up a policy change on technical grounds until the current policymaker is changed. In one such instance of good judgment dating back to the Watergate era, the U.S. Department of Labor secretary George Shultz ordered the Internal Revenue Service to "do nothing" in response to Nixon counsel John Dean's illegitimate order to investigate the president's "enemies list."

Those who feel that their colleagues, clients, or checkbooks are being exploited have a variety of remedial tactics at their disposal. The dated receipt for a warranty a day or two past expiration can accidentally be misread to the client's benefit—and to the bureaucrat's gratification in terms of a warm "thank you." However, accepting a gratuity or gift in return moves the action from compassionate to corrupt. A working welfare mother who is no longer permitted funds for transportation to a job under new legislation might instead be granted a greater allowance in another category in order to keep her employed instead of seeing her incentive to work destroyed. A job applicant might be given hints about completing an application rather than having it rejected for insufficient information. A maintenance supervisor might quietly fix a customer's small problem (no charge, no paper trail), although the request was rejected in short order by the short-tempered general manager. In every such case, flexible common sense triumphs over bureaucratic rigidity.

If the top brass have not listened privately to reason, chances are they will have to hear public objections to their organization's unreasonable actions. Policies are rarely written in full enough detail to fully paralyze policy implementers. A popular saying among bureaucrats in the nation's capital is that the "D.C." after "Washington" stands for "Discretion Central." When Washington (under the administration of Republican president Ronald Reagan) ordered a cut in the size of school lunches, an "objective" bureaucratic decision to count ketchup as a vegetable lit a destructive fire under the entire school lunch cutback effort. Likewise, when Washington ordered schools not to feed students who had failed to file new re-eligibility forms, a decision by one school administrator to feed leftovers to hungry students attracted Page One attention, embarrassing the order-givers into becoming order-rescinders.

Channeling Complaints to Conscience: Sore Throat, Deep Throat, Cutthroat

It is a healthy sign that more organizations have created self-correcting mechanisms for possible mistakes and abuses. Such mechanisms do not include suggestion boxes, which we suspect are linked to wastebaskets. Rather, they are home remedies for bureaucratic sore throats, remedies that should always be tried before going public. They are the embodiment of the organizational conscience through which we can "blow the whistle," bringing to the surface urgent questions that regular channels have ignored: "Why were bids for project A solicited only from bidders B and C?" "Is official X being transferred in retaliation for speaking out?" "Does the organization secretly discriminate against females or older males?" "Are minorities blacklisted on promotion lists?" Even when promised anonymity or protection, public servants who speak up against such wrongs and abuses are likely to be identified and may even earn the label of "troublemaker" or "pest" as stories travel through the grapevine.

> "If ethics are poor at the top, that behavior is copied down through the organization."
>
> **ROBERT NOYCE**
> Co-inventor, Microchip; Co-founder, Intel Corporation (1927–1990)

If home remedies do not work, public servants can try "whistling" from home or a pay phone—playing the anonymous role of "Deep Throat" for surrogates ranging from reporters to legislators to crusaders. As the administration of President Richard Nixon learned in the Watergate scandal, a very effective way of blowing the whistle is to blow it anonymously. For decades, many observers speculated as to the identity of the Deep Throat source that blew the Republican break-in of Democratic headquarters wide open and supplied so much damaging evidence against Nixon. In May 2005, the former deputy director of the Federal Bureau of Investigation William Mark Felt revealed himself as the real "Deep Throat."

If an ethically conscience bureaucrat's story is not as spectacular as presidential guilt or public danger, the press may not be interested in it. Most cases of questionable ethics in the field of public administration are far more mundane, involving, for instance, evidence that indicts a controller for charging his beach house to the entertainment fund, or questions an illegal campaign contribution, or produces examples of blatant nepotism.

Whistleblowing

Although bureaucratic lore commonly holds that uncovering unlawful waste, fraud, or abuse will result in chilling isolation, impossible job transfers, or other cruel and unusual forms of recrimination, there are still ways to fight back. There are means with which public servants can force a change in an organization's course without being forced out of a job. Not all government workers with information that threatens the status quo are in danger of losing their jobs; occasionally, they may even be rewarded for speaking up. But too often they may be warned in subtle ways that such behavior is not a "team" strategy, not an "acceptable" avenue to problem solving. Superiors and even coworkers may go so far as to imply that whistleblowers are "letting their friends down," that they are "disloyal," that they are "squealing." Such suggestions are powerful squelchers. Government workers who are truth-pushers may be warned by being cold-shouldered, overloaded, or having their work sabotaged. Unfortunately, many accede to the pressure and quickly adopt the self-serving norm: They "go along to get along." Tangible cooperation, friendship, and promotions loom larger than what they rationalize as far more distant organizational or public interests. However, more and more public servants are stepping out of the bureaucratic shadows and acting in the interest of ethics. Daniel Ellsberg, who released the top secret "Pentagon Papers" to the *New York Times* during the Vietnam War may be the most well-known bureaucrat to have put his ethics over his self interest, inspiring untold numbers of public servants to do so over the intervening decades.

> "In practice, whistleblowing can be a solution to some of our problems. We should be permitted to tell the truth without fearing that it is something dangerous."
>
> **BILL BUSH**
> NASA Aerospace Engineer; Whistleblower

Sometimes, whistleblowers recruit allies in the form of the press, politicians, professional organizations, private lawyers, or public prosecutors. After the whistle is blown, the bureaucracy oftentimes buries the charger and charges. It politely pretends to listen, to follow-up, consider, and take corrective action. But complaints, at times, are buried in bureaucratic backwaters in the expectation that they will be forgotten. If they resist fading away, most bureaucracies are large enough to transfer them away. Ironically, those bureaucrats who are most adept at such discreet burials are sometimes rewarded by discreet promotions. In contrast, whistleblowers are disdainfully rewarded by becoming the butt of bureaucratic humor; by being assigned to "make work" or "no work" jobs; by being shunned, transferred or ignored; by being frozen out of anything sensitive. The organization reasons that we will become discouraged, that we will lose the interest of fickle allies, that we will be reduced to insignificant blemishes on the bureaucratic body.

Although the heat of whistleblowing can be intense, the rewards of going public include the highs of:

1. Enhancing our self-respect;
2. Gaining and maintaining the esteem of our family and friends;
3. The chance of vindication by forcing responsible actions.

Resignation as a Test and Protest

In the game of organizational power, an effective hand for forcing change may be to threaten a parting of the ways. Drawing up a letter of resignation may compel higher-ups to pay attention. The bureaucracy's desire to deal with complaints frequently hinges on the importance of the complainant to the overall organization. For example, one individual with specialized knowledge of an organization's books, files, or procedures possesses tremendous leverage. In contrast, an individual who is one of ten specialists serving under a grossly unethical and incompetent administrator has significantly less leverage. If the organization calls a public servant's bluff and accepts his or her resignation, often an effective way to protest is to sound off while taking off. If their subordinates care about the issue, they may join in resignation. (But, applying pressure to do so is, of course, unethical.)

Unfortunately and traditionally, though, most bureaucrats who resign because they are at odds with the organization never say so publicly. That is, most resignations are "discreet." If, however, a bureaucrat views his or her resignation as a matter of conscience, then that individual can draft a statement underscoring the basis for his or her disillusion, distrust, or dismay, distributing it widely with the introduction "I am resigning effective immediately because. . . ." Bureaucrats who have faith in their eventual resurrection can "destroy and search," resigning and then looking elsewhere for employment, perhaps even in another field. If they consider their

EXERCISE 11.3

Your Values and Ethics—A BBC Tool (Simulation)

Students will take this test and identify where they fall on the values/ethics continuum. After completing this inventory, students will summarize their results and explain whether or not they believe this tool should be used in the workplace and, if so, how.

www.thinkingethics.typepad.com/thinkingethics/games

present environment unhealthy, chances are that forcing a job search will land them a better position—one more in keeping with their commitment to public service.

Having something to say is not necessarily sufficient reason to say it—until one has the right platform, the right position, and the right placement. A public servant may attract more attention for change as the new commissioner of Agency X than the ex-commissioner of Agency Y. In other words, patience may prove useful for those looking to evoke positive changes ethically. The press regularly reports critiques and exposés by bureaucrats who left politely and quietly, but who had second thoughts about the knowledge they harbored. Those without access to the press could write letters to the editor, inspectors general, ombudsmen, and regulators. Admittedly, some post-resignation complaints may be cases of sour grapes, some may be self-serving, but many are legitimate attempts to right what is still wrong.

Resigned, Retired, or Fired

Most bureaucrats are turned out to pasture when they are too "old," but some of them are forced to depart because they are too bold. They understand the fatal flaws in decisions everyone else has rubber-stamped, and they say so. That verbal action, no matter how politely put, is often sufficient reason to cut them from the team. They become expendable, and neat methods of disposal are used to force their "voluntary" resignation or retirement. The implicit deal is that their professional reputation and pension will be protected if their silence and acquiescence protect the team.

> "In a civilized life, law floats in a sea of ethics."
>
> **EARL WARREN**
> Chief Justice of the U.S. Supreme Court (1891–1974)

There are many examples of whistleblowing success stories, though some are bittersweet. For instance, it took Ernie Fitzgerald, a Nixon-era government budget analyst who blew the whistle on Pentagon cost overruns, a decade of grief, but with the help of an organized committee, members of Congress, the press, and the courts he regained his position plus promotion, his reputation, and even civil damages from the government. Hugh Kaufman, who was harassed and rated unfavorably by the Environmental Protection Agency after blowing the whistle on mismanagement of toxic waste programs, successfully sued to right his record and land a suitable reassignment. Cyril Lang successfully reversed his suspension for teaching the unauthorized classics of Machiavelli and Aristotle from Charles W. Woodward High School, in Rockville, MD (*TIME* magazine, 1980). Another strategy for fighting back is to do something on the way out. If organizational life is limited, one may still be able to breathe new life into the organization or issue by doing the unexpected. Shortly before ending his career in government as special counsel to the Department of Energy, Paul Bloom (1939–2009) arranged to donate $4 million to pay the heating bills of low-income families out of $2 billion he and his colleagues had recovered from oil company overcharges.

CORRUPTION LEVELS AND CULTURAL DIFFERENCE

According to corruption perception index released by transparency international, Korea (South) was ranked 43rd(5.4 points) out of 182 countries, while the US was ranked 24th(7.1 points).

Do you think this corruption level is associated with national culture that has deeply been rooted in each county? For example, the Western culture upon which the US is founded can be called a rule-based culture, while the Korean culture which is grounded in Confucian values and which has a strong military government history can be termed a relationship-based culture (Hooker 2008). Do you think these different cultures shape different corruption behaviors? Do you think strategies to reduce corruption levels should be different according to different national cultures? How are these strategies different in each country? Please discuss.

Source: Hooker, J.(2008). Corruption from a Cross-Cultural Perspective, http://ba.gsia.cmu.edu/jnh/corruption08s.pdf

FIGURE 11.1 – CORRUPTION PERCEPTIONS INDEX 2001

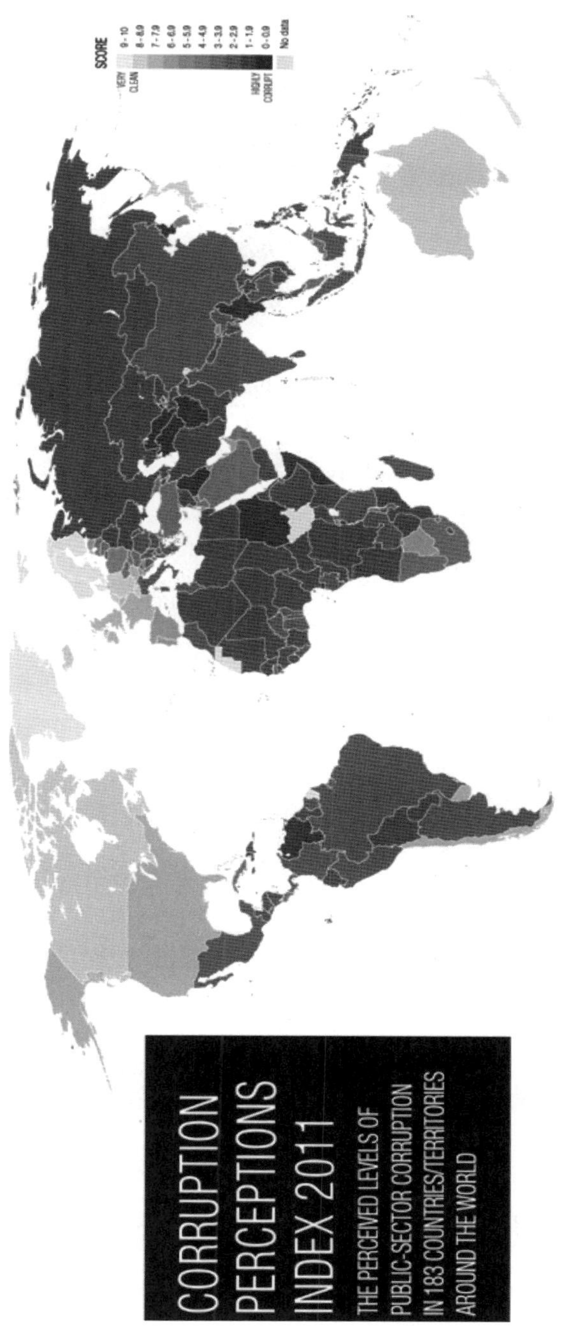

RANK	COUNTRY/TERRITORY	SCORE
1	New Zealand	9.5
2	Denmark	9.4
2	Finland	9.4
4	Sweden	9.3
5	Singapore	9.2
6	Norway	9.0
7	Netherlands	8.9
8	Australia	8.8
8	Switzerland	8.8
10	Canada	8.7
11	Luxembourg	8.5
12	Hong Kong	8.4
13	Iceland	8.3
14	Germany	8.0
14	Japan	8.0
16	Austria	7.8
16	Barbados	7.8
16	United Kingdom	7.8
19	Belgium	7.5
19	Ireland	7.5
21	Bahamas	7.3
22	Chile	7.2
22	Qatar	7.2
24	United States	7.1
25	France	7.0
25	Saint Lucia	7.0
25	Uruguay	7.0
28	United Arab Emirates	6.8
29	Estonia	6.4
30	Cyprus	6.3
31	Spain	6.2
32	Botswana	6.1
32	Portugal	6.1
32	Taiwan	6.1
35	Slovenia	5.9
36	Israel	5.8
36	Saint Vincent and the Grenadines	5.8
38	Bhutan	5.7
39	Malta	5.6
39	Puerto Rico	5.6
41	Cape Verde	5.5
41	Poland	5.5
43	Korea (South)	5.4
44	Brunei	5.2
44	Dominica	5.2
46	Bahrain	5.1
46	Macau	5.1
46	Mauritius	5.1
49	Rwanda	5.0
50	Costa Rica	4.8
50	Lithuania	4.8
50	Oman	4.8
50	Seychelles	4.8
54	Hungary	4.6
54	Kuwait	4.6
56	Jordan	4.5
57	Czech Republic	4.4
57	Namibia	4.4
57	Saudi Arabia	4.4
60	Malaysia	4.3
61	Cuba	4.2
61	Latvia	4.2
61	Turkey	4.2
64	Georgia	4.1
64	South Africa	4.1
66	Croatia	4.0
66	Montenegro	4.0
66	Slovakia	4.0
69	Ghana	3.9
69	Italy	3.9
69	FYR Macedonia	3.9
69	Samoa	3.9
73	Brazil	3.8
73	Tunisia	3.8
75	China	3.6
75	Romania	3.6
77	Gambia	3.5
77	Lesotho	3.5
77	Vanuatu	3.5
80	Colombia	3.4
80	El Salvador	3.4
80	Greece	3.4
80	Morocco	3.4
80	Peru	3.4
80	Thailand	3.4
86	Bulgaria	3.3
86	Jamaica	3.3
86	Panama	3.3
86	Serbia	3.3
86	Sri Lanka	3.3
91	Bosnia and Herzegovina	3.2
91	Liberia	3.2
91	Trinidad and Tobago	3.2
91	Zambia	3.2
95	Albania	3.1
95	India	3.1
95	Kiribati	3.1
95	Swaziland	3.1
95	Tonga	3.1
100	Argentina	3.0
100	Benin	3.0
100	Burkina Faso	3.0
100	Djibouti	3.0
100	Gabon	3.0
100	Indonesia	3.0
100	Madagascar	3.0
100	Malawi	3.0
100	Mexico	3.0
100	Sao Tome and Principe	3.0
100	Suriname	3.0
100	Tanzania	3.0
112	Algeria	2.9
112	Egypt	2.9
112	Kosovo	2.9
112	Moldova	2.9
112	Senegal	2.9
112	Vietnam	2.9
118	Bolivia	2.8
118	Mali	2.8
120	Bangladesh	2.7
120	Ecuador	2.7
120	Ethiopia	2.7
120	Guatemala	2.7
120	Iran	2.7
120	Kazakhstan	2.7
120	Mongolia	2.7
120	Mozambique	2.7
120	Solomon Islands	2.7
129	Armenia	2.6
129	Dominican Republic	2.6
129	Honduras	2.6
129	Philippines	2.6
129	Syria	2.6
134	Cameroon	2.5
134	Eritrea	2.5
134	Guyana	2.5
134	Lebanon	2.5
134	Maldives	2.5
134	Nicaragua	2.5
134	Niger	2.5
134	Pakistan	2.5
134	Sierra Leone	2.5
143	Azerbaijan	2.4
143	Belarus	2.4
143	Comoros	2.4
143	Mauritania	2.4
143	Nigeria	2.4
143	Russia	2.4
143	Timor-Leste	2.4
143	Togo	2.4
143	Uganda	2.4
152	Tajikistan	2.3
152	Ukraine	2.3
154	Central African Republic	2.2
154	Congo Republic	2.2
154	Côte d'Ivoire	2.2
154	Guinea-Bissau	2.2
154	Kenya	2.2
154	Laos	2.2
154	Nepal	2.2
154	Papua New Guinea	2.2
154	Paraguay	2.2
154	Zimbabwe	2.2
164	Cambodia	2.1
164	Guinea	2.1
164	Kyrgyzstan	2.1
164	Yemen	2.1
168	Angola	2.0
168	Chad	2.0
168	Democratic Republic of the Congo	2.0
168	Libya	2.0
172	Burundi	1.9
172	Equatorial Guinea	1.9
172	Venezuela	1.9
175	Haiti	1.8
175	Iraq	1.8
177	Sudan	1.6
177	Turkmenistan	1.6
177	Uzbekistan	1.6
180	Afghanistan	1.5
180	Myanmar	1.5
182	Korea (North)	1.0
182	Somalia	1.0

Source: http://cpi.transparency.org/cpi2011/results/

Country	(Region)	PSM	Politics and policy	Compassion	Self-sacrifice
Australia	(AUS)	5.25	5.20	5.36	5.12
Austria	(WEU)	5.16	4.84	5.48	5.08
Brazil	(SAM)	5.49	5.15	6.35	4.36
Bulgaria	(EEU)	4.17	3.90	5.12	2.57
Canada	(NAM)	5.31	5.45	5.34	4.98
Cyprus	(SEU)	5.09	5.06	5.49	4.34
Czech Republic	(EEU)	3.97	3.74	4.40	3.59
Denmark	(NEU)	4.90	4.65	5.28	4.61
Finland	(NEU)	4.22	3.77	4.66	4.14
Flanders	(WEU)	4.40	4.18	4.81	4.10
France	(WEU)	4.84	4.83	5.03	4.54
Germany	(WEU)	4.72	4.49	5.13	4.32
Great Britain	(WEU)	4.58	4.30	4.96	4.28
Hungary	(EEU)	4.13	3.90	4.34	4.25
Ireland	(WEU)	5.28	4.99	5.81	4.79
Israel	(MEA)	5.10	5.27	5.46	4.00
Japan	(ASI)	4.74	4.82	4.86	4.33
Latvia	(EEU)	4.34	4.08	4.85	3.74
Mexico	(SAM)	5.50	5.39	6.34	4.02
Netherlands	(WEU)	4.94	4.90	5.29	4.27
New Zealand	(AUS)	4.65	4.67	4.73	4.42
Norway	(NEU)	4.83	4.83	5.17	4.13
Philippines	(ASI)	5.56	5.82	5.63	4.87
Poland	(EEU)	5.03	4.88	5.66	3.85
Portugal	(SEU)	5.63	5.33	5.93	5.53
Republic of Chile	(SAM)	5.33	4.89	6.27	4.13
Russia	(EEU)	4.57	4.69	4.74	3.94
Slovak Republic	(EEU)	4.59	4.08	5.30	4.17
Slovenia	(EEU)	4.83	4.29	5.33	4.87
South Africa	(AFR)	5.51	5.41	5.62	NA
South Korea	(ASI)	4.93	5.03	4.71	5.15
Spain	(SEU)	5.40	4.85	5.94	5.36
Sweden	(NEU)	4.77	4.68	4.96	4.55
Switzerland	(WEU)	4.98	4.61	5.38	4.91
Taiwan	(ASI)	5.00	4.86	5.24	4.78
United States	(NAM)	5.29	5.38	5.43	4.81
Uruguay	(SAM)	5.42	5.18	6.11	4.46
Venezuela	(SAM)	5.44	5.20	6.55	3.47

Source: Wouter Vandenabeele and Steven Van de Walle (2008). International Differences in Public Service Motivation: Comparing Regions across the World (pp.223–244) in James Perry and Hondeghem Annie (Eds.), Motivation in Public Management. The Call of Public Service, Oxford: Oxford University Press.

KEY TERMS

Administrative ethics

Athenian oath

Deontological theories

Ethics

Machiavellianism

Teleological theories

Tuskegee Experiment

Whistleblowing

REFERENCES

Bloomberg, M.R. 2001. *Bloomberg by Bloomberg*. Hoboken, NJ: Wiley.

Bottorff, Dean L. 1997. "How Ethics Can Improve Business Success." *Quality Progress* 30, no. 2 (February): 57–60.

Clinton, William. 1997. "Apology for Study Done in Tuskegee." The White House Office of the Press Secretary, May 16.

Ferrell, O.C., and S.J. Skinner. 1988. "Ethical Behavior and Bureaucratic Structure in Marketing Research Organizations." *Journal of Marketing Research* 25: 103–9.

Frederickson, H. George, and Jeremy David Walling. 1999. "Editors' Introduction: Ethics in Contemporary Human Resources Management." *Public Personnel Management* 28: 501.

French, W. and J. Granrose. 1995. *Practical Business Ethics*. Englewood Cliffs, N.J.: Prentice-Hall.

Healy, M. 1996. "Max Weber's Comeback, Wearing Topical Hats." *People Management*, January.

Heller, Jean. 1972. "Syphilis Victims in U.S. Study Went Untreated for 40 Years." *New York Times*. July 26, p. 1.

Krohe, J. 1997. "Ethics Are Nice, But Business Is Business." *Across the Board*, April, 16–17.

Litwak, Eugene, 1961. "Models of Bureaucracy Which Permit Conflict." *American Journal of Sociology* 67: 177–84.

Machiavelli, N. 1532. *The Prince*. Trans. D. Donno, New York: Bantam Dell Classics, 1984.

National League of Cities Official Website. *The Athenian Oath*. http://www.nlc.org/about_cities/cities_101/146.aspx.

Roberts, R.N. 2007. "History of the Legalization of Executive Branch Ethics Regulation: Implications for the Management of Public Integrity." *Public Integrity* 9, 4 (Fall): 313–32.

Strait, Patricia Bellin. 1998. "Unethical Actions of Public Servants: A Voyeur's View." *Public Management* 80: 12–18.

Thompson, Dennis F. 1985. "The Possibility of Administrative Ethics." *Public Administrative Review* 45, no. 5: 555–61.

———. 1987. *Political Ethics and Public Office.* Cambridge, MA: Harvard University Press.

TIME magazine. 1980. *Education: How to Protect Tender Minds.* http://www.time.com/time/magazine/article/0,9171,922234-2,00.html, accessed October 8, 2010.

Van Wart, M. 1996. "The Sources of Ethical Decision Making for Individuals in the Public Sector." *Public Administration Review* 56: 525–33.

———. 1998. *Changing Public Sector Values.* Hamden, CT: Garland Publishing.

Weber, Max. 1947. *The Theory of Social and Economic Organization.* Translated by A.M. Henderson and Talcott Parsons. London: Collier Macmillan Publishers.

Zinkhan, G.M., D.E. Delorme, C.O. Peters, and R.T. Watson. 2007. "Information Sources and Government Research: Ethical Conflicts and Solutions." *Public Integrity* 9, no. 4: 363–76.

SUPPLEMENTARY READINGS

Adams, G.B., and D.L. Balfour. 2004. *Unmasking Administrative Evil.* Armonk, NY: M.E. Sharpe.

Bowman, J.S., and C. Connolly Knox. 2008. "Ethics in Government: No Matter How Long and Dark the Night." *Public Administration Review* 68, no. 4 (June): 627–39.

Cooper, T. 1998. *The Responsible Administrator: An Approach to Ethics for the Administrative Role.* San Francisco: Jossey-Bass.

Denhardt, K.G. 1988. *The Ethics of Public Service: Resolving Moral Dilemmas in Public Organizations.* Westport, CT: Greenwood Press.

Frederickson, G., and R.K. Ghere. 2005. *Ethics in Public Management.* Armonk, NY: M.E. Sharpe.

Gawthrop, L.C. 1993. "The Ethical Foundations of American Public Administration." *International Journal of Public Administration* 16, no. 2: 139–63.

Lewis, C.W., and S.C. Gilman. 2005. *The Ethics Challenge in Public Service: A Problem-Solving Guide*. San Francisco: Jossey-Bass.

Madsen, P., and J.M. Shafritz, eds. 1992. *Essentials of Government Ethics*. New York: New American Library.

Roberts, R.N. 2001. *Ethics in U.S. Government: An Encyclopedia of Investigations, Scandals, Reforms, and Legislation*. Westport, CT: Greenwood Press.

Rohr, J. 1989. *Ethics for Bureaucrats: An Essay on Law and Values*. 2d ed. New York: Marcel Dekker.

ELECTRONIC RESOURCES

Centre for Applied Ethics—applied ethics resources on the web, including public sector and government ethics, environmental ethics, and ethical decision making: http://www.ethicsweb.ca/resources/

Citizens' Circle for Accountability—a Canadian website that provides an international forum on strategies to help citizens hold their government officials fully accountable for their actions: http://accountabilitycircle.org/index.html

Government Accountability Project—a nonprofit public interest group that promotes government and corporate accountability and advocates greater protection of whistleblowers: http://www.whistleblower.org

National Institutes of Health Ethics Program—focuses on standards of ethical conduct for federal employees: http://ethics.od.nih.gov/default.htm

Organisation for Economic Co-operation and Development (OECD)'s Fighting Corruption webpage:
http://www.oecd.org/about/0,3347,en_2649_34135_1_1_1_1_37447,00.html

Transparency International—the global coalition against corruption: http://www.transparency.org/

U.S. Department of Defense Standards of Conduct Office (SOCO)—Ethics Resource Library that also contains Ethics Resources on the Web, an electronic library of federal and nonfederal websites devoted to ethics; statutes, regulations, and executive orders; and a plethora of other materials on the topic: http://www.dod.mil/dodgc/defense_ethics/

U.S. Department of the Interior Ethics Office: http://www.doi.gov/ethics/

U.S. Department of the Navy—The Ethics Compass: http://www.ethics.navy.mil

U.S. House of Representatives, Committee on Standards of Official Conduct: http://www.house.gov/ethics

U.S. Office of Government Ethics (OGE): http://www.usoge.gov/

U.S. Office of Government Ethics—Standards of Ethical Conduct for Employees of the Executive Branch: http://www.usoge.gov/ethics_docs/publications/reference_publications/rfsoc_02.pdf

U.S. Senate Select Committee on Ethics: http://ethics.senate.gov

EXERCISE ANSWER KEY

Exercise 11.1

Across

2. You can't use __________ information to further your own private interest or that of another.

You cannot use **nonpublic** information to further your own private interest or that of another. For example, if you learn on the job that a company will be awarded a government contract, you may not take any action to purchase stock in the company or its suppliers and you may not advise friends or relatives to do so until after public announcement of the award. It makes no difference whether you heard about the contract award as a result of your official duties or at the lunch table.

5 C.F.R. § 2635.703(a) states:

> Prohibition. An employee shall not engage in a financial transaction using nonpublic information, nor allow the improper use of nonpublic information to further his own private interest or that of another, whether through advice or recommendation, or by knowing unauthorized disclosure.

5. Generally, you can't use your government title or position to __________ any product, enterprise, or service.

Generally, you cannot use your government title or position to **endorse** any product, enterprise, or service. That could imply that your agency or the government sanctions or endorses your personal opinion. Of course, if it is part of your agency's mission to promote products or document compliance, that would be permitted.

5 C.F.R. § 2635.702(c) states:

> Endorsements. An employee shall not use or permit the use of his Government position or title or any authority associated with his public office to endorse any product, service or enterprise except:
>
> (1) In furtherance of statutory authority to promote products, services or enterprises; or
>
> (2) As a result of documentation of compliance with agency requirements or standards or as the result of recognition for achievement given under an agency program of recognition for accomplishment in support of the agency's mission.

7. Generally, you can't use your position, title, or __________ associated with your public office to imply that your agency sanctions your outside activities.

You generally cannot use your government position, title, or **authority** associated with your job to imply that your agency or the government sanctions or endorses your outside activities. Even though your government authority may give you clout within the community, you are not to use this to your own personal benefit.

An excerpt from 5 C.F.R. § 2635.702(b) states:

> An employee shall not use or permit the use of his Government position or

EXERCISE ANSWER KEY

> title or any authority associated with his public office in a manner that could reasonably be construed to imply that his agency or the Government sanctions or endorses his personal activities or those of another.

9. You can't use government property, including the services of __________, for unauthorized purposes.

You may not use any government property, including the services of **contractors**, supplies, photocopying equipment, computers, telephones, mail, records, or government vehicles for purposes other than doing your job (unless your agency has rules permitting some types of incidental use).

5 C.F.R. § 2635.704(b)(1) states:

> Government property includes any form of real or personal property in which the Government has an ownership, leasehold, or other property interest as well as any right or other intangible interest that is purchased with Government funds, including the services of contractor personnel. The term includes office supplies, telephone and other telecommunications equipment and services, the Government mails, automated data processing capabilities, printing and reproduction facilities, Government records, and Government vehicles.

11. Unless authorized, playing games on your office computer is a misuse of official __________ and government property.

It is misuse of your official **time** and government property to play games on your office computer. If you do not have any work to do, ask your supervisor for something to work on. You are expected to put in a full day's work and use government property for authorized purposes only. Some agencies may permit you to use your office computer for nonofficial purposes for a limited amount of time, such as during lunch or after work. Check with your ethics official to see if your agency has a limited use policy.

An excerpt from 2635.705(a) states:

> Use of an employee's own time. Unless authorized in accordance with law or regulations to use such time for other purposes, an employee shall use official time in an honest effort to perform official duties.

12. Widely used and misused piece of government equipment.

The **copier** is a widely used and misused piece of government equipment. You must conserve and protect Government property. You cannot use Government property or allow its use, other than for authorized purposes. You may not use the photocopying machine, or any other Government property, including supplies, computers, telephones, mail, records or Government vehicles for purposes other than doing your job (unless your agency has rules permitting incidental use).

5 C.F.R. § 2635.704(b)(1) states:

EXERCISE ANSWER KEY

> Government property includes any form of real or personal property in which the Government has an ownership, leasehold, or other property interest as well as any right or other intangible interest that is purchased with Government funds, including the services of contractor personnel. The term includes office supplies, telephone and other telecommunications equipment and services, the Government mails, automated data processing capabilities, printing and reproduction facilities, Government records, and Government vehicles.

Down

1. You are to protect and __________ government property.

You are to protect and **conserve** government property and use it properly. Remember that all government property is paid for by the public. The public expects you to use their resources wisely.

5 C.F.R. § 2635.704(a) states:

> Standard. An employee has a duty to protect and conserve Government property and shall not use such property, or allow its use, for other than authorized purposes.

3. Your __________ can't ask you to shop for his wife's birthday present during duty hours.

Your **supervisor** cannot ask you to shop for his wife's birthday present during work hours. Official time is to be used for the performance of official duties. You can only use your work hours to perform your job. Shopping for the present would be misuse of your official time.

5 C.F.R. § 2635.705(b) states:

> Use of a subordinate's time. An employee shall not encourage, direct, coerce, or request a subordinate to use official time to perform activities other than those required in the performance of official duties or authorized in accordance with law or regulation.

4. Recommending your neighbor for a federal job on agency __________ is ok if you have personal knowledge of his abilities or character.

You may use agency **letterhead** to write a letter of recommendation for your neighbor if you have personal knowledge of his abilities or character. You may also use your official title. This also applies to letters of recommendation for a person you've dealt with in your federal job as long as you have personal knowledge of that person's ability or character.

An excerpt from 5 C.F.R. § 2635.702(b) states:

> [An employee] may sign a letter of recommendation using his official title only in response to a request for an employment recommendation or char-

> acter reference based upon personal knowledge of the ability or character of an individual with whom he has dealt in the course of Federal employment or whom he is recommending for Federal employment.

6. You can't use your public office for private __________.

You cannot use your position with the Government for your own personal **gain** or for the benefit of others. This includes family, friends, neighbors, and persons or organizations that you are affiliated with outside the government. Your job is not an opportunity to obtain special treatment for yourself and others, but to serve the public.

An excerpt from 5 C.F.R. § 2635.702 states:

> An employee shall not use his public office for his own private gain, for the endorsement of any product, service or enterprise, or for the private gain of friends, relatives, or persons with whom the employee is affiliated in a nongovernmental capacity, including nonprofit organizations of which the employee is an officer or member, and persons with whom the employee has or seeks employment or business relations.

8. Don't use your public office to __________ yourself or others.

You are not to use your public office to **benefit** yourself or others. That includes your friends, relatives, or people you are associated with outside the government. You are serving the public, not yourself and people you know.

5 C.F.R. § 2635.702(a) states:

> Inducement or coercion of benefits. An employee shall not use or permit the use of his Government position or title or any authority associated with his public office in a manner that is intended to coerce or induce another person, including a subordinate, to provide any benefit, financial or otherwise, to himself or to friends, relatives, or persons with whom the employee is affiliated in a nongovernmental capacity.

10. You learn on the job that Company X found the cure for a major disease. You may not buy __________ in Company X before your agency announces the company found the cure.

You are never permitted to use nonpublic information to get a jump on purchasing **stock** for yourself, family members, friends, or anyone else. That would be taking advantage of your government position for your own gain or the gain of others. Nonpublic information remains nonpublic until that announcement is made.

5 C.F.R. § 2635.703(a) states:

> Prohibition. An employee shall not engage in a financial transaction using nonpublic information, nor allow the improper use of nonpublic information to further his own private interest or that of another, whether through advice or recommendation, or by knowing unauthorized disclosure.

CHAPTER 12

Technology and Public Administration

This chapter co-authored by Alan R. Shark, D.P.A.

Chapter 12 examines the growing use of technology in public organizations. After reading this chapter, students will understand the evolution of the technology organization, knowledge and database management, the use of geospatial information systems, and broadband deployment. Of particular emphasis are the use of Internet applications in the context of citizen participation in governance and the delivery of public services. This chapter further discusses the widespread integration of 311 hotlines and concludes by examining Baltimore's and New York City's computer pin mapping systems.

"The new information technology—Internet and e-mail—have practically eliminated the physical costs of communications."

PETER DRUCKER
Economist; Management Guru; Author
(1909–2005)

A CitiStat session with then Baltimore Mayor Martin O'Malley

Source: Perez, Teresita and Reese Rushing. 2007. "The CitiStat Model: How Data-Driven Government Can Increase Efficiency and Effectiveness." Center for American Progress. http://www.americanprogress.org/issues/2007/04/pdf/citistat_report.pdf.

HIGH TECH GOVERNMENT

Today more than ever, federal, state, and local governments depend on technology to provide greater efficiencies in collecting, validating, processing, analyzing, reporting, protecting, and storing data. As of late 2010, over $71 billion was being spent per year in the United States by civilian federal agencies, as coordinated by the nation's first formally appointed chief information officer (CIO). When you add defense and national security spending, the federal government spends well over $200 billion on technology each year. Military and national defense agencies spend billions more dealing with national security issues at the highest levels. The Pentagon has reported that it receives thousands of security probes and intrusions into its many data networks every single day; if left unprotected, these breaches could lead to serious violations of national security. It is no small wonder that the U.S. Air Force modified its mission several years ago to read " . . . to fly and win in the air, space *and cyberspace*" (emphasis added).

> "The number one benefit of information technology is that it empowers people to do what they want to do. It lets people be creative. It lets people be productive. It lets people learn things they didn't think they could learn before, and so in a sense it is all about potential."
>
> **STEVE BALLMER**
> CEO, Microsoft

At the state and local levels of government, according to Washington Technology, $52.8 billion was spent on technology in 2010 (Lipowicz, 2010). Research groups like Input, Inc., had predicted a 45 percent increase in technology spending for state and local governments within the next five years over and above the $50 billion figure—depending on economic conditions (Dixon 2009). Whether or not those lofty spending numbers are reached, they are indeed illustrative of the demand for greater technology applications and solutions.

The need to embrace and better understand technology and the solutions it can provide has never been more important to the public administration practitioner. When used properly, technology applications can dramatically save time and money; in addition, technology can improve the decision-making process, as well as the speed of collecting, analyzing, and processing data, with advanced analytical tools. When not used properly, however, sensitive data can be compromised with ease, leading to identity theft, fraud, and the disruption of vital services.

Understanding how technology is organized within government is important because what were once considered stand-alone systems are converging or being consolidated into shared databases and support systems. Every new and legacy government program or system entails some form of technology infrastructure and support. In the past, public managers were mostly beholden to technology support managers and did not need to know much more than how to operate their own desktop computer and voice mail system. However, as technology has grown in complexity and scope, so too has the need for public managers to better understand and embrace technology. One way or another, technology is being integrated into almost everything that public administrators do. Managers must commit to learning more about how technology can be better applied through various tools, applications, and solutions in the workplace, as well as how policy drives technology and vice versa.

In today's political environment, one cannot discuss technology and how it benefits public managers and elected officials without also recognizing the important role technology plays in benefiting citizens. Government trust has been waning for almost four decades. According to results revealed in the American National Election Studies (ANES) surveys from 1958 to 2008, trust in government peaked in 1966, while 1994 marked the lowest level of trust. In 1964, 62 percent of Americans felt as though they could trust the federal government "most of the time." This compares to only 25 percent in 2008. In 1966, 17 percent felt that they could "just about always" trust the federal government, which compares to only 5 percent in 2008 (American National Election Studies, 2010).

> "I think it's fair to say that personal computers have become the most empowering tool we've ever created. They're tools of communication, they're tools of creativity, and they can be shaped by their user."
>
> **BILL GATES**
> Microsoft Creator; Philanthropist

Berman (1997) argues that citizens are cynical of government because of several factors. First, people feel that elected officials and bureaucrats abuse their powers for their own personal interests. Second, citizens feel overly detached from government. Third, the delivery of government services is viewed as substandard. With the hope of reversing these perceptions, Berman describes strategies that target "cynical citizens"—strategies for which emphasis is placed on publicizing the benefits of government, improving service delivery, and, perhaps most important, giving individuals a means of influencing public policy and government decision making. Government accountability and responsiveness are concerns of public managers, citizens, the media, and advocacy groups. Finding appropriate ways to monitor government performance, to provide mechanisms for citizen feedback and complaints, and to document government responsiveness in terms of timeliness and service quality has a long history in public administration. Technologies provide viable alternatives for increasing citizen access to government and improving government responses to the issues of greatest concern to its citizens.

This chapter will first provide a brief overview of how technology is organized at all levels of government and review some of the key types of internal applications governments use. Next, we move to the network and look in particular at network security and the government's responsibilities in keeping information safe. We then

FIGURE 12.1 – A PERILOUS TREND: THE EROSION OF TRUST IN GOVERNMENT

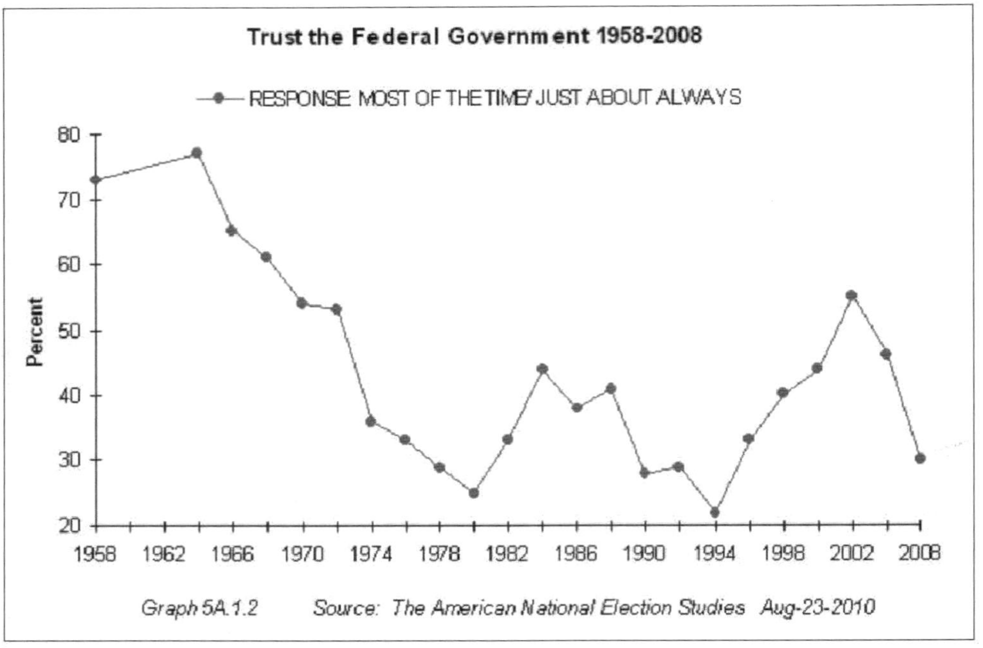

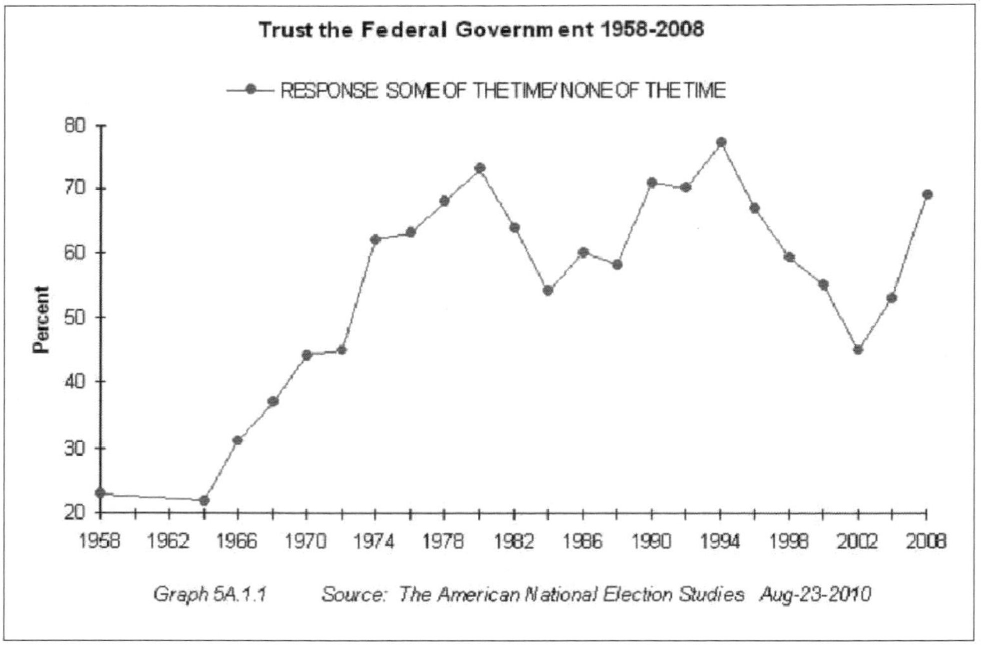

Source: The American National Election Studies (www.electionstudies.org). 2010. "Trust in the Federal Government, 1958-2008." In The ANES Guide to Public Opinion and Electoral Behavior. Ann Arbor, MI: University of Michigan, Center for Political Studies. http://www.electionstudies.org/nesguide/toptable/tab5a_1.htm

cover the growth of the database and its evolving applications—including visualization—and proceed to a discussion of how convergence and innovation benefits public managers in their quest to provide more effective and efficient services to their citizens. Finally, we focus on the technological advances that are allowing citizens to participate in government in ways never before possible.

Technology Organization

Every federal agency has a chief information officer (CIO) and often a chief technology officer (CTO) responsible for coordinating secure and uniform technology systems. To help coordinate the technology applications across federal agencies and departments, the Chief Information Officers Council was established. The CIO Council was created by Congress via the E-Government Act of 2002, and it is the chief interagency vehicle for enhancing practices in the development, improvement, utilization, sharing, and performance of federal information resources. The CIO Council recommends IT management policies; identifies opportunities for information sharing; and evaluates the government's IT workforce needs. The council is now headed by the CIO for the federal government—a position that resides in the administration's Office of Management and Budget (OMB).

The federal government collects trillions of megabits of data every year. Some of the information gathering is mandated by agencies' missions or charters, and some is the result of administration initiatives or congressional mandates. For example, every ten years, the U.S. Department of Commerce provides the apparatus for the U.S. Census. The Department of Education tracks trends in schools and universities—including standardized test results—and student placement and enrollment statistics. The U.S. Department of Labor tracks unemployment figures and jobless benefits as well as the number of new jobs created or lost. The U.S. Department of Agriculture tracks food supplies and crop yields, imports and exports, and much more. For every agency and commission, there is an intense data-gathering system, as well as a data analyzing and reporting responsibility.

Until recently, most of the raw data collected by the government has been considered confidential, leaving citizens unable to conduct critical reviews of summaries and reports. As you will see later in this chapter, all that is changing.

At the state level, nearly every state has a CIO reporting to the governor. Like the federal government, states collect and analyze a lot of information and administer many critical programs. A sampling of state agency functions appears in Figure 12.2. Each of these agencies utilizes a high degree of technology to carry out its mandated services.

Technology-related roles and responsibilities for cities and counties is an evolving responsibility. Local governments only recently began to consider such titles as CIO or CTO. Traditionally, the person mainly responsibility for technology might be called director of technology, or director of the office of information and technology.

Typically, a CIO leads, manages, coordinates, and integrates all applications related to communication and information technology. The CIO is responsible for the entire enterprise. The CTO position, by contrast, is more concerned with technology solutions, and is less concerned about dealing with the political and administrative arenas. In practice, though, these titles have been used with little distinction between them. Knowing this, do titles matter? While the answer is yes and no, questions surrounding the duties and expectations of the senior technology staff person are ultimately more important. Important questions include: How many people does this person manage? What is the size of the budget? Does the department or agency operate as a stand-alone unit or as part of a federated structure? Who makes decisions and at what levels are given decisions made?

The stature of the CIO and/or CTO within city and county governments has grown with the ever-increasing sophistication of managing communications and information technology. As of 2010, there were over 3,000 counties and 36,000 cities and townships in the United States. The CIO and/or CTO are believed to be the most essential "new" positions in local government, and there is every reason to believe that the importance of this positions will continue to grow.

The Network and Its Security

The network is the core for all data transactions, storing all vital data, including e-mails, website information, and more. Networks are systems that allow groups of interconnected computers (or workstations) to work together. These computers can access the network in several ways: directly through cables, remotely, or wirelessly. The network hub usually resides in a data center where security is often very tight and the temperature and humidity are carefully regulated. Some data centers support remote data storage facilities and are linked to other data centers. A more complex type of network is known as the "cloud" (or "cloud computing"). In the cloud, computing functions—including storage, processing, and software applications—

FIGURE 12.2 - SAMPLE OF STATE GOVERNMENT FUNCTIONS

- Budget and Administration
- Community Affairs
- Corrections (prisons)
- Education (state systems)
- Environmental Protection
- Employment Services
- Health Systems and Human Services
- Highways and Maintenance
- Insurance Administration
- Licensing (vehicles, registration, titles)
- Justice and Courts Systems
- Lottery
- Parks and Recreation
- Pension Systems
- Prisons
- Public Safety (police and emergency)
- State Judicial Systems
- Social Services
- Transportation
- Taxation
- Vital Health Records
- Voter Registration

run on the Internet instead of being housed in any one particular data center owned and operated by a company or government. Questions regarding network security, redundancy, and access are legitimate concerns of cloud computing. However, companies such as Amazon, Google, Microsoft, IBM, and many more are making the move to the cloud very compelling—especially for local governments. This is because up-front and ongoing costs to build and maintain network systems are usually dramatically lower in a cloud environment. It also means that wherever you have access to the Internet, you have access to your applications as well. As a result, governments may no longer need to own and operate their own equipment and storage facilities, as more companies are offering cloud computing as an alternative.

> "Speech has allowed the communication of ideas, enabling human beings to work together to build the impossible. Mankind's greatest achievements have come about by talking, and its greatest failures by not talking... With the technology at our disposal, the possibilities are unbounded. All we need to do is make sure we keep talking."
>
> **STEPHEN HAWKING**
> Theoretical Physicist; Author, *"A Brief History of Time"*

Whether networks are in a building or in a cloud, all federal, state, and local government employees have a responsibility to ensure the integrity of data that is collected and stored by their agency. There are numerous examples of security breaches—most of them unintentional. For example, a town in Michigan inadvertently printed the social security numbers of more than 70,000 residents on mailing labels. This was not a breach in technology; it was human error. Unfortunately, there was no senior policy overseer to check what was actually being printed on the labels. Inevitably, personal records stored online may be made visible inadvertently, showing records containing social security numbers, a mother's maiden name, and other information that could expose someone to identity theft. Other examples include people losing laptops or USB storage drives containing sensitive data in unencrypted files. Again, this is not a technology issue as much as a public management issue.

Network security is every public administration employee's responsibility, whether one works from the field, at home, or in the office. According to the Federal Trade Commission (FTC), in 2007 they received over 800,000 complaints of consumer fraud and identity theft, which cost consumers roughly $1.2 billion in losses. Today's networks are constantly under attack, and some local governments report receiving 20,000 or more serious threats a day on average—with well over 50 percent of them coming from foreign nations. As security threats from the "outside" increase in frequency and sophistication, there is also an alarming trend of even greater threats coming from "within"—some of it knowingly and some of it unknowingly.

Four interrelated areas are vulnerable to network threats, but separate strategies are necessary to protect each one. The areas are (1) network security, (2) web security, (3) e-mail security, and (4) mobile workforce security. The network is the information hub of all computer activities. Therefore, protecting the hub requires a multilayered approach that includes smart firewalls, intrusion protection systems, secure and encrypted virtual private networks (VPN), and updated and secure user validation. The Internet has become the dominant source of two-way communication between all levels of government, as well as the various publics they serve. Web security includes virus protection, content filtering, and spyware protection. E-mail security measures include virus protection, phishing protection, and spam protection. The mobile environment encompasses remote systems such as satellite offices and employees working from their home offices or offsite in the field. Wireless communications would also be included where workers have laptops, portable storage devices, and personal digital assistants (PDAs)—also referred to as smart phones. The mobile environment requires the same protections as the other forms of computer technology, except that in the mobile environment there is less control over the devices themselves. Additionally, in the wireless arena, special precautions are needed to address encryption and remote monitoring.

Twenty-first-century security systems employ sophisticated network and traffic monitoring devices that help data managers see exactly how the network is functioning at any given point in time. Ongoing vulnerability scanner or penetration tests are also used. Policies must be updated continually, and well-trained employees are vital to any sound security plan.

When public administration employees access government systems, most adhere to what is referred to as the triple As—Access, Authentication, and Authorization. Some favor the three "Ds"—Deter, Detect, and Defend. Regardless of preference,

FIGURE 12.3 – NETWORK SECURITY: EXAMPLES OF USER TRAINING AND EDUCATION

- Data classification—public and nonpublic data
- Rules for adding "unauthorized" content or programs
- Rules for file sharing
- Rules for social networking websites—dos and don'ts
- Files, backups and storage of data and how to ensure copies of your data
- Ethics and computer misuse
- Wireless communications technologies and security
- Rules for creation of passwords and changing passwords regularly
- Using the Internet—explanations of "Phishing," "Spyware" and other vulnerabilities
- Uses of e-mail, when to avoid e-mail and the use of attachments
- Physical security
- Rules governing use of peripherals such as USB drives, etc.
- Rules for laptop data protection and encryption
- Providing users with lists of the most frequently asked questions

the rules are quite similar. Some localities issue physical devices that help in user authentication. Here the emphasis is on controlling who has permission to enter a network and verifying the identity of whomever tries to access files. Keeping employees up-to-date with the latest information on security developments is also tantamount to the success of any written policy. Ongoing training and education is a continuous process that requires written guidelines, updates, and hands-on demonstrations. Some will argue there is simply no time—experts will argue that it is necessary and time well spent.

Not too long ago, most networks were relatively insulated from the outside environment and operated as closed systems. In the current environment—with so many employees having network access and with a mounting number of public interfaces due to enhanced e-government services—networks face a heightened threat due to unprecedented exposure risks. The growing use of videos and other forms of social media have introduced new security issues concerning network capacity and bandwidth. How can today's networks manage the predicted and dramatic increase in the need for more network bandwidth? By all accounts, network use and storage capacity will grow exponentially as new technologies require. Early in the administration of President Barack Obama, the president and his staff learned firsthand what happens when a huge group of citizens tries to visit the White House website at the same time. Obama had asked Americans to offer input on his proposed policies via the web, and the overwhelming response resulted in the crash of the White House e-mail system. It took several days to repair. The White House system was simply unprepared for the enormous amount of traffic—both legitimate and illegitimate.

Network threats begin with people. The best lines of defense involve having sound policies in place, a well-trained staff, and state-of-the-art detection and prevention systems. The mobile workforce is growing in complexity and number. A police chief in a mid-sized western city, with the best of intentions, purchased new PDAs for his entire force without getting input from the technology manager or anyone outside of the police department. The concern here was that the new devices lacked sufficient security features and were not supported by the city's network or IT staff; a time-consuming workaround for security and back-ups was needed to remedy the situation. Unfortunately, situations like this happen all too often when departments make computer equipment or software purchases without the knowledge or consent of IT security officials. Only after seeking post-purchase support do buyers realize the need for better purchasing policies, greater security integration, and guaranteed oversight. As more local government employees access applications from their homes or on the road, the level of security on any employee's wireless communications becomes key. Additionally, the increasing popularity of peer-to-peer networking calls for greater scrutiny of authentication protocols and encryption systems to protect both the data communications and entry into the network itself. Network security affects everybody and is therefore everyone's responsibility as a user, a manager, or a supervisor.

Knowledge Management

One area that is gaining attention in the information technology arena is knowledge management. Knowledge management involves either basic internal administrative procedures or more comprehensive, enterprise-wide policies and procedures. Internal procedures focus mainly on factors such as what happens when an employee is terminated or goes on leave for a long period of time. Job turnover has become more common than ever before—and so too has the need to safeguard critical documents, contacts, and records. What happens to a departing employee's voice mail account, e-mail records, personal office files, shared files, reports, spreadsheets, and other forms of data? Does the public manager/supervisor have an up-to-date record of every employee password for voice mail, network, and computer workstations in his or her group? How are files moved to new folders and over to a new or replacement employee? Are critical reports and documents stored in a familiar central area?

> "There are managers so preoccupied with their e-mail messages that they never look up from their screens to see what's happening in the nondigital world."
>
> **MIHALY CSIKSZENTMIHALYI**
> Psychology Professor

The aforementioned questions are best answered by enterprise policies regarding knowledge management. These policies dictate how major pieces of critical information are stored and indexed so that they can be found easily when needed. This is especially important in light of recent Freedom of Information Act and E-Discovery requirements. The length of time that certain files must be kept is federally mandated and, in many cases, subject to additional local or state laws. Because storing and preserving records are viewed as central IT functions, knowledge management is often overlooked, as the IT staff must rely on program staff to manage content. Ideally, institutional records and legal documents should be indexed and stored by those closest to the substance and origin of the data. Knowledge management also involves creating and maintaining a sharing and learning environment.

The Basics: Database Evolution

While the network is the core of most technological activity, the database is how things are logically stored and retrieved. Every work procedure involves some form of database interaction. Every time you search for a word, article, e-mail, or website, your request is being sent instantly and electronically to a database.

Computing emerged from the laboratory and entered government as a tool in the early 1970s. It began with what amounted to advanced electric typewriters, then grew into stand-alone systems called word processors. For the first time, written documents could be typed and saved to a disk. Technology was also making its debut in government accounting, where records were first stored and kept, and checks were printed—and the rest is history.

Increasingly complex databases will continue to grow rapidly and exponentially. Database management systems were designed to control, store, manage, and retrieve data. Databases are not only about transactions; they are about relationships—tying certain record fields together. Programmers and database managers are concerned with data structure, which might be a field, a record, a file, or an object. Currently we have added layers of security that allow access for specific classifications of employees. This is where passwords, fingerprint scans, and eye retina scans can become necessary: An employee database may be designed to allow certain employees to view human resource and financial data, while allowing others to view the medical record portion of that same record. Some will be able to view one or the other depending on their clearance, and some may be able to see both. Logs are kept to further safeguard data; in this way, it is possible to track who accessed what records and when they did so. Advances in the network, network security, and database management have improved public managers' ability to plan, keep records, and extrapolate data into visual forms that enhance the interpretation of raw data.

Geospatial Information Systems (GIS)—Data Visualizing

Geospatial information systems (GIS) can best be described as visual and graphic interfaces that combine (from a database source) and organize various forms of data and overlay that information onto a map of a city, county, state, or any other geographic area. As databases have grown in sophistication, so too has the need to better understand the various relationships of a city or county's infrastructure. According to Environmental Systems Research Institute, Inc. (ESRI, 2010), GIS "integrates hardware, software, and data for capturing, managing, analyzing, and displaying all forms of geographically referenced information." GIS allows for the visualization of information for the purpose of revealing data patterns and trends, which can be shared quickly and easily through maps and charts.

After 9/11, when terrorists attacked the World Trade Center in New York City, there was an immediate need to better understand the area of the city that had been affected. A team of NYC officials were tasked with creating an emergency GIS system that stands today as a model for the world to see. Aerial maps of the city were obtained, and a database was created with latitude and longitude overlays on top of the aerial maps. From there, additions to the map were made, including every subway system, every affected building, and all gas mains, fire hydrants, water and sewer pipe systems, electrical cables, telephone lines, fiber cables, hospitals, closed streets, major transportation lines, and so on. With access to this data, emergency planners could obtain precise information on services and locations with the touch of a button. Maps were given to TV stations and posted on the city's website to alert citizens to street and road closings and rerouted active transportation routes. The city could also see what parts of the infrastructure needed immediate attention. Without the integrated approach utilizing GIS systems, the time and effort needed to rebuild New York City would have multiplied tenfold.

In the early twenty-first century, most local jurisdictions utilize GIS systems for strategic planning that involves zoning, transportation planning, crime reporting, land improvements, water and sewer infrastructure, and more. While this type of technology has become a necessity for city and county government, ordinary citizens are making increasing use of it as well; for instance, parents can access bus routes to determine where their child's school bus is at any given moment. Some localities are posting public transportation updates that allow passengers to know where a bus or train is located on a real-time basis. Businesses can use GIS mapping systems to see where population growth or shifts are occurring, thus facilitating the process of planning for new locations. Global Positioning System (GPS) technology is very much related to GIS in that they both rely on geographic mapping and databases and are visual and interactive—some even "talk" to the user in the voice and language of choice.

Public managers who use GIS systems have a new set of tools for planning and sharing in a dynamic and interactive environment. Once a GIS system is in place, it is relatively easy to add what is referred to as "layers" of new data points for a particular

FIGURE 12.4 – NYC SAMPLE GIS MAP

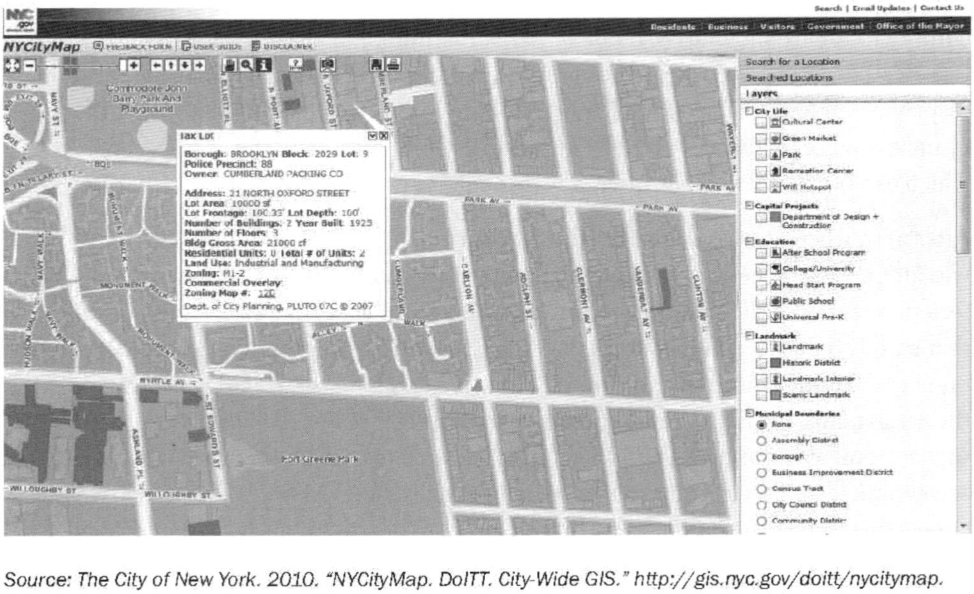

Source: The City of New York. 2010. "NYCityMap. DoITT. City-Wide GIS." http://gis.nyc.gov/doitt/nycitymap.

application or inquiry. Furthermore, the addition of "mashups" enables data from one area to be integrated and used with another set of data. An example of a mashup would be taking an existing map from a web site such as Google Earth and adding the street addresses of every library or fire station or pizza joint in your area. The coordinates of, say, any reported crimes could be added as well. The plotting process is easy: A map of your community appears with a list of buttons on the side of the map. When you click on any one button, a mashup group is plotted on the map. You might then add directions, or telephone numbers, or information on hours of operation. Once you understand how these tools work, you will realize the power of planning and information sharing—and see that it is something you could probably do yourself.

Convergence and Innovation

Geospatial Information Systems is a prime example of the convergence of many technologies into one application. Many people remain unaware of the amazing progress that has taken place regarding our data networks. Like GIS, the advances

FIGURE 12.5 – A SAMPLE OF SMARTPHONE FEATURES AND APPLICATIONS

1. Phone
2. Answering machine
3. Recording machine/tape recorder
4. Address book
5. Calendar
6. Caller ID
7. Video clips
8. MP3 player
9. Camera—still
10. Video camera
11. GPS tracking
12. Web browser
13. E-mail
14. IM
15. Games (3-D)
16. Calculator (tip calculator)
17. Clock/world clock
18. Timer
19. Wireless modem
20. Computer
21. Word processor
22. Stopwatch
23. Currency converter
24. Note pad
25. Appointment calendar (real-time)
26. Speaker phone
27. Picture viewer
28. "Walkie-talkie"
29. Bluetooth enabled
30. Enterprise applications
31. USB connectivity
32. TV
33. Video conferencing
34. Voice recognition
35. News, weather, traffic report alerts
36. Wi-Fi
37. Flashlight
38. GPS directions
39. Book reader
40. Bio-hazard detector
41. Smart cards (transportation)
42. Video LCD projector
43. Medical record and monitoring
44. Remote TV "clicker"
45. Bar code reader
46. Airline boarding pass
47. Bio feedback monitor
48. White noise appliance

Source: PDA example (Shark 2008).

in desktop computing are noteworthy, as well, with many more choices in available power, features, and size. As laptops have given way to the original desktop in sales, units continue to get smaller, lighter, and loaded with more features such as longer battery life, built-in cameras, and greater storage and memory capacities. Additionally, with all these advances, the relative price per device keeps going down. On the software front, we no longer are at the mercy of computer programmers and engineers. While they still have their place in any enterprise, tremendous flexibility has been provided to the general user for anyone who can afford a computer of their own—or a system they have access to at work or perhaps a library. Some schools require laptops for their students, and some private institutions actually provide them as part of their tuition.

> "The key is the Internet. The United States is by far the most advanced country in this new digital culture, so we have to be there. The Internet is the heart of this new civilization, and telecommunications are the nervous system, or circulatory system."
>
> **CARLOS SLIM HELU**
> Named Richest Man in the World, *Forbes* Magazine, 2010

Moore's Law, which is not really a law, states that technology innovation will double every two years. Some critics predict that Moore's Law will actually succumb to new laws of change because the "law" is no longer applicable to the fast pace of technological change. The law was named after Gordon Moore, the cofounder of Intel. In 1965 Moore wrote a paper explaining that with exponential growth, technology doubles approximately every two years. He based his observations on the number of transistors that could be placed inexpensively on an integrated circuit board. Moore's Law best describes the advances in size, memory, features, and pixels that over the years have grown exponentially without causing an increase in the price of new devices. Although Moore's law held up for nearly 50 years, experts in computer technology are beginning to see change occurring more rapidly than Moore's two-year cycle.

The greatest technological advances to date are best illustrated by the declining cost of data storage per megabyte or gigabyte.—This growth in computer-processing power allows us to better multitask and perform considerably more functions for less money. Miniaturization is another outcome of exponential growth. By 2010, smart phones had emerged on the scene that were more powerful and feature-rich than a desktop computer of just a few years earlier. An example of features that can be found in a state-of-the-art smart phone are listed in Figure 12.5, and there is little doubt the list will grow every year.

In 2007, Apple dazzled the world with its first iPhone. The phone contained hundreds of clever features and marked the first successful foray into the cell phone market by a computer manufacturer. The iPhone raised the bar for all manufacturers and sparked a huge competitive rush by other companies to develop new and better smart phones that could outperform the iPhone. Many observers expected there would be a convergence of the smart phone and the computer—it was only a matter of time—but it is occurring more quickly than anyone imagined.

Computers have morphed into cell phones and laptops, notebooks and netbooks; likewise, cell phones have morphed into computers. Customers around the world now see and hear things differently—and instantly. Convergence has enabled voice, data, and video to be brought together through digital technologies. According to the Pew Internet and American Life Project (2008) 62 percent of all Americans are part of a wireless, mobile population.

A growing number of Americans now receive supplemental news of the day through a small screen—be it handheld or a computer screen. Consequently, since the turn of the twenty-first century, print newspapers and magazines have been facing an uphill battle as advertisers follow their customer base to the digital market and, to a growing extent, so too is government. Members of today's younger generations, "Digital Natives," are more apt to get news from their handheld device or computer. Marc Prensky introduced the concept "Digital Natives" to describe today's students, K through College, who grew up with the new technology, and thus are "native speakers" of the dialect of personal computers, electronic games and the Internet (Prensky 2001). Digital Natives are less likely to own a landline phone, opting instead for cell phones and perhaps a voice over IP phone (VoIP). Additionally, they typically use a cell phone as a wristwatch and, when traveling, are more likely to turn to their phone as a wake-up alarm instead of a portable alarm clock.

Everyone serving in the field of public administration must be aware of—and embrace—these changes in technology. It is vital that public managers examine how people communicate and how they receive and process news and information.

The Connected Society: Trends and Opportunities Facing Public Managers

Societal growth has always been predicated on the exploitation of food, energy, shelter, and transport. Most historic cities throughout the world were built near waterways. Newer cities sprang up near train stations or airports. Today, however, all anyone needs to stay connected is a reliable energy supply, a good computer, and a high-speed broadband connection.

According to data from the Pew Internet and American Life Project (2008), 55 percent of American adults have high-speed Internet connections in their homes, and nearly one-third of broadband users are willing to pay more for speedier connections. When it comes to age groups, 78 percent of adults over 64 years old use the Internet primarily for sending and receiving e-mails. This technology comes with a price—even with all its efficiencies of scale. Federal, state, and local government IT spending is rising exponentially, just as demands for new upgrades, new hardware, and new software applications are needed. This has created enormous pressure to do more with less and may alter the way we view technology in government.

Thus far, this chapter has focused on the evolutionary path of technology: its background, the changing nature of networks and security, changes in the information infrastructure, and how citizens are embracing technology in general terms. Now that the Internet is so well entrenched in American society, enlightened government leaders are seeking new and improved ways of providing information to the public. This process involves creating new internal and external tools that improve the decision-making process, providing the public with unprecedented amounts of online information and options, and actually engaging citizens in what some refer to as digital democracy.

Building upon the new fiscal realities and the rapidly emerging connected society, there are three broad trends facing public managers at all levels of government:

1. Governance—regionalism/shared services as a necessity, not a luxury
2. Broadband deployment mobility and applications
3. Social networking (Web 2.0) beyond e-government

Governance: Regionalism/Shared Services

State and local government are facing economic pressures to do more with less—and technology spending is no exception. The need for greater cost-benefit justification plans and better performance-measurement criteria and reporting has grown significantly. The U.S. Office of Personnel Management (OPM) has been instrumental in developing plans and best practices for an integrated approach to performance measurement. President Obama, realizing the need for greater performance measurement applied across the board among all federal agencies, has created an Office of Performance & Personnel Measurement (OPPM), which is part of the Office of Management and Budget (OMB). At the city and county levels, performance-measurement techniques are not necessarily common or uniformly applied throughout the local enterprise.

In most communities, one will find at least five different public entities in any given geographic area, which might include a city, a county, a library system, a court system, an election system, a health care system, and a school system. Each of these public entities typically has some form of technology support system. Unfortunately, these same entities rarely interact with one another in terms of sharing expertise, staff, resources, or pooling of purchasing requirements—at least until now. Local government managers facing painful budget decisions have a tremendous opportunity to meet, convene, study, and explore ways of sharing technology support systems among public agencies within a given geographic area or region. This could take the form of shared data centers, GIS systems, IT staff, and other applications that lend themselves to sharing.

Broadband Deployment Mobility and Applications

A mayor was once quoted as saying, "I don't give a darn about broadband—all we want is high-speed Internet!" "Broadband" is a relative term; its definition is complicated and usually means different things to different people. For our purposes, we will refer to broadband as an always-on Internet connection—either wired or wireless—that supports many bandwidth-intensive programs such as large downloads, basic video conferencing, music and video downloads, and other popular applications. The term broadband refers to a wide degree of bandwidth—a collection of frequencies that are "pumped" through the Internet at varying degrees of speed. The wider and faster the connection, the more applications can be carried on it—like high definition video conferencing. Popular options include DSL, cable modem, 3G and 4G cellular phone connectivity, and T1 lines. As technology progresses, we will see greater speeds followed by greater bandwidth-intensive applications.

As mentioned earlier, more than 55 percent of Americans have broadband at home (Pew Internet and American Life Project 2008). According to data from the 2008 Pew project, 74 percent of Americans had access to the Internet; 91 percent sent or read e-mail; 89 percent used the Internet to search for general information; 86 percent have searched for directions; and 59 percent had visited a local, state, or federal website.

Local governments were slow to recognize the opportunities they had in providing even basic information and services to their citizens via their websites. Debate arose around the question of the appropriate role for local government regarding broadband deployment and government's possible function as a provider of broadband service to the public. There is little disagreement, though, as to the growing need for internal wireless systems used exclusively by cities and counties for public safety, critical communication, and mobile workforce applications. Applications include requests for construction permits, safety inspections for buildings, health IT, surveillance cameras, and monitoring devices. Some cities and counties are reporting that their workforce is increasingly more mobile—both in terms of applications and workers.

In 2009 the federal government entered the broadband arena with an unprecedented series of legislative mandates and funding to map the U.S. broadband infrastructure, providing targeted funds for rural broadband deployment and committing over $5 billion to broadband-related projects. The United States has fallen behind most Western nations in broadband deployment, leading some experts to speculate that a weak or inconsistent broadband infrastructure will further hurt American workers and productivity and make the nation less competitive on a global scale.

While critics may debate the appropriate role for government to play in broadband public policy, government offices at the city, county, and state levels depend on it and are one of its largest users—especially when it comes to internal operations. It makes sense that if governments wish to continue moving greater amounts of vital information and transactions to the Internet, then they must ensure that citizens are well connected "on the other end." This requires more than having access to the Internet—it means understanding how to use the technology interfaces.

Social Networking (Web 2.0) Beyond e-Government

Advances in broadband accessibility and Web 2.0 have created a number of interesting and exciting opportunities for increasing citizen participation in government. Web 2.0 refers to "second generation" Internet-based applications and it promises a much higher level of participation through greater public interface, "digital democracy," and perhaps even online voting. According to Alan Shark, "Web 2.0 is all about social networking and bringing people together in common forums and experiences" (Shark 2008), and governments at all levels are just beginning to realize the amazing opportunities that this new technology is providing. Other developments of high importance in connecting government and citizens include non-emergency 311 systems, customer relationship management (CRM) software, and other information and communications technologies (ICTs). These concepts and the implications that Web 2.0 and social networking may have on government services and the role of public managers are discussed in greater detail next.

The Public Interface and Online Services

The Internet has provided governments with the opportunity to develop and maintain web portals that continue to evolve; many have won awards for innovative services and easy-to-find information. A government website is the new public interface of government. Most government websites began small, providing static information such as office hours, calendars of events, directions, web addresses of elected officials, and basic city or county information. They now offer a multitude of online communications, enabling users to perform credit card transactions, fill out forms, pay off parking fines, reserve meeting rooms, renew licenses, search budget data, view and apply for job postings, and even see webcasts of meetings.

Innovation lays the foundation for most key government integration of Internet-

FIGURE 12.6 – LOCAL GOVERNMENTS: ADVANTAGES OF E-GOVERNMENT

- Always open (24-hour City Hall)
- Locality-neutral
- Faster transactions
- No lines
- Saves government money
- Citizen satisfaction
- Business satisfaction
- Improved security applications
- Accessibility (can be almost anywhere)
- Language options
- Greater citizen participation
- Competitive advantages over other localities

based applications, non-emergency 311 systems, and other *information and communications technologies (ICTs)* that enhance the responsiveness, effectiveness, and efficiency of government entities endeavoring to provide better services to citizens. At the same time, innovation is helping to restore a measure of trust in government by facilitating more direct communication between citizens and government.

The Internet and ICTs

Internet-based applications may prove ideal in reducing cynicism in government, as these applications can help make information more available, make people feel more in touch with government, and enable citizens to participate in the government process with greater ease. These changes may help restore faith in our bureaucratic and political institutions. Traditional methods of policy formation and decision making do not value the participation of citizens. The development of ICTs has presented alternative options. Proponents of "e-government" and "digital democracy" believe that ICTs will engender direct interaction between citizens and government—in other words, increased citizen participation. Some would argue that increased citizen participation exposes policymakers to a wider range of issues and information, and that this, in turn, will improve policy decisions. Having been applied extensively throughout the United States and Europe (Tsagarousianou, Tambini, and Bryan 1998; Holzer and Kim 2005), ICTs afford citizens greater participation in the policy discourse. They demonstrate the potential to provide citizens greater opportunities to influence public policy, thereby better connecting citizens and decision makers.

Digital Democracy

ICTs afford citizens a way of contributing to the public decision-making process. A new term has emerged, this being "digital democracy." *Digital democracy* encompasses using ICTs in democratic processes (Jankowski and van Selm 2000). In a democracy, citizens hold influence over the policies that have impact on their lives. Central to a digital democracy are the processes and structures that characterize the government-citizen relationship. Hacker and van Dijk (2000, p. 1) define digital democracy as "a collection of attempts to practice democracy without the limits of time, space and other physical conditions, using ICTs or computer-mediated communication instead, as an addition [to], not a replacement for, traditional 'analogue' political practices." Digital democratic applications, then, are nontraditional ways of participating in government. Nugent (2001, p. 223) defines digital democracy as "processes carried out online—communicating with fellow citizens and elected representatives about politics." Digital democracy entails the use of ICTs to improve democratic values. Government transparency is essential to digital democracy, and transparency is based on improving access to government information.

Digital democracy is presented in terms of static and dynamic forms of information dissemination and citizen deliberation. *Static information dissemination* most resembles obtaining information from read-only websites. Citizens simply obtain information about government policies and operations, usually provided through an official government website. *Dynamic information dissemination* resembles two-way communication between citizens and public officials, an example being e-mail communications initiated by citizens, resulting in a question-and-answer dialogue. *Static citizen deliberation* resembles a web-based poll without a public dialogue or a virtual bulletin board where citizens can post complaints or recommendations. *Dynamic citizen deliberation* includes electronic town halls, electronic policy forums, and web-based polls with the opportunity to discuss issues. These types of public spaces on the Internet must include all major stakeholders—namely citizens, elected officials, bureaucrats, interest and advocacy groups, and the media. In these spaces, O'Looney (2002) characterizes digital deliberation as providing:

- Balanced information
- Adequate time to deliberate the issues
- Freedom from coercion
- Predetermined rules that guide the discussion
- Inclusive participation
- Inclusiveness with regard to ideas

Regulations.gov: Opening Federal Regulations to the Masses

Regulations.gov is a web-based application (http://www.regulations.gov) where citizens can read and submit electronic comments on proposed federal regulations for 35 departments and agencies. Simplification and access are key components of this system. According to Mark Forman, former associate director for Information Technology and E-Government for the Office of Management and Budget, "the guiding principles for achieving our e-government vision are also about simplifying the process and unifying operations to better serve citizen needs; that is, 'uncom-

FIGURE 12.7 – STAGES OF DIGITAL DEMOCRACY

Stage		Characteristics
Information Dissemination	Static (Passive)	• Information Portal Sites
		• Information Search Method
		• Notice of Information Openness
		• Links to Related Websites
	Dynamic (Active)	• E-Mail Communication to Request Information
		• Newsletters or Newsgroups
		• E-mail lists
Citizen Deliberation	Static (Passive)	• Online Poll (Instant Results, Presentation of Previous Polls)
		• Bulletin Board for Complaints
		• Bulletin Board for Recommendations
	Dynamic (Active)	• Digital Town Hall Meeting
		• Digital Policy Forum
		• Online Voting with Deliberation

FIGURE 12.8A – REGULATIONS.GOV: EXAMPLE OF SEARCH RESULTS SCREEN

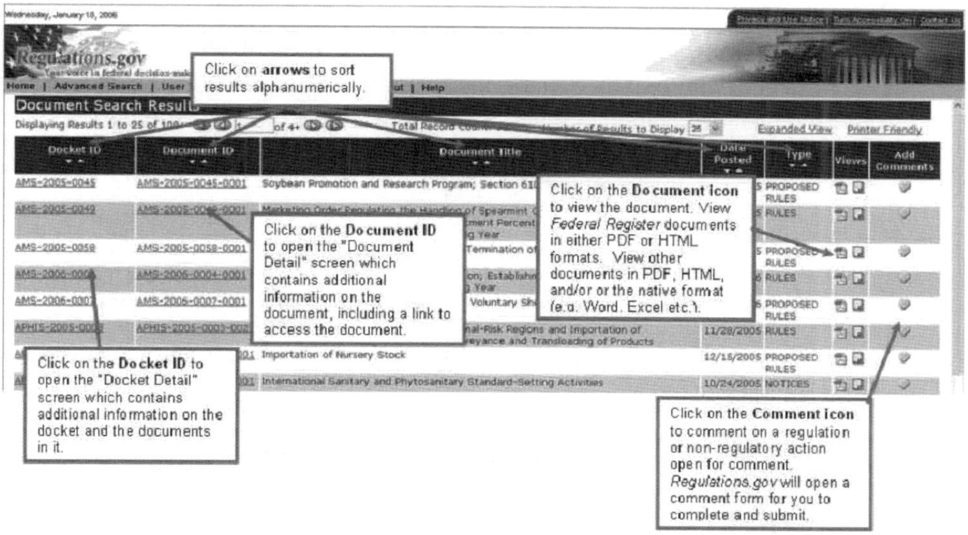

FIGURE 12.8B – REGULATIONS.GOV: ELECTRONIC COMMENT FORM

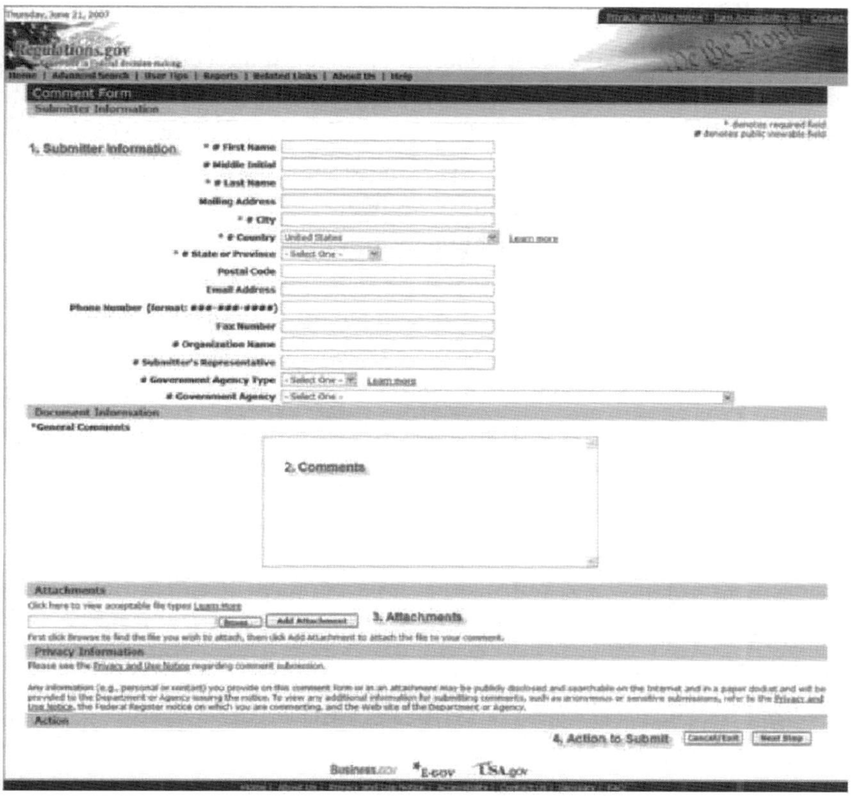

plicating' government" (Forman 2002). Forman stresses that accessing government information "should not take a citizen more than three 'clicks' of a mouse." Through Regulations.gov, anyone can track regulations open for comment via a keyword search or by selecting a federal agency from a drop-down menu. After performing a keyword or agency search, clicking on a proposed regulation will provide the user with a detailed description of the proposal. The following information is shown in the description of a regulation open for public comment:

1. *Full text* of the proposed regulation (text and PDF);
2. *Code of Federal Regulations (CFR) citation*, which corresponds to the section of the CFR that an agency is amending or proposing to amend;
3. *Date published* refers to the date on which the proposed rule was published in the Federal Register;
4. *Comments due* refers to the closing date of a consultation period;
5. *Add comments* directly forwards an individual to an electronic comment form when clicked;
6. *How to comment* guides citizens through the comment process, both electronically and paper-based.

Champions of Regulations.gov believe it has opened up federal rulemaking to individuals outside of the Washington, D.C., elite and special interest lobbyists. In a perfect world, Regulations.gov will be an egalitarian tool that gives the rank and file a way of influencing public policy. Skeptics, however, argue that Regulations.gov will become yet another tool for the powerful. For example, labor unions might provide its members with a comment template, or an electronic comment form containing pre-packaged comments that support or oppose a proposed regulation. Gary Bass, executive director of OMB Watch—a public interest group dedicated to promoting government accountability and citizen participation—believes that special interest groups are positioned to benefit from applications like Regulations.gov in the short term because of their access to technology and ability to organize. In the long run, however, Regulations.gov may be central to empowering diverse groups of constituencies (Skrzycki 2003).

The AmericaSpeaks Model

While town hall meetings and hearings afford individuals opportunities to convey their opinions, they do not foster a meaningful dialogue among citizens and decision makers (Uchimura 2002). Lukensmeyer and Brigham (2002, p. 351) note, "Public hearings and typical town hall meetings are not a meaningful way for citizens to engage in governance and to have an impact on decision making. They are speaker focused, with experts simply delivering information or responding to questions." Carolyn Lukensmeyer, founder and president of America*Speaks*, argues that ordinary citizens do not have access to the policymaking process—a process that has been dominated by the special interest elite. The America*Speaks* 21st Century Town Meeting was therefore created as a way of overcoming this challenge by using ICTs to bring together large numbers of citizens.

The 21st Century Town Meeting brings people together using networked computers, electronic keypads, and movie-theater-sized video screens. Intimate group dialogues are essential to this process. Groups of 10 to 12 individuals discuss predetermined policy issues. Group dialogues are steered by trained moderators, who ensure that the discussions remain focused and that everyone within the group has a chance to speak. Networked computers collect and communicate each group's viewpoints to a main computer. Each group's viewpoints are organized into broader themes, and each individual uses a keypad (similar to a television remote control) to vote on each of the themes.

> "We have technology, finally, that for the first time in human history allows people to really maintain rich connections with much larger numbers of people."
>
> **PIERRE OMIDYAR**
> Founder, e-Bay; Philanthropist

A noteworthy example of this process took place in November 2003, when 2,800 residents from Washington, D.C., participated in a 21st Century Town Meeting known as Citizen Summit III. Participants discussed three important city challenges: providing better education, improving neighborhood safety, and creating employment opportunities. The opinions expressed by these 2,800 citizens helped create a "Citywide Strategic Plan." The input from the Citizen Summit meetings was used to formulate goals for several city departments (Citizen Summit III: Real Challenges, Real Choices 2004).

E-Government: Enhancing Service Delivery

As defined by Calista and Melitski (2007, p. 12), e-government "provides governmental services electronically, usually over the Internet to customers, to reduce their physical character by recreating them virtually." Scholars such as Fanie Cloete (2003) maintain that to be effective, government must implement technological innovations. Recent e-government applications are service delivery in nature. For example, residents or proprietors are able to apply for government permits or licenses online. More and more frequently, taxes, utilities, and fines are being paid online. Citizens are able report service complaints by visiting their city website. E-government services have received increasing interest from governments at all levels. This added interest in e-government can be attributed to citizens expecting government websites to provide a range of services similar to those of commercial websites. Advanced e-government websites allow users to:

- Pay utilities (e.g., tap water, sewage, gas, electricity)
- File or pay taxes

- Pay fines or tickets
- Apply for permits (or register) and track the status of permits online
- Apply for licenses
- Look up property assessments
- Access searchable databases
- File service complaints
- Customize the main homepage based on users' interests or needs

Hot Hotlines: 311 Systems

The Origins and Demand for 311

Between 50 and 90 percent of 911 emergency calls are, in fact, not emergencies

FIGURE 12.9 – STAGES OF E-GOVERNMENT COMPLEXITY

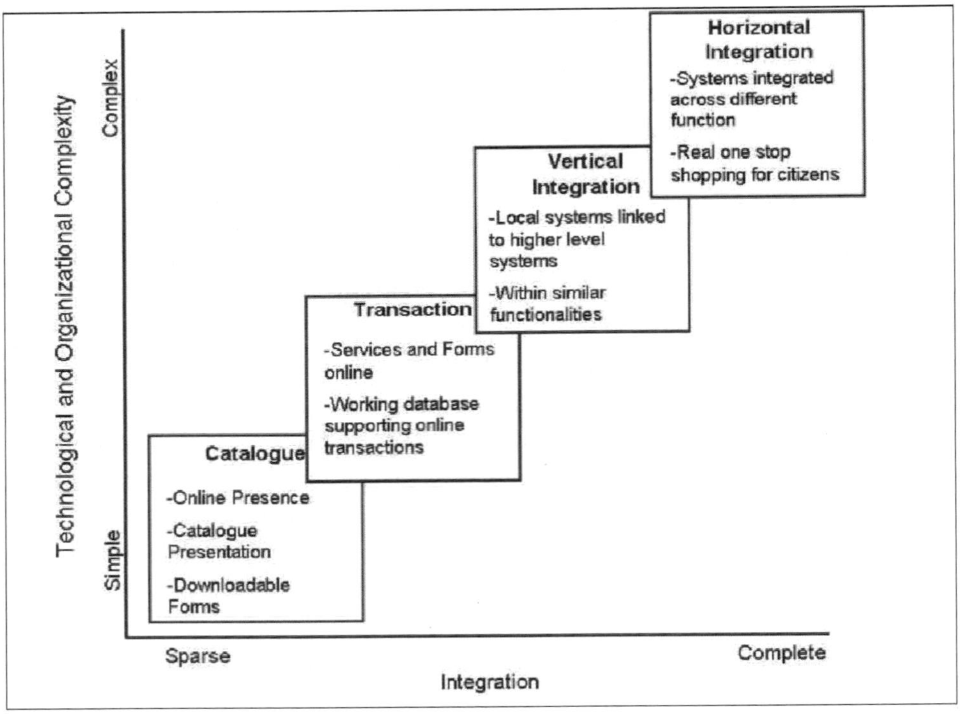

Source: Stephen H. Holden, Donald F. Norris, and Patricia D. Fletcher .2003. "Electronic Government at the Local Level: Progress to Date and Future Issues." Public Productivity and Management Review 26(4): 328. Reprinted by permission of Sage Publications.

(U.S. Department of Justice 2006). Non-emergency calls to 911 cause backlogs that delay police, fire, and other emergency services, the consequences of which range from frustration to the loss of life. As a result of this growing problem, in 1996 President Bill Clinton requested that the Department of Justice (DOJ) devise a way of relieving 911 systems of unnecessary calls. The Office of Community Oriented Policing Services (COPS Office) of the DOJ pursued this, requesting that the Federal Communications Commission (FCC) designate the number 311 as a non-emergency help number (Solomon and Uchida 2003). The FCC in 1997 established the 311 number for non-emergency local government services (City of Oakland 2002). Baltimore, Maryland, was the first U.S. city to implement a 311 system specifically designed to reduce non-emergency 911 calls (Mazerolle et al. 2003). The Baltimore Police attributed the following improvements to 311:

- Amount of time needed to answer 911 calls decreased by 50 percent.
- Number of abandoned 911 calls decreased by 50 percent.
- Number of 911 calls receiving a recorded message decreased by 14 percent.
- Amount "total position busy" time decreased by 169 hours monthly.
- Percentage of time 911 operators were busy with calls decreased by 18 percent.

311 systems are also changing the way governments and citizens interact, serving as a means of enhancing access to public services. By expanding its original "police nonemergency" role, 311 embodies a movement toward community-oriented government. Through an easy to remember number, 311 provides a direct link to government service agencies and provides citizens with the power to monitor their requests (COPS Fact Sheet 2006). Frustrations with government services have generated demand for 311. Customer service complaints, by and large, deal with ease of use, timeliness, service, and accessibility.

- Ease of Use: A frequent complaint of people is the trouble they have determining whom to contact whenever they have a question, complaint, or service request. The City of Los Angeles determined that 50 percent of all calls required at least two transfers before the caller was connected with the right department.
- Timeliness: Often, it takes too much time for a citizen to receive follow-up information subsequent to making a request.
- Service: Citizens want the "personal touch" of speaking with a live person—not an automated, computer voice that offers an excess options and little chance of finding the correct one quickly.

- Accessibility: Citizens want to know when their service request will be fulfilled. As FedEx has discovered, giving customers the ability to check the whereabouts of their packages is a meaningful way of demonstrating a commitment to accountability.

Service Enhancement and Government Efficiency

According to Martin (2004), 311 systems have the potential to improve government efficiency by centralizing the contact point between government and citizens.

- 311 is viewed as a management tool. Public managers are able to monitor the volume and types of calls received. Information from incoming calls can be analyzed with what is referred to as customer relationship management (CRM) software. This information can be used to pinpoint service problems (e.g., persistent illegal dumping problems, missed trash pickups) and set service standards.
- Significantly reducing the phone-answering duties for government workers is a direct benefit of 311 call centers. The 311 system frees up workers, enabling them to handle essential functions rather than serving as a telephone operator, transferring citizens to whomever they need to contact.
- Savings and efficiencies resulting from 311 are more easily recognized over time. For example, the Chicago water department used information collected via 311 to identify the most regularly opened fire hydrants. Locking caps were eventually placed on those hydrants to ensure sufficient water pressure.
- 311 systems have resulted in revenue enhancement. An example of this is how the Baltimore water department now deals with leaks. In the past, when a water meter was discovered to have a leak, a bypass pipe would be installed and another division in the water department would be called in to replace the meter. In conjunction with Baltimore's CitiStat program (discussed later), 311 managers discovered thousands of cases where individuals were waiting for meters to replace the bypasses. Now, upon the installation of a bypass, the CRM tool promptly makes a request to the division responsible for replacing the meters. This has resulted in a significant decrease in the number of bypass pipes, which equates to millions of dollars of water revenue for the city that otherwise would have been lost.
- The instantaneous nature of 311 allows for quicker government responses. For instance, in inclement weather, 311 enables officials to identify areas where there is more water and, therefore, helps predict and avert possible flooding problems.

Hampton, Virginia: A Citizen-Centered 311 System

In an effort to improve service delivery and government responsiveness to the needs of its residents, the city of Hampton, Virginia, established a 311 call center in 1999. Prior to Hampton's implementation of a 311 system, residents often found it very difficult to contact city departments. Residents with questions or concerns were all too frequently bounced from one department to another. In instances where a concern or question was interdepartmental, there was a significant likelihood of confusion as to which department should handle a specific service request or problem. In short, contacting the government proved more difficult than it should have been. Hampton's 311 system was envisioned as a means of streamlining the service request and delivery process, giving residents the luxury of calling when they want, telling one story (one time), and feeling assured that their requests and/or problems would reach the necessary department. For example, a resident with a solid waste complaint (e.g., trash was not picked up), simply places a 311 call, registers the complaint, and a truck is dispatched to pick up the trash within a specified time period.

One perceived obstacle to integrating Hampton's 311 systems centered on concerns that the call center personnel would not be able to handle the responsibilities of more technical departments. Hampton's assessor department expressed concerns in this regard. However, personnel training and the user-friendly nature of the 311 software make it possible for the call center personnel to handle the responsibilities and field questions regarding all departments. The software uses a keyword search that routes the call taker to approximately 3,400 Frequently Asked Questions (FAQs) relevant to an inquiry of problem. If by chance a resident has an inquiry that is not covered by any of the 3,400 departmental FAQs, the 311 call center representative will take that person's name and number and obtain a response in a timely manner. Once resolved, this request (or piece of information) is then added to the departmental list of FAQs. Each department started with roughly 1,200 FAQs. Hampton's 311 system includes an Internet-based component that allows residents to request information and services. Individuals simply complete a short electronic form that is forwarded to the call center. Users are promised a response within one business day. Individuals are also able to search the call center FAQs. For example, typing "trash collection" into the FAQ "question description" box would provide an individual with 25 FAQs on that topic.

Citizen Satisfaction and 311

Since the inception of 311, impressions regarding customer service in Hampton have improved. Data covering the period July 1, 2006, to December 19, 2006, indicate that 93 percent of residents rate Hampton's 311 customer service as very good or excellent, while 91 percent of users rate the convenience of the call center as very good or excellent. These impressions are further bolstered given that 20 percent of residents use 311 to conduct business with the city after hours, on weekends, and holidays. Moreover, 94 percent of users indicated that 311 met their needs, and 55 percent of 311 users were left with an improved impression of Hampton's services.

Overall, the perception of efficiency has improved. According to the Hampton call center manager (City of Hampton, Virginia 2006), even though the quality of Hampton's service delivery has not changed per se (the city maintains that it provided quality service delivery prior to its 311 system), perceptions of service delivery quality in terms of effectiveness and efficiency have changed for the better. The call center manager attributes this to the fact that 311 is publicized at the grassroots level; that is, all city departments have public meetings and use such forums to advertise 311. Hampton's 311 system is successful insofar as it has (1) customer-service-driven employees, and (2) interdepartmental cooperation. Hampton has a culture of working together and understanding that getting things done depends on cooperation. Call center staff have a great relationship with the government leaders (council-manager system), and the council and city manager's office pay strict attention to what people want.

The Future of Hampton's 311 Call Center

An effort is under way to implement a robust integration feature to Hampton's cur-

FIGURE 12.10 – ELECTRONIC SERVICE REQUEST FORM, HAMPTON (VA) 311 CALL CENTER

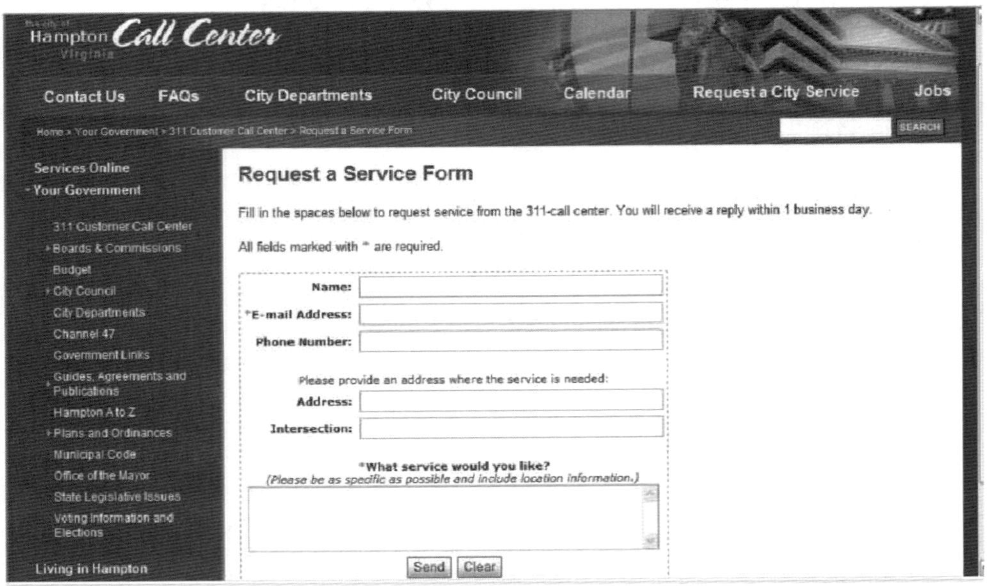

Source: The City of Hampton. 2010. "City of Hampton, 311Customer Call Center, Request a Service Form." http://www.hampton.gov/311/request_service_form.php.

rent 311 call center. Consider, for example, that resident x wants to apply for permit y. When the department in change of issuing permit y runs resident x's name, they find that this person has outstanding parking tickets, and thus they will not issue the permit until all fines have been paid. Or, suppose resident z calls 311 for the third time to report that her trash has not been picked up. A fully integrated 311 system would recognize that this is a recurring problem for this particular resident and take steps to ensure that it no longer happens. Moreover, a fully integrated system may offer person specific reminders, such as reminders as to when the next council or planning meeting is scheduled. Hampton hopes to create a more comprehensive view of customer service (City of Hampton, Virginia 2006).

New York City's 311 System

New York City's 311 system was spearheaded in 2002 by Mayor Michael Bloomberg. He envisioned this system as a way of learning what citizens thought of government services. As a very successful member of the international business community, Bloomberg's style of public management mirrors that of his private sector management style; that is, emphasis is placed on customer satisfaction. From the government point of view, citizens are the customers, as they are the consumers of public services. Bloomberg planned the development of New York's 311 system soon after he took office.

FIGURE 12.11 – ELECTRONIC FAQS, HAMPTON (VA) 311 CALL CENTER

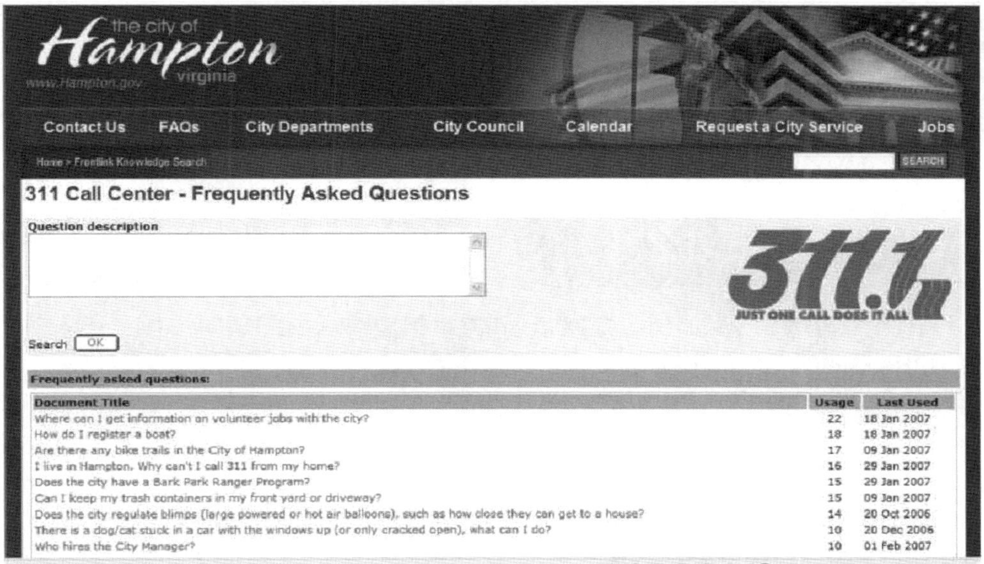

Source: The City of Hampton. 2010. "City of Hampton. Frequently Asked Questions." http://www.hampton.gov/faq.html.

Bloomberg stressed the need for callers to be put in contact with a live representative as quickly as possible. At the behest of Bloomberg, the 311 system was developed and implemented by the Department of Information Technology and Telecommunications (DOITT) in eight months, and this process had the full cooperation of the other city agency commissioners.

Four years after its launch, New York City's 311 system surpassed expectations. The system answered 13.2 million calls in fiscal year (FY) 2006, far more than was expected. The wait time to speak with a live representative averaged 14 seconds in FY2006, far less than target goal of 30 seconds.

Given the initial success of New York City's 311 system, greater emphasis will be placed on how 311 can drive agency performance. Internet, cell phone, twitter, and Skype have been integrated into 311. This allows citizens to submit and track service requests via the Internet without the need for call operators. Citizen satisfaction surveys are also planned, with the hope that this information will improve the system. Another new development is that DOITT, the agency that manages 311, will establish service level agreements (SLAs) with the city agencies. Take the issue of potholes, for example. The Department of Transportation will commit to an SLA whereby 85 percent of reported potholes are repaired within a specific time period. SLAs within other city agencies will be created in accordance with the agency's responsibilities. The SLAs will ultimately serve as a means of standardizing agency performance in areas that are most important to the citizens. Doing so makes government more responsive. Data gathered from the SLAs can be incorporated into the city's performance management tool, the Mayor's Management Report. This is a semi-annual report on the performance of all city agencies.

In August 2007, New York City announced a 311 application called SCOUT—the Street Conditions Observation Unit. This is a 15-member team charged with pin-

EXERCISE 12.1

SimProcess: Modeling and Simulations (Simulation)

In this exercise, students will have an opportunity to experience firsthand how technology can be utilized to improve efficiency and effectiveness in public administration. Students will (1) visit the SimProcess website; (2) choose a simulation from one of the following areas: Business Process Management, Health Care, Human Resources, or Call Centers; (3) access the demonstration model site; and (4) complete the trial. Following this exercise, students will create a one-page executive summary demonstrating how technology has improved the effectiveness and the efficiency of the process chosen.

http://www.simprocess.com/solutions/solutions.html

pointing street problems like potholes, broken bus shelters, and graffiti. Using BlackBerry technology and global positioning software, identified street problems will be processed and tracked using 311.

Computer Pin Mapping: Baltimore's CitiStat

Baltimore's CitiStat is an accountability tool designed around computer pin mapping and weekly accountability sessions. CitiStat is derivative of the New York City Police Department's CompStat program, which was the brainchild of Jack Maple (former Deputy Commissioner for Crime Control Strategies). CompStat was credited with dramatically reducing crime, and similar programs have been employed by police departments around the world. The former mayor of Baltimore, Martin O'Malley (elected governor of Maryland in November 2006), was convinced that the CompStat program could be applied to all city agencies—from Public Works to Health to Police and Fire. In short, CitiStat is how the O'Malley administration ran Baltimore. How exactly does CitiStat work? Agency or bureau heads meet at CitiStat meetings every two weeks. These biweekly meetings include the mayor, deputy mayors, and key members of the mayor's administration. Prior to each meeting, each bureau or agency submits data to the "CitiStat team," which, in turn, examines the data and puts together the presentation for the meeting. Precise and timely data is essential to the CitiStat process. The CitiStat team has the responsibility of making sure that the data submitted by the various bureaus and agencies make sense; in other words, that the data are "true." This is done by going out into the field and investigating, in addition to choosing cases randomly. The team also compares all collected data to previous reports, which further serves to identify problem areas. These problem areas are then geographically coded (geocoded) and plotted on a computer map.

Using 311 Data to Feed Computer Pin Mapping Programs

For citizens, 311 help lines create a single point of access between residents and their local government. 311 systems are responsive to citizen needs; they eliminate endless call forwarding mazes and "not my job" responses from municipal employees ill equipped to handle people's inquiries. Because 311 operators work directly with citizens to solve problems, they become citizen advocates within local government. In the most effective systems, 311 operators work with citizens to see inquiries through to completion, rather than forwarding calls into voice mail systems. 311 operators increase trust in government because they are trained to interact with the public and are evaluated based on the number of calls resolved. In the event that calls are not resolved immediately, citizens who call 311 receive a case number for tracking their issue. Tracking numbers are used to determine the number of open cases and, when tracked over time, can establish how long it takes to resolve similar cases.

For managers, 311 help lines create performance data that can be used to evaluate departments over time. Call resolutions are tracked over time, and managers can use the data to predict future needs based on geographic or seasonal variances. When 311 data are incorporated into an agency's management practices, the information helps in the evaluation of management processes and the search for operational efficiencies. Fully integrated 311 systems demonstrate that the performance of departments can be effectively evaluated using citizen-driven performance measurement. Again, Baltimore provides a good example of how 311 can be used as a direct feed to its CitiStat program. Using 311 to feed computer pin mapping has great potential, particularly when organized by neighborhoods or districts. For example, as reported in the *New York Times* (Hu 2003), "large and small, city officials are using information gathered through the 311 system to reexamine how city agencies carry out their jobs." This information has the potential to empower citizens and elected officials and to help build constructive dialogues between them and public managers.

The integration of technology is an effective problem-solving tool that has had a profound impact on public administration. 311 systems are better connecting government with citizens by providing a single point of access between residents and their local government. The systems have also become a source of information that feeds computer pin mapping programs like Baltimore's CitiStat, which are designed to improve public services and solve problems quickly. By reconnecting citizens to government, trust in government may be restored to levels more appropriate to our democracy.

Public organizations are experimenting with new Internet-driven methods for deliberating proposed regulations and policies between citizens and public agencies. But despite the potential benefits, the Internet as a communications medium presents some difficulties, particularly the "digital divide" between those with web access and web-based skills and those without such access and skills. While the online population is becoming more representative of communities in general, the reality of a digital divide means that certain segments of the population are effectively excluded from online deliberation, and the excluded populations tend to consist of historically disenfranchised individuals. A parallel criticism of digital policy deliberation is that it is skewed toward technical experts who effectively speak the "language" of public policy, thereby alienating average citizens. There is no doubt that experts, by and large, influence public policy dialogues. Some fear that this influence might be more pronounced through digital and Internet-based mediums. Clearly, expert knowledge is very important to policy development, but citizens' knowledge and intuition are key to the policy process as well. In addition, the Internet as a communication medium benefits individuals with better cultivated writing skills. These individuals tend to be in the upper echelon financially and educationally as well. These are some of the issues that need to be considered as public organizations become more reliant on technology.

E-GOVERNMENT AND CITIZENS' WILLINGESS TO MOVE

Like the US, Korea has been a leading country in e-government initiatives, and success stories are found in many areas (See the following three articles).

What are the opportunities and challenges in an era of E-government?

Information technology became a critical factor in operating governmentat all levels and is closely related to both transparency and trust issues. Among others, e-government initiatives enabled both countries to respond to the demand from citizens in more effective, efficient ways. There are many success stories in both countries. Please compare New York City's 311 system with Seoul City's 120 Dasan call system. What are differences and similarities between the two systems?

Please visit the website at http://120.seoul.go.kr/ for Dasan call center and visit the web site at http://www.nyc.gov/apps/311/ for NY City's 311 system.

Korea's e-People wins U.N. Public Service Awards

By Chun Sung-woo

The Anti-Corruption and Civil Rights Commission said Friday that its online portal on civil complaints and proposals, "e-People," had won a United Nations Public Service Award.

On June 23, U.N. Public Service Day on June 23, the U.N. honors creative and innovative administrative achievements every year.

The commission had entered the "e-People system, knowledge management for people's voice" in the category of "advancing knowledge management in government," and was told it had won on April 30.

The panel says that e-People is an integrated website (www.epeople.go.kr) that deals with civil complaints and proposals to central and provincial governments and public organizations. It is utilized as a venue for free and open discussion. About 100,000 people visit the portal daily.

The commission analyzes some 800,000 complaints filed through the portal to identify problems and improve related systems.

"We will offer unstinted cooperation and support to developing countries with a great interest in e-People, and help them adopt our process for resolving civil complaints," an official of the commission said.

(continued)

(continued)

The awards ceremony is scheduled to take place in Dar es Salaam, Tanzania from June 20–23.

The portal had been cited as the Online Politics Trophy Top 10 at the World eGov Forum 2006 and the Best Demonstration Stand Award at the eChallenges 2008.

Source: http://www.koreaherald.com/national/Detail.jsp?newsMLId=20110506000 526

The People's Voice is the Voice of Heaven

Sinmoongo(Big Drum), the system of handling complaints against the government during the Joseon Dynasty, was the first step towards giving the people a say in government affairs.

Driven by our ancestors' lofty ideals, Sinmoongo is reborn as "e–People" by integrating all channels of administrative organization to the people to upgrade the whole function of administrative judgment and corruption reporting as well as petition, proposal and policy discussion services.

e–People, available everywhere in the world, will take the lead to make a new face of Korea by resolving even trivial complaints after listening closely to the voices of the people and accepting their creative ideas positively.

FIGURE 12.12 – CONSTRUCTION OF WORLD'S BEST ONLINE PORTAL FOR PEOPLE

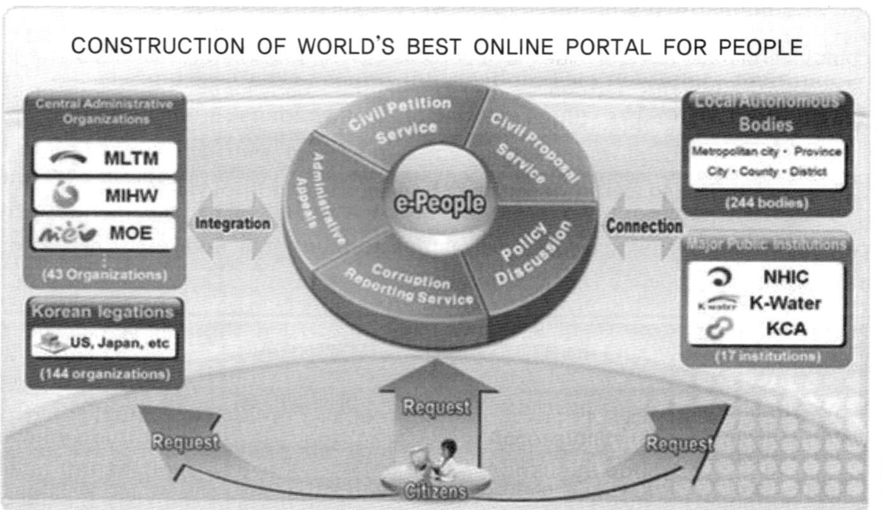

Source: http://www.epeople.go.kr/jsp/user/on/eng/intro01.jsp

FIGURE 12.13 – 120 DASAN CALL CENTER OFFERING SNS SERVICES

| 120 Dasan Call Center offering the SNS Service

| Celebrating the 40-millionth call at the 120 Dasan Call Center

Source: http://www.epeople.go.kr/jsp/user/on/eng/intro01.jsp

120 Dasan Call Center Offering SNS Services

The information provided by the call center ranges from traffic, transportation and public utility issues, including subway breakdowns, power outages, water supply disruptions, traffic advice on heavy snowfall or rain, and the extended operation of public transport, to the great variety of events taking place in Seoul.

(continued)

(continued)

Citizens have so far shown a very positive response to the service, stating that it is faster and more up-to-date than any other news or information media. This resounding success has been made possible by feeding the latest data required for the provision of an up-to-the-minute information service directly into the center on a real-time basis.

In the meantime, the Dasan Call Center received its 40 millionth telephone inquiry on April 18, some five years and three months after the service was launched in January 2007.

- The individual who made that historic call at 15:30 on April 16 was inquiring about a fee charged for late payment of a water bill, which she thought was unjustified. She said, "I am very satisfied with the 120 Center service. The service was quick and accurate, and the representative was very kind."
- The 120 Dasan Call Center is staffed with 524 service representatives (as of March 2012) who provide 24-hour call services using information supplied from more than 25,000 databases. The number of telephone calls to the center has increased sharply, rising from 1,184 a day immediately following the center's launch to 38,000 a day at present, representing a 32-fold increase. The level of satisfaction with the city government's call service has also improved significantly, rising from a score of 41.6 before the establishment of Dasan Call Center to over 95 out of 100 at present.

Source: http://english. seoul.go.kr/gtk/news/news_view.php?idx=18043

KEY TERMS

311 call centers
Broadband
Customer Relationship Management (CRM)
Digital democracy
Digital divide
Dynamic citizen deliberation
Dynamic information dissemination
E-government
Geospatial Information Systems
Information and communications technologies (ICTs)
Static citizen deliberation
Static information dissemination

REFERENCES

American National Election Studies (ANES). 2010. "Trust the Federal Government, 1958–2008." In *The ANES Guide to Public Opinion and Electoral Behavior*. Ann Arbor, MI: University of Michigan, Center for Political Studies. http://www.electionstudies.org/nesguide/toptable/tab5a_1.htm.

Berman, Evan M. 1997. "Dealing with Cynical Citizens," *Public Administration Review*, 57, no. 2 (March–April): 105–12.

Calista, Donald, and James Melitski. 2007. "E-Government and E-Governance: Converging Constructs of Public Sector Information and Communications Technologies." *Public Administration Quarterly* 32, no. 1.

Citizen Summit III: Real Challenges Real Choices. 2004. Executive Summary and Data Analysis Prepared by the Executive Office of Neighborhood Action.

City of Hampton, Virginia. 2006. Information and Data on Hampton's 311 Call Center Provided by Elizabeth Nisley, Call Center Manager, and Through the Call Center's Website, http://www.hampton.gov/311/.

City of Oakland. (2002). "Moving Oakland Forward." City Manager Summit Recommendations. http://www.oaklandnet.com/movingforward/8CRecommendationsDetailed.pdf.

Cloete, Fanie. 2003. "Assessing Governance with Electronic Policy Management Tools." *Public Performance and Management Review* 26, no. 3: 276–90.

Dixon, C. 2009. *INPUT State & Local IT Market Forecast, 2009-2014*. Input, Inc. June 2009. http://www.input.com/corp/analysis/state_IT_spending.cfm.

Environmental Systems Research Institute, Inc. (ESRI). "What is GIS? Geographic Information Systems." http://www.esri.com/what-is-gis/index.html.

Environmental Systems Research Institute, Inc. (ESRI). 2002. "Lessons Learned from 9/11.Good Metadata is Key." www.esri.com/library/fliers/pdfs/lessons-learned.pdf.

Federal Trade Commission (FTC). 2007. "Consumer Fraud and Identity Theft Complaint Data." http://www.ftc.gov/opa/2008/02/fraud.pdf.

Forman, Mark. 2003. "Statement of Mark Forman, Associate Director for Information Technology and E-Government, Office of Management and Budget, Before the Subcommittee on Technology and Procurement Policy of the Committee on Government Reform." March 21. http://www.whitehouse.gov/omb/legislative_testimony_default_prior2009.

———. 2003. "Statement of Mark Forman, Associate Director for E-Government and Information Technology, Office of Management and Budget, Before the Subcommittee on Technology, Information Policy, Intergovernmental Relations, and the Census. Committee on Government Reform. United States House of Representatives." March 13. http://www.whitehouse.gov/omb/legislative_testimony_forman031303/.

Hacker, Kenneth L., and Jan van Dijk. 2000. "What Is Digital Democracy?" In *Digital Democracy: Issues of Theory and Practice,* ed. Kenneth L. Hacker and Jan van Dijk, 1–9. Thousand Oaks, CA: Sage Publications.

Holzer, Marc, and Seang-Tae Kim. 2005. *Digital Governance in Municipalities Worldwide: A Longitudinal Assessment of Municipal Websites Throughout the World.* Newark, NJ: National Center for Public Productivity.

Hu, W. 2003. "New Yorkers Love to Complain, and Hotline Is Making the Most of It." *New York Times,* December 1.

Jankowski, Nicholas W., and Martine van Selm. 2000. "The Promise and Practice of Public Debate in Cyberspace." In *Digital Democracy: Issues of Theory and Practice,* ed. Kenneth L. Hacker and Jan van Dijk, 149–65. Thousand Oaks, CA: Sage Publications.

Lipowicz, A. 2010. "State, Local Agencies Will Increase IT Spending Through 2015." *Washington Technology.* September 2, 2010. http://washingtontechnology.com/articles/2010/09/02/state-and-local-agencies-forecasted-for-increase-in-it-spending.aspx.

Lukensmeyer, C.J., and S. Brigham. 2002. "Taking Democracy to Scale: Creating a Town Hall Meeting for the Twenty-first Century." *National Civic Review* 91, no. 4: 351–66.

Martin, W. Eric. 2004. "Point of Contact." *Government Technology*, May 12. www.public-cio.com/story.print.php?id=90220.

Mazerolle, L., D. Rogan, J. Frank, C. Famega, and J.E. Eck. 2003. "Managing Citizen Calls to the Police: An Assessment of Non-Emergency Call Systems." Research Report Submitted to the U.S. Department of Justice, National Institute of Justice, October. www.ncjrs.gov/pdffiles1/nij/grants/199060.pdf.

National Center for Public Performance. E-Governance Institute. 2007. "Developing a Statewide 311 System in New Jersey. A Feasibility Study." School of Public Affairs and Administration, Rutgers University, Newark. www.911dispatch.com/reference/nj_statewide_311.pdf.

Nugent, John D. 2001. "If E-Democracy Is the Answer, What's the Question?" *National Civic Review* 90, no. 3: 221–23.

O'Looney, John A. 2002. *Wiring Governments: Challenges and Possibilities for Public Managers.* Westport, CT: Quorum Books.

Shark, Alan. 2008. "Reconnecting America: The Role of Government With Technology and Policy at the Crossroads." In *Beyond e-Government and e-Democracy: A Global Perspective*, ed. Shark, Alan and Sylvianne Toporkoff. 1–10. Charleston, SC: Public Technology Institute and ITEMS International, Booksurge Llc.

Skrzycki, Cindy. 2003. "U.S. Opens Online Portal to Rulemaking; Web Site Invites Wider Participation in the Regulatory Process." *Washington Post*, January 23, E01.

Solomon, S.E., and C.D. Uchida. 2003. "Building a 311 System for Police Non-Emergency Calls: A Process and Impact Evaluation." Report. 21st Century Solutions, Inc., and the U.S. Department of Justice, September. www.cops.usdoj.gov/files/ric/Publications/buildinga311systemaustinevaluation.pdf.

The White House. "OMB Leadership Bios." http://www.whitehouse.gov/omb/organization_office.

Tsagarousianou, Roza, Damian Tambini, and Cathy Bryan. 1998. *Cyberdemocracy: Technology, Cities, and Civic Networks.* London, UK: Routledge.

Uchimura, Y. 2002. "The Citizen Summit: Integrating Technology and Democracy in the Nation's Capitol." *The Public Manager* 21, no. 2.

U.S. Air Force. 2010. "Learn About the Air Force." http://www.airforce.com/learn-about/our-mission/.

U.S. Department of Justice. 2006. "COPS Fact Sheet: 311 for Non-Emergencies." Washington, DC: Office of Community Oriented Policing Services. www.cops.usdoj.gov/files/ric/Publications/e01060007.pdf.

SUPPLEMENTARY READINGS

Carrizales, Tony, Marc Holzer, Seang-Tae Kim, and Chan-Gon Kim. 2006. "Digital Governance Worldwide: A Longitudinal Assessment of Municipal Websites." *International Journal of Electronic Government Research* 2, no. 4.

Mayer-Schönberger, Viktor, and David Lazer, eds. 2007. *Governance and Information Technology*. Cambridge, MA: MIT Press.

Moon, M.J. 2002. "The Evolution of E-government Among Municipalities: Rhetoric or Reality?" *Public Administration Review* 62, no. 4: 424–33.

Norris, P. 2001. *Digital Divide: Civic Engagement, Information Poverty, and the Internet Worldwide*. Cambridge, UK: Cambridge University Press.

Scott, James K. 2006. "'E' the People: Do U.S. Municipal Government Web Sites Support Public Involvement?" *Public Administration Review* 66, no. 3: 341–53.

ELECTRONIC RESOURCES

America*Speaks*—Engaging Citizens in Governance: a nonpartisan organization based in Washington, DC, http://www.americaspeaks.org/

Digital Divide Institute—Social Justice Through Digital Convergence, http://www.digitaldivide.org

ECommerce-Guide, http://www.ecommerce-guide.com/

E-Gov Link—e-government solutions for local governments, http://www2.egov-link.com/

Federal Chief Information Officers (CIO) Council, http://www.cio.gov

GovTech—Government Technology, http://govtech.com

Net Valley—provider of Internet history, http://www.netvalley.com

Pew Internet and American Life Project—A Project of the Pew Research Center, http://www.pewinternet.org/

Public Technology Institute, http://www.pti.org

Regulations.gov—Your Voice in Federal Decision Making, http://www.regulations.gov

CHAPTER 13

Public Service and Popular Culture

Chapter 13 examines the people who work for the public—public servants. Although they are often depicted as inefficient members of an inefficient bureaucracy, this chapter demonstrates the value and effectiveness of public servants. It provides examples of public servants in action in both the government and nonprofit sectors. Furthermore, it describes the mechanisms that government uses to help engage more citizens in public service and the various modes by which public information is conveyed to the citizenry. Finally, this chapter provides helpful resources for people interested in engaging with government and professional networks that address issues of public concern.

"Service is the rent we pay to be living.
It is the very purpose of life and not
something you do in your spare time."

MARIAN WRIGHT EDELMAN
Attorney; Activist;
Founder, *Children's Defense Fund*

Franklin Delano Roosevelt Memorial, Washington, DC.

PUBLIC SERVANTS

Public service embodies the ethical principles of the common good—service to others and social equity. Public service is important because the essential purposes of our society are carried out largely in the public sphere: public education, public health, justice and security, environmental protection, museums, universities, etc. Many organizations—profit and nonprofit—are government's partners in building our necessary infrastructure, as well as developing and applying our emerging technologies. A strong public service ethic is, then, a common thread that spans a wide spectrum of disciplines and sectors, ranging from government to the not-for-profit and for-profit sectors.

Public service attracts a special kind of individual (Holzer 1999; Pattakos 2004; Perry 1996). The calling to public service is at the heart of public administration (Frederickson 1997) and is based on a "duty . . . or an intense inner commitment to a cause that extends beyond the exigencies of the moment" (Gawthrop 1998, p. 74). Public servants are people who achieve internal satisfaction by making a contribution to a society (Houston 2006; Perry 1996) as opposed to a self-serving commitment to achieving personal goals. As such, monetary gain and other external rewards are often not primarily significant; instead, those who enter public service do so out of a desire to serve the public interest (Hart 1989). Theirs is a vocation that links them to "fellow workers and the larger community," thereby making public service a transcendent act (Wolf and Bacher 1990, p. 178).

> "I can assure you, public service is a stimulating, proud and lively enterprise. It is not just a way of life, it is a way to live fully."
>
> **LEE H. HAMILTON**
> Former U.S. Congressman; Vice Chairman, 9/11 Commission

The roots of public service can be traced back to the Athenian Oath, first sworn by citizens of ancient Athens to serve their fellow citizens. In an American context, James Madison expressed this sentiment in *The Federalist Papers:* "The public good, the real welfare of the great body of the people, is the supreme object to be pursued" (Madison 1788/1961, "Federalist #45"). The root of the common good stems from an acknowledged interconnectedness of individuals who rely on one another, providing the basis of community (Frederickson 1997; Gawthrop 1998; Hart 1989).

In the mid-nineteenth century, the French historian Alexis de Tocqueville was fascinated with the strong American cooperative spirit between the citizenry and the government. He wrote in *Democracy in America* (cited in Klein 1990):

> In no country in the world do the citizens make such exertions for the common weal. I know of no people who have established schools so numerous, places of public worship better suited to the wants of the inhabitants, or roads kept in better repair.

Tocqueville was equally impressed with the willingness of citizens to build public improvements by voluntary association, "of the people, by the people, for the people" (cited in Ellis 1999).

As the embodiment of an ethic of service, increased volunteerism has been a goal of public policy since at least the 1960s, regardless of the political party in power (Brudney 1990). Most famously, President John F. Kennedy, at his inauguration in 1961, stated, "Ask not what your country can do for you—ask what you can do for your country" (cited in Ellis 1999).

In this chapter, we explore the idea of public service and the public servant. We discuss some of the common generalizations about public servants' work ethics and their images within society as portrayed in popular culture. We also shed light on

The Athenian Oath

We will never bring disgrace to this our city, by any act of dishonesty or cowardice; nor ever desert our suffering comrades in the ranks; we will fight for the ideal and sacred things of the city, both alone and with many; we will revere and obey the city's laws and do our best to incite a like respect in those above us who are prone to annul or set them at naught; we will strive unceasingly to quicken the public's sense of civic duty. Thus, in all these ways, we will transmit this city not only, not less, but greater and more beautiful than it was transmitted to us.

some actual public servants by exploring a few noteworthy cases. We discuss efforts to attract youth into the public sector and highlight some of the current incentive programs that exist, as well as efforts to rectify the image of public service and initiatives that might be pursued to do so. Finally, we provide some practical information about public service networks and ways in which people might connect.

The Image of the Public Servant

Critics argue that bureaucracy is epitomized by the sufficiency of mediocrity, by the adage "don't rock the boat," and by a significant loss of independence. Popular culture has reinforced the contrast between the new public employee's wide-eyed eagerness to serve—to make a difference—versus the well-entrenched bureaucrat who stereotypically overemphasizes formality, rules, and regulations. Popular culture has also painted a proverbial picture of the public organization where individuals become stifled, losing all sense of independence, pride, and initiative. They seem to no longer care, only to go through the motions, only to count down the years until retirement.

Government's critics are equally concerned that the energies of workers and managers may be corrupted, not merely suppressed. Without the possibility of making a real difference or the incentive to solve problems of productivity and performance, they direct their energies toward personal promotion, playing office politics, discrediting fellow employees, and diverting resources. In W.S. Gilbert and Arthur Sullivan's comedic opera *H.M.S. Pinafore* (1878), musical lyrics imprinted negative bureaucratic images on the public consciousness. That message is embodied in the protagonist Sir Joseph Porter's observation that he rose through a hierarchy from office boy to the post of First Lord of the Admiralty by merely "going along." He explains that he identified so entirely and predictably with the Navy's interests—regardless of whether truth or logic contradicted such interests—that he ended up in a position of command: "Stick close to your desks and never go to sea, and you all may be Rulers of the Queen's Navee."

Bureaucratic behavior is not harmless. Critics also argue that the unproductive forces of bureaucracy ultimately have a negative impact on the client. In many cases, bureaucracy has degenerated into a vehicle that is too impersonal and too insensitive for effective response to public demands. The clerk who interprets a rule with unnecessary narrowness and the official who mindlessly defers to the computer are examples of the unproductive nature of bureaucratic thinking. They are the symptoms of a mindset that creates more problems than it solves. Beginning with the earliest readers, the cartoonist's assault on bureaucracy has been incessant and overwhelming. Nationally syndicated cartoons reinforce a negative image of public service throughout the daily papers.

In some instances, government's clients are not merely inconvenienced or discouraged. Some of the most depressing anti-client tales are those of the Austrian existentialist Franz Kafka, as in *The Trial,* which he wrote between 1914 and 1915 (publ. 1925). Perhaps the most recognized critic of bureaucracy, even to the extent of the generally accepted adjective "Kafkaesque," Kafka suggests that the impersonal often shades into the unjust.

Movies serve as a more powerful vehicle than the stage, if only because the audience is much wider. For example, in the 1984 Ivan Reitman film *Ghostbusters,* which underscored the popular image of "bureaucrat as buffoon," an official of the Environmental Protection Administration (EPA) obnoxiously demands to inspect a storage facility for ghostly spirits. Turned away by ghostbuster Dr. Peter Venkman (played by Bill Murray) because he did not use the magic word "please," the EPA official returns with a court order. After being told that closing the ghost-holding office would allow the spirits to run amok, surely endangering the public, the EPA official blindly opts to follow rules and regulations, ordering the facility to be shut down. Even as his actions lead almost to disaster, the agitated bureaucrat still clings to the letter of the law. He is finally removed by the mayor, who opts for live, grateful voters over mindless procedures. The message is that bureaucrats can be unthinkingly and dangerously incompetent.

> "It is a grand mistake to think of being great without goodness and I pronounce it as certain that there was never a truly great man that was not at the same time truly virtuous."
>
> **BENJAMIN FRANKLIN**
> American Statesman; Ambassador; Patriot

The classroom, in particular, is often portrayed as suffering from the bumbling actions of educational bureaucrats. In the 1988 biopic *Stand and Deliver,* Jaime Escalante, a dedicated math teacher in an inner-city high school, overcomes the skepticism of burned-out colleagues and the harassment of the disbelieving, bureaucratic Educational Testing Service. Fortunately, he prevails and his students succeed, but only due to his David-like efforts versus the bureaucratic Goliath.

The image of civil servants also suffers from guilt by association, from confusion with the misdeeds of political superiors. Although the public service in the United States is among the most honest in the world, the reputation of appointed civil servants has been diminished by the ineptitude and inefficiency of those elected to serve. The press features charges of misconduct under headlines such as "Local Official Indicted" or "Public Servant Accused." But the official in question often may have been an elected or appointed politician, not a civil servant. Such simple headlines taint the entire public service by association with their sometimes unethical political taskmasters.

A reinforcing problem is misapplication of the term "bureaucracy." In Boston, Massachusetts, for example, *The Globe* reported that "A Simple Park Is No Match for

City Bureaucracy." Although years of delays in building a park were apparently blamed on the bureaucracy—implying career officials were negligent—a more careful reading reveals that an elected official, city councilor David Scondras, was the source of the delay. From Washington, D.C., a story headlined "Bush Transforms an Emergency into a Bureaucracy" deals not with an agency action but an environmental policy decision emanating from the White House. Another Washington report, "How Bureaucrats Pad Their Pensions" focuses not on civil servants but on pension laws passed by U.S. Congress that served their own interests. And "Bureaucracy Stifles Biotechnology" argues that a major public organization was understaffed and underequipped, but it is not until well into the story that the reader sees the source of the problems are attributable not to bureaucratic negligence but to budget-cutting priorities in the White House and in Congress.

Thus, as the media dutifully chronicle charges of misconduct against elected officials and politicians, they also unintentionally taint the character of career civil servants. Broad labels suggest that all individuals who publicly aspire to the calling of public service secretly aspire to private gain. The average reader is not likely to differentiate between elected and appointed public officials. Because corruption anywhere in government tarnishes the image of everyone in government, the reputation of civil servants is diminished by misidentification with less-than-ethical politicians, and public servants take a beating throughout the media. Seemingly without exception, artists and writers confirm a pessimistic view of bureaucracy's impact on its clients and even its own employees. Our society has established a mistaken image of public servants as untrustworthy, inept, entangled in red tape, and incapable of applying the common sense possessed by the average American citizen. The popular view of the public bureaucracy is a weak system that produces profoundly negative behaviors—stifling, demoralizing, corrupting, impersonal, and unjust. Some of those complaints are valid and deserve attention. Government needs to be improved—as does every organization. One obstacle to improvement, however, is the ceaseless and unbalanced nature of the attack on public organizations. Journalists, writers, and artists have overworked and exploited that image. It would be naive to criticize the government's critics for failing to seek evidence of excellent public-sector performance, but that evidence is extensive and available.

The Real Public Servant

The negative image of the public servant is likely to remain dominant, as it has such deep roots in our popular culture. Nevertheless, the truth about public servants is far from this negative depiction. Certainly, like any other field, public service has some employees that lack the appropriate motivations and skill sets, but many public servants are dedicated, innovative professionals dealing with a unique set of challenges and working in about 87,000 units of local government that deliver necessary and critical services.

> For Census Bureau statistical purposes, a government is defined as an organized entity subject to public accountability, whose officials are popularly elected or are appointed by public officials, and which has sufficient discretion in the management of its affairs to distinguish it as separate from the administrative structure of any other government unit. The Census Bureau recognizes five basic types of local governments—counties, municipalities, townships, school districts, and special districts (U.S. Census Bureau 2002).

The federal government represents only one unit of government, and the states another fifty. Some 35,000 of units of government are on the local level—such as municipalities or townships. School districts, business districts, fire districts, water districts, and many other special purpose organizations comprise another 50,000+

A worker at the National Cancer Institute (NCI), which is part of the National Institutes of Health (NIH), one of 11 agencies that compose the Department of Health and Human Services (HHS).

City Manager Ed Everett Receives Top Annual Honor from International City/County Management Association "Award for Career Excellence"

Redwood City, CA—June 19, 2007—The International City/County Management Association (ICMA) has awarded its most-prestigious annual award, the Award for Career Excellence, to Ed Everett, City Manager of Redwood City. Each year, this much sought-after award recognizes individual professional achievement by "an outstanding chief local government administrator who has fostered representative democracy by enhancing the effectiveness of local elected officials, and by consistently initiating creative and successful programs." The award will be formally presented to Mr. Everett at ICMA's annual conference in October. Mr. Everett informed the City Council recently that he will be retiring in September of this year.

Among the elements that led to Mr. Everett being awarded this prominent honor is his remarkable 34 years in public service and 15 years as Redwood City's manager, earmarked by innovation, integrity, and inspiration. His innovation in the many internal and external programs and projects he's led to success in Redwood City; his integrity in making the right decisions, not necessarily the easy decisions, in empowering others at all levels of the organization to make decisions, and in informing, guiding, debating, and supporting the members of the city council in their decision-making; and his inspiration, which has infected the City staff and elected officials, as well as an expanding portion of the community—all traits of a true leader who actively promotes a culture of achievement, productivity, and fulfillment.

Mr. Everett has dedicated his career to going beyond the standard of working toward "just" a well-managed city government; instead, he has set the standard for new heights of community involvement and engagement, and inspired a genuine dedication in staff and in elected officials. Mr. Everett's efforts extend beyond the City's borders to other cities and organizations, where he is a recognized leader in the concepts of Community Building.

During his tenure as City Manager, a number of ground-breaking Community Building programs were developed and have matured into respected, valued, and sought-after elements contributing to our community's quality of life; other cities have used this model to provide similar programs—Partnership Academy for Community Teamwork, Community Builders speakers series, Neighborhood Liaison and Community Task Forces, and more.

ICMA (www.icma.org) is the professional and educational organization for chief appointed managers, administrators, and assistants in cities, towns, counties, and regional entities throughout the world. Since 1914, ICMA has provided technical and management assistance, training, and information resources to its members and the local government community. The management decisions made by ICMA's nearly 8,000 members affect more than 100 million individuals in thousands of communities--from small towns with populations of a few hundred to metropolitan areas serving several million.

Source: Redwood City, California. 2007b. "City Manager Ed Everett Receives Top Annual Honor from International City/County Management Association – 'Award for Career Excellence.'" Redwood City, CA, June 19. http://www.redwoodcity.org/manager/news/2007/pr_mgr_icma.html.

government units. In total, these local governmental units employ about 14 million public servants. Therefore, the local level of government is a likely starting point to highlight some of the real efforts taken by public servants to quash the familiar stereotypical depictions.

Comparable innovations are evident at the county level of government, which, according to the National Association of Counties, includes more than 3,000 American counties.

States hold a unique position within the United States. They serve as conduits between the federal government and the local governments. With their special set of distinctive powers and responsibilities, the 50 states channel substantial federal funding to counties, municipalities, and school districts. In total, states employ more than 5 million public servants.

Typecast bureaucrats would have had no interest in innovating and saving the state large sums. But directors such as Kevin Concannon and Jeff Vonk proved otherwise:

> The Department of Human Services implemented the Preferred Drug List for Medicaid and saved the state $1.7 million in 2005. They also increased the number of children with health insurance by 33 percent. . . .
>
> The Department of Natural Resources reduced the amount of time it takes to obtain air quality, wastewater construction, and landfill permits without sacrificing any environmental standards or quality. . . .
>
> The Department of Revenue increased the number of income tax returns filed electronically from 55 percent to 67 percent. They also improved the number of income tax refunds issued within 45 days from 75 percent to 94 percent (Democratic Leadership Council 2008).

2008 Strategic Leadership and Governance Program Excellence Award: The Case of Polk County

In 2003, a new administration came to Polk County. Among the several strategic initiatives it identified as critical to the organization's success, one initiative—a renewed commitment to excellence in customer service, both internal and external—identified three challenges:

- Develop a high-performing workforce that delivers top-quality customer service
- Engender a commitment to excellence within that workforce
- Foster a culture that recognizes that achieving these objectives is the key to organizational excellence.

Believing that the only way to successfully attain these goals is to invest in the organization's most valuable resource, its employees, County Manager Herr created an entirely new division, Organization and Employee Development (OED). OED's mission is to achieve organizational excellence through the engagement, development, and recognition of employees, and to stimulate a culture shift that values employees as critical to organizational success. To support its mission, OED developed and implemented the following programs:

Employee Development Program

Developed from an organization-wide needs assessment, this program offers over 110 classroom sessions within four certificate concentration programs of study (communications skills, professional development, customer services provider, and supervisory skills) all directly related to the organization's strategic objectives. The courses are taught by both in-house talent and outsourced subject experts. Since the program began, course offerings have increased significantly, with subject matter chosen in response to employee feedback. To date, more than 1,300 employees have participated in the program, and almost 150 certificates have been awarded to those who have completed a program of study.

New Employee Orientation (NEO)

NEO is a two-day program that presents an overview of the county's mission, vision, values, services, strategic objectives, and diversity goals, followed by a half-day course devoted to customer service. An "Information Fair" allows new employees to meet and question various benefit and service providers one-on-one. The program also provides worksite orientation to help employees transition into their new work life. An orientation coordinator is designated for each work division, and each new hire is assigned to a sponsor within his or her work group for a two-week period. The success of the NEO is evident in employee response: nearly 100 percent of employees reported that they felt welcomed to the organization, 97 percent believed that they had made a positive career choice, and after 90 days, 92 percent felt that the orientation had helped them assimilate into their new workplace. NEO won the National Association of Counties Award for Excellence in 2007.

Emerging Leaders Program (ELP)

ELP has three goals: to identify top performers in the organization, to develop and prepare them for leadership roles, and to enable them to qualify for consideration in upcoming supervisory/management vacancies. After top-performing nonsupervisory employees are identified through a competitive application process, a select group is given the chance to develop their leadership capabilities and skills by participating in a high-visibility personal and professional development program. Participants are provided with opportunities for organization-wide exposure through a communications package that showcases their talents and abilities.

Succession Planning Program

Anticipating the possible retirement of up to 37 percent of senior leaders by 2011, this program identifies potential candidates for positions considered critical to organizational success, and ensures that they all have targeted, individual development plans to prepare them for candidacy. This program is the first formal process initiated that aligns strategic career development with future organizational leadership needs.

SHINE Employee Suggestion Program

The SHINE (Suggestions Help Increase & Nurture Excellence) program recognizes that employees represent an unlimited source of ingenuity in developing ideas to reduce costs and improve processes. Adopted ideas can earn the suggester anywhere from $25 to $3,000. SHINE has become a part of the county's work culture, encouraging employee involvement and fostering employee recognition. Since its inception, SHINE has generated almost 1,800 suggestions and saved more than $6 million through improved county operations and services. The program has been recognized by the Employee Involvement Association, and has received awards for excellence in the performance of an employee suggestion program, for savings per 100 eligible employees in an employee suggestion program, and for an evaluator's exceptional performance in evaluating suggestions and promoting employee involvement.

(continued)

(continued)

REACHIS/Kudos Program

For the first time, employees were given the responsibility for selecting the organizational mission, vision, and values. After more than 60 managers and directors joined together to develop the mission statement ("We enhance the quality of life for people throughout Polk County"); vision statement ("Polk County, where people excel"); and values (Results-oriented, Excellence, Accountability, Collaboration, Honesty, Integrity, Stewardship—REACHIS), a campaign was launched to convey the message to the entire organization of over 2,200 employees. Employees received a REACHIS wallet card with the mission and values defined. A team of OED specialists then visited every work unit, explaining the purpose and meaning of the information, and County Manager Herr followed up, visiting and speaking personally with every group to reinforce the concepts. This highly popular and versatile recognition tool has been incorporated into the award and celebration programs of the various work groups, divisions, and departments.

Employee Survey

An organization-wide employee satisfaction survey was designed as a tool for open communication. For the first time, employees had the opportunity to voice their feelings and to analyze the results of their opinions. Each survey question was tied to an organizational value, and responses were used to identify strengths and weaknesses of each division based on employee opinion. Results were shared with employees, and discussion of problem areas provided the basis for developing strategies for improvement.

Better, Faster, Cheaper

An organization-wide initiative used employee teams to identify and develop process improvement strategies for targeted service areas, such as health care claims processing, e-payment options, capital improvement projects, board agenda, and hiring/on-boarding processes. Participation in the program developed leadership skills, such as active listening, critical thinking, facilitation, team building, and process improvement methodologies. In an organization proud of its history, conservative in its spending, and cautious in its decisions, the creation of a new kind of division was a major departure for the executive team. County Manager Herr knew that to achieve the goals defined by strategic objectives and achieve a high level of performance throughout the organization, employees would have to become a focus for development. To that end, the OED division was placed under the Financial and Strategic Planning Department—an indication that OED programs would have a global effect on the organization and would tie directly to organizational strategies. At first this small but dedicated team spent a lot of time establishing an identity for the division, whose initial project was a training needs assessment. For the first time, employees were given choices about the skills they wanted to master and the developmental goals they wanted to pursue to improve their performance. Giving employees a real voice in the process established a precedent for OED programs, and sent a powerful message to the entire organization: employees are the focus and employee development is a priority. Over time, the professional diligence that creates a consistent level of quality began to permeate the minds of both management and employees. OED began to establish an identity as a resource for innovation and problem solving. Its hard-won reputation for excellence was borne out by the high level of quality that its programs and staff members exhibited. OED has made incredible strides in changing the way employees think about themselves, their future, and their workplace. The work that lies ahead for this division remains a challenge, but the foundation of quality and dedication to excellence will serve OED well as it continues to grow and strive toward organizational greatness, one employee at a time.

Source: International City/County Management Association (ICMA). 2008. "Strategic Leadership and Governance. Populations of 50,000 and Greater. Polk County, Florida." Alliance for Innovation Case Studies. http://transformgov.org/Documents/Document/Document/5824.

The charter agencies exceeded their original goals by at least 50 percent and saved the state about $22 million (Public Strategies Group 2009).

Although Iowa's charter agencies are just one set of examples of responsible government—and were recognized with Harvard University's Kennedy School of Government Innovation Award in 2005—thousands of parallels are operating in governments across the country.

The nonprofit sector is another often invisible part of the public service delivery system. Nonprofits fill a special role our society. They are not considered formal government entities but often receive government funding and deliver government services. They are not part of the market economy but often provide services similar to their for-profit counterparts. Many citizens view nonprofit organizations as the threads that hold our society together. They are mission-driven organizations, which means their main motivation is not to increase profit but to achieve their service goals. They serve thousands of communities in areas ranging from the arts to education, from health care to social services, from museums to orphanages, and they provide assistance at the local, state, national, and international levels.

According to the Urban Institute, there are approximately 1.4 million nonprofit organizations in the United States (Urban Institute 2010). And according to the Foun-

The Case of Iowa

If the typical depiction of government is that of a static system—an unchanging bureaucracy that is not willing or likely to change—then Iowa has challenged this misconception, and its public servants have won that challenge. In 2003 the Iowa State Assembly passed into law a statute permitting six charter agencies: "These agencies have agreed to be held accountable to produce better, measurable results for Iowans through the services they provide, and they have either cut spending or will generate new revenue as part of their agreements. In exchange, the Charter Agencies exercise greater flexibility in such administrative matters as agency personnel, procurement, and information technology decision-making. These agencies will identify new, more efficient and innovative ways to achieve results" (State of Iowa 2004, p. 3).

Finding agencies that were willing to participate in the charter agency initiative was not an easy task. J. Chrisinger and B. Armajani (2008) note that "many directors and staff remained skeptical. Many did not want to gamble on the new deal because they were unsure it was 'real.' Some felt they could not justify the fiscal obligation. Others had not made the transformation into a results-based organization a priority. But six directors who were running into roadblocks on the road to results saw enough potential to literally pay for charter status with budget cuts or new revenue contributions from their agencies." These directors headed up the following agencies: Alcoholic Beverages Division of the Department of Commerce; Department of Corrections; Department of Human Services; Department of Natural Resources; Department of Revenue; and the Iowa Veterans Home.

Jeff Vonk was the director of Iowa's Department of Natural Resources (DNR). He had been a public servant for over 30 years, working for the Natural Resources Conservation Service and the Department of Agriculture. Vonk believed that a charter agency would give him an opportunity to turn the DNR into a "world class" organization.

Kevin Concannon, director of the Iowa Department of Human Services, believes that the charter status has allowed his agency to achieve its goals and exceed expectations. Additionally, the greater flexibility has given the agency more control over its staffing (Chrisinger 2007). Concannon knew a good opportunity when he saw one in the field of health and human services. Since 1980, he has served in four different posts as a health-related government administrator. Prior to becoming the director of the Iowa Department of Human Services in 2003, he served as the commissioner of Maine's Department of Human Services from 1995 to 2003, the director of Oregon's Department of Human Services from 1987 to 1995, and the Commissioner of the Maine Department of Mental Health and Mental Retardation from 1980 to 1987 (U.S. Department of Agriculture 2009).

dation Center, about 12.5 million people were employed by nonprofit organizations in 2001 (Foundation Center 2010). They work with millions of others who volunteer with those organizations. Nearly 100 million Americans volunteer each year to assist public, nonprofit, and informal organizations. In 2009 the Corporation for National and Community Service reported that in 2008 about 61.8 million Americans volunteered their time to organizations. According to the corporation, they gave, "8.1 billion hours of service worth approximately $162 billion to America's communities." This figure remained relatively steady during the economic downturn in comparison with the previous year (Corporation for National and Community Service 2009).

According to the Federal Bureau of Justice, about 67 percent of U.S. prisoners who are released are rearrested within three years (Carnegie Mellon University 2009). Support services that work to prevent prisoner reincarceration typically are operated by nonprofits organizations such as Family Justice and its La Bodega de la Familia/The Partner Project.

Many public services are delivered by private organizations (both for-profit and not-for-profit). In 2007 the federal government spent about $450 billion on contracts. Those service delivery arrangements utilized about 189,000 contracting organizations. Paul Light, a scholar at the Brookings Institution and professor at New York University's Robert F. Wagner School of Public Service, estimated that the total number of federal contractor employees working with the government was around 7.63 million in 2005 (Lee 2006). If one includes those employed under federal grants, the number of employees supporting federal programs but not directly on the payroll increases to over 10 million (Lee 2006). It is challenging to estimate these numbers on the state and local level, primarily because consistent data is not available; however, it is safe to assume that the state and local contracting workforce is at least as great as that of the federal government.

In addition to contracted companies, government also disburses a large amount of funding through grants. The federal government defines a grant as "an award of financial assistance from a federal agency to a recipient to carry out a public purpose of support or stimulation authorized by a law of the United States" (Grants.gov 2009). In 2008 the federal government expended about $500 billion in grants. Funding went to states, which then distributed the money to localities and private companies to serve a public purpose. Medical assistance programs received the greatest portion of this funding, at about $175 billion. Grants provide states and localities with the opportunities to develop highly successful programs that other governments might emulate (Executive Office of the President of the United States 2009; USA Government Grants 2010).

Community Care of North Carolina (CCNC) is a "public-private partnership between the State of North Carolina and 14 not-for-profit networks that are comprised

A Conversation with Cas Holloway, Commissioner, New York City Department of Environmental Protection

As we continue to engage government executives who are changing the way government does business, we had the pleasure of taking The Business of Government Hour on the road to a variety of U.S. cities. New York City, perhaps more than any other, represents a complex ecosystem that requires and consumes a vast array of natural resources. Protecting such resources and the environmental health and welfare of its residents is essential for the City—for all cities to exist and thrive. We spoke with Cas Holloway, commissioner of the NYC Department of Environmental Protection (DEP), about his efforts in this area that includes an overview of the City's water system, how the City ensures its water system is viable for the next 100 years, innovative ways of managing a major capital construction portfolio, NYC's sustainability efforts, and protection of its watersheds.

On New York City's Sustainability Agenda and PlaNYC

Mayor Bloomberg probably has the most ambitious urban environmental agenda in the country, if not the world— PlaNYC. It sets 127 goals for 2030, which range from reducing the city's greenhouse gas emissions by 30 percent to opening up 90 percent of the city's waterways to recreation. In order to do that, you have to have high water quality. In order to have high water quality, you have to meet treatment standards, while always looking to do better either through technology or operating efficiency. DEP has a central role in PlaNYC. One of the first things I did when I became commissioner was to create a new position, the deputy commissioner for sustainability. Our deputy commissioner, Carter Strickland, is looking at how we can bring in a more aggressive, green infrastructure approach. The basic idea is, how do we capture storm water from the buildings or the streets, and can we do it with infrastructure that also has ancillary public benefit? DEP is ahead of the curve on sustainable methods of dealing with things like storm water. This is a really exciting area. It's going to take open-mindedness on the part of our regulators for us to be successful, but we think we can capture more storm water, and do a better job overall.

Source: IBM Center for The Business of Government. 2010. "Conversations with Leaders. A Conversation with Cas Holloway, Commissioner, New York City Department of Environmental Protection." The Business of Government. Fall/Winter 2010, pp. 23-27. www.businessofgovernment.org.

of the majority of local healthcare providers; primary care physicians, hospitals, health departments, social service agencies and safety net organizations" (Dobson 2009). The program receives most of its funding from Medicaid dollars distributed among the various partners in the network and provides a strong network for Medicaid patients. As of 2010, about a million of the 1.4 million North Carolinians receiving Medicaid are enrolled in CCNC (North Carolina Division of Medical Assistance 2010). North Carolina has also taken steps to include individuals with disabilities and those who are enrolled in the state's Children Health Insurance Program (SCHIP).

CCNC is a networked model. This means that the state has organized a number of responsible parties to assist in providing services to patients in need. Each of its 14 networks "employs a full-time program director, a part-time medical director, and a team of case managers. Some networks have hired additional staff to help with data analysis and other network initiatives. Each network is guided by a steering committee that consists of physicians and representatives from the local hospitals, health departments, and departments of social services" (Steiner 2008). In total, the network is comprised of 3,500 primary care physicians and 1,200 medical homes, and provides coverage in all of North Carolina's 100 counties (Dobson 2009). Each of the 14 networks has a "medical home" in which care can be organized and coordinated among the team members. According to Grover and Conroy (2009), a medical home is a "concept of care delivery that includes an ongoing relationship with patients and their families, around the clock access to medical consultation, respect for cultural and religious beliefs, comprehensive approach to care, and coordination of care among providers and community services." Every patient is assigned a case manager who can ensure that proper care is provided and the network's resources are used properly.

CCNC uses quality data to evaluate the progress of the networks and focuses on data analysis to provide a clear understanding of benchmarks achieved. According to a study conducted by the Mercer Group, "Using conservative model-

EXERCISE 13.1

Rutgers Newark Public Service, RUPubserve Channel—A Career in Public Service—UALR Faculty Awards of Excellence (Video)

Base upon the vignettes presented in this video, students will create a statement about popular culture and public service. Why is public service important? How can they contribute?

www.youtube.com/RUPubServe

ing, CCNC saved the State of North Carolina $60 million in fiscal year 2003. By 2006, savings had increased to $161 million annually. More liberal modeling puts the cost saving at more than $300 million annually by 2006. The largest savings were achieved in emergency department utilization (23 percent less than projected), outpatient care (25 percent less than projected), and pharmacy (11 percent less than projected)" (cited by Steiner 2008). As this case demonstrates, public servants both inside and outside of government are professionals contributing to the public good. Government and its partners are efficiently providing quality services.

Capturing the Attention of Youth

Public service is not provided solely by those who work for the state. In addition to nonprofit and private-sector partners, the government has made a concerted effort to engage young people in public service. Since the terrorist attack on the World Trade Center in New York City on September 11, 2001, a significant increase has been noted in service among youth between the ages of 18 and 24. In order to encourage college graduates to embark on a lifetime of service, the Corporation for Na-

FIGURE 13.1 – VOLUNTEER RATES BY STATE

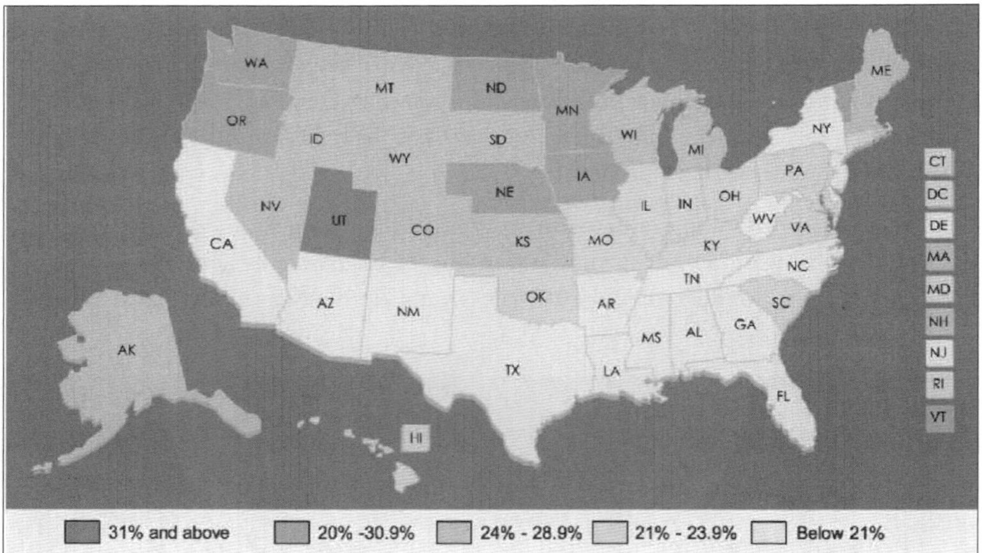

Young Adult Volunteer Rate (ages 16–24): Between 2006 and 2008, the average national volunteer rate was 26.4 percent per year. During the same time frame, average Young Adult volunteer rates for states ranged from 13.8 percent to 37.4 percent. Rankings are based on a three-year moving average.

Source: Volunteering in America, April 27, 2008. www.volunteeringinamerica.gov/rankings.cfm.

tional and Community Service provides volunteer opportunities for dedicated college students across the country. Cultivating an ethic of civic responsibility, America's colleges and universities increasingly and explicitly promote service-oriented studies, facilitating and encouraging a culture of service. Many universities have instituted public service honors for students who complete at least 100 hours of service during their college careers, and others have required public service as part of the general university requirements for graduation.

Between September 2004 and September 2005, nearly 3.3 million college students (ages 16–24) participated in volunteer activities throughout the United States. From 2002 to 2005, the number of college students who volunteered their time to not-for-profit groups increased by nearly 20 percent, or almost 600,000, from 2.7 million to almost 3.3 million. The number of adult volunteers increased by perhaps half that rate. In 2005 the volunteer rate among college students was much higher than that of the general population aged 16 to 24. At 30.2 percent, the college-student volunteer rate exceeded the national volunteer rate of 28.8 percent, the rate for 25 to 34 year olds (25.3 percent), and the rate for those over 65 (24.8 percent) (Corporation for National and Community Service 2006).

Nearly 32 percent of college students volunteer with educational or youth service organizations, and almost 23 percent of college student volunteers serve with religious organizations (Corporation for National and Community Service 2006). College students' commitment to serve has even helped redefine spring break from "party time" to "volunteer time." Six months after Hurricane Katrina, more than 31,000 students took alternative, service-oriented spring breaks. The following year, that number increased by 16 percent. In March 2007, approximately 36,000 students from 300 schools spent their spring break cleaning up debris and painting houses in the Gulf or around the world (Johnston 2007). "So many young people were sitting in school watching the horrible devastation and wondering what they could do about it. . . . Because they're students . . . they just can't write checks and feel like they did something. In order to contribute, they have to do it with their physical labor" (United Way spokesperson Shelia Consaul, quoted in Johnston 2007).

The willingness and "can-do" spirit exemplified by students who take public service-oriented spring breaks is critical to securing America's democratic future in the twenty-first century. Such commitment helps to maintain the openness and optimism that make a democracy work (Friedman 2007). As the class of 2007 entered the workforce, they were asked to demonstrate that service matters beyond their college service experience: "Do you have a purpose? Do you have a calling?" (Rev. Peter J. Gomes, Augustana College 2007 Commencement Speech, quoted in Finder 2007). These graduates are being encouraged to make a commitment to serve others by getting involved and becoming "part of the solution." Former first lady Laura Bush, in a commencement speech at Pepperdine University, encouraged the Class of 2007 to make the most of their tremendous energy and idealism by entering public service:

> Today starts a period of incredible liberty and adventure—a time to demand the most of your life. . . . And as you work to make the most of what you received, I can tell you one thing for sure: You won't waste your talents and education if you "freely give" them in service to others (Bush, quoted in Finder 2007).

Speaker of the House Nancy Pelosi, in her 2007 Webster University commencement speech, emphasized the importance of service during a "time when international cooperation will be critical to solving the world's most pressing problems" (Webster University 2007).

The appeal of community involvement continues to rise. According to the Higher Education Research Institute (2006), more than two-thirds of the 2005 freshman class at institutions of higher education in the United States expressed a desire to serve others—the highest rate in a generation. In the 11th Biannual Youth Survey on Politics and Public Service, conducted by the Harvard Institute of Politics in the fall of 2006, more than 80 percent of the 18 to 24 year olds surveyed indicated that volunteerism is an effective way of solving important issues facing their communities (Harvard University Institute of Politics 2006).

"It is one of the most beautiful compensations of this life that no man can sincerely try to help another without helping himself. "

RALPH WALDO EMERSON
Essayist; Philosopher; Poet

College students also contribute their time through more structured programs such as service learning. Service learning is defined as a method of teaching and learning that combines academic work with meaningful service to the community. Students "learn by doing" through a clear application of skills and knowledge while helping to meet specific needs in neighboring schools and the community. Service learning enriches the learning experience, teaches civic responsibility, and strengthens communities (State of New Jersey 2006).

An estimated 10.6 million students nationwide (38.6 percent) participate in community service as part of a school activity or requirement (Corporation for National and Community Service 2006). Seventy-eight percent of students who participate in school-based service learning report their experience as positive, and 87 percent of students believe they learned skills they will use in the future. Service-learning students participate in diverse community programs. For example, in California, a group of 60 students from San Diego State University teach in the City Heights Schools and develop exams or new courses. And in a short-term service-learning relief effort organized by the University of South Carolina, 100 students served in Biloxi, Mississippi, after Hurricane Katrina. Working closely with Salvation Army volunteers, these students contributed hands-on work that included cleanup, home restoration, the delivery of water and food, and the preparation of care packages. The Student Hurricane Network (SHN) was founded by Morgan Williams, a Tulane University law school student, in response to community needs after Hurricane Katrina. The SHN provides ongoing legal assistance to communities affected by Katrina and creates and coordinates volunteer opportunities in the Gulf Coast region. As of 2006, it was affiliated with more than 60 law schools nationwide and averages 175 volunteers per month (Student Hurricane Network 1999–2010).

Community service among teenagers is substantial. The Corporation for National and Community Service, in collaboration with the U.S. Census Bureau and the non-profit coalition Independent Sector, conducted a major federal survey of teenage volunteerism in early 2005. Results indicate that an estimated 15.5 million youth—or 55 percent of youth ages 12 to 18—participate in volunteer activities; the teen volunteer rate is nearly twice the adult volunteer rate of 29 percent (Corporation for National and Community Service 2006). Moreover, youth contribute more than 1.3 billion hours of community service each year.

In addition to the Corporation for National and Community Service, other agencies provide opportunities for younger citizens looking to participate. Internationally, since 1961, about 200,000 volunteers have worked for the Peace Corps. The average age of Peace Corps volunteers is 27. The three main goals of the program are:

1. To help the people of interested countries in meeting their need for trained men and women.
2. To help promote a better understanding of Americans on the part of the peoples served.

EXERCISE 13.2

American Public Media Public Insight Journalism—Consumer Consequences: Find Out if You Are Living a Sustainable Life (Simulation)

In this simulation, students will learn how to become more socially and environmentally responsible. See how your consumption decisions affect the planet's sustainability. You may decide to live in a more cooperative way and enhance your appreciation of the limits of consumable resources. After completing this simulation, identify the decisions you made to live more sustainably and show how these decisions have a positive impact on the environment. Answer these questions: Why is sustainability an important contemporary public policy issue? What other issues should be included?

http://sustainability.publicradio.org/consumerconsequences

3. To help promote a better understanding of other peoples on the part of Americans (Peace Corps 2008).

The Peace Corps provides education, health, business development, agriculture, environmental, and youth development services, and many of its volunteers are recent college graduates. That same age group also provides young teachers for urban public schools through the Baltimore City Teaching Residency, the New York City Teaching Fellows, and the Washington, D.C., Teaching Fellows. Each of these programs provides extended support for new recruits and enrolls them in a local master's degree program. Since 1991, the nationwide fellowship program Teach for America has placed more than 25,000 recent graduates in 35 cities and rural areas across the United States. It also involves alumni in policy and leadership roles after serving in the classroom: "Alumni are a powerful and growing force for change. By exerting leadership from inside and outside education, our alumni leverage their corps experience to improve outcomes and opportunities for low-income students and to fight for systemic reform" (Teach for America 2009).

Public Information

Informing the public about the accomplishments of the public sector and public servants is an essential but often neglected duty of government. Government agencies and their staffs are under constant scrutiny from politicians, the private sector, and the media. As discussed earlier, an inaccurate, distorted portrayal of public servants characterizes them as inept and inefficient. To the extent that society perpetuates these misconceptions and erroneous images remain unchallenged, the job of the public servant becomes even more difficult. Public administration needs to emphasize the value of service as a form of "intangible income." Public servants who are dedicated to serving their fellow citizens are motivated by desires, in many small ways, to make our society a better place in which to live. Although many award-winning public servants work in environments that challenge even the most optimistic, creative, and industrious personalities, they are motivated by a calling to contribute to improving the lives of their fellow citizens and by a compelling desire to address social problems. Public servants must bring that sense of mission and commitment into the classroom and the living room, providing students and citizens with more balanced views of public service.

Public administration must attract the attention of government's critics (such as MBAs), some of whom might consider temporary public service, if not career changes, in the spirit of the Populist movement of the nineteenth century. Populists were suspicious of government and concerned about abuses of power by large private institutions such as banks, railroads, political machines, and corporations. They recognized that for individuals and communities to retain any real power in modern society, they would need the help of an energetic government staffed with some of the country's best and brightest people, who would work in concert with an active citizenry in order to counter the inherent power of these private interests.

The public service must communicate commitment as a series of positive images. By no means is the public sector dead or moribund. Public servants are typically productive, successful, and professional, and when citizens are asked to evaluate specific public servants with whom they come into personal contact, they are generally complimentary. Negative images do not usually withstand careful scrutiny: government does a good job, often an outstanding job, in difficult circumstances. The public sector must present evidence that public servants function well, despite the constant barrage of negative images, superficial criticism, and less-than-ideal levels of public support. It is imperative to communicate to the citizenry how committed public organizations and public employees have developed systematic problem-solving strategies and a remarkable capacity for innovation.

Public administration's "target" audience must be multifaceted. The primary goal should be to capture the imagination of present and future students in the field (graduates, and perhaps undergraduates specializing in public administration, health, law enforcement, education, nonprofit administration, etc.), with the goal of attracting more of the top minds to government service. Public administration programs in colleges and universities are encouraged to develop the strategies necessary to defend public workers and eradicate the prevailing view of stereotypical "bureaucrats."

Beyond government, it is important to educate government's most ardent critics. Many highly educated professionals, such as doctors, lawyers, and accountants, are not certain about what the field of public administration encompasses. They might confuse it with business administration, engineering, or city planning. It is important for government's stakeholders to realize that there is a field of study dedicated to the management of our public organizations. To foster such an education, a collaborative effort on the part of various professional communities might be helpful.

Networks and Professional Organizations

An important aspect of the public service community is the ability of its members to connect. With the popularity of websites such as Facebook, MySpace, and LinkedIn, it is clear that networking is an important aspect of our professional and social lives. Fortunately, within the field of public administration, a number of networks and professional organizations exist to fulfill this need. The foci of these groups differ, based upon members' needs and responsibilities. Some foster relationships within a content-specific community, while others provide support for the field in general. A list and brief description of the typical networks for students and practitioners in the field of public administration follows.

American Society for Public Administration (ASPA)

ASPA is one of the broadest-serving organizations in the field of public administration. With some 9,000 members, ASPA provides services to practitioners, scholars, educators, and students in both government and the nonprofit sectors.

ASPA is the leading public service organization that:

- Advances the art, science, teaching, and practice of public and non-profit administration
- Promotes the value of joining and elevating the public service profession
- Builds bridges among all who pursue public purposes
- Provides networking and professional development opportunities to those committed to public service values
- Achieves innovative solutions to the challenges of governance.

ASPA publishes *Public Administration Review (PAR)*, the *PA Times*, and *The Bridge*. *PAR* is a leading academic journal with over 60 volumes of articles. The *PA Times* is a bimonthly newspaper that focuses on key issues facing practitioners, and *The Bridge* is an online newsletter that offers frequent updates and much-needed information about various networking opportunities. ASPA hosts an annual conference with more than a thousand people in attendance and a number of smaller conferences and professional development opportunities. The organization also features content-specific subsections along with a number of regional affiliates to make membership more accessible and applicable to members' daily activities.

Web: www.aspanet.org

Alliance 4 Public Service

The Alliance 4 Public Service is a network that aims to engage a broad range of citizens, public interest organizations, governments, and not-for-profit service providers in the active promotion of public service and personal responsibility at the local level. Through the alliance, individuals can learn how to make a difference through public service and receive information about career and volunteer opportunities, grants currently available, and conferences and meetings.

The activities of the Alliance 4 Public Service include:

- Collaboration on issues concerning the quality of life of the public and the civic society

- Capacity-building programs to facilitate the education and ongoing professional development of current and future leaders in public service
- Communications networks between individuals involved in providing and promoting civic engagement
- Advocacy of public service through media channels, print, and online publications, conference presentations, and other opportunities
- Partnerships with organizations that are building capacities for civic engagement.

Web: http://publicservice.newark.rutgers.edu

The International City/County Management Association (ICMA)

ICMA is a nonprofit 501(c)(3) member-based organization offering services to over 9,000 managers across the world. ICMA's "mission is to create excellence in local governance by developing and fostering professional local government management worldwide." ICMA offers a number of professional services, including publications, opportunities for professional development, and conferences throughout the year. Their network of managers is highly professional and offers a strong resource for other members to access.

Web: http://icma.org

IMAGES OF PUBLIC SERVANT AND CURRENT SITUATION IN KOREA

How would you evaluate the images of public service in your country? Is public service something that deserves your effort and time for the rest of your life? Please read the following article about Korea. It does not seem that young people are looking for public service jobs simply because public service is meaningful. According to public service motivation theories, people choose the public sector because they are committed to the welfare of the society and they will be productive employees in the workplace. But the following article does not seem to support the PSM theory. Once they entered the public sector, are they committed to public service or are they committed to their jobs? Do you think there are some different factors between the two countries in choosing the public sector as a career?

Ivory Tower turns into a Training Camp for State Exams

By Kang Hyun-kyung

A tough labor market after the Asian financial crisis, which hit the nation in 1997, has changed the landscape of college campuses with a new post-crisis cohort of college students, dubbed "seven-to-eleven" people.

This refers to undergraduates aspiring to become public officers through state exams, who hone their exam skills in the library from early morning till late at night.

Experts say the presence of seven-to-eleven students is a reflection that Koreans, who were accustomed to life-time employment before the crisis, are longing for permanent jobs, amid growing employment instability.

Joining the cohort are students from all departments, even engineering majors and those who study arts and sciences.

To eliminate their competitors in the heavy competition, applicants for the state exams spend as much time at library as they can to secure permanent positions that are to die for.

Kongdan (Katy) Oh, a non-resident senior fellow at the Brookings Institute, told *The Korea Times* that the guarantee of a life-time career in government has prompted smart college students to consider these jobs as more attractive than those in the private sector.

"The job market is tight and nobody guarantees life-time employment. Once you enter public service, including a foreign career service, you may retain the job and be promoted based on seniority and experience. So retirement and stability is guaranteed," the Korea watcher said.

"The paycheck may not be large or lucrative, but will be a steady and guaranteed source of income."

As the trend of smart students heading for government jobs in the quest for life-time careers continues, concerns are growing over a possible brain drain in the engineering, science and technology fields.

In a statement posted on the website of Seoul National University (SNU) in 2007, professor Kang Myung-koo warned of the deleterious effect of this on the nation's future.

Given that an average SNU student's scholastic aptitude test score is a 99 percentile ranking, their heading for public service jobs could lead to a shortage of a quality workforce in the engineering, science and technology areas that are crucial to the competitiveness of the country, Kang said.

Gypsy Graduates

A brain drain in other fields is not the sole factor raising concerns.

The rising social costs on post-graduate applicants are another problem.

Some people prepare for the exams for several years after graduation. They are called "gypsy applicants" as they tend to travel from one study studio to another until they either quit or pass the exams.

Their full-time preparation for the exams after graduation entails spending large amounts of money.

The Law Journal survey of 808 people out of 997 who passed the state bar exam last yearfound they spent an average of 800,000 won (approximately $690) per month on housing, books, and taking courses at private institutes.

The vast majority of them (73 percent) said their parents sponsored their preparation for the exam.

The survey showed 27.7 percent studied for six years or more. Given the four-year university system, this indicates that they studied fulltime to prepare for the exam even after graduation due to the fierce competition.

Oh said the phenomenon of gypsy applicants was the combined result of the Koreans' traditionally positive attitude toward government jobs and the worsening

(continued)

(continued)

employment market after the Asian Financial Crisis.

"The so-called Kwan (the public sector) has been viewed as more powerful and influential than Min (the private sector) since Korea adopted a central and authoritarian government from its last dynasty to today," she said.

"Plus, the old system of social class concepts may still be pervasive."

In this system, the court's nobility and selected high-level civil servants topped the class ladder, followed by the literati and learned class, farmers, technical workers and merchants.

"Many Koreans tend to regard diplomats and government officials of high rank to be the most powerful elite group even today," Oh said.

Gosi-vill

Sillim-dong, southwestern Seoul near Seoul National University, is a Mecca for aspiring lawyers, prosecutors, judges and government officials. This district is called Gosi-vill — a village to which applicants of the state exams (Gosi) flock from across the nation.

The area is filled with studio apartments, bookstores selling and buying used books, stationary stores displaying copies of theses and documents useful for test-takers, and private academies.

Test-takers began going there in 1975 when SNU relocated from Hyehwadong.

These people live in studios, and go to reading rooms nearby to focus on previewing and reviewing what they learned and take courses at private academies.

They have breakfast, lunch and dinner at nearby cafeterias with prepaid coupons priced at 3,000 won or below.

Industry experts project the number of applicants preparing for the state exams in this town has reached approximately 40,000 people.

However, the Gosi-vill may be subject to change as the state exams are to be scrapped in the very near future.

Source: http://www.koreatimes.co.kr/www/news/nation/2010/09/116_73297.html

KEY TERMS

Federal government

Grant

Local government

Public-private partnership

Public servants

REFERENCES

Brudney, Jeffrey L. 1990. *Fostering Volunteer Programs in the Public Sector: Planning, Initiating, and Managing Voluntary Activities.* San Francisco, CA: Jossey-Bass.

Carnegie Mellon University. 2009. "Alum Offers Innovative Solutions." FamilyJustice.org. www.cmu.edu/homepage/innovation/2007/fall/familyjustice.org.shtml.

Chrisinger, Jim. 2007. "The Charter Agencies Initiative." Pioneer Institute, Roe Paper No. 1. www.pioneerinstitute.org/pdf/ROE1.pdf.

Chrisinger, Jim, and Babak Armajani. 2008. "Reinventing Bureaucracy with Charter Agencies." www.mncounties.org/scrai/Iowa%20Charter%20Agency%20article.pdf.

Corporation for National and Community Service. 2006. "AmeriCorps State Commission Performance Report." Washington, DC: August.

———. 2009. "Volunteering in America Research Highlights." http://www.volunteeringinamerica.gov/assets/resources/VolunteeringInAmericaResearch-Highlights.pdf.

Democratic Leadership Council (DLC). 2008. "Charter Agencies." June 30. www.dlc.org/ndol_ci.cfm?kaid=450015&subid=900152&contentid=253941 .

Dobson, L.A., Jr. 2009. "State Initiatives That Improve Health and Control Costs." Statement of L. Allen Dobson, Jr., MD FAAFP, Chairman, North Carolina Community Care Networks, Inc., on behalf of Community Care of North Carolina and the North Carolina Department of Health and Human Services, January 22.

Ellis, Richard, ed. 1999. *Founding the American Presidency.* Lanham, MD: Rowman and Littlefield.

Executive Office of the President of the United States. Office of Management and Budget. 2009. "Federal Financial Management Report, FY 2009." www.whitehouse.gov/sites/default/files/omb/assets/about . . . /2009_fin.pdf.

Finder, Alan. 2007. "Commencement Speeches; With Iraq War as a Backdrop, Speakers Reflect on the Future." *New York Times*, June 10.

Foundation Center. 2010. "Frequently Asked Questions. How Many People Are Employed in the Nonprofit Sector?" http://foundationcenter.org/getstarted/faqs/html/employed.html.

Frederickson, H. George. 1997. *The Spirit of Public Administration*. San Francisco, CA: Jossey-Bass.

Friedman, Thomas. 2007. *The World Is Flat: A Brief History of the Twenty-First Century*. New York: Farrar, Straus, and Giroux.

Gawthrop, Louis C. 1998. *Public Service and Democracy: Ethical Imperatives for the 21st Century*. New York: Chatham House.

Gilbert, W.S. and Arthur Sullivan. 1878. *Her Majesty's Ship Pinafore; or, the Lass That Loved a Saylor*. Boston,: Alfred Mudge and Son, Printers.

Grants.gov. 2009. "What Is a Grant?" www.grants.gov/aboutgrants/grants.jsp.

Grover, Atul, and Joanne Conroy. 2009. "The Medical Home: A New Model of Care." Association of American Medical Colleges. www.aamc.org/meetings/orr/presentations09/conroygrover.pdf.

Hart, David K. 1989. "A Partnership in Virtue Among All Citizens: The Public Service and Civic Humanism." *Public Administration Review* 49, no. 2: 101–7.

Harvard University Kennedy School of Government. 2005. Government Innovators Network. http://www.innovations.harvard.edu/awards.html?id=3666.

Harvard University Institute of Politics. 2006. "Executive Summary: The 11th Biannual Youth Survey on Politics and Public Service." November 1. http://www.iop.harvard.edu/Research-Publications/Survey/Fall-2006-Youth-Survey/Executive-Summary.

Higher Education Research Institute. 2006. "The America Freshman. National Norms for Fall 2005." Los Angeles: University Of California. www.heri.ucla.edu/PDFs/ResearchBrief05.pdf.

Holzer , Marc. 1999. "Communicating Commitment: Public Administration as a Calling." *Public Administration and Management: An Interactive Journal* 4, no. 2: 184–207.

Houston, D.J. 2006. "'Walking the Walk' of Public Service Motivation: Public Employees and Charitable Gifts of Time, Blood, and Money." *Journal of Public*

Administration Research and Theory 16, no. 1: 67–86.

International City/County Management Association (ICMA). 2007a. "Celebrate the Value of Professional Management: ICMA's Annual Awards Program, 2007. 2007 Annual Awards Program Commemorative Booklet." http://icma.org/en/icma/members/awards/annual_awards.

———. 2007b. "ICMA Leaders at the Core of Better Communities. Manager In Residence Profiles." http://icma.org/en/Page/998/Manager_In_Residence_Profiles.

Iowa, State of. 2004. "State of Iowa. Charter Agencies Quarterly Report. FY 2003–04 Quarter 3. January 1–March 31 2004." Public Strategies Group, April 30, 2004. http://staffweb.legis.state.ia.us/lfb/docs/GAweb/Reinvent/docs_other%5CCharter%20Agency%20FY%202004%20Third%20Quarter%20Report.pdf.

Johnston, Laura. 2007. "Forfeiting the Sun, Gaining Awareness." *Star Ledger*, March 28.

Klein, Daniel. 1990. "The Voluntary Provision of Public Goods? The Turnpike Companies of Early America." *Economic Inquiry* 28, no. 4 (October): 788–812.

Lee, Christopher. 2006. "Big Government Gets Bigger: Study Counts More Employees, Cites Increase in Contractors." *Washington Post*, October 6.

Madison, James. 1788/1961. "Federalist #45." Reprinted in *The Federalist Papers*, ed. Clinton Rossiter. New York: New American Library.

New Jersey, State of. Department of Education. 2006. "Learn and Serve America—New Jersey." http://www.state.nj.us/education/lsa/whatis.htm.

North Carolina Division of Medical Assistance. 2010. "CCNC Workgroup Minutes." January 19. www.ncdhhs.gov/dma/casemgmt/CMCCNCMinutes01192010.pdf.

Pattakos, A.N. 2004. "The Search for Meaning in Government Service." *Public Administration Review* 64, no. 1: 106–12.

Peace Corps. 2008. "About Us: Mission." http://www.peacecorps.gov/index.cfm?shell=about.mission.

Perry, James L. 1996. "Measuring Public Service Motivation: An Assessment of Construct Reliability and Validity." *Journal of Public Administration Research and Theory* 6, no. 1: 5–22.

Polk County. 2008. "Polk County's Stewardship: Saving Through Productivity

Improvements." Comparing Polk County Productivity Improvements to Statewide Initiatives Cited in Florida TaxWatch Special Report–September 2007. Updated November 2008. http://www.polk-county.net/WorkArea/linkit.aspx?LinkIdentifier=id&ItemID=11690.

Public Strategies Group. 2009. "Iowa's Charter Agencies Win Prestigious Innovations in American Government Award." http://www.psg.us/resources/newscharteragencywins.html.

Redwood City, California. 2009. "Partnership Academy for Community Teamwork (PACT)." http://www.redwoodcity.org/manager/initiatives/pact.html.

———. 2007a. "City Manager Ed Everett Announces Retirement from Redwood City," Redwood City, CA—April 9. http://www.redwoodcity.org/manager/news/2007/pr_mgr_everettretire.html.

———. 2007b. "City Manager Ed Everett Receives Top Annual Honor from International City/County Management Association - "Award for Career Excellence." Redwood City, CA - June 19. http://www.redwoodcity.org/manager/news/2007/pr_mgr_icma.html.

———. 2006. "Redwood City E-News. Building a Great Community Together." Issue # 39. November. http://classic.redwoodcity.org/e-news/issue39.html#communitybuilders.

Steiner, D.D. 2008. "Community Care of North Carolina: Improving Care Through Community Health Networks." *Annals of Family Medicine* 6, no. 4: 361–67.

Student Hurricane Network. 1999–2010. "Law Students Working for Justice in the Gulf Coast." http://www.studentjustice.org/.

Teach for America. 2009. "Our Impact." www.teachforamerica.org/mission/our_impact/our_impact.htm.

Urban Institute. 2010. "Nonprofits." http://www.urban.org/nonprofits/index.cfm.

U.S. Census Bureau. 2002. "Government Units in 2002." GC02–1(P), July. www2.census.gov/govs/cog/2002COGprelim_report.pdf.

U.S. Department of Agriculture. 2009. "President Obama, Secretary Vilsack Announce Intent to Nominate Kevin Concannon as Under Secretary for Food, Nutrition and Consumer Services at USDA." Food and Nutrition Service, News Release No. 0116.09, April 17. www.fns.usda.gov/cga/pressreleases/2009/PR-0116.htm.

USA Government Grants. 2010. "Government Grants 2010." http://www.usagovernmentgrants.org/Government_Grants.html.

Webster University. 2007. "Address to Webster University Graduating Class." Saturday May 12. http://www.webster.edu/commencement/media/pelosispeech.shtml.

Wolf, James F., and Robert N. Bacher. 1990. "The Public Administrator and Public Service Occupations." In *Refounding Public Administration*, ed. Gary L. Wamsley et al., 163–181. Newbury Park, CA: Sage Publications.

SUPPLEMENTARY READINGS

Adams, Guy B., and Danny L. Balfour. 2005. "Public Service Ethics and Administrative Evil: Prospects and Problems." In *Ethics in Public Management*, ed. H. George Frederickson and Richard Ghere. Armonk, NY: M.E. Sharpe.

Bloomfield, P. 2006. "The Challenging Business of Long-Term Public–Private Partnerships: Reflections on Local Experience." *Public Administration Review* 66: 400–11.

Brewer, Gene A. 2003. "Building Social Capital: Civic Attitudes and Behavior of Public Servants." *Journal of Public Administration Research & Theory* 13, no. 1: 5-26.

Denhardt, Janet Vinzant, and Robert B. Denhardt. 2007. "The New Public Service: Serving, Not Steering." Armonk, New York: M.E. Sharpe.

Denhardt, Robert B., and Edward T. Jennings, Jr. 1989. "Image and Integrity in the Public Service." *Public Administration Review* 49, no. 1: 74-77.

Evans, Don S. 2003. "The Public Interest in Private Water." In *Revisiting the Public Interest in Private Water*, ed. Alex Tsybine, 4–5. Los Angeles, CA: Reason Public Policy Institute.

Forrer, John, and James Edwin Kee. 2004. "Public Servants as Contract Managers." *Public Contract Law Journal* 33, no. 2: 361–68.

Forrer, J., Kee, J. E., Newcomer, K. E., and E. Boyer. 2010. "Public–Private Partnerships and the Public Accountability Question." *Public Administration Review* 70: 475–84.

Ghere, Richard K.1996."Aligning the Ethics of Public-Private Partnership: The Issue of Local Economic Development." *Journal of Public Administration Research & Theory* 6 no. 4: 599–621.

Kee, James Edwin, Kathryn E. Newcomer, Deborah L. Trent, Valerie Oster, and Sasha Rosen. 2007. "Keeping the Public Interest in Public–Private Partnerships." Working Paper no. 5, Center for Innovation in Public Service. George Washington University.

Wettenhall, Roger. 2003. The Rhetoric and Reality of Public–Private Partnerships. *Public Organization Review* 3, no. 1: 77–107.

Koppenjan, J. F. M., and Enserink, B. 2009. "Public-Private Partnerships in Urban Infrastructures: Reconciling Private Sector Participation and Sustainability." *Public Administration Review* 69: 284–96.

Portillo, S., and DeHart-Davis, L. 2009. "Gender and Organizational Rule Abidance." *Public Administration Review* 69: 339–47.

Vigoda, Eran. 2002. "From Responsiveness to Collaboration: Governance, Citizens, and the Next Generation of Public Administration." *Public Administration Review* 62, no. 5: 527–40.

ELECTRONIC RESOURCES

Rich Anderson. 2003."Urban Water Council Meets to Discuss Public/Private Partnerships." The United States Conference of Mayors Website, http://www.usmayors.org/uscm/us_mayor_newspaper/documents/02_03_03/urban_water.asp

National Council for Public-Private Partnerships (NCPPP). 2002. "For the Good of the People: Using Public-Private Partnerships to Meet America's Essential Needs," http://ncppp.org/presskit/ncpppwhitepaper.pdf

United Nations Department of Economics and Social Affairs Division for Public Economics and Public Administration. 2000. "Professionalism and Ethics in the Public Service: Issues and Practices in Selected Regions," http://unpan1.un.org/intradoc/groups/public/documents/un/unpan000112.pdf

CHAPTER 14

The Future of Public Administration

This chapter focuses on the future of public administration. Is that future any different from the past? Decidedly, yes: Significant shifts over recent decades have changed the face of government in the United States and throughout the world. Domestically, three major shifts directly affected public administration. First, a great deal of administrative responsibility shifted from the federal level to the states, and then to local government. Second, we saw large increases in the number of private-sector partners providing public services. Lastly, the growth of the global economy plays a significant role in public administration. Discussed is the changing structure of government, in addition to performance measurement, citizen participation, and e-governance as accountability tools.

"The future is not fixed, it's fluid...
It's waiting for you to hammer it into shape."

BONO
Musician; Activist

Technology is playing an increasingly important role in enabling citizen participation.

THE EVOLUTION OF PUBLIC ADMINISTRATION

The very structure of government has changed. Rather than simply understanding the bureaucratic structure, we must also grasp the concept of governance networks as structures that incorporate multiple partners in the delivery of public services. This structure operates via horizontal relationships rather than a vertical, hierarchical chain of command. Consequently, processes of top-down control and accountability—from agency leadership all the way to street-level bureaucrats—are diminishing. This shift creates ambiguity in the accountability structure that was so firmly entrenched within the traditional bureaucratic framework. The development of new modes of control and coordination are designed to ensure that public agencies are run responsibly. Results-based accountability places an emphasis on the outcome of government services rather than the processes utilized to reach that outcome. Performance measurement is often identified as a tool with which to achieve results-based accountability.

> "Never doubt that a small group of thoughtful committed citizens can change the world; indeed, it's the only thing that ever has."
>
> **MARGARET MEAD**
> Cultural Anthropologist

Accountability may be achieved through citizen participation and government transparency. Advocates of citizen participation believe that citizens need to take a more active role in the day-to-day activities of government. Such participation creates a more representative form of government and develops a strong relationship between government and its citizens. Government transparency and accessibility go hand in hand. Are agencies accessible to the average citizen? If so, then they are most likely committed to accountability as well. E-governance—or government information and services delivered via websites—also provides access to government in ways that were previously unavailable. Those capabilities are growing very rapidly.

Governance Networks

The structures of government are changing, and new mechanisms are being put into place to respond to such changes. One definition of a governance network is provided by the Center for Democratic Network Governance:

> 1) A horizontal articulation of interdependent, but operationally autonomous actors; 2) who interact through negotiations; 3) transpiring within a regulative, normative, cognitive and imaginary framework; 4) that to a certain extent is self-regulating; and 5) which contribute to the production of public purpose within a particular area. (Marcussen and Torfing 2003, p. 7)

Keast, Mandell, Brown, and Woolcock (2004) articulate the difference between formal network structures and informal associations often linked to the word "network." Unlike networks and networking, network structures are unified by a single mission—a mission that all actors work together to achieve. Rather than operating through command-and-control directives, network structures feature horizontal relationships; they are dependent upon "exchange-based interpersonal relations" (Keast et al. 2004, p. 365). One of the purposes of a network structure is to develop a "holistic" approach in which the entire picture may be seen from a new, unified perspective (Keast et al. 2004, p. 365). Network structures frequently form when other structures fail to reach a proposed goal.

As previously mentioned, governance networks no longer use the traditional command-and-control relationship exemplified in bureaucratic systems (Salamon 2002). Rather, network actors cooperate "because they trust that the other actors will also play their part" and fulfill their responsibilities (Marcussen and Torfing 2003). Networks are formed based upon interdependent relationships in which members are "highly committed" to the goals at hand. In order to reach network goals, all partners must fulfill their duties. Unlike traditional hierarchical or market relationships, networks are based upon ideals of "complementary strengths," and they resolve conflicts through relations of "reciprocity" (Lowndes and Skelcher 1998. Although networks are not perceived as being quite as flexible as market

TABLE 14.1 – FIVE EXAMPLES OF GOVERNMENT-ACTIVATED NETWORKS

Network type	Definition	Example/use
Service Contract	Government's use of a contract to activate a network.	Mental health, welfare, defense
Supply Chain	Deliver complex products to government	Department of Defense, Department of Transportation, space shuttle, helicopter
Ad-Hoc	Activated as a response network to a specific situation—typically an emergency	Emergency network for natural disasters or an infectious disease outbreak
Channel Partnership	Companies conduct transactions on behalf of government agency	Car dealer handles registration of new cars; sporting good stores sell fishing licenses
Information Dissemination	A partnership activated to disseminate information	Recycling information is distributed by nonprofit organization

Source: Goldsmith, S., and W.D. Eggers. 2004. "Governing by Network: The New Public Management Imperative." Harvard University, Ash Institute for Democratic Governance and Innovation. http://ash.harvard.edu/Home/Programs/Innovations-in-Government/21stCentury/Governing-By-Network.

relationships, they are seen as being more flexible than traditional bureaucratic structures (Lowndes and Skelcher 1998).

A contemporary understanding of governance points to changing realities in which public administrators hold a great deal of responsibility. Government officials are no longer expected to work exclusively within their bureaucratic agency or department; rather, they must work with multiple organizations both inside and outside of government (Agranoff and McGuire 2003). "Through partnerships, networks, contractual relationships, alliances, committees, coalitions, consortia, and councils, managers in public and private agencies jointly develop strategies and produce goods and services on behalf of their organizations" (Agranoff and McGuire 2003, p. 2). Collaborative relationships are being developed to help managers pursue both "political" and "economic objectives" (Agranoff and McGuire 2003, p. 3).

> "Citizen service is the very American idea that we meet our challenges not as isolated individuals but as members of a true community, with all of us working together. Our mission is nothing less than to spark a renewed sense of obligation, a new sense of duty, a new season of service."
>
> **WILLIAM J. CLINTON**
> 42nd President of the United States

There are many reasons for which a network might be activated. According to Goldsmith and Eggers (2004), "The job of [a] network designer and activator is to see how all the pieces of the network should work together, identify possible partners, bring all the relevant stakeholders to the table, and determine what resources will be used to keep the network together" (p. 11). Goldsmith and Eggers provide a framework for understanding different types of networks that may be activated by government. Table 14.1 provides five examples of government-activated networks.

Much of government management—routine or crisis driven—already takes place in networked structures. It is important, then, that this trend is acknowledged in policy formulation. According to Keast et al. (2004), "Unless policy makers have a fuller understanding of what it means to work through network structures, they will continue to develop traditional policies and management techniques that mitigate against the positive attributes of networked arrangements" (p. 364). Additionally, the appropriate safeguards will not be fully realized until governance networks are clearly articulated and understood by those responsible for their activation. Public managers need to go beyond simply acknowledging the existence of governance networks and become expert at utilizing these structures to promote specific policy goals.

Governance networks provide exciting opportunities for the future. The cooperative arrangements of networks may serve to enhance a civility that is necessary for effective governance. Networks provide opportunities for citizen participation, more effective regulatory control, and the expression of public-sector values within the marketplace. Due to the shared sense of responsibility and the dependent relationships of network partners, each participant helps to develop a common sense of goals.

Performance Measurement

Government performance is an important concern for many stakeholders. Performance measurement is dedicated to developing systems that effectively measure the efficiency and efficacy of government. Ultimately, measuring government performance becomes a challenging, but rewarding, endeavor.

Measuring government performance is not a new concept. From the early part of the twentieth century, governments have measured their activities (Streib and Poister 1999). According to Williams (2003), performance measurement emerged in the early twentieth century as a mode of "reconciling" the conflicting views of supporters of two opposing forms of government: a strong executive type and a commission type. Williams notes, "Through the instrument of reporting, the executive could be given broad discretion while retaining more inclusive democracy of legislative decision making, or at least its appearance" (p. 645). Therefore, from its original conception, performance measurement was used as a mechanism for accountability.

Throughout the 1960s and 1970s, significant contributions were made to the theory of performance measurement in the form of both plans and practical guides for fair and accurate measurement. A renewed importance on performance measurement occurred again in the 1990s. In particular, Osborne and Gaebler in *Reinventing Government* (1992) and the National Performance Review chaired by Vice President Al Gore called for a more results-oriented government (cited in Streib and Poister 1999).

Performance measurement systems rely on indicators and analyses dealing with improvement. Tracking and improving organizational outcomes over time is essential to identifying successful areas of operation or areas where performance is slipping, as evidenced by work backlogs, high employee turnover, or citizen complaints. Typically, performance measurement systems include the following indicators.

Input Indicators

According to the Government Accounting Standards Board (GASB), input indicators are designed "to report the amount of resources, either financial or other (especially personnel), that have been used for a specific service or program. Input indicators are ordinarily presented in budget submissions and sometimes external management reports" (Hatry et al. 1990). For example, the number of employees within an organization or the amount of money spent on a project is an input.

Output/Workload Indicators

Output/workload indicators center on the amount of work produced or services provided by a program or organization. A measure that would exemplify an output or workload measure might be the number of applications processed by a government agency.

Outcome/Effectiveness Indicators

Outcome/effectiveness indicators deal with the results or quality of the services being measured. Essentially, they measure how well the organization is meeting its goals. Outcome indicators have both quantitative and qualitative aspects. They might be measured as larger community goals such as the overall crime rate, or by surveying community members. For example, a survey question might ask if community members feel safe, indicating the overall sense of security in a town or municipality.

Efficiency (and Cost-Effectiveness) Indicators

Efficiency measures focus not on what is being achieved but on how it is being achieved. Essentially, we are interested in whether the desirable ends are achieved with minimal input of resources, or that the resources we employ bring the maximum amount of desirable goal attainment. Therefore, an efficiency measure might look at the quantity of work completed based upon the number of people doing that work, as in the number of tons of waste collected per sanitation worker.

Productivity Indicators

According to David N. Ammons (1996), productivity indicators combine elements of efficiency and effectiveness. For instance, meters fixed per hour is an efficiency indicator, and the percentage of meters fixed properly (i.e., meters needing no further repair for at least six months) is an effectiveness indicator. Labor costs per effective meter repair is a productivity indicator. Both the costs to fix faulty meters and the costs of effective repairs are combined and included in the numerator of this productivity calculation. However, only proper repairs are included within the denominator. An indicator such as this encourages both efficiency and effectiveness among the meter repair personnel.

Seven Step Methodology

There are many measurement methodologies. For example, the National Center for Public Performance at the Rutgers-Newark School of Public Affairs and Administration utilizes the Seven Step Methodology in its development of performance measurement systems (National Center for Public Performance 2004). Each step allows for greater specification of the system and continued performance improvement.

Step 1: Identification of a Program

A clear definition of a program is necessary to develop performance measures. Programs are identified as separate units made up of distinct activities to accomplish specific goals. A good example is a crime prevention program.

Step 2: Statement of Purpose

Each program has a specific purpose that must be articulated in a clear and concise manner. It is imperative to know the purpose of a program in order to measure its progress. In continuing our example from step one, the purpose of this program is to reduce and prevent crime.

Step 3: Identification of Program Inputs, Outputs, Efficiency, and Productivity Indicators

As described above, indicators can be identified throughout a program's activities, often by documents and systems already in place. For example, input indicators can be identified in program budgets and staffing plans. Output or workload measures can be identified through daily service delivery activities such as the number of applications processed by an agency. The key to developing performance indicators, however, is in determining meaningful measures that may be useful for managers and employees at all levels of the organization. Measurement development is a process that should include employees throughout the organization in order to create their "buy in" and a sense of purpose in performance measurement and improvement actions.

Step 4: Setting Targets for Accomplishment

This step identifies specific targets in which we can say we have accomplished our program's goals. Targets can be developed based upon internal goals, or they might be more broadly based upon regional or national standards. Oftentimes, during initial phases of performance measurement, organizations simply benchmark (or compare themselves) to their own historical organizational performance. This gauges progress over time. They can also compare their performance to similar jurisdictions. Setting a lower target for the crime rate might be one way to quantify this.

> "You must be the change you wish to see in the world."
>
> **MAHATMA GANDHI**
> Global Humanitarian

Step 5: Monitoring

Performance measurement is an ongoing process that requires frequent monitoring to ensure that appropriate management interventions take place. Performance measurement is not an end in itself. It is a tool to aid management in increasing the efficiencies and effectiveness of service delivery. Through timely monitoring, managers can assess program effectiveness and determine appropriate modifications to both delivery processes and performance measures.

Step 6: Performance Reporting

Performance reporting is an essential but often-neglected step in performance measurement. It is discussed at length in the next section of this chapter.

Step 7: Analysis and Action

Although not always included in a performance measurement system, design analysis and action are essential to performance measurement. This step promotes the utilization of performance data by organizational management in order to make logical, data-driven decisions that can enhance overall organizational performance.

Performance Reporting

Performance reporting is an essential link between performance measurement and improvement. It provides stakeholders—citizens, elected officials, community and interest groups, businesses, the media—with necessary information on organizational activities. Proper methods of reporting can enhance organizational communications with citizens, ultimately resulting in greater understanding between the organization and its users. Furthermore, performance reporting helps managers generate a search for appropriate interventions that might increase efficiency and effectiveness.

Performance reports should be accessible to the reader and include the following information:

- Program name, jurisdiction, and purpose statement
- Inputs, outputs, productivity and/or efficiency ratios
- Achievement targets for effectiveness and efficiency indicators

Performance reports should also include brief synopses of additional explanatory information. The National Center for Public Performance has developed a "Ten Point Readability Criteria" to aid managers in creating accessible, functional performance reports (see Figure 14.2).

FIGURE 14.1 – STRONG EXAMPLE OF PERFORMANCE REPORTING

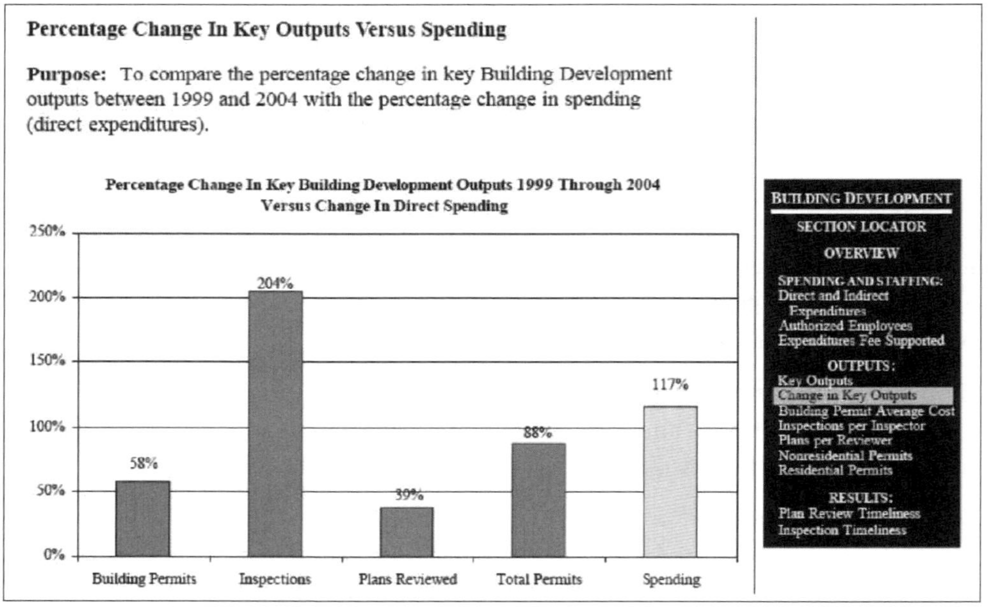

Source: Prince William County. 2004. Prince William County 2004 Building Development SEA Report. Virginia: Budget & Accountability Reports Archive http://www.pwcgov.org/docLibrary/PDF/003246.pdf

FIGURE 14.2 – NCPP'S TEN POINT CRITERIA FOR PERFORMANCE REPORTS

#	Indictors	Explanation	0	1	2	Score
1	Are images included in the report?	0 = No 1 = Images are included but do not relate to the text 2 = Images relate to the text				
2	Are the colors attractive?	0 = No 1 = Color contrast OR comfort 2 = Color contrast AND comfort				
3	Is there appropriate spacing (leading space) between the lines?	0 = Leading space below 5 mm 1 = Leading space above 5 mm 2 = Leading space above 5 mm AND margin provided				
4	Is the report brief or comprehensive?	0 = More than 20 pages 1 = Bewtween 10-20 pages 2 = Less than 10 pages				
5	Does the report use measurement tools like bar graphs, tables, pie charts?	0 = No 1 = Yes but do not relate to the text 2 = Images relate to the text (size does not exceed 1/3 of page)				
6	Are too many technical words, jargon used?	0 = More than 7 words per page 1 = Between 3-7 words per page 2 = Less than 3 words per page				
7	Does the report offer contact information for agencies/departments or employees/public officials?	0 = No 1 = Phone contact of advocacy group OR agency 2 = Phone contact of advocacy group AND agency				
8	Is the survey / research methodology provided?	0 = No 1 = Methodology is provided				
9	Are the sources for data collection and verification providded?	0 = No 1 = Sources of data provided				
10	Is there a multi-year comparison of data?	0 = No 1 = Data for last 3 years				

Source: National Center for Public Performance (NCPP) at Rutgers University, A Brief Guide For Performance Measurement in Local Government, February 2004.

Government Performance vs. Private-Sector Performance

Unlike private-sector entities, government cannot simply measure its performance against a predetermined bottom line. In measuring performance, public administrators balance an array of values and numerous goals. Government must endorse democratic modes of decision making and look to its stakeholders to understand what constitutes high government performance. Joseph Wholey (1999), in his article "Performance-Based Management: Responding to the Challenges," wrote: "Managers first must achieve a reasonable level of agreement with senior officials and other key stakeholders on agency or program goals and on the resources, activities, and processes required to meet those goals" (p. 289).

Key among these stakeholders are U.S. citizens, whose participation, according to Holzer and Kloby (2005), is fundamental to the decision-making and performance measuring process. Citing the Alfred P. Sloan Foundation, Holzer and Kloby (2005) note that "citizen involvement is necessary to ensure that what is measured is what matters to citizens and that the data are not corrupted by the natural desire of officeholders to report favorable outcomes." Similarly, according to Julnes (2006), citizen participation in performance measurement "not only implies that the appropriate values are represented, but also that more meaningful performance measures are likely to be developed."

The results-oriented model of government associated with the so-called Reinvention Movement was often more focused on private-sector values (such as customer service), rather than democratic values (such as accountability to citizens). This emphasis, aimed at making government more efficient and businesslike, raised questions concerning citizens' roles within our current systems of governance—including those of performance measurement. Citizen-centric ideas discussed in the performance measurement literature, as well as in governance networks, have spurred a revitalized concept of citizen participation in government.

Citizen Participation

The idea of applying a private-sector customer service mentality in a democratic system of government has raised concerns in the public administration field. The customer service model assumes "citizens are passive consumers" who purchase government services "in the same way they purchase consumer products" (Smith and Huntsman 1997, p. 311). According to Richard Box (1999), unlike citizens, "customers . . . are people to be persuaded and sold an image, a product, or a service rather than people who deliberate and decide" (p. 36). Box goes on to say, "Gone is the image of citizens determining public policy and its implementation to shape a better future because customers do not actively participate in governance" (pp. 19–20).

Some observers feel that it is the responsibility of the public administrator to take advantage of the changing structures of governance to increase collaborative arrangements and citizen participation. Bingham, Nabatchi, and O'Leary (2005) write: "Public administrators have a unique opportunity to become the direct conduit for the public's voice in policy making, implementation, and enforcement" (p. 550). Smith and Ingram (2002) suggest that "American democracy is an unfinished and open-ended project," adding, "Especially during times in which patterns of governance are undergoing fundamental change, it is important to examine carefully whether expansion or contraction of democracy is taking place" (p. 567).

As the government turns more frequently to market mechanisms, citizens will likely turn to community organizations to engender trust and responsiveness (Brown and Keast 2003). This may further isolate citizens from government and create feelings of distrust. By examining government as an active and engaged partner, and ensuring that managers utilize participatory mechanisms, public administrators may then engender trust among the citizenry. Holzer (2005) notes that "there is substantial value, in terms of improving citizens' trust in government, of involving citizens in the measurement of government performance" (p. 5).

> "I always wondered why somebody didn't do something about that. Then I realized I was somebody."
>
> **LILY TOMLIN**
> Actress; Comedian; Writer

In a discussion of the impact of collaboration on responsiveness in public administration, Vigoda (2002) wrote: "Because the needs and demands of a heterogeneous society are dynamic, it is vital to develop systematic approaches to understanding it" (p. 528). Unlike the old Weberian tradition of closed hierarchical systems, an ideal collaborative system operates through "negotiation, participation, cooperation, free and unlimited flow of information, innovation, agreements based on compromises and mutual understanding, and a more equitable distribution and redistribution of power and resources" (Vigoda 2002, p. 529).

Citizen participation does not have one agreed-upon definition. Generally, observers who believe in increasing citizen participation see it as a means of reconnecting the public to government and developing a relationship that allows citizens to play a "meaningful role" in shaping their community (Lando 1999, p. 116). According to Rosener (1978), the meaning of citizen participation varies with the perspective of each individual. For example, a political actor may have an entirely different perspective than that of an administrative actor. Likewise, a citizen may view the situation from a completely different standpoint than a politician or an administrator (Rosener 1978). For the purpose of this text, citizen participation will be defined as "the process by which members of a society (those not holding office or administrative positions in government) share power with public officials in making substantive decisions" and in taking actions related to the community (Roberts 2004, p. 320).

The notion of citizen participation can be traced back hundreds of years to the very roots of America's democratic ideals. Undoubtedly, levels of citizen participation were of great concern to the framers of the U.S. Constitution, and much thought was given to citizen representation. For instance, the Federalist Papers—a series of unsigned essays penned by Alexander Hamilton, John Jay, and James Madison between 1787 and 1788 and published in New York newspapers—argued for the adoption of the Constitution (Lando 1999). Since the 1960s, citizen participation has reemerged as a consequential topic in terms of definition, implementation, and evaluation.

The federal government renewed its attempts to increase citizen participation during the burgeoning civil rights movement. Social awareness and issues of equality dominated the political landscape throughout the 1960s and 1970s; at the same time, groups such as Community Action Agencies and the Model Cities Program began taking shape (Rosener 1978; Crosby, Kelly, and Schaefer 1986). Although the successes of the Community Action Agencies and the Model Cities Program are not considered entirely effective modes of enabling citizen participation (Crosby, Kelly, and Schaefer 1986), it is clear that their purpose was to empower citizens who lacked power.

The growing disenchantment with government (and its bureaucratic structures) that occurred during the 1960s and 1970s sparked a movement to empower the unempowered (Arnstein 1969). However, as Stenberg (1972) points out, such empowerment presented a contradiction to the values of the middle-class bureaucrat whose upward progression was based upon the merits of his actions. Stenberg demonstrates one of the many possible reasons that citizen participation at that point in history may not have reached levels of true empowerment. The challenge of empowering citizens remains a concern even in the twenty-first century.

Citizen participation efforts of past decades are not much different from many of the calls for greater citizen participation today. In 1969, when Sherry Arnstein wrote "A Ladder of Citizen Participation," she focused on empowering citizens to overcome social inequality. Now, if anything, citizen participation is a much broader concept, but the basic premise has remained the same. Citizen participation is an attempt to empower citizens so they may provide input and contribute to the functioning of

EXERCISE 14.1

City Creator (Simulation)

Students will access the city creator site and build a city. After completing this exercise, students will graph the city and include brief explanations as to their choices for locating roads, homes, green spaces, medical facilities, schools, and shops.

www.citycreator.com

their government. As Daniel Fiorino (1990) puts it, citizen participation theory "accepts that people are the best judge of their interests and can acquire the political skills needed to take part in governance" (p. 229).

Globalization: The Internationalization of Public Administration

"Whatever it is, you can get it here." That is the slogan for eBay, the online auction site. "Here" is the indistinguishable word that exemplifies globalization. Traditionally, the word *here* connotes a specific physical space; in today's world, however, that is no longer the case. In a global community, physical space is no longer of consequence. Globalization has given us a borderless world.

Some scholars indicate (Farazmand 1999; Kettl 2000) that globalization does not have one universal definition. Globalization can conjure up different ideas from different people with different perspectives. Farazmand (1999), in his article "Globalization and Public Administration," defines globalization from six different perspectives. These range from an isolated economics perspective to a perspective that sees globalization as a "transcending phenomenon and a process" (Farazmand 1999, p. 512). Kettl (2000) writes, "Most often, the term is synonymous with the galloping expansion of the global marketplace. However, globalization is much more. It includes political, technological, and cultural forces. It is more than a description—it is an ideology that defines basic expectations about the roles and behaviors of individuals and institutions" (p. 490). Similar themes arise from each definition, yet the complexity of the term and its associations makes it difficult to boil it down to one universal concept.

> "Service to others is the payment you make for your space here on earth."
>
> **MOHAMMAD ALI**
> World Champion Boxer

Huddleston (2000) explains globalization in a broad sense, to avoid limiting its understanding. His definition serves as a solid foundation to continue this discussion. Globalization starts from three "empirical observations" (Huddleston 2000, p. 668). First, it asserts that no economic activities are merely local. Second, it assumes that physical space and time have been fundamentally changed due to revolutions in the telecommunication sciences. Third, it suggests that human social relations have changed significantly in reaction to these developments, making communities possible on a global level (Huddleston 2000). These three premises capture the global community in which we currently live; however, they do not necessarily speak to the growing changes that must be made within the public sector to properly address such changes.

The consequences of globalization are being felt at the federal, state, and local levels. In each level of government, public administrators are faced with new challenges and opportunities pressing them to develop the infrastructure and capacities to meet these growing needs. For instance, on the local level, communities can no longer rely on multinational corporations to be a secure source of revenue and employment (Farazmand 1999). Due to lower employment wages in overseas locations, multinational and transnational corporations are likely to close locally run U.S. manufacturing sites and establish infrastructures in developing nations. According to Farazmand, public administrators should build a stronger sense of community and promote public involvement at the local level (1999). This, however, will not necessarily attract economic development and secure tax revenues. Public administrators must develop alternate infrastructures that will support further economic growth.

Public administrators must invest in building their communities' educational resources. Rondinelli, Johnson, and Kasarda (1998) believe that "the most competitive cities recognize that global enterprises must be located near or have access to knowledge centers" (p. 87). By investing in education, municipalities are developing capacities that will always be attractive to corporations. Educational investments can fulfill multinationals' research and development needs or help provide information technology support. Nontechnical education is equally important to corporate growth. "Salt Lake City is an attractive labor market because Utah has the highest literacy rate in the United States and because so many of Salt Lake City's residents have participated in Mormon missions overseas and are therefore more fluent in foreign languages than residents of most other American cities" (Rondinelli, Johnson, and Kasarda 1998, p. 88). Public administrators must consider alternate infrastructure developments to continue to compete in a growing global economy.

On the state level, similar themes exist. Public administrators can no longer rely on national foreign policy to deal with international relations. Due to globalization and the devolution of government, "more responsibility for both making and implementing policy has flowed to the state" (Kettl 2000, p. 489). Public administrators at the state level are working with foreign governments to "promote trade and attract foreign investment" (Kettl 2000, p. 489). State investment in overseas programs to attract trade has grown dramatically since the 1980s. In 1984, 54 overseas state offices existed to attract trade and investment. In 2000, that number had grown to 233 offices (Chernotsky and Hobbs 2001). State-level public administrators now have the opportunity to operate in almost every realm of public service. As transnational corporations challenge the borders of national sovereignty, state agents will increasingly be involved in the global economy.

Globalization's impacts and consequences at the federal level are much broader and more complex, encompassing not only the factors affecting local and state-level agencies but addressing additional structural concerns that remain at the core of their operations. The federal government, originally structured for a fixed world, will have to continue evolving in order to deal with a world in which transnational corporations stretch the borders of national sovereignty and telecommunication technologies displace time and space. Increasingly, public administrators at the federal level must be trained to work within an international community while creating national policy. According to Kettl (2000), "More decisions have flowed from the national to the international level, and the international level to both ad-hoc and multinational organizations" (p. 489). The rise of international bodies such as the European Union, or "regional collaborations" as seen in Italy, Portugal, and Spain, have even replaced national policymaking (Farazmand 1999, p. 515). As globalization continues to evolve, federal-level public administrators will have to learn to embrace a global world while simultaneously holding on to national values and public accountability.

Creating a balance between national and international interests could be the greatest challenge for public administrators in the coming years. With an increase on international regulatory reliance and a decrease in national sovereignty, the public administrator will have to develop modes for sustaining international relations while protecting national interests. Often, these national interests are mistaken as being solely economic in nature, but our national values play an equally important role in developing international treaties and organizations. Although economic growth is integral to national sustainability, economic growth in lieu of national values is unacceptable.

FIGURE 14.3 – WORLD INTERNET USAGE, 2000 VERSUS 2008

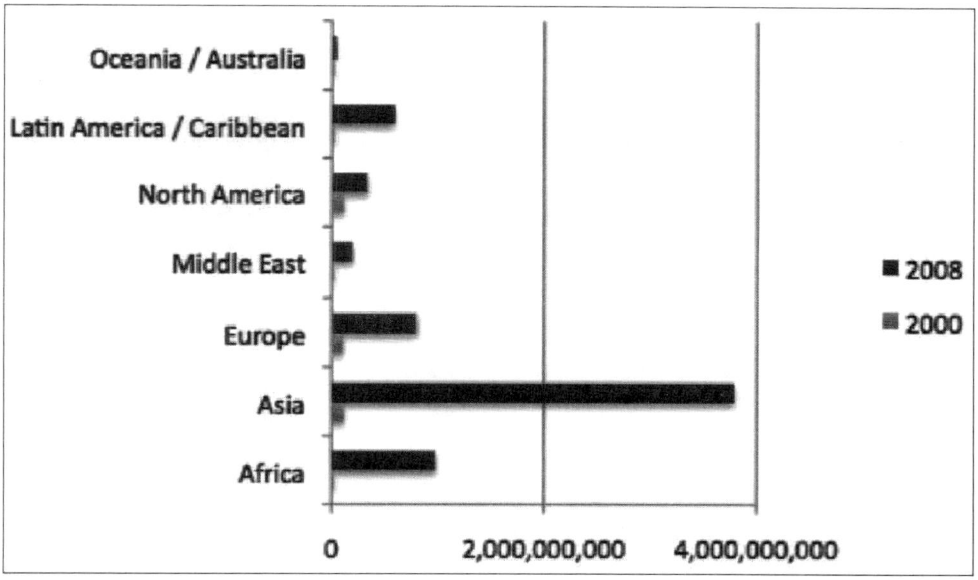

Source: Internet World Stats, www.internetworldstats.com/. Copyright © 2000-2010 Miniwatts Marketing Group.

This challenging balance presents public administrators with an opportunity. Over the past century, our country has made historic strides in promoting fair labor practices and environmental protections. Although room for improvement always exists, it is imperative that we promote these national practices throughout the world. Public administrators have the responsibility to take hold of this opportunity and develop an international framework that respects the human rights of every world citizen.

E-Governance

Technological advances have changed the way that all of us go about our daily activities. Whether it is checking our e-mail in the morning or texting on the go, mobile communication has grown steadily, and our ability to navigate the World Wide Web has improved dramatically. We use the Internet to shop, check the weather, do research, and connect with networks. According to the Internet World Stats (Figure 14.3), usage has grown exponentially across the world in a very short time.

Usage within North America during this period did not grow as rapidly as in the rest of the world. One can assume that there is less room for growth in developed countries such as the United States. Figure 14.4 shows the breakdown of Internet users in North America. As of 2010, there were about 240 million Internet users in the United States.

Those 250 million Internet users make up about 17 percent of the world's total usage as displayed in Figure 14.5.

FIGURE 14.4 – INTERNET USERS IN NORTH AMERICA

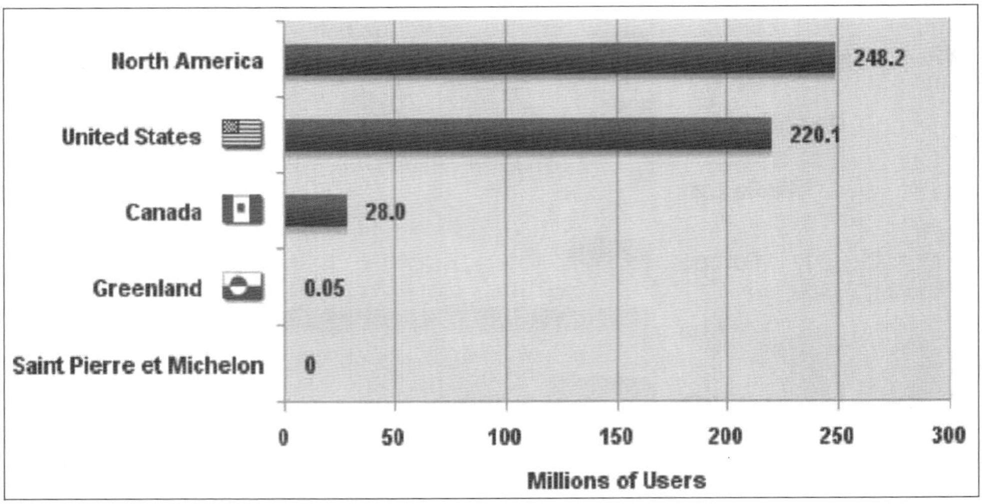

Source: Internet World Stats, http://www.internetworldstats.com/stats14.htm. Copyright © 2001-2010 Miniwatts Marketing Group.

What does this have to do with public administration? As Internet usage grows, and the use of technology in general grows, so too does the use of technology and the Internet by government. E-governance is the general term used to describe the government's use of technology in performing its multiple responsibilities. According to the United Nations Educational, Scientific and Cultural Organization (UNESCO): "E-governance is the public sector's use of information and communication technologies with the aim of improving information and service delivery, encouraging citizen participation in the decision-making process, and making government more accountable, transparent, and effective." The principles of e-governance, according to the E-Governance Institute at the School of Public Affairs and Administration at Rutgers University in Newark, are to:

- Build services with citizen choices in mind
- Increase government accessibility
- Foster social inclusion
- Disseminate information in a responsible fashion
- Use taxpayer resources effectively and efficiently

E-governance offers some exciting possibilities for the future. First, it may enhance access to government by citizens (Garson 2004). It may also increase access by those who work within government and those who work with government. Take, for example, the payment of a parking ticket. In the past, we would either have to go through the trouble of mailing in a payment or going directly to the payment office to submit our parking violation fee. Now, citizens across the country have access to

FIGURE 14.5 – NORTH AMERICAN INTERNET USERS

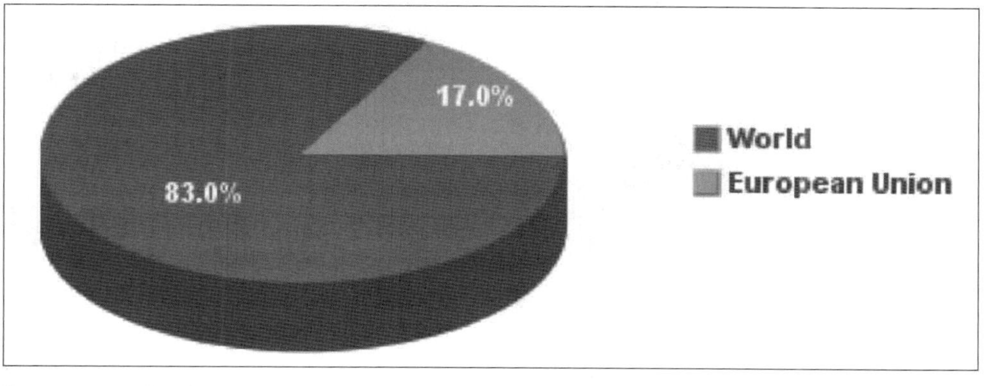

Source: Internet World Stats, http://www.internetworldstats.com/stats14.htm. Copyright © 2000-2010 Miniwatts Marketing Group.

a government website 24 hours a day, 7 days a week, during which they can make that payment electronically. This access is available for a number of government services that previously required a visit to a physical location such as a local police department, courthouse, or office of the Secretary of State.

Internally, for government employees, e-governance also provides access to services that were previously unavailable. Take, for example, government buildings. Obviously, governments need office space to provide their services, and the federal government alone maintains office space totaling 354 million square feet. Other government agencies need access to this inventory to determine the best space to lease for their needs. In the past, when information was not available online, the task of securing space was cumbersome. Now the General Services Administration (GSA) can post the entire inventory online. A manager can go to the GSA website, select a location on a map, and view all available properties. Figure 14.6 illustrates the beginning of this search capacity.

Following the selection of a state, managers can select a particular district or city in

FIGURE 14.6 – GENERAL SERVICES ADMINISTRATION (GSA) INVENTORY OF OWNED AND LEASED PROPERTY

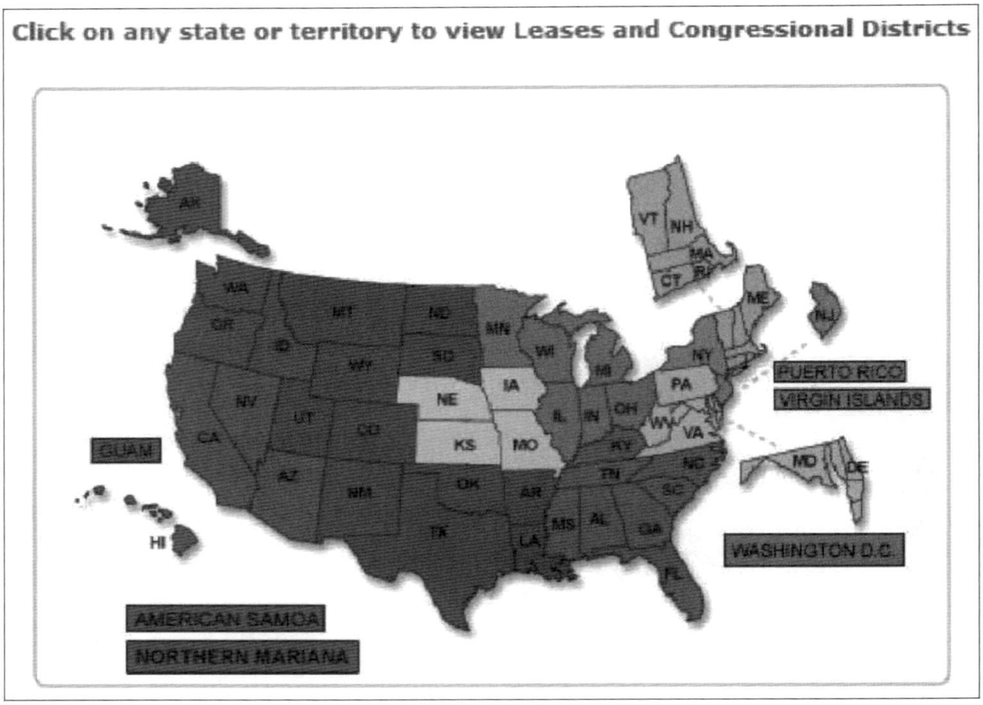

Source: U.S. General Services Administration. 2010. "General Services Administration (GSA) Inventory of Owned and Leased Property." http://www.iolp.gsa.gov/iolp/NationalMap.asp.

which they want to locate their agency. This is displayed in the image in Figure 14.7.

Although such access to real estate seems commonplace, one can imagine the challenge this might have presented just ten years ago.

E-governance also helps government's partners. In the past, cumbersome lists of available government contracts were printed out, and government contractors had to wait to receive them. Now, they can now log on to Business.gov, "the official busi-

FIGURE 14.7 – GENERAL SERVICES ADMINISTRATION (GSA) INVENTORY OF OWNED AND LEASED PROPERTY: COLORADO

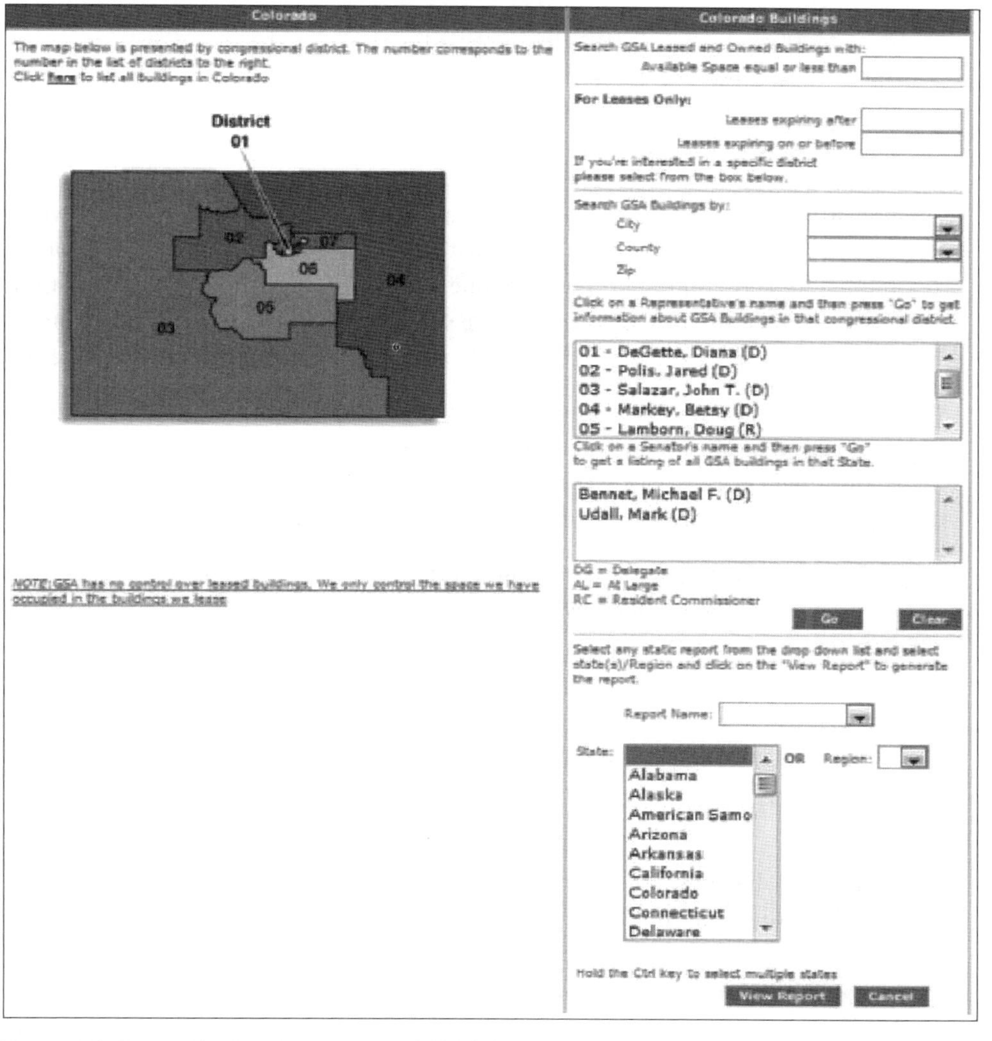

Source: U.S. General Services Administration. 2010. "General Services Administration (GSA) Inventory of Owned and Leased Property: Colorado." http://www.iolp.gsa.gov/iolp/StateDetail.asp?sID=8.

ness link to the U.S. government." This easy-to-use website allows contractors to register as government vendors, view current jobs, and gain an understanding of the laws that regulate such transactions. Having instant access to government business provides vendors with a clear advantage in supporting government services.

Beyond access, e-governance also reduces government costs considerably. Garson (2004) explains, "It is hoped that e-government will allow for flatter organizational structures as government is re-engineered to eliminate process pass-offs, which are better handled through online process control, and this, too, promises to yield impressive cost saving." Think about filing taxes. As we shift to an electronic system to file taxes, immediate reductions will be seen in the cost of mailing supplies. The real savings, though, comes with the decrease in processing costs that accompanies the transition to an electronic submission system.

Another advantage of e-governance is how it may shift the role of the citizen to build greater social capital within a society (Garson 2004). Social capital typically refers to the strength of the connection between members of a specific network. In this case, it is argued that e-governance can increase the level of social capital between citizens and their governments. E-governance presents opportunities for government to engage citizens in a manner that has previously been impossible. For example, similar to filing a tax return online, imagine if citizens could file suggestions to government online. In 2008 Virginia Governor Tim Kaine launched an online community for citizens to share ideas. As posted in a government news release:

> The community portal at www.ideas.virginia.gov enables constituents to share their ideas, engage in discussions and play a role in improving government service. This new community will strengthen the Commonwealth's commitment to performance by:
>
> - Inviting members to submit ideas so that others can comment and vote on them;
> - Allowing members to discuss ideas with each other and collaborate;
> - Encouraging members to vote on other ideas and help promote them for implementation consideration. (Virginia Municipal League 2008)

While many benefits arise from the use of e-governance, many challenges remain. The more we interact on the Internet or through web portals, the greater the amount of personal information floating about online. The protection of this information has become an urgent concern of those in the field of e-governance. According to Mullen (2004), there are three areas in which personal protection and Internet security are focused—personal privacy, confidentiality, and security. To abate concerns over personal privacy, the federal government is required to post privacy policies

(Mullen 2004). Additionally, giving users the ability to control more of their personal information online might help to reduce concerns. Confidentiality, according to Mullen (2004), is based on one or more of the following statements:

- Promises made to keep information confidential
- A legal obligation to protect confidentiality
- A duty to protect personal information, especially if the disclosure of the information would be harmful to the data provider

Finally, there is the issue of security. There are four areas in which security can be implemented:

- Physical safeguards such as locks and security personnel
- System and accountability safeguards such as passwords and audit trails
- Data transfer safeguards such as encryption
- Stipulated rules and procedures for handling information

If these areas of protection are considered, the use of e-governance will continue to flourish.

Transparency

According to the United Nations, government transparency is based upon "citizens' access to information" and "facilitating their understanding of decision-making processes." Garrett and Vermeule (2006) note, "Transparency can promote public-spirited behavior by constraining bargaining based on self-interest, promoting principled deliberation instead." Examples of transparency are freedom of information acts, administrative procedure laws, televised or radio access to legislative debates, published data or reports, and online information sources.

Within the United States, the Freedom of Information Act (FOIA) was an important step in providing open access to government information. Passed in 1966, FOIA provides citizens access to government documents and records. Each federal government agency is required to provide FOIA reports on its website so that interested citizens can submit requests for information. States also have open records laws, although they differ throughout the country.

There are many different aspects to transparency in practice, some of which focus on fiscal transparency or transparency within the budgeting process. According to the Organisation for Economic Co-operation and Development (OECD), "The budget is the single most important policy document of governments, where policy objectives are reconciled and implemented in concrete terms. Budget transparency is defined as the full disclosure of all relevant fiscal information in a timely and systematic manner." According to an OECD report on best practices in budget transparency, among those practices are (1) publishing regular budget reports, (2) disclosing obscure information such as tax expenditures and any economic assumptions, and (3) providing information on the integrity and accountability of the budget documents.

The U.S. federal budgeting process has aspects of transparency as well as some features that are obscured from the citizenry. According to Garrett and Vermeule (2006), the process of developing the budget is hidden from citizens' view under executive privilege laws. Therefore, those that work in the executive branch can craft the budget with little input or oversight from external groups. However, once the budget reaches Congress, the process tends to be open to the public (Garrett and Vermeule 2006). Most of this is simply based upon the rules of Congress, which allow public access in many respects.

Certain critics are concerned with transparency in government procurement. Understandably, procurement can be a process in which corruption thrives. To ensure transparency in procurement practices, the United Nations suggests there should be:

- Clearly defined and transparent rules and procedures
- Uniform tender documents
- Fairness in the bidding process

By following the aforementioned procurement policies, the government can save money, promote economic growth, and strengthen disadvantaged groups (United Nations 1999).

As discussed above, technology can serve to assist government in making information readily available to its citizenry. E-governance may provide a system for accessing government documents and records. According to Brito (2008), the availability of such information online can help the entire citizenry: "Making government information available online would not only benefit individual users of government Web sites, it would also make it simpler for third parties to aggregate government data. By aggregating data, Web sites can present government information in innovative and useful ways. For example, federal spending data gathered from a government Web site could be presented by a third party as an interactive map that shows the locations of funding recipients. Such applications make data exponentially more valuable."

KEY TERMS

Citizen participation

E-governance

Performance measurement

Transparency

REFERENCES

Agranoff, R., and M. McGuire. 2003. *Collaborative Public Management*. Washington, DC: Georgetown University Press.

Ammons, D.N. 1996. *Municipal Benchmarks: Assessing Local Performance and Establishing Community Standards*. Thousand Oaks, CA: Sage Publications.

Arnstein, S. 1969. "A Ladder of Citizen Participation." *Journal of the American Institute of Planners* 35: 216–24.

Bingham, L., T. Nabatchi, and R. O'Leary. 2005. "The New Governance: Practices and Processes for Stakeholder and Citizen Participation in the Work of Government." *Public Administration Review* 65: 547–58.

Brito, J. 2008. "Improving Government Transparency Online." *The Public Manager* 37, no. 1: 22–26.

Brown, K., and R. Keast. 2003. "Citizen-Government Engagement: Community Connection Through Networked Arrangements." *Asian Journal of Public Administration* 25: 107–31.

Box, R. 1999. "Running Government Like a Business: Implications for Public Administration Theory and Practice." *American Review of Public Administration* 29, no. 1: 19–43.

Chernotsky, H., and H. Hobbs. 2001. "Responding to Globalization: State and Local Initiatives in the Southern United States." *Passages* 3, no. 1: 57–82.

Crosby, N., J. Kelly, and P. Schaefer. 1986. "Citizen Panels: A New Approach to Citizen Participation." *Public Administration Review* 46, no. 2: 170–78.

Farazmand, A. 1999. "Globalization and Public Administration." *Public Administration Review* 59, no. 6: 509–22.

Fiorino, D. 1990. "Citizen Participation and Environmental Risk: A Survey of Institutional Mechanisms." *Science, Technology, and Human Values* 15: 226–43.

Garson, D. 2004. "The Promise of Digital Government." *In Digital Government:*

Principles and Best Practices, ed. Alexei Pavlichev and G. David Garson, 2–15. Hershey, PA: Idea Publishing.

Garrett, E., and A. Vermeule. 2006. "Transparency in the Budget Process." Public Law Working Paper No. 115. University of Chicago, January. http://papers.ssrn.com/so13/papers.cfm?abstract_id=877951.

Goldsmith, S., and W.D. Eggers. 2004. "Governing by Network: The New Public Management Imperative." Harvard University, Ash Institute for Democratic Governance and Innovation. http://ash.harvard.edu/Home/Programs/Innovations-in-Government/21stCentury/Governing-By-Network.

Hatry, H. P., J.R. Fountain, Jonathan M. Sullivan and Lorraine Kremer (eds). 1990. "Service Efforts and Accomplishments: Its Time Has Come—An Overview." Governmental Accounting Standards Board (GASB), Norwalk, CT.

Holzer, M., and K. Kloby. 2005. "Public Performance Measurement: An Assessment of the State-of-the-Art and Models for Citizen Participation." *International Journal of Productivity and Performance Management* 54, no. 7: 517–32.

Huddleston, M.W. 2000. "Onto the Darkling Plain: Globalization and the American Public Service in the Twenty-first Century." *Journal of Public Administration Research and Theory* 10, no. 4: 665–84.

Julnes, P.D.L. 2006. "Performance Measurement: An Effective Tool for Government Accountability? The Debate Goes On." *Evaluation* 12, no. 2: 219–35.

Keast, R., M.P. Mandell, K. Brown, and G. Woolcock. 2004. "Network Structures: Working Differently and Changing Expectations." *Public Administration Review* 64, no. 3: 363–71.

Kettl, D.F. 2000. "The Transformation of Governance: Globalization, Devolution, and the Role of Government." *Public Administration Review* 60, no. 6: 488–97.

Lando, T. 1999. "Public Participation in Local Government: Points of View." *National Civic Review* 88: 109–22.

Lowndes, V., and C. Skelcher. 1998. "The Dynamics of Multi-Organizational Partnerships: An Analysis of Changing Modes of Governance." *Public Administration* 76, no. 2: 313–33.

Marcussen, M., and J. Torfing. 2003. "Grasping Governance Networks." Working Paper 2003:5. Center for Democratic Network Governance. http://rudar.ruc.dk/bitstream/1800/4139/1/Working_Paper_2003_5.pdf.

Mullen, P. 2004. "Digital Government and Individual Privacy." In *Digital Gov-*

ernment: Principles and Best Practices, ed. Alexei Pavlichev and G. David Garson, 134–48. Hershey, PA: Idea Publishing.

National Center for Public Performance. 2004. "Citizen-Driven Government Performance: A Brief Guide for Performance Measurement in Local Government." http://andromeda.rutgers.edu/~ncpp/cdgp/teaching/brief-manual.html.

Osborne, D., and Ted Gaebler. 1992. *Reinventing Government: How the Entrepreneurial Spirit Is Transforming the Public Sector*. New York: Addison-Wesley.

Roberts, N. 2004. "Public Deliberation in an Age of Direct Citizen Participation." *American Review of Public Administration* 34: 315–53.

Rondinelli, Dennis A., James H. Johnson, and John D. Kasarda. 1998. "The Changing Forces of Urban Economic Development: Globalization and City Competitiveness in the 21st Century." *Cityscape* 3, no. 3: 71–105.

Rosener, J. 1978. "Citizen Participation: Can We Measure Its Effectiveness?" *Public Administration Review* 38, no. 5: 457–63.

Salamon, L. 2002. "The New Governance and the Tools of Public Action." In *The Tools of Government: A Guide to the New Governance*, ed. L.M. Salamon, 1–47. New York: Oxford University Press.

Smith, G., and C. Huntsman. 1997. "Reframing the Metaphor of the Citizen-Government Relationship: A Value-Centered Perspective." *Public Administration Review* 57, no. 4: 309–18.

Smith, S., and H. Ingram. 2002. "Policy Tools and Democracy." In *The Tools of Government: A Guide to the New Governance*, ed. L.M. Salamon, 565–84. New York: Oxford University Press.

Stenberg, C. 1972. "Citizens and the Administrative State: From Participation to Power." *Public Administration Review* 32, no. 3: 190–98.

Streib, G.D., and Theodore H. Poister. 1999. "Assessing the Validity, Legitimacy, and Functionality of Performance Measurement Systems in Municipal Governments." *American Review of Public Administration* 29, no. 2: 107–23.

United Nations. 1999. "Transparency in Government." Presentation for ILEA Seminar. July 20. http://unpan1.un.org/intradoc/groups/public/documents/un/unpan012062.pdf.

Vigoda, E. 2002. "From Responsiveness to Collaboration: Governance, Citizens, and the Next Generation of Public Administration." *Public Administration Review* 62: 527–40.

Virginia Municipal League. 2008. "Update. The Newsletter of the Virginia Municipal League." September 19.
www.vml.org/UP/PDFUPs/UP08/UPSep1908.pdf.

Williams, D. 2003. "Measuring Government in the Early Twentieth Century." *Public Administration Review* 63, no. 6: 643–58.

Wholey, J.S. 1999. "Performance-Based Management." *Public Productivity and Management Review* 22, no. 3: 288–307.

SUPPLEMENTARY READINGS

Beckett, Julia, and Cheryl Simrell King. 2002. "The Challenge to Improve Citizen Participation in Public Budgeting: A Discussion." *Journal of Public Budgeting, Accounting and Financial Management* 14, no.3: 463–85.

Carrizales, Tony. 2009. "The Internet Citizenry: Access and Participation." *Public Administration Review* 69, no. 2: 350-353

Frederickson, David G., and H. George Frederickson. 2006. *Measuring the Performance of the Hollow State.* Washington, DC: Georgetown University Press.

Government Performance Project. 2003. *Paths to Performance in State and Local Government.* Syracuse, NY: Maxwell School of Citizenship and Public Affairs, Syracuse University.

Ho, Alfred Tat-Kei. 2002. "Reinventing Local Governments and the E-Government Initiative." *Public Administration Review* 62, no. 4: 434–44.

Holzer, Marc, and Seang-Tae Kim. 2003. *Digital Governance in Municipalities Worldwide: An Assessment of Municipal Web Sites throughout the World.* Newark, NJ: National Center for Public Productivity.

Julnes, De Lancer Patria and Marc Holzer. 2001. "Promoting the Utilization of Performance Measures in Public Organizations: An Empirical Study of Factors Affecting Adoption and Implementation." *Public Administration Review* 61, no. 6: 693–708.

Thompson, Frank J. 2008. "Public State and Local Governance Fifteen Years Later: Enduring and New Challenges." *Public Administration Review* 68, no. 1: S8–S19.

Tolbert, C. J., and K. Mossberger. 2006. "The Effects of E-Government on Trust and Confidence in Government." *Public Administration Review* 66: 354–69.

Wang, XiaoHu. 2001. "Assessing Public Participation in U.S. Cities." *Public Performance and Management Review* 24, no. 4: 322–36.

ELECTRONIC RESOURCES

Center for Accountability and Performance, "Performance Measurement at the State and Local Levels: A Summary of Survey Results," http://64.91.242.87/cap/survey_results.html

Ohio State University Fact Sheet, "Citizen Participation in Community Development," http://ohioline.osu.edu/cd-fact/l700.html

Oak Ridge Associated Universities Performance-Based Management Special Interest Group, "Performance Measurement Documents," http://www.orau.gov/pbm/documents/documents.html

United Nations Division for Public Economics and Public Administration, and American Society for Public Administration. 2001. "Benchmarking E-Government: A Global Perspective," http://unpan1.un.org.proxy.libraries.rutgers.edu/intradoc/groups/public/documents/un/unpan021547.pdf

CASE STUDIES

A Broadband World: The Promise of Advanced Services
Matthew D. Bennett, Alliance for Public Technology and the Benton Foundation. 2003. This study has cases on the use of broadband technology in various service areas. http://www.benton.org/publibrary/broadband/broadband-world.pdf.

Use and the Effects of Using Performance Measures for Budgeting, Management, and Reporting
Diane Artrip, Deputy City Auditor, City of Phoenix. January 2004. www.seagov.org/sea_gasb_project/local_phoenix.pdf.

Technology and Poverty Reduction: Text Messages Boost Competitiveness for Armenian Farmers
The Millennium Challenge Corporation, *Results on the Ground,* August 28, 2009. http://www.mcc.gov/documents/press/successstory-082909-results-armenia.pdf.

INDEX

Italic page references indicate boxed text, tables, graphs, and photographs.

C

D

E

F

G

H

I

J

K

L

M

N

O

P

Q

R

S

T

U

V

W

Z